A SOURCE BOOK

IN

AMERICAN HISTORY

TO 1787

COLLECTED AND EDITED

BY

WILLIS MASON WEST

SOMETIME PROFESSOR OF HISTORY AND HEAD OF THE
DEPARTMENT AT THE UNIVERSITY OF MINNESOTA

—◦◦❈◦◦—

ALLYN AND BACON

Boston   New York   Chicago

COPYRIGHT, 1913,
BY WILLIS MASON WEST.

Norwood Press
J. S. Cushing Co. — Berwick & Smith Co.
Norwood, Mass., U.S.A.

FOREWORD

EARLY American history is especially suited for "source work" in secondary schools and undergraduate college classes. After the year 1800, there are too many documents and many of them are too long. The student can get no systematic survey nor any sense of continuity; and source work is therefore merely illustrative of particular incidents. But, for the early period, it is possible, by careful selection and exclusion, to lay a basis for a fairly connected study.

To do this, it is necessary to combine in one volume selections which are usually grouped separately, as "Documents" and as "Readings," — such, for instance, as the Massachusetts charter, on the one hand, and Winthrop's letters to his wife, on the other. Rigid scholarship may object to the inclusion of such different sorts of sources between the same covers. But students cannot be expected to own or use more than one volume of sources in American history; and the practical educational advantages of the combination seem to me to outweigh all possible objections — besides which, something might be said for the arrangement in itself, for young students, on the side of interest and convenience.

A number of admirable collections of sources for schools are already in use. And yet, in preparing my *American History and Government*,[1] I found no single volume which contained the different kinds of source material desirable for illustration, while much of the most valuable material was still inaccessible in any collection. Some two-thirds of the selections in the present volume, I believe, have not previously appeared in

---

[1] Allyn and Bacon. 1913.

FOREWORD

Source Books; and, for many of the customary documents, I have found it desirable to print parts not usually given. Thus, for Gorges' Patent for Maine, instead of reproducing the territorial grant (which is all that is given in the only Source Book which touches on that document), I have chosen rather to give the portion authorizing a degree of popular self-government (the reference to the "parliament in New England").

In a few cases, documents which might have been expected are not given, because extracts from them are used freely in the *American History and Government*, to which this is a companion volume. The most important cases of this character are noted at appropriate points. In general, in the selection and arrangement of documents, special emphasis has been given to the following topics: (1) the idealistic motives back of American colonization in Virginia as well as in Puritan New England; (2) the evolution of political institutions in Virginia and in typical Northern colonies, — especially of representative government and of the town meeting, and of such details as the use of the ballot; (3) the very imperfect nature of democracy, political and social, in colonial America, — so that the student may better appreciate our later growth; (4) social conditions, — necessarily a rather fragmentary treatment; (5) the evolution of commonwealths out of colonies in the Revolution; and (6) the breakdown of the Confederation and the making of the Constitution.

Many typical documents are given entire. Other selections are excerpted carefully. In such cases, omissions are indicated, of course, and the substance of the omitted matter is usually indicated in brackets. In the case of a few selections, like those from Winthrop's *History*, the original document has already been published in standard editions with modernized spelling. Such editions have been followed. The text of all other documents has been reproduced faithfully, except for such departures as are authorized in the American Historical Association's *Suggestions for the Printing of Documents*; *i.e.*, regarding the spelling out of abbreviations, and the modern usage for the consonantal *i* and *u,* and the modernizing of punctuation when absolutely needful to prevent ambiguity. Some students may find a slight difficulty at first in the vagaries of seventeenth century orthography. But this difficulty is quickly surmounted; and, apart from the added flavor that comes from the quaintness of the original, and from the consciousness that the copy has been strictly adhered to, there is often a distinct historical advantage in the practice. The falling away in book-culture in the second generation of New England colonization can hardly be suggested so forcibly in any other way as by following the degeneration of spelling by town officials — as in the Watertown records in Number 83. The peculiarities of type in printed documents have been preserved so far as possible, but here I have taken a greater liberty than in any other matter of this kind. Italics and black-faced type have been introduced freely, to call attention to matter of special importance for instruction. Sometimes this practice has been noted in the respective introductions; and in other cases there will be little difficulty in deciding which passages owe their prominence of this sort to the editor.

I have tried also to add to the teaching value of the book by a free use of introductions to the various extracts, and by footnotes and addenda, with occasional "Hints for Study."

WILLIS MASON WEST.

WINDAGO FARM,
   November, 1913.

TABLE OF CONTENTS

NUMBER PAGE
I. England in the Century of Colonization
1. Classes of Englishmen; by William Harrison; from Holinshed's *Chronicles* (1577) 1

A. SOUTHERN COLONIES TO 1660

II. Motives for Early Colonization
2. Sir George Peckham's "True Report" (1582) of Gilbert's expedition; from Richard Hakluyt's *Voyages and Discoveries of the English Nation*. 4
3. Richard Hakluyt's *Discourse on Western Planting* (1584); from the *Maine Historical Society Collections* . . . 4
4. Michael Drayton's *Ode* to the Virginian Voyage (1606) . . 7
5. "Goodspeed to Virginia" (1609); by Robert Gray; from Brown's *Genesis of the United States* 7
6. "Nova Britannia" (1609); anonymous; from Peter Force's *Historical Tracts* 10
7. The "True and Sincere Declaration" by the London Company (1609), with a "Table of such [colonists] as are required"; from Brown's *Genesis of the United States* . 12
8. Marston's *Eastward Hoe!* (1605) 15
9. Crashaw's "Daily Prayer" for use in Virginia (1609); from Force's *Historical Tracts* 15
10. Crashaw's "Sermon" before Lord Delaware's Expedition (1610); from Brown's *Genesis of the United States* . 16
11. A letter by Sir Edwin Sandys (1612) to stockholders of the London Company; from Neill's *Virginia and Virginiola* . 17
12. The glories of Virginia; from a letter from Sir Thomas Dale (governor in Virginia) to Sir Thomas Smith (head of the London Company), in 1613; from the *Records of the Virginia Company of London*, edited by Susan Kingsbury . 17

TABLE OF CONTENTS

NUMBER	PAGE
13. A defense of the London Company (declared not mercenary) by Captain John Smith (1616); from Smith's *Generall Historie of Virginia*	18
14. A plea for colonization on patriotic and religious grounds (1631), by Captain John Smith; *Works*	18

III. Virginia (1606-1619), to the Introduction of Self-government

15. The charter of Sir Humphrey Gilbert (1578); from Hakluyt's *Voyages and Discoveries*	20
16. The Virginia charter of 1606; from the Appendix to Stith's *History of Virginia*	23
17. Instructions by King James to the London Company (November 20/30, 1606); from Hening's *Statutes at Large* . .	29
18. Instructions from the Council of the Virginia Company to the first Jamestown expedition (December, 1606); from Neill's *Virginia Company*	32
19. The early settlers and their sufferings:	
a. A "Discourse" by Master George Percy (1607); from "Purchas his Pilgrimes" (1625) . . .	35
b. An account of "gentlemen" in Virginia, by Amos Todkill (1608); from Smith's *Works* . . .	36
20. The Virginia charter of 1609 (with hints for study); from the Appendix to Stith's *History of Virginia*	37
21. The Virginia charter of 1612 (the portions relating to a more democratic organization of the Company and its powers); *ib.*	44
22. The danger from Spanish attack: correspondence of Spanish and English ambassadors with their respective governments; from Brown's *Genesis of the United States* . .	47

IV. Virginia under the Liberal Company, 1619-1624

23. Rules of the Virginia Company (1619); from Force's *Historical Tracts*	51
24. An "Order" of the Company authorizing temporary self-government in its plantations (February 2/12, 1619/1620); from Susan Kingsbury's *Records of the Virginia Company of London*	53
25. Records of the Assembly of 1619; from Wynne and Gilman's *Colonial Records of Virginia*	53

TABLE OF CONTENTS

NUMBER		PAGE
26.	The "Declaration" by the Company (drawn by Sandys), June 22/July 2, 1620, justifying the liberal management; from Susan Kingsbury's *Records of the Virginia Company of London*	63
27.	The Ordinance of 1621, — a grant of limited self-government by the Company to the settlers, with authorization of a representative Assembly; from the Appendix to Stith's *History of Virginia*	70
28.	Attempts by King James to control the elections in the Company in favor of the "court party" in 1620 and 1622; from Susan Kingsbury's *Records of the Virginia Company of London*	73

V. Virginia a Royal Province: Struggle to save the Assembly

29.	Royal Commission to Governor Wyatt and his Council (1624), ignoring the Assembly; from Hazard's *State Papers*.	80
30.	Royal commission to Governor Yeardley (1625), to like purpose; from Hazard's *State Papers*	82
31.	Protests in the Colony:	
	a. The Assembly's precautionary "bill of rights," with statement of the principle, "No taxation without representation" (three laws from the session of March, 1624); from Hening's *Statutes at Large*.	83
	b. Requests from the colony for aid, and, indirectly, for an Assembly:	
	1. Letter from the Governor and Council to the Special Commission in England (April, 1626); from the Aspinwall Papers, in *Massachusetts Historical Society Collections*.	84
	2. Letter from the same to the same (May, 1626); from the *Virginia Magazine of History*	85
32.	Restoration of the Assembly by royal authority (1629):	
	a. Captain Harvey's "Propositions" (after appointment as governor); *ib.*	86
	b. The King's answer to the same; *ib.*	86
	c. Royal instructions to Governor Berkeley (1641); *ib.*	87
33.	Virginian legislation, financial and moral; from Hening's *Statutes at Large*	87

TABLE OF CONTENTS

VI. Virginia under the Commonwealth

NUMBER · PAGE
34. Terms of settlement between Parliamentary Commissioners and the Assembly (1652); from Hening's *Statutes at Large* . 90
35. Legislation restricting the franchise, and restoring it to the old basis; *ib.* 92

VII. Maryland to 1660

36. Lord Baltimore's letter to Charles I (1629), describing the hardships of the Avalon colony and asking for a grant in "Virginia"; from Scharf's *History of Maryland* . . . 93
37. The Maryland charter of 1632; from Bacon's *Laws of Maryland* 94
38. Extracts from the Avalon charter of 1623 (with comparison with the Maryland grant); from Scharf's *History of Maryland* 99
39. Excursus: Extracts from the Plowden grant of New Albion of 1634, and the Gorges grant of Maine of 1639 (for comparison with the foregoing, in tracing the development of royal approval of representative institutions in the colonies); the documents from Hazard's *State Papers* . . 100
40. The "Toleration Act" of 1649; from the *Maryland Archives* . 102

B. NEW ENGLAND TO 1660

VIII. An Early Exploration

41. Captain George Weymouth's "True Relation" of his voyage in 1605 to the coast of Maine; from the *Massachusetts Historical Society Collections* 106

IX. The First Source of New England Land Titles

42. The charter of 1620 for the Plymouth Council (sometimes called the Council for New England); from Hazard's *State Papers* 109

X. Plymouth Colony

43. Negotiations between the Pilgrims and the Virginia Company for the Wincob charter: Cushman's letter explaining the delay; from Bradford's *Plymouth Plantation* . . . 113
44. Articles of Partnership between Pilgrims and London merchants; *ib.* 114

TABLE OF CONTENTS

NUMBER	PAGE
45. The "farewell letter" from Pastor Robinson: the Pilgrims a "body politic" with power of self-government; *ib.*	116
46. The Mayflower Compact; *ib.*; with addendum — The Exeter Agreement; from Hazard's *State Papers*	116
47. The Peirce charter of June, 1621, from the New England Council; from the *Massachusetts Historical Society Collections*	118
48. Early history and hardships:[1]	
a. Edward Winslow's letter of December, 1621, to a friend in England; from Arber's *Story of the Pilgrim Fathers*	120
b. Captain John Smith's account, in 1624; *Works*	122
49. The final source of Plymouth land titles:	
a. Bradford's Patent of 1630; from Hazard's *State Papers*	124
b. Bradford's surrender of the same to the colony; *ib.*	126
50. Extracts from the "Fundamental Laws" of 1636; *ib.*	127

XI. The Founding of Massachusetts Bay

51. The Gorges claim:	
a. The charter from the New England Council to Robert Gorges (1622); from Sir Ferdinando Gorges' "Briefe Narration," in Hazard's *State Papers*	129
b. The Gorges expedition of 1623; *ib.*, in *Massachusetts Historical Society Collections*	131
52. The founding of Salem and Charlestown: White's "Relation" (1630); from Young's *Massachusetts Chronicles*	132
53. The Massachusetts Company's charter of 1629; from the *Records of the Governor and Company of Massachusetts Bay*, edited by Nathaniel Shurtleff (usually quoted here as the *Massachusetts Colonial Records*)	137
54. The docket of the above charter, as it was presented for royal approval (showing the King's expectation that the charter was to remain in England; from the *Massachusetts Historical Society Proceedings* for 1869–1870	144

---

[1] Bradford's *Plymouth Plantation*, the main source for this topic, is quoted so extensively in the *American History and Government* that it is not used here in this connection.

NUMBER	PAGE
55. Excursus: discussion of the original intention of the grantees in the Massachusetts charter as to removing to America, with illuminating extracts from the "Charter of the Company of Westminster for the Plantation of Providence Isle"; (the document from the manuscript in British Record Office)	146
56. Agreement between the Massachusetts Company in England and the Rev. Francis Higginson, on his removal to America; from Young's *Chronicles of Massachusetts* . .	148
57. Establishment of a subordinate government in the colony (April, 1629), by order of the Company in England; from the *Massachusetts Colonial Records*	150

XII. The Colony Becomes Puritan

58. The decision to transfer the government and charter to the colony:	
a. The first official proposal, by Governor Cradock, at a meeting of the Company in London (July 28, 1629); from the *Massachusetts Colonial Records* . .	153
b. The Cambridge Agreement; from Young's *Chronicles of Massachusetts*	154
c. The final decision by the Company; from the *Colonial Records*	156
59. Decision of Puritan gentlemen to settle in the colony:	
a. John Winthrop's argument for a Puritan colony; from Winthrop's *Life and Letters of John Winthrop*	157
b. Winthrop's reasons for himself coming to America; *ib.*	159
c. The decision of John Winthrop, Jr.; *ib.* . . .	160
d. Higginson's "News from New England"; from Young's *Chronicles of Massachusetts* . . .	161
60. The attitude of the early Puritan colonists toward the Church of England:	
a. Winthrop's farewell letter to the Church of England; *Life and Letters*	162
b. Captain John Smith's opinion of the Puritans in 1630 (not Separatists); from Smith's *Works* . . .	164
61. Political principles of the Puritan leaders (distrust of democracy): illustrated by extracts from Calvin's *Institutes* .	164

NUMBER		PAGE
62.	Early hardships and religious tendencies:	
	a. From Winthrop's *History of New England*, 1630–1631	168
	b. From Winthrop's letters to his wife; *Life and Letters*	171
	c. From Thomas Dudley's letter to the Countess of Lincoln (1631); from Young's *Chronicles of Massachusetts*	174

XIII. Development of Democracy

63.	Oligarchic usurpations in 1630–1631; from the *Colonial Records*	178
64.	The "Watertown Protest" against taxation without representation (the first popular movement), in 1632, and the consequent resumption by the democracy of some of their rights; from Winthrop's *History of New England*	180
65.	Sample legislation under aristocratic rule, 1630–1633; from the *Colonial Records*	183
66.	The beginning of town government, at Dorchester; from the *Dorchester Records*	188
67.	The development of representative government:	
	a. Winthrop's account; from his *History of New England*	189
	b. The official records of the revolutionary General Court of 1634; from the *Colonial Records*	191
68.	Political reaction: the magistrates demand a "negative voice"; from Winthrop's *History of New England*	194
69.	The Puritan government denies free speech in political matters; *ib.*	195
70.	The adoption of the ballot in elections in the General Court; *ib.*	196
71.	The first use of the ballot in local elections; *ib.*	197
72.	A military commission with power of martial law; from the *Colonial Records*	198
73.	Winthrop's account of various political actions: a "Life Council"; extension of the ballot by the use of proxies; restriction of "churches" to the organizations recognized by the government; from Winthrop's *History of New England*	199
74.	The Wheelwright controversy, with special reference to political phases; *ib.*	199
75.	Political and social conditions in Massachusetts in 1636:	
	a. "Proposals" of Lords Say and Brooke, with the answers of John Cotton; from the Appendix to Hutchinson's *History of Massachusetts Bay*	201

TABLE OF CONTENTS

NUMBER		PAGE
	b. Legislation of 1651 regarding dress of different classes; from the *Colonial Records*	205
76.	Attack upon the charter:	
	a. An order in Council in England for its surrender; from Hutchinson's *Original Papers*	206
	b. The defiant refusal of the Colony; from Winthrop's *History of New England*	207
77.	Democratic discontent with aristocratic privilege in 1639 (Winthrop's denial of the right of petition; the abolition of Life Council; delay in conceding a written code); *ib.*	210
78.	The "Body of Liberties"; from Whitmore's *Bibliographical Sketch of the Laws of Massachusetts Colony*	214
79.	A Puritan view of the rules of fair trade (Cotton's sermon upon the conviction of a shopkeeper for exacting exorbitant profits); from Winthrop's *History of New England*	225
80.	The separation of the General Court into two Houses (the first two-chambered legislature in America); the story from Winthrop's *History of New England*, and the preamble of the act of 1644 from the *Colonial Records*	226
81.	A town code of school laws (1645); from the *Dorchester Records*	230
82.	Colonial school laws (1642 and 1647); from the *Colonial Records*	233
83.	Representative town records (*Watertown Records*, 1634–1678)	236

XIV. Massachusetts and Religious Persecution

84.	Puritan arguments for and against persecution:	
	a. From Nathaniel Ward's *Simple Cobbler of Aggawamm* (1647)	246
	b. From Captain Edward Johnson's *Wonder-working Providence of Sions Saviour in New England* (1654)	248
	c. The discussion between Saltonstall and Cotton (about 1650); from Hutchinson's *Original Papers*	249
85.	Criticism of the Massachusetts way, by a moderate Episcopalian and royalist (Lechford's *Plaine Dealing*; 1641)	252
86.	A Presbyterian demand for the franchise in 1646 (the letter of Dr. Robert Child and others to the Governor and General Court); from Hutchinson's *Original Papers*	255

NUMBER	PAGE
87. Trial and punishment of nonconformists for not attending approved churches; from the *Colonial Records*	259
88. Quaker Persecutions:	
a. Edward Burrough's appeal to King Charles (1660); from Burrough's *Sad and Great Persecution and Martyrdom of Quakers in New England*	260
b. Trial of the Quaker, Wenlock Christison (1661); from Besse's *Collection of the Sufferings of the People called Quakers*	263

XV. Rhode Island to 1660

89. The first covenant at Providence (1636): a compact in "*civil* things only"; from the *Early Records of the Town of Providence*	267
90. Roger Williams' argument that religious freedom is consonant with civil order (the ship illustration); from Arnold's *History of Rhode Island*	268
91. The Patent for Providence Plantation from the Council of the Long Parliament (1644), restricting the government to *civil* matters; from the *Rhode Island Colonial Records*	269
92. Rhode Island's answer to the demand of Massachusetts (a refusal to exclude Quakers); from the Appendix to Hutchinson's *Massachusetts Bay*	270

XVI. Connecticut before 1660

93. The Fundamental Orders of 1639; from the *Connecticut Colonial Records*	273

XVII. The New England Confederation

94. The constitution (Articles of Confederation); from the *New Haven Colonial Records*	280
95. The demand of Massachusetts for more weight in the union, with the answer of the Congress of the Confederation; from the *Plymouth Colony Records*	285
96. Nullification by Massachusetts, with the protest of the Congress of the Confederation; *ib.*	287

C. COLONIAL AMERICA

XVIII. Liberal Charters

97. The Connecticut charter of 1662; from the *Connecticut Colonial Records*	290

TABLE OF CONTENTS

NUMBER		PAGE
98.	The Rhode Island charter of 1663 (parts referring especially to religious liberty) ; from the *Rhode Island Colonial Records*	293

XIX. An English Colonial System

99.	Royal instructions for the "Councill appointed for Forraigne Plantations" (1660) ; from O'Callaghan's *Documents relative to the Colonial History of New York*	298
100.	The English commercial policy:	
	a. The "first" Navigation Act (1660), regarding shipping and "enumerated" colonial exports, with note from the Act of 1662 explaining that "English" ships include colonial; from *Statutes of the Realm*	300
	b. The Navigation Act of 1663 (regarding colonial imports); *ib.*	301
	c. The Sugar Act of 1733; *ib.*	303
101.	The Duke of York's charter for New York (1664); from O'Callaghan's *Documents relative to Colonial History of New York*	305
102.	Penn's grant of Pennsylvania (1680); from the *Charters and Laws of Pennsylvania*	307
103.	Penn's grants to the Pennsylvanians :	
	a. "Laws agreed upon in England" (1683); from Hazard's *Annals of Pennsylvania*	311
	b. The "Charter of Privileges" of 1701 ; from *Votes and Proceedings of the House of Representatives of Pennsylvania*	314
104.	Berkeley's Report on Virginia in 1671; from Hening's *Statutes*	319
105.	The franchise in Virginia restricted (the Act of 1670) ; *ib.*	324
106.	"Bacon's Laws" (the legislation of the revolutionary Assembly of 1676) ; *ib.*	325
107.	The proclamation of July, 1676, by Nathaniel Bacon, "Generall by Consent of the People"; from the *Massachusetts Historical Society Collections*	328
108.	Testimony by various county courts showing that democratic political discontent was a chief cause of Bacon's Rebellion; from the *Virginia Magazine of History*	329

NUMBER		PAGE
109.	The abolition of Bacon's reforms:	
	a. The royal order; from Hening's *Statutes at Large* .	330
	b. The repeal of "Bacon's Laws" by the Assembly of 1677; ib.	331
110.	Self-government in Massachusetts restricted:	
	a. Randolph's report to the Lords of Trade; from Hutchinson's *Original Papers*	331
	b. The Massachusetts charter of 1691; from *Acts and Resolves of the Province of Massachusetts Bay* .	333
111.	Attempts by England at closer control:	
	a. Recommendation of the Board of Trade (1701) that all charter colonies be transformed into royal provinces by act of parliament; from the *North Carolina Colonial Records*	339
	b. The feeling of the colonists (extracts from a pamphlet by John Wise, minister of Ipswich) . .	342
	c. The action of a Boston town meeting relative to a proposed permanent salary for the colonial Governor; from the *Boston Town Records* . .	343
	d. Connecticut's refusal to obey a royal officer commissioned to command her militia (a private letter of Governor Fletcher, describing his repulse); from the *New York Colonial Documents* . . .	347
112.	The commission of a royal governor (from George III to Benning Wentworth); from the *New Hampshire Provincial Papers*	349
113.	Freedom of speech vindicated: the trial of John Peter Zenger for criticising the governor of New York; from Zenger's *Brief Narrative of the Case and Tryall* . . .	352
114.	Franklin's "Albany Plan" for the union of the colonies under the crown:	
	a. An account of the motives for the proposal; from *Franklin's Works*	358
	b. The document; from *New York Colonial Documents*	359

XX. Harsh Phases of Colonial Life

115.	Legal punishments in Virginia: "pillory and ducking stoole" in 1662–1748; from Hening's *Statutes at Large* . .	364

TABLE OF CONTENTS

NUMBER		PAGE
116.	White "servants" (indentured and others) in 1774; from Eddes' *Letters from America*	364
117.	Advertisements for runaway servants; newspaper extracts for the years 1770–1771, from the *New Jersey Archives*	366

D. THE REVOLUTION

XXI. Preliminary Period — to 1774

118.	The Sugar Act of 1764; from the *Statutes of the Realm*	369
119.	The Stamp Act of 1765; *ib.*	373
120.	Reception of the Stamp Act in America:	
	a. Patrick Henry's Resolutions; from the *Journals of the House of Burgesses of Virginia*	374
	b. A Virginia County Association against the Act; *ib.*	375
	c. The stamp distributor for Virginia persuaded to resign (the letter from Governor Fauquier to the Lords of Trade); *ib.*	377
	d. Threat of violence against any who should use stamped paper; a notice in the *New York Gazette* of February 27, 1766; reproduced in the *New Jersey Archives*	380
121.	Origin of the Virginia non-importation agreement:	
	a. Protest of the Burgesses against the proposal of the English government to send Americans to England for trial (May 16, 1769); from the *Journals of the House of Burgesses*	380
	b. The "association" of the ex-Burgesses (May 18, 1769); *ib.*	383
122.	The origin of the Massachusetts town-committees of correspondence; from the *Boston Town Records*	387
123.	The creation of Intercolonial Committees of Correspondence:	
	a. Jefferson's later account; from *Jefferson's Writings*	390
	b. The action of the Virginia House of Burgesses; from the *Journals*	391
	c. Letters from other colonies received by the Virginia Committee, approving the recommendation; *ib.*	392
124.	Intimidation of the owners of tea ships (a Philadelphia handbill by "The Committee for Tarring and Feathering"); from Scharf and Westcott's *History of Philadelphia*	394

XXII. The Rise of Revolutionary Governments

125. The Virginia Burgesses suggest an annual Congress (1774):
    a. Extract from a letter by a member of the Assembly; from Force's *American Archives* . . . 396
    b. Jefferson's account of the plan for declaring a day of prayer and fasting, on receipt by the Burgesses of the news of the Boston Port Bill; from *Jefferson's Works* 397
    c. Resolution of the Burgesses appointing June 1, 1774, a day of prayer and fasting; from the *Journals* . 398
    d. The consequent dissolution of the Assembly by the Governor; *ib.* 399
    e. The ex-Burgesses suggest an annual Continental Congress; *ib.* 399
    f. Letters from the Virginia Committee of Correspondence to the other colonies, conveying Virginia's suggestion for an annual Congress; *ib.* . . 401
    g. The answer of Rhode Island to Virginia, with the appointment of delegates to the proposed Congress; *ib.* 403
126. A "call" for the Continental Congress from the Massachusetts Assembly (June 17) 405
127. A Virginia county (Frederick) suggests a Continental Congress and a "General Association" of the colonies (June 8); from Force's *American Archives* . . . 406
128. Virginia issues the first call for a provincial convention (to elect delegates to the Continental Congress); *ib.*:
    a. Suggestion from the ex-Burgesses, May 30, 1774 . 407
    b. Sample notice of the call by an ex-Burgess to his county (a letter from Thomas Mason of June 16) 408
    c. Typical call (June 27) by a county committee for a county meeting (Norfolk) to instruct delegates to the coming provincial convention 409
129. Typical Instructions by Virginia county meetings:
    a. Westmoreland County 410
    b. George Washington's county (Fairfax) . . . 412
    c. Nansemond County 416

TABLE OF CONTENTS

NUMBER		PAGE
	d. York County	417
	e. Middlesex County (disapproval of the Boston Tea Party)	417
130.	The First Continental Congress:	
	a. The decision upon how the colonies should vote; from John Adams' "Diary" in his *Works*	418
	b. Adams' impressions of the meeting at its close; *ib.*	420
	c. The Declaration of Rights; from Ford's *Journals of the Continental Congress*	421
	d. The Act of Association; *ib.*	427
131.	Typical resolutions by a Virginia county (Prince William) approving the Association of the Continental Congress; from Force's *American Archives*	432
132.	Virginia county conventions become de facto governments (typical action by Fairfax County, organizing a Revolutionary militia (January 17, 1775); *ib.*	433
133.	The Virginia Provincial Convention becomes a government:	
	a. Cumberland County instructs delegates for preparation for war; *ib.*	435
	b. The Second Virginia Convention arms and taxes the colony; *ib.*	436
	c. The Third Convention (June, 1775) assumes the forms of a government; from *Virginia Calendar of State Papers*	442

XXIII. Independence

134.	Charlotte County, Virginia, instructs delegates (April 23, 1776) to the coming Fourth Virginia Convention to favor independence and an independent State constitution; Force's *American Archives*	443
135.	The Virginia Convention, May 15, instructs for independence and adopts resolutions for a bill of rights and a constitution; *ib.*	445
136.	The Virginia Bill of Rights; from Poore's *Charters and Constitutions*	446
137.	Virginia's Declaration of Independence, June 29, 1776; from *Jefferson's Writings*	450

138. Revolutionary State Governments :
    a. The recommendation of Congress of May 15, 1776; from Ford's *Journals of Congress* . . . 452
    b. John Adams' comment; from *John Adams' Letters to Abigail Adams* 453

139. The Maryland Convention instructs its delegates in Congress against independence; from *Proceedings of the Conventions of Maryland* 454

140. Lee's motion for Independence in Congress; from Ford's *Journals* 458

141. The Declaration of Independence of July 4, 1776; from Ford's *Journals of Congress* 459

142. Anti-social tendencies of pre-Revolutionary measures :
    a. The effect of closing the courts (Adams' account of his welcome by his horse-jockey client); from *John Adams' Works* 463
    b. A Tory's protest against mob violence, in a parody on Hamlet's soliloquy; from Moore's *Diary of the American Revolution* 464
    c. Correspondence between a Tory and a Committee, showing how the Tory was induced to sign a recantation; from Niles' *Principles and Acts of the Revolution* 464

143. An oath of allegiance to a new State (Pennsylvania): a facsimile, from Scharf and Westcott's *History of Philadelphia* 466

144. A Loyalist's pretended "diary" of the year 1789 (written in 1778), to show the danger of French conquest; from Tyler's *Literary History of the American Revolution* . 467

145. A statement of how the Revolution set free social forces; from David Ramsey's *History of the American Revolution* . 468

E. CONFEDERATION AND CONSTITUTION

XXIV. The Articles of Confederation

146. Debates in the Congress on the Articles; from *John Adams' Works* 470
147. The Articles; from the *Revised Statutes of the United States* . 475

XXV. The National Domain

148. The desire for Statehood in the West, and Western self-confidence; a statement by a convention of the proposed State of Frankland 485
149. Organization of the Western Territory by Congress:
    a. The Ordinance of 1784; from the *Journals of Congress* 486
    b. The Northwest Ordinance (1787); *ib.* . . . 488

XXVI. Drifting toward Anarchy

150. Gouverneur Morris to John Jay, on the prospect of a military dictator; from Sparks' *Life and Works of Gouverneur Morris* 497
151. Shays' Rebellion:
    a. A statement of grievances by Hampshire County; from Minot's *History of the Insurrection in Massachusetts* 497
    b. Washington's alarm; letters to Henry Lee and to Madison; from *Washington's Writings* . . 500
152. A shrewd foreigner's view of the social conflict over the adoption of a new Constitution (Otto's letter to Vergennes, on the failure of the Annapolis Convention); from the Appendix to Bancroft's *History of the Constitution* . . 502

XXVII. Making the Constitution

153. The call issued by the Annapolis Convention for a Federal Convention; from the *Documentary History of the Constitution* 506
154. Typical credentials of delegates to the Federal Convention (the Georgia credentials); from Farrand's *Records of the Federal Convention* 510
155. George Mason's account of the preliminaries at Philadelphia (a letter to George Mason, Jr., May 20, 1787); *ib.* . . 512
156. The "Virginia Plan"; *ib.* 514
157. George Mason on aristocratic and democratic forces in the Convention at its opening (letter to George Mason, Jr., June 1); *ib.* 517
158. The "New Jersey Plan"; *ib.* 518

NUMBER		PAGE
159.	Hamilton's plan; from *Hamilton's Works*	521
160.	Character sketches of men of the Convention, by William Pierce, a delegate from Georgia; from Farrand's *Records of the Federal Convention*	522
161.	One day in the Convention,— the critical day's debate on the Connecticut Compromise; *ib.*	532

XXVIII. Ratifying the Constitution

162.	George Mason's objections to the Constitution; from Kate Mason Rowland's *Life of George Mason*	543
163.	Mason's explanation of the preparation of his "Objections"; from Farrand's *Records of the Federal Convention*	546
164.	A Federalist account of how John Hancock was induced finally to support the Constitution in the Massachusetts ratifying convention; by Stephen Higginson, in *Writings of Laco*	547
165.	The Federal Constitution	551

INDEX OF SOURCES 576

SUBJECT INDEX 580

A SOURCE BOOK IN AMERICAN HISTORY

I. ENGLAND IN THE SIXTEENTH CENTURY

1. Classes of Englishmen

William Harrison, in Holinshed's *Chronicle* (1577). Cf. No. 75 on like social divisions in early New England; and see *American History and Government*, § 65.

We in England divide our people commonlie into foure sorts, as gentlemen, citizens or burgesses, yeomen, . . . or [and] laborers. Of gentlemen the first and chéefe (next the king) be the prince, dukes, marquesses, earls, viscounts, and barons: and these are called gentlemen of the greater sort, or (as our common usage of spéech is) lords and noblemen: and next unto them be knights, esquiers, and last of all they that are simplie called gentlemen, . . . Who soever studieth the lawes of the realme, who so abideth in the universitie giving his mind to his booke, or professeth physicke and the liberall sciences, or beside his service in the roome of a capteine in the warres, or good counsell given at home, whereby his commonwealth is benefited, can live without manuell labour, and thereto is able and will beare the port, charge, and countenance of a gentleman, he shall for monie have a cote and armes bestowed upon him by heralds (who in the charter of the same doo of custome pretend antiquitie and service, and manie gaie things) and, thereunto being made so good cheape, be called master, which is the title that men give to esquiers and gentlemen, and reputed for a gentleman ever after. . . .

. . . our merchants [are] to be installed, as amongst the citizens (although they often change estate with gentlemen, as gentlemen doo with them, by a mutuall conversion of the one into the other). . . .

Yeomen are . . . free men, borne English, and [who] may dispend of their owne free land in yearelie revenue, to the summe of fortie shillings sterling, or six pounds as monie goeth in our times. . . . This sort of people have a certeine preheminence, and more estimation than labourers and the common sort of artificers, and commonlie live wealthilie, keepe good houses, and travell to get riches. They are also for the most part farmers to gentlemen . . . or at the leastwise artificers, and with grasing, frequenting of markets, and keeping of servants (not idle servants as the gentlemen doo, but such as get both their owne and part of their master's living) do come to great welth, in somuch that manie of them are able and doo buie the lands of unthriftie gentlemen, and often setting their sonnes to the schooles, to the universities, and to the Ins of the court, or otherwise leaving them sufficient lands whereupon they may live without labour, doo make them by those means to become gentlemen. *These were they that in times past made all France afraid.* . . .

The fourth and last sort of people in England are daie labourers, poore husbandmen, and some retailers (which have no frée land) copie holders, and all artificers, — as tailers, shomakers, carpenters, brickmakers, masons, etc. As for slaves and bondmen we have none, naie such is the privilege of our countrie by the especiall grace of God, and bountie of our princes, that if anie come hither from other realms, so soone as they set foot on land they become so free of condition as their masters. . . . This fourth and last sort of people therefore have neither voice nor authoritie in the common wealth, but are to be ruled, and not to rule other; yet they are not altogither neglected, for in cities and corporat townes, for default of yeomen they are faine to make up their inquests [juries] of such maner of people. And in villages they are commonlie made churchwardens, sidemen, aleconners, now and then constables, and manie times injoie the name of hedboroughes. Unto this sort also may our great swarmes of idle serving men be referred, of whome there runneth a proverbe; 'Young serving men, old beggers,' bicause service is none heritage. . . .

A. SOUTHERN COLONIES TO 1660

II. MOTIVES FOR EARLY ENGLISH COLONIZATION

2. From Sir George Peckham's "True Report"

Richard Hakluyt's *Voyages . . . and Discoveries* (1589), III, 167 ff. Peckham was a partner in Gilbert's enterprise. His *Report*, a considerable pamphlet, was written in 1582.

. . . To conclude, since by Christian dutie we stand bound chiefly to further all such acts as do tend to the encreasing the true flock of Christ by reducing into the right way those lost sheepe which are yet astray: And that we shall therein follow the example of our right vertuous predecessors of renowned memorie, and leave unto our posteritie a divine memoriall of so godly an enterprise: Let us, I say, for the considerations alledged, enter into judgement with our selves, whether this action may belong to us or no. . . . Then shal her Majesties dominions be enlarged, her highnesse ancient titles justly confirmed, all odious idlenesse from this our Realme utterly banished, divers decayed townes repaired, and many poor and needy persons relieved, and estates of such as now live in want shall be embettered, the ignorant and barbarous idolaters taught to know Christ, the innocent defended from their bloodie tyrannical neighbours, the diabolicall custome of sacrificing humane creatures abolished. . . .

3. A Discourse on Western Planting by Richard Hakluyt, 1584

Maine Historical Society Collections, Second Series, II (1877).

This pamphlet was written by Hakluyt, an English clergyman and an ardent advocate of American colonization, at Raleigh's request, to influence Queen Elizabeth. It fills 107 pages of the volume of the Maine collections.

CHAPTER I. *That this Westerne discoverie will be greately for thinlargemente of the gospell of Christe, whereunto the princes of the Refourmed Relligion are chefely bounde, amongeste whome her Majestie ys principall.*

* * * * * * *

Nowe the meanes to sende suche as shall labour effectually in this busines ys, by plantinge one or tuoo colonies of our nation upon that fyrme, where they may remaine in safetie, and firste learne the language of the people nere adjoyninge (the gifte of tongues beinge nowe taken awaye), and by little and little acquainte themselves with their manner, and so with discretion and myldeness distill into their purged myndes the swete and lively liquor of the gospel. Otherwise for preachers to come unto them rashly with oute some suche preparation for their safetie, yt were nothinge els but to ronne to their apparaunte and certaine destruction, as yt happened unto those Spanishe ffryers, that, before any plantinge, withoute strengthe and company, landed in Fflorida, where they were miserablye massacred by the savages.

* * * * * * *

Now yf they [Romanists], in their superstition, by means of their plantinge in those partes, have don so greate things in so shorte space, what may wee hope for in our true and syncere relligion, *proposinge unto ourselves in this action not filthie lucre nor vaine ostentation, as they in deede did,* but principally the gayninge of the soules of millions of those wretched people, the reducinge of them from darkenes to lighte, from falsehoodde to truthe, from dombe idolls to the lyvinge God, from the depe pitt of hell to the highest heavens.

* * * * * * *

And this enterprise the princes of the relligion (amonge whome her Majestie ys principall) oughte the rather to take in hande, because the papistes confirme themselves and drawe other to theire side, shewinge that they are the true Catholicke churche because they have bene the onely converters of many millions of infidells to Christianttie. Yea, I myselfe have bene demannded of them, how many infidells have been by us converted? ... Yet in very deede I was not able to name any one infidell by them converted. But God, quoth I, hath his tyme for all men, whoe calleth some at the nynthe, and some at the eleventh houer. And if it please him to move the harte of her Majestie to put her helpinge hande to this godly action, she shall finde as willinge subjectes of all sortes as any other prince in all Christendome.

* * * * * * *

CHAPTER V. *That this voyadge will be a greate bridle to the Indies of the Kinge of Spaine* . . .

* * * * * * *

But the plantinge of tuoo or three stronge fortes upon some goodd havens (whereof there is greate store) betwene Florida and Cape Briton, woulde be a matter in shorte space of greater domage as well to his flete as to his westerne Indies; for wee shoulde not onely often tymes indannger his flete in the returne thereof, but also in fewe yeres put him in hazarde in loosinge some parte of Nova Hispania.

* * * * * * *

Nowe if wee (beinge thereto provoked by Spanishe injuries) woulde either joyne with these savages, or sende or give them armor, as the Spaniardes arme our Irishe rebells, wee shoulde trouble the Kinge of Spaine more in those partes, than he hath or can trouble us in Ireland, and holde him at suche a bay as he was never yet helde at.[1]

---

[1] Sir Philip Sydney urged his countrymen "to check the dangerous and increasing power of Spain and Rome in the New World by planting English protestant settlements there, which will increase until they extend from ocean to ocean." (Brown, *First Republic*, 1, 2.)

4. Drayton's Ode to the Virginian Voyage

This poem was written by Michael Drayton in 1606, in honor of the proposed Virginian voyage that founded Jamestown. The complete Ode contains twelve stanzas, as printed in Drayton's *Poems* in 1619. It is reprinted in full in Brown's *Genesis of the United States*, I, 86-87.

* * * * *

You brave heroique minds,
Worthy your countries name,
That honour still pursue,
Goe, and subdue,
Whilst loyt'ring hinds
Lurk here at home with shame.

* * * * *

And cheerefully at sea,
Successe you still intice,
To get the pearle and gold,
And ours to hold,
Virginia,
Earth's only Paradise.

* * * * *

And in regions farre,
Such heroes bring yee forth
As those from whom we came;
And plant our name
Under that starre
Not knowne unto our north.

5. Goodspeed to Virginia, 1609

This pamphlet (by Robert Gray) contains about 9000 words. It was never printed. Extracts are given in Brown's *Genesis of the United States*, 293 ff. It was written to encourage the reorganization of the Virginia Company in 1609. (Cf. *American History and Government*, § 25.) The first of the extracts below comes from the "Epistle Dedicatory."

To the Right Noble and Honorable Earles, Barons, and Lords, and to the Right Worshipfull Knights, Merchants, and Gentlemen,

Adventurers for the plantation of Virginea, all happie and prosperous successe, which may either augment your glorie, or increase your wealth, or purchase your eternitie.

Time . . . consumes both man and his memorie. It is not brasse nor marble that can perpetuate immortalitie of name upon the earth. [But] A right sure foundation . . . have you (My Lords and the rest of the most Worthie Adventurers for Virginia) laid for the immortalitie of your names and memorie, which, for the advancement of Gods glorie, the renowne of his Majestie, and the good of your Countrey, have undertaken so honourable a project, as all posterities shall blesse: and Uphold your names and memories so long as the Sunne and Moone endureth: Whereas they which preferre their money before vertue, their pleasure before honour, and their sensuall securitie before heroicall adventures, shall perish with their money, die with their pleasures, and be buried in everlasting forgetfulnes. . . .

And therefore we may justly say, as the children of Israel say here to Joshua, we are a great people, and the lande is too narrow for us; so that whatsoever we have beene, now it behooves us to be both prudent and politicke, and not to deride and reject good powers of profitable and gainefull expectation; but rather to embrace every occasion which hath any probabilitie in its future hopes: And seeing there is neither preferment nor employment for all within the lists of our Countrey, we might justly be accounted as in former times, both imprudent and improvident, if we will yet sit with our armes foulded on our bosomes, and not rather seeke after such adventers whereby the Glory of God may be advanced, the teritories of our Kingdome inlarged, our people both preferred and employed abroad, our wants supplyed at home, His Majesties customes wonderfully augmented, and the honour and renown of our Nation spread and propagated to the ends of the World. . . .

The report goeth, that in Virginia the people are savage and incredibly rude, they worship the divell, offer their young children in sacrifice unto him, wander up and downe like beasts, and in manners and conditions, differ very little from beasts, having no Art, nor science, nor trade, to imploy themselves, or give themselves unto, yet by nature loving and gentle, and desirous to imbrace a better condition. Oh how happy were that man which could reduce this people from brutishness to civilitie, to religion, to Christianitie, to the saving of their souls. . . .

Farre be it from the hearts of the English, they should give any cause to the world to say that they sought the wealth of that Countrie above or before the glorie of God, and the propagation of his Kingdome.

Their second objection is [the argument of opponents of colonization] that this age will see no profit of this plantation. Which objection admit it were true, yet it is too brutish, and bewraies their neglect and incurious respect of posteritie: we are not borne like beasts for ourselves, and the time present only. . . . What benefit or comfort should we have enjoyed in things of this world, if our forefathers had not provided better for us, and bin more carefully respective of posteritie than for themselves? We sow, we set, we build, not so much for ourselves as for posteritie; . . . They which onely are for themselves, shall die in themselves, and shall not have a name among posterity; their rootes shall be dried up beneath, and above shall their branches bee cut down, their remembrance shall perish from the earth, and they shall have no name in the street. Job xviii; 16, 17.

Others object to the continuall charges [assessments] which will prove in their opinion very heavie and burdensome to those that shall undertake the said Plantation. These like the dog in the manger, neither eate hay themselves, neither will they suffer the Oxe that would. They never think any charge too much that may any way increase their owne private estate. They have thousands to bestow about the ingrossing of a commoditie, or upon a morgage, or to take their neighbors house over his head, or to lend upon usurie; but if it come to a publicke good, they grone under the least burden of charges that can bee required of them. *These men should be used like sponges; they must be squeased, seeing they drink up all,* and will yeeld to nothing, though it concerne the common good never so greatly. But it is demonstratively prooved in Nova Britannia, that the charges about this Plantation will be nothing, in comparison of the benefit that will grow thereof. And what notable thing I pray you can be brought to passe without charges? . . . *Without question, he that saves his money*, where Gods glory is to be advanced, Christian religion propagated and planted, the good of the commonwealth increased, and the glorious renowne of the King inlarged is subject to the curse of Simon Magus, *his money and he are in danger to perish together.* Let none therefore find delaies, or faine excuses to withhold them from this imployment for Virginia, seeing every opposition against it is an opposition against God, the King, the Church, and the Commonwealth. . . .

6. Nova Britannia, 1609

Peter Force's *Historical Tracts*, I (Washington, 1836).
This tract of some 12,000 words (equivalent to thirty-five pages of this volume) was written in 1609 for the same purpose as No. 5 above.

So I wish and intreat all well affected subjects, some in their persons, others in their purses, cheerefully to adventure, and joyntly take in hand this high and acceptable worke, tending to advance and spread the kingdome of God, and the knowledge of the truth, among so many millions of men and women, Savage and blind, that never yet saw the true light shine before their eyes . . . as also for the honor of our King, and enlarging of his kingdome, and for preservation and defence of that small number our friends and countrimen already planted, least for want of more supplies we become a scorne to the world, subjecting our former adventures to apparent spoile and hazard, and our people (as a prey) to be sackt and puld out of possession, as were the French out of *Nova Francia*, not many yeares ago; and, *which is the lest and last respect* (yet usuallie preferred), for the singular good and benefite that will undoubtedly arise to this whole nation, and to everie one of us in particular, that will adventure therein.

It is knowne to the world [reference to attempts of Raleigh and Gilbert] how the present generation, scorning to sit downe by their losses, made newe attempts, not induring to looke on whilst so huge and spacious countries (the fourth part of the world) and the greatest and wealthiest part of all the rest, should remain a wilderness, subject (for the most part) but to wild beasts and fowles of the ayre, and to savage people, which have no Christian nor civill use of any thing; and that the subjects onely of one Prince *Christian* [Spaniards], which but within the memorie of man began first to creepe upon the face of those Territories, and now by meanes of their remnants settled here and there, do therefore imagine the world to be theirs, shouldring out all other nations, accounting themselves Kings and Commanders, not onely in townes and places where they have planted, but over all other partes of *America*, which containe sundrie vast and barbarous Regions, many of which (to this day) they never knew, nor did ever setle foote therein: which notwithstanding, if it were yeelded them as due, yet their strength and meanes, farre inferiour to their aspires, will never stretch to compasse . . . the hundredth part.

But seeing we so passed by their dwellings, that in seating ourselves, wee sought not to unsettle them, but by Gods mercy, after many stormes, were brought to the Coast of another countrie, farre distant and remote from their habitations: why should any frowne or envie at it; or if they doe, why should wee (neglecting so faire an opportunitie) faint or feare to enlarge our selves? Where is our force and aunciant vigour? Doth our late reputation sleepe in the dust? No, no, let not the world deceive it selfe; we still remaine the same, and upon just occasion given, we shall quickly shew it too:

. . . But wee must beware that . . . that bitter root of greedy gaine be not so settled in our harts, that béeing in a golden dreame, if it fall not out presently to our expectation, we slinke away with discontent, and draw our purses from the charge. If any shew this affection, I would wish his baseness of minde to be noted. What must be our direction then? No more but this: if thou dost once approve the worke, lay thy hand to it cheerfully, and withdraw it not till thy taske bee done. In all assayes and new supplies of money be not lagge, nor like a dull horse thats alwaies in the lash; for héere lies the poison of all good attempts, when as men without halling and pulling, will not be drawne to performance, for by this, others are discouraged, the action lies undone, and the first expence is lost: But are wee to looke for no gaine in the lewe of all adventures? Yes undoubtedly, there is assured hope of gaine, as I will shew anon in due place; *but look it be not chiefe in your thoughts.* God, that hath said by *Solomon: Cast thy bread upon the waters, and after many daies thou shalt find it:* he will give the blessing.

. . . Two things are especially required herein, *people* to make the plantation, and *money* to furnish our present provisions and shippings now in hand: For the first, wee neede not doubt, our land abounding with swarmes of idle persons, which having no meanes of labour to reléeve their misery, doe likewise swarme in lewd and naughtie practises, so that if we seeke not some waies for their forreine employment, wee must provide shortly more prisons and corrections for their bad conditions, for it fares with populous common weales as with plants and trees that bee too frolicke, which not able to sustaine and feede their multitude of branches, doe admit an engrafting of their buds and sciences into some other soile, accounting it a benefite for preservation of their kind, and a disburdening their stocke of those superfluous twigs that suck away their nourishment.

7. Statement of the Virginia Company, 1609

Brown's *Genesis of the United States*, I, 377 ff. This is one of the pamphlets put forth by the Company to stimulate stock subscription and emigration. As to the motives set forth in it, and in Nos. 2–6 above, cf. *American History and Government*, § 17.

A True and Sincere Declaration of the Purposes and Ends of the Plantation in Virginia. By Authority of the Governor and Councillors, December 14, 1609.[1]

... If all these be yet too weake to confirm the doubtfull, or awake the drousie, then let us come nearer, and arise from their *reasons* and *affections* to their *soules* and *consciences:* remember that what was at first but of *conveniency*, and for *Honour* is now become a case of *necessity* and *piety:* let them consider, that they have promised to adventure and not performed it; that they have encouraged and exposed many of *Honorable* birth, and which is of more consequence 600 of our *Bretheren* by our common mother the *Church*, Christians of one *Faith* and one *Baptisme*, to a miserable and inevitable death. Let not any man flatter himself, that it concernes not him, for he that forsakes whome he may safely releeve, is as guilty of his death as he that can swim, and forsakes himself by refusing, is of his owne. Let every man look inward, and disperse that cloud of avarice, which darkeneth his spiritual sight and he will finde there that when he shall appear before the *Tribunall of Heaven*, it shall be questioned him what he hath done? Hath he fed and clothed the hungry and naked? It shall be required, what he hath done for the advancement of that Gospell which hath saved him; and for the releefe of his makers Image, whome he was bound to save: O let there be a vertuous *emulation* betweene us and the *Church* of *Rome*, in her owne *Glory*, and *Treasury of Good Workes!* And let us turn all our contentions upon the common enemy of the *Name* of Christ. How farre hath *she* sent out her *Apostles* and thorough how *glorious dangers?* How is it become a marke of Honor to her Faith, to have converted Nations, and an obloquie cast upon us, that we, having the better Vine, should have worse dressers and husbanders of it? ...

---

[1] Nos. 5–7 are taken from the voluminous literature of like character in *one* year, in order to make more vivid the amount available.

APPENDIX. — To render a more particular satisfaction and account. . . . And to avoyde both the scandall and peril of accepting idle and wicked persons; such as shame or fear compels into this action (and such as are the weedes and ranknesse of this land; who, being the surfet of an able, healthy, and composed body must needes be the poison of one so tender, feeble, and as yet unformed); And to divulge and declare to all men, what kinde of persons, as well for their religion and conversations, as Faculties, Arts and Trades, we propose to accept of: — We have thought it convenient to pronounce that for the first provision, we will receive no man that cannot bring or render some good testimony of his religion to God, and civil manners and behaviour to his neighbor with whom he hath lived; And for the second, we have set downe in a Table annexed, the proportion, and number we will entertaine in every necessary Arte, upon proofe and assurance that every man shall be able to performe that which he doth undertake, whereby such as are requisite to us may have knowledge and preparation to offer themselves. And we shall be ready to give honest entertainment and content, and to recompence with extraordinary reward, every fit and industrious person respectively *to his Paines and quality.*

The Table of such as are required to This *Plantation.*

Foure honest and learned Ministers.
2. Surgeons.
2. Druggists.
10. Iron men for the Furnace and Hammer.

2. Armorers.
2. Joyners.
2. Sope-ashe men.
6. Ship-wrights.
2. Planters of Sugar-Cane.
2. Pearle Drillers.
2. Brewers.
6. Fowlers.

2. Salt-makers.
6. Coopers.
2. Coller-makers for draught.
2. Plow-wrights.
4. Rope-makers.
6. Vine-dressers.

2. Presse-makers.
6. Blacksmiths.
6. Carpenters.
2. Minerall men.
2. Silke-dressers.
2. Bakers.
2. Tile-makers.
10. Fishermen.

2. Gun-Founders.
10. Sawyers.
4. Pitch Boylers.
6. Gardeners.
4. Turners.
4. Brickmakers.
2. Colliers.
4. Sturgeon dressers.

8. Marston's "Eastward Hoe"

Marston published this play in 1605 to caricature the intended Virginian colonization. The name is a survival of the idea that Columbus had found the East. In the extract, the mate, Sea Gull, at a tavern meeting, is persuading some young blades to embark for the venture.

* * * * * * *

Sea Gull. Come boyes, Virginia longs till we share the rest of her . . .

Spendall. Why, is she inhabited alreadie with any English?

Sea Gull. A whole countrie of English is there, men bread of those that were left there in '79 [Ralegh's colony of '87 is meant]; they have married with the Indians . . . [who] are so in love with them that all the treasure they have they lay at their feete.

Scape Thrift. But is there such treasure there, Captaine . . . ?

Sea Gull. I tell thee, golde is more plentifull there then copper is with us; and for as much redde copper as I can bring, Ile have thrise the waight in gold. Why, man, all their dripping pans . . . are pure gould; and all the chaines with which they chaine up their streets are massie gold; all the prisoners they take are fettered in gold; and for rubies and diamonds they goe forth on holydayes and gather 'em by the seashore to hang on their childrens coates, and sticke in their children's caps, as commonly as our children wear saffron-gilt brooches. . . . Besides, there wee shall have no more law than consceince, and not too much of eyther.

* * * * * * *

9. Crashaw's "Daily Prayer"

Force's *Historical Tracts*, III (1844), page 67.

The ardent clerical advocates of expansion, like Hakluyt and Crashaw, resented bitterly such "jests of prophane players" as No. 8 above; and Crashaw retorted by this passage in his form for "A Prayer duly said [at Jamestown] Morning and Evening . . . either by the Captaine of the watch himselfe, or by some one of his principall officers." This form was drawn up in 1609, before Delaware's expedition, and was incorporated afterward in Dale's Code of Laws. The prayer would fill some twelve pages of this volume.

And whereas we have by undertaking this plantation undergone the reproofs of a base world, insomuch that many of our oune brethren laugh us to scorne, O Lord, we pray thee fortifie us against this temptation. Let . . . Papists and *players* and such other . . . scum and dregs of the earth, let them mocke such as helpe to build up the wals of Jerusalem, and they that be filthy, let them be filthy still; and let such swine still wallow in their mire. . . .

10. Crashaw's Sermon, March 3/13, 1609/10

Brown's *Genesis of the United States*, page 360 ff.
This sermon was preached before Lord Delaware's Expedition, on the point of departure. The extract below was intended especially to refute such insinuations as those in No. 8. Cf. also the introduction to No. 9.

Text (*Luke 22–32*). "*But I have praied for thee that thy faith faile not: therefore when thou art converted, strengthen thy brethren.*"

Oh but those that goe in person are rakte up out of the refuse, and are a number of disordered men, unfit to bring to passe any good action: So indeed say those **that lie and slander.** But I answer for the generalitie of them that goe, they be such as offer themselves voluntarily . . . and be like (for ought that I see) to those [that] are left behind,—men of all sorts, better and worse. But for manie that go in person, let these objectors know, they be as good as themselves, and it may be, many degrees better. . . .

This enterprise hath only three enemies. 1. The Divell, 2. The Papists, and 3. The Players. [Then, after paying respects to the first two] As for Plaiers: (pardon me, right Honorable and beloved, for wronging this place and your patience with so base a subject) they play with Princes and Potentates, Magistrates, and Ministers, nay, with God and Religion, and all holy things: nothing that is good, excellent, or holy can escape them: how then can this action? But this may suffice, that they are *Players*. They abuse Virginia, but they are but *Players:* they disgrace it: true, but they are but *Players*. . . . The divell hates us, because wee purpose not to suffer Heathens; and the Pope, because we have vowed to tolerate no Papists. [Cf. Charter of 1609.] So doe the Players, because wee resolve to suffer no Idle persons in Virginea, which course, if it were taken in England, they know *they* might turn to new occupations.

11. Sir Edwin Sandys, 1612

Neill's *Virginia and Virginiola* (1878), page 44.

Sandys, then a member of the Council of the London Company, wrote to delinquent stockholders, urging the payment of subscriptions (April 8/18, 1612).

. . . presuming greatly of your affectionate Redines to aid . . . so worthy an Enterprise, tending so greatly to the Enlargement of the Christian Truth, the Honour of our Nation, and Benefit of the English People. . . .

12. Governor Dale to the London Company, 1613

Records of the Virginia Company of London (edited by Susan Kingsbury; Washington, 1906), II, 399-400.

Sir Thomas Dale wrote the following exhortation to Sir Thomas Smith, "Treasurer" of the Company, on June 13/23, 1613. This extract was read ten years later in a meeting of the Company.

Lett me tell you all at home this one thinge, and I pray remember it, — if you give over this Country and loose it, you with your wisedomes will leape such a gugion as our state hath not done the like since they lost the Kingdome of ffraunce: be not gulled with the clamorous reports of base people . . . if the glory of god hath noe power with them, and the conversion of these poore Infidells, yet lett the rich Mammon's desires egge them on to inhabite these Countries. I protest unto you by the faith of an honest man, the more I range the Country, the more I admire it. I have seene the best Countries in Europe. I protest unto you before the Living God, put them altogether, this Country will be equivalent unto them if it be inhabited with good people.

[The *Records* continue, that, when this letter had been read, two members added that they had heard Dale say " that in his judgment out of foure of the best Kingdomes in Europe there could not be picked out soe much good ground as was in Virginia."]

13. The London Company not Mercenary

From Captain John Smith's *Generall Historie of Virginia* (Birmingham edition of the *Works*, 1884, page 527). The passage was published in 1616, when Smith was at odds with the Company; but he defends that body gallantly against unjust charges.

This deare bought Land, with so much bloud and cost, hath onely made some few rich, and all the rest losers [which fate, however, does not deter their efforts, Smith explains] . . . For the Nobilitie and Gentrie, there is scarce any of them expects anything but the prosperitie of the Action [success of the colony]; and there are some Merchants . . . I am confidently persuaded, doe take more care and paines, nay, and at their continuall great charge, than they could be hired to for the love of money; so honestly regarding the generall good of this great Worke, they would hold it worse than sacrilege to wrong it but a shillinge.

14. John Smith's Last Plea for Colonization, 1631

Captain John Smith's *Works* (Birmingham edition), 935, 962.

. . . and what hath ever beene the worke of the best great Princes of the world, but planting of Countries, and civilizing barbarous and inhumane Nations to civility and humanity; whose eternall actions fils our histories with more honour than those that have wasted and consumed them by warres.

. . . the *Portugals* and *Spaniards* that first began plantations in this unknowne world of *America* [their "everlasting actions"] will testifie our idlenesse and ingratitude to all posterity, and neglect of our duty and religion we owe our

God, our King, and Countrey. . . . Having as much power and meanes as others, why should English men despaire, and not doe as much as any ? . . . Seeing honour is our lives ambition, and our ambition after death to have an honourable memory of our life . . . let us imitate their vertues, to be worthily their successors.

* * * * * * *

I speak not this to discourage any with vaine feares, but could wish every English man to carry alwaies this Motto in his heart,— Why should the brave Spanish Souldiers brag, The Sunne never sets in the Spanish dominions, but ever shineth on one part or other we have conquered for our King: . . . but to animate us to doe the like for ours, who is no way his inferior.

And truly there is no pleasure comparable to a generous spirit as good imploiment in noble actions, especially amongst Turks, Heathens, and Infidels; to see daily new Countries, people, fashions, governments, stratagems; releeve the oppressed, comfort his friends, passe miseries, subdue enemies, adventure upon any feazable danger for God and his Country.

[The fine, idealistic motives of colonization, which have been treated in this Division (Nos. 2-14), are touched upon in many other documents. See especially the missionary purpose in No. 26 c, below.]

III. ILLUSTRATIVE OF VIRGINIA HISTORY TO THE INTRODUCTION OF SELF-GOVERNMENT (1606–1619)

15. The Gilbert and Raleigh Charters

Queen Elizabeth's charter to Sir Humphrey Gilbert (June, 1578) was first printed in Hakluyt's *Voyages . . . and Discoveries of the English Nation* (1589). The Goldsmid edition of Hakluyt gives it, I, 360 ff. After Gilbert's death, Elizabeth reissued the charter to Sir Walter Raleigh (1584), with changes only in names and date. The Raleigh grant is easily accessible in Poore's *Charters and Constitutions*, under the head of North Carolina, or in Thorpe's *American Charters and Constitutions*.

The Letters Patents *graunted by her Maiestie to Sir Humfrey Gilbert, knight, for the inhabiting and planting of our people in America.*

I. — Elizabeth by the grace of God Queene of England, . . . To all people to whom these presents shall come, greeting. Know ye that . . . we . . . by these presents . . . do give and graunt to our trustie and welbeloved servant Sir Humfrey Gilbert of Compton, in our Countie of Devonshire knight, and to his heires and assignes for ever, free libertie and licence from time to time and at all times for ever hereafter, to discover, . . . remote, heathen and barbarous lands . . . not actually possessed of any Christian prince or people . . . and the same to have, hold, occupie and enjoy to him, his heires and assignes for ever, with all commodities, jurisdictions, and royalties both by sea and land: . . . And wee doe likewise by these presents . . . give full authoritie and power to the saide Sir Humfrey, his heires and assignes, . . . that hee and they . . . shall and may at all and every time and times hereafter, have, take, and lead in the same voyages, to travell thitherward, and to inhabite there . . . so many of our subjects as shall willingly accompany him . . . with sufficient shipping, and furniture for their transportations, — so that none of the same persons . . . be such as hereafter shall be specially restrained by us, . . . And further, that he, the said Humfrey, his heires and assignes . . . shall have, hold, occupy, and enjoy for ever, all the soyle of all such lands, countries, and territories so to be discovered or possessed as aforesaid, and of all Cities, Townes, and Villages, and places, in the same, with rites, royalties and jurisdictions, as well marine as other, within the sayd lands or countreys . . . with ful power to dispose thereof, and of every part thereof, in fee simple or otherwise, according to the order of the laws of England, as nere as the same conveniently may be, paying unto us, for all services, dueties and demaunds, the fift part of all the oare of gold and silver, that from time to time, . . . shall be there gotten; all which lands, countreys, and territories, shall for ever bee holden by the sayd Sir Humfrey, his heires and assignes of us, our heires and successours by homage, and by the sayd payment of the sayd fift part before reserved onely, for all services.

II. — And moreover, we doe by those presents . . . give and graunt licence to the sayde Sir Humfrey Gilbert, his heires or assignes . . . that hee and they . . . shall and may from time to time and all times for ever hereafter, for his and their defence, encounter, expulse, repell, and resist, as well by Sea, as by land, and by all other wayes whatsoever, all, and every such person and persons whatsoever, as *without the speciall licence and liking* of the sayd Sir Humfrey, and of his heires and assignes, shall attempt to inhabite within the sayd countreys, . . . or that shall enterprise or attempt at any time hereafter unlawfully to annoy either by Sea or land, the said sir Humfrey, his heires and assignes, or any of them:

III. — . . . And wee doe graunt to . . . all . . . persons, being of our allegiance, whose names shall be noted or entred in some of our courts of Record, within this our Realme of England, and that with the assent of the said sir Humfrey, his heires or assignes, shall travel to such lands, . . . and to their heires : that **they and every or any of them, . . . shall, and may have, and enjoy all privileges of free denizens and persons native of England, and within our allegiance: any law, custome, or usage to the contrary notwithstanding.**

IV. — And forasmuch as upon the finding out, discovering and inhabiting of such remote lands, countreys and territories, as aforesayd, it shall be necessarie for the safetie of all men that shall adventure themselves in those journeys and voiages, to determine to live together in Christian peace and civill quietnesse each with other, whereby every one may with more pleasure and profit enjoy that whereunto they shall attaine with great paine and perill: wee, for us, our heires and successours, are likewise pleased and contented, and by these presents do give and graunt to the sayd sir Humfrey and his heires and assignes for ever, that he and they, and every or any of them, shall and may from time to time for ever here after within the sayd mentioned remote lands and countreys, and in the way by the Seas thither, and from thence, have full and meere power and authoritie to correct, punish, pardon, govern and rule by their, and every or any of their good discretions and pollicies, as well in causes capitall or criminall, as civill, both marine and other, all such our subjects and others, as shall from time to time hereafter adventure themselves in the sayd journeys or voyages . . . or that shall at any time hereafter inhabite any such lands, countreys or territories as aforesayd, . . . according to such statutes, lawes and ordinances, as shall be by him the said sir Humfrey, his heires and assignes, or every or any of them, devised or established for the better government of the said people as aforesayd: so alwayes that the sayd statutes, lawes, and ordinances may be, as neere as conveniently may, agreeable to the forme of the lawes and pollicy of England : and also, that they be not against the true Christian faith or religion now professed in the church of England, nor in any wise to withdraw any of the subjects or people of those lands or places from the allegiance

FIRST CHARTER FOR COLONIZING VIRGINIA

of us, our heires or successours, as their immediate Soveraignes under God. . . .

Hints for Study. — 1. Observe that no exact district is granted; why? 2. Note the power of the proprietor: (*a*) to regulate settlement; (*b*) to repel invasion; (*c*) to administer the government; (*d*) to make laws. 3. Note the guarantee of rights to the settlers; could it have been meant to cover the "right to vote," when taken in connection with the rest of the charter? 4. What church is established for the colony? Read and criticise Fiske's amazing misstatement in *Old Virginia*, I, 31, regarding this charter.

16. First Charter for Colonizing Virginia; April 10/20,[1] 1606

This charter was first printed by Stith in his *History of Virginia* (1747). Stith compiled carefully the four manuscript copies discoverable by him, and his text is usually followed. The text here given is taken from his work (Sabin's Edition, 1865). For secondary accounts, see *American History and Government*, § 22, and references for the same.

I. — JAMES, by the grace of God, King of England, Scotland . . . etc. **Whereas** our loving and well-disposed Subjects, Sir *Thomas Gates*, and Sir *George Somers*, Knights, *Richard Hackluit*, Clerk, Prebendary of *Westminster*, and *Edward-Maria Wingfield*, *Thomas Hanham*, and *Ralegh Gilbert*, Esqrs., *William Parker*, and *George Popham*, Gentlemen, and divers others of our loving Subjects, have been humble Suitors unto us, that We would vouchsafe unto them our Licence to make Habitation, Plantation, and to deduce a Colony of sundry of our People into that Part of *America*, commonly called VIRGINIA, . . . situate, lying, and being all along the Sea Coasts, between four and thirty Degrees of *Northerly* Latitude from the Equinoctial Line, and five and forty Degrees of the same Latitude, . . .

II. — AND to that End, and for the more speedy Accomplishment of their said intended Plantation and Habitation there, are desirous to divide themselves into two several Colonies and Companies; The one consisting of certain Knights, Gentlemen, Merchants, and other Adventurers, of our City of *London* and

---

[1] See explanation of this form on page 44.

elsewhere, . . . which do desire to begin their Plantation and Habitation in some fit and convenient Place, between four and thirty and one and forty Degrees of the said Latitude, alongst the Coasts of *Virginia* and Coasts of *America* aforesaid ; And the other consisting of sundry Knights, Gentlemen, Merchants, and other Adventurers, of our Cities of *Bristol* and *Exeter*, and of our Town of *Plimouth*, and of other Places, . . . which do desire to begin their Plantation and Habitation in some fit and convenient Place, between eight and thirty Degrees and five and forty Degrees of the said Latitude, . . .

III. — WE, greatly commending and graciously accepting of their Desires for the Furtherance of so noble a Work, which may, by the Providence of Almighty God, hereafter tend to the Glory of his Divine Majesty, in propagating of *Christian* Religion to such People, as yet live in Darkness and miserable Ignorance of the true Knowledge and Worship of God, and may in time bring the Infidels and Savages living in those Parts to human Civility, and to a settled and quiet Government; DO, by these our Letters Patents, graciously accept of, and agree to, their humble and well-intended Desires;

IV. — AND do therefore, for Us, our Heirs, and Successors, GRANT and agree, that the said Sir *Thomas Gates*, Sir *George Somers*, *Richard Hackluit*, and *Edward-Maria Wingfield*, Adventurers of and for our City of *London*, and all such others, as are, or shall be, joined unto them of that Colony, shall be called the *first Colony;* And they shall and may begin their said first Plantation and Habitation, at any Place upon the said Coast of *Virginia* or *America*, where they shall think fit and convenient between the said four-and-thirty and one-and-forty Degrees of the said Latitude; And that they shall have all the Lands, Woods, Soil, Grounds, Havens, Ports, Rivers, Mines, Minerals, Marshes, Waters, Fishings, Commodities, and Hereditaments, whatsoever, from the said first Seat of their Plantation and Habitation by the Space of fifty Miles of *English* Statute Measure, all along the said Coast of *Virginia* and *America*, towards the *West* and *Southwest*, as the Coast lyeth, with all the Islands within one hundred Miles directly over against the same Sea Coast; And also all the Lands, Soil, Grounds, [etc.] . . . from the said Place of their first Plantation and Habitation for the space of fifty like *English* Miles, . . . towards the *East* and *Northeast*, or towards the *North*, as the Coast lyeth, together with all the Islands within one hundred Miles, directly over against the said Sea Coast; And also all the Lands, Woods, Soil, Grounds, [etc.] . . . from the same fifty Miles every way on the Sea Coast, directly into the main Land by the Space of one hundred like *English* Miles; And shall and may inhabit and remain there; and shall and may also build and fortify within any the same, for their better Safeguard and Defence, according to their best Discretion, and the Discretion of the Council of that Colony. . . .

V. — AND we do likewise, for Us, our Heirs, and Successors, by these Presents, GRANT and agree, that the said *Thomas Hanham*, and *Ralegh Gilbert, William Parker*, and *George Popham*, and all others of the Town of *Plimouth* in the County of *Devon*, or elsewhere, which are, or shall be, joined unto them of that Colony, shall be called the *second Colony;* And that they shall and may begin their said Plantation and Seat of their first Abode and Habitation, at any Place upon the said Coast of *Virginia* and *America*, where they shall think fit and convenient, between eight and thirty Degrees of the said Latitude, and five and forty Degrees of the same Latitude; And that they shall have all the Lands [Here follows a passage duplicating the corresponding part of section IV for the other subcompany.]

VI. — PROVIDED always . . . that the Plantation and Habitation of such of the said Colonies as shall last plant themselves, as aforesaid, shall not be made within one hundred like English miles of the other of them that first began to make their Plantation, as aforesaid.

VII. — AND we do also ordain, establish, and agree, for Us, our Heirs, and Successors, that each of the said Colonies shall have a Council, which shall govern and order all Matters and

Causes, which shall arise, grow, or happen, to or within the same several Colonies, according to such Laws, Ordinances, and Instructions, as shall be, in that behalf, given and signed with Our Hand or Sign Manual, and pass under the Privy Seal of our Realm of *England;* Each of which Councils shall consist of thirteen Persons, to be ordained, made, and removed, from time to time, according as shall be directed and comprised in the same instructions. [Provision for "seals" for the councils.]

VIII. — AND that also there shall be a Council established here in *England,* which shall, in like Manner, consist of thirteen Persons, to be, for that Purpose, appointed by Us, our Heirs and Successors, which shall be called our *Council of Virginia;* And shall, from time to time, have the superior Managing and Direction, only of and for all Matters, that shall or may concern the Government, as well of the said several Colonies, as of and for any other Part or Place within the aforesaid Precincts of four and thirty and five and forty Degrees, abovementioned [Provision for a seal.]

IX. — [Grant of right to mine for precious metals, yielding to the monarch the fifth part of gold and silver and the fifteenth part of copper.]

X. — [Right to coin money in the colonies.]

XI. — AND we do likewise, for Us, our Heirs, and Successors, by these Presents, give full Power and Authority to the said Sir *Thomas Gates,* Sir *George Somers, Richard Hackluit, Edward-Maria Wingfield, Thomas Hanham, Ralegh Gilbert, William Parker,* and *George Popham,* and to every of them, and to the said several Companies, Plantations, and Colonies, that they, and every of them, shall and may, at all and every time and times hereafter, have, take, and lead in the said Voyage, and for and towards the said several Plantations and Colonies, and to travel thitherward, and to abide and inhabit there in every the said Colonies and Plantations, such and so many of our Subjects, as shall willingly accompany them, or any of them, in the said Voyages and Plantations; . . .

FIRST CHARTER FOR COLONIZING VIRGINIA

PROVIDED always that none of the said Persons be such as shall hereafter be specially restrained by Us, our Heirs, or Successors.

XII. — MOREOVER, we do, by these Presents, for Us, our Heirs, and Successors, GIVE AND GRANT Licence unto the said Sir *Thomas Gates*, Sir *George Somers*, *Richard Hackluit*, *Edward-Maria Wingfield*, *Thomas Hanham*, *Ralegh Gilbert*, *William Parker*, and *George Popham*, and to every of the said Colonies, that they, and every of them, shall and may, from time to time, and at all times for ever hereafter, for their several Defences, encounter, expulse, repel, and resist, as well by Sea as by Land, by all Ways and Means whatsoever, all and every such Person and Persons, as without the especial Licence of the said several Colonies and Plantations, shall attempt to inhabit within the said several Precincts and Limits of the said several Colonies and Plantations, or any of them, or that shall enterprise or attempt, at any time hereafter, the Hurt, Detriment, or Annoyance, of the said several Colonies or Plantations:

XIII. — [A peculiarly obscure section, which provides that the governing bodies in the colonies may collect tariffs on imported goods, — 2½ per cent on English goods and 5 per cent on foreign goods; the proceeds to go to the proprietary Companies for 21 years, and afterward to the crown.]

XIV. — AND we do further, by these Presents, for Us, our Heirs, and Successors, GIVE AND GRANT unto the said Sir *Thomas Gates*, Sir *George Somers*, *Richard Hackluit*, and *Edward-Maria Wingfield*, and to their Associates of the said first Colony and Plantation, and to the said *Thomas Hanham*, *Ralegh Gilbert*, *William Parker*, and *George Popham*, and their Associates of the said second Colony and Plantation, that they, and every of them, by their Deputies, Ministers, and Factors, may transport the Goods, Chattels, Armour, Munition, and Furniture, needful to be used by them, for their said Apparel, Food, Defence, or otherwise in Respect of the said Plantations, out of our Realms of *England* and *Ireland*, and all other our

Dominions, from time to time, for and during the Time of seven Years, next ensuing the Date hereof, for the better Relief of the said several Colonies and Plantations, without any Custom, Subsidy, or other Duty, unto Us, our Heirs, or Successors, to be yielded or paid for the same.

XV. — ALSO we do, for Us, our Heirs, and Successors, DECLARE, by these Presents, that all and every the Persons, being our Subjects, which shall dwell and inhabit within every or any of the said several Colonies and Plantations, and every of their children, which shall happen to be born within any of the Limits and Precincts of the said several Colonies and Plantations, shall HAVE and enjoy all Liberties, Franchises, and Immunities, within any of our other Dominions, to all Intents and Purposes, as if they had been abiding and born within this our Realm of *England,* or any other of our said Dominions.[1]

XVI. — MOREOVER, our gracious Will and Pleasure is, and we do, by these Presents, for Us, our Heirs, and Successors, declare and set forth, that if any Person or Persons, which shall be of any of the said Colonies and Plantations, or any other, which shall traffick to the said Colonies and Plantations, or any of them, shall, at any time or times hereafter, transport any Wares, Merchandises, or Commodities, out of any our Dominions, with a Pretence to land, sell, or otherwise dispose of the same, within any the Limits and Precincts of any the said Colonies and Plantations, and yet nevertheless, being at Sea, or after he hath landed the same within any of the said Colonies and Plantations, shall carry the same into any other Foreign Country, with a Purpose there to sell or dispose of the same, without the Licence of Us, our Heirs, and Successors, in that Behalf first had and obtained; That then, all the Goods and Chattels of such Person or Persons so offending and transporting, together with the said Ship or

---

[1] Observe that this important section of the charter is sandwiched in between two sections which ought not to have been separated.

Vessel wherein such Transportation was made, shall be forfeited to Us, our Heirs, and Successors.

[Paragraph XVII reserves to the crown the right to disavow any unauthorized violence used by the Companies or their agents toward the subjects of other European countries; so that England need not be drawn into war by the colony if the king choose instead to leave it to its fate. The remaining paragraphs have to do mainly with landholding. They provide for a simpler method of transfer than was then common in England, and provide also that all land should be held as a freehold, not by military service, — "To be Holden of Us, our Heirs, and Successors, as of our Manor at *East-Greenwich* in the County of *Kent*, in free and common Soccage only, and not in Capite."]

17. Instructions issued by King James

Hening's *Statutes* (1809, 1823), I, 67 ff.

The following instructions for the guidance of the colonizing companies were issued by King James, November 20/30, 1606, in accordance with power reserved by him in the charter. They do not merit the ridicule which has been heaped upon them.

[Recital of the grant in preceding charter.]

Wee, according to the effect and true meaning of the same letters pattents, doe by these presents, . . . establish and ordaine, that our trusty and well beloved Sir William Wade, knight, our Lieutenant of our Tower of London, Sir Thomas Smith, knight, Sir Walter Cope, knight, Sir Gorge Moor, knight, Sir Francis Popeham, knight, Sir Ferdinando Gorges, knight, Sir John Trevor, knight, Sir Henry Montague, knight, recorder of the citty of London, Sir William Rumney, knight, John Dodderidge, Esq., Sollicitor General, Thomas Warr, Esqr., John Eldred of the citty of London, merchant, Thomas James of the citty of Bristol, merchant, and James Bagge of Plymouth, in the county of Devonshire, merchant, shall be our councel for all matters which shall happen in Virginia of any the territories of America, between thirty-four and forty-five degrees from the æquinoctial line northward, and the Islands to the several collonies limited and assigned, and that they shal be called the King's Councel of Virginia, which councel or the most part of them shal have full power and authority, att our pleasure, in our name, and under us, our heires and successors, *to give directions to the councels of the several collonies* which shal be within any part of the said country of Virginia and America, within the degrees first above mentioned, with the Islands aforesaid, for the good government of the people to be planted in those parts, and for the good ordering and disposing of all causes happening within the same, and the same to be done for the substance thereof, as neer to the common lawes of England, and the equity thereof, as may be, and to passe under our seale, appointed for that councel, which councel, and every or any of them shall, from time to time be increased, altered or changed, and others put in their places, att the nomination of us, our heires and successors, and att our and their will and pleasure; *And the same councel of Virginia, or the more part of them, for the time being shall nominate and appoint the first several councellours of those several councells which are to be appointed for those two several colonies*, which are to be made plantations in Virginia . . . according to our said letters pattents in that behalfe made; And that each of the same councels of the same several colonies shal, by the major part of them, choose one of the same councel, not being the minister of God's word, to be president of the same councel, and to continue in that office by the space of one whole year, unless he shall in the mean time dye or be removed from that office; and wee doe further hereby establish and ordaine that it shal be lawful for the major part of either of the said councells, upon any just cause, either absence or otherwise, to remove the president or any other of that councel, . . . from being either president or any of that councel, and upon the deathes or removal of any of the presidents or councel, it shal be lawfull for the major part of that councel to elect another in the place of the party soe dying or removed, so alwaies as they shal not be above thirteen of either of the said councellours, and we doe establish and ordaine, that the president shal not continue in his office of presidentship above the space of one year; and wee doe specially ordaine, charge, and require the said presidents and councells, and the ministers of the said several colonies respectively, within their several limits and precincts, that they, with all diligence, care, and respect, doe provide, that the true word and service of God and Christian faith be preached, planted, and used, not only within every of the said several colonies and plantations, but alsoe as much as they may amongst the salvadge people which doe or shall adjoine unto them, or border upon them, according to the doctrine, rights, and religion now professed and established within our realme of England; . . . and moreover wee doe hereby ordaine and establish for us, our heires and successors, . . . that the offences of tumults, rebellion, conspiracies, mutiny and seditions in those parts which may be dangerous to the estates there, together with murther, manslaughter, incest, rapes, and adulteries committed in those parts within the precincts of any the degrees above mentioned (and noe other offences) shal be punished by death, and that without the benefit of the clergy, except in case of manslaughter, in which clergie is to be allowed; and that the said several presidents and councells . . . shall have full power and authority, to hear and determine all and every the offences aforesaid, within the precinct of their several colonies, in manner and forme following, that is to say, by twelve honest and indifferent persons sworne upon the Evangelists, to be returned by such ministers and officers as every of the said presidents and councells, or the most part of them respectively shall assigne, and the twelve persons soe returned and sworne shall, according to the evidence to be given unto them upon oath and according to the truth, in their consciences, either convict or acquit every of the said persons soe to be accused and tried by them, . . . and that every the said presidents and councells, within their several limits and precincts, shall have power and authority by these presents, to hear and determine all and every other wrongs, trespasses, offences, and misdemeanors whatsoever, other than those before mentioned, upon accusation of any person, and proofe thereof made, by sufficient witnesse upon oath; and that in all those cases the said president and councel . . . shall have power and authority to punish the offender, either by reasonable corporal punishment and imprisonment, or else by a convenient fine, awarding damages or other satisfaction to the party grieved, as to the same president and councell shall be thought fitt and convenient, having regard to the quality of the offence, or state of the cause; and that alsoe the said president and councel, shall have power and authority, by virtue of these presents, to punish all manner of excesse, through drunkennesse or otherwaise, and all idle loytering and vagrant persons, which shall be found within their several limits and precincts, according to their best discretions, and with such convenient punishment, as they or the most part of them shall think fitt; . . . Alsoe our will and pleasure is, and wee doe hereby establish and ordaine, that the said several collonies and plantations, . . . shall . for the space of five years, next after their first landing upon the said coast of Virginia and America, trade together all in one stocke (or devideably, but in two or three stocks at the most), and bring not only all the fruits of their labours there, but alsoe all such other goods and commodities which shall be brought out of England, or any other place, into the same collonies, into severall magazines or store houses, for that purpose to be made and erected there, and that in such order, manner, and form, as the councel of that collony, or the more part of them, shall sett downe and direct . . .

18. Instructions by the Council in England to the Expedition to Virginia; December, 1606

Printed first in Neill's *Virginia Company* (1869) from the manuscript records of the Company at Washington. Reprinted in full in Brown's *Genesis*, I, 79 ff. About a third of the paper is given here.

*   *   *   *   *   *   *

When it shall please God to send you on the coast of Virginia, you shall do your best endeavour to find out a safe port in the entrance of some navigable river making choice of such a one as runneth farthest into the land, and if you happen to discover divers portable rivers, and amongst them any one that hath two main branches, if the difference be not great, make choice of that which bendest most to the North-West, *for that way you shall soonest find the other sea.*

When you have made choice of the river on which you mean to settle, be not hasty in landing your victuals and munitions, but first let Captain Newport discover how far that river may be found navigable, that you make election of the strongest, most wholesome and fertile place; for if you make many removes, besides the loss of time, you shall greatly spoil your victuals and your casks, and with great pain transport it in small boats.

* * * * * * *

When you have discovered [explored] as far up the river as you mean to plant yourselves, and landed your victuals and munitions, to the end that every man may know his charge, you shall do well to divide your six score men into three parts, whereof one party of them you may appoint to fortifie and build, of which your first work must be your store-house for victual; the other you may imploy in preparing your ground and sowing your corn and roots; [but] ten of these forty you must leave as centinel at the haven's mouth. The other forty you may imploy for two months in discovery of the river above you, and on the country about you, . . .

* * * * * * *

In all your passages you must have great care not to offend the naturals, if you can eschew it, and imploy some few of your company to trade with them for corn and all other lasting victuals, if they have any, and this you must do before that they perceive you mean to plant among them; for not being sure how your own seed corn will prosper the first year, to avoid the danger of famine, use and endeavour to store yourselves of the country corn.

* * * * * * *

And how weary soever your soldiers be, let them never trust the country people with the carriage of their weapons, for if they run from you with your shott, which they only fear, they will easily kill them all with their arrows. And whensoever any of yours shoots before them, be sure that they be chosen out of your best marksmen, for if they see your learners miss what they aim at, they will think the weapon not so terrible, and thereby will be bould to assault you.

Above all things do not advertize the killing of any of your men, that the country people may know it; if they perceive that they [you] are but common men, and that with the loss of many of theirs, they may deminish any part of yours, they will make many adventures upon you. If the country be populous, you shall do well also not to let them see or know of your sick men, if you have any, which may also encourage them to many enterprises. You must take especial care that you choose a seat for habitation that shall not be over burthened with woods near your town, for all the men you have shall not be able to cleanse twenty acres a year, besides that it may serve for a covert for your enemies round about.

Neither must you plant in a low or moist place because it will prove unhealthfull. You shall judge of the good air by the people, for some part of that coast where the lands are low have their people blear eyed, and with swollen bellies and legs; but if the naturals be strong and clean made, it is a true sign of a wholesome soil.

* * * * * * *

It were necessary that all your carpenters and other such like workmen about building do first build your store house and those other rooms of publick and necessary use before any house be set up for any private persons; yet let them all work together first for the company and then for private men.

* * * * * * *

Lastly and chiefly the way to prosper and achieve good success is to make yourselves all of one mind for the good of your country and your own, and to serve and fear God the Giver of all Goodness, for every plantation which our Heavenly Father hath not planted shall be rooted out.

19. Exploration and Sufferings

a. *Percy's Discourse*

"That Honorable Gentleman, Master George Percy," wrote a detailed narrative of the first months in Virginia. The manuscript is lost, but extended extracts from it (such as would fill some twenty-five pages of this volume) are preserved in the fourth volume of "Purchas his Pilgrimes" (1625).

. . . The six and twentieth day of Aprill about foure a clocke in the morning, wee descried the Land of Virginia: the same day wee enterd into the Bay of Chesupioc without any let or hinderance; there wee landed and discovered a little way, but we could find nothing worth the speaking of but faire meddowes and goodly tall Trees, with such Fresh-waters runninge through the woods as I was almost ravished at the first sight thereof.

At night, when wee were going aboard, there came the Savages creeping upon all foure, from the Hills, like Beares, with their Bowes in their mouthes, [and] charged us very desperately . . . After they had spent their Arrowes and felt the sharpnesse of our shot, they retired into the Woods with a great noise, and so left us.

The [28th] day . . . we went further into the Bay, and saw a plaine plot of ground where we went on Land . . . we saw nothing there but a Cannow, which was made out of the whole tree, which was five and fortie foot long, by the Rule. Upon this plot of ground we got good store of Mussels and Oysters, which lay upon the ground as thicke as stones: wee opened some and found in many of them Pearles. . . . We passed through excellent ground full of Flowers of divers kinds and colours, and as goodly trees as I have seene, as cedar, cipresse, and other kindes. Going a little farther, we came into a little plot full of fine and beautifull strawberries, foure times bigger and better than ours in England.

* * * * * * *

[The closing pages are in the main a list of deaths, through August and September.] Our men were destroyed with cruell diseases, as Swellings, Fluxes, Burning fevers, and by warres; and some departed suddenly, but for the most part they died of meere famine. There were never Englishmen left in a forreigne Countrey in such miserie as wee were . . . Wee watched every three nights, lying on the bare cold ground, what weather soever came; [and] warded all the next day, which brought our men to bee most feeble wretches. Our feed was but a small can of Barlie sod in Water to five men a day; our drinke, cold water taken out of the River, which was at a flood verie Salt, at a low tide full of slime and filth, which was the destruction of many of our men. Thus we lived for the space of five months in this miserable distresse, not having five able men to man our Bulwarkes upon any occasion. If it had not pleased God to have put a terrour in the Savages heartes, we had all perished by those vild and cruell Pagans, being in that weake estate . . . our men night and day groaning in every corner of the Fort most pittiful to heare. If there were any conscience in men, it would make their harts to bleede to heare the pittifull murmurings and outcries of our sick men without reliefe every night and day for the space of sixe weekes, some departing out of the World, many times three or foure in a night, in the morning their bodies trailed out of their Cabines like Dogges to be burried.

b. "Gentlemen" in Virginia in 1608

From an account written probably by Captain Todkill, a rough soldier, and published in Smith's *Works* (Birmingham edition), 439.

But 30 of us he [Smith] conducted doune the river some 5 myles from James toune, to learne to make Clapbord, cut doune trees, and lye in the woods. Amongst the rest he had chosen Gabriel Beadle, and John Russell, the onely two gallants of this last Supply, and both proper Gentlemen. Straunge were these pleasures to their conditions; yet lodging, eating, and drinking, working or playing, they [were] but doing as the President did himselfe. All these things were carried so pleasantly as within a weeke they became Masters: making it their delight to heare the trees thunder as they fell; but the Axes so oft blistered their tender fingers that many times every third blow had a loud othe to droune the eccho; for remedie of which sinne, the President devised how to have every mans othes numbred, and at night for every othe to have a Cann of water poured doune his sleeve, with which every offender was so washed (himselfe and all) that a man should scarce heare an othe in a weeke.

By this, let no man thinke that the President and these Gentlemen spent their times as common Wood haggers at felling of trees, or such other like labour, or that they were pressed to it as hirelings, or common slaves; for what they did, after they were but once a little inured, it seemed . . . onely as a pleasure and recreation: yet 30 or 40 of such voluntary Gentleman would doe more in a day than 100 of the rest that must be prest to it by compulsion; but twentie good workemen had beene better than them all.

20. Second Charter of Virginia; May 23 / June 2, 1609

The text is printed in Stith's *History of Virginia;* cf. introduction to No. 16.

I. — [A recital of the grant of 1606.]

II. — Now, forasmuch as divers and sundry of our loving Subjects, as well Adventurers, as Planters, of the said first Colony, which have already engaged themselves in furthering the Business of the said Colony and Plantation, and do further intend, by the Assistance of Almighty God, to prosecute the same to a happy End, have of late been humble Suitors unto Us, that (in Respect of their great Charges and the Adventure of many of their Lives, which they have hazarded in the said Discovery and Plantation of the said Country) We would be pleased to grant them a further Enlargement and Explanation of the said Grant, Privileges, and Liberties, and that such Counsellors, and other Officers, may be appointed amongst them, to manage and direct their affairs, as are willing and ready to adventure with them, as also whose Dwellings are not so far remote from the City of *London* but that they may, at convenient Times, be ready at Hand to give their Advice and Assistance upon all Occasions requisite.

III. — WE, greatly affecting the effectual Prosecution and happy Success of the said Plantation, and commending their good Desires therein, for their further Encouragement in accomplishing so excellent a Work, much pleasing to God, and profitable to our Kingdom, Do . . . GIVE, GRANT, and CONFIRM, to our trusty and well-beloved Subjects, *Robert*, Earl of *Salisbury*[1] . . . ; AND to such, and so many, as they do, or shall hereafter, admit to be joined with them, in Form hereafter in these Presents expressed, whether they go in their Persons, to be Planters there in the said Plantation, or whether they go not, but adventure their Monies, Goods, or Chattels ; THAT they shall be one Body or Commonalty perpetual, and shall have perpetual Succession, and one common Seal, to serve for the said Body or Commonalty ; And that they, and their Successors, shall be KNOWN, CALLED, and INCORPORATED by the Name of, *The Treasurer and Company of Adventurers and Planters of the City of London for the first Colony in Virginia:*

---

[1] Here follow the names of 659 persons and 56 gilds. The lists would fill some ten pages. It includes 21 of the greatest lords in England, 96 knights and some 90 other country gentlemen, 53 "captains," and a number of "sadlers," "drapers," "grocers," etc., with some professional men and others not classified. Fifty of the incorporators were members of the existing parliament, and fifty more were members of Parliament at one time or another. Among the 659 incorporators were Robert Cecil (the minister of Elizabeth and of James), the Earl of Southampton (Shakspere's friend), Sir Oliver Cromwell (uncle to the great Oliver), Francis Bacon, Richard Hakluyt, George Calvert (afterward Lord Baltimore), and Sir Edwin Sandys, soon to be the great Puritan leader in Parliament.

SECOND CHARTER OF VIRGINIA 39

IV. — AND that they, and their Successors, shall be, from henceforth, for ever enabled to TAKE, ACQUIRE, and PURCHASE, by the Name aforesaid (Licence for the same, from Us, our Heirs or Successors, first had and obtained) any Manner of Lands, Tenements, and Hereditaments, Goods, and Chattels, within our Realm of *England* and Dominion of *Wales:*

V. — AND that they, and their Successors, shall likewise be enabled, by the Name aforesaid, to PLEAD, and BE IMPLEADED, before any of our Judges or Justices, in any of our Courts, and in any Actions or Suits whatsoever.

VI. — AND we do also . . . GIVE, GRANT and CONFIRM, unto the said Treasurer and Company, and their Successors, under the Reservations, Limitations, and Declarations, hereafter expressed, all those Lands, Countries, and Territories, situate, lying, and being, in that Part of *America* called VIRGINIA, from the Point of Land, called Cape or *Point Comfort,* all along the Sea Coast, to the *Northward* two hundred Miles, and from the said Point of *Cape Comfort,* all along the Sea Coast, to the *Southward* two hundred Miles, and all that Space and Circuit of Land, lying from the Sea Coast of the Precinct aforesaid, up into the Land, throughout from Sea to Sea, West and Northwest; And also all the Islands lying within one hundred Miles along the Coast of both Seas of the Precinct aforesaid; . . .

VII. — [Right to dispose of lands.]

VIII. — AND forasmuch, as the good and prosperous Success of the said Plantation cannot but chiefly depend, next under the Blessing of God, and the Support of our Royal Authority, upon the provident and good Direction of the whole Enterprize by a careful and understanding Council, and that it is not convenient that all the Adventurers shall be so often drawn to meet and assemble, as shall be requisite for them to have Meetings and Conference about the Affairs thereof; Therefore we DO ORDAIN, establish, and confirm, that there shall be perpetually one COUNCIL here resident, according to the Tenour of our former Letters-patents; Which Council shall have a Seal, for the better Government and Administration of the said Plantation, besides the legal Seal of the Company or Corporation, as in our former Letters-patents is also expressed.

IX. — [Names of the members of the council appointed.]

X. — AND the said Sir *Thomas Smith* we do ORDAIN to be Treasurer of the said Company; which Treasurer shall have Authority to give Order for the Warning of the Council, and summoning the Company, to their Courts and Meetings.

XI. — AND the said Council and Treasurer, or any of them, shall be from henceforth, nominated, chosen, continued, displaced, changed, altered, and supplied, as Death, or other several Occasions, shall require, out of the Company of the said Adventurers, by the Voice of the greater Part of the said Company and Adventurers, in their Assembly for that Purpose: PROVIDED always, That every Counsellor, so newly elected, shall be presented to the Lord Chancellor of *England*, or to the Lord High Treasurer of *England*, or to the Lord Chamberlain of the Household of Us, our Heirs, and Successors, for the time being, to take his Oath of a Counsellor to Us, our Heirs, and Successors, for the said Company of Adventurers and Colony in *Virginia*.

XII. — [Provision for a Deputy Treasurer.]

XIII. — AND further . . . we do, by these Presents, GIVE and GRANT full Power and Authority to our said Council, here resident, as well at this present Time, as hereafter from time to time, to nominate, make, constitute, ordain, and confirm, by such Name or Names, Stile or Stiles, as to them shall seem good, And likewise to revoke, discharge, change, and alter, as well all and singular Governors, Officers, and Ministers, which already have been made, as also which hereafter shall be by them thought fit and needful to be made or used, for the Government of the said Colony and Plantation:[1]

---

[1] Hannis Taylor (in his *English Constitution*, I, 21), in a passage abounding in blunders, regards this Council as made up of Virginians and exercising local self-government. Unhappily there are other instances of the same error in standard works.

XIV. — And also to make, ordain, and establish all Manner of Orders, Laws, Directions, Instructions, Forms, and Ceremonies of Government and Magistracy, fit and necessary, for and concerning the Government of the said Colony and Plantation; And the same, at all times hereafter, to abrogate, revoke, or change, not only within the Precincts of the said Colony, but also upon the Seas in going and coming to and from the said Colony, as they, in their good Discretion, shall think to be fittest for the Good of the Adventurers and Inhabitants there.

XV. — [Previous authorities in Virginia supplanted by these new arrangements.]

XVI. — And we do further, by these Presents, Ordain and establish, that the said Treasurer and Council here resident, and their Successors, or any four of them, being assembled (the Treasurer being one) shall, from time to time, have full Power and Authority, to admit and receive any other Person into their Company, Corporation, and Freedom; And further, in a General Assembly of the Adventurers, with the Consent of the greater Part, upon good Cause, to disfranchise and put out any Person or Persons, out of the said Freedom or Company.

XVII. — [Right to minerals, as in First Charter, section IX, paying to the king the fifth part, etc.]

XVIII. — [Right to transport willing colonists to Virginia.]

XIX. — [Certain exemptions from English customs duties, in favor of the Company.]

XX. — [Grant to the Company and to its officers in Virginia that it may expel unwelcome settlers and outsiders who "enterprise" destruction, hurt, or annoyance. The language is taken from the First Charter, section XII.]

XXI. — [Right to levy import duties, as in First Charter.]

XXII. — [Rights of settlers. Repeated from First Charter, section XV.]

XXIII. — And forasmuch, as it shall be necessary for all such our loving Subjects as shall inhabit within the said Precincts of *Virginia*, aforesaid, to determine to live together, in the Fear and true Worship of Almighty God, Christian Peace, and civil Quietness, each with other, whereby every one may, with more Safety, Pleasure, and Profit, enjoy that whereunto they shall attain with great Pain and Peril; WE . . . do GIVE and GRANT unto the said Treasurer and Company, and their Successors, and to such Governors, Officers, and Ministers, as shall be, by our said Council, constituted and appointed, according to the Natures and Limits of their Offices and Places respectively, that they shall and may, from time to time for ever hereafter, within the said Precincts of *Virginia*, or in the way by Sea thither and from thence, have full and absolute Power and Authority, to correct, punish, pardon, govern, and rule, all such the Subjects of Us . . . as shall, from time to time, adventure themselves in any Voyage thither, or that shall, at any time hereafter, inhabit in the Precincts and Territories of the said Colony, as aforesaid, according to such orders, Ordinances, Constitutions, Directions, and Instructions, as by our said Council, as aforesaid, shall be established; And in Defect thereof, in case of Necessity, according to the good Discretions of the said Governor and Officers, respectively, as well in Cases capital and criminal as civil, both marine and other; So always, as the said Statutes, Ordinances, and Proceedings, as near as conveniently may be, be agreeable to the Laws, Statutes, Government, and Policy of this our Realm of *England*.

XXIV. — AND we do further . . . GRANT, DECLARE, and ORDAIN, that such principal Governor, as, from time to time, shall duly and lawfully be authorised and appointed, in Manner and Form in these Presents heretofore expressed, shall have full Power and Authority, to use and exercise Martial Law, in Cases of Rebellion or Mutiny, in as large and ample Manner as our Lieutenants in our Counties, within this our Realm of *England*, have, or ought to have. . . .

XXV. — [Penalty for trying to evade English revenue laws under color of transporting goods to the colony, as in section XVI of the First Charter.]

XXVI. — And further our will and pleasure is, that in all questions and doubts that shall arise upon any difficulty of construction or interpretation of anything contained either in this or in our said former letters patents, the same shall be taken and interpreted in most ample and beneficial manner for the said treasurer and company . . .

XXVII. — [Confirms all privileges granted in the first charter and not herein altered or revoked.]

XXVIII. — [Provides that anyone who will adventure the necessary money shall be received in full equality as a member of the Company.]

XXIX. — AND lastly, because the principal Effect which we can desire or expect of this Action, is the Conversion and Reduction of the People in those Parts unto the true Worship of God and Christian Religion, in which Respect we should be loath that any Person should be permitted to pass that we suspected to affect the superstitions of the Church of *Rome;* We do hereby DECLARE, that it is our Will and Pleasure, that none be permitted to pass in any Voyage, from time to time to be made into the said Country, but such as first shall have taken the Oath of Supremacy; For which Purpose, we do, by these Presents, give full Power and Authority, to the Treasurer for the time being, and any three of the Council, to tender and exhibit the said Oath to all such Persons as shall at any time be sent and employed in the said Voyage. . . .

[It is a profitable exercise to read some of the sections in a more logical order. Thus the political provisions are seen better if arranged in the following sequence : XIV, XIII, XV, XXIII, XXIV, XXII. Certainly, too, XXVIII should follow, or be combined with, XVI. The utterly meaningless arrangement of many of these great documents, together with the unpardonable carelessness of the copiers, account partly for their needless length and largely for their obscurity.

Nova Britannia (No. 6 above) contains also an explanation of the method of "industry in common" and of the proposed method of sharing profits, — all of which was continued ten years more under this charter : —

"Wee call those *Planters* that goe in their persons to dwell there, and those *Adventurers* that adventure their money and go not in person; and both doe make the members of one Colonie. We do account twelve pound ten shillings to be a single share adventured. Every ordinary man or woman, if they will goe and dwell there, and every childe above tenne yeares that shall be carried thither to remaine, shall be allowed for each of their persons a single share, as if they had adventured twelve pound ten shillings in money. [Extraordinarie men, as Divines, Governors, . . . Knights, Gentlemen, Physitions, and such as be men of worth for special services, to be rated higher, — as the Council may value them.] And likewise, if any that goe to bee planters will lay downe money to the Treasurer, it shall be also registered and their shares inlarged, accordingly, be it for more or lesse. All charges of setling and maintaining the Plantation, and of making supplies, shall be borne in a joint stock of the adventurers for seven yeares after the date of our new enlargement: during which time there shall be no adventure nor goods returned in private from thence, neytheir by Master, Marriner, Planter, nor Passenger."]

21. Third Charter for Virginia. March 12/22, 1611/1612 [1]

First printed in Stith (cf. introduction to No. 16); found also in the collections of Poore and Thorpe (cf. introduction to No. 15).

The greater part of this document is given (1) to an enlargement of territory (by inclusion of the Somers islands), (2) to extraordinary rights of jurisdiction to compel fulfilment of contracts and to prevent slander of the Company, and (3) to provisions for lotteries for the Company's support. These parts are omitted. Only those clauses are given here

---

[1] England in the seventeenth century still used the "Old Style" dates, instead of the "New" or Gregorian Style. The year began March 25, instead of January 1, and all dates between these two (from January 1 to March 25) were then given in the year previous to the one in which our "New Style" puts them. Moreover, the New Style moved all dates forward ten days. Therefore *March 12, 1611*, as the charter was dated at the time, means to us *March 22, 1612.*

which bear upon the reorganization of the Company and upon its powers of government.

VII. — AND We do hereby ORDAIN and GRANT, by these Presents, that the said Treasurer and Company of Adventurers and Planters aforesaid, shall and may, once every Week, or oftener, at their Pleasure, hold and keep a Court and Assembly, for the better Order and Government of the said Plantation, and such things, as shall concern the same; And that any five Persons of our Council for the said first Colony in *Virginia*, for the time being, of which Company the Treasurer, or his Deputy, to be always one, and the Number of fifteen others, at the least, of the Generality of the said Company, assembled together in such Manner as is and hath been heretofore used and accustomed, shall be said, taken, held, and reputed to be, and shall be a *sufficient Court* of the said Company, for the handling, and ordering, and dispatching [dispatching] of all such casual and particular Occurrences, and accidental Matters, of less Consequence and Weight, as shall, from time to time, happen, touching and concerning the said Plantation:

VIII. — AND that nevertheless, for the handling, ordering, and disposing of Matters and Affairs of greater Weight and Importance, and such, as shall or may, in any Sort, concern the Weal Publick and General Good of the said Company and Plantation, as namely, the Manner of Government from time to time to be used, the Ordering and disposing of the Lands and Possessions, and the Settling and Establishing of a Trade there, or such like, there shall be held and kept, every Year, upon the last *Wednesday*, save one, of *Hillary* Term, *Easter*, *Trinity*, and *Michaelmas* Terms, for ever, one great, general, and solemn Assembly, which four Assemblies shall be stiled and called, *The four Great and General Courts of the Council and Company of Adventurers for Virginia;* In all and every of which said Great and General Courts, so assembled . . . the said Treasurer and Company, or the greater Number of them, so assembled, shall and may have full Power and Authority, from time to time, and at all times hereafter, to elect and chuse discreet Persons, to be of our said Council for the said first Colony in *Virginia*, and to nominate and appoint such officers, as they shall think fit and requisite for the Government, Managing, Ordering, and Dispatching of the Affairs of the said Company; And shall likewise have full Power and Authority, to ordain and make such Laws and Ordinances, for the Good and Welfare of the said Plantation, as to them, from time to time, shall be thought requisite and meet: *So always*, as the same be not contrary to the Laws and Statutes of this our Realm of *England*. . . .

X. — And we do . . . further grant . . . that the said Treasurer and Company, or the greater Part of them . . . so in a full and general Court assembled . . . shall and may . . . admit into their Company . . . any Person or Persons . . .

XI. — And We do further . . . grant . . . that it shall be lawful and free for them . . . out of our Dominions . . . to take, lead, carry and transport . . . for and toward the said Plantation of our said . . . Colony of Virginia all and so many of our loving Subjects . . . as shall willingly accompany them. . . .

XII. — And We do further . . . grant . . . that the said Treasurer of that Company, or his Deputy . . . or any two other of the said Council . . . have full power and authority to minister and give the Oath and Oaths of Supremacy and Allegiance, or either of them, to all and every Person and Persons, which shall at any Time or Times . . . go or pass to the said Colony.

XX. — And further, our Will and Pleasure is, that in all Questions and Doubts, that shall arise, upon any Difficulty of Construction or Interpretation of any Thing, contained in these, or any other our former Letters-patents, the same shall be taken and interpreted, in most ample and beneficial Manner for the said Treasurer and Company, and their Successors, and every Member thereof.

XXI. — And lastly, we do, by these Presents, RATIFY AND CONFIRM unto the said Treasurer and Company, and their

DANGER FROM SPANISH ATTACK

Successors, for ever, all and all Manner of Privileges, Franchises, Liberties, Immunities, Preheminences, Profits, and Commodities, whatsoever, granted unto them in any our former Letters-patents, and not in these Presents revoked, altered, changed, or abridged.

Hints for Study.— 1. Compare the clauses relating to the oath of supremacy in the second and third charters. (The passage given above contains all such matter found in the third charter.) When the third charter was issued, James had broken with his first parliament, and probably wished to draw the great Catholic lords nearer to himself.

2. Compare the provisions for the meeting of the whole Company in the second charter with the more specific provisions in the third.

3. The most important sections are VII and VIII. Observe that no regular meetings of the Council are provided. That body had lost all controlling power; it remained merely a preconsidering body, to prepare business for the meetings of the stockholders. Five of the Council, however, had to be of the small quorum necessary for one of the minor "courts" (VII), and, in fact, those minor courts were *usually* little more than Council meetings.

From the general tenor of this charter and the preceding one, it would seem as though "Planters" from Virginia, if present in London, might attend the "Courts" and vote. But in practice, when this question was raised, it was decided against the visiting Planters (*Company Records*, II, 301). *Only holders of shares of stock could vote*, and, in practice, stock certificates were not issued for emigration to America.

22. Danger from Spanish Attack (1607-1614)

The following extracts from the correspondence between Zuñiga, the Spanish ambassador at London, and the King of Spain are taken from the documents printed in Brown's *Genesis*. These letters were usually in cypher. The translations, of course, are in modern English. Cf. *American History and Government*, § 24.

a. Zuñiga to the King of Spain; London, October 16, 1607

Those who urge the colonization of Virginia become every day more eager . . . and before Nativity there will sail from here [London] and from Plymouth five or six ships. *It will be serving God and Your Majesty to drive these villains out from there, hanging them.*

[In this same letter, Zuñiga says that he has found a man to inform him of all the secret doings of the Council for Virginia; and, November 10, he advises that the Spanish "Windward fleet" be used at once to drive out the colonists. The Spanish Council at Madrid reported, however, that the fleet was not in state of preparation.]

[December 6.] As to Virginia, I hear that three or four other ships will return there. *Will your Majesty give orders that measures be taken in time* [to destroy the settlement]; because now it will be very easy, and quite difficult afterwards, when they have taken root; and if they are punished in the beginning, the result will be that no more will go there.

[December 22.] It appears that there will be more people there after Nativity than those I have written of. Wherefore Your Majesty will see how necessary it is to act with vigor *and hasten the remedy.*

[After reading these letters, the Spanish Council made the following record: "The Council says that having informed Your Majesty . . . Your Majesty was pleased to command that there should be prepared whatever was necessary to drive out the people who are in Virginia." This report is indorsed by the King: "Not to let anyone know what is being done."

Similar matter is found in letters from Zuñiga under date of March 28, 1608; November 8, 1608.]

[March 5, 1609.] The Baron de Arundel [an English Catholic who had been a candidate for the governorship of Virginia, and who now apparently was playing traitor] offers to leave here whenever Your Majesty may command, under pretext of a voyage of discovery, and that in the Canaries or Porto Rico he will take on board the person Your Majesty will send, as a man fleeing out of Spain, and will carry him to Virginia, and instruct him as to . . . the parts which the English hold . . . and that soon he will tell Your Majesty by what means those people may be driven out without violence.[1] [But Zuñiga urges immediate and violent action, since King James is sure to acquiesce *after* the fact.] *Hence*

---

[1] A long report upon the state of Virginia, its geography and resources, by an Irishman in Spanish pay, is given in Brown's *Genesis*, I, 393–399.

Your Majesty will command that they be destroyed with the utmost possible promptness.

[April 12, 1609. After describing a new English expedition to Virginia, — Lord Delaware's.] Your Majesty will see the great importance of this matter for your Royal Service, and thus, I hope, **will give orders to have these insolent people quickly annihilated.**

b. *Velasco (Zuñiga's Successor at the English Court) to the King of Spain; June 14, 1610*

[After reporting the news of the terrible winter of 1609 in Virginia] Thus it looks as if the zeal for this enterprise was cooling off, **and it would be easy to make an end of it altogether by sending out a few ships to finish what might be left in that place.**

[The Spanish Council report upon this letter to the King, and add: "It appears to the Council that this should be communicated to the Council of War . . . and that it be asked to state what will be right and proper to do, the supply of ships and whatever else may be needful for that purpose. Y. M. will command what shall be done." This is indorsed, with the King's signature, "*It is well.*"

c. *Digby (English Ambassador at Madrid) to King James*

[September 22, 1612.] There is nothing so generally spoken of in the Courte as their intent to remove Our plantation from Virginia. And, for myne owne parte, I am of beliefe that the Spaniards will serve us as thei did the Frenchmen in Florida [Ribault's colony] unless wee undertake the business much more thoroughly and roundely then hitherto wee have donne.[1]

[November 12, 1612.] I got a view of his [Zuñega's] dispatch [by bribing some Spanish official, of course]. The chief matters were . . . that there was no cause to apprehend so much danger in Virginia . . . that he held it not unlikely *the*

---

[1] For more such exhortation and warning from Digby, see Brown's *Genesis*, 539, 588, 592-3, 787.

Business might sinke of itselfe, since it was maynteyned but by these shifts, which could last but for a yeare or two. . . .

[For some months after the above, however, Digby sends frequent warnings of a Spanish expedition which he thinks is preparing against Virginia (Brown, *Genesis,* 603, 609, 623); but May 13, 1613, he writes again to James I:]

. . . theire resolution is not to stirre therein until they shall be better informed . . . they are yet in a greate hope that the businesse will fall of itselfe. [Cf. other letters to the same effect, May 22, May 26, Aug. 15, in Brown's *Genesis,* 634, 635, 656.]

IV. THE LIBERAL LONDON COMPANY AND SELF-GOVERNMENT IN VIRGINIA (1619–1624)

23. From the Rules of the Virginia Company in London

Peter Force's *Historical Tracts*, III (Washington, 1844), No. 6.

These rules, one hundred thirty-two in number, and bulky enough to fill fifty pages of this volume, were adopted by the London Company shortly after it came under Liberal control, in June, 1619. For the history of the struggle in the Company, cf. a brief statement in *American History and Government*, § 27.

XV. — At the great and generall Court, commonly called the Quarter Court, in Easter Terme, all offices of this Company (excepting the Counseil) shall be void: And the Court shall proceede to an election of new Officers, in manner following.

XVII. — After the choise of a Treasuror, a Deputie shall be chosen; then the Auditors, and Comitties; and lastly the Secretarie, Bookekeeper, Husband, and Bedle.

XVIII. — At the choise of each Officer, the persons nominated for the election, shall withdraw themselves till the party chosen be publiquely so pronounced. And generally no man shall be present in the Court whilst himselfe or his matter passeth the judgement of the Court.

XX. — It is for weighty reasons thought very expedient, that no man continue in the place of Treasurer or Deputie, above three yeares at once.

XXI. — For the avoiding of divers inconveniences, It is thought fit that all elections of principall Officers in or for[1] Virginia as also of the Treasurer and Deputie here, be performed by a *Ballating box, as in some other Companies*.

---

[1] This means *for*, not *in*; cf. Rule CI.

XXVI. — He [the Treasurer] is to propound and put all things to the question which the Court requires, under paine of being immediately put from his Office, if he refuse. In which case the Deputie shall doo it, under the like paine. And if he refuse, then any of the Council there present.

LXXXIX. — Every man speaking in Court, shall addresse his speech to the Treasuror, or deputie in his absence, as representing the Court: And all private speeches, or directed to particular persons, shall be forborne.

XCI. — No man with his speech shall interrupt the speech of another, before he have finished: Except the Treasurer, or in his absence the Deputie, (with approbation of the Court) see cause to put any to silence, for impertinency, or other unseemely speaking.

XCIV. — Whosoever shall attempt by private solicitation to packe the Court to any unjust or unlawfull end, shall, upon complaint, be convented before the Counseil, and, being convicted, shall be disfranchized.

CI. — All principal Officers in [for] Virginia, namely the Governour, Lieutenant Governour, Admirall, Marshal, chiefe Justice, and Treasuror, shall be chosen **here** *by Ballating* in a Quarter-Court.

CII. — The Counseil established in Virginia, and all other Officers there reserved to the choise of the Companie here, shall be chosen in a Quarter-Court by onely erection of hands; *unlesse the Court desire to have it passe by Ballating.*

[The frequent reference to the ballot in these rules is a sufficient answer to an absurd claim that the English colonies had to learn that device from Holland. Cf. *American History and Government*, § 77. The use of the ballot is referred to frequently in the Company's *Records*, in accounts of elections under these rules, as in *Records*, I, 315, 368, 385, 440, 468, 471, 474, 489 ; II, 28, 29, 154, 536, 537.]

FIRST REPRESENTATIVE ASSEMBLY IN AMERICA 53

24. An Order of the London Company as to Self-government
February 2/12, 1619/20

Records of the Virginia Company in London (edited by Susan Kingsbury; Washington, 1906), I, 303.

This order, to provide for temporary self-government in new colonies under the jurisdiction of the Company, was adopted on the same day that the Company made four grants of land to companies expecting to settle in "Virginia." One of these grants was to John Pierce and his Associates. Pierce was one of the London partners of the Mayflower Pilgrims. The order below *may* therefore have suggested to the Pilgrims the Mayflower Compact (No. 52 below).

It was ordered by generall Consent that such Captaines or Leaders of Perticulerr Plantacions that shall goe there to inhabite . . . in Virginia, shall have liberty, till a forme of Goverment bee here settled for them, Associatinge unto them divers of the gravest and discreetes of their companies, to make Orders, Ordinances, and Constitucions for the better orderinge and dyrectinge of their Servants and buisines, Provided they be not Repugnant to the Lawes of England.

25. The First Representative Assembly in America
July 30/August 9, 1619

Stith and Hening (Nos. 16, 17), those early and zealous explorers in Virginian records, both believed that no record of this great Assembly was extant. George Bancroft, however, found a copy in the London Record Office, in 1856, and published it in the *New York Historical Society Collections* of 1857. A somewhat more critical text was published in 1874 by Wynne and Gilman, in their thin volume of *Colonial Records of Virginia*. The record was made by John Twine, Clerk of the Assembly. It is printed here almost in full.

A reporte of the manner of proceeding in the General assembly convented at James city in Virginia, July 30, 1619, consisting of the Governo^r, the Counsell of Estate and two Burgesses elected out of eache Incorporation and Plantation, and being dissolved the 4th of August next ensuing.

First. Sir George Yeardley, Knight, Governo^r and Captaine general of Virginia, having sente his sumons all over the Country, as well to invite those of the Counsell of Estate that were absente as also for the election of Burgesses, there were chosen and appeared

For James citty
    Captaine William Powell,
    Ensigne William Spense.

For Charles citty
    Samuel Sharpe,
    Samuel Jordan.

For Martin Brandon — Capt. John Martin's Pla'tation
    Mr. Thomas Davis,
    Mr. Robert Stacy.

For Smythes hundred
    Captain Thomas Graves,
    Mr. Walter Shelley.

For Martins hundred
    Mr. John Boys,
    John Jackson.

For the city of Henricus
    Thomas Dawse,
    John Polentine.

For Kiccowatan
    Captaine William Tucker,
    William Capp.

For Argall's guiffe
    Mr. Pawlett,
    Mr. Gourgaing.

For Flowerdieu hundred
    Ensigne Rossingham,
    Mr. Jefferson.

For Captain Lawne's plantation
    Captain Christopher Lawne,
    Ensigne Washer.

For Captaine Warde's plantation
    Captaine Warde,
    Lieutenant Gibbes.

The most convenient place we could finde to sitt in was the Quire of the Churche Where Sir George Yeardley, the Governour, being sett down in his accustomed place, those of the Counsel of Estate sate nexte him on both handes, excepte onely the Secretary then appointed Speaker, who sate right before him, John Twine, clerke of the General assembly, being placed nexte the Speaker, and Thomas Pierse, the Sergeant, standing at the barre, to be ready for any Service the Assembly should comaund him. But forasmuche as men's affaires doe little prosper where God's service is neglected, all the Burgesses tooke their places in the Quire till a prayer was said by Mr. Bucke, the Minister, that it would please God to guide and sanctifie all our proceedings to his owne glory and the good of this Plantation. Prayer being ended, to the intente that as we had begun at God Almighty, so we might proceed with awful and due respecte towards the Lieutenant, our most gratious and dread Soveraigne, all the Burgesses were intreatted to retyre themselves into the body of the Churche, which being done, before they were fully admitted, they were called in order and by name, and so every man (none staggering at it) tooke the oathe of Supremacy, and then entred the Assembly. . . .

These obstacles removed, the Speaker, who a long time had bene extreame sickly and therefore not able to passe through long harrangues, delivered in briefe to the whole assembly the occasions of their meeting. Which done, he read unto them the commission for establishing the Counsell of Estate and the general Assembly, wherein their duties were described to the life.

Having thus prepared them, he read over unto them the greate Charter, or commission of priviledges, orders and lawes, sent by Sir George Yeardly out of Englande. Which for the more ease of the Committies, having divided into fower books, he read the former two the same forenoon, for expeditious sake, a second time over, and so they were referred to the persuall of twoe Comitties, which did reciprocally consider of either, and accordingly brought in their opinions. But some men may here objecte to what ende we should presume to referre that to the examination of the Comitties which the Counsell and Company in England had already resolved to be perfect, and did expecte nothing but our assente thereunto? To this we answere that we did it not to the ende to correcte or controll anything therein contained, but onely in case we should finde ought not perfectly squaring with the state of this Colony, or any lawe which did presse or binde too harde, that we might, by waye of humble petition, seeke to have it redressed, *especially because this great Charter is to binde us and our heyers for ever.* . . .

After dinner the Governor and those that were not of the Comitties sate a seconde time, while the said Comitties were employed in the perusall of those twoe bookes. And whereas the Speaker had propounded fower severall objects for the Assembly to consider on: namely, first, the great charter of orders, lawes, and priviledges; Secondly, which of the instructions given by the Counsel in England to my [Lord De La Warre], Captain Argall, or Sir George Yeardley, might conveniently putt on the habite of lawes; Thirdly, what lawes might issue out of the private conceipte of any of the Burgesses, or any other of the Colony; and lastly, what petitions were fitt to be sente home for England. It pleased the Governour for expedition sake to have the second objecte of the fower to be examined and prepared by himselfe and the Non-Comitties. Wherin after having spente some three howers conference, the twoe Committies brought in their opinions concerning the twoe former bookes, (the second of which beginneth at these words of the Charter: And foreasmuche as our intente is to establish one equall and uniforme kinde of government over all Virginia etc.,) which the whole Assembly, because it was late, deffered to treatt of till the next morning.

SATTURDAY, July 31. — The nexte daye, therefore, out of the opinions of the said Comitties, it was agreed these Petitions ensuing should be framed, to be presented to the Treasurer, Counsel and Company in England. . . .

These petitions thus concluded on, those twoe Comitties broughte me a reporte what they had observed in the two latter bookes, which was nothing else but that the perfection of them was suche as that they could finde nothing therein subject to exception. . . .

At the same time, there remaining no farther scruple in the mindes of the Assembly, touching the said great Charter of lawes, orders and priviledges, the Speaker putt the same to the question, and so it had both the general assent and the applause of the whole assembly, who, as they professed themselves in

FIRST REPRESENTATIVE ASSEMBLY IN AMERICA 57

the first place most submissivily thankfull to almighty god, therefore so they commaunded the Speaker to returne (as nowe he doth) their due and humble thankes to the Treasurer, Counsell and company for so many priviledges and favours, as well in their owne names as in the names of the whole Colony whom they represented.

This being dispatched we fell once more debating of suche instructions given by the Counsell in England to several Governors as might be converted into lawes, the last whereof was the Establishment of the price of Tobacco, namely, of the best at 3 d and the second at 18 d the pounde, . . .

SUNDAY, Aug. 1. — Mr. Shelley, one of the Burgesses, deceased.

MUNDAY, Aug. 2. — . . . , the Committies appointed to consider what instructions are fitt to be converted into lawes, brought in their opinions, and first of some of the general instructions.

> Here begin the lawes drawen out of the Instructions given by his Majesties Counsell of Virginia in England to my lo: la warre [Lord Delaware] Captain Argall and Sir George Yeardley, knight.

By this present Generall Assembly be it enacted, that no injury or oppression be wrought by the Englishe against the Indians whereby the present peace might be disturbed and antient quarrells might be revived. . . .

Against Idleness, Gaming, durunkenes, and excesse in apparell, the Assembly hath enacted as followeth:

First, in detestation of Idlenes be it enacted, that if any men be founde to live as an Idler or renagate, though a freedman, it shalbe lawfull for that Incorporation or Plantation to which he belongeth to appoint him a Mr [Master] to serve for wages, till he shewe apparant signes of amendment.

Against gaming at dice and Cardes be it ordained by this present assembly that the winner or winners shall lose all his or their winninges and both winners and loosers shall forfaicte ten shillings a man, one ten shillings whereof to go to the discoverer, and the rest to charitable and pious uses in the Incorporation where the faulte is comitted.

Against drunkenness be it also decreed that if any private person be found culpable thereof, for the first time he is to be reprooved privately by the Minister, the second time publiquely, the thirde time *to lye in boltes 12 howers* in the house of the Provost Marshall and to paye his fee, and if he still continue in that vice, to undergo suche severe punishment as the Governor and Counsell of Estate shall thinke fitt to be inflicted on him. [Provision for milder penalty for drunken officials.]

Against excesse in apparell, that every man be cessed in the churche for all publique contributions, if he be unmarried according to his owne apparell, if he be married according to his owne and his wives, or either of their apparrell. . . .

Be it enacted by this present assembly that for laying a surer foundation of the conversion of the Indians to Christian Religion, eache towne, citty, Borrough, and particular plantation do obtaine unto themselves by just means a certaine number of the natives' children to be educated by them in the true religion and civile course of life — of which children the most towardly boyes in witt and graces of nature to be brought up by them in the first elements of litterature, so to be fitted for the Colledge intended for them, that from thence they may be sente to that worke of conversion.

As touching the business of planting corne this present Assembly doth ordaine that yeare by yeare all and every householder and householders have in store for every servant he or they shall keep, and also for his or their owne persons, whether they have any Servants or no, one spare barrell of corne, to be delivered out yearly, either upon sale or exchange as need shall require. For the neglecte of which duty he shalbe subjecte to the censure of the Governor and Counsell of

Estate. Provided alwayes that the first yeare of every newe man this lawe shall not be of force.

About the Plantation of Mulberry trees, be it enacted that every man as he is seatted upon his division, doe for seven years together every yeare plante and maintaine in growte six Mulberry trees at the least, and as many more as he shall thinke conveniente and as his virtue and Industry shall move him to plante, and that all suche persons as shall neglecte the yearly planting and maintaining of that small proportion shalbe subjecte to the censure of the Governour and the Counsell of Estate.

Be it farther enacted as concerning Silke-flaxe, that those men that are upon their division or setled habitation doe this next yeare plante and dresse 100 plantes, which being founde a comedity, may farther be increased. And whosoever do faill in the performance of this shalbe subject to the punishment of the Governour and Counsell of Estate.

For hempe also both Englishe and Indian, and for Englishe flax and Anniseeds, we do require and enjoine all householders of this Colony that have any of those seeds to make tryal thereofe the nexte season.

Moreover be it enacted by this present Assembly, that every householder do yearly plante and maintaine ten vines untill they have attained to the art and experience of dressing a Vineyard either by their owne industry or by the Instruction of some Vigneron . . . upon what penalty soever the Governor and Counsell of Estate shall thinke fitt to impose upon the neglecters of this acte.

Be it also enacted that all necessary tradesmen, or so many as need shall require, suche as are come over since the departure of Sir Thomas Dale, or that shall hereafter come, shall worke at their trades for any other man, each one being payde according to the quality of his trade and worke, to be estimated, if he shall not be contented, by the Governor and officers of the place where he worketh.

Be it further ordained by this General Assembly, and we doe by these presents enacte, that all contractes made in England between the owners of lande and their Tenants and Servantes which they shall sende hither, may be caused to be duely performed, and that the offenders be punished as the Governour and Counsell of Estate shall thinke just and convenient.

Be it established also by this present Assembly that no crafty or advantagious means be suffered to putt in practise for the inticing awaye the Tenants or Servants of any particular plantation from the place where they are seatted. And that it shalbe the duty of the Governor and Counsell of Estate most severely to punishe both the seducers and the seduced, and to returne these latter into their former places. . . .

TUESDAY, Aug. 3, 1619.— . . . Captaine William Powell presented a Petition to the generall Assembly against one Thomas Garnett, a servant of his, not onely for extreame neglect of his business to the great loss and prejudice of the said Captaine, and for openly and impudently abusing his house, . . . but also for falsely accusing him to the Governor both of Drunkenes and Thefte, and besides for bringing all his fellow servants to testify on his side, wherein they justly failled him. It was thought fitt by the general assembly (the Governour himselfe giving sentence), that he should stand fower dayes with his eares nayled to the Pillory, viz: Wednesday, Aug 4th, and so likewise Thursday, fryday and Satturday next following, and every of those fower dayes should be publiquely whipped. Now, as touching the neglecte of his worke, what satisfaction ought to be made to his Mr. for that is referred to the Governor and Counsell of Estate.

The same morning the lawes abovewritten, drawen out of the instructions, were read, and one by one thoroughly examined, and then passed once again. . . .

WEDNESDAY Aug. 4th. — This daye (by reason of extream heat, both paste and likely to ensue, and by that meanes of the alteration of the healthes of diverse of the general Assembly) the Governour, who himselfe also was not well, resolved should

FIRST REPRESENTATIVE ASSEMBLY IN AMERICA 61

be the last of this first session; so in the morning the Speaker (as he was required by the Assembly) redd over all the lawes and orders that had formerly passed the house, to give the same yett one reviewe more, and to see whether there were any thing to be amended or that might be excepted againste. This being done, the third sorte of lawes which I am nowe coming to sett downe, were read over [and] thoroughly discussed, which together with the former, did now passe the last and finall consente of the General Assembly.

A third sorte of lawes, suche as may issue out of every man's private conceipte.

. . . All Ministers in the Colony shall once a year, namely, in the moneth of Marche, bring to the Secretary of Estate a true account of all Christenings, burials and marriages, upon paine, if they faill, to be censured for their negligence by the Governor and Counsell. . . .

No man, without leave of the Governor, shall kill any Neatt Cattle whatsoever, young or olde, especially kine . . . upon penalty of forfeiting the value of the beast so killed.

Whosoever shall take any of his neighbors' boates, oares, or canvas, without leave from the owner, shall be held and esteemed as a felon, and so proceeded against.[1]

All ministers shall duly read divine service, and exercise their ministerial function according to the Ecclesiastical lawes and orders of the churche of Englande, and every Sunday in the afternoon shall Catechize suche as are not yet ripe to come to the Com. And whosoever of them shalbe found negligent or faulty in this kinde shalbe subject to the censure of the Governor and Counsell of Estate. . . .

For reformation of swearing, every freeman and Master of a family, after thrice admonition [by church wardens], shall give 5 s . . . to the use of the church . . . and every servant . . . except his Mr discharge the fine, shalbe subject to whipping.

---

[1] Water was the only means of travel and trade. To steal a boat was equivalent to horse-stealing in a cow-boy country today. "Felony" was punishable by death.

Provided that, the payment of the fine notwithstanding, the said servant shall acknowledge his faulte publiquely in the Churche.

All persons whatsoever upon the Sabaoth daye shall frequente divine service and sermons both forenoon and afternoon, and all suche as beare arms shall bring their pieces, swordes, poulder and shotte. And every one that shall trangresse this lawe shall forfaicte three shillinges a time to the use of the churche, all lawful and necessary impediments excepted. But if a servant in this case shall wilfully neglecte his Mr's commande he shall suffer bodily punishmente.

No maide or woman servant, either now resident in the Colonie or hereafter to come, shall contract herselfe in marriage without either the consente of her parents, or of her Master or Mistress, or of the magistrat and minister of the place both together. And whatsoever minister shall marry or contracte any suche persons without some of the foresaid consentes shalbe subjecte to the severe censure of the Governor and Counsell of Estate.

Here ende the lawes.

. . . Captain Henry Spellman was called to the barre to answere to certain misdemeanors . . . whereupon the General Assembly, having thoroughly heard and considered his speeches [evidence had been taken and defense put in], did constitute the following order [For exposing the colony to disturbance from the Indians by inciting them to disrespect of the government, Spellman was "degraded of his title of Captaine" and "condemned to performe seven yeares service to the Colony" as an interpreter to the governor.]

[Provision that every male in the colony over 16 years of age shall be taxed "one pound of the best tobacco" for pay to the officers of the Assembly.]

* * * * * * * * * * *

Thirdly, the General Assembly doth humbly beseech the . . . Treasurer, Counsell and Company that, albeit it belongeth

THE LONDON COMPANY'S "DECLARATION" 63

to them onely to allowe or to abrogate any lawes which we shall here make . . . yet that it would please them not to take it in ill parte if these lawes . . . do passe currant and be of force till suche time as we may knowe their farther pleasure. . . .

Their last humble suite is that the said Counsell and Company would be pleased, so soon as they shall find it convenient, to make good their *promise sett downe at the conclusion of their commission for establishing the Counsel of Estate and the General Assembly, namely that they give us power to allowe or to disallowe of their orders of Courts, as his Majesty hath given them power to allowe or reject our lawes.*

In sume, Sir George Yeardley, the Governor, prorogued the said general Assembly till the firste of Marche, which is to fall out this present yeare of 1619 [1620. New Style; cf. note, page 44], and in the mean season dissolved the same.

26. The London Company's "Declaration," June, 1620

Peter Force's *Historical Tracts* (Washington, 1844), III, No. 5.

Sandys resigned his "Treasurership" at the Court of the Company in May, 1620. The statistics of his report, with an enthusiastic general statement to introduce them, were published soon afterward by the Company as "A Declaration of the State of the Colonie and Affaires in Virginia." Sandys' report is now printed in full in the *Records* of the Company, edited by Susan Kingsbury (Washington, 1906).

After the many disasters wherewith it pleased Almighty God to suffer the great Enemy of all good Actions to encounter and interrupt this noble Action for the planting of Virginia with the Christian Religion and English people, it having pleased him now, contrarily, of his especiall great grace, so to blesse and prosper our late carefull endeavors . . . that [the colony] hath as it were growne to double that height, strength, plenty, and prosperity which it had in former times. . . . We have thought it now the peculiar duety of our place . . . to Summon, as it were, by a kinde of loving invitement, the whole body of the Noble and other worthy Adventurors, as well to the . . . perfecting of this happy worke as to the reaping of the fruit of their great expenses and travailes.

. . . [And first, to remove the effect of slanders upon Virginia, the Company declares] the Countrey is rich, spacious, and well watered; temperate as for the Climate; very healthfull after men are a little accustomed to it; abounding with all Gods naturall blessings: The Land replenished with the goodliest Woods in the world, and those full of *Deere*, and other Beasts of sustenance: The Seas and Rivers (whereof many are exceeding faire and navigable) full of excellent Fish, and of all sorts desireable; both Water and Land yeelding Fowle in very great store and variety: In Summe, a Countrey too good for ill people; and wee hope reserved by the providence of God for such as shall apply themselves faithfully to his service and be a strength and honour to our King and Nation. . . .

The rich Furres, Caviary, and Cordage, which we draw from *Russia* with so great difficulty, are to be had in *Virginia*, and the parts adjoining, with ease and plenty. The Masts, Planckes, and Boords, the Pitch and Tarre, the Pot-ashes and Sope-ashes, the Hempe and Flax (being the materials of Linnen) which now we fetch from *Norway*, *Denmarke*, *Poland*, and *Germany*, are there to be had in abundance and great perfection. The *Iron*, which hath so wasted our *English* Woods,[1] that it selfe in short time must decay together with them, is to be had in *Virginia* (where wasting of Woods is a benefit) for all good conditions answerable to the best in the world. The Wines, Fruite, and Salt of *France* and *Spaine*, The Silkes of *Persia* and *Italie*, will be found also in *Virginia*, and in no kinde of worth inferior. Wee omit here a multitude of other naturall Commodities, dispersed up and downe the divers parts of the world: of Woods, Rootes, and Berries, for excellent Dyes: Of Plants and other Drugges, for Physicall service: Of sweet Woods, Oyles, and Gummes, for pleasure and other use: Of Cotton-wooll, and Sugar-Canes: all which

---

[1] Wood was the fuel then used to smelt iron ore.

may there also be had in abundance, with an infinity of other more: And will conclude with these three, Corne, Cattle, and Fish, which are the substance of the foode of man. The Graines of our Countrey doe prosper there very well: Of Wheate they have great plenty: But their *Maze*, being the naturall Graine of that Countrey, doth farre exceede in pleasantnesse, strength, and fertility. The Cattle which we have transported thither (being now growne neere to five hundred) become much bigger of Body then the breed from which they came: The Horses also more beautifull, and fuller of courage. And such is the extraordinary fertility of that *Soyle*, that the *Does* of their *Deere* yeelde two Fawnes at a birth, and sometimes three. The Fishings at *Cape Codd*, being within those Limits, will in plenty of Fish be equall to those of *Newfound Land*, and in goodnesse and greatnesse much superiour. To conclude, it is a Countrey, which nothing but ignorance can thinke ill of, and which no man but of a corrupt minde and ill purpose can defame.

Now touching the present estate of our Colony in that Country, Wee have thought it not unfit thus much briefly to declare. There have beene sent thither this last yeare, and are now presently in going, twelve hundred persons and upward, as particularly appeareth in the note above [below] specified: and there are neere one thousand more remaining of those that were gone before. *The men lately sent, have beene most of them choise men, borne and bred up to labour and industry. Out of Devonshire, about an hundred men, brought up to Husbandry. Out of Warwickshire and Staffordshire, above one hundred and ten; and out of Sussex about forty; all framed to Iron-workes: the rest dispersedly out of divers Shires of the Realme. There have been also sundry persons of good quality, much commended for sufficiency, industry and honesty, provided and sent to take charge and government of those people.* The care likewise that hath beene taken by directions, Instructions, Charters, and Commissions to reduce the people and affaires in *Virginia* into a regular course, hath beene such and so great that the Colony beginneth now to have the face and fashion of an orderly State, and such as is likely to grow and prosper. The people are all divided into severall Burroughs; each man having the shares of Land due to him set out, to hold and enjoy to him and his Heires. The publique Lands for the Company here, for the Governor there, for the College, and for each particular Burrough, for the Ministers also, and for divers other necessary Officers, are likewise laid out by order, and bounded. The particular Plantations for divers private Societies, are settled in their Seates, being allotted to their content, and each in convenient distance. *The rigour of Martiall Law, wherewith before they were governed, is reduced within the limits prescribed by his Majesty: and the laudable forme of Justice and government used in this Realme [is] established and followed as neere as may be. The governour is so restrained to a Counseil joyned with him that hee can doe no wrong to no man who may not have speedy remedy.* . . .

In summe, they [the colonists] are now so full of alacritie and cheerefulnesse, that, in a late generall Assembly, they have, in the name of the Colony, presented their greatest possible thankes to the Company. . . .

[After enumerating recent grants]

These and other like Planters, having priority of time, will have priority also in choise of the Seat of their Plantations. Seeing therefore the onely matter of retribution to the Adventurors, is by a faire proportion of Land to them and their heires; namely of one hundred acres for every share of twelve pounds and ten shillings, upon a first division; and as much more upon a second, the first being peopled; with fiftie acres for every person (to be doubled in like manner) which at their owne charges they shall transport to inhabit in *Virginia* before the 24th day of *June* 1625 [therefore, quite after the fashion of modern land companies, intending "adventurers" are urged to invest promptly, before the choice land is all taken].

THE LONDON COMPANY'S "DECLARATION"

Note of the Shipping, Men, and Provisions sent to Virginia, by the Treasurer and Company *in the yeere*, 1619.

a. Ships.

The *Bona Nova* of 200. Tun sent in August 1619. with 120 persons.
The *Duty*, of 70. Tunne, sent in January 1619. with 51. persons.
The *Jonathan*, of 350. Tun, sent in February, 1619. with 200. persons.
The *Triall*, of 200. Tun, sent in February, 1619. with 40. persons, and 60. Kine.
The *Faulcon*, of 150. Tun, sent in February, 1619. with 36. persons, and 52. Kine, and 4. Mares.
The *London Merchant*. of 300. Tun, sent in March, 1619. with 200. persons.
The *Swan of Barnstable*, of 100. Tun, in March, 1619. with 71. persons.
The *Bonaventure*, of 240. Tun, sent in Aprill, 1620. with 153. persons.

Besides these, sent out by the *Treasurer* and Company, ther have been sennt outt by particularr adventurers for private *Plantations*.

The *Garland*, of 25. Tunne, sent in June, 1619, for Mr. *John Ferrars* Plantation, with 45. persons. Who are yet deteyned in the *Summer Islands*.

A Ship of *Bristoll*, of 80. Tunne, sent in Septemb. 1619. for Mr. *Barkleys* Plantation, with 45. persons.

Ther are allso two Ships in providinge to be shortlie gone, for about 300 Personnes more, to be sent by priyvate Adventurers to *Virginia*.

	Summe
Summe of the Persons	1261
Whereof in eight Ships sett out by the Treasurer and Company	871

[The other 390 came in other vessels, not sent by the Company.]

Of these [871], there were sent for Publique and other Pious uses these ensuinge.

Tenants for the governors Land	080
Tenants for the Companies Land	130
Tenants for the Colledge Land	130
Tenants for the Mynisters gleab Land	050
Young Maydens to make wives	090
Boyes to make Apprentises	100
Servants for the Publique	050
Men sent to beare up the Charge of bringinge upp thirty of the Infidles Children in true religion and Civilitie	050
Summe of the Persons for Publique use is	650 [680]

b. *Commodities.*

The Commodities which these people are dyrected principally to apply (next to their owne necessary mayntenance) are these ensuinge.

Iron, for which are sent 150 persons to sett upp three Iron works; proofe haveinge beene made of the extraordinary goodnes of that Ironn.

Cordage . . . .

Pitch and Tarr, Pott Ashes, and Sope Ashes, — for the makinge whereof the *Polackers* are returned to their workes.

TIMBER of all sorts, with Masts, Plankes and Boordes for provision of Shippinge, etc.; ther beinge not so good Timber for all uses in any one knowne Countrey whatsoever. And for the ease and encrease of divers of these workes, provision is sent of men and materiales for the settinge upp of Sundry Sawinge Mills.

SILKE: for which that Country is exceedinge proper, haveing innumerable store of Mulberie Trees of the best, and some Silke-wormes naturally found upon them [caterpillars?] producing excellent Silke: some whereof is to be seene. For the setting up of which Comoditie, his Majesty hath beene gratiouslie pleased now the second time (the former haveing miscarried) to bestowe uppon the Company plenty of Silkewormes seed of his owne store, being the best.

VINES: whereof the Countrey yeeldeth naturally greate store, and of sundry sorts: which by Culture wilbe brought to excellent perfection. For the effectinge whereof, divers skillful *Vignerons* are sent, with store allso from hence of *Vine* plantes of the best sort.

SALT: which workes haveinge been lately suffered to decay, are now ordered to be sett upp in so great plenty, as not onely to serve the Collony for the present; but as is hoped in short time allso the great Fishinge on those Coastes.

For the followinge, workinge, and perfectinge of these *Commodities,* all provisions necessary for the present are sent in good aboundance. As likewise the people that goe, are plentifully furnished with Apparell, Beddinge, Victuall for six monethes : Implements both for House and labour, Armour, weapons, tooles, and sundry other necessaries. And a supply of Armour, Powder, and many necessary provisions is made for those of the Colonie which were there before; yet without any prejudice to the former *Magazine*.

c. Gifts.[1]

There have beene given to the Collonie this yeere, by Devoute Persons, these guifts ensuinge.

Two Persons, unknowne, have given faire Plate and other rich Ornaments for two Communion Tables; whereof one for the Colledge, and the other for the Church of Mistress Mary Robinson's foundinge : who in the former yeere by her Will gave 200. pounds towards the foundinge of a Church in *Virginia*.

Another unknowne person[2] (together with a goodly letter) hath lately sent to the Treasurer 550. pounds in gold, for the bringing up of Children of the *Infidels*: first in the Knowledge of God and true Religion; and next, in fitt Trades whereby honestly to live.

Master *Nicolas Ferrar* deceased, hath by his Will given 300. pounds to the College in *Virginia*, to be paid, when there shall be ten of the *Infidels* children placed in it. And in the meane time foure and twenty pounds by yeere, to be distributed unto three discreet and Godlie men in the Colony, which shall honestly bring up three of the *Infidels* children in Christian Religion, and some good course to live by.

An unnamed person sent to the *Treasurer* the summe of ten pounds, for advancing the *Plantation*.[3]

---

[1] This part of the appendix to the Declaration is taken from Sir Edwin Sandys' report in May, and his wording is followed here (*Records*, I, 353, 354). It is plain that such gifts were made because the Company had the character of a foreign missionary society.

[2] This person in his letter to the Company signs himself "Dust and Ashes," and, in a *later* communication, "D.& A."

[3] The entry in the *Records* of the Company (I, 335) speaks of this gift "for some good uses in Virginia."

In 1622, "a person not willinge as yet to be knowne" sent £ 25 " to helpe

27. The Ordinance of 1621 for Virginia

Stith's *History of Virginia*, App. IV; Hening's *Statutes*, I, 110 ff.

The *Records* of the Virginia Assembly of 1619 (see No. 25 above) show that the London Company had given to the settlers a "great charter." No copy of it exists; but apparently its political features were repeated in this document, issued by the Company July 24/Aug. 3, 1621, on the appointment of a new governor. This great Ordinance has sometimes been called, mistakenly, The First Charter to the Virginian Colonists. It is the *second* such charter. Cf. *American History and Government*, § 30.

An Ordinance and Constitution of the Treasurer, Council, and Company in England, *for a Council of State and General Assembly.*

I. — To all People, to whom these Presents shall come, be seen, or heard, The Treasurer, Council, and Company of Adventurers and Planters for the city of *London* for the first Colony of *Virginia* send Greeting. KNOW YE, that we, the said Treasurer, Council, and Company, taking into our Consideration the present State of the said Colony of Virginia, and intending, by the Divine Assistance, to settle such a Form of Government there, as may be to the greatest Benefit and Comfort of the People, and whereby all Injustice, Grievances, and Oppression may be prevented and kept off as much as possible from the said Colony, have thought fit to make our Entrance, by ordering and establishing such Supreme Councils as may not only be assisting to the Governor for the time being, in the Administration of Justice, and the Executing of other Duties to this Office belonging, but also, by their vigilant Care and and Prudence, may provide as well for a Remedy of all Inconveniences, growing from time to time, as also for the advancing of Increase, Strength, Stability, and Prosperity of the said Colony:

---

forward the 'East India' Schoole." I count up twelve entries of such gifts in three years' *Records*. In 1623 the Company reported that in the past four years there had been contributed "towards the forwardinge of this glorious Worke, . . . presents to the value of fifteen hundred pounds, by zealous and devoute Persons, most of them refusing to be named."

II. — WE therefore, the said Treasurer, Council, and Company, by Authority directed to us from his Majesty under the Great Seal [section xiii of the Second Charter; p. 40 above], upon Mature Deliberation, do hereby order and declare, that, from hence forward, there shall be TWO SUPREME COUNCILS in *Virginia*, for the better Government of the said Colony aforesaid.

III. — THE one of which Councils, to be called THE COUNCIL OF STATE (and whose Office shall chiefly be assisting, with their Care, Advice, and Circumspection, to the said Governor) shall be chosen, nominated, placed, and displaced, from time to time, by Us, the said Treasurer, Council, and Company, and our Successors: Which Council of State shall consist, for the present, only of these persons, as are here inserted, *viz.* Sir *Francis Wyat*, Governor of *Virginia*, Captain *Francis West*, Sir *George Yeardley*, Knight, Sir *William Neuce*, Knight Marshal of *Virginia*, Mr. George *Sandys*, Treasurer, Mr. George *Thorpe*, Deputy of the College, Captain *Thomas Neuce*, Deputy for the Company, Mr. *Pawlet*, Mr. *Leech*, Captain *Nathaniel Powel*, Mr. *Christopher Davison*, Secretary, Dr. *Pots*, Physician to the Company, Mr. *Roger Smith*, Mr. *John Berkeley*, Mr. *John Rolfe*, Mr. *Ralph Hamer*, Mr. *John Pountis*, Mr. *Michael Lapworth*, Mr. *Harwood*, Mr. *Samuel Macock*. Which said Counsellors and Council we earnestly pray and desire, and in his Majesty's Name strictly charge and command, that (all Factions, Partialities, and sinister Respect laid aside) they bend their Care and Endeavours to assist the said Governor; first and principally, in the Advancement of the Honour and Service of God, and the Enlargement of his Kingdom amongst the Heathen People; and next, in erecting of the said Colony in due Obedience to his Majesty, and all lawful Authority from his Majesty's Directions; and lastly, in maintaining the said People in Justice and *Christian* Conversation amongst themselves, and in Strength and Ability to withstand their Enemies. And this Council to be always, or for the most Part, residing about or near the Governor.

IV. — THE other Council, more generally to be called by the

Governor once Yearly, and no oftener but for very extraordinary and important Occasions, shall consist, for the present, of the said Council of State, and of two Burgesses out of every Town, Hundred, or other particular Plantation, to be respectively chosen by the Inhabitants: Which Council shall be called THE GENERAL ASSEMBLY, wherein (as also in the said Council of State) all Matters shall be decided, determined, and ordered, by the greater Part of the Voices then present; reserving to the Governor always a Negative Voice. And this General Assembly shall have free Power to treat, consult, and conclude, as well of all emergent Occasions concerning the Publick Weal of the said Colony and every Part thereof, as also to make, ordain, and enact such general Laws and Orders for the Behoof of the said Colony, and the good Government thereof, as shall, from time to time, appear necessary or requisite;

V. — WHEREAS in all other Things, we require the said General Assembly, as also the said Council of State, to imitate and follow the Policy of the Form of Government, Laws, Customs, and Manner of Trial, and other Administration of Justice, used in the Realm of *England*, as near as may be, even as ourselves, by his Majesty's Letters Patent are required.

VI. — PROVIDED, that no Law or Ordinance, made in the said General Assembly, shall be or continue in Force or Validity, unless the same shall be solemnly ratified and confirmed in a General Quarter Court of the said Company here in *England*, and so ratified, be returned to them under our Seal; It being our Intent to afford the like Measure also unto the said Colony, that after the Government of the said Colony shall once have been well framed, and settled accordingly, which is to be done by Us, as by Authority derived from his Majesty, and the same shall have been so by us declared, no Orders of Court afterwards shall bind the said Colony, unless they be ratified in like Manner in the General Assemblies [1] . . .

---

[1] Such a promise in the preceding "great charter" is plainly referred to in the "last humble suite" of the Assembly of 1619; see p. 63 above.

28. Royal Attempts to Control the Company, 1620-1622

Records of the Virginia Company, I and II, under dates given. These Records were first published in full in 1908 by the Government Printing Office at Washington. For a brief outline of the history, with references to some other source material, cf. *American History and Government*, § 32.

(1) *A Quarter Courte held for Virginia at Mr Ferrars in St Sithes Lane the 17th of May 1620.*

Present — [The list includes 172 names with the addenda " and many others." The first eight named were Lords ; the next thirty, knights.]

Uppon request of some of the generallytie itt was ordered that frome hence forth before the Company proceed to the choyce of their Officers the Chapter or title of election [*i.e.*, the company's rules regarding elections] shall allwaies be red before.

* * * * * * *

Imeadiately after, and before they proceeded in any buisines, one mr Kerkham agent, sent from the King, presented himselfe to the boord and signified to the Courte that his Majestie, understandinge of the Eleccion of their Treasuror, which they intended this day to make choyce of, out of an especiall care and respect hee hath to that Plantacion, hath required him to nominate unto them ffower, outt of which his pleasure is the Company should make choyce of one to be their Treasurer; That was, Sir Thomas Smith, Sir Thomas Roe, Mr. Alderman Johnson, and Mr. Maurice Abbott, *and noe other*.

* * * * * * *

These buisines beinge thus ordered mr Treasurer accordinge to the standing Lawes of the Company before the giveinge upp of his place proceeded to declare unto this Courte the State of the Colony together with the Supplies of this yeare, and the present State of the Treasury, how both hee found itt and now should leave itt.   [See No. 26 above.]

Lastly hee concluded with his respective thanks, first to the Company in generall for their love in chosinge him, and then particularly to the Lords for their so frequent presence to the graceinge of the Courte and great assistance in the buisines; to the Officers for their faythfull joyninge with him in the supportinge of his burthen; and againe to the Courte in generall for their patience in bearringe with his unwillinge errors and other naturall infirmities. So deliveringe upp his Office togeather with the Sealls, hee desyred the Courte to proceed in Eleccion of their Treasuror, accordinge to the message lately receaved from his Majesty: and theruppon withdrew himselfe out of the Courte.

Uppon which this great and generall Courte found themselves uppon a deliberate consideracion of the matter att an exceedinge pinch: for if they should not doe as the Kinge had commaunded they might incurre suspicion of defect in poynte of duety, — from which they protested they were and would be free; on the other side, if they should proceed accordinge to the lymitts of that message they suffered a greate breach into their Prevyledge of free Eleccion graunted to them by his Majestys letters Pattents, which they held fitt rather to lay downe with all dutie and submission att his Majesties ffeet then to be depryved of their pryveledge. And theruppon perusing the said letters Pattents, after longe arguinge and debatinge, itt was concluded by generall ereccion of hands, that the eleccion might and should be adjourned to the next Quarter Courte notwithstanding any order made by the Company to the contrarie.

Wheruppon forasmuch as itt manyfestly appeared that his Majestie hadd beene much misinformed of the menaginge of their buisines this last yeare, Itt was agreed accordinge to the opynion aforesaide that the day of Eleccon should be putt of till the next generall Courte some six weeks hence in Midsomer Tearme, and till they understood the Kings farther pleasure, And in the intrym they humbly entreated the Right Honorable the Lord of Southampton, Vyscount Doncaster, The Lord Cavendish, the Lord Sheffield, Sir John Davers, Sir Nicholas Tufton, Sir Lawrence Hide, mr Christopher Brook, mr Gibbes, mr Herbert, mr Keightley, and mr Cranmer to meet uppon ffryday morninge att Southampton house to determine of an humble answere unto his Majesties message and to deliver to him a true informaccon as well of the former as of this latter years government of the buisines for Virginia, beseechinge allso that his Majestie would be pleased not to take from them the Pryveledge of their letters Pattents, butt that itt might be in their owne choyce to have free eleccion.

Uppon which, till his Majesties pleasure were knowne, Sir Edwin Sandys, after much and ernest refusall, att length uppon ernest request of the whole Courte hee yeilded to sett down in his former place, yett forbearinge to receave the Seales againe or to putt any thinge to Question; and all other Officers were likewise continued till the same time.

(2) *A Great and Generall Quarter Courte helde in the afternoone at Mr. Ferrars House. 28th July 1620.*

*   *   *   *   *   *   *

The Earle of Southampton acquainted this Courte that himselfe with the rest of the Lords and gentlemen requested therunto by the last Quarter Courte had presented their humble desires unto his Majestie for the free eleccon of their Treasurer, wherunto his Majestie had most gratiously condiscented, signyfyinge unto them that it would be pleasinge to him they made choyce of such a one as might att all times and occasions have free accesse unto his royall personn. And further declaringe that itt was the mistakinge of the messenger, haveinge not receaved his message imeadiately from his owne royall mouth, to exclud them from the libertie of choosinge any butt the fower nominated, whom his Majesties intent was indeed to recommend butt not so as to barr the Company from the choyse of any other.

Wheruppon the wholl Courte rendred to his Majestie all humble thanks and ordered that by writinge itt should be signified unto his Majestie:

Then mr Herbert delivered unto the Company that wheras by some distractions and discentions in the Company the buisines much suffered in the reputaccon and otherwise, they should now think uppon some Person of such worth and authoritie as might give full remedie therunto, which since itt could not be performed by the late Treasurer a man of that greate habilitie and sufficiencie together with his industrie and integritie as of his ranke ther could not be found any to passe him, there was now lefte noe hope except itt might please some of those Honorable personages [Lords] then present to vouchsaffe to accept of the place, who by adiccon of Nobilitie might effect that which others by meere habillytie could not doe.

Which moccon beinge exceedinglie approved, the whole Courte imeadiately with much joy and applause nominated the Earle of Southampton, with much ernestnes beseechinge his Lordship that for the redeeminge of this Noble Plantaccon and Company from the ruines that seemed to hange over itt hee would vouchsaffe to accept of the place of Treasurer.

Which itt pleased him after some finale pause in fine to doe in very noble manner out of the worthie love and affeccon that hee bare to the Plantaccon. And the Courte in testimoniall of their bounden thankfullnes and of the great honoure and respect they ought him, did resolve *to surcease the ballatinge box;* and without nominaccon of any other, by ereccon of hands, his Lordship was chosen Treasurer and tooke his Oath. Which done, his Lordship desyred the Company that they would all putt on the same myndes with which hee hadd accepted that place.

(3) *At a great and generall Quarter Courte held for Virginia in the Afternoone the 22 of May 1622.*

Imediately after these things were thus ordered, as the Court were proceedinge after their accustomed manner to the eleccon of their Treasurer Deputy and other Officers for this present yeare accordinge to the direccon of his Majesties Letters Patents, mr Alderman Hamersly rose upp and havinge first excused his seldome comminge to Courts by reason of the Officers negligent warninge of him, he said That himselfe and mr Bell were both commaunded by mr Secretary Calvert to deliver a Message in his Majesties name unto this Court, namely to signifie, that although it was not his Majesties desire to infringe their liberty of free elleccon yet it would be pleasing unto him, if they made choise for Treasuror and Deputy any of those gentlemen (commended for their Sufficiency), whose names were mencioned in the paper nowe presented in open Court which were these that followe vizt. [The names of five gentlemen nominated by the King for Treasurer, and five more for Deputy.] . . .

Mr Bell, beinge also entreated to deliver the Message he had receaved from mr Secretary Calvert, said that he was not present when mr Secretary Calvert imparted this Message to mr Alderman Hamersley, but that there came a Messenger to him over night to require him to attend mr Secretary Calvert at his Chamber; and beinge there, mr Secretary told him that his Majestie commaunded him to signifie his pleasure that out of his good wishes (for the good of the Company and the Plantation) he had recommended to this Court certaine Gentlemen (named in the paper nowe presented) if the Company so thought good: But it was not his meaning to infringe the liberty of their free choise; And beinge desirous to have had his Message in writing, mr Secretary said it needed not for it was but short.

Both which Messages agreeing in substance, and **beinge a full remonstrance of his Majesties well wishing unto the Plantation and of his graceous meaninge not to infringe the priviledge of the Companie and liberty of their free eleccon,** was receaved with great love and contentment of the whole Court; and therupon proceedinge to the eleccon of their Treasuror (for which onely three by the orders of the Company could stand). It was generally agreed that out of the five formerly proposed by his Majestie for Treasuror, choise should be made of two of them to stand in eleccon with one that the Companie should name:

Wherupon the former five beinge severally put to the question, it appeared by ereccon of most hands that mr Clethero and mr Hanford were to stand for it: Then the Companie named the Lord of Southampton; who beinge all three accordingly ballated, the place fell to the Lord of Southampton by havinge 117 balls, mr Clethero 13 and mr Hanford 7. In like manner out of the five formerly named by his Majestie for Deputy, by ereccion of most hands, mr Leat and mr Bateman were to stand for it; ûnto whome the Companie havinge added mr Nicholas ffarrer, they were all three put to the Ballatinge Boxe, and thereupon choise was made of mr Nicholas ffarar by havinge 103, mr Bateman 10: and mr Leate 5.

* * * * * * *

Itt beinge moved that there might be some presentaccon of the Companies humble thankfullnes unto his Majestie in respect of the graceous Message formerly delivered, after some deliberaccon had thereuppon, the Court conceaved it fitt to be sett downe in these words (vizt) That the Lord Cavendish the Lord Padgett, the Lord Haughton are humbly requested by the Court to present their most humble thanks to his Majestie for his graceous remembrance and good wishes to their affaires out of which he was graceously pleased to recommend certaine persons for Treasuror and Deputy if they so thought fitt, but without any infringement of their liberty of free eleccon; and they were further humbly requested to signify and testifie unto his Majestie the great respect and reverence wherewith his message was receaved and howe in conformity thereunto, although they had formerly accordinge to their custome in their Praeparative Court nominated the Earle of Southampton for Treasuror, yet out of the persons recommended by his Majestie they choose fower who had most voices and put them in eleccon with two nominated by the Company, — upon whom the places were conferred by an unanimous consent of the Company, havinge founde the Plantation to prosper every of these three last yeares more then in ten before, and [more] found to have bin donn with Ten thousand pounds, then formerly with fower score thousand. . . .

[The language of the *Records*, of course, is decorous and courtly; but the student ought to be able to see a certain grim humor along with the steadfast determination not to permit royal usurpation. The Ferrars' Papers report that, when this last communication was delivered to the King, he "flung away in a furious passion," — not unnaturally. Some of the other episodes in this connection told in those papers are given in *American History and Government*.]

V. A ROYAL PROVINCE

(Representative Government in Danger)

29. The Royal Commission of 1624 for the First Royal Governor in Virginia

Hazard's *State Papers* (1792), I, 189 ff. The first part of the extract here given presents King James' view of recent troubles with the Virginia Company.

. . . And whereas Wee, out of our zeal and affection to the furthering of the said Plantations, having still a watchfull and carefull eye to the same, and finding the courses taken for the setling thereof, had not taken the good effect which Wee intended and so much desired, did, by our Commission lately graunted to certaine Persons of Qualitie and Trust, cause the state of the said country of *Virginia* be to examined how it stood, as well in point of livelihood as government; . . . to the end, yf good cause were, Wee might by our royall hand, supply what should be defective. And whereas our Commissioners, after much care and paines expended in execution of our said Commissions, did certifie us, that our Subjects and People sent to inhabite there, and to plant themselves in that country, were most of them by God's visitations, sickness of bodie, famine, and by massacres of them by the native savages of the land, dead and deceased, and those that were living of them lived in necessitie and want, and in danger by the Savages: but the Country, for any thing appeared to the said Commissioners to the contrary, they conceaved to be fruitfull and healthfull after our People had been some time there; and that if industry were used it would produce divers good and staple Commodities, though in the sixteene years government past, it had yealded fewe or none; . . . and that yf our first graunt herein mentioned, and our most prudent and princely instructions given in the beginning of the Plantation, for the direction of the affaires thereof . . . had bin pursued, much better effect had bin produced than had bin by the alteration thereof, into soe popular [democratic] a course . . .: Whereupon Wee entring into mature and deliberate consideration of the premisses, did, by the advise of the Lords of our Privie Counsell, resolve, by altering the Charters of the said Company, as to the point of government wherein the same might be found defective, to settle such a course as might best secure the safetie of the People there, and cause the said Plantation to flourish, and yet with the preservation of the interest of every Planter or Adventurer, soe far forth as their present interests shall not prejudice the publique Plantations; But because the said *Treasurer and Company* did not submitt their Charters to be reformed, our proceedings therein were stayed for a tyme, untill, uppon a *Quo Warranto* . . . by due course of Lawe, the said charters were avoyded; [And whereas the King intends to prepare another charter, and in the interval, by a commission of July 15, 1629, has established a supervising council in England for the Colony (composed of members of the Privy Council), now, according to advice from this council] . . . untill some other constant . . . course be resolved upon . . . Knowe yee . . . that Wee reposing assured trust and confidence in the understanding, care, fidelitie, experience, and circumspection of you, . . . Sir Francis Wyatt, Francis West, Sir George Yardeley, George Sandys, Roger Smith, Ralph Hamor, John Martin, John Harvy, Samuell Mathews, Abraham Perrey, Isaacke Madison, and William Clayborne, have nominated and assigned, and do hereby nomynate and assigne you the said Sir Francis Wyatt, to bee the present Governor, and you the said Francis West, Sir George Yardeley, and the rest before mentioned, to be our present Councell of and for the said Colonye and Plantation in *Virginia:* Giving and granting unto you, and the greater nomber of you, by theis presents respectively, full power and authoritie to performe and execute the places, powers, and authorities incident to a Governor and Councell in *Virginia*, respectively, and to direct and governe, correct and punish our Subjects nowe inhabiting or being, or which hereafter shall inhabite or be in *Virginia*, or in any the Isles, portes, havens, creaks, or territories thereof, either in tyme of peace or warre, and to order and direct the affaires touching or concerning that Colonie or Plantation in those forraigne partes onely;[1] *and [to] doe, execute and performe all and every other matters and things concerning that Plantation, as fullye and amplye as any Governor and Councell resident there, at any tyme within the space of five yeares now last past* . . . Nevertheless, our will and pleasure is, that yee proceed therein according to such instructions as yee, or such of you as have bene heretofore of our Councell there, have received, or according to such instructions as you shall hereafter receave from Us, or our Commissioners here. . . . And lastly, our will and pleasure is, that this our commission shall continue in force untill such tyme as Wee by some other writing under our Signett, privie Seale, or greate Seale, shall signify our pleasure to the contrary. . . .

30. Yeardley's Commission from Charles I, March 4/14, 1624/5

Hazard's *State Papers* (1792), I, 230–234. This commission, so far as concerns the powers of the governor, followed the commission given in No. 29 above. Cf. *American History and Government*, § 34.

[The King, Charles I,] reposing assured Truste and Confidence in the Understanding, Care, Fidelitie, Experience, and Circumspection of you the said Sir *George Yardeley, Francis West, John Hervey, George Sandys, John Pott, Roger Smith, Ralph Hamor, Samuell Matthews, Abraham Percey, William Clayborne, William Tucker, Jabes Whitacres, Edward Blaney*, and *William Farrar*, have nominated and assigned . . . you the said Sir *George Yardeley*, to be the present Governour, and you

---

[1] The English Council, previously named, remained in supreme charge in England.

the said John Harvey, and the rest before mentioned to be the present Councell of and for the said *Collony and Plantation in Virginia,* giveing ... unto you full Power and authority to performe and execute the Places, Powers, and Authorities incident to a Governour and Councell of Virginia respectively ; and to direct and governe, correct and punish our Subjects ... in Virginia, eyther in tyme of Peace or Warr; and to order and direct the Affaires touching or concerneing that Collony or Plantation in those forreigne parts only ; and to execute and performe all and every other Matters and Things concerneing that Plantation, *as fully and amply as any Governour and Councell resident there, at anie time within the Space of Five Years now last past, had or might performe or execute:* ...

[*Observe* that there is no reference to the Assembly in this document or in the preceding one.]

31. The Colony favors the Policy of the Company

a. *The Assembly enacts a precautionary "Bill of Rights," March, 1624*

Hening's *Statutes at Large, being a Collection of the Laws of Virginia* (1823). Cf. *American History and Government,* § 34.

It had become apparent that the King was about to destroy the Company and take over the colony. This Assembly enacted some thirty brief statues. Three are of interest in this connection.

8. — *That the Governor shall not lay any taxes or ympositions upon the colony their lands or comodities other way than by the authority of the General Assembly, to be levyed and ymployed as the said Assembly shall appoynt.*[1]

9. — The governor shall not withdraw the inhabitants from their private labors to any service of his own upon any colour whatsoever; and in case the publick service require yimployments of many hands before the holding a General Assemblie to give order for the same, in that case the levying of men shall be done by order of the governor and whole body of the coun-

---

[1] This law was reënacted in the same words in *1632 and 1642.*

sell, and that in such sorte as to be least burthensome to the people and most free from partiality.

11. — That no burgesses of the General Assembly shall be arrested during the time of the assembly, a week before and a week after, upon pain of the creditors forfeiture of his debt and such punishment upon the officer as the court shall award.[1]

b. *Requests for Aid (and, indirectly, for an Assembly)*

(1) *Letter from Governor and Council to the Special Commission mentioned in No. 29 above.*

Aspinwall Papers, in *Massachusetts Historical Society Collections*, 4th series, IX, 74–81. About a third of the letter is given here.

Right Honorable, — . . . .

Nothing hath bine longe more earnestly desired then the setling of the affaires of the Collony, as well for the government as other wayes, neither could ther have bine a greater incouragement to the Planter then to understand it to bee his Majesties gratious pleasure that no person of whom they have heretofore justlie complayned should have any hand in the government, either here or their [in Virginia or in England]. And wee humbly desire your Lordshipps to solicitt his Majestie (if it bee not alreadie done) for the speedie accomplishment thereof, the rather because the Governors necessary occasions require his present retourne [to England].

His Majesties gratious assurance that every man shall have his perticuler right preserved and inlarged, with Addicion of reasonable imunities, wilbe a singular meanes of inviting many people hither, and setling themselves here . . .

Those greate important workes of suppressing the Indians, discoveries by sea and land, and Fortificacion against a forren enemy, that they may be thoroughly and effectually performed, will require no less numbers then Five hundred soldiers, to bee yearely sent over, for Certaine yeares, with a full yeares

---

[1] This immunity is copied from that of members of the English Parliament for some centuries preceding.

provision of Victuall, aparrell, armes, Munition, tooles, and all necessaries, to which Worthie designes the Collony wilbe alwayes readie to yeald ther best furtherance and assistance, as they have bine very forward since the Massacre, notwithstanding ther great losse then sustayned. And wee Conceive soe great expence, will have the better successe, if the ordering therof be refered to the Governor and Counsell here residing, **with the advise (in speciall Cases) of the Generall Assembly.** Both Concerning this, and alother things which may Conduce to the setling of the Plantacion, wee have formerly given your Lordshipps Advertisement, in the generall Assemblies answere to the ffowre propositions propounded by your Lordshipps to the Commissioners sent hither, and wee doubt not but Sir George Yardly hath given your Lordshipps full information of all things necessary. . . .

Your Lordshipps very humble Servants,

FRANCIS WYATT.
FRANCIS WEST.
RAPHE HAMOR.
ROGER SMITH.
ABRAHAM PERSEY.
WILLIAM CLAYBOURNE.

James Cittie the 6th. of Aprill, 1626.

(2) *The Same to the Same, May 17, 1626.*

Virginia Magazine of History, II, 50–55. An abstract is printed in the *Colonial State Papers*.

But the groundwork of all is, that their bee a sufficient publique stock to goe through with soe greate a worke, which wee cannot compute to bee lesse then £20,000 a yeare, certaine for some yeares; for by itt must be mainetained the goverser and counsell and other officers here, the forrest wonne and stockt with cattle, fortifications raysed, a running armye mainetayned, discoveries made by Sea and land, and all other things requisitt in soe mainefould a business. And because [of the difficulty of administering such sums wisely from England], wee humbly desire that a good proporcion thereof may bee whollie att the disposall of the governer, Counsell, *and generall Assembly in Virginia.* . . .

32. Royal Restoration of the Virginia Assembly, 1629

a. *Harvey's Propositions Touching Virginia (without date; 1629)*

Virginia Magazine of History, VII, 369.

For explanation, see *American History and Government*, § 34. Sir John Harvey had been appointed governor a few months before, with a commission *which made no mention of an Assembly.* The extract is No. 2 of the seven "propositions" submitted by him to King Charles.

2. That his Ma[jes]tie wilbe pleased gratiously to extend his favour to the planters, for a new confirmation of their lands and goods by charter under the great seale of England, and therein to authorize the Lords to consider what is fitt to be done for the ratifying of the privileges formerly granted, *and holding of a general assembly*, to be called by the Governor upon necessary occasions, therein to propound laws and orders for the good government of the people; and for that it is most reasonable that his ma[jes]ties subjects should be governed only by such laws as shall have their originall from his ma[jes]ties royall approbation, it be therefore so ordered that those laws, so there made, only stand as propositions, until his ma[jes]tie shalbe pleased, under his great seal or privy seal, or by the Lords of his noble privy council, to ratify the same.

b. *Certaine Answeres (by Charles I) to Capt. Harveye's Proposicons Touching Virginia*

Virginia Magazine of History, VII, 370.

2. The sett[l]ing of Lands and goods and privileges is to be done here, and may be done by calling in the former books and charters at a convenient time. *But the governor may be authorized shortly after his first coming into Virginia to call a*

grand assembly and there to set down an establishment of the Government, and ordaine laws and orders for the good thereof, and those to send hither to receive allowance [i.e., to be ratified]; and such as shall be soe allowed to be returned thither under the great seal and put in execution, the same to be temporary and changeable at his ma[jes]ties pleasure, signified under the like great seal.

[This is the formal restoration of the Virginia Assembly. The meeting in 1628 had been with special sanction for that particular occasion.]

c. *Assembly Authorized in a Governor's Instructions, 1641*

Virginia Magazine of History, II, 281 ff.

These instructions in the matter of the Assembly are said to have been given in the same form to Wyatt in 1639, — the governor who came between Harvey and Berkeley. For the significance of these papers, see *American History and Government*, §§ 34–35.

Instructions to Sir Wm. Berkeley, Knt., Governor of Virginia

* * * * * * *

4. That you and the Councillors as formerly once a year or oftener if urgent occasion shall require, Do summon the Burgesses of all and singler Plantations there, which together with the Governor and Council makes the Grand Assembly, and shall have Power to make Acts and Laws for the Government of that Plantation, correspondent, as near as may be, to the Laws of England, in which assembly the Governor is to have a negative voice, as formerly.

* * * * * * *

33. Legislation by the Virginia Assembly as to Morals and Taxes

Hening's *Statutes at Large* (1823).

(1) [*March, 1623/4.*]

19. — The proclamations for swearing and drunkenness sett out by the governor and counsell are confirmed by this As-

sembly; — and it is further ordered that the church-wardens shall be sworne to present them to the commanders of every plantation and that the forfeitures shall be collected by them to be for publique uses.

33. — That for defraying of such publique debts our troubles have brought upon us. There shall be levied 10 pounds of tobacco upon every male head above sixteen years of adge now living (not including such as arrived since the beginning of July last).

(2) [*October, 1629.*]

Act VI. — It is further concluded and ordered that every master of a family, and every freeman that is to pay five pounds of tobacco per pol as aforesaid for the defraying of publique charges, shall bring the same unto the Houses of the Burgesses of the plantations within two dayes after notice thereof given unto them. And if any shall faile to bring in the same, it is thought fitt that by virtue of this order the said Burgesses shall have power to levy the same by distresse, upon the goods of the delinquents, and to make sale of the said goods, and to detaine such tobacco which shall be due by this order, and for their ffees in making this distresse, restoring to the owner of the said goods the residue and remainder. And if the Burgesses shall make neglecte herein they shall be fined by the governour and Council.

(3) [*February, 1631/2.*]

Act XI. — Mynisters shall not give themselves to excesse in drinkinge, or riott, spendinge theire tyme idellye by day or night, playinge at dice, cards, or any other unlawfull game; but at all tymes convenient they shall heare or reade somewhat of the holy scriptures, or shall occupie themselves with some other honest study or exercise, alwayes doinge the thinges which shall apperteyne to honesty, and endeavour to profitt the church of God, alwayes haveinge in mynd that they ought to excell all others in puritie of life, and should be examples to the people to live well and christianlie.

(4) [*March, 1643.*]

Act XXXV. — Be it also enacted and confirmed, for the better observation of the Sabbath, that no person or persons shall take a voyage[1] upon the same, except it be to church, or for other cause of extreme necessitie, upon the penalty of the forfeiture for such offense of twenty pounds of tobacco, being justly convicted for the same.

(5) [*October, 1644.*]

Act VIII. — Noe debts made for wines or strong waters shall be pleadable or recoverable in any court of justice.[2]

---

[1] Travel was mainly by water. To "take a voyage" was equivalent to "make a journey."

[2] This finds its modern parallel in our custom that prevents the collection of gambling debts by legal process.

VI. THE ASSEMBLY DURING THE COMMONWEALTH

34. Virginia and the Parliamentary Commissioners, 1652

Hening's *Statutes*, I, 363 ff.
Cf. *American History and Government*, § 337, for the supremacy of the Assembly during the Commonwealth.

Articles agreed on and concluded at James Cittie in Virginia for the surrendering and settling of that plantation under the obedience and government of the Common Wealth of England, by the commissioners of the Councill of State, by authoritie of the Parliament of England, and by the Grand Assembly of the Governour, Councill, and Burgesses of that countrey.

First. It is agreed and consented that the plantation of Virginia, and all the inhabitants thereof, shall be and remain in due obedience and subjection to the common wealth of England, according to the lawes there established, And that this submission and subscription bee acknowledged a voluntary act, not forced nor constrained by a conquest upon the countrey. And that they shall have and enjoy such freedomes and priviledges as belong to the free borne people of England, and that the former government by the commissioners and instructions be void and null.

2dly. — *Secondly*, that the Grand Assembly, as formerly, shall convene and transact the affairs of Virginia, wherein nothing is to be acted or done contrarie to the government of the common wealth of England and the lawes there established.

3dly. — That there shall be a full and totall remission and indempnitie of all acts, words, or writings done or spoken against the parliament of England in relation to the same.

4thly. — That Virginia shall have and enjoy the antient bounds and lymitts granted by the charters of the former Kings. And that we shall seek a new charter from the parliament to that purpose against any that have intrencht upon the rights thereof.[1]

5thly. — That all the pattents of land granted under the collony seale, by any of the precedent Governours, shall be and remaine in their full force and strength.

7thly. — That the people of Virginia have free trade, as the people of England do enjoy, to all places and with all nations according to the lawes of that common-wealth, and that Virginia shall enjoy all priviledges equall with any English plantations in America.

8thly. — That Virginia shall be free from all taxes, customes, and impositions whatsoever, and none to be imposed on them without the consent of the Grand Assembly, and soe that neither ffortes nor castles bee erected or garrisons maintained without their consent.

10thly. — That for the future settlement of the countrey in their due obedience, the engagement shall be tendred to all the inhabitants according to act of parliament made to that purpose; that all persons who shall refuse to subscribe the said engagement, shall have a yeares time if they please to remove themselves and their estates out of Virginia, and in the meantime during the said yeare to have equall justice as formerly.

11thly. — That the use of the booke of common prayer shall be permitted for one yeare ensueinge with reference to the consent of the major part of the parishes, Provided that things which relate to kingshipp or that government be not used publiquely; and the continuance of ministers in their places, they not misdemeaning themselves: And the payment of their accustomed dues and agreements made with them respectively shall be left as they now stand dureing this ensueing yeare.

---

[1] This article was not ratified by Parliament.

16thly. — That the comissioners for the parliament subscribing these articles engage themselves and the honour of the parliament for the full performance thereof: And that the present Governour and the Councill and the Burgesses do likewise subscribe and engage the whole collony on their parts.

35. The Franchise Restricted and Restored, 1655, 1656

Hening's *Statutes at Large.* Cf. *American History and Government,* § 103 and note.

(1) [*March, 1654/5.*]

Act VII. — Be it enacted by this present Grand Assembly . . . That the persons who shall be elected to serve in Assembly shall be such and no other then such as are persons of knowne integrity and of good conversation and of the age of one and twenty yeares — That all housekeepers whether ffreeholders, lease holders, or otherwise tenants, shall onely be capeable to elect Burgesses, and none hereby made uncapable shall give his subscription to elect a Burgesse upon the pennalty of four hundred pounds of tobacco and cask, to be disposed of by the court of each county where such contempt shall be used: Provided that this word housekeepers repeated in this act extend no further than to one person in a ffamily.

(2) [*March, 1655/6.*]

> Act XVI. — **Whereas we conceive it something hard and unagreeable to reason that any persons shall pay equall taxes and yet have no votes in elections, Therefore it is enacted by this present Grand Assembly, That soe much of the act for chooseing Burgesses be repealed as excludes freemen from votes, Provided allwaies that they fairly give their votes by subscription and not in a tumultuous way,**[1] . . .

---

[1] This was reënacted in 1658. Hening, I, 475. But cf. Nos. 105–109 for later developments.

VII. MARYLAND

36. Lord Baltimore to King Charles, August 19/29, 1629

Scharf's *Maryland*, I, 44, 45. The letter was written from Avalon (No. 38), in Nova Scotia. Only the second half is given here; the first half defends the writer against certain "slanders" by Protestant enemies.

Most Gracious and Dread Sovereign : —

. . . So have I met with greater difficultys . . . here, which in this place are no longer to be resisted, but enforce me presently to quitt my residence and to shift to some other warmer climate of this new world, where the wynter be shorter and less rigorous. For here Your Majesty may please to understand that I have found by too deare bought experience, [what] other men for their private interests always concealed from me, that from the middlest of October to the middlest of May there is a sadd fare of wynter upon all this land; both sea and land so frozen, for the greater part of the tyme, as they are not penetrable, no plant or vegetable thing appearing out of the earth; . . . nor fish in the sea, besides the ayre so intolerable cold as it is hardly to be endured. By means whereof, and of much salt meate, my house hath been an hospital all this wynter; of 100 persons, 50 sick at a time, myself being one; and nyne or ten of them dyed. Hereupon I have had strong temptations to leave all proceedings in plantations, and, being much decayed in my strength, to retire myselfe to my former quiett. But my inclination carrying me naturally to these kynd of workes, and not knowing how better [to use] the poore remaynder of my dayes, than . . . to further . . . the enlarging your majesty's empire in this part of the world, I am determined to committ this place to fisherman (that are able to encounter stormes and hard weather) and to remove myselfe with some 40 persons to your majesty's dominion Virginia; where, if your majesty will please to grant me a precinct of land with such privileges as the king your father, my gracious master, was pleased to grante me here, I shall endeavor, to the utmost of my power, to deserve it. . . .

37. Charter of Maryland, June 20/30, 1632

The text in Latin and English is given in Bacon's *Laws of Maryland*. For explanation of events leading to this grant, see *American History and Government*, § 38. The document is in Latin.

I. — CHARLES, by the grace of GOD, of *England*, *Scotland*, *France*, and *Ireland*, King, Defender of the Faith, etc. To ALL to whom these Presents shall come, GREETING.

[II, III, and first part of IV, recite the petition of Cecilius, Baron of Baltimore, the determination of the King to "encourage the pious and noble purpose," and the grant of land, with confused geographical description.]

IV. — Also WE do GRANT . . . unto the said Baron of BALTIMORE, his heirs and assigns, . . . the PATRONAGES, and ADVOWSONS of all Churches which (with the increasing Worship and Religion of CHRIST) within the said Region . . . hereafter shall happen to be built, together with Licence and Faculty of erecting and founding Churches, Chapels, and Places of Worship, in convenient and suitable Places, within the Premises, and of causing the same to be dedicated and consecrated according to the Ecclesiastical Laws of our Kingdom of *England;* with[1] all, and singular such, and as ample Rights, Jurisdictions, Privileges, Prerogatives, Royalties, Liberties, Immunities, and royal Rights, and temporal Franchises whatsoever, as well by Sea as by Land, within the Region . . . aforesaid, to be had, exercised, used, and enjoyed, as any Bishop of *Durham*, within the Bishoprick or County Palatine of *Durham*, in our Kingdom of *England*, ever heretofore hath had, held, used, or enjoyed, or of Right could or ought to have, hold, use, or enjoy.

---

[1] This word "with" should properly be "and"; it begins a new grant — the *feudal* powers of the proprietor.

CHARTER OF MARYLAND, JUNE 20/30, 1632

[V. — Tenure by Baltimore to be in free and common soccage, and not *in capite*, or by "Knight's Service," "yeilding therefore to Us . . . two Indian Arrows of these parts every year," and the fifth part of gold and silver ore.]

VI. — Now, That the aforesaid Region, thus by us granted and described, may be eminently distinguished above all other Regions of that Territory, and decorated with more ample Titles, KNOW YE, that WE . . . have thought fit that the said Region and Islands be erected into a PROVINCE, as out of the plenitude of our royal power and prerogative, WE do . . . ERECT and INCORPORATE the same into a PROVINCE, and nominate the same MARYLAND, by which name WE will that it shall from henceforth be called.

VII. — And forasmuch as WE have above made and ordained the aforesaid now Baron of *BALTIMORE*, the true LORD and *Proprietary* of the whole PROVINCE aforesaid, KNOW YE therefore further, that WE . . . do grant unto the said now Baron, (in whose Fidelity, Prudence, Justice, and provident Circumspection of Mind, WE repose the greatest Confidence) and to his Heirs, for the good and happy Government of the said PROVINCE, free, full, and absolute Power, by the tenor of these Presents, to Ordain, Make, and Enact LAWS, of what kind soever, according to their sound Discretions, whether relating to the Public State of the said PROVINCE, or the private Utility of Individuals, of and with the Advice, Assent, and Approbation of the Free-Men of the same PROVINCE, or of the greater Part of them, or of their Delegates or Deputies, whom WE will shall be called togther for the framing of LAWS, when, and as often as Need shall require, by the aforesaid now Baron of *BALTIMORE*, and his Heirs, and in the Form which shall seem best to him or them, and the same to publish under the Seal of the aforesaid now Baron of *BALTIMORE*, and his Heirs, and duly to execute the same upon all Persons, for the Time being, within the aforesaid PROVINCE, and the Limits thereof, or under his or their Government and Power, in Sailing towards *MARYLAND*, on thence Returning, Outward-bound, either to *England*, or elsewhere, whether to any other Part of Our, or of any foreign Dominions, wheresoever established, by the Imposition of Fines, Imprisonment, and other Punishment whatsoever; even if it be necessary, and the Quality of the Offence require it, by Privation of Member, or Life, by him the aforesaid now Baron of *BALTIMORE*, and his Heirs, or by his or their Deputy, Lieutenant, Judges, Justices, Magistrates, Officers, and Ministers, to be constituted and appointed according to the Tenor and true Intent of these Presents, and to constitute and ordain Judges, Justices, Magistrates, and Officers, of what Kind, for what Cause, and with what Power soever, within that Land, and the Sea of those Parts, and in such Form as to the said now Baron of *BALTIMORE*, or his Heirs, shall seem most fitting: And also to Remit, Release, Pardon, and Abolish, all Crimes and Offences whatsoever against such Laws, whether before, or after Judgment passed; and to do all and singular other Things belonging to the Completion of Justice, and to Courts, Prætorian Judicatories, and Tribunals, judicial Forms and Modes of Proceeding, although express Mention thereof in these Presents be not made; and, by Judges by them delegated, to award Process, hold Pleas, and determine in those Courts, Prætorian Judicatories, and Tribunals, in all Actions, Suits, Causes, and Matters whatsoever, as well Criminal as Personal, Real and Mixed, and Prætorian: ... So NEVERTHELESS, that the Laws aforesaid be consonant to Reason and be not repugnant or contrary, but (so far as conveniently may be) agreeable to the Laws, Statutes, Customs and Rights of this Our Kingdom of *England*.

VIII. — AND FORASMUCH as, in the Government of so great a PROVINCE, sudden Accidents may frequently happen, to which it will be necessary to apply a Remedy before the Freeholders of the said PROVINCE, their Delegates, or Deputies, can be called together for the framing of Laws; neither will it be fit that so great a Number of People should immediately, on such emergent Occasion, be called together, WE THEREFORE, for the better Government of so great a PROVINCE, ... do

CHARTER OF MARYLAND, JUNE 20/30, 1632

grant . . . that the aforesaid now Baron of *BALTIMORE;* and his Heirs, by themselves, or by their Magistrates and Officers, thereunto duly to be constituted as aforesaid, may, and can make and constitute fit and wholesom Ordinances from Time to Time, to be kept and observed within the PROVINCE aforesaid, as well for the Conservation of the Peace, as for the better Government of the People inhabiting therein, and publickly to notify the same to all Persons whom the same in any wise do or may affect . . . : so that the same Ordinances do not, in any Sort, extend to oblige, bind, change, or take away the Right or Interest of any Person or Persons, of or in Member, Life, Freehold, Goods or Chattels.

IX, X — [Permission to English subjects to emigrate to Maryland, and X, to enjoy (with their descendants) the rights of Englishmen at home.]

XI. — [Certain exemptions from export duties, as in earlier charters.]

XII. — [Authorization for the proprietor or his officers to make war, if needful, upon savages and pirates or other invaders.]

XIII. — [Authorization for martial law, under the usual restrictions.]

XIV. — [Authority for Baltimore to confer titles of nobility (not such as in England), to incorporate towns, etc.]

XV–XVI. — [Regulations regarding ports and temporary exemptions from English custom duties.]

XVII. — MOREOVER, We will, appoint, and ordain, and by these Presents, for US, our Heirs and Successors, do grant unto the aforesaid now Baron of *BALTIMORE*, his Heirs and Assigns, that the same Baron of *BALTIMORE*, his Heirs and Assigns, from Time to Time, for ever, shall have, and enjoy the Taxes and Subsidies payable, or arising within the Ports, Harbours, and other Creeks and Places aforesaid, within the PROVINCE aforesaid, for Wares bought and sold, and Things there to be laden, or unladen, to be reasonably assessed by them on emergent Occasion, and the People there as aforesaid;

to whom WE grant Power by these Presents, for US, our Heirs and Successors, to assess and impose the said Taxes and Subsidies there, upon just Cause, and in due Proportion.

XVIII. — AND FURTHERMORE . . . , WE . . . do give . . . unto the aforesaid now Baron of *BALTIMORE*, his Heirs and Assigns, full and absolute License, Power, and Authority . . . [to] assign, alien, grant, demise, or enfeoff so many, such, and proportionate Parts and Parcels of the Premises, to any Person or Persons willing to purchase the same, as they shall think convenient, to have and to hold . . . in Fee-simple, or Fee-tail, or for Term of Life, Lives, or Years; to hold of the aforesaid now Baron of *BALTIMORE*, his Heirs and Assigns, by . . . such . . . Services, Customs and Rents OF THIS KIND, as to the same now Baron of *BALTIMORE*, his Heirs and Assigns, shall seem fit and agreeable, and not immediately of US . . . [notwithstanding the English law *Quia Emptores* or other statutes to the contrary].

XIX. — WE also, . . . do . . . grant Licence to the same Baron of *BALTIMORE*, and to his Heirs, to erect any Parcels of Land within the PROVINCE aforesaid, into Manors, and in every of those Manors, to have and to hold a Court-Baron, and all Things which to a Court-Baron do belong; and to have and to keep View of Frank-Pledge, for the Conservation of the Peace and better Government of those Parts, by themselves and their Stewards, or by the Lords, for the Time being to be deputed, of other of those Manors when they shall be constituted, and in the same to exercise all Things to the View of Frank-Pledge belonging.

XX. — And further We will, and do . . . grant . . . that we, our heirs and successors, at no time hereafter, will impose any impositions, customs, or other taxations . . . whatever, in or upon the residents . . . of the province, for their goods, lands, or tenements . . . or in or upon any goods or merchandizes within the province or within the ports or harbors of the said province [this declaration to be a sufficient quittance to all English officers].

XXI. — [Maryland not to be reputed a part of Virginia but to be immediately dependent upon the crown.]

XXII. — [Baltimore and his heirs to be entitled to the most generous interpretation of any indefinite clause in the charter] "provided always that no interpretation be made thereof whereby God's holy and true Christian religion, nor the allegiance due to us . . . may in any wise suffer . . . prejudice or diminution."

38. Comment on the Avalon Charter of 1623

With the addition of two of its sections, with the necessary changes of names, and with three or four other slight modifications, the Maryland Charter of 1632 is an exact transcript of the *Charter of Avalon*, given in 1623 by James I to George Calvert (afterward, the first Lord Baltimore). The Avalon Charter has been printed, the editor believes, only in Scharf's *Maryland* (I, 34 ff.).

The sections of the two documents correspond up to XVIII. Sections XVIII and XIX of the Maryland Charter (relating to subinfeudation and manorial courts) are not found in the earlier document. Sections XVIII–XX of the Avalon Charter correspond to XX–XXII of the Maryland patent.

Other changes, aside from names, etc., are:

1. — (Section IV.) In the granting of advowsons and other ecclesiastical powers, there is no reference in the Avalon Charter to the "ecclesiastical laws of the kingdom of England." This phrase is added in the Maryland Charter, since Baltimore has now (1624) been converted to Catholicism, *probably* as a safeguard.

2. — Baltimore's tenure in Avalon (§ 5) is to be "*in Capite, by Knight's Service*" [not so, but in free socage, in Maryland], "yielding therefor . . . a white horse, so often as we or our successors shall come into the said region," together with the usual "fifth part of gold and silver ore."

3. — The Avalon Charter does not refer directly to *representative* government. The authorization to Baltimore to publish laws runs, — "with the advice, assent, and approbation of the Freeholders of the said Province, or the greater part of them," while the Maryland Charter says the assent of "the *Free Men* of the said Province, or the greater part of them, *or their delegates, or deputies*"; but the earlier like the later charter leaves it to the proprietor to assemble the people "in such form as to him shall seem best," and this probably looked to a representative gathering.

4. — (XVII.) The Avalon Charter does not *mention* the participation of the popular assembly in granting taxes. Given such an assembly, however, and the renunciation by the English government (Section XVIII) of that power, then the possession of the power by the Assembly would inevitably follow. In the Maryland Charter it is *expressed*.

The Avalon Charter then, is the first *royal* patent to give to settlers in America *political rights*, in addition to the private common-law privileges. It is followed (as to sections VII and VIII) *in exact detail* by the Heath Charter for Carolina (1629), the Baltimore Charter (1632), and the Plowden Charter for New Albion (1634).[1]

Of the four grants just mentioned, that of Maryland in 1632 was the only one under which a successful colony was established, but the others help to show that that document was no prodigy. The student may like to notice here one of the rare slips of Dr. Channing (*History of the United States*, I, 245), when he ascribes the likeness between the charters of 1629, 1632, and 1634 to Sir Robert Heath's influence in that of 1629, instead of to the earlier Avalon Charter of 1623.

39. Excursus: Charters for New Albion and Maine

The "governing" clauses only are given, — for comparison with corresponding parts of the Maryland and Avalon grants.

a. Grant of Charles I to Edmund Plowden, Earl Palatine of Albion, of the Province of New Albion in America

Hazard's *State Papers* (Washington, 1792), I, 162 ff. New Albion was to lie north of Maryland. No settlement was effected.

. . . And forasmuch, as We have above made and ordained the before-named Edmund Plowden, Knight, true lord and proprietor of all the province aforesaid. THEREFORE further know ye, that We, for Us, our heirs, and successours, to the same Edmund, (of whose fidelity, prudence, justice and providence, and circumspection of mind, we have full confidence) and to his heirs, for the good and happy government of the said province, [grant power to make, ordain, and establish] whatsoever laws, whether concerning the public estate of the same province, or the private utility of individuals, according to their wise discretions, and with the council, approbation, and assents of the free tenants of the same province, or the

---

[1] Indeed, until the grant of "New York" to James, Duke of York, in 1664, every subsequent royal patent to an *individual* proprietor contains such provision, whether or not it be an exact and formal copy of the Avalon document. New York was a conquered province settled by Dutch, — which may explain the omission there.

major part of them who shall be called together by the aforesaid Edmund Plowden, and his heirs, to make laws when, and as often as there shall be occasion, in such form as to him or them shall seem best. . . . And because, in so large a province it may often happen, that there will be a necessity to provide a remedy in a number of cases, before the free tenants of the said province can be assembled to make laws, nor will it be proper to delay in a case of emergency, until so many people can be called together. THEREFORE, for the better government of the said province, we will, and ordain, and by these presents, for Us, our heirs, and successors, grant unto the before-named Edmund Plowden, and to his heirs, that the aforesaid Edmund Plowden, and his heirs, by themselves, or by magistrates and officers in that behalf, to be duly constituted as aforesaid, fit and wholesome ordinations from time to time, shall and may be able to make and constitute, to be kept and preferred within the province aforesaid, as well for keeping the peace as for the better government of the people there living or inhabiting, and to give public notice of them to all persons whom the same doth or may concern; which said ordinations We will, shall be inviolably observed within the said province, under the penalties in the same expressed. So that the same ordinances be consonant to reason, and be not repugnant nor contrary, but as much agreeable as may be to the laws, statutes, and rights of our kingdoms of England and Ireland. And so as that the same ordinances do not extend themselves to the right or interest of any person or persons, of, or in free tenements, or the taking, distraining, binding, or charging any of their goods or chattles. . . .

b. *Grant of Charles I to Sir Ferdinando Gorges for the Province of Maine, 1639*

Hazard's *State Papers* (1792), I, 442–455.

The members of the Plymouth Council surrendered the charter of 1620 back to the King in 1634, having first divided the territory among themselves. The King confirmed Gorges' allotment ("The Province of Maine") and gave him the usual proprietary jurisdiction in a lengthy charter (April 3/13, 1639), from which come the following clauses.

. . . And wee doe for us, our heirs and successors, give and graunte unto the saide Sir Ferdinando Gorges, his heirs and assignes, power and authoritie, **with the assent of the greater parte of the freeholders of the said Province and premisses for the time being,** when there shalbe any to be called therunto from time to time, when and as often as shall be requisite, to make and ordeyne and publish lawes, ordinances and constitucons, reasonable, and not repugnant and contrary, but agreable as nere as conveniently may bee, to the lawes of England, for the publique good of the said Province and premisses, and of the inhabitants thereof, by imposing of penalties, imprisonment or other corections, or, if the offence shall requier, by taking away of life or member; the said lawes and constitucons to extend aswell to such as shalbe passing unto or returning from the said Province or premisses as unto the inhabitants or residents of or within the same, and the same to be put into execucon by the said Sir Ferdinando Georges, his heirs or assignes, or by his or there depputies, liftenants, judges, officers or ministers in that behalfe, lawfully authorized; and the same lawes ordinances and constitucons, or any of them, to alter, change, and revoke, or to make voide and to make new, not repugnant nor contrary, but agreable as nere as may bee, to the lawes of England, as the said Sir Ferdinando Georges his heires and assignes, together with the said freeholders, or the greater part of them for the time being, shall from time to time thinke fitt and convenient: . . .

40. The Maryland Toleration Act of 1649

Maryland Archives, I, 244 ff.
For explanation, cf. *American History and Government*, § 43.

. . . **Forasmuch** as in a well governed and Christian Common Wealth, matters concerning Religion and the honor of God ought in the first place to bee taken into serious consederacion . . . Be it therefore ordered and enacted by the Right Honorable Cecilius Lord Baron of Baltemore, absolute Lord and Proprietary of this Province, with the advise and consent of this Generall Assembly: That whatsoever person or persons within this Province and the Islands thereunto belonging shall from henceforth blaspheme God, — that is, Curse him, — or deny our Saviour Jesus Christ to bee the sonne of God, or shall deny the holy Trinity, the ffather sonne and holy Ghost, or the Godhead of any of the said Three persons of the Trinity, or the Unity of the Godhead, or shall use . . . any reproachfull Speeches, . . . concerning the said Holy Trinity, or any of the three persons thereof, *shall be punished with death and confiscation of all his or her lands and goods* . . . And be it also Enacted . . . That whatsoever person or persons shall from henceforth use . . . any reproaching words or speeches concerning the blessed Virgin Mary, the Mother of our Saviour, or the Holy Apostles or Evangelists ... shall in such case for the first offence forfeit ... the summe of ffive pound sterling ... but in case such Offender or Offenders shall not then have goods and chattells sufficient for the satisfyeing of such forfeiture, or that the same bee not otherwise speedily satisfyed, that then such Offender or Offenders shalbe publiquely whipt and bee ymprisoned during the pleasure of the Lord Proprietary or ... chiefe Governor of this Province for the time being. And that every such Offender or Offenders for every second offence shall forfeit tenne pound sterling or the value thereof to bee levyed as aforesaid, or in case such offender or Offenders shall not then have goods and chattells within this Province sufficient for that purpose then to bee publiquely and severely whipt and imprisoned as before is expressed. And that every person or persons before mentioned offending herein the third time, shall for such third Offence forfeit all his lands and Goods and bee for ever banished and expelled out of this Province. And be it also further Enacted ... that whatsoever person or persons shall from henceforth uppon any occasion of Offence or otherwise in a reproachful manner or Way declare call or denominate any person or persons whatsoever ... an heritick, Scismatick, Idolator, puritan, Independant, Prespiterian, popish prest, Jesuite, Jesuited papist, Lutheran, Calvenist, Anabaptist, Brownist, Antinomian, Barrowist, Roundhead, Seperatist, or any other name or terme in a reproachfull manner relating to matter of Religion shall for every such Offence forfeit and loose the some or [of] tenne shillings sterling or the value thereof, to bee levyed on the goods and chattells of every such Offender and Offenders, the one half thereof to be forfeited and paid unto the person and persons of whom such reproachfull words are or shalbe spoken or uttered, and the other half thereof to the Lord Propriuetary and his heires Lords and Proprietaries of this Province. But if such person or persons who shall at any time utter or speake any such reproachfull words or Language shall not have Goods or Chattells sufficient and overt within this Province to bee taken to satisfie the penalty aforesaid, or that the same bee not otherwise speedily satisfyed, that then the person or persons soe offending shalbe publickly whipt, and shall suffer imprisomnt without baile or maineprise untill hee, shee, or they respectively shall satisfy the party soe offended or grieved by such reproachfull Language by asking him or her respectively forgivenes publiquely for such his Offence before the Magistrate or cheife Officer or Officers of the towne or place where such Offence shalbe given. And be it further likewise Enacted . . . That every person and persons within this Province that shall at any time hereafter prophane the Sabbath or Lords day, called Sunday, by frequent swearing, drunkennes, or by any uncivill or disorderly recreacon, or by working on that day when absolute necessity doth not require it, shall for every such first offence forfeit $2^s\ 6^d$ sterling or the value thereof, and for the second offence 5^s sterling or the value thereof, and for the third offence and soe for every time he shall offend in like manner afterwards, 10^s sterling or the value thereof. And in case such offender and offenders shall not have sufficient goods or chattells within this Province to satisfy any of the said Penalties reecsptively hereby imposed . . . That in Every such case the partie soe offending shall for the first and second offence in that kinde be imprisoned till hee or shee shall publickly in open Court before the cheife Commander Judge or Magistrate of that County Towne or precinct where such offence shalbe committed acknowledg the Scandall and offence he hath in that respect given against God and the good and civill Governmt of this Province; And for the third offence and for every time after, shall also bee publickly whipt. *And whereas the inforceing of the conscience in matters of Religion hath frequently fallen out to be of dangerous Consequence in those commonwealthes where it hath been practised, And for the more quiett and peaceable governmt of this Province, and the better to preserve mutuall Love and amity amongst the Inhabitants thereof. Be it Therefore also by the Lord Proprietary with the advise and consent of this Assembly Ordeyned and enacted (except*

THE MARYLAND TOLERATION ACT OF 1649

as in this present Act is before Declared and sett forth) that noe person or persons whatsoever within this Province, or the Islands, Parts, Harbors, Creekes, or havens thereunto belonging, professing to beleive in Jesus Christ, shall from henceforth bee any waies troubled, Molested or discountenanced for or in respect of his or her religion nor in the free exercise thereof within this Province or the Islands thereunto belonging nor any way compelled to the beleife or exercise of any other Religion against his or her consent, soe as they be not unfaithfull to the Lord Proprietary, or molest or conspire against the civill Government established or to bee established in this Province under him on his heires. And that all and every person and persons that shall presume Contrary to this Act and the true intent and meaning thereof directly or indirectly either in person or estate wilfully to wrong disturbe trouble or molest any person whatsoever within this Province professing to beleive in Jesus Christ for or in respect of his or her religion, or the free exercise thereof, within this Province . . . that such person or persons soe offending shall be compelled to pay trebble damages to the party soe wronged . . . and for every such offence shall also forfeit 20 s. sterling . . . [or, in default of payment, shall make satisfaction by public whipping, and imprisonment during the pleasure of the Governor]. . . .

B. NEW ENGLAND TO 1660

VIII. AN EARLY EXPLORATION IN MAINE

41. Weymouth's Voyage, 1605

From *A True Relation of Captain George Waymouth, His Voyage* (1605), reprinted in Massachusetts Historical Society Collections, Vol. VIII. Weymouth's voyage was a precursor of the attempt at settlement on the Kennebec in 1607 by one branch of the Virginia Company.

Upon Tuesday, *the 5th day of March*, about ten o'clock before noon, we set sail from Ratcliffe, and came to an anchor that tide about two o'clock before Gravesend. . . .

Friday, *the 17th of May*, about six o'clock at night, we descried the land. . . . It appeared a mean high land, as we after found it, being an island of some six miles in compass, but I hope the most fortunate ever yet discovered. . . .

This island is woody grown with fir, birch, oak and beech, as far as we saw along the shore; and so likely to be within. On the verge grow gooseberries, strawberries, wild pease, and wild rose bushes. The water issued forth down the rocky cliffe in many places: and much fowl of divers kinds breed upon the shore and rocks.

While we were at shore, our men aboard, with a few hooks, got above thirty great cods and haddocks, which gave us a taste of the great plenty of fish which we found afterward wheresoever we went upon the coast. From hence we might discern the main land from the west-south-west to the east-north-east; and a great way (as it then seemed, and we after found it,) up into the main we might discern very high mountains, though the main seemed but low land; . . .

The profits and fruits which are naturally on these islands are these:

All along the shore, and some space within, where the wood hindereth not, grow plentifully, raspberries, gooseberries, strawberries, roses, currants, wild vines, angelica.

Within the islands grow wood of sundry sorts, some very great, and all tall, as birch, beech, ash, maple, spruce, cherry tree, yew, oak, very great and good, fir tree, out of which issueth turpentine in so marvellous plenty, and so sweet as our chirurgeon and others affirmed they never saw so good in England. We pulled off much gum, congealed on the outside of the bark, which smelled like frankincense. This would be a great benefit for making tar and pitch.

We staid the longer in this place, not only because of our good harbor (which is an excellent comfort,) but because every day we did more and more discover the pleasant fruitfulness; insomuch as many of our company wished themselves settled here, not expecting any further hopes, or better discovery to be made.

Here our men found abundance of great muscles among the rocks; and in some of them many small pearls: and in one muscle (which we drew up in our net) was found fourteen pearls, whereof one of pretty bigness and orient; in another above fifty small pearls: and if we had had a drag, no doubt we had found some of great value, seeing these did certainly shew that here they were bred; the shells all glittering with mother of pearl. . . .

Our captain had in this small time discovered up a great river, trending alongst into the main about forty miles. The pleasantness whereof, with the safety of harbor for shipping, together with the fertility of ground and other fruits, which were generally by his whole company related, I omit till I report of the whole discovery thereinafter performed. . . .

The next day being Saturday and the first of June, I traded with the savages all the forenoon upon the shore, where were eight-and-twenty of them; and because our ship rode nigh, we were but five or six; where for knives, glasses, combs, and other trifles to the value of four or five shillings, we had forty good beavers' skins, otters' skins, sables, and other small skins, which we knew not how to call . . . Here are more good harbors for ships of all burthens, than England can afford, and far more secure from all winds and weathers, than any in England, Scotland, France, or Spain. . . .

As we passed with a gentle wind up with our ship in this river, any man may conceive with what admiration we all consented in joy. Many of our company who had been travellers in sundry countries, and in most famous rivers, yet affirmed them not comparable to this they now beheld. Some that were with Sir Walter Raleigh in his voyage to Guiana, in the discovery of the river Orenoque, which echoed fame to the world's ears, gave reasons why it was not to be compared with this, which wanteth the dangers of many shoals, and broken ground, wherewith that was incumbered. Others before that notable river in the West Indies called Rio Grande; some before the river of Loire, the river Seine, and of Bourdeaux in France; which although they be great and goodly rivers, yet it is no detraction from them to be accounted inferior to this, which not only yieldeth all the foresaid pleasant profits, but also appeared infallibly to us free from all inconveniences.

I will not prefer it before our river of Thames, because it is England's richest treasure: . . .

The excellency of this part of the river, for his good breadth, depth, and fertile bordering ground, did so ravish us all with variety of pleasantness, as we could not tell what to commend, but only admired; some compared it to the river Severn, (but in a higher degree) and we all concluded (as I verily think we might right) that we should never see the like river in every degree equal, until it pleased God we beheld the same again. . . .

The temperature of the climate (albeit a very important matter) I had almost passed without mentioning, because it afforded to us no great alteration from our disposition in England; somewhat hotter up into the main, because it lieth open to the south; the air so wholesome, as I suppose not any of us found ourselves at any time more healthful, more able to labor, nor with better stomachs to such good fare as we partly brought and partly found . . .

IX. THE FIRST SOURCE OF LAND TITLES IN NEW ENGLAND

42. Charter of the Plymouth Council
[Often called The Council for New England]
November 3/12, 1629

Hazard's *State Papers* (Washington, 1792), I, 103–118.

The "Second Colony" of the Charter of 1606 (No. 16 above) sent out an expedition to the coast of Maine in 1607. This failed; and the Company made no further efforts until 1620, save for the vain attempt of Sir Ferdinando Gorges, one of the leading members. In March of 1619/20, Gorges and other members petitioned for a reorganization of the Company, and this prayer was granted by the King in this charter. This document stands to the "Second Colony" of 1606 (the Plymouth branch) as do the charters of 1609 and 1612 to the "First Colony" (the London branch).

[The charter begins by reciting the grant of the Virginia Charter of 1606, the grant of 1609 to one branch of the original Company, and the petition of Gorges and others of the Plymouth branch for a similar enlargement and for a monopoly of the northern fisheries.]

And also for that We have been further given certainly to knowe, that within these late Yeares there hath by God's Visitation raigned a wonderfull Plague, together with many horrible Slaughters, and Murthers, committed amoungst the Savages and bruitish People there heertofore inhabiting, in a Manner to the utter Destruction, Devastacion, and Depopulacion of that whole Territorye . . . whereby We in our Judgment are persuaded and satisfied that the appointed Time is come in which Almighty God in his great Goodness and Bountie towards Us and our People, hath thought fitt and determined that those large and goodly Territoryes, deserted as it were by their naturall inhabitants, should be possessed and enjoyed by such of our Subjects and People as heertofore have and hereafter shall by his Mercie and Favour, and by his Powerfull Arme, be directed and conducted thither. In Contemplacion and serious Consideracion whereof, Wee have thougt it fitt according to our Kingly Duty, soe much as in Us lyeth, to second and followe God's sacred Will, rendering reverend Thanks to his Divine Majestie for his gracius favour in laying open and revealing the same unto us before any other Christian Prince or State, by which Meanes without Offence, . . . Wee therefore . . . Do . . . grant . . . that all that Circuit, Continent, Precincts, and Limitts in America, lying and being in Breadth from Fourty Degrees of Northerly Latitude, from the Equinoticall Line, to Fourty-eight Degrees of the said Northerly Latitude, and in Length by all the Breadth aforesaid throughout the Maine Land, from Sea to Sea, . . . shall be the Limitts . . . of the second Collony : And to the End that the said Territoryes may forever hereafter be more particularly and certainly known and distinguished, our Will and Pleasure is, that the same shall from henceforth be nominated, termed, and called by the Name of New-England, in America. . . . And for the better Plantacion, ruling, and governing of the aforesaid New-England in America, We . . . ordaine . . . that from henceforth, there shall be . . . in our Towne of Plymouth, in the County of Devon, one Body politicque and corporate, which shall have perpetuall Succession, which shall consist of the Number of fourtie Persons, and no more, which shall be, and shall be called and knowne by the Name of the Council established at Plymouth, in the County of Devon, for the planting, ruling, ordering, and governing of New-England, in America; [The names of the Council. They have power to fill vacancies in their membership, and the usual rights of a corporation ; they are to choose a "President," etc.; and to control trade with New England and the ownership of land.]

And further . . . Wee . . . grant full Power and Authority to the said Councill . . . [to] nominate, make, constitute, ordaine, and confirme by such Name or Names, Style or Styles, as to them shall seeme Good ; and likewise to revoke, discharge, change, and alter, as well all and singular, Governors, Officers, and Ministers, which hereafter shall be by them thought fitt and needful to be made or used, as well to attend the Business of the said Company here, as for the Government of the said Collony and Plantation, and also to make . . . all Manner of Orders, Laws, Directions, Instructions, Forms, and Ceremonies of Government and Magistracy fitt and necessary for any concerning the Government of the said Collony and Plantation, so always as the same be not contrary to the Laws and Statutes of this our Realme of England; and the same att all Times hereafter to abrogate, revoke, or change, not only within the Precincts of the said Collony, but also upon the Seas in going and coming to and from the said Collony, as they in their good Discretions shall thinke to be fittest for the good of the Adventurers and Inhabitants there.

[Clauses similar to those in the London Company's charter of 1609 regarding martial law; the forfeiture of goods fraudulently transported to a foreign country; landholding by free socage, etc.; the right "to take, load, carry, and transport . . . out of our Realmes to New England all such . . . of our loveing Subjects . . . as shall willingly accompany them"; exemption from duties on goods exported from England for seven years; and from all taxes for twenty-one years, except the five per cent customs duty for imports to be reëxported; right to dispose of lands.]

And Wee do also . . . grant to the said Councell . . . that they . . . shall, and lawfully may, . . . for their . . . Defence and Safety, encounter, expulse, repel, and resist by Force of Arms, as well by Sea as by Land, and all Ways and Meanes whatsoever, all such . . . Persons, as without the speciall Licence of the said Councell . . . shall attempt to inhabitt within the said severall Precincts and Limitts of the said Collony and Plantation. And also all . . . such . . . Persons . . . as shall enterprize or attempt att any time hereafter Destruction, Invasion, Detriment, or Annoyance to the said Collony and Plantation.

112 SOURCE OF LAND TITLES IN NEW ENGLAND

[A like provision for use of force to prevent traders visiting the territory without the "License and consent of the said Councill . . . first had and obtained in Writing." Authority for two of the Council to administer the oaths of allegiance and supremacy (as in the charter of 1612); a long passage giving the Councill extraordinary jurisdiction as a safeguard against its being defrauded or libeled (as in the charter of 1612); English subjects settling in the colony and their descendants there to have all the rights of Englishmen. None to be permitted to go to New England except such as first take the oath of supremacy, — this provision intended to exclude Catholics (wording taken from the charter of 1609; not found in 1612); etc. etc. etc. — Privileges granted in 1606, and not altered in this charter, are confirmed.]

X. PLYMOUTH PLANTATION

43. Delays in securing the Wincob Charter
Robert Cushman to Pastor Robinson, May 8/18, 1619

Bradford's *Plymouth Plantation* (Original Narratives edition), 58, 59. Cushman was the agent of the Pilgrims, sent from Holland to secure a charter from the London Company for some district in "Northern Virginia." The negotiations had been going on more than a year when this letter was written.

. . . The maine hinderance of our proseedings in the Virginia bussines is the dissentions and factions as they terme it among the Counsell and Company of Virginia; which are such as that ever since we came up no busines could by them be dispatched. The occasion of this trouble amongst them is, for that a while since Sir Thomas Smith, repining at his many offices and troubles, wished the Company of Virginia to ease him of his office. . . . Wereupon the Company tooke occasion to dismisse him and choose Sir Edwin Sands Treasurer and Goverr of the Company. He having 60 voyces, Sir John Worstenholme 16 voices, and Alderman Johnson 24.[1] But Sir Thomas Smith when he saw some parte of his honour lost, was very angrie, and raised a faction to cavill and contend aboute the election, and sought to taxe Sir Edwin with many things that might both disgrace him, and allso put him by his office of Governour. In which contentions they yet stick and are not fit nor readie to intermedle in any bussines; and what issue things will come to we are not yet certaine. It is most like Sir Edwin will carrie

---

[1] The correct vote, according to the Company's *Records* (I, 212), is 59, 23, and 18 (No. 28 below). This, of course, was the election in April, 1619, by which the Liberals came into power. Cf. *American History and Government*, §§ 27, 49 and note.

113

it, and if he doe, things will goe well[1] in Virginia, if otherwise, they will goe ill enough allways. We hope in some 2 or 3 Court days things will settle.[1]

44. Agreement between the Pilgrims in Holland and the Merchant Adventurers in London
July 1/11, 1620

Bradford's *Plymouth Plantation* (Original Narratives edition), 66, 67. The following "articles" outline the business partnership by which the Pilgrims secured funds to come to America.

1. — The adventurers and planters doe agree that every person that goeth, being aged 16 years and upward, be rated at 10 £, and ten pounds to be accounted a single share.

2. — That he that goeth in person, and furnisheth him selfe out with 10 £ either in money or other provissions, be accounted as having 20 £ in stock, and in the devission shall receive a double share.

3. — The persons transported and the adventurers shall continue their joynt stock and partnership togeather the space of 7 years (excepte some unexpected impedimente doe cause the whole company to agree otherwise), during which time all profits and benefits that are gott by trade, traffick, trucking, working, fishing, or any other means of any person or persons, remaine still in the commone stock untill the division.

4. — That at their comming ther, they chose out such a number of fitt persons, as may furnish their ships and boats for fishing upon the sea; imploying the rest in their severall faculties upon the land; as building houses, tilling, and

---

[1] Things did "settle" rapidly. Bradford's narrative continues: "But at last after all these things and their long attendance, they had a Patent granted them and confirmed under the Companies seale [June 9/19, according to *Records* of the Virginia Company for May 26 and June 9, 1619]. . . . By the advice of some of their friends, this pattente was not taken in the name of any of their owne, but in the name of Rev. John Wincob (a religious gentleman then belonging to the Countess of Lincoline), who intended to goe with them. But God so disposed as he never went, nor they ever made use of this patente, which had cost them so much labour and charge. . . ."

planting the ground, and makeing shuch commodities as shall be most usefull for the collonie.

5. — That at the end of the 7 years, the capitall and profits, — viz. the houses, lands, goods and chatles, — be equally devided betwixte the adventurers and planters; which done, every man shall be free from other of them of any debt or detrimente concerning this adventure.

6. — Whosoever cometh to the colonie herafter, or putteth any into the stock, shall at the ende of the 7 years be alowed proportionably to the time of his so doing.

7. — He that shall carie his wife and children, or servants, shall be alowed for everie person now aged 16 years and upward, a single share in the devision, or if he provid them necessaries, a duble share, or if they be between 10 year old and 16, then 2 of them to be reconed for a person, both in transportation and devision.

8. — That such children as now goe, and are under the age of ten years, have noe other shar in the devision but 50 acers of unmanured land.

9. — That such persons as die before the 7 years be expired, their executors to have their parte or sharr at the devison, proportionably to the time of their life in the collonie.

10. — That all such persons as are of this collonie, are to have their meate, drink, apparell, and all provissions out of the common stock and goods of the said collonie.

[Bradford adds : "The cheefe and principall differences between these and the former conditions [*i.e.* articles proposed at first by the Pilgrims] stood in these 2 points; that the houses and lands improved, espetialy gardens and home lotts, should remain undevided wholly to the planters at the 7 years end [*i.e.* not go into the common stock of the partnership] 2ly, that they should have had 2 days in a weeke for their own private imploymente."

These points are made in a letter of John Robinson, the Pilgrim pastor, to John Carver, the agent in England, dated July 14, 1620 (Bradford, 69, 70).

"Aboute the conditions . . . let this spetially be borne in minde; that the greatest parte of the collonie is like to be imployed constantly, not upon dressing ther perticuler [individual] land, and building houses, *but upon fishing, trading*, etc. So as the land and house will be but a trifell for advantage to the adventurers [London capitalists] ; and yet the devission of it a great discouragemente to the planters [colonists], who would with singuler care make it comfortable with borowed houres from their sleep."

For the fallacy in this view, cf. *American History and Government*, §§ 49, 52.]

45. From the Farewell Letter of John Robinson

Bradford's *Plymouth Plantation* (Original Narratives edition), 84–86.

Robinson was the pastor of the Separatist congregation at Leyden. This letter was written to that part of the congregation which had just embarked for America, soon to found Plymouth colony. It is not dated. Bradford gives the full text. This extract shows that the charter which the Pilgrims had secured from the London Company, but which they were never to use (No. 43 note, and *American History and Government*, § 51 note), had guaranteed them a large measure of self-government. The letter would fill some five pages of this book.

. . . Lastly, whereas you are become a body politik, using amongst yourselves civill governmente, and are not furnished with any persons of spetiall eminence above the rest, to be chosen by you into office, let your wisdome and godlines appear, not only in chusing shuch persons as do entirely love and will promote the commone good, but also in yeelding unto them all due honour and obedience . . . and this dutie you may the more willingly . . . performe, because you are at least for the present to have onely them for your ordinarie governours which your selves shall make choyse of for that worke.

46. The Mayflower Compact
November 11/21, 1620

Bradford's *Plymouth Plantation* (Original Narratives edition), 107. The original document is lost. Bradford gives no signatures. However, another copy, in Mourt's *Relation*, has the signatures, forty-two in number.

In the name of God, Amen. We whose names are under writen, the loyall subjects of our dread soveraigne Lord, King

James, by the grace of God, of Great Britaine, Franc, and Ireland king, defender of the faith, etc., haveing undertaken, for the glorie of God, and advancemente of the Christian faith, and honour of our king and countrie, a voyage to plant the first colonie in the Northerne parts of Virginia, doe by these presents solemnly and mutualy in the presence of God, and one of another, covenant and combine our selves togeather into a civill body politick, for our better ordering and preservation and furtherance of the ends aforesaid; and by vertue hearof to enacte, constitute, and frame such just and equall lawes, ordinances, acts, constitutions, and offices, from time to time, as shall be thought most meete and convenient for the generall good of the Colonie, unto which we promise all due submission and obedience. In witnes whereof we have hereunder subscribed our names at Cap-Codd the 11. of November, in the year of the raigne of our soveraigne lord, King James, of England, France, and Ireland the eighteenth, and of Scotland the fiftie fourth. Anno: Dom. 1620.

For a discussion of this document, see *American History and Government*, § 51. Here it should be noted that it is not a "constitution" so much as a preliminary "social compact." Nineteen years later, Wheelwright and his followers (banished from Massachusetts) settled on the New Hampshire coast and adopted an agreement similar to the Mayflower document in occasion and character. Western mining camps have taken like action many times in later days.

The Wheelwright document follows from Hazard's *State Papers*, I, 463.

COMBINATION OF SETTLERS AT EXETER

Whereas it hath pleased the Lord to move the Heart of our dread Sovereign Charles by the Grace of God King etc. to grant Licence and Libertye to sundry of his subjects to plant themselves in the Westerne parts of America. We his loyal Subjects, Brethren of the Church in Exeter, situate and lying upon the River Pascataqua, with other Inhabitants there, considering with ourselves the holy Will of God and our own Necessity that we should not live without wholesom Lawes and Civil Government among us, of which we are altogether destitute; do in the name of Christ and in the Sight of God combine ourselves together to erect and set up among us such Government as shall be to our best discerning agreeable to the Will of God, professing ourselves Subjects to our Sovereign Lord King Charles according to the Libertyes of our English Colony of Massachusetts, and binding ourselves solemnly by the Grace and help of Christ, and in his Name and fear, to submit ourselves to such Godly and Christian Lawes as are established in the realm of England to our best Knowledge, and to all other such Lawes which shall upon good grounds be made and enacted among us according to God, that we may live quietly and peaceably together in all godliness and honesty. Mo. 8. D. 4. 1639, as attests our Hands.

John Wheelwright [and thirty-four other names].

47. The Peirce Charter, June, 1621

Massachusetts Historical Society Collections, Fourth Series, II, 158 ff.
Finding themselves within the jurisdiction of the newly reorganized Plymouth Council (or New England Council), the Pilgrims secured from that body the following grant through their London partners. Peirce was intended to act as trustee while the partnership lasted. Cf. *American History and Government*, § 55, and (for the documents regarding Peirce's later attempt to steal the colony) Arber's *Story of the Pilgrim Fathers*, 259, 260.

This Indenture made the First Day of June, *1621,* Betwene the *President and Counsell of New England* of the one partie, And *John Peirce* Citizen and Clothworker of London *and his Associates* of the other partie, Witnesseth that whereas the said John Peirce and his Associates have already transported and undertaken to transporte at their cost and chardges themselves and dyvers persons into New England and there to erect and build a Towne and settle dyvers Inhabitantes for the advancement of the generall plantacion of that Country of New England, Now the sayde President and Counsell, in consideracion thereof and for the furtherance of the said plantacion and incoragement of the said Undertakers, have agreed to graunt, assigne, allott, and appoynt to the said John Peirce and his associates and every of them, his and their heires and assignes, one hundred acres of grownd for every person so to be transported, besides dyvers other pryviledges, Liberties, and commodyties hereafter mencioned. . . .

The same land to be taken and chosen by them, their deputies or assignes, in any place or places wheresoever not already inhabited by any English. . . .

And forasmuch as the said John Peirce and his associates intend and have undertaken to build Churches, Schooles, Hospitalls, Toune houses, Bridges, and such like workes of Charytie, As also for the maynteyning of Magistrates and other inferior Officers (In regard whereof and to the end that the said John Peirce and his Associates, his and their heires and assignes, may have where withall to beare and support such like charges), Therefore the said President and Councell aforesaid do graunt unto the said Undertakers, their heires and assignes, Fifteene hundred acres of Land moreover and above the aforesaid proporcion of one hundred the person for every undertaker and Planter, to be imployed upon such publique uses as the said Undertakers and Planters shall thinck fitt. . . .

And shall also at any tyme within the said terme of Seaven Yeeres upon request unto the said President and Counsell made, graunt unto them (the said John Peirce and his Associates, Undertakers, and Planters, their heires and assignes) Letters and Grauntes of Incorporacion by some usuall and fitt name and tytle, *with Liberty to them and their successors from tyme to tyme to make orders, Lawes, Ordynaunces, and Constitucions, for the rule, governement, ordering, and dyrecting of all persons to be transported and settled upon the landes hereby graunted, intended to be graunted, or hereafter to be granted.* . . . *And in the meane tyme untill such graunt made, It shalbe lawfull for the said John Peirce, his Associates, Undertakers, and Planters, their heires and assignes, by consent of the greater part of them, To establish such Lawes and ordynaunces as are for their better government, and the same, by such Officer or Officers as they shall by most voyces elect and choose, to put in execucion.*

[The above grant was the first charter issued by the Plymouth Council of 1620 (No. 42 above). It is sometimes said that these patents from the Council had no legal force, so far as *political features* were concerned. It is true that such grants had no force, as against the royal government; but, as long as the royal grant to the Council stood, grants from that body were valid, — certainly valid as against any later claim from that proprietary body. The king's patent of 1620 authorized the Council to arrange the government of colonies in its New England territories as it pleased. In carrying out this provision for the Pilgrims, the Council saw fit to permit a large share of self-government, — just as the London Company had done, in less degree, for the Virginians, and as Penn was to do for the Pennsylvanians in his famous charter to them in 1701 (No. 109 below). As to the overthrow of the validity of the charters to the Pilgrims in 1634, cf. *American History and Government*, § 55 close.]

48. Early Descriptions of Plymouth [1]

a. *Edward Winslow's Letter (to a friend in England), December 11/21, 1621*

Arber's *Story of the Pilgrim Fathers*, 488–494. (The spelling is modernized in all printed copies.)

Loving and Old Friend, —

Although I received no letter from you by this ship, yet forasmuch as I know you expect the performance of my promise, which was, to write unto you truly and faithfully of all things, I have therefore at this time sent unto you accordingly, referring you for further satisfaction to our more large Relations [Winslow's *Relations*, a considerable volume].

You shall understand that in this little time [less than one year] that a few of us have been here, we have built seven dwelling-houses and four for the use of the plantation, and have made preparation for divers others. We set the last spring some twenty acres of Indian corn, and sowed some six acres of barley and pease; and according to the manner of the Indians, we manured our ground with herrings, or rather shads, which we have in great abundance, and take with great ease at our doors. Our corn did prove well; and, God be praised, we had a good increase of Indian corn, and our barley

---

[1] Bradford's longer accounts are omitted here, because they are quoted so freely in *American History and Government*.

indifferent good, but our pease not worth the gathering, for we feared they were too late sown. They came up very well, and blossomed; but the sun parched them in the blossom. . . .

When it pleaseth God we are settled and fitted for the fishing business and other trading, I doubt not but by the blessing of God the gain will give content to all. In the mean time, that we have gotten we have sent by this ship; and though it be not much, yet it will witness for us that we have not been idle, considering the smallness of our number all this summer. We hope the merchants will accept of it, and be encouraged to furnish us with things needful for further employment, which will also encourage us to put forth ourselves to the uttermost.

Now because I expect your coming unto us, with other of our friends, whose company we much desire, I thought good to advertise you of a few things needful. Be careful to have a very good bread-room to put your biscuits in. Let your cask for beer and water be iron-bound, for the first tire, if not more. Let not your meat be dry-salted; none can better do it than the sailors. Let your meal be so hard trod in your cask that you shall need an adz or hatchet to work it out with. Trust not too much on us for corn at this time, for by reason of this last company that came, depending wholly upon us, we shall have little enough till harvest. Be careful to come by some of your meal to spend by the way; it will much refresh you. Build your cabins as open as you can, and bring good store of clothes and bedding with you. Bring every man a mussket or fowling-piece. Let your piece be long in the barrel, and fear not the weight of it, for most of our shooting is from stands. Bring juice of lemons, and take it fasting; it is of good use. For hot waters, aniseed water is the best; but use it sparingly. If you bring anything for comfort in the country, butter or sallet oil, or both is very good. Our Indian corn, even the coarsest, maketh us pleasant meat as rice; therefore spare that, unless to spend by the way. Bring paper and linseed oile for your windows, with cotton yarn for your lamps. Let

your shot be most for big fowls, and bring store of powder
and shot. I forbear further to write for the present, hoping
to see you by the next return. So I take my leave, commending you to the Lord for a safe conduct unto us, resting in him,

Your loving friend,
E. W.

b. *Captain John Smith's Account, 1624*

Smith's *Works* (Birmingham edition), 782 ff.

At New-Plimoth there is [1624] about 180 persons, some cattell and goats, but many swine and poultry; 32 dwelling houses, whereof 7 were burnt the last winter [1623], and the value of five hundred pounds in other goods; the Towne is impailed about halfe a mile [in] compasse. In the toune upon a high Mount they have a Fort well built with wood, lime, and stone, where is planted their Ordnance: Also a faire Watch-tower, partly framed for the Sentinell. The place it seemes is healthfull, for in these last three yeeres [1621–4], notwithstanding their great want of most necessaries, there hath not one died of the first planters. They have made a saltworke, and with that salt preserve the fish they take; and this yeare [1624] hath fraughted a ship of 180 tunnes.

The Governour is one Master William Bradford;

* * * * * * *

The most of them live together as one family or household, yet every man followeth his trade and profession both by sea and land, and all for a generall stocke: out of which they have all their maintenance, untill there be a divident betwixt the Planters and the Adventurers.

Those Planters are not servants to the Adventurers here, but have onely councells of directions from them, but no injunctions or command; and all the masters of families are partners in land or whatsoever, setting their labours against the stocke, till certaine yeeres be expired for the division;

they have young men and boies for their Apprentises and servants, and some of them speciall families, as Ship-carpenters, Salt-makers, Fish-masters, yet as servants upon great wages.

The Adventurers which raised the stocke to begin and supply this Plantation were about 70 :[1] some Gentlemen, some Merchants, some handy-crafts men, some adventuring great summes, some small, as their estates and affection served. The generall stocke already imploied is about 7000 l.; by reason of which charge and many crosses, many of them would adventure no more: but others that knowes so great a designe cannot bee effected without both charge, losse, and crosses, are resolved to goe forward with it to their powers; which deserve no small commendations and encouragement. These [The Adventurers generally] dwell most[ly] about London. They are not a Corporation, but [are] knit together by a voluntary combination in a society without constraint or penalty, aiming to doe good and to plant Religion; they have a President and Treasurer, every yeere newly chosen by the most voices, who ordereth the affaires of their Courts and meetings, and with the assent of the most of them, undertaketh all ordinary business; but in more weighty affaires, the assent of the whole Company is required.

There hath beene a fishing this yeere [1624] upon the Coast about 50. English ships: . . . and though I promise no Mines of gold, yet the warlike Hollanders let us imitate but not hate, whose wealth and strength are good testimonies of their treasury gotten by fishing; and New-England hath yeelded already [up to 1624] by generall computation one

---

[1] Bradford gives forty-two names, — those still interested in 1626. (Bradford's *Letter Book, Massachusetts Historical Society Collections,* First Series, III, 48.) In his latest work (*Advertisements*, etc., 1630) Smith implies that the London merchants lost far the greater part of their investment, — "being out of purse six or seven thousand pounds," and accepting in lieu of this the promise of the Planters in 1627 "to pay them for nine years two hundred pounds yearely, without any other account [settlement]." Smith, no doubt, heard only the merchants' side and exaggerates their loss. Bradford's *History* shows that the accounts were badly muddled.

hundred thousand pounds at the least. Therefore, honourable and worthy Country men, let not the meannesse of the word fish distaste you, for it will afford as good gold as the Mines of Guiana or Potassie, with lesse hazard and charge, and more certainty and facility.

49. Final Source of Plymouth Land Titles

a. The Bradford Charter, January 13/23, 1629/30

Hazard's *State Papers* (Washington, 1792), I, 298 ff.
Cf. *American History and Government*, § 55.

[Recital of grant of New England by James I to the Council for New England in charter of 1620.]

Now know yee that the said Councell, by Vertue and Authority of his said late Majestie's Letters pattents, and . . . in Consideration that William Bradford and his Associates have for these nine Yeares lived in New-Englande . . . and have there . . . planted a Towne . . . att their owne proper Costs . . . and now seeinge that by the speciall Providence of God and [by] their extraordinary Care and Industry, they have encreased their Plantacion to neere three hundred People . . . Have given . . . and sett over . . . unto the said William Bradford, his Heires, *Associates*, and Assigns, all that Parte of New England [boundaries of the Colony]

. . . Alsoe it shalbe lawfull and free for the said William Bradford, his Associats, his Heires and Assignes, att all tymes hereafter, to incorporate by some usuall or fitt Name and Title, him or themselves, or the People there inhabitinge under him or them, with Liberty to them and their Successours, from tyme to tyme to frame and make Orders, Ordinances, and Constitucons, as well for the better Governemente of their Affaires here, and the receaving or admitting any to his or their Society, as alsoe for the better Government of his or their People and Affaires in *New Englande*, or his and their People att Sea in goeinge thither, or returninge from thence, and the same to putt or cause to be putt in Execucon by such

Officers and Ministers as he and they shall authorise and depute; Provided that the said Lawes and Orders bee not repugnante to the Lawes of Englande, or the Frame of Governmente by the said Presidente and Councell here after to be established. . . . And the said Councell doe hereby covenante and declare, that it is their Intente and Meaninge for the good of this Plantacon, that the said William Bradford his Associats, or their Heires or Assignes, shall have and enjoy whatsoever Priveledge or Priveledges of what kinde soever, as are expressed or intended to be graunted by his said late Majestie's Letters-Pattents, and that in as large and ample manner as the said Councell thereby now may or hereafter can graunte (coyninge of Money excepted). . . . And lastly, know yee that wee the said Councell have made and . . . appointed Captaine Myles Standish, or, in his absence, Edward Winslowe, . . . and John Alden, or *any of them,* to be our true and lawfull Attorney . . . in our Name and Stead, to enter into the said Tracte . . . of Lande . . . or into some parte thereof . . . and in our Names to take possession and seizin thereof, . . . and after such possession and seizin, . . . then . . . in our Names to deliver the full and peaceable possession of all . . . the said mencioned . . . premises unto the said William Bradford. . . .

[The Plymouth copy of this grant is indorsed: —

"The within named John Alden, authorised as Attorney for the within mentioned Counsill, haveing in their name . . . entered into some parte of the within mentioned tracts of Land . . . and in their Names taken possession and seazin thereof, did in the name of the said Counsill, deliver the full and peacable possession and seazin of all . . . the within mentioned . . . premises unto William Bradford, for him, his Heires, Associates, and Assignes. . . .

"In Presence of
    James Cudworth
    William Clark
    Nathaniel Mortan, *Secretary.*"]

b. *Surrender of the Bradford Patent to the Plymouth Freemen, March 2/12, 1640/1641*

This document was first printed by Hazard in his *State Papers* (I, 468, 469). The text as given later (1855) in the *Plymouth Records* has the same spelling in nearly every case, but is somewhat more economical of capital letters. The Hazard text is followed here.

WHEREAS . . . the said William Bradford and divers others the first Instruments of God in the beginninge of this greate work of Plantacon together with such as the Alorderinge God in his Providence soone added unto them have beene at very greate charges to procure the said lands priveledges and freedomes from all entanglements . . . by reason whereof the title to the day of this present remayneth in the said William his heires associats and assignes now for the better setling of the state of the said land aforesaid the said William Bradford and those first Instruments termed and called in sondry orders upon publick Record the Purchasers or Old Comers . . . whereby they are distinguished from other the freemen and Inhabitants of the said Corporation Be it known unto all men therefore by these presents That the said William Bradford for himself his heires together with the said purchasers do onely reserve unto themselves their heires and assignes those three tracts of land . . . together with such other smale percells of lands as they or any of them are personally possessed of or interessed in by vertue of any former titles or graunts whatsoever and the said William Bradford doth by the free and full consent approbacon and agreement of the said Old Planters or Purchasers together with the likeing approbacon and acceptacon of the other part of the said Corporacon surrender into the hands of the whole Court consisting of the Freemen of this Corporacon of New-Plymouth all that ther right and title power authorytie priveledges immunities and freedomes graunted in the said Letters Patents by the said Right Honorable Councell for New England reserveing his and their personall Right of Freemen . . . declaring the

Freemen of this present Corporacon together with all such as shall be legally admitted into the same his associates . . . In witnes whereof the said William Bradford hath in Publicke Court surrendered the said Letters Patents actually into the hands and power of the said Court bynding himselfe his heires executors administrators and assignes to deliver up whatsoever specialties are in his hands that do or may concerne the same.

Memorand. That the said surrender was made by the said William Bradford in publicke Court to Nathaniell Sowther especially authorized by the whole Court to receive the same together with the said Letters Patents in his name and for the use of the whole Body of Freemen. . . .

50. First Code of Laws in America
Plymouth " Fundementals," 1636.

Hazard's *State Papers* (Washington, 1792), I, 404–410.

The following extracts come from a code (much resembling a bill of rights) drawn up for Plymouth Colony in 1636 by the first representative gathering of that colony. Cf. *American History and Government*, § 54.

1. — WEE the associates of the Colony of New-Plymouth, coming hither as free born subjects of the kingdom of England, endowed with all and singular the priveleges belonging to such: Being assembled,

Do enact, ordain and constitute; that no act, imposition, law or ordinance be made or imposed on us at present, or to come, but such as shall be enacted by consent of the body of freemen or associates, or their representatives legally assembled; which is according to the free liberties of the free born people of England.

2. — And for the well governing this Colony: It is also resolved and ordered, that there be a free election annually of Governor, Deputy Governor, and assistance, by the vote of the freemen of this corporation . . .

4. — It is also enacted, that no person in this government shall suffer or be indamaged, in respect of life, limb, liberty,

good name or estate, under color of law, or countenance of authority, but by virtue or equity of some express law of the general court of this Colony, or the good and equitable laws of our Nation, suitable for us, in matters which are of a civil nature (as by the court here hath been accustomed) wherein we have no particular law of our own. And that none shall suffer as aforesaid, without being brought to answer by due course and process of Law.

5. — And that all cases, whether capital, criminal, or between man and man, be tried by a jury of twelve good and lawful men, according to the commendable custom of England, except where some express law doth refer it to the judgement of some other judge or inferior court where jury is not; in which case also any party aggrieved, may appeal and have trial by a jury.

And it shall be in the liberty of any person, that is to be tried by a jury to challenge any of the jurors, and if the challenge be found just and reasonable by the bench, it shall be allowed; and others without just exception shall be impanelled in their room: And if it be in case of life and death, the prisoner shall have liberty (according to the law of England) to except against twenty of the jury without giving any reason for the same.

* * * * * * *

7. — And it is enacted; being the privelege of our charter; that all persons of the age of 21 years, of right understanding and memory, whether excommunicated, condemned or other, having any estate properly theirs to dispose of, shall have full power and liberty to make their reasonable wills and testaments, and other lawful alienations of their lands and estates; be it only here excepted, That such as are sentenced for Treason . . . or other capitall crimes, shall forfeit . . . for the carrying on the charge of government, their personal estate: Their lands and real estate being still at their disposal.

* * * * * * *

XI. THE FOUNDING OF MASSACHUSETTS

51. The Gorges Claim to Massachusetts

a. *Charter from the New England Council to Robert Gorges. December 30/January 9, 1622/3*

Hazard's *State Papers* (1792), I, 152 ff. Reprinted from Sir Ferdinando Gorges' *Briefe Narration of the Originall Undertakings . . . of Plantations into . . . America* (1658). Gorges' *Briefe Narration* is reprinted in full in the *Massachusetts Historical Society Collections*, Third Series, V, 45–93.

The Gorges Charter is short, and is given almost in full below.

[Recital of the grant of 1620 to the Council of New England] Now know all Men by these Presents, that We the Councell of *New-England,* for, and in respect of the good and speciall Service done by Sir *Ferdinando Gorges,* Knight, to the Plantation, from the first Attempt thereof unto this present, as also for many other causes us hereunto moving, and likewise for and in Consideration of the Payment of one hundred and sixty pounds of lawfull English Money unto the Hands of our Treasurer, by *Robert Gorges,* Sonne of the said Sir Ferdinando Gorges, Knight, whereof, and of every Part and Parcell whereof, the said *Robert Gorges,* his Heires, Executors, and Assignes, are for ever acquitted and discharged, by these Presents; have given, granted and confirmed, and by these Presents do give, grant, and confirme, unto the said *Robert Gorges,* his Heires and Assignes for ever, all that part of the Main Land in *New-England* aforesaid, commonly called or known by the name of *Messachusiack,* situate, lying and being upon the North-East side of the Bay called or knowne by the the Name of *Massachuset,* or by what other Name or Names soever it be, or shall be called or knowne, together with all the Shoars and Coasts along the Sea, for ten *English* Miles, in a streight line towards the North-East, accounting one thousand, seven hundred and sixty yards to the Mile, and thirty *English* Miles (after the same rate) unto the Main Land through all the Breadth aforesaid, together with all the Islets and Islands, lying within three Miles of any Part of the said Lands (except such Islands as are formerly granted): together also with all the Lands, Rivers, Mines and Mineralls, Woods, Quarryes, Marshes, Waters, Lakes, Fishings, Huntings, Fowlings, and Commodities, and Hereditaments whatsoever, with all and singular their Appurtenances, together with all Prerogatives, Rights, Jurisdictions and Royalties, and Power of Judicature in all Causes and Matters whatsoever, Criminal, Capital, and Civil, arising, or which may hereafter arise, within the Limits, Bounds, and Precincts aforesaid, *to be executed according to the great Charter of England, and such Lawes as shall be hereafter established by Publique Authority of the State assembled in Parliament in New-England*, to be executed and exercised by the said *Robert Gorges*, his Heires and Assignes, or his or their Deputies, Lieutenants, Judges, Stewards, or other Officers, thereunto by him or them assigned, . . . saving and alwayes reserving unto the said Councell, and their Successours, and to the Court of Parliament hereafter to be in *New-England* aforesaid, and to either of them, power to receive, heare and determine all and singular Appeale and Appeales, of every Person and Persons whatsoever, dwelling or inhabiting within the said Territories and Islands, or either or any of them, to the said *Robert Gorges* granted as aforesaid, of and from all Judgments and Sentences whatsoever given within the said Territories; . . .

[Sir Ferdinando Gorges was one of the original patentees of the "Northern Colony" of 1606. More than any other one man, he was instrumental in keeping that enterprise alive and in finally securing its reorganization as the Council of New England in 1620 (No. 42 above). He continued to be prominent in the meetings and business of that Company until its dissolution in 1634. He drew up a plan of government for all New England, in accordance with which the New England Council appointed his son Robert "generall Governor." This governor was to be assisted by a "Councill" consisting of heads of any individual colonies established or to be established. The Governor and Council were to make laws with the assent of a central "Parliament" to be chosen from the several colonies.

Thus Robert Gorges came to America in this double capacity, — patentee of his own small grant on Massachusetts Bay, and General Governor (or "Lieutenant General") of all New England. It was this last position that brought upon him the dislike of Governor Bradford of Plymouth, as noted in *American History and Government*, § 45, note.]

b. Robert Gorges, Lieutenant General of New England
(1623)

From Sir Ferdinando Gorges' "Briefe Narration" (1658), reprinted in *Massachusetts Historical Society Collections*, Third Series, VI, 74–75.

My son Captain Robert Gorges sent by authority of the Council for those Affairs, as their Lieutenant General.

The several complaints made to the council of the abuses committed by several the fishermen, and other interlopers, who without order from them frequented those coasts, tending to the scorn of our nation . . . to the overthrow of our trade, and dishonor of the government, —

For reformation whereof, and to prevent the evils that may ensue, they were pleased to resolve of the sending some one into those parts as their Lieutenant, to regulate the estate of their affairs and those abuses. Hereupon my son Robert Gorges being newly come out of the Venetian war, was the man they were pleased to pitch upon, being one of the Company, and interested in a proportion of the land with the rest of the Patentees in the Bay of the Majechewsett, containing ten miles in breadth and thirty miles into the main land; who, between my Lord Gorges and myself, was speedily sent away into the said Bay of Massechewset, where he arrived about the beginning of August following, anno 1623, that being the place he resolved to make his residence, as proper for the public as well as for his private [affairs]; where landing his provisions and building his storehouses, he sent to them of New Plymouth (who by his commission were authorized to be his assistants) to come unto him, who willingly obeyed his order, and as carefully discharged their duties; by whose experience he suddenly understood what was to be done with the poor means he had, believing the supplies he expected would follow according to the undertakings of divers his familiar friends who had promised as much. But they, hearing how I sped in the House of Parliament, withdrew themselves; and myself and friends were wholly disabled to do any thing to purpose. The report of these proceedings with us coming to my son's ears, he was advised to return home till better occasion should offer itself unto him.

52. The Beginning of Salem Colony

Extracts from the *Brief Relation* by the Reverend John White, 1630. For explanation of White's connection with the Company, see *American History and Government*, § 57 and note.

The ensuing faithful and impartial narration of the first occasions, beginning, and progress of the whole work, is laid before the eyes of all that desire to receive satisfaction, by such as have been privy to the very first conceiving and contriving of this project of planting this Colony. . . .

About ten years since, a company of English, part out of the Low Countries, and some out of London and other parts, associating themselves into one body, with an intention to plant in Virginia, in their passage thither being taken short by the wind, in the depth of winter, the whole ground being under snow, were forced with their provisions to land themselves in New-England, upon a small bay beyond Mattachusets, in the place which they now inhabit, and call by the name of New Plymouth. The ground being covered a foot thick with snow, and they being without shelter, and having amongst them divers women and children, no marvel if they lost some of their company; it may be wondered how they saved the

THE BEGINNING OF SALEM COLONY

rest. But notwithstanding this sharp encounter at the first, and some miscarriages afterward, yet, conceiving God's providence had directed them unto that place, and finding great charge and difficulty in removing, they resolved to fix themselves there; and being assisted by some of their friends in London, having passed over most of the greatest difficulties that usually encounter new planters, they began to subsist at length in a reasonably comfortable manner; being, notwithstanding, men but of mean and weak estates of themselves; and after a year's experience or two of the soil and inhabitants, sent home tidings of both, and of their well-being there, which occasioned other men to take knowledge of the place, and to take it into consideration.

About the year 1623, some western merchants, who had continued a trade of fishing for cod and bartering for furs in those parts for divers years before, conceiving that a Colony planted on the coast might further them in those employments, bethought themselves how they might bring that project to effect, and communicated their purpose to others, alleging the conveniency of compassing their project with a small charge, by the opportunity of their fishing trade, in which they accustomed to double-man their ships, that, by the help of many hands, they might dispatch their voyage and lade their ship with fish while the fishing season lasted; which could not be done with a bare sailing company. Now it was conceived that, the fishing being ended, the spare men that were above their necessary sailors, might be left behind with provisions for a year; and when that ship returned the next year, they might assist them in fishing, as they had done the former year; and, in the mean time, might employ themselves in building, and planting corn, which, with the provisions of fish, fowl, and venison, that the land yielded, would afford them the chief of their food. This proposition of theirs took so well, that it drew on divers persons to join with them in this project; the rather because it was conceived, that not only their own fishermen, but the rest of our nation that went thither on the same errand, might be much advantaged, not only by fresh victual, which that Colony might spare them in time, but withal, and more, by the benefit of their ministers' labors, which they might enjoy during the fishing season; whereas otherwise, being usually upon those voyages nine or ten months in the year, they were left all the while without any means of instruction at all. Compassion towards the fishermen, and partly some expectation of gain, prevailed so far that for the planting of a Colony in New England there was raised a stock of more than £3000, intended to be paid in in five years, but afterwards disbursed in a shorter time.

How this stock was employed, and by what errors and oversights it was wasted, is, I confess, not much pertinent to this subject in hand. Notwithstanding, because the knowledge there of may be of use for other mens' direction, let me crave leave, in a short digression, to present unto the reader's view the whole order of the managing of such moneys as were collected, with the success and issue of the business undertaken. [Here follows an account of mismanagement and losses, and the failure of the Company.]

But to return to our former subject, from which we digressed. Upon the manifestation of the Western Adventurers' resolution to give off their work, most part of the land men, being sent for, returned. But a few of the most honest and industrious resolved to stay behind, and to take charge of the cattle sent over the year before; which they performed accordingly. And not liking their seat at Cape Anne, chosen especially for the supposed commodity of fishing, they transported themselves to Nahum-Keike, about four or five leagues distant to the south-west from Cape Anne.

Some then of the Adventurers, that still continued their desire to set forward the plantation of a Colony there, conceiving that if some more cattle were sent over to those few men left behind, they might not only be a means of the comfortable subsisting of such as were already in the country, but of inviting some others of their friends and acquaintance to come

THE BEGINNING OF SALEM COLONY 135

over to them, adventured to send over twelve kine and bulls more; and, conferring casually with some gentlemen of London, moved them to add unto them as many more. By which occasion, the business came to agitation afresh in London, and being at first approved by some and disliked by others, by argument and disputation it grew to be more vulgar; insomuch that some men showing some good affection to the work, and offering the help of their purses if fit men might be procured to go over, inquiry was made whether any would be willing to engage their persons in the voyage. By this inquiry it fell out that among others they lighted at last on Master Endecott, a man well known to divers persons of good note, who manifested much willingness to accept of the offer as soon as it was tendered; which gave great encouragement to such as were upon the point of resolution to set on this work of erecting a new Colony upon the old foundation. Hereupon divers persons having subscribed for the raising of a reasonable sum of money, a patent was granted with large encouragements every way by his most excellent Majesty. Master Endecott was sent over Governor [1] assisted with a few men, and arriving in safety there in September, 1628, and uniting his own men with those which were formerly planted in the country into one body, they made up in all not much above fifty or sixty persons.

His prosperous journey, and safe arrival of himself and all his company, and good report which he sent back of the country, gave such encouragement to the work, that more adventurers joining with the first undertakers, and all engaging themselves more deeply for the prosecution of the design, they sent over the next year about three hundred persons more, most servants, with a convenient proportion of rotherbeasts, to the number of sixty or seventy, or there about, and some mares and horses; of which the kine came safe for the most part, but the greater part of the horses died, so that there remained not above twelve or fourteen alive.

---

[1] White gets the order of events wrong here. Endicott came before the charter was secured.

By this time the often agitation of this affair in sundry parts of the kingdom, the good report of Captain Endecott's government, and the increase of the Colony, began to waken the spirits of some persons of competent estates, not formerly engaged. Considering that they lived either without any useful employment at home, and might be more serviceable in assisting the planting of a Colony in New England, [they] took at last a resolution to unite themselves for the prosecution of that work. And, as it usually falls out, some other of their acquaintance, seeing such men of good estates engaged in the voyages, some for love to their persons, and others upon other respects, united unto them; which together made up a competent number, (perhaps far less than is reported,) and embarked themselves for a voyage to New-England, where I hope they are long since safely arrived [a reference to John Winthrop's expedition].

This is an impartial though brief relation of the occasion of planting of this Colony. The particulars whereof, if they could be entertained, were clear enough to any indifferent judgment, that the suspicious and scandalous reports raised upon these gentlemen and their friends, (as if, under the color of planting a Colony, they intended to raise and erect a seminary of faction and separation,) are nothing else but the fruits of jealousy of some distempered mind, or, which is worse, perhaps, savor of a desperate malicious plot of men ill affected to religion, endeavoring, by casting the undertakers into the jealousy of State, to shut them out of those advantages which otherwise they do and might expect from the countenance of authority. Such men would be intreated to forbear that base and unchristian course of traducing innocent persons under these odious names of Separatists and enemies to the Church and State, for fear lest their own tongues fall upon themselves by the justice of His hand who will not fail to clear the innocency of the just, and to cast back into the bosom of every slanderer the filth that he rakes up to throw in other men's faces. As for men of more indifferent and better tempered minds, they would be seriously advised to beware of entertaining and admitting, much more countenancing and crediting such uncharitable persons as discover themselves by their carriage, and that in this particular, to be men ill affected towards the work itself, if not to religion, at which it aims, and consequently unlikely to report any truth of such as undertake it.

53. The First Charter for Massachusetts Bay
March 4/14, 1628/1629

The text follows the copy of the charter in the *Massachusetts Colonial Records*, I, 3–19. The charter had been printed earlier (1769) in Hutchinson's *Collections of Original Papers*, but with a somewhat less faithful text. The document is more than usually verbose, and, if printed in full, it would occupy six times the space given it in this volume. Every grant and provision of any importance, however, is given or summarized in the following pages.

[Recital of the patent of 1620 to the Council for New England, and the subsequent grant[1] by the Council, in March, 1627/8, to Sir Henry Rosewell and others, which grant is by this present charter confirmed.]

AND FURTHER know yee, That . . . Wee . . . by theis presents doe . . . give and graunt unto the said Sir Henry Rosewell, Sir John Younge, Sir Richard Saltonstall, Thomas Southcott, John Humfrey, John Endecott, Symon Whetcombe, Isaack Johnson, Samuell Aldersey, John Ven, Mathewe Cradock, George Harwood, Increase Nowell, Richard Pery,

---

[1] This grant included the territory granted by the New England Council to Gorges in 1623. This was due, no doubt, to geographical ignorance. Ferdinando Gorges ("Briefe Narration," in *Mass. Hist. Soc. Coll.*, Third Series, V, 80), after explaining how the new Company came to ask for a grant from the New England Council, adds: "to which it pleased the thrice honored Lord of Warwick to write to me [from London], then at Plymouth, to condescend that a Patent might be granted. . . . Whereupon I gave my approbation *so far forth as it might not be prejudicial to my son Robert Gorges' interests, whereof he had a patent.*" Gorges always felt that the grant to the Massachusetts Bay Company had worked a great injustice to his family. Cf. *American History and Government*, §§ 57, note, 61.

Richard Bellingham, Nathaniel Wright, Samuell Vassall, Theophilus Eaton, Thomas Goffe, Thomas Adams, John Browne, Samuell Browne, Thomas Hutchins, William Vassall, William Pinchion, and George Foxcrofte, theire heires and assignes, All that parte of Newe England in America which lyes and extendes betweene a great river there commonlie called Monomack river, alias Merrimack river, and a certen other river there called Charles river, being in the bottome of a certen bay there commonlie called Massachusetts, alias Mattachusetts, alias Massatusetts bay: And also all and singuler those landes and hereditaments whatsoever, lyeing within the space of three Englishe myles on the south parte of the saide river called Charles river, or of any or every parte thereof: And also all and singuler the landes and hereditaments whatsoever lyeing and being within the space of three Englishe myles to the southward of the southernmost parte of the said baye called Massachusetts . . . : And also all those landes and hereditaments whatsoever which lye and be within the space of three English myles to the northward of the saide river called Monomack, alias Merrymack, or to the northward of any and every parte thereof, and all landes and hereditaments whatsoever, lyeing within the lymitts aforesaide, north and south, in latitude and bredth, and in length and longitude, of and within all the bredth aforesaide, throughout the mayne landes there from the Atlantick and westerne sea and ocean on the east parte, to the south sea on the west parte: . . . [with mines and fisheries, to be held in free soccage, paying one-fifth part of gold and silver ore. Incorporation, "by the name of the Governor and Company of the Mattachusetts Bay in New England," with succession and rights at law common to corporations, and with a seal.]

And wee doe hereby . . . graunte, That . . . there shalbe one Governor, one Deputy Governor, and eighteene Assistants . . . to be from tyme to tyme . . . chosen out of the freemen of the saide Company, for the tyme being, in such manner and forme as hereafter in theis presents is expressed. Which said officers shall applie themselves to take care for the best disposeing and ordering of the generall buysines and affaires of . . . the saide landes and premisses . . ., and the plantacion thereof, and the government of the people there.

[Appointment of Craddock and Goffe as first Governor and Deputy, and of eighteen of the others named in the opening of the grant as Assistants, " to continue in their offices for such time . . . as in these presents is hereafter declared," Governor or Deputy to call meetings of the Company.] And that the said Governor, Deputie Governor, and Assistants . . . shall or maie once every moneth, or oftener at their pleasures, assemble, and houlde, and keepe a Courte or Assemblie of themselves, for the better ordering and directing of their affaires. [Seven or more Assistants, with the Governor or Deputy Governor, to be a sufficient Court] and that there shall or maie be held . . . upon every last Wednesday in Hillary, Easter, Trinity, and Michas termes respectivelie for ever, one greate, generall, and solemne Assemblie, which foure Generall Assemblies shalbe stiled and called the Foure Greate and Generall Courts of the saide Company: IN all and every or any of which saide Greate and Generall Courts soe assembled, WEE DOE . . . graunte . . . That the Governor, or, in his absence, the Deputie Governor . . . and such of the Assistants and freemen . . . as shalbe present, or the greater nomber of them soe assembled, whereof the Governor or Deputie Governor and six of the Assistants, at the least to be seaven, shall have full power and authoritie to choose, nominate, and appointe such and soe many others as they shall thinke fitt, and that shall be willing to accept the same, to be FREE of the said Company and Body, and them into the same to admitt, and to elect and constitute such officers as they shall thinke fitt and requisite for the ordering, mannaging, and dispatching of the affaires of the saide Governor and Company. And to make Lawes and Ordinances for the Good and Welfare of the saide Company and for the government and ordering of the saide Lands and Plantacions, and the People inhabiting

... the same ... soe as such Lawes ... be not contrary or repugnant to the Lawes and Statutes of this our Realm of England. ... And wee doe ... ordeyne, That yearely once in the yeare for ever hereafter, namely, the last Wednesday in Easter tearme yearely, the Governor, Deputy Governor, and Assistants ... and all other officers of the saide Company shalbe, in the Generall Court or Assembly to be held for that day or tyme, newly chosen for the yeare ensueing by such greater parte of the said Company for the tyme being, then and there present, as is aforesaide.

[Vacancies caused by the death or removal of any officer of the Company may be filled by new elections. All officers are required to take an oath for the faithful performance of their duties. Permission, in the usual terms, to transport to America English subjects who offer themselves and who are not especially restrained by the King, with the usual guarantee of the rights of Englishmen to such emigrants and their descendants, and with the usual long clauses granting certain tariff privileges to the Company.]

And that the Governor or Deputie Governor ... or either of them, and any two or more of such of the saide Assistants as may be there unto appointed ... shall and maie at all Tymes, and from Tyme to Tyme hereafter, have full Power and Authority to minister and give the Oathe and Oathes of Supremacie and Allegiance, or either of them, to all and everie Person and Persons which shall at any Tyme ... pass to the Landes ... hereby mencioned. ...

AND wee doe ... graunt ..., That it shall ... be lawfull to and for the Governor or Deputie Governor and such of the Assistants and Freemen of the said Company ... as shalbe assembled in any of their Generall Courts aforesaide, or in any other Courtes to be specially summoned and assembled for that purpose, or the greater parte of them, (whereof the Governor or Deputie Governor and six of the Assistants, to be alwaies seaven,) from tyme to tyme to make, ordeine, and establishe all manner of wholesome and reasonable orders, lawes, statutes,

FIRST CHARTER FOR MASSACHUSETTS BAY

and ordinances, directions, and instructions not contrarie to the lawes of this our realme of England, aswell for setling of the formes and ceremonies of government and magistracy fitt and necessary for the said plantation and the inhabitants there, and for nameing and stiling of all sortes of officers, both superior and inferior, which they shall finde needefull for that governement and plantation, and the distinguishing and setting forth of the severall duties, powers, and lymytts of every such office and place, and the formes of such oathes warrantable by the lawes and statutes of this our realme of England as shalbe respectivelie ministred unto them, for the execution of the said severall offices and places, as also for the disposing and ordering of the elections of such of the said officers as shalbe annuall, and of such others as shalbe to suceede in case of death or removeall, and ministring the said oathes to the newe elected officers, and for impositions of lawfull fynes, mulcts, imprisonment, or other lawfull correction, according to the course of other corporations in this our realme of England, and for the directing, ruling, and disposeing of all other matters and things whereby our said people, inhabitants there, maie be soe religiously, peaceablie, and civilly governed, as their good life and orderlie conversation maie wynn and incite the natives of [that] country to the knowledg and obedience of the onlie true God and Savior of mankinde, and the Christian fayth, which, in our royall intention and the adventurers free profession, is the principall ende of this plantation.

AND WEE DOE further ... graunte to the saide ... Company ... that it may be lawful [for the Company and its officers] from Tyme to Tyme, and at all Tymes hereafter, for their speciall Defence and Safety, to incounter, expulse, repell, and resist by Force of Armes, as well by Sea as by Lande, and by all fitting Waies and Meanes whatsoever, all such Persons as shall at any Tyme hereafter attempt or enterprise the Destruction, Invasion, Detriment, or Annoyance to the saide Plantation ... [with the usual clause reserving to the English King the privilege of disavowing wrongful acts by the colony if he prefer to put it out of his allegiance, and *without* the usual half of the "expulse" clause relating to *settlers* who "may attempt to inhabit" in the colony without the permission of the Company; provided further that other Englishmen may fish on the coasts of the colony; and with the usual clause promising the Company the most favorable construction of any disputed clause.]

[**Hints for Study.**— 1.— Early New England historians *assumed* that this charter gave unusual powers. A comparison with the Virginia Company charters of 1609 and 1612, or with the New England Council charter of 1620, shows this assumption wholly false. Students may be asked to find four important powers given to those earlier corporations and not contained in this grant (noting the *limited* authority here in the inflictions of punishment, and the omission of the power to regulate settlement in connection with the usual "expulse, repel, etc." clause). The charter is not "very liberal," but very limited. This is more apparent when we notice that all these powers missing in this charter (or vaguely phrased here) *reappear* in the usual explicit form in the charter granted a few months later to the company for planting Providence Isle (No. 55, below).

2. — American historians (*e. g.* John Fiske, in *Beginnings of New England*) have often assumed that this charter used loose language as to the oath of supremacy *in order that* the Puritans might set up their own form of worship. *The wording, however, is practically identical with that of the Virginia Company charter of 1612 — from which unquestionably it was copied*, with only the necessary changes of names. (Let students verify this statement.)

3. — With the overthrow of these false assumptions goes another (in great measure) founded upon them, — *i.e.* that the Puritans intended, when they were securing this charter, to bring it to America and use it as a constitution for a free state. This assumption, however, is worth further investigation by the student, because it offers so admirable a lesson in historical criticism.

A single sentence of Governor John Winthrop's has been taken often as sufficient proof that the grantees so intended. Indeed (except for the groundless assumptions of 1 and 2 above, and for the equally worthless consideration discussed in 4 below) there is *no other evidence*.[1] Win-

---

[1] The very obscure sentence of Sir Ferdinando Gorges, written even later than Winthrop's one sentence, carries a like implication; but it contains

FIRST CHARTER FOR MASSACHUSETTS BAY 143

throp states that, in drawing up the charter, there was at first a clause which would have fixed the Company in England, "and, with much difficulty, *we* got it abscinded." Winthrop is high authority. But this sentence was written **fifteen years after the event**, and it is interjected hastily, *as a parenthesis*, in a bitter controversy (*Life and Letters*, II, p. 443). It could have been only "hearsay" at the best; since Winthrop did not belong to the Company until some months after the charter was secured (though he seems to have forgotten that for the moment when he says "we"). Such evidence would prove little in a law court, even if there were no evidence on the other side.

But there is evidence on the other side, — abundant, conclusive, unimpeachable.

(1) The abstract of the charter (docket) presented to the king by his legal advisors shows with absolute certainty that they and the grantor expected the charter powers to be exercised "here in England" (No. 54 below).

(2) The official records of the Company, *made at the time*, declare explicitly that Governor Cradock's proposal to transfer the charter to America (five months after it was granted) was "conceived by himself." Further, *the general tenor* of those records for those five intervening months agree wholly with the idea that the Company then had no thought of leaving England (see some extracts, No. 57 below), and they contain, in their fifty odd pages, no single suggestion of the other sort. Most conclusive of all, the *Records* show that even after the surprised Company had come to look with approval upon Cradock's proposal, they could not easily adjust their plans and financial interests to the new movement. (Advanced students will find the proof in the *Records*. It is impossible to represent them here in the necessary complete detail to show this. It may be added, however, that Cradock's proposal of July 28 was first debated, then deferred a month for *secret* consideration; then debated, in two meetings, by assigned sets of debaters for the two sides of the argument; then legal advice was sought, with what result, we don't know; and afterwards many plans were discussed as to how the transfer *could* be made without "prejudicing" the interests of the majority of the Company[1]. See Nos. 57, 58, for some of the evidence.)

Of the 110 members of the Company in England, only about one

---

such gross errors of chronology about external events that it can carry no weight at all **as to motives of his adversaries** (Mass. Hist. Society Collections, Third Series, VI, 80).

[1] Curiously, even Osgood, almost infallible in colonial history, refers only to Winthrop's sentence (with justifiable caution, to be sure), without any reference to the contrary evidence in the *Records*.

fourth ever came to America. Cradock himself never came, — though he had lands and servants here. Most of the members, who stayed in England, lost all their investment eventually. Indeed, in the summer of 1629, the Company was already in serious financial straits. A special inventory, in the fall, rated the stock at only one-third the face value. This condition may have inclined some stockholders to favor Cradock's proposition in July. The funds paid in for stock by Winthrop and other new members made it possible for old members to draw out (on this reduced scale). In this sense, the new members "bought" out some of the old ones.

4. — *No place of meeting* is suggested in the charter. This probably resulted from the fact that the Company was made up partly of Londoners, partly of Dorchester men (from the West of England; cf. *American History and Government*, § 57). All such previous colonizing corporations for America had been designated geographically (probably for convenient descriptions, rather than for limitation). But the "Council of Plymouth in the County of Devon" had never held a meeting at Plymouth: its records show that all its meetings were held at London. This fact may have helped to make the even more composite Massachusetts Company wary about having a place of meeting mentioned in their fundamental law. If John Winthrop is right in his statement of fifteen years later (above) that such a limitation was at first put into this document and that "with much difficulty we got it abscinded," then we may be sure that the Company desired that elision, not in order that they might hold meetings in America (as Winthrop afterward assumed), but to prevent their being hampered in England. This view is made practically certain when we observe the clause regarding place of meeting in the charter of the Providence Isle Company (below). That company certainly never expected to hold its meetings out of England, but it guards against being hampered, not by mere silence, but by express provision that it may meet where it likes.]

54. Docket of the Massachusetts Charter, 1629

When the king granted a charter, an exact copy, known as "the King's Bill," was presented to him, with a *docket*, or abstract, approved by his Attorney-General. This docket was what the king, or his council, read.

The following docket, now attached to the King's Bill of this charter in the London Record Office, is printed in the *Massachusetts Historical Society Proceedings* for 1869–1870, pages 172–173. The italics are used in this reproduction to call attention to important matters.

DOCKET OF THE MASSACHUSETTS CHARTER

May it please your most Excellent Majestie.

Whereas your Majesties most deare and royall father did, by his letteres Patents in the 18th yeare of his raigne, incorporate divers noblemen and others by the name of the Councell for the planting of New England in America and did thereby grant unto them all that part of America which lyeth betweene 40 degrees of Northerly latitude and 48 inclusive, — with divers priviledges and immunities. . . . Which said Councell have sithence by theire Charter in March last [1628] granted a part of that Continent to Sir Henrie Rosewell and others, their heires and associates, for ever, with all jurisdiccions, rightes, priviledges, and commodities of the same.

This Bill conteineth your Majesties confirmacion and Grant to the said Sir Henry Rosewell and his partners and their Associates and to their heires and assignes for ever of the said part of New England in America, with the like tenure in socage and reservacion of the fifth part of gould and silver oare, — Incorporating them also by the name of the Governor and Company of the Mattachusetts Bay in New England in America, — with such clauses for the electing of Governors and Officers *here* in England for the said Company, and powers to make lawes and Ordinances for setling the Governement and Magistracie of the plantacion *there,* and with such exempcions from Customes and Imposicions and some [such?] other priviledges as were originallie granted to the Councell aforesaid and are *usuallie allowed to Corporacions in England.*

And is done by direccion from the Lord Keeper upon your Majesties pleasure therein signified to his Lordship by Sir Ralph Freeman.

(Signed)   Ri. Shilton.

55. Excursus: For a Comparative Study of Charters

Notes upon the Charter for the Company of Westminster for the Plantation of the Island of Providence

December 4/14, 1630

This very important charter has never been printed. An abstract in the *Colonial State Papers* seemed so significant that the editor of this volume secured a complete transcript of the charter from the manuscript in the British Record Office. On that transcript, the notes below are based.

The colony of Providence Isle was of little weight, and the charter of the proprietary Company, accordingly, has received scant attention. That document, however, issued twenty-one months later than that of the Massachusetts Bay Company, is in many ways the culmination of the series of grants to English corporations for colonizing purposes. All the powers granted to proprietaries in earlier charters, including those which were dropped out in the Massachusetts charter, reappear here; and in some important matters there is much new detail. A study of this document removes the last possible basis for the claims of the older New England historians that the Massachusetts charter was in any peculiar way adapted to the purpose of a transfer to America.

1. *Puritan membership.* — The incorporators comprise the Earl of Warwick, Lord Say and Sele, Sir Nathaniel Rich, Oliver St. Johns, and John Pym, — all prominent leaders of the Puritan party, more prominent than any Puritans in the Massachusetts Company.

2. *Sectarianism.* — The Company is given the "Patronages and Advowsons" of "all" churches and chapells, — without even a restriction as to the customs of the Church of England (such as is found in the Baltimore charter). If this provision had been in the Massachusetts charter, Puritan historians would have found it certain proof of an intention to build a non-conformist state. The passage conferring authority to impose the oath of supremacy is copied from the charters of 1612 and 1629. No other sectarian restriction occurs.

3. *Place of meeting.* — The Company are to govern themselves and their settlement (as the Virginia Company of 1612 and the Massachusetts Bay Company) in four " General Courts " each year; but these courts are to be held "*in any place or places by themselves to be appointed.*" (And, again, the Company is authorized to hold its courts "*in any place or*

A COMPARATIVE STUDY OF CHARTERS 147

places convenient"). Surely, this disposes of the ancient argument that the omission of a specific place of meeting in the Massachusetts charter suggests an intention to establish some place out of England.

The facts as to a specific meeting place for a colonizing corporation in England seem to be as follows:

a. The charter of 1606 establishes two sub-companies, which necessarily are designated geographically to distinguish one from the other; and the charters of 1609, 1612, and 1620 use geographical designations, necessarily, to show to which one of those sub-companies they respectively apply.

b. But the " Plymouth Council " (charter of 1620) did not regard its geographical designation as fixing its place of meeting, or else it found it necessary to ignore the restriction. All its meetings were held, not at Plymouth, but in London.

c. The Massachusetts Bay Company was made up of two bodies of men, one from the east, one from the west of England. This fact, together with the experience of the Plymouth Council, probably made them unwilling to have a place of meeting fixed in their charter.

d. The Providence Isle charter carries this development, as suggested above, to its logical conclusion, permitting the Company itself to fix the places for its meetings. But this last Company certainly never expected to leave England. So the old argument from the omission of a specific place in the charter of the Massachusetts Company falls to the ground.

4. *Law making.* — In the General Courts the Company is empowered "to ordaine frames of Government, *with all things thereto incident;* and to make reasonable lawes . . . not being contrarie to the Lawes of this our Realme of England . . . for the Government of the Company . . . and of all Collonyes which shall be planted . . . in the said Islands . . . and to appoint, by such title as they . . . shall thinke good, such . . . offices and officers . . . for such Times and with such powers, as they shall thinke good, both for the Company here within our Realme of England and for the Collonies in the said Islands . . . and the said Offices and Officers . . . to alter . . . and displace, and in their places, to appoint others . . . and the said Lawes . . . to put into execution." . . .

5. Admiralty jurisdiction conferred.

6. Local Government. Power to divide the territory into " Provinces, Counties . . . Hundreds, Mannors," or other units, and to erect and fortify villages, etc., and *to grant letters of incorporation* to towns and burroughs, " with all Liberties and things unto Corporations requisite and usual within this our Realme of England " ; and to set up markets ; and to constitute and appoint magistrates and all manner of officers for all local units, with fit legislation for them.

7. Power of punishment to extend to "life and members," with authority to exercise martial law.

8. Right to settle restricted to those having a license from the Company.

9. Rights of Englishmen guaranteed to settlers and their posterity.

10. Company to coin money (not gold or silver).

11. Repetition of the usual privileges granted in earlier charters, and a "blanket clause" promising the Company "all such Prerogatives," etc., as have ever been granted to any colonizing Company in England.

56. The Massachusetts Company's Agreement with Mr. Higginson

Alexander Young's *Chronicles of Massachusetts* (1846), 209 ff. Young modernized the spelling. On March 19, at a meeting of the Company, it had been decided to try to secure Higginson for the coming voyage.

A true note of the allowance that the New-England [Massachusetts Bay] Company have, by common consent and order of their Court and Council, granted unto Mr. Francis Higginson, Minister, for his maintenance in New-England, April 8, 1629.

1. — Imprimis, that 30 pounds in money shall be forthwith paid him by the Company's treasurer towards the charges of fitting himself with apparel and other necessaries for his voyage.

2. — Item, that 10 pounds more shall be paid over by the said treasurer towards the providing of books for present use.

3. — Item, that he shall have 30 pounds yearly paid him for three years, to begin from the time of his first arrival in New-England, and so to be accounted and paid him at the end of every year.

4. — Item, that during the said time, the Company shall provide for him and his family necessaries of diet, housing and firewood, and shall be at charges of transporting him into New-England; and at the end of the said three years, if he shall not like to continue there any longer, to be at the charge of transporting him back for England.

5. — Item, that in convenient time a house shall be built, and certain lands allotted thereunto; which, during his stay in the country, and continuance in the ministry, shall be for his use; and after his death or removal, the same to be for succeeding ministers.

6. — Item, at the expiration of the said three years, a hundred acres of land shall be assigned to him and his heirs forever.

7. — Item, that in case he shall depart this life in that country, the said Company shall take care for his widow during her widowhood and abode in that country and Plantation; and the like for his children whilst they remain upon the said Plantation.

8. — Item, that the milk of two kine shall be appointed towards the charges of diet for him and his family as aforesaid, and half the increase of calves during the said three years; but the said two kine, and the other half of the increase, to return to the Company at the end of the said three years.

9. — Item, that he shall have liberty of carrying over bedding, linen, brass, iron, pewter, of his own, for his necessary use during the said time.

10. — Item, that if he continue seven years upon the said Plantation, that then a hundred acres of land more shall be allotted him for him and his forever. . . .

Further,[1] though it was not mentioned in the Agreement, but forgotten, Mr. Higginson was promised a man-servant, to take care and look to his things, and to catch him fish and fowl, and provide other things needful, and also two maid-servants, to look to his family.

---

[1] This item is added by Higginson in his written acceptance of the above terms.

57. First Government in Massachusetts Bay under the Company in England; April, 1629

Records of the Governor and Company of Massachusetts Bay (1853; edited by Nathaniel Shurtleff), I, 361 ff.

The early records were kept very informally, — more so than would pass with a high school debating society to-day. This particular entry is placed by the editor far out of its chronological order, preserved as it was on a loose sheet of manuscript. Previous to the transfer of the Company to America, the records as printed would fill about one hundred pages of this volume.

> *A generall Court, holden at London, the 30th Day of Aprill, 1629, by the Governor and Company of the Mattachusetts Bay in New England.*

Whereas the Kings most excellent Majesty hath bin gratiously pleased to erect and establish us, by his lettres pattents, under the great seale of England, to bee a body corporate, entytuled the Governor and Company of the Mattachusetts Bay in New England, and therby hath endowed us with many large and ample priviledges and immunities, with power to make good and wholsome lawes, and ordinances for the better maintenance and support of the said priviledges and for the better and more orderly and regular government, to bee observed in the prosecucion and propagacion of our intended voyages and the plantacion there, authorising us to nominate and appoint and select fitt persons amoungst ourselves for the managing, ordering, and governing of our affaires, both in England and in the places speyed and graunted unto us by vertue of his majestys said charter, wee have, in the prosecucion of the said power and authoritie given us . . . thought fitt to settle and establish an absolute government at our plantacion in the said Mattachusetts Bay in New England, which, by the vote and consent of a full and ample Court now assembled, is . . . ordered as followeth, viz.: —

That thirteene of such as shalbe reputed the most wyse, honest, expert, and discreete persons resident upon the said

FIRST GOVERNMENT IN MASSACHUSETTS BAY

plantacion, shall from tyme to tyme, and at all tyme hereafter, have the sole managing and ordering of the government and our affaires there, who, to the best of their judgments, are to endeavor soe to settle the same as may make most to the glory of God, the furtherance and advancement of this hopeful plantacion, the comfort, encouragement, and future benefitt of us and others, the beginners and prosecutors of this soe laudable a worke. The said 13 persons soe appointed to bee entytled by the name of the Governor and Councell of **Londons Plantacion in the Mattachusetts Bay in New England.**

And having taken into due consideracion the meritt, worth, and good desert of Captain John Endecott, and others lately gone over from hence with purpose to resyde and continue there, wee have, with full consent and authoritie of this Court, and by ereccion of hands, chosen and elected the said Captain John Endecott to the place of present Governor in our said plantacion.

Also, by the same power, and with the like full and free consent, wee have chosen and elected Mr. Francis Higgeson, Mr. Samuel Skelton, Mr. Francis Bright, Mr. John Browne, Mr. Samuel Browne, Mr. Thomas Graves, and Mr. Samuell Sharpe, these seaven, to bee of the said councell, and doe hereby give power and authoritie to the said Governor and those seaven to make choice of 3 others, such as they, or the greater nomber of them, in their discrecions, shall esteeme and conceive most fitt thereunto, to bee also of the said councell.

And to the end that the former planters there may have noe just occasion of excepcion, as being excluded out of the priviledges of the Company, this Court are content, and doe order, by ereccion of hands, that such of the said former planters as are willing to live within the lymitts of our plantacion shalbe enabled, and are hereby authorized, to make choice of 2 such as they shall thinke fitt, to supply and make upp the nomber of 12 of the said councell, one of which 12 is, by the Governor and councell, or the major part of them, to bee chosen Deputie to the Governor for the tyme being. . . .

It is further concluded on and ordered by this Court, that the said Governor, Deputie, and councell, before named, soe chosen and established in their severall places, shall continue and bee confirmed therin for the space of one whole yeare from and after the taking the oath, or untill such time as this Court shall thinke fitt to make choice of any others to succeed in the place or places of them or any of them. . . .

And it is further agreed on and ordered, that the Governor for the tyme beeing shall have power, and is heereby authorized, to call courts and meetings in places and at tymes convenyent, as to his discrecion shall seeme meete, which power is also conferred upon the Deputie in the absence of the said Governor; and the said. Governor or Deputie, togeather with the said councell, being chosen and assembled as aforesaid, and having taken their oaths respectively to their severall places, they, or the greater nomber of them, whereof the Governor or Deputie to bee always one, are authorized by this act, grounded on the power derived from his majestys charter, to make, ordaine, and establish all manner of wholsome and reasonable lawes, orders, ordinances and constitucions, (soe as the same bee noe way repugnant or contrary to the lawes of the realme of England) for the administring of justice upon malefactors, and inflicting condigne punishment upon all other offendors, and for the furtherance and propagating of the said plantacion, and the more decent and orderly government of the inhabitants resydent there.

[This establishment of a subordinate government in Massachusetts corresponds to the government in Virginia in 1614, perhaps, — before the Virginia Company granted self-government to the settlement. There is no hint, here, be it noted, that this arrangement was soon to be superseded by the transfer of the English Company itself to America. Ten meetings are recorded between the one when these orders were taken and the one (next given here) in which that suggestion first appears.]

XII. THE COLONY BECOMES A PURITAN ENTERPRISE

58. Decision to Transfer the Charter to the Colony

a. First Official Proposition to Transfer the Charter to America

Records of the Governor and Company of Massachusetts Bay, I, 47–51.

A Generall Court, holden for the Company of the Mattachusetts Bay, in New England, at Mr. Deputies House, on Tewsday, the 28 of July, 1629.

Present,
MR. MATTHEW CRADOCK, *Governor,*
MR. THOMAS GOFF, *Deputie,*
MR. GEORGE HARWOOD, *Treasurer,*
MR. THOMAS ADAMS,
MR. NATHANIELL WRIGHT,
MR. THEOPHILUS EATON,
MR. RICHARD PERRY,
MR. JOSEPH BRADSHAWE,
MR. BURNELL,
MR. RIVET,
MR. DANIEL BALLARD,
MR. SPURSTOWE,
MR. INCREASE NOELL,
MR. SYMON WHETCOMBE,
MR. JOHN POCOCKE,
MR. COLSON,
MR. HUTCHINS,
MR. WILLIAM PINCHON,
MR. SAMUEL VASSAIL,
Assistants,
MR. THOMAS HEWSON,
MR. WOODGATE,
MR. WEB,
MR. CRANE, *Generalitie.*

... [A long meeting with much business]

And lastly, Mr. Governor read certaine proposicions *conceived by himselfe,* viz, that for the advancement of the plantacion, *the inducing and encouraging persons of worth and qualitie to transplant themselves and famylyes thether,*[1] and for

---

[1] No doubt the movement that culminated in *b* below was already under way.

other weighty reasons therein contained, to transferr the government of the plantacion to those that shall inhabite there, and not to continue the same in subordinacion to the Company heer, as it now is. This business occasioned some debate; but by reason of the many great and considerable consequences therupon depending, it was not now resolved upon; but those present are desired privately and seriously to consider hereof, and to sett down their particular reasons in wryting, pro and contra, and to produce the same at the next Generall Court, where, they being reduced to heads and maturely considered of, the Company may then proceede to a fynall resolucion there [on]; and in the meane tyme *they are desired to carry this businesse secretly, that the same bee not divulged.*

b. *The Cambridge Agreement*

Hutchinson's *Collection of Original Papers* (1769), 25, 26. Cf. *American History and Government*, §§ 58, 59.

The True Copy of the Agreement at Cambridge, August 26, 1629.

Upon due consideration of the state of the Plantation now in hand for New-England, wherein wee whose names are hereunto subscribed, have engaged ourselves, and have weighed the greatnes of the worke in regard of the consequence, God's glory, and the Churches good; as also in regard of the difficultys and discouragements which in all probabilityes must be forecast upon the execution of this businesse; Considering withall that this whole adventure grows upon the joynt confidence we have in each other's fidelity and resolution herein, so as no man of us would have adventured it without assurance of the rest: Now, for the better encouragement of ourselves and others that shall joyne with us in this action, and to the end that every man may without scruple dispose of his estate and affayres as may best fit his preparation for this voyage; it is fully and faithfully agreed amongst us, and every of us doth hereby freely and sincerely promise and bind himselfe in the word of a christian and in the presence of God, who is the searcher of all hearts, that we will so really endeavour the prosecution of this worke, as by God's assistance, we will be ready in our persons, and with such of our several familyes as are to go with us, and such provision as we are able conveniently to furnish ourselves withall, to embarke for the said Plantation by the first of March next, at such port or ports of this land as shall be agreed upon by the Companie, to the end to passe the seas, (under God's protection,) to inhabite and continue in New-England: *Provided always, that, before the last of September next, the whole government, together with the patent for the said Plantation, be first, by an order of Court, legally transferred and established to remain with us and others which shall inhabit upon the said Plantation:* and provided also, that if any shall be hindered by such just and inevitable lett or other cause, to be allowed by 3 parts of four of these whose names are hereunto subscribed, then such persons, for such tymes and during such letts, to be discharged of this bond. And we do further promise, every one for himselfe, that shall fayle to be ready through his own default by the day appointed, to pay for every day's default the sum of £3, to the use of the rest of the Companie who shall be ready by the same day and time.

Richard Saltonstall,	Thomas Sharpe,
Thomas Dudley,	Increase Nowell,
William Vassall,	John Winthrop,
Nicholas West,	William Pinchon,
Isaac Johnson,	Kellam Broune,
John Humfrey,	William Colburn.

[Several of these signers did not come to America.]

c. Decision by the Company

Records of the Governor and Company of Massachusetts Bay, I, 49 ff.

(1) *A Generall Court, holden at Mr. Deputyes House, the 28 of August, 1629.*

[Present: 25 Names given.]

Mr. Deputie acquainted this Court, that the espetiall cause of their meeting was to give answere to divers gentlemen,[1] intending to goe into New England, whether or noe the chiefe government of the plantacion, togeather with the pattent, should bee settled in New England, or heere.

Wherupon it was ordered, that this afternoone Mr. Wright, Mr. Eaton, Mr. Adams, Mr. Spurstowe, and such others as they should thinke fitt to call unto them, whether they were of the Company or not, to consider of arguments against the setling of the chiefe government in New England.

And, on the other syde, Sir Richard Saltonstall, Mr. Johnson, Captain Venn, and such others as they should call unto them, to prepare arguments for the setling of the said government in New England; and that tomorrow morning, being the 29th of August, at 7 of the clock, both sydes should meete and conferr and weigh each others arguments, and afterwards, at 9 of the clock, (which is the tyme appointed of meeting for a General Court,) to make report therof to the whole Company, who then will determine this business.

(2) *A General Court, at Mr. Deputyes House, the 29th of August, 1629.*

This day the committees which were appointed to meete yesterday in the afternoone to consider of arguments pro and contra touching the setling of the government of the Companyes plantacion in New England, being according to the order of the last Court mett togeather, debated their arguments and reasons

---

[1] See *b* above.

on both sydes; where were present many of the Assistants and generalitie; and after a long debate, Mr. Deputie put it to the question, as followeth:

As many of yow as desire to have the pattent and the government of the plantacion to bee transferred to New England, *soe as it may bee done legally*, hold up your hands: Soe many as will not, hold upp your hands.

Where, by ereccion of hands, it appeared by the generall consent of the Company, that the government and pattent should bee setled in New England, and accordingly an order to bee drawne upp.

[This by no means settled the matter. The question arose as to how to protect the property rights of those stockholders who were to remain in England, and several meetings were devoted to consideration of various plans proposed.]

59. Decision of Puritan Gentlemen to Settle in the Colony [1]

a. *Winthrop's Argument for a Puritan Colony*

Robert Winthrop's *Life and Letters of John Winthrop*, I, 309 ff.

This argument is generally ascribed to John Winthrop, and one manuscript of it at least is said to be in his handwriting. The first printed copy was made by Hutchinson in his *Collections*, but from a different manuscript.

Reasons *to be considered for justifieinge the undertakeres of the intended Plantation in New England, and for incouraginge such whose hartes God shall move to joyne with them in it.*

1. — It will be a service to the Church of great consequence to carry the Gospell into those parts of the world, to helpe on the comminge of the fullnesse of the Gentiles, and to raise a Bulworke against the Kingdome of Ante Christ which the Jesuites labour to reare up in those parts.

2. — All other churches of Europe are brought to desolation, and our sinnes, for which the Lord beginnes allreaddy to frowne

---

[1] The first document under this number should logically be a repetition of the Cambridge Agreement, above.

upon us and to cutte us short, doe threatne evill times to be comminge upon us, and whoe knowes but that God hath provided this place to be a refuge for many whome he meanes to save out of the generall callamity; and seeinge the Church hath noe place lefte to flie into but the wildernesse, what better worke can there be, then to goe and provide tabernacles and foode for her against she comes thither:

3. — *This Land growes weary of her Inhabitants, soe as man, whoe is the most pretious of all creatures, is here more vile and base then the earth we treade upon, and of less prise among us then an horse or a sheepe:* masters are forced by authority to entertaine servants, parents to mainetaine there oune children, all tounes complaine of the burthen of theire poore, though we have taken up many unnessisarie yea unlawfull trades to mainetaine them, and we use the authoritie of the Law to hinder the increase of our people, as by urginge the Statute against Cottages, and inmates; and thus it is come to passe, that children, servants, and neighboures, especially if they be poore, are compted the greatest burthens, which if thinges weare right would be the cheifest earthly blessinges.

4. — The whole earth is the Lords garden and he hath given it to the Sonnes of men with a general Commission: Gen: 1: 28: "Increace and multiplie, and replenish the earth and subdue it," which was againe renewed to Noah: the end is double and naturall, that man might enjoy the fruits of the earth, and God might have his due glory from the creature: why then should we stand striving here for places of habitation, etc. (many men spending as much labour and coste to recover or keepe sometimes an acre or tuoe of Land, as would procure them many and as good or better in another Countrie) and in the meane time suffer a whole Continent as fruitfull and convenient for the use of man to lie waste without any improvement?

5. — We are groune to that height of Intemperance in all excesse of Riott, as noe mans estate allmost will suffice to keepe saile with his aequalls: and he whoe failes herein, must live in scorne and contempt. Hence it comes that all artes and

Trades are carried in that deceiptfull and unrighteous course as it is allmost impossible for a good and upright man to mainetayne his charge and live comfortablie in any of them.

6. — The ffountaines of Learning and Religion are soe corrupted as (besides the unsupportable charge of there education) most children (even the best witts and of fairest hopes) are perverted, corrupted, and utterlie overthroune by the multitude of evill examples and the licentious government of those seminaries, where men straine at knatts and swallowe camells, use all severity for mainetaynance of cappes and other accomplyments, but suffer all ruffianlike fashions and disorder in manners [morals] to passe uncontrolled.

b. *Winthrop's Argument for Coming Himself to America*

John Winthrop sent the following " Considerations " relating to himself to various friends for their advice. *Life and Letters*, I, 327.

Particular Considerations in the case of J : W :

1 : It is come to that issue as (in all probabilitye) the wellfare of the Plantation dependes upon his goeinge, for divers of the Chiefe Undertakers (upon whom the reste depende) will not goe without him.

2 : He acknowledges a satisfactorye callinge, outwarde from those of the Plantation, inwardly by the inclination of his oun hearte to the worke, and bothe approved by godly and juditious Devines (whereof some have the first interest in him), and there is in this the like mediate call from the Kinge, which was to his former imployment.

3 : Though his means be sufficient for a comfortable subsistence in a private condition heere, yet the one halfe of them being disposed to his 3: elder sonnes, who are now of age, he cannot live in the same place and callinge with that which remains; his charge being still as great as before, when his means were double : and so if he should refuse this opportunitye, that talent which God hath bestowed upon him for publike service, were like to be buried.

4: His wife and suche of his children, as are come to years of discreation, are voluntarylye disposed to the same Course.

5: Most of his friends (upon the former considerations) doe consent to his change.

c. *Decision of John Winthrop, Jr.*

JOHN WINTHROP, JR., TO HIS FATHER

Winthrop's *Life and Letters of John Winthrop*, I, 306–307.

Sir, — My humble duty remembered to you and my mother. . . .

For the business of New England, I can say no other thing but that I believe confidently, that the whole disposition thereof is of the Lord, who disposeth all alterations, by his blessed will, to his own glory and the good of his; and, therefore, do assure myself, that all things shall work together for the best therein. And for myself, I have seen so much of the vanity of the world, that I esteem no more of the diversities of countries, than as so many inns, whereof the traveller that hath lodged in the best, or in the worst, findeth no difference, when he cometh to his journey's end; and I shall call that my country, where I may most glorify God, and enjoy the presence of my dearest friends. Therefore herein I submit myself to God's will and yours, and, with your leave, do dedicate myself (laying by all desire of other employments whatsoever) to the service of God and the Company herein, with the whole endeavors, both of body and mind.

The CONCLUSIONS, which you sent down, I showed to my uncle and aunt, who liked them well. I think they are unanswerable; and it cannot but be a prosperous action, which is so well allowed by the judgments of God's prophets, undertaken by so religious and wise worthies of Israel, and indented to God's glory in so special a service.

. . . So, desiring your prayers and blessing, I commend you to the Almighty's protection, and rest   Your obedient son,

JOHN WINTHROP.

LONDON, August 21, 1629.

d. News from New England, 1629

Higginson's *Relation* is the name under which his *New-England's Plantation* is commonly quoted. Apparently he sent back the manuscript in the early fall (September, presumably) of 1629, some four months after his arrival. The little book was printed in London in 1630, but before that time it (together with earlier letters) had had much influence in leading to the main Puritan migration. The selections below are taken from Young's *Chronicles of Massachusetts*, where the spelling is modernized.

* * * * * * *

The fertility of the soil is to be admired at, as appeareth in the abundance of grass that groweth everywhere, both very thick, very long, and very high in divers places. But it groweth very wildly, with a great stalk, and a broad and ranker blade, because it hath never been eaten with cattle, nor mowed with a scythe, and seldom trampled on by foot. It is scarce to be believed how our kine and goats, horses and hogs do thrive and prosper here, and like well of this country.

In our Plantation we have already a quart of milk for a penny. But the abundant increase of corn proves this country to be a wonderment. Thirty, forty, fifty, sixty, are ordinary here. Yea, Joseph's increase in Egypt is outstripped here with us. Our planters hope to have more than a hundredfold this year. And all this while I am within compass; what will you say of two hundred fold, and upwards? It is almost incredible what great gain some of our English planters have had by our Indian corn. Credible persons have assured me, and the party himself avouched the truth of it to me, that of the setting of thirteen gallons of corn he hath had increase of it fifty-two hogsheads, every hogshead holding seven bushels of London measure, and every bushel was by him sold and trusted to the Indians for so much beaver as was worth eighteen shillings; and so of this thirteen gallons of corn, which was worth six shillings eight pence, he made about 327 pounds of it the year following, as by reckoning will appear; where you may see how God blesseth husbandry in this land. There is not such great and plentiful ears of corn I suppose any where else to be found but in this country, being also of variety of colors, as red, blue, and yellow, etc.; and of one corn there springeth four or five hundred. I have sent you many ears of divers colors, that you might see the truth of it.

Little children here, by setting of corn, may earn much more than their own maintenance.

The temper of the air of New-England is one special thing that commends this place. Experience doth manifest that there is hardly a more healthful place to be found in the world that agreeth better with our English bodies. Many that have been weak and sickly in Old England, by coming hither have been thoroughly healed, and grown healthful and strong. For here is an extraordinary clear and dry air, that is of a most healing nature to all such as are of cold, melancholy, phlegmatic, rheumatic temper of body . . . and therefore I think it is wise course for all cold complexions to come to take physic in New-England; for a sup of New-England's air is better than a whole draught of Old England's ale.

60. Early Attitude of the Puritan Colony to the Church of England

It is certain that the Puritans did not expect, at first, to separate so far and so definitely from the Church of England as they very soon did separate. On this, cf. *American History and Government*, § 82, and observe also, besides *a* and *b* below, passages in No. 52, close, and No. 62 *c*, close.

a. Winthrop's Farewell Letter to the Church of England
April 7/17, 1630

Hutchinson's *Massachusetts Bay*, Appendix I (1769). About two thirds the letter is here reproduced. Winthrop is supposed to be the author.

THE HUMBLE REQUEST *of his Majesties Loyall Subjects, the Governour and the Company late gone for* **New England;** *for the obtaining of their Prayers, and the Removall of Suspicions and Misconstructions of their Intentions.*

... And howsoever your Charitie may have met with some Occasion of Discouragement through the Misreport of our Intentions, or through the Disaffection or Indiscretion of some of us, or rather amongst us: for we are not of those who dreame of Perfection in this World; yet wee desire you would be pleased to take Notice of the Principals and Body of our Company, as those who esteeme it our honour to call the *Church* of *England*, from whence wee rise, our deare Mother; and cannot part from our native Countrie, where she specially resideth, without much Sadness of Heart, and many Tears in our Eyes, ever acknowledging that such Hope and Part as we have obtained in the common Salvation, we have received in her Bosome, and suckt it from her Breasts: wee leave it not therefore as loathing that milk wherewith we were nourished there, but blessing God for the Parentage and Education, [and] as Members of the same Body, [we] shall alwaies rejoice in her Good, and unfeignedly grieve for any Sorrow shall ever betide her, and while we have Breath, sincerely desire and indeavour the Continuance and Abundance of her Welfare, with the Inlargement of her Bounds in the Kingdome of CHRIST JESUS.

Be pleased therefore, *Reverend* FATHERS *and* BRETHREN, to helpe forward the Worke now in Hand; which if it prosper, you shall be the more glorious. [A fervent request for prayers.] ...

What Goodness you shall extend to us in this or any other Christian Kindnesse, wee, *your Brethren in Christ Jesus*, shall labor to repay ... promising, so farre as God shall enable us, to give him no Rest on your Behalfes, wishing our Heads and Hearts may be Fountains of Tears for your everlasting Welfare, when we shall bee in our poor Cottages in the Wildernesse ... And so commending you to the Grace of GOD *in* CHRIST, wee shall ever rest,

Your assured Friends and Brethren,

From Yarmouth, aboard
the Arabella, April 7, 1630.

John Winthrop, Gov. [and six other signatures].

164 THE COLONY BECOMES A PURITAN ENTERPRISE

b. *Opinion of Captain John Smith, 1630*

Smith's *Works* (Birmingham edition), 926, 958.

The following passages come from the introduction to Smith's "Pathway to the Inexperienced," his last pamphlet, written in 1631, to support the Massachusetts Bay Colony. Smith wrote at the home of a brother of John Winthrop's first wife, and seems to have been well acquainted with the Puritan leaders.

Pardon me if I offend in loving that [which] I have cherished truly, by the losse of my prime fortunes, meanes, and youth. If it over-glad me to see Industry her selfe adventure now to make use of my aged ende[a]vours, *not by such (I hope) as rumour doth report, a many of discontented Brounists, Anabaptists, Papists, Puritans, Separatists, and such factious Humorists: for no such they will suffer among them, if knowne, as many of the chiefe of them (John Winthrop etc.) have assured mee; and the much conferences I have had with many of them, doth confidently perswade me to write thus much in their behalfe.* . . .

They have . . . God's true Religion (they say) taught amongst themselves, the Sabbath day observed, the common Prayer (as I understand) and Sermons performed, and diligent catechising . . . and commendable good orders to bring those people [natives] with whom they have to deale . . . into a Christian conversation . . . which done, in time, . . . may grow **a good addition to the Church of England.**

[Smith evidently had some doubts on the matter, as his parenthetical expressions show. But he had confidence enough *to dedicate this booklet to the two Archbishops of Canterbury and York.*]

61. Political Principles of the Puritans

From John Calvin's *Institutes* (1559; translation of 1813, III, 517-551).

a. [*Attempt to justify a union of church and state*]

III.—Nor let anyone think it strange that I refer to human polity the due maintenance of religion . . . I do not allow

men to make laws respecting religion and the worship of God
... though I approve of civil government which provides
that the true religion, ... contained in the law of God, be
not violated and poluted.

b. [Of the parts of government and the supremacy of magistrates]

These are three. The Magistrate, who is the guardian and
conservator of the laws: The Laws, according to which he
governs: The People, **who are governed by the laws, and obey
the magistrate.** ...

IV. — The Lord hath not only testified that the function of
magistrates has his approbation and acceptance, but hath
eminently commended it to us, by dignifying it with the most
honourable titles. ... This is just as if it had been affirmed,
that the authority possessed by kings and other governors over
all things upon earth is not a consequence of the perverseness
of men, but of the providence and holy ordinance of God. ...

VII. — Those who are not restrained by so many testimonies
of Scripture, but still dare to stigmatize this sacred ministry
[magistrates] as a thing incompatible with religion and Christian piety, do they not offer an insult to God himself, who
cannot but be involved in the reproach cast upon his ministry?
And in fact **they do not reject magistrates, but they reject God,**
" that he should not reign over them." ...

VIII. — **And for private men, who have no authority to deliberate on the regulation of any public affairs, it would surely be
a vain occupation to dispute which would be the best form of
government in the place where they live.** ... Indeed if these
three forms of government, which are stated by philosophers
[Monarchy, Aristocracy, and Democracy], be considered in
themselves, I shall by no means deny, that either aristocracy
or a mixture of aristocracy and democracy far excell all
others; and that indeed not of itself, but because it very

rarely happens that kings regulate themselves so that their will is never at variance with justice and rectitude; or in the next place, that they are indued with such penetration and prudence, as in all cases to discover what is best. The vice or imperfection of men therefore renders it safer and more tolerable for the government to be in the hands of many, that they may afford each other mutual assistance and admonition, and that if any one arrogate to himself more than is right, the many may act as censors and masters to restrain his ambition. . . . **But if those, to whom the will of God has assigned another form of government, transfer this to themselves so as to be tempted to desire a revolution, the very thought will be not only foolish and useless, but altogether criminal.** . . .

XIV. — From the magistracy we next proceed to the laws, which are the strong nerves of civil polity, or, according to an appellation which Cicero has borrowed from Plato, the souls of states, without which magistracy cannot subsist.

* * * * * * *

XXII. — The first duty of subjects towards their magistrates is to entertain the most honourable sentiments of their function, **which they know to be a jurisdiction delegated to them from God,** and on that account to esteem and reverence them as *God's ministers and vicegerents.* For there are some persons to be found, who shew themselves very obedient to their magistrates, and have not the least wish that there were no magistrates for them to obey, because they know them to be so necessary to the public good; but who, nevertheless, consider the magistrates themselves as no other than necessary evils. But something more than this is required of us by Peter, when he commands us to "honour the king;" and by Solomon when he says, "Fear thou the Lord and the King:" for Peter, under the term honour, comprehends a sincere and candid esteem; and Solomon, by connecting the king with the Lord, attributes to him a kind of sacred veneration and dignity. . . . The obedience which is rendered to princes and magistrates is rendered to God, from whom they have received their authority.

XXIII. — Hence follows another duty: that, with minds disposed to honour and reverence magistrates, subjects approve their obedience to them, in submitting to their edicts, in paying taxes, in discharging public duties and bearing burdens which relate to the common defence, and in fulfilling all their other commands. . . . For, **as it is impossible to resist the magistrate without, at the same time, resisting God himself**, though an unarmed magistrate may seem to be despised with impunity, yet God is armed to inflict exemplary vengeance on the contempt offered to himself. Under this obedience I also include the moderation which private persons ought to prescribe to themselves in relation to public affairs, **that they do not, without being called upon, intermeddle with affairs of state**, or rashly intrude themselves into the office of magistrates, or undertake any thing of a public nature. If there be anything in the public administration which requires to be corrected, let them not raise any tumults, or take the business into their own hands, which ought to be all bound in this respect, but let them refer it to the cognizance of the magistrate, **who is alone authorized to regulate the concerns of the public.**

XXV. — But, if we direct our attention to the word of God, it will carry us much further; even to submit to the government, not only of those princes who discharge their duty to us with becoming integrity and fidelity, but of all who possess the sovereignty, **even though they perform none of the duties of their function.** For though the Lord testifies that the magistrate is an eminent gift of his liberality to preserve the safety of men, and prescribes to magistrates themselves the extent of their duty; yet he, at the same time, declares, that whatever be their characters, they have their government only from him; that those who govern for the public good are true specimens and mirrors of his beneficence; and that those who rule in an unjust and tyrannical manner are raised up by him to punish the iniquity of the people; **that all equally possess that sacred majesty which he hath invested with legitimate authority.** . . .

XXIX. — But it will be said, that rulers owe mutual duties to their subjects. That I have already confessed. **But he who infers from this that obedience ought to be rendered to none but just rulers, is a very bad reasoner.** For husbands owe mutual duties to their wives, and parents to their children. Now, if husbands and parents violate their obligations, if parents conduct themselves with discouraging severity and fastidious moroseness towards their children, whom they are forbidden to provoke to wrath: if husbands despise and vex their wives, whom they are commanded to love and to spare as the weaker vessels; does it follow that children should be less obedient to their parents; or wives to their husbands? They are still subject, even to those who are wicked and unkind. . . .

XXXII. — But in the obedience which we have shewn to be due to the authority of governors, it is always necessary to make one exception, and that is entitled to our first attention, that it do not seduce us from obedience to him, to whose will the desires of all kings ought to be subject, to whose decrees all their commands ought to yield, to whose majesty all their scepters ought to submit. . . .

62. Early Hardships and Religious Matters, 1630–1631

a. *Extracts from Winthrop's "History of New England"*

John Winthrop, leader of the great Puritan migration of 1630, while on board ship, began a "Journal," which gradually merged into a great contemporary "History." The work was printed first in 1790. A better edition appeared in 1853; and, that edition having long been "out of print," the work was reëdited by Dr. James K. Hosmer in 1907 ("Original Narratives" Series). The spelling and punctuation have been modernized in all these editions.

EARLY HARDSHIPS AND RELIGIOUS MATTERS

(1) [*The Voyage.*]

April 6, 1630. [Eight days on board, but still delayed at Yarmouth in the English Channel] . . .

Our captain called over our landmen, and tried them at their muskets, and such as were good shot among them were enrolled to serve in the ship, if occasion should be.

The lady Arbella[1] and the gentlewomen, and Mr. Johnson and some others went on shore to refresh themselves. . . .

Thursday, 8. . . . The wind continued N. [blank] with fair weather, and after noon it calmed, and we still saw those eight ships to stand towards us; having more wind than we, they came up apace, so as our captain and the masters of our consorts were more occasioned to think they might be Dunkirkers,[2] (for we were told at Yarmouth, that there were ten sail of them waiting for us;) whereupon we all prepared to fight with them, and took down some cabins which were in the way of our ordnance, and out of every ship were thrown such bed matters as were subject to take fire, and we heaved out our long boats, and put up our waste cloths, and drew forth our men, and armed them with muskets and other weapons, and instruments for fireworks; and for an experiment our captain shot a ball of wild-fire fastened to an arrow out of a cross-bow, which burnt in the water a good time. The lady Arbella and the other women and children were removed into the lower deck, that they might be out of danger. All things being thus fitted, we went to prayer upon the upper deck. It was much to see how cheerful and comfortable all the company appeared; not a woman or child that showed fear, though all did apprehend the danger to have been great, if things had proved as might well be expected, for there had been eight against four, and the least of the enemy's ships were reported

---

[1] Observe the setting off of this "lady" from the women of the gentry families. A like sequence occurs below. Hawthorne's *Grandfather's Chair* has acquainted all young people with the story of Lady Arbella.

[2] Dunkirk was held by Spain, with whom England was still practically at war. Ships from Dunkirk preyed upon English commerce in the Channel.

to carry thirty brass pieces; but our trust was in the Lord of Hosts; and the courage of our captain, and his care and diligence, did much encourage us. [The fleet prove to be friends.]

Saturday, 10. . . . This day two young men, falling at odds and fighting, contrary to the orders which we [1] had published and set up in the ship, were adjudged to walk upon the deck till night with their hands bound behind them, which accordingly was executed; and another man, for using contemptuous speeches in our [1] presence, was laid in bolts till he submitted himself, and promised open confession of his offence.

Lord's day, [May] 2. The tempest continued all the day, with the wind W. and by N., and the sea raged and tossed us exceedingly; yet, through God's mercy, we were very comfortable, and few or none sick, but had opportunity to keep the Sabbath, and Mr. Phillips preached twice that day. . . .

Friday, 21. . . . A servant of one of our company had bargained with a child to sell him a box worth 3 $d.$ for three biscuit a day all the voyage, and had received about forty . . . We caused his hands to be tied up to a bar, and hanged a basket, with stones, about his neck, and so he stood for two hours.

(2) [*Early Religious Practices.*]

July 27. We, of the congregation [at Boston] kept a fast, and chose Mr. Wilson our teacher,[2] and Mr. Nowell an elder, . . . We used imposition of hands, but with this protestation by all, that it was only as a sign of election and confirmation, not of any intent that Mr. Wilson should renounce his ministry that he received in England.[3]

---

[1] Winthrop uses the official plural, for the dignity of his office. The first person was soon discarded for the third.

[2] Two ministers, a *teacher* and a *pastor*, were customary. The differences in duties were not very important.

[3] But cf. the entry for November 22, 1632, when no such protestation is made: "A fast was held by the congregation of Boston, and Mr. Wilson (formerly their teacher) was chosen pastor and —— Oliver a ruling elder; and both *were ordained* by imposition of hands." This illustrates the gradual tendency to separate from the Church of England.

EARLY HARDSHIPS AND RELIGIOUS MATTERS

[1631. April 12.]

At a court holden at Boston, (upon information to the governour that they of Salem had called Mr. Williams to the office of a teacher), a letter was written from the court to Mr. Endecott to this effect: That whereas Mr. Williams had refused to join with the congregation at Boston, because they would not make a public declaration of their repentance for having communion with the churches of England while they lived there; and, besides, had declared his opinion, that the magistrate might not punish the breach of the Sabbath, nor any other offence, as it was a breach of the first table; therefore, they marvelled they would choose him without advising with the council; and withal desiring him [Endicott] that they would forbear to proceed till they had conferred about it. . . .

b. *Winthrop's Letters*

JOHN WINTHROP FROM NEW ENGLAND TO HIS WIFE,
SEPTEMBER 9/19, 1630

Winthrop's *Life and Letters of John Winthrop*, II, 48–49 and 53–55.

My Dear Wife, — The blessing of God all-sufficient be upon thee and all my dear ones with thee forever.

I praise the good Lord, though we see much mortality, sickness and trouble, yet (such is his mercy) myself and children, with most of my family, are yet living, and in health, and enjoy prosperity enough, if the affliction of our brethren did not hold under the comfort of it. The lady Arbella is dead, and good Mr. Higginson, my servant, old Waters of Neyland, and many others. Thus the Lord is pleased to humble us; yet he mixes so many mercies with his corrections, as we are persuaded he will not cast us off, but, in his due time, will do us good, according to the measure of our afflictions. He stays but till he hath purged our corruptions, and healed the hardness and error of our hearts, and stripped us of our vain confidence in this arm of flesh, that he may have us rely wholly upon himself.

The French ship, so long expected, and given for lost, is now come safe to us, about a fortnight since, having been twelve weeks at sea; and yet her passengers (being but few) all safe and well but one, and her goats but six living of eighteen. So as now we are somewhat refreshed with such goods and provisions as she brought, though much thereof hath received damage by wet. I praise God, we have many occasions of comfort here, and do hope, that our days of affliction will soon have an end, and that the Lord will do us more good in the end than we could have expected, that will abundantly recompense for all the trouble we have endured. Yet we may not look for great things here. It is enough that we shall have heaven, though we should pass through hell to it. We here enjoy God and Jesus Christ. Is not this enough? What would we have more? I thank God, I like so well to be here, as I do not repent my coming; and if I were to come again, I would not have altered my course, though I had foreseen all these afflictions. I never fared better in my life, never slept better, never had more content of mind, which comes merely of the Lord's good hand; for we have not the like means of these comforts here which we had in England. But the Lord is all-sufficient, blessed be his holy name. If he please, he can still uphold us in this estate; but, if he shall see good to make us partakers with others in more affliction, his will be done. He is our God, and may dispose of us as he sees good.

I am sorry to part with thee so soon, seeing we meet so seldom, and my much business hath made me too oft forget Mondays and Fridays. I long for the time, when I may see thy sweet face again, and the faces of my dear children. But I must break off, and desire thee to commend me kindly to all my good friends, and excuse my not writing at this time. If God please once to settle me, I shall make amends. . . . The good Lord bless thee and all our children and family. So I kiss my sweet wife and my dear children, and rest

Thy faithful husband,
JO. WINTHROP.

I would have written to Maplestead, if I had time. Thou must excuse me, and remember me kindly to them all.

This is the third letter I have written to thee from New England.

[November 29/December 9, 1630.]

. . . Thou shalt understand by this, how it is with us since I wrote last, (for this is the third or fourth letter I have written to thee since I came hither,) that thou mayest see the goodness of the Lord towards me, that, when so many have died and so many yet languish, myself and my children are yet living and in health. Yet I have lost twelve of my family,[1] viz. Waters and his wife, and two of his children: Mr. Gager and his man: Smith of Buxall and his wife and two children: the wife of Taylor of Haverill and their child: my son H. makes the twelve. And, besides many other of less note, as Jeff. Ruggle of Sudbury, and divers others of that town, (about twenty,) the Lord hath stripped us of some principal persons, Mr. Johnson and his lady, Mr. Rossiter, Mrs. Phillips, and others unknown to thee. We conceive, that this disease grew from ill diet at sea, and proved infectious. I write not this to discourage thee but to warn thee and others to provide well for the sea, and, by God's help, the passage will be safe and easy, how long soever. Be careful (I entreat thee) to observe the directions in my former letters; and I trust that that God, who hath so graciously preserved and blessed us hitherto, will bring us to see the faces of each other with abundance of joy. My dear wife, we are here in a paradise. Though we have not beef and mutton etc., yet (God be praised) we want them not; our Indian corn answers for all. Yet here is fowl and fish in great plenty. I will here break off, because I hope to receive letters from thee soon, and to have opportunity of writing more largely. I will say nothing of my love to thee, and of my longing desires towards thee. Thou knowest my heart. Neither can I men-

---

[1] This is an old use of the word family, to include Winthrop's many dependents, even married servants.

tion salutations to my good friends, other than in general. In my next, I hope to supply all. Now the Lord, our good God, be with thee and all my children and company with thee. Grace and peace be with you all. So I kiss my sweet wife and all my dear children, and bless you in the Lord. Farewell.

Thy faithful husband,   Jo. WINTHROP.

c. Thomas Dudley to the Countess of Lincoln March, 1631

Force's *Historical Tracts* (1638), II, No. 4.

To the righte honourable, my very good Lady,
the Lady Brydget, Countesse of Lincoln

Your letters (which are not common or cheape) following mee hether into New-England, and bringeing with them renewed testimonies of the accustomed favours you honoured me with in the old, have drawne from mee this narrative retribucion (which in respect of your proper interest in some persons of great note amongst us)[1] was the thankfullest present I had to send over the seas. Therefore I humblie intreat your honour this bee accepted as payment from him, who neither hath nor is any more than your honours old thankful servant,

THOMAS DUDLEY.

BOSTON IN NEW ENGLAND,
    March 12th 1630 [March 22, 1631].

[A narrative of the beginnings of the colony, through the sending of Higginson's company in the spring of 1629.]

Theis by their too large comendacions of the country . . . invited us soe strongly to goe on that Mr. Wenthropp of Soffolke (who is well knowne in his owne country and well approved heere for his pyety, liberality, wisdome, and gravity) comeing into us, wee came to such resolution that in April, 1630, wee sett sail from Old England with 4 good shipps. And in May following, 8 more followed, 2 haveing gone be-

---

[1] The Lady Arbella was of the house of Lincoln.

fore in February and March, and 2 more following in June and August besides another set out by a private merchant. Theis 17 Shipps arrived all safe . . . but made a long, a troublesome, and a costly voyage. . . . Our four shipps which set out in Aprill arrived here in June and July, wheere we found the colony in a sadd and unexpected condicion; above 80 of them beeing dead the winter before and many of those alive, weake and sicke; all the corne and bread amongst them all hardly sufficient to feed them a fortnight, insoemuch that the remainder of 180 servants wee had the 2 years before sent over, comeing to us for victualls to sustaine them, wee found ourselves wholly unable to feed them . . . whereupon necessity enforced us, to our extreme loss, to give them all libertie, who had cost us about 16 or 20 pounds a person furnishing and sending over. But bearing theis things as we might, wee beganne to consult of the place of our sitting downe: for Salem, where wee landed, pleased us not. [They decide upon six new settlements, besides the already established Salem and Charlestown.] This dispersion troubled some of us; but helpe it wee could not, wanting ability to remove to any place fit to build a towne upon, and the time too short to deliberate longer, least the winter should surprise us before we had builded our houses. . . . So, ceasing to consult further for that time, they who had health to labour fell to building, wherein many were interrupted with sicknes, and many dyed weekely, yea almost dayley. . . . Insomuch that the shipps being now uppon their returne . . . there was, as I take it, not much less than an hundred (some think many more) partly out of dislike of our government which restrained and punished their excesses, and partly through fear of famine (not seeinge other means than by their labour to feed themselves), which returned back againe. And glad were wee so to bee ridd of them. Others also, afterwards hearing of men of their owne disposition which were planted at Piscataway, went from us to them; whereby though our numbers were lessened, yet wee accounted ourselves nothing weakened by their removall.

Before the departure of the shipps, wee contracted with Mr. Peirce, Mr. [Master] of the Lyon . . . to returne to us with speed with fresh supplies of victualls. . . .

The shipps beeinge gone, victualls wastinge, and mortality increasinge, wee held diverse fasts in our severall congregations, but the Lord would not yet bee deprecated [A long list of deaths] And of the people who came over with us . . . [from Aprill to December] there dyed by estimacion about 200 at the least. . . .

If any come hether to plant for worldly ends, that canne live well at home, hee comits an errour of which hee will soon repent him. But if for spirittuall, and that noe particular obstacle hinder his removeall, he may finde here what may well content him: viz., materialls to build, fewell to burn, ground to plant, seas and rivers to ffish in, a pure ayer to breath in, good water to drinke till wine or beare canne be made, — which, toegether with the cowes, hoggs, and goates brought hether allready, may suffice for food; for as for foule and venison, they are dainties here as well as in England. Ffor cloaths and beddinge they must bringe them with them, till time and industry produce them here. In a word, wee yett enjoy little to bee envyed, but endure much to bee pytyed in the sicknes and mortalitye of our people. And I do the more willingly use this open and plaine dealinge, least other men should fall short of their expectations when they come hether, as wee to our great prejudice did, by means of letters sent us from hence into England, wherein honest men, out of a desire to draw over others to them, wrote somewhat hyperbolically of many things here. If any godly men out of religious ends will come over to helpe us . . . I thinke they cannot dispose of themselves or their estates more to Gods glory . . . but they must not bee of the poorer sort yett for diverse yeares. Ffor we have found by experience that they have hindered, not furthered the worke. And for profaine and deboshed persons, their oversight in comeinge hether is wondered at, where they shall finde nothing to content them.

If there bee any endued with grace and furnished with meanes to feed themselves and theirs for 18 months, and to build and plant, — lett them come into our Macedonia to helpe us.

[Record of disasters; the return of the Lyon] . . . Also, to increase the heape of our sorrows, wee received advertisement by letters from our friends in England and by the reports of those who came hether in this shipp to abide with us . . . that those who went discontentedly from us last yeare, out of their evill affections towards us, have raised many false and scandelous reports against us, affirminge us to be Brounists in religion and ill affected to our state at home, and that theis vile reports have wonne creditt with some who formerly wished us well. But wee doe desire, and cannot but hope, that wise and impartiall men will at length consider that such malcontents have ever pursued this manner of casting dirt to make others seeme as fowle as themselves, and that our godly friends to whom wee have ben knowne will not easily believe that wee are soe soon turned from the profession wee soe long have made in our native Country. And for our further clearing, I truely affirme that I know noe one person who came over with us the last yeare to bee altered in his judgment and affection eyther in ecclesiasticall or civill respects since our comeinge hether; but wee doe continue to pray dayley for our soveraigne lord the Kinge, the Queene, the Prince, the royal blood, the counsaile, and the whole state, as dutye bindes us to doe and reason persuades others to believe. For how ungodly and unthankfull should wee be if wee should not thus doe . . . Lett our friends therefore give no creditt to such malicious aspersions, but bee more ready to answer for us than wee heare they have bene. Wee are not like those which have dispensation to lye. . . .

XIII. DEVELOPMENT OF DEMOCRACY, 1630–1644

63. The Oligarchic Usurpation

Records of the Governor and Company of Massachusetts Bay, I (under dates given). Cf. Introduction to No. 57.

(1) [*The First Court of Assistants, Charlestown, August 23/ September 2, 1630.*]

. . . It was ordered that the Governor and Deputy Governor, for the tyme being, shall alwaies be justices of the peace, and that Sir Rich: Saltonstall, Mr. Johnson, Mr. Endicott, and Mr. Ludlowe shalbe justices of the peace for the present tyme, in all things to have like power that justices of the peace hath in England for reformacion of abuses and punishing of offenders; and that any justice of the peace may imprison an offender, but not inflict any corporall punishment without the presence and consent of some one of the Assistants.[1]

(2) [*October 19/29, 1630.*]

A General Court, holden att Boston.
[The first General Court in America.]

Present, THE GOVERNOR [*Winthrop*]   CAPT. ENDICOTT
DEPUTY GOVERNOR [*Dudley*]   MR. NOWELL
SIR RICHARD SALTONSTALL   MR. PINCHON
MR. LUDLOWE   MR. BRADSTREETE
[all magistrates]

For establishinge of the government. It was propounded if it were not the best course that the ffreemen should have the power of chuseing Assistants, **when there are to be chosen,**

---

[1] Had the Assistants legal right, under the charter, to appoint such officers and define their powers? It is worthy of note, that, Nov. 30/Dec. 9, 1630, Sir Richard Saltonstall was "fyned V £ for whipping 2 severall persons without the presence of another Assistant, contrary to an act of Court formerly made."

and the Assistants from amongst themselves to chuse a Governor and Deputy Governor, whoe with the Assistants should have the power of makeing lawes and chuseing officers to execute the same. This was fully assented unto by the generall vote of the people and ereccion of hands.

[Two charter provisions are here violated. The italicized clause was further explained the next May by another unconstitutional decree of the Assistants making themselves life-officers, unless removed for cause ((4) below).

There were present, qualified to vote, the eight magistrates named above, and certainly not more than one or two other "freemen," — probably *no one except the Assistants*. The "people" referred to in the final sentence were probably the 109 men who came to this Court to ask to be admitted "freemen." Apparently *they* were asked, in turn, whether they would agree to this new law; and (not knowing the charter rights of freemen, anyway) they consented. Even so, they were not admitted until May of the next year. Cf. *American History and Government*, § 62.]

(3) [*March 8/18, 1630/31.*]
    Att a Court [of Assistants] att Waterton

... Further, (in regard the number of Assistants are but fewe; and some of them goeing for England,) it was therefore ordered that whensoever the number of Assistants resident within the lymitts of this jurisdiccion shalbe fewer than 9, it shalbe lawfull for the major parte of them to keepe a Court, and whatsoever orders or acts they make shalbe as legall and authenticall as if there were the full number of 7 or more. ...

[Queries: What charter provision did this law "violate"? Why did not the government instead increase the number of Assistants toward the number prescribed in the charter?]

(4) [*May 18/28, 1631.*]
    A General Court, holden att Boston

[Old governor and deputy reëlected.]
For explanacion of an order made the last Generall Court ... it was ordered nowe, with full consent of all the commons

then present, that once in every yeare, att least, a Generall Court shalbe holden; att which Court it shalbe lawfull for the commons to propound any . . . persons whom they shall desire to be chosen Assistants [provision for voting on such new nominations by "poll," — vive-voce]. *The like course [of voting] to be holden when they, the said commons, shall see cause for any defect or misbehavior to remove any one or more of the Assistants.* And, to the end the body of the commons may be preserved of honest and good men, it was likewise ordered . . . that, for time to come, noe man shalbe admitted to the freedome of this body polliticke but such as are members of some of the churches within the lymitts of the same. . . .

[The italicized clause in the above entry is the one which indirectly established a life-tenure for Assistants, contrary to the charter provision for annual reëlection of all such officers. The "commons" were to be permitted to suggest and choose new Assistants (since the charter-number of eighteen was far from full), *but, once elected, the Assistant held until deposed for cause.*

At this same court, 116 freemen were elected, including those who had so applied in the preceding October. Whether this admission was before or after the legislation given above is wholly uncertain from the *Records;* but the natural inference is that the applicants were asked to assent to these changes also as a prerequisite to admission. After this meeting, voters are always referred to as "freemen." The words "people" and "commons" used in these records of October, 1630, and May, 1631, refer, presumably, to people not yet admitted to the political corporation.]

64. The First "Popular" Movement — Watertown Protest, 1632

Winthrop's *History of New England* (under dates given).
Cf. introductory statements to No. 62 *a* above.

Winthrop's bias for aristocratic organization in politics and in industry appears always in most naïve unconsciousness;[1] but his fine candor and magnanimity make his book as attractive as it is valuable.

---

[1] Cf. *American History and Government*, §§ 62, 64, 77, note, etc., for several illustrative quotations not given in this volume.

[November 23, 1631.] The congregation at Watertown (whereof Mr. George Phillips was pastor) had chosen one Richard Brown for their elder, before named, who, persisting in his opinion of the truth of the Romish church, and maintaining other errors withal, and being a man of a very violent spirit, the court wrote a letter to the congregation, directed to the pastor and brethren, to advise them to take into consideration, whether Mr. Brown were fit to be continued their elder or not; to which, after some weeks, they returned answer to this effect: That if we would take the pains to prove such things as were objected against him, they would endeavour to redress them.

[The dissensions in the Watertown church soon led to a more active interference by the government of the colony. The party of the elder and pastor plainly resented this interference. There may be some connection between that fact and the following famous "remonstrance" in the matter of taxation.]

[1631/2. February 17.] The governour and assistants called before them, at Boston, divers of Watertown; the pastor and elder by letter, and the others by warrant. The occasion was, for that a warrant being sent to Watertown for levying of £8, part of a rate of £60, ordered for the fortifying of the new town, the pastor and elder, etc., assembled the people and delivered their opinions, that it was not safe to pay moneys after that sort, for fear of bringing themselves and posterity into bondage. Being come before the governour and council, after much debate, they acknowledged their fault, confessing freely, that they were in an error, and made a retractation and submission under their hands, and were enjoined to read it in the assembly the next Lord's day. The ground of their error was, for that they took this government to be no other but as of a mayor and aldermen, who have not power to make laws or raise taxations without the people; but understanding that this government was rather in the nature of a parliament, and that no assistant could be chosen but by the freemen, who had power likewise to remove the assistants and put in others, and therefore at every general court (which was to be held once every year) they had free liberty to consider and propound anything concerning the same, and to declare their grievances, without being subject to question, or, etc., they were fully satisfied; and so their submission was accepted, and their offence pardoned.

[Winthrop was overconfident. The Watertown men must soon have recovered from the browbeating he had given them. May 1, Winthrop called together the Assistants informally at his house, and warned them "that he had heard the people intended at the next court to desire that the Assistants might be chosen anew every year, and that the governor might be chosen by the whole court, and not by the Assistants only. Upon this, *Mr. Ludlow grew into a passion, and said that then we should have no government, but there would be an interim wherein every man might do what he pleased.*" The others, however, did not anticipate quite such deplorable results, and wisely concluded to submit. The results appear in the following entry.]

[May 8, 1632.] A general court at Boston. Whereas it was (at our first coming) agreed, that the freemen should choose the assistants, and they the governour, the whole court agreed now, that the governour and assistants should all be new chosen every year by the general court, (the governour to be always chosen out of the assistants;) and accordingly the old governour, John Winthrop, was chosen; accordingly all the rest as before, and Mr. Humfrey and Mr. Coddington also, because they were daily expected. . . .

. . . A proposition was made by the people that every company of trained men might choose their own captain and officers; but the governor giving them reasons to the contrary, they were satisfied without it.

Every town chose two men to be at the next court, to advise with the governour and assistants about the raising of a public stock, so as what they should agree upon should bind all, etc.

[The facts about this meeting of the General Court are given even more briefly in the *Records*, but in agreement with these statements of

Winthrop. The *Records* omit, naturally, all reference to the preceding action at Watertown, which explains these reforms. The freemen had now recovered the right to choose all magistrates annually, together with some direct local control over taxation; but the law-making power was still retained, unconstitutionally, by the Assistants.]

65. Legislation and Administration by the "Assistants," 1630-1633

Records of Governor and Company of Massachusetts Bay, I (under dates given).

These extracts show the moral and economic ideas of the ruling class. The extracts are all taken from records of the *Courts of Assistants*, meeting at Charlestown or Boston.

(1) [*August 23/September 2, 1630.* The first "court" after the arrival of Winthrop.]

. . . It was ordered that carpenters, joyners, brickelayers, sawers, and thatchers shall not take above 2 s. a day, nor any man shall give more, under paine of X s. . . .

(2) [*September 28/October 8, 1630.*]

. . . It is ordered that labourers [*i.e.*, unskilled] shall not take above 12 d. a day for their worke, and not above 6d. and meate and drinke, under paine of X s. . . .

(3) [*November 30/December 10, 1630.*]

. . . It is ordered that John Baker shalbe whipped for shooteing att fowle on the Sabbath day, etc.

[No law had been made regarding such an offense. This is an instance of an *ex post facto* law, made by the magistrates in imposing sentence.]

(4) [*March 1/11, 1630/1631.*]

. . . It is ordered that Mr. Aleworth, Mr. Weaver, Mr. Plastowe, Mr. Shuter, Cobbett, and Wormewood shalbe sent into England by the shipp Lyon, or soe many of them as the ship can carry, the rest to be sent thither by the 1th of May nexte, if there be opportunitie of shipping, if not, by the nexte shipp that returnes for England, **as persons unmeete to inhabit here**; and that Sir Christopher Gardner and Mr. Wright shalbe sent as prisoners into England by the shipp Lyon, nowe returneing thither.

[The two last named had been "tried" after a fashion. For the others, apparently, there was not even a form of trial, with or without a jury. The banishment was executive, not judicial.]

(5) [*March 22/April 1, 1630/1631.*]

... It is ordered, (that whereas the wages of carpenters, joyners, and other artificers and workemen, were by order of Court restrayned to particular sommes) [wages] shall nowe be lefte free and att libertie as men shall reasonably agree.

Further, it is ordered, that every toune within this pattent shall, before the 5th of Aprill nexte, take espetiall care that every person within their toune, (except magistrates and ministers,) as well servants as others, [be] furnished with good and sufficient armes allowable by the captain or other officers, those that want and are of abilitie to buy them themselves, others that are unable to have them provided by the toune, for the present, and after to receive satisfacion for that they disburse when they shalbe able.

It is likewise ordered that all persons whatsoever that have cards, dice, or [gaming] tables in their howses, shall make away with them before the nexte Court. . .

(6) [*May 3/13, 1631.*]

It is ordered, that John Legge, servant to Mr. Humfry, shalbe severely whipped this day att Boston, and afterwards, soe soone as conveniently may be, att Salem, for strikeing Richard Wright, when hee came to give him correccion for idleness in his maisters worke.

[Apparently Wright (who was not even the "master" of Legge) had struck first (that being the usual meaning of "give correction"); but a servant must not strike back.]

(7) [*June 14/24, 1631.*]

It is ordered, that Phillip Ratliffe shalbe whipped, have his eares cutt of, fyned 40 £, and banished out of the lymitts of this jurisdiccion, for uttering mallitious and scandulous speeches against the government and the church of Salem, etc., as appeareth by a particular thereof, proved upon oath.

[Apparently no jury trial was permitted in this case (or in several other equally serious cases noted in the early *Records*). For the definite establishment of the jury, see No. 67 *b*, below. It was already in use, however, in capital trials. (Cf. *American History and Government*, § 80.) The extracts from the Massachusetts *Records* regarding those early cases are too long to give here.]

(8) [*July 26/August 5, 1531.*]

. . . It is ordered, that Josias Plaistowe shall (for stealing 4 basketts of corne from the Indians) returne them 8 basketts againe, be ffined V£, and hereafter to be called by the name of Josias, and not Mr., as formerly hee used to be; and that William Buckland and Thomas Andrewe shalbe whipped for being accessary to the same offence.

[These two men were servants of Plaistowe. Cf. *American History and Government*, § 65, on the exemption of gentlemen from corporal punishment; and also No. 78, note 43, below.]

(9) [*July 2/12, 1633.*]

. . . It is ordered, that it shalbe lawfull for any man to kill any swine that comes into his corne: the party that ownes the swine is to have them, being kild, and allowe recompence for the damage they doe, etc. . . .

(10) [*September 3/13, 1633.*]

Roberte Coles is ffined X £, and enjoyned to stand with a white sheete of paper on his back, wherein *a drunkard* shalbe written in greate letteres, and to stand therewith soe longe as the Court thinks meete, for abuseing himselfe shamefully with drinke.

[Cowles did not reform. A Court of March 4/14, 1633/34, passed the following sentence upon him: —

"It is ordered, that Roberte Coles, for drunkeness by him committed att Rocksbury, shalbe disfranchized, weare about his necke, and soe to hange upon his outward garment, a D, made of redd cloath, and sett upon white; to contynue this for a yeare, and not to leave it of att any tyme when hee comes amongst company, under the penalty of XI s for the first offence, and V £ the second, and after to be punished by the Court as they thinke meete; also, hee is to weare the D outwards, and is enjoyned to appeare att the nexte Generall Court, and to contynue there till the Court be ended."

Cowles seems to have been one of the early democratic agitators. The *Records* show that he was one of the deputies chosen in May, 1632, to help assess taxes. Possibly he had made himself obnoxious in such fashion to these aristocratic judges.]

(11) [*October 1/11, 1633.*]

It is ordered, that maister carpenters, sawers, masons, clapboard-ryvers, brickelayers, tylars, joyners, wheelwrights, mowers, etc., shall not take above 2 s. a day, findeing themselves dyett, and not above 14 d. a day if they have dyett found them, under the penalty of V s., both to giver and receaver, for every day that there is more given and receaved. Also, that all other inferior workemen of the said occupacions shall have such wages as the constable of the said place, and 2 other inhabitants, that hee shall chuse, shall appoynet.

Also, it is agreed, that the best sorte of labourers shall not take above 18 d. a day if they dyett themselves, and not above 8 d. a day if they have dyett found them, under the aforesaid penalty, both to giver and receaver.

Likewise, that the wages of inferior labourers shalbe referd to the constable and 2 other, as aforesaid.

Maister taylours shall not take above 12d. a day, and the inferior sorte not above 8d. if they be dyeted, under the aforesaid penalty; and for all other worke they doe att home proporcionably, and soe for other worke that shalbe done . . . by any other artificer.

Further, it is ordered, that all workemen shall worke the whole day, alloweing convenient tyme for foode and rest. This order to take place the 12th of this present moneth. [The "whole day" was from sun-rise to sun-set.]

It is further ordered, that noe person, howse houlder or other, shall spend his time idlely or unproffitably, under paine of such punishment as the Court shall thinke meete to inflicte; and for this end it is ordered, that the constable of every place shall use spetiall care and deligence to take knowledge of offenders in this kinde, espetially of common coasters, unproffittable fowlers, and tobacco takers, and to present the same to the 2 nexte Assistants, whoe shall have power to heare and determine the cause, or, if the matter be of importance, to transferr it to the Court.

[The following entries from Winthrop's *History* show the desperate feeling of the servants and the attitude of the gentry class at this time : —

"August 6, 1633. Two men servants to one Moodye, of Roxbury, returning in a boat from the windmill, struck upon the oyster bank. They went out to gather oysters, and, not making fast their boat, when the flood came, it floated away, and they were both drowned, although they might have waded out on either side ; but it was an evident judgment of God upon them, for they were wicked persons. One of them, a little before, being reproved for his lewdness, and put in mind of hell, answered, that if hell were ten times hotter, he had rather be there than he would serve his master, etc. The occasion was, because he had bound himself for divers years, and saw that, if he had been at liberty, he might have had greater wages, though otherwise his master used him very well.

"November, 1633. . . . The scarcity of workmen had caused them to raise their wages to an excessive rate, so as a carpenter would have three shillings the day, a laborer two shillings and sixpence, etc. ; and accordingly those who had commodities to sell advanced their prices sometime double to that they cost in England, so as it grew to a general complaint, which the court, taking knowledge of, as also of some further evils, which were springing out of the excessive rate of wages, they made an order, that carpenters, masons, etc., should take but two shillings the day, and laborers but eighteen pence, and that no commodity should be sold at above four pence in the shilling more than it cost for ready money in England; oil, wine, etc., and cheese (in regard of the hazard of bringing, etc.,) excepted. . . ."

Winthrop, no doubt, put the cart before the horse. The increased cost of all European goods, due to high freights, necessitated higher wages; but Winthrop resents any attempt of the laborers to ask more than their old European wages.]

66. The Beginning of Town Government in Massachusetts, 1633

Dorchester Town Records, p. 3.

For some three years after the great migration of 1630, the eight Massachusetts "towns" were governed wholly by the central colonial authority, — the courts of Assistants and the General Courts, — and by officers appointed by this central authority. The entry below marks the beginning of local self-government. The Dorchester *Records*, it is true, contain notice of four earlier meetings to regulate pasturage or the division of town lands (cf. one such Boston meeting later; No. 73 *b*); but here we have *a formal assumption of government by periodic town meetings and "select men."* The next town to act in a like way was Watertown (cf. No. 83, opening). *Later* (cf. No. 78, law 66), the central government accepted this establishment of local government, giving it the sanction of law. On the history of this movement, see *American History and Government*, §§ 71–74.

An agreement made by the whole consent and vote of the Plantation made Mooneday 8th of October, 1633.

Inprimus it is ordered that for the generall good and well ordering of the affayres of the Plantation their shall be every Mooneday before the Court by eight of the Clocke in the morning, and presently upon the beating of the drum, a generall meeting of the inhabitants of the Plantation att the meeteing house, there to settle (and sett downe) such orders as may tend to the generall good as aforesayd; and every man to be bound thereby without gaynesaying or resistance. It is also agreed that there shall be twelve men selected out of the Company that may or the greatest part of them meete as aforesayd to determine as aforesayd, yet so as it is desired that the most of the Plantation will keepe the meeteing constantly and all that are there although none of the Twelve shall have a free voyce as any of the 12 and that the greate[r] vote both of the 12 and the other shall be of force and efficasy as aforesayd. And it is likewise ordered that all things concluded as aforesayd shall stand in force and be obeyed untill the next monthely meeteing and afterwardes if it be not contradicted and other wise ordered upon the sayd monthley meete[ing] by the greatest parts of those that are present as aforesayd.

67. Representative Central Government Established, 1634

a. *Winthrop's Account*

Winthrop's *History of New England*, under dates given. Cf. Introduction to No. 64 for Winthrop's bias.

For the outline of the whole story, cf. *American History and Government*, § 64.

[April 1, 1634.] . . . Notice being sent out of the general court to be held the 14th day of the third month, called May, the freemen deputed two of each town to meet and consider of such matters as they were to take order in at the same general court; who, having met, desired a sight of the patent, and, conceiving thereby that all their laws should be made at the general court, repaired to the governour to advise with him about it, and about the abrogating of some orders formerly made, as for killing of swine in corn,[1] etc. He told them, that, when the patent was granted, the number of freemen was supposed to be (as in like corporations) so few, as they might well join in making laws; but now they were grown to so great a body, as it was not possible for them to make or execute laws, but they must choose others for that purpose: and that howsoever it would be necessary hereafter to have a select company to intend that work, yet for the present they were not furnished with a sufficient number of men qualified for such a business; neither could the commonwealth bear the loss of time of so many as must intend it. Yet this they might do at present, viz., they might, at the general court, make an order, that, once in the year, a certain number should be appointed (upon sum-

---

[1] Cf. No. 65 (9).

mons from the governour) to revise all laws, etc., and to reform what they found amiss therein; but not to make any new laws, but prefer their grievances to the court of assistants; and that no assessment should be laid upon the country without the consent of such a committee, nor any lands disposed of. . . .

[May 14.] At the general court, Mr. Cotton preached, and delivered this doctrine, that a magistrate ought not to be turned into the condition of a private man without just cause, and to be publicly convict, no more than the magistrates may not turn a private man out of his freehold, etc., without like public trial, etc. This falling in question in the court, and the opinion of the rest of the ministers being asked, it was referred to further consideration.

The court chose a new governour, viz., Thomas Dudley,[1] Esq., the former deputy; and Mr. Ludlow was chosen deputy; and John Haines, Esq., an assistant, and all the rest of the assistants chosen again.

At this court it was ordered, that four general courts should be kept every year, and that the whole body of the freemen should be present only at the court of election of magistrates, etc., and that, at the other three, every town should send their deputies, who should assist in making laws, disposing lands, etc. Many good orders were made by this court. It held three days, and all things were carried very peaceably, notwithstanding that some of the assistants were questioned by the freemen for some errors in their government, and some fines imposed, but remitted again before the court broke up. The court was kept in the meeting house at Boston, and the new governour and the assistants were together entertained at the house of the old governour, as before.

---

[1] A marginal note in the manuscript, in Winthrop's handwriting, adds "chosen by papers." This election of Winthrop's rival, by a secret ballot, was the democratic answer to Cotton's argument above.

b. The Colony Records

(1) [*An Attempt of the Oligarchic Government to hold the Allegiance of all Inhabitants by an Oath.*]

The Oath for all Inhabitants prescribed at a Court of Assistants at Boston, April 1/11, 1634.

I doe heare sweare, and call God to witnes, that, being nowe an inhabitant within the lymitts of this jurisdiccion of the Massachusetts, I doe acknowledge myselfe lawfully subject to the aucthoritie and goverment there established and doe accordingly submit my person, family, and estate, to be protected, ordered, and governed by the lawes and constitucions thereof, and doe faithfully promise to be from time to time obedient and conformeable thereunto, and to the aucthoritie of the Governor, and all other the magistrates there, and their successors, and to all such lawes, orders, sentences, and decrees, as nowe are or hereafter shalbe lawfully made, decreed, and published by them or their successors. And I will always indeavor (as in duty I am bound) to advance the peace and wellfaire of this body pollitique, *and I will* (to my best power and meanes) *seeke to devert and prevent whatsoever may tende to the ruine or damage thereof, or of the Governor, Deputy Governor, or Assistants, or any of them or their successors, and will give speedy notice to them, or some of them, of any sedicion, violence, treacherie, or other hurte or evill which I shall knowe, heare, or vehemently suspect to be plotted or intended against them or any of them*, or against the said Commonwealth or goverment established. Soe helpe mee God.

(2) [*The Revolutionary General Court of May 14/24, 1634.*]

This court opens with a list of those present, giving, after the names of the Assistants, twenty-four other names written in different columns, *before* the usual word *Generalitie*. These twenty-four seem to have come, by threes, from each of the eight towns. It is quite certain that they were "deputies" sent for the purpose by the towns. Cf. *American History and Government*, § 64.

Oath of Freemen

I (*A. B.*), being, by Gods providence, an inhabitant and ffreeman within the jurisdiccion of this commonweale, doe freely acknowledge my selfe to be subject **to the goverment** there of, and therefore doe heere sweare, by the greate and dreadfull name of the everlyveing God, that I wilbe true and faithfull to the same, and will accordingly yeilde assistance and support thereunto, with my person and estate, as in equity I am bound, and will also truely indeavor to mainetaine and preserve **all the libertyes and previlidges thereof**, submitting my selfe to the wholesome lawes and orders made and established by the same; and further, that I will not plott nor practise any evill against *it*, nor consent to any that shall soe doe, but will timely discover and reveale the same to lawful aucthority nowe here established, for the speedy preventing thereof. *Moreover, I doe solemnely bynde myselfe, in the sight of God, that when I shalbe called to give my voice touching any such matter of this state, wherein ffreemen are to deale, I will give my vote and suffrage, as I shall judge in myne oune conscience may best conduce and tend to the publique weale of the body, without respect of persons, or favor of any man.* Soe helpe mee God, in the Lord Jesus Christ.[1]

Further, it is agreed, that none but the Generall Court hath power to chuse and admitt ffreemen.

That none but the Generall Court hath power to make and establishe lawes, nor to elect and appoynct officers, as Governor, Deputy Governor, Assistants, Tresurer, Secretary, Captain, Leiuetenants, Ensignes, or any of like moment, or to remove such upon misdemeanor, as also to sett out the dutyes and powers of the said officers.

That none but the Generall Court hath power to rayse moneyes and taxes, and to dispose of lands, viz. to give and confirme proprietyes.

---

[1] For the significance of the difference between this oath and that in (1) above, cf. *American History and Government*, § 64.

Thomas Dudley, Esq. was chosen Governor for this yeare nexte ensueing, and till a newe be chosen, and did, in presence of the Court, take an oath to his said place belonginge. . . .

It is agreed, that there shalbe ten pounds ffine sett upon the Court of Assistants, and Mr. Mayhewe, for breach of an order of Court against imployeing Indeans to shoote with peeces, the one halfe to be payde by Mr. Pinchon and Mr. Mayhewe, offending therein, the other halfe by the Court of Assistants then in being, who gave leave thereunto.

It was further ordered, that the constable of every plantacion shall, upon process receaved from the Secretary, give timely notice to the ffremen of the plantacion where hee dwells to send soe many of their said members as the process shall direct, to attend upon publique service; and it is agreed that no tryall shall passe upon any, for life or banishment, but by a jury soe summoned, or by the Generall Courte.

It is likewise ordered that there shalbe foure Generall Courts held yearely, to be summoned by the Governor, for the tyme being, and not to be dissolved without the consent of the major parte of the Court.

It was further ordered that it shalbe lawfull for the ffremen of every plantacion to chuse two or three of each towne before every Generall Court, to conferre of and prepare such publique busines as by them shalbe thought fitt to consider of att the nexte Generall Court, and that such persons as shalbe hereafter soe deputed by the ffreemen of [the] severall plantacions, to deale in their behalfe, in the publique affayres of the commonwealth, shall have the full power and voyces of all the said ffreemen, deryved to them for the makeing and establishing of lawes, graunting of lands, etc., and to deale in all other affaires of the commonwealth wherein the ffreemen have to doe, the matter of election of magistrates and other officers onely, excepted, wherein every freeman is to gyve his owne voyce.[1]

---

[1] This enactment is the formal establishment of representative government in the colony, — in accordance with the character of this Court which so decreed. Cf. Introduction, above, to this No. 67 *b*. (2).

All former orders concerneing swine are repealed. And it is agreed that every towne shall have liberty to make such orders aboute swine as they shall judge best for themselves, and that if the swine of one towne shall come within the the lymitts of another, the owners thereof shalbe lyeable to the orders of that towne where their swine soe trespasseth. . . .

68. Reaction: The Aristocratic Veto

Winthrop's *History of New England.*

[September 4, 1634.] The general court began at Newtown, and continued a week, and then was adjourned fourteen days. Many things were there agitated. . . . But the main business, which spent the most time, and caused the adjourning of the court, was about the removal of Newtown [to Connecticut]. . . .

Upon these and other arguments the court being divided, it was put to vote; and, of the deputies, fifteen were for their departure, and ten against it. The governour and two assistants were for it, and the deputy and all the rest [1] of the assistants were against it, (except the secretary, who gave no vote;) whereupon no record was entered, because there were not six assistants in the vote,[1] as the patent requires. Upon this grew a great difference between the governour and assistants, and the deputies. They would not yield the assistants a negative voice, and the others (considering how dangerous it might be to the commonwealth, if they should not keep that strength to balance the greater number of the deputies) thought it safe to stand upon it. So, when they could proceed no farther, the whole court agreed to keep a day of humiliation to seek the Lord, which accordingly was done, in all the congregations, the 18th day of this month; and the 24th the court met again. Before they began, Mr. Cotton preached, (being desired by all the court, upon Mr. Hooker's instant excuse of his unfitness for that occasion). He took his text out of Hag.

---

[1] Not more than four, so the vote stood probably 18 for, and 15 against. But the new claim of the Assistants that at least six magistrates must be "in the vote" (*i.e.* vote yes) prevents action.

ii, 4, etc., out of which he laid down the nature or strength (as he termed it) of the magistracy, ministry, and people, viz., — the strength of the magistracy to be their authority; of the people, their liberty; and of the ministry, their purity; and showed how all of these had a negative voice, etc., and that yet the ultimate resolution, etc., ought to be in the whole body of the people, etc., with answer to all objections, and a declaration of the people's duty and right to maintain their true liberties against any unjust violence, etc., which gave great satisfaction to the company. And it pleased the Lord so to assist him, and to bless his own ordinance, that the affairs of the court went on cheerfully; and although all were not satisfied about the negative voice to be left to the magistrates, yet no man moved aught about it, and the congregation of Newtown came and accepted of such enlargement as had formerly been offered them by Boston and Watertown; and so the fear of their removal to Connecticut was removed. . . . At this court were many laws made against tobacco, and immodest fashions, and costly apparel,[1] etc., as appears by the Records: and £600 raised towards fortifications and other charges. . . .

69. Right of Free Speech Denied

Winthrop's *History of New England*.

March 4, 1634 [1635] . . . At this court, one of the deputies was questioned for denying the magistracy among us, affirming that the power of the governour was but ministerial, etc. He had also much opposed the magistrates, and slighted them,

---

[1] It is refreshing to see that the gentle Puritan women were not to be controlled in the matter. In 1638, four years later, Winthrop has the following item:

"The court, taking into consideration the great disorder general through the country in costliness of apparel, and following new fashions, sent for the elders of the churches, and conferred with them about it, and laid it upon them, as belonging to them, to redress it, by urging it upon the consciences of their people, which they promised to do. But little was done about it; *for divers of the elders' wives, etc., were in some measure partners in this general disorder.*"

and used many weak arguments against the negative voice, as himself acknowledged upon record. He was adjudged by all the court to be disabled for three years from bearing any public office. . . .

[This was Israel Stoughton, deputy from Dorchester (see No. 70, below). Afterward Stoughton was an officer in Cromwell's original regiment of Ironsides.

Winthrop wrote a pamphlet *in favor* of the negative voice; but for this he was not called to account.]

70. Formal Adoption of the Ballot in Elections in the General Court

Winthrop's *History of New England*. For the one earlier instance, cf. No. 67 *a* and note.

[May 6/16, 1635.] A general court was held at Newtown, where John Haynes, Esq., was chosen governour, Richard Bellingham, Esq., deputy governour, and Mr. Hough and Mr. Dummer chosen assistants to the former; and Mr. Ludlow, the late deputy, left out of the magistracy. The reason was, partly, because the people would exercise their absolute power, etc., and partly upon some speeches of the deputy, who protested against the election of the governour as void, for that the deputies of the several towns had agreed upon the election before they came, etc.[1] But this was generally discussed, and the election adjudged good.

Mr. Endecott was also left out, and called into question about the defacing the cross in the ensign. . . .

The governour and deputy were elected by papers, wherein their names were written; but the assistants were chosen by papers, without names, viz. the governour propounded one to the people; then they all went out, and came in at one door, and every man delivered a paper into a hat. Such as gave their vote for the party named, gave in a paper with some figures or scroll in it; others gave in a blank.

* * * * * * *

---

[1] Cf. Ludlow's extreme fear of democracy in No. 64, above.

A petition was preferred by many of Dorchester, etc., for releasing the sentence against Mr. Stoughton the last general court; but it was rejected, and the sentence affirmed by the country to be just. . . .

71. Secret Ballot in a Local Election, because of Democratic and Aristocratic Jealousies

Winthrop's *History of New England.*
The use of the ballot noted in No. 70 was not the first in New England. An earlier instance in the General Court of the year before has been noted (No. 67 *a*, note), and the following extract shows an instance of its use in a town election, along with other interesting political data. On the matter of the ballot, cf. *American History and Government*, § 77.

December 11, 1634. This day after the lecture,[1] the inhabitants of Boston met to choose seven men who should divide the town lands among them. They chose *by papers*, and, in their choice, left out Mr. Winthrop, Coddington, and other of the chief men; only they chose one of the elders and a deacon, and the rest of the inferior sort, and Mr. Winthrop had the greater number before one of them by a voice or two. This they did, as fearing that the richer men would give the poorer sort no great proportions of land, but would rather leave a great part at liberty for new comers and for common, which Mr. Winthrop had oft persuaded them unto, as best for the town, etc. Mr. Cotton and divers others were offended at this choice, because they declined the magistrates; and Mr. Winthrop refused to be one upon such an election as was carried by a voice or two, telling them, that though, for his part, he did not apprehend any personal injury, nor did doubt of their good affection towards him, yet he was much grieved that Boston should be the first who should shake off their magistrates, especially Mr. Coddington, who had been always

---

[1] The mid-week (Thursday) religious service, then held in the morning, of which our Thursday evening " prayer meetings " are a survival. Boston had no town government, as yet, with regular town meetings; but the gathering for this religious purpose was utilized for a special governmental purpose.

so forward for their enlargement; adding further reason of declining this choice, to blot out so bad a precedent. Whereupon, at the motion of Mr. Cotton, who showed them, that it was the Lord's order among the Israelites to have all such businesses committed to the elders, and that it had been nearer the rule to have chosen some of each sort, etc., they all agreed to go to a new election, which was referred to the next lecture day.[1]

72. Martial Law

Records of the Governor and Company of Massachusetts Bay.

Att a Generall Court holden at NeweTowne, March 11th, 1634 [March 21, 1635.]

It is ordered, that the present Governor, Deputy Governor, John Winthrop, John Humfry, John Haynes, John Endicott, William Coddington, William Pinchon, Increase Nowell, Richard Bellingham, Esquire, and Simon Birdstreete, or the major parte of them, whoe are deputed by this Court to dispose of all millitary affaires whatsoever, shall have full power and aucthority to see all former lawes concerneing all military men and municion executed, and also shall have full power to ordeyne or remove all millitary officers, and to make and tender to them an oathe suteable to their places, to dispose of all companyes, to make orders for them, and to make and tender to them a suteable oath, and to see that strickt dissipline and traineings be observed, and to command them forth upon any occacion they thinke meete, to make either offensive or defensive warr, as also to doe whatsoever may be further behoofefull, for the good of this plantacion, in case of any warr that may befall us, and also that the aforesaid commissioners, or the major parte of them, shall have power to imprison or confine any that they shall judge to be enemyes to the commonwealth, and such as will not come

---

[1] The aristocratic protest won; at the second election, the usual gentlemen were placed upon the committee.

under command or restrainte, as they shalbe required, it shalbe lawfull for the said commissioners to putt such persons to death. This order to continue till the end of the next Generall Court.

[At the next Court (May, 1635; the same to which Winthrop refers in No. 70, above), this committee with its authority was continued for one year, though this power was wholly unauthorized by the charter. The reason was a desire to be prepared to resist a "General Governor" from England. Cf. *American History and Government*, § 61.]

73. Life Council; Proxies; "Approved" Churches

Winthrop's *History of New England*.

April 7, 1636. At a general court it was ordered that a certain number of the magistrates should be chosen for life (the reason was, for that it was showed from the word of God, etc., that the principal magistrates ought to be for life).[1] . . . It was likewise ordered . . . that, in regard of the scarcity of vituals, the remote towns should send their votes by proxy to the court of elections,[2] and that no church . . . should be allowed . . . that was gathered without consent of the churches and magistrates.[3]

74. The Wheelwright Controversy (Political Aspects)

Winthrop's *History of New England*.

May 17, 1637. Our court of elections was at Newtown. So soon as the court was set, being about one of the clock, a petition was preferred by those of Boston. The governour would have read it, but the deputy said it was out of order; it was a court for elections, and those must first be despatched,

---

[1] The immediate occasion was the desire to satisfy Lord Say. and Lord Brooke. Cf. No. 75, below.

[2] This provision for "proxies," or written ballots (as the men of that day used the term "proxy" often), was soon extended to all towns at all annual elections.

[3] The regulation regarding churches was needful to supplement the restriction of the franchise to church members (No. 63 (4)).

and then their petitions should be heard. Divers others also opposed that course, as an ill precedent, etc.; and the petition, being about pretence of liberty, etc., (though intended chiefly for revoking the sentence given against Mr. Wheelwright,) would have spent all the day in debate, etc.; but yet the governour and those of that party would not proceed to election, except the petition was read. Much time was already spent about this debate, and the people crying out for election, it was moved by the deputy, that the people should divide themselves, and the greater number must carry it. And so it was done, and the greater number by many were for election. But the governour [Vane] and that side kept their place still, and would not proceed. Whereupon the deputy [Winthrop] told him, that, if he would not go to election, he and the rest of that side would proceed. Upon that, he came from his company, and they went to election; and Mr. Winthrop was chosen governour, Mr. Dudley deputy, and Mr. Endecott of the standing council; and Mr. Israel Stoughton and Mr. Richard Saltonstall were called in to be assistants; and Mr. Vane, Mr. Coddington, and Mr. Dummer, (being all of that faction,) were left quite out.

There was great danger of a tumult that day; for those of that side grew into fierce speeches, and some laid hands on others; but seeing themselves too weak, they grew quiet. They expected a great advantage that day, because the remote towns were allowed to come in by proxy; but it fell out, that there were enough beside. But if it had been otherwise, they must have put in their deputies, as other towns had done, for all matters beside elections. Boston, having deferred to choose deputies till the election was passed, went home that night, and the next morning they sent Mr. Vane, the late governour, and Mr. Coddington, and Mr. Hoffe, for their deputies; *but the court, being grieved at it, found a means to send them home again, for that two of the freemen of Boston*[1] *had*

---

[1] Presumably Winthrop and Cotton, who had stayed at Newtown for the Court.

not notice of the election. So they went all home, and the next morning they returned the same gentleman again upon a new choice; and the court *not finding how they might reject them,* they were admitted. . . .

75. Political and Social Conditions in New England before 1660

a. *Correspondence between Cotton and Certain English Lords, 1636*

Thomas Hutchinson's *History of Massachusetts Bay* (1769), App. II.

In 1636, certain Puritan lords in England sent to John Cotton in Massachusetts a series of conditions upon which they might come to live in the colony. Cotton prepared the answers, with "such leading men as [he] thought meete to consult."

CERTAIN Proposals made by LORD SAY, LORD BROOKE, and other Persons of quality, as conditions of their removing to NEW-ENGLAND, with the answers thereto.

Demand 1. That the Commonwealth should consist of two distinct ranks of men, — whereof the one should be (for them *and their heirs*) gentlemen of the country; the other (for them and their heirs) freeholders.

Answer. Two distinct ranks we willingly acknowledge, from the light of nature and scripture; the one of them called Princes or Nobles, or Elders (amongst whom *gentlemen* have their place); the other, *the people.* Hereditary dignity or honours we willingly allow to the former, unless by the scandalous and base conversation of any of them, they become degenerate. Hereditary liberty, or estate of freemen, we willingly allow to the other, unless they also, by some unworthy and slavish carriage, do disfranchize themselves.

Dem. 2. That in these gentlemen and freeholders, assembled together, the chief power of the Commonwealth shall be placed, both for making and repealing laws.

Ans. So it is with us.

Dem. 3. That each of these two ranks should, in all public assemblies, have a negative voice, so as without a mutuall consent nothing should be established.

Ans. So it is agreed among us.

Dem. 4. That the first rank (consisting of gentlemen) should have power, for them and their heirs, to come to the parliaments or public assemblies, and there to give their free votes *personally;* the second rank (of freeholders) should have the same power for them and their heirs of meeting and voting, *but by their deputies.*

Ans. Thus far this demand is practiced among us. The freemen meet and vote by their deputies; the other rank give their votes personally, only with this difference, there be no more of the gentlemen that give their votes personally but such as are chosen to places of office, either governors, deputy governors, councellors, or assistants. All gentlemen in England have not that honour to meet and vote personally in parliament, much less all their heirs. But of this more fully, in an answer to the ninth and tenth demand.

Dem. 5. That for facilitating and dispatch of business, and other reasons, the gentlemen and freeholders should sit and hold their meetings in two distinct houses.

Ans. We willingly approve the motion, only as yet it is not so practiced among us, but in time, the variety and discrepancy of sundry occurrences will put them upon a necessity of sitting apart.

* * * * * * *

Dem. 8. [*The governor to be chosen from "gentlemen."*]

Ans. We never practice otherwise, chusing the governor either out of the assistants, which is our ordinary course, or out of approved known gentlemen, as this year, Mr. Vane.

Dem. 9. That for the present, the Right Honorable the Lord Viscount Say and Seale, the Lord Brooke, who have already been at great disbursements for the public works in New-England, and such other gentlemen of approved sincerity and worth, as they, before their personal remove, shall take into their number, should be admitted for them and their heirs, gentlemen of the country. But for the future, none shall be admitted into this rank but by the consent of both houses.

Ans. The great disbursements of these noble personages and worthy gentlemen we thankfully acknowledge, because the safety and presence of our brethren at Connecticut is no small blessing and comfort to us. But, though that charge had never been disbursed, the worth of the honorable persons named is so well known to all, and our need of such supports and guides is so sensible to ourselves, that we do not doubt the country would thankfully accept it, as a singular favor from God and from them, if he should bow their hearts to come into this wilderness and help us. As for accepting them and their heirs into the number of gentlemen of the country, the custom of this country is, and readily would be, to receive and acknowledge, not only all such eminent persons as themselves and the gentleman they speake of, but others of meaner estate, so be it is of some eminency, to be for them and their heirs, gentlemen of the country. Only, thus standeth our case. Though we receive them with honor and allow them pre-eminence and accomodations according to their condition, yet we do not, ordinarily, call them forth to the power of election, or administration of magistracy, until they be received as members into some of our churches, a privelege, which we doubt not religious gentlemen will willingly desire (as David did in Psal. xxvii. 4) and christian churches will as readily impart to such desirable persons. Hereditary honors both nature and scripture doth acknowledge (Eccles. x. 17.) but hereditary authority and power standeth only by the civil laws of some commonwealths, and yet even amongst them, the authority and power of the father is nowhere communicated, together with his honors, unto all his posterity. Where God blesseth any branch of any noble or generous family, with a spirit and gifts fit for government, it would be a taking of God's name in vain to put such a talent under a bushel, and a sin against the honor of magistracy to neglect such in our public elections. But if God should not delight to furnish some of their posterity with gifts fit for magistracy, we would expose them rather to reproach and prejudice, and the commonwealth with them, than exalt them to honor, if we should call them forth, when God doth not, to public authority. . . .

[In Cotton's personal letter to Lord Say and Sele and Lord Brooke (Hutchinson's *Massachusetts Bay* (1765), App. III), a fuller statement as to some features of Massachusetts practice and theory is given. The English lords evidently objected to the restriction of citizenship to church members. They wanted less of theocracy and more of aristocracy. Cotton defends the middle course of the colony as follows:

. . . "Your Lordships advertisement touching the civill state of this colony, as they doe breath forth your singular wisdome, and faithfulness, and tender care of the peace, so wee have noe reason to misinterprite, or undervalue your Lordships eyther directions or intentions therein. I know noe man under heaven (I speake in Gods feare without flattery) whose counsell I should rather depend upon, for the wise administration of a civill state according to God, than upon your Lordship, and such confidence have I (not in you) but in the Lords presence in Christ with you, that I should never feare to betrust a greater commonwealth than this (as much as in us lyeth) under such a *perpetuâ dictaturâ* as your Lordship should prescribe. For I nothing doubt, but that eyther your Lordship would prescibe all things according to the rule, or be willing to examine againe, and againe, all things according to it. . . . It is very suitable to Gods all-sufficient wisdome, and to the fulnes and perfection of Holy Scriptures, not only to prescribe perfect rules for the right ordering of a private mans soule to everlasting blessednes with himselfe, but also for the right ordering of a mans family, yea, of the commonwealth too, so farre as both of them are subordinate to spiritual ends, and yet avoide both the churches usurpation upon civill jurisdictions . . . and the commonwealths invasion upon ecclesiasticall administrations . . . Gods institutions (such as the government of church and of commonwealth may be) may be close and compact, and coördinate one with another, and yet not confounded. God hath so framed the state of church government and ordinances, that they may be compatible to any common-wealth, though never so much disordered in his frame. But yet when a commonwealth hath liberty to mould his owne frame . . . I conceyve the scripture hath given full direction for the right ordering of the same. . . . Mr. Hooker doth often quote a saying out of Mr. Cartwright (though I have not read it in him) that noe man fashioneth his house to his hangings, but his hangings to his house. It is better that the commonwealth be fashioned to the setting forth of Gods house, which is his church: than to accommodate the church frame to the civill state. Democracy, I do not conceyve that ever God did ordeyne as a fitt government eyther for church or commonwealth. If the people be governors, who shall be governed? As for monarchy, and aristocracy, they are both of them clearely approved, and directed in scripture, yet so as referreth the soveraigntie to himselfe, and setteth up

Theocracy in both, as the best forme of government in the commonwealth as well as in the church.

"The law, which your Lordship instanceth in [that none shall be chosen to magistracy among us but a church member] was made and enacted before I came into the country; but I have hitherto wanted sufficient light to plead against it. . . . Your Lordship's feare that this will bring in papal excommunication, is just, and pious: but let your Lordship be pleased againe to consider whether the consequence be necessary. . . .

"When your Lordship doubteth that this corse will draw all things under the determination of the church . . . (seeing the church is to determine who shall be members, and none but a member may have to doe in the government of a commonwealth) be pleased (I pray you) to conceyve, that magistrates are neyther chosen to office in the church. . . . Nor neede your Lordship feare (which yet I speake with submission to your Lordships better judgment) that this corse will lay such a foundation, as nothing but a mere democracy can be built upon it. Bodine confesseth, that though it be *status popularis*, where a people choose their owne governors, **yet the government is not a democracy, if it be administered, not by the people, but by the governors**, whether one (for then it is a monarchy, though elective) or by many, for then (as you know) it is aristocracy. . . . Mean while two of the principall of [the requirements of the Lords], the generall cort hath already condescended unto. 1. In establishing a standing councell, who, during their lives, should assist the governor in managing the chiefest affayres of this little state. They have chosen, for the present, onely two (Mr. Winthrope and Mr. Dudley) nor willing to choose more, till they see what further better choyse the Lord will send over to them, that so they may keep an open doore for such desireable gentlemen as your Lordship mentioneth. 2. They have graunted the governor and assistants a negative voyce, and reserved to the freemen the like liberty also." . . .]

b. Social Legislation, October 14, 1651

Records of Massachusetts Colony, IV, Pt. I, pages 60–61.

. . . "though we acknowledge it to be a matter of much difficultie, in regard of the blindnes of mens mindes and the stubbornes of their willes, to sett downe exact rules to confine all sorts of persons, yett wee cannot but account it our duty . . . to declare our utter detestation . . . that men or weomen *of meane condition* should take uppon them the garbe of gentlemen, by wearing gold or silver lace or buttons, or points at their knees, or to walk in great bootes, or weomen of the same rancke to weare silke or tiffany hoodes or scarfes, which though allowable to persons of greater estates or more liberall education, yett we cannot but judge it intollerable in persons of such like condition: it is therefore ordered by this Courte ... that no person ... whose visible estates ... shall not exceed ... two hundred pounds, shall weare any gold or silver lace [etc.] uppon the penaltie of tenn shillings for every such offence, and every such delinquent to be presented by the graund jury," [with long and detailed provisions for enforcement].

76. Some Relations with England, 1638

a. *Attack upon the Massachusetts Charter*

Thomas Hutchinson's *Collection of Original Papers* (1769), 105–106. This is the last of several demands for the return of the charter between the years 1634 and 1638. Winthrop refers to it as " a very strict order." For the reasons why the colony " thought it safe " to disregard the order, and for the earlier history, cf. *American History and Government*, § 61.

A Coppie of a Letter sent by the appointment of the Lords of the Council to Mr. Winthrop, for the Patent of this Plantation to be sent to them.

At Whitehall April 4th 1638. Present,

Lord Archbishop of Canterbury	Earle of Holland
Lord Keeper	Lord Cottington
Lord Treasurer	Mr. Treasurer
Lord Privy Seale	Mr. Controuler
Earle Marshall	Mr. Secretary Cooke
Earle of Dorset	Mr. Secretary Windebank

This day the Lords Commissioners for foreign Plantations, taking into consideration that the petitions and complaints of his Majestys subjects, planters and traders in New-England, grow more frequent than heretofore for want of a settled and

orderly government in those parts, and calling to mind that
they had formerly given order about two or three years since
to Mr. Cradock a member of that plantation, to cause the
grant or letters patent of that plantation (alleadged by him to
be there remaining in the hands of Mr. Winthrop) to be sent
over hither, and that notwithstanding the same, the said
letters patent were not as yet brought over: And their Lordships being now informed by Mr. Attorney General that a Quo
Warranto had been by him brought according to former order
against the said patent, and the same was proceeded to judgment against so many as had appeared, and that they which
had not appeared, were outlawed.

Their lordships well approving of Mr. Attorney's care and
proceeding therein did now resolve and order, that Mr.
Meawtis, clerk of the council attendant upon the said commissioners for foreign plantations, should in a letter from
himselfe to Mr. Winthrop inclose and convey this order unto
him. And their Lordships hereby in his Majestys name, and
according to his express will and pleasure, strictly require and
enjoine the said Winthrop or any other in whose power and
custody the said letters patent are, that they fail not to
transmit the said patent hither by the returne of the ship in
which the order is conveyed to them, it being resolved that in
case of any further neglect or contempt by them shewed
therein, their lordships will cause a strict course to be taken
against them, and will move his Majesty to reassume into his
hands the whole plantation.

b. *The Refusal of the Colony*

Hutchinson's *Massachusetts Bay* (1765), App. V. See introductory
matter to *a*, above.

*An Addresse of the General Court
To the Right Honourable the Lords Commissioners for foreigne
Plantations* [*September 6/16, 1638*]

The humble Petition of the Inhabitants of the Massachusets
 in New England, of the Generall Court there assembled,

the 6th day of September, in the 14th yeare of the Reigne of our Soveraigne Lord King CHARLES.

Whereas it hath pleased your Lordships, by order of the 4th of April last, to require our patent to be sent unto you, wee do hereby humbly and sincerely professe, that wee are ready to yield all due obedience to our soveraigne Lord, the King's majesty, and to your Lordships under him, and in this minde wee left our native countrie, and according thereunto, hath been our practice ever since, so as wee are much grieved, that your Lordships should call in our patent, there being no cause knowne to us, nor any delinquency or fault of ours expressed in the order sent to us for that purpose, our government being according to his Majestyes grant, and wee not answerable for any defects in other plantations, etc.

This is what his Majesties subjects here doe believe and professe, and thereupon wee are all humble suitors to your Lordships, that you will be pleased to take into further consideration our condition, and to affoord us the liberty of subjects, that we may know what is layd to our charge; and have leaive and time to answer for ourselves before we be condemned as a people unworthy of his Majesties favour or protection; as for the quo warranto mentioned in the said order, wee doe assure your Lordships wee were never called to answer to it, and if wee had, wee doubt not but wee have a sufficient plea to put in.

It is not unknowne to your Lordships, that we came into these remote parts with his Majesties licence and encouragement, under his great seale of England, and in the confidence wee had of that assurance, wee have transported our families and estates, and here have wee built and planted, to the great enlargement and securing of his Majesties dominions in these parts, so as if our patent should now be taken from us, we shall be looked on as runnigadoes and outlawed, and shall be enforced, either to remove to some other place, or to returne into our native country againe; either of which will put us to unsupportable extremities, and these evils (among others) will necessarily follow: (1.) Many thousand souls will be exposed to ruine, being layd open to the injuries of all men. (2.) If wee be forced to desert this place, the rest of the plantations (being too weake to subsist alone) will, for the most part, dissolve and goe with us, and then will this whole country fall into the hands of the French or Dutch, who would speedily imbrace such an opportunity. (3.) If we should loose all our labour and costs, and be deprived of those liberties which his Majesty hath granted us, and nothing layd to our charge, nor any fayling to be found in us in point of allegiance (which all our countrymen doe take notice of and will justify our faithfulness in this behalfe) it will discourage all men heereafter from the like undertakings upon confidence of his Majestyes royal grant. *Lastly, if our patent be taken from us (whereby wee suppose wee may clayme interest in his Majestyes favour and protection) the common people here will conseive that his Majesty hath cast them off, and that, heereby, they are freed from their allegiance and subjection, and, thereupon, will be ready to confederate themselves under a new government, for their necessary safety and subsistance, which will be of dangerous example to other plantations, and perillous to ourselves of incurring his Majestyes displeasure, which wee would by all means avoyd.*[1]

Upon these considerations wee are bold to renew our humble supplications to your Lordships, that wee may be suffered to live here in this wilderness, and that this poore plantation, which hath found more favour from God than many others, may not finde lesse favour from your Lordships [so] that our liberties should be restreyned, when others are enlarged, that the doore should be kept shutt unto us, while it stands open to all other plantations, that men of ability should be debarred from us, while they give incouragement to other colonies.

---

[1] Observe the plain threat, cloaked in this language, that the colony would rebel rather than surrender its charter. The real leaders of revolt would have been, not "the common people," but Winthrop and his friends, who drew up this paper.

77. Democratic Discontent, 1639

(Winthrop's Denial of the Right of Petition; Abolition of the Life Council; Delay in the Written Code)

Winthrop's *History of New England*.

May 22, 1639. The court of elections was: at which time there was a small eclipse of the sun. Mr. Winthrop was chosen governour again, though some laboring had been, by some of the elders and others, to have changed, not out of any dislike of him (for they all loved and esteemed him), but out of their fear lest it might make way for having a governour for life, which some had propounded as most agreeable to God's institution and the practice of all well-ordered states. But neither the governour nor any other attempted the thing; though some jealousies arose, which were increased by two occasions. The first was, there being want of assistants, the governour and other magistrates thought fit (in the warrant for the court) to propound three, amongst which Mr. Downing, the governour's brother-in-law, was one, which they conceived to be done to strengthen his party, and therefore, though he were known to be a very able man, etc., and one who had done many good offices for the country for these ten years, yet the people would not choose him. Another occasion of their jealousy was, the court, finding the number of deputies to be much increased by the addition of new plantations, thought fit, for the ease both of the country and the court, to reduce all towns to two deputies. This occasioned some to fear, that the magistrates intended to make themselves stronger, and the deputies weaker, and so, in time, to bring all power into the hands of the magistrates; so as the people in some towns were much displeased with their deputies for yielding to such an order. Whereupon, at the next session, it was propounded to have the number of deputies, restored; and allegations were made, that it was an infringement of their liberty; so as, after much debate, and such reasons given for diminishing the number of deputies, and clearly proved that their liberty consisted not in the number, but in the thing, divers of the deputies, who came with intent to reverse the last order, were, by force of reason, brought to uphold it; so that, when it was put to the vote, the last order for two deputies only was confirmed. Yet, the next day, a petition was brought to the court from the freemen of Roxbury, to have the third deputy restored. Whereupon the reasons of the court's proceedings were set down in writing, and all objections answered, and sent to such towns as were unsatisfied with this advice, that, if any could take away those reasons, or bring us better for what they did desire, we should be ready, at the next court, to repeal the said order.

The hands of some of the elders (learned and godly men) were to this petition, though suddenly drawn in, and without due consideration. For the lawfulness of it may well be questioned: for when the people have chosen men to be their rulers, and to make their laws, and bound themselves by oath to submit thereto, now to combine together (a lesser part of them) in a public petition to have any order repealed, which is not repugnant to the law of God, savors of resisting an ordinance of God; for the people, having deputed others, have no power to make or alter laws, but are to be subject; and if any such order seem unlawful or inconvenient, they were better prefer some reasons, etc., to the court, with manifestation of their desire to move them to a review, than peremptorily to petition to have it repealed, which amounts to a plain reproof of those whom God hath set over them, and putting dishonor upon them, against the tenor of the fifth commandment.

There fell out at this court another occasion of increasing the people's jealousy of their magistrates, viz.: One of the elders, being present with those of his church, when they were to prepare their votes for the election, declared his judgment, that a governour ought to be for his life, alleging for his authority the practice of all the best commonwealths in Europe, and especially that of Israel by God's own ordinance. But this was opposed by some other of the elders with much zeal, and so notice was taken of it by the people, not as a matter of dispute, but as if there had been some plot to put it in practice.

June 9, 1639 . . . The people had long desired a body of laws, and thought their condition very unsafe, while so much power rested in the discretion of magistrates. Divers attempts had been made at former courts, and the matter referred to some of the magistrates and some of the elders; but still it came to no effect; for, being committed to the care of many, whatsoever was done by some, was still disliked or neglected by others. . . . Two great reasons there were, which caused most of the magistrates and some of the elders not to be very forward in this matter. One was, want of sufficient experience of the nature and disposition of the people, considered with the condition of the country and other circumstances, which made them conceive, that such laws would be fittest for us, which should arise *pro re nata* upon occasions, etc., and so the laws of England and other states grew (and therefore the fundamental laws of England are called customs, consuetudines). 2. For that it would professedly transgress the limits of our charter, which provide, we shall make no laws repugnant to the laws of England, and that we were assured we must do. But to raise up laws by practice and custom had been no transgression; as in our church discipline, and in matters of marriage, to make a law, that marriages should not be solemnized by ministers, is repugnant to the laws of England: but to bring it to a custom by practice for the magistrates to perform it, is no law made repugnant, etc. At length (to satisfy the people) it proceeded . . .[1]

November, 1639. Some of the freemen, without the consent of the magistrates or governour, had chosen Mr. Nathaniel Ward to preach at this court, pretending that it was a part of their liberty. The governour (whose right indeed it is, for till the court be assembled the freemen are but private persons) would not strive about it, for though it did not belong to them, yet if they would

---

[1] For a brief history of this proceeding, cf. *American History and Government*, § 81. The code was established in 1641. See No. 78, below.

have it, there was reason to yield it to them. . . . In his sermon he delivered many useful things, but in a moral and political discourse, grounding his propositions much upon the old Roman and Grecian governments, which sure is an error, for if religion and the word of God makes men wiser than their neighbors, and these times have the advantage of all that have gone before us in experience and observation, it is probable that by all these helps, we may better frame rules of government for ourselves than to receive others upon the bare authority of the wisdom, justice, etc. of those heathen commonwealths. Among other things, he advised the people to keep all their magistrates in an equal rank, and not give more honor or power to one than to another, which is easier to advise than to prove, seeing it is against the practice of Israel (where some were rulers of thousands, and some but of tens) and of all nations known or recorded. Another advice he gave, that magistrates should not give private advice, and take knowledge of any man's cause before it came to public hearing. This was debated after in the general court, where some of the deputies moved to have it ordered. [Successfully resisted by the magistrates.]

[Wood's sermon shows that he regarded himself as put forward to champion democratic doctrine: cf. Cotton's sermons for the magistrates, noted in former entries. An entry of Winthrop's, dated May 10, 1643, shows a continuance of this democratic purpose.

"Our court of elections was held, when Mr. Ezekiel Rogers, pastor of the church in Rowley, preached. He was called to it by a company of freemen, whereof the most were deputies chosen for the court. . . . Mr. Rogers, hearing that exception was taken to this call, as unwarrantable, wrote to the governour for advice, etc., who returned him answer: That he did account his calling not to be sufficient, yet the magistrates were not minded to strive with the deputies about it, but seeing it was noised in the country, and the people would expect him, and that he had advised with the magistrates about it, he wished him to go on. In his sermon he described how the man ought to be qualified whom they should choose for their governour, yet dissuaded them earnestly from choosing the same man twice together, and expressed his dislike of that with such vehemency as gave offence. But when it came to trial, the former governour, Mr. Winthrop, was chosen again."]

78. The Body of Liberties, 1641

Whitmore's *Bibliographical Sketch of the Laws of the Massachusetts Colony* gives the text in facsimile.

For the history and significance, see *American History and Government*, § 81. Cf. also No. 77, above. The starred numbers each contain some important advance upon English custom or law of the day, and italic type is used to call attention to provisions that especially justify the name, **Body of Liberties**.

A Coppie of the Liberties of the Massachusets Collonie in New England

The free fruition of such liberties, Immunities, and priveledges, as humanitie, Civilitie, and Christianitie call for as due to every man in his place and proportion, without impeachment and Infringement, hath ever bene and *ever will be the tranquillitie and Stabilitie of Churches and Commonwealths. And the deniall or deprivall thereof, the disturbance if not the ruine of both.* . . .

Wee doe therefore this day religiously and unanimously decree and confirme these following Rites, liberties, and priveledges concerneing our Churches and Civill State, to be respectively impartiallie and inviolably enjoyed and observed throughout our Jurisdiction for ever.

1. No mans life shall be taken away, no mans honour or good name shall be stayned, no mans person shall be arested, restrayned, banished, dismembred, nor any wayes punished, no man shall be deprived of his wife or children, no mans goods or estaite shall be taken away from him, nor any way indammaged under Coulor of law, or Countenance of Authoritie, *unlesse it be by vertue or equitie of some expresse law of the Country warranting the same, established by a generall Court and sufficiently published*, or, *in case of the defect of a law* in any partecular case, by the word of god. *And in Capitall cases*, or in cases concerning dismembring or banishment, *according to that word to be judged by the Generall Court.*

*2. Every person within this Jurisdiction, whether Inhabitant or forreiner shall enjoy the same justice and law, that is generall for the plantation, which we constitute and execute one towards another, without partialitie or delay.

* * * * * * *

5. No man shall be compelled to any publique worke or service unlesse the presse be grounded upon some act of the generall Court, and [he] have reasonable allowance therefore.

* * * * * * *

8. No mans Cattell or good of what kinde soever shall be pressed or taken for any publique use or service, unlesse it be by warrant grounded upon some act of the generall Court, nor without such reasonable prices and hire as the ordinarie rates of the Countrie do afford. . . .

*9. No monopolies shall be granted or allowed amongst us, but of such new Inventions that are profitable to the Countrie, and that for a short time.

*10. All our lands and heritages shall be free from all fines and licences upon Alienations, and from all hariotts, wardships, Liveries, Primerseisens, yeare day and wast, Escheates, and forfeitures, upon the deaths of parents, or Ancestors, be they naturall, casuall, or Juditiall.

*11. All persons which are of the age of 21 yeares, and of right understanding and meamories, *whether* [even if] *excommunicate or condemned* shall have full power and libertie to make there wills and testaments, and other lawfull alienations of theire lands and estates.

12. *Every man whether Inhabitant or fforreiner, free or not free shall have libertie to come to any publique Court, Councell or Towne meeting, and either by speech or writing to move any lawfull, seasonable, and materiall question, or to present any necessary motion, complaint, petition, Bill or information, whereof that meeting hath proper cognizance, so it be done in convenient time, due order, and respective manner.*

* * * * * * *

16. Every Inhabitant that is an howse holder shall have free fishing and fowling in any great ponds and Bayes, Coves and Rivers, so farre as the sea ebbes and flowes within the presincts of the towne where they dwell, unless the free men of the same Towne or the Generall Court have otherwise appropriated them, provided that this shall not be extended to give leave to any man to come upon others proprietie without there leave.

*17. Every man of or within this Jurisdiction shall have free libertie, not with standing any Civill power, to remove both himselfe and his familie at their pleasure out of the same, provided there be no legall impediment to the contrarie.

Rites Rules and Liberties concerning Juditiall proceedings

18. *No mans person shall be restrained or imprisoned by any Authority what so ever, before the law hath sentenced him thereto,* if he can put in sufficient securitie, bayle, or mainprise, for his appearance, and good behaviour in the meane time, unlesse it be in Crimes Capitall, and Contempts in open Court, and in such cases where some expresse act of Court doth allow it.

19. If in a generall Court any miscariage shall be amongst the Assistants when they are by themselves that may deserve an Admonition or fine under 20 sh, it shall be examined and sentenced amongst themselves, If amongst the Deputies when they are by themselves, It shall be examined and sentenced amongst themselves, If it be when the whole Court is togeather, it shall be judged by the whole Court, and not severallie as before.[1]

* * * * * * *

*25. No Summons pleading Judgement, or any kinde of proceeding in Court or course of Justice shall be abated, arested, or reversed, upon any kinde of cercumstantiali errors or mistakes, if the person and cause be rightly understood and intended by the Court.

* * * * * * *

---

[1] This law shows that in 1641 the two orders of the Assembly had come to sit by themselves frequently. For the final separation, see No. 80.

29. In all Actions at law it shall be the libertie of the plantife and defendant by mutual consent to choose whether they will be tryed by the Bench or by a Jurie, unlesse it be where the law upon just reason hath otherwise determined. The like libertie shall be granted to all persons in Criminall cases.

30. It shall be in the libertie both of plantife and defendant, and likewise every delinquent (to be judged by a Jurie) to challenge **any of the Jurors.** And if his challenge be found just and reasonable by the Bench,[1] or the rest of the Jurie, as the challenger shall choose, it shall be allowed him. . . .

34. If any man shall be proved and Judged a commen Barrator vexing others with unjust frequent and endlesse suites, It shall be in the power of Courts both to deny him the benefit of the law, and to punish him for his Barratry.

* * * * * * *

36. It shall be in the libertie of every man . . . sentenced in any cause in any Inferior Court, to make their Appeale to the Court of Assistants, provided they tender their appeale and put in securitie to prosecute it before the Court be ended wherein they were condemned, and within six dayes next ensuing put in good securitie before some Assistant to satisfie what his Adversarie shall recover against him ; And if the cause be of a Criminall nature, for his good behaviour and appearance. And everie man shall have libertie to complaine to the Generall Court of any Injustice done him in any Court of Assistants or other.

* * * * * * *

40. No Conveyance, Deede, or promise what so ever shall be of validitie, If it be gotten by Illegal violence, imprisonment, threatenings, or any kinde of forcible compulsion called Dures.

41. Everie man that is to Answere for any Criminall cause, whether he be in prison or under bayle, his cause shall be heard and determined at the next Court that hath proper Cognizance thereof, And [i.e., if it] may be done without prejudice of Justice.

---

[1] The "peremptory challenge" of the Plymouth Code does not appear here.

42. No man shall be twise sentenced by Civill Justice for one and the same Crime, offence, or Trespasse.

43. No man shall be beaten with above 40 stripes, nor shall any true gentleman, nor any man equall to a gentleman be punished with whipping,[1] unles his crime be very shamefull, and his course of life vitious and profligate.

*44. No man condemned to dye shall be put to death within fower dayes next after his condemnation, unles the Court see spetiall cause to the contrary, or in case of martiall law; nor shall the body of any man so put to death be unburied 12 howers, unlesse it be in case of Anatomie.

45. No man shall be forced by Torture to confesse any Crime against himselfe nor any other unlesse it be in some Capitall case where he is first fullie convicted by cleare and suffitient evidence to be guilty, After which, if the cause be of that nature That it is very apparent there be other conspiratours, or confederates with him, Then he may be tortured, yet not with such Tortures as be Barbarous and inhumane.

46. For bodilie punishments we allow amongst us none that are inhumane, Barbarous, or cruell.[2]

47. No man shall be put to death without the testimony of two or three witnesses, or that which is equivalent there unto.

49. No free man shall be compelled to serve upon Juries above two Courts in a yeare, except grand Jurie men, who shall hould two Courts together at the least.

*50. **All Jurors shall be chosen continuallie by the freemen of the Towne where they dwell.**

*   *   *   *   *   *   *

54. When so ever anything is to be put to vote, any sentence to be pronounced, or any other matter to be proposed, or read

---

[1] Cf. No. 65 (8).

[2] These terms are relative. Winthrop describes, after this date, the cruel flogging of a woman for a matter of opinion, and says that she had her tongue put in "a cleft stick" for half an hour, for "abusing" the magistrates who punished her.

in any Court or Assembly, If the president or moderator thereof shall refuse to performe it, the Major parte of the members of that Court or Assembly shall have power to appoint any other meete man of them to do it, And, if there *be just cause, to punish* him that should and would not.[1]

* * * * * * *

57. When so ever any person shall come to any very suddaine untimely and unnaturall death, Some Assistant, or the Constables of that Towne shall forthwith summon a Jury of twelve free men to inquire of the cause and manner of their death, and shall present a true verdict thereof to some neere Assistant, or the next Court to be helde for that Towne upon their oath.[2]

Liberties more peculiarlie concerning the free men

58. Civill Authorie hath power and libertie to see the peace, ordinances and Rules of Christ observed in every church according to his word, so it be done in a Civill and not in an Ecclesiastical way.

* * * * * * *

60. No church censure shall degrade or depose any man from any Civill dignitie, office, or Authoritie he shall have in the Commonwealth.

* * * * * * *

62. Any Shire or Towne shall have libertie to choose their Deputies whom and where they please for the General Court, So be it they be free men, and have taken there oath of fealtie, and [be] Inhabiting in this Jurisdiction.

* * * * * * *

66. The Freeman of everie Township shall have power to make such by laws and constitutions as may concerne the

---

[1] This is a protest against the occasional arbitrary action of the Massachusetts governor in past years. Both Winthrop and Vane had been guilty of refusing to put motions to the General Court.

[2] The coroner's jury had existed by custom in the colony from the first.

wellfare of their Towne, provided they be not of a Criminall, but onely of a prudentiall nature, And that their penalties exceede not 20 sh. for one offence. And that they be not repugnant to the publique laws and orders of the Countrie. And if any Inhabitant shall neglect or refuse to observe them, they shall have power to levy the appointed penalties by distresse.[1]

* * * * * * *

68. It is the libertie of the freemen to choose such deputies for the Generall Court out of themselves, either in their owne Townes or elsewhere as they judge fitest. And because we cannot forsee what varietie and weight of occasions may fall into future consideration, and what counsells we may stand in neede of, we decree: *That the Deputies* (to attende the Generall Court in the behalfe of the Countrie) *shall not any time be stated or inacted, but from Court to Court, or at the most but for one yeare,* — that the Countrie may have an Annuall libertie to do in that case what is most behoofefull for the best welfaire thereof.

69. *No Generall Court shall be desolved or adjourned without the consent of the Major parte thereof.*[2]

70. All Freemen called to give any advise, vote, verdict, or sentence in any Court, Counsell, or Civill Assembly, shall have full freedome to doe it according to their true Judgements and Consciences, So it be done orderly and inofensively for the manner.

* * * * * * *

74. The freemen of every Towne or Towneship, shall have full power to choose yearly or for lesse time out of themselves a convenient number of fitt men to order the planting or prudentiall occasions of that Towne, according to Instructions

---

[1] This recognized existing local practice. Cf. No. 66.
[2] This democratic advance had been taken two years earlier in Connecticut. Cf. No. 93.

given them in writeing, Provided nothing be done by them contrary to the publique laws and orders of the Countrie, provided also the number of such select persons be not above nine.[1]

Liberties of Woemen

*79. If any man at his death shall not leave his wife a competent portion of his estaite, upon just complaint made to the Generall Court, she shall be relieved.

*80. Everie marryed woeman shall be free from bodilie correction or stripes by her husband, unlesse it be in his owne defence upon her assalt. If there be any just cause of correction complaint shall be made to Authoritie assembled in some Court, from which onely she shall receive it.

Liberties of Children

81. When parents dye intestate, the Elder sonne shall have a doble portion of his whole estate reall and personall, unlesse the Generall Court upon just cause alleadged shall Judge otherwise.

82. When parents dye intestate, having noe heires males of their bodies, their Daughters shall inherit as Copartners, unles the Generall Court upon just reason shall judge otherwise.

83. If any parents shall wilfullie and unreasonably deny any childe timely or convenient mariage, or shall exercise any unnaturall severitie towards them, Such children shall have free libertie to complain to Authoritie for redresse.

84. No Orphan dureing their minoritie which was not committed to tuition or service by the parents in their life time, shall afterwards be absolutely disposed of by any kindred, friend, Executor, Towneship, or Church, nor by themselves, without the consent of some Court, wherein two Assistants at least shall be present.

---

[1] Actual practice disregarded this limitation to nine, and also the attempt to restrict the "select men" and the voters to "freemen." 74 should have followed 66.

Liberties of Servants

* * * * * * *

87. If any man smite out the eye or tooth of his man servant, or maid servant, or otherwise mayme or much disfigure him, unlesse it be by meere casualtie, he shall let them goe free from his service.[1] And shall have such further recompense as the Court shall allow him.

88. Servants that have served deligentlie and faithfully to the benefitt of their maisters seaven yeares, shall not be sent away emptie. And if any have bene unfaithfull, negligent or unprofitable in their service, notwithstanding the good usage of their maisters, they shall not be dismissed till they have made satisfaction according to the Judgement of Authoritie.

Liberties of Forreiners and Strangers

* * * * * * *

91. There shall never be any bond slaverie villinage or Captivitie amongst us,[2] unles it be lawfull Captives taken in just warres, and such strangers as willingly selle themselves or are sold to us. And these shall have all the liberties and Christian usages which the law of god established in Israell concerning such persons doeth morally require. This exempts none from servitude who shall be Judged thereto by Authoritie.

Off [of] the Bruite Creature

92. No man shall exercise any Tirranny or Crueltie towards any bruite Creature which are usuallie kept for mans use.

* 93. If any man shall have occasion to leade or drive Cattel from place to place that is far of, So that they be weary, or hungry, or fall sick, or lambe, It shall be lawful to rest or refresh them, for a competent time, in any open place that is not Corne, meadow, or inclosed for some peculiar use.

---

[1] This with the first half of the next law is based upon the Jewish law.
[2] This noble provision soon became a dead letter.

94. *Capitall Laws*

1

Dut. 13. 6. 10
Dut. 17. 2. 6
Ex. 22. 20

If any man after legall conviction shall have or worship any other god, but the lord god, he shall be put to death.

2

Ex. 22. 18.
Lev. 20. 27.
Dut. 18. 10.

If any man or woeman be a witch, (that is hath or consulteth with a familiar spirit,) They shall be put to death.

3

Lev. 24. 15. 16

If any person shall Blaspheme the name of god, the father, Sonne or Holie ghost, with direct, expresse, presumptuous or high handed blashemie, or shall curse god in the like manner, he shall be put to death.

4

Ex. 21. 12.
Numb. 35. 13.
14. 30. 31.

If any person comitt any wilfull murther, which is manslaughter, comitted upon premeditated mallice, hatred, or Crueltie, not in a mans necessarie and just defence, nor by meere casualtie against his will, he shall be put to death.

5

Numb. 25. 20.
21.
Lev. 24. 17.

If any person slayeth an other suddainely, in his anger or Crueltie of passion, he shall be put to death.

6

Ex. 21. 14.

If any person shall slay an other through guile, either by poysoning or other such divelish practice, he shall be put to death.

* * * * * * *

10

Ex. 21. 16. If any man stealeth a man or mankinde, he shall surely be put to death.

11

Dut. 19. 16.
18. 19.
If any man rise up by false witnes, wittingly and of purpose to take away any man's life, he shall be put to death.

12

If any man shall conspire and attempt any invasion, insurrection, or publique rebellion against our commonwealth, or shall indeavour to surprize any Towne or Townes, fort or forts therein, or shall treacherously and perfediouslie attempt the alteration and subversion of our frame of politie or Government fundamentallie, he shall be put to death.

95. *A declaration of the Liberties the Lord Jesus hath given to the Churches*

1. All the people of god within this Jurisdiction who are not in a church way, and be orthodox in Judgement, and not scandalous in life, shall have full libertie to gather themselves into a Church Estaite. Provided they doe it in a Christian way, with due observation of the rules of Christ revealed in his word.

2. Every Church hath full libertie to exercise all the ordinances of god, according to the rules of Scripture.

3. Every Church hath free libertie of Election and ordination of all their officers from time to time, provided they be able, pious and orthodox.

4. Every Church hath free libertie of Admission, Recommendation, Dismission, and Expulsion, or deposall of their officers, and members, upon due cause, with free exercise of the Discipline and Censure of Christ according to the rules of his word.

10. Wee allowe private meetings for edification in religion amongst Christians of all sortes of people. So it be without just offence both for number, time, place, and other cercumstances.

*   *   *   *   *   *

98. Lastly because our dutie and desire is to do nothing suddainlie which fundamentally concerne us, we decree that these rites and liberties,

shall be Audably read and deliberately weighed at every Generall Court that shall be held, within three yeares next insueing, And such of them as shall not be altered or repealed they shall stand so ratified, That no man shall infringe them without due punishment.

And if any Generall Court within these next thre yeares shall faile or forget to reade and consider them as abovesaid. The Governor and Deputie Governor for the time being, and every Assistant present at such Courts shall forfeite 20 sh. a man, and everie Deputie 10 sh. a man for each neglect, which shall be paid out of their proper estate, and not by the Country or the Townes which choose them. And when so ever there shall arise any question in any Court amonge the Assistants and Associates thereof about the explanation of these Rites and liberties, The Generall Court onely shall have power to interprett them.

79. A Puritan View of Trade

Winthrop's *History of New England*.

November, 1639. At a general court holden at Boston, a great complaint was made of the oppression used in the country in sale of foreign commodities; and Mr. Robert Keaine, who kept a shop in Boston, was notoriously above others observed and complained of; and, being convented, he was charged with many particulars; in some, for taking above sixpence in the shilling profit; in some, eight pence; and, in some small things, above two for one; and being hereof convict, (as appears by the records,) he was fined £ 200, which came thus to pass: The deputies considered, apart, of his fine, and set it at £ 200; the magistrates agreed but to £ 100. So, the court being divided, at length it was agreed, that his fine should be £ 200, but he should pay but £ 100, and the other should be respited to the further consideration of the next general court. By this means the magistrates and deputies were brought to an accord, which otherwise had not been likely, and so much trouble might have grown, and the offender escaped censure. For the cry of the country was so great against oppression, . . .

And sure the course was very evil, especial circumstances considered: 1. He being an ancient professor of the gospel:

2. A man of eminent parts . . . 4. Having come over for consciences sake . . .

These things gave occasion to Mr. Cotton, in his public exercise the next lecture day, to lay open the error of . . . false principles, and to give some rules of direction in the case.

Some false principles were these: —

1. That a man might sell as dear as he can, and buy as cheap as he can.

2. If a man lose by casualty of sea, etc., in some of his commodities, he may raise the price of the rest.

3. That he may sell as he bought, though he paid too dear, etc., and though the commodity be fallen, etc.

4. That, as a man may take the advantage of his own skill or ability, so he may of another's ignorance or necessity.

5. Where one gives time for payment, he is to take like recompense of one as of another.

The rules for trading were these: —

1. A man may not sell above the current price, i. e., such a price as is usual in the time and place, and as another (who knows the worth of the commodity) would give for it, if he had occasion to use it . . .

2. When a man loseth in his commodity for want of skill, . . . he must look at it as his own fault or cross, and therefore must not lay it upon another.

3. Where a man loseth by casualty of sea, . . . it is a loss cast upon himself by providence, and he may not ease himself of it by casting it upon another; for so a man should seem to provide against all providences, that he should never lose; but where there is a scarcity of the commodity, there men may raise their price; for now it is a hand of God upon the commodity, and not the person.

80. The Separation of the Legislature into Two Houses

Winthrop's *History of New England.* Cf. *American History and Government,* §§ 69, 70.

June 4, 1642. . . . At the same general court there fell out a great business upon a very small occasion. Anno 1636, there was a stray sow in Boston, which was brought to Captain Keayne: he had it cried divers times, and divers came to see it, but none made claim to it for near a year. He kept it in his yard with a sow of his own. Afterwards one Sherman's wife, having lost such a sow, laid claim to it, but came not to see it, till Captain Keayne had killed his own sow. After being showed the stray sow, and finding it to have other marks than she had claimed her sow by, she gave out that he had killed her sow. The noise hereof being spread about the town, the matter was brought before the elders of the church as a case of offence; many witnesses were examined, and Captain Keayne was cleared. [The case was then brought before the county court], — when, upon a full hearing, Capt. Keayne was again cleared, and the jury gave him £3 for his costs. [Keayne then recovers £20 damages for slander.] Story [friend of "Sherman's wife"[1]], upon this, searcheth town and country to find matter against Captain Keayne . . . and got one of his witnesses to come into Salem court and to confess there that he had foresworn himself [in the former trial]; and upon this he petitions in Sherman's name to this *general court* to have the cause heard again; which was granted, and the best part of seven days were spent in examining witnesses and debating of the [case]. And yet it was not determined; for there being nine magistrates and thirty deputies, no sentence could by law pass without the greater number of both, which neither [side] had; for there were for the plaintiff two magistrates and fifteen deputies, and for the defendant [Keayne] seven magistrates and eight deputies. . . .

There was great expectation in the country, by occasion of Story's clamours against him, that the cause would have passed against the captain, but falling out otherwise, gave occasion to many to speak unreverently of the court, especially of the

[1] To give the prefix Mrs. (Mistress) to this poor woman would be wholly out of keeping with the usage of that day.

magistrates, and the report went, that their negative voice had hindered the course of justice, and that these magistrates must be put out, that the power of the negative voice might be taken away.

June 12, 1643. . . . The sow business not being yet digested in the country [even Bellingham, ex-governor, urging a new trial without a negative voice for the magistrates, — Winthrop gives over three pages here to a review of the controversy. Then follows :]

The sow business had started another question about the magistrates' negative vote in the general court. The deputies generally were very earnest to have it taken away; whereupon one of the magistrates [Winthrop?] wrote a small treatise, wherein he laid down the original of it from the patent, and the establishing of it by order of the general court in 1634, showing thereby how it was fundamental to our government, which, if it were taken away, would be a mere democracy. He showed also the necessity and usefulness of it by many arguments from scripture, reason, and common practice, etc. Yet this would not satisfy, but the deputies and common people would have it taken away; and yet it was apparent (as some of the deputies themselves confessed) the more did not understand it. An answer also was written (by one of the magistrates as was conceived) to the said treatise, undertaking to avoid all the arguments both from the patent and from the order, etc. This the deputies made great use of in this court, supposing they had now enough to carry the cause clearly with them, so as they pressed earnestly to have it presently determined. But the magistrates told them the matter was of great concernment, even to the very frame of our government; it had been established upon serious consultation and consent of all the elders; it had been continued without any inconvenience or apparent mischief these fourteen years; therefore it would not be safe nor of good report to alter on such a sudden, and without the advice of the elders: offering withal, that if upon such advice and consideration it should appear to be inconvenient, or not warranted by the patent and the said order, etc., they should be ready to join with them in taking it away. Upon these propositions they were stilled, and so an order was drawn up to this effect, that it was desired that every member of the court would take advice, etc., and that it should be no offence for any, either publicly or privately, to declare their opinion in the case, so it were modestly, etc., and that the elders should be desired to give their advice before the next meeting of this court. It was the magistrates' only care to gain time, that so the people's heat might be abated, for then they knew they would hear reason, and that the advice of the elders might be interposed; . . .

. . . One of the elders [Winthrop himself] also wrote a small treatise wherein he handled the question, laying down the several forms of government, both simple and mixt, and the true form of our government, **and the unavoidable change into a democracy if the negative voice were taken away.** . . .

March, 1644. . . . At the same court in the first month, **upon the motion of the deputies,** it was ordered that the court should be divided in their consultations, the magistrates by themselves and the deputies by themselves. What the one agreed upon, they should send to the other; and if both agreed, then to pass, etc. This order determined the great contention about the negative voice.

[The *Records of the Governor and Company of Massachusetts Bay* (II, 58-59) give this act which established the first two-chambered legislature in America (An Act of the Generall Court at Boston, March 7/17, 1644). The preamble contains an interesting reference to English precedent: —

"For as much as after long experience wee find divers inconveniences in the manner of our proceeding in Courts, by Magistrates and deputies siting together, and accounting it wisdome to follow the laudable practice of other states who have layd groundworks for government and order in the issuing of busines of greatest and highest consequence, . . ."

See also an interesting prophecy of the change to two Houses in Cotton's letter, No. 75 *a*, above.]

81. A Town Code of School Law

Dorchester Town Records, 54–57. Cf. *American History and Government*, § 123.

Upon a generall and lawfull warning of all the Inhabitants the 14th of the 1st moneth 1645 these rules and orders following presented to the Towne Concerning the Schoole of Dorchester are Confirmed by the major parte of the Inhabitants then present.

First, It is ordered that three able, and sufficient men of the Plantation shalbe Chosen to bee wardens or overseers of the Schoole above mentioned who shall have the Charge oversight and ordering thereof and of all things Concerneing the same in such manner as is hereafter expressed and shall Continue in their office and place for Terme of their lives respectively, unlesse by reason of any of them removing his habitation out of the Towne, or for any other weightie reason the Inhabitants shall see cause to Elect or Chuse others in their roome in which cases and upon the death of any of the sayd wardens the Inhabitants shall make a new Election and choice of others.

And Mr. Haward, Deacon Wiswall, Mr. Atherton are elected to bee the first wardens or overseers.

Secondly, the said Wardens shall have full power to dispose of the Schoole stock. . . .

Thirdly, the sayd Wardens shall take care, and doe there utmost and best endeavor that the sayd Schoole may from tyme to tyme bee supplied with an able and sufficient Schoolemaster who nevertheless is not to be admitted into the place of Schoolemaster without the Generall consent of the Inhabitants or the major parte of them. . . .

Fivethly, the sayd wardens shall from tyme to tyme see that the Schoole howse bee kept in good, and sufficient repayre, the Charge of which reparacion shalbe defrayed and payd out of such rents, Issues and profitts of the Schoole stock, if there be sufficient, or else of such rents as shall arise and grow in time of the vacancy of the Schoolemaster —

if there bee any such and in defect of such vacancy the wardens shall repayre to the 7 men of the Towne for the tyme beeing who shall have power to taxe the Towne with such somme, or sommes as shalbe requisite for the repayring of the Schoole howse as aforesayd.

Sixthly, the sayd Wardens shall take Care that every yeere at or before the end of the 9th moneth their bee brought to the Schoolehowse 12 sufficient Cart, or wayne loads of wood for fewell, to be for the use of the Schoole master and the Schollers in winter the Cost and Chargs of which sayd wood to bee borne by the Schollers for the tyme beeing who shalbe taxed for the purpose at the discretion of the sayd Wardens.

Lastly, the sayd Wardens shall take care that the Schoolemaster for the tyme beeing doe faythfully performe his dutye in his place, as schoolmasters ought to doe, as well in other things as in these in which are hereafter expressed, viz.

First, that the Schoolemaster shall diligently attend his Schoole and doe his utmost indeavor for Benefitting his *Schollers* according to his best discretion without unnecessaryly absenting himself to the prejudice of his schollers, and hindering there learning.

2ly, that from the beginning of the first moneth [March] untill the end of the 7th he shall every day begin to teach at seaven of the Clock in the morning and dismisse his schollers at fyve in the afternoone. And for the other five moneths that is from the beginning of the 8th moneth untill the end of the 12th moneth he shall every day begin at 8th of the Clock in the morning and [end] at 4 in the afternoone.

3ly, every day in the yeare the usual tyme of dismissing at noone shall be at 11 and to beginn agayne at one except that

4ly, every second day in the weeke he shall call his schollers togeither betweene 12 and one of the Clock to examin them what they have learned on the saboath day preceding at which tyme also he shall take notice of any misdemeanor or disorder that any of his skollers shall have Committed on the saboath to the end that at somme convenient tyme due Admonition and Correction may bee admistred by him according as the nature, and qualitie of the offence shall require at which sayd examination any of the elders or other Inhabitants that please may bee present to behold his religious care herein and to give there Countenance, and approbation of the same.

5ly, hee shall equally and impartially receive and instruct such as shalbe sent and Comitted to him for that end whither their parents bee poore or rich not refusing any who have Right and Interest in the Schoole.

6ly, such as shalbe Comitted to him he shall diligently instruct as they shalbe able to learne both in humane learning, and good literature and likewise in poynt of good manners, and dutifull behaviour towards all specially their superiors as they shall have ocasion to bee in their presence whether by meeting them in the streete or otherwise.

7ly, every 6 day of the weeke at 2 of the Clock in the afternoone hee shall Chatechise his schollers in the principles of Christian religion either in somme Chatechism which the Wardens shall provide and present, or in defect thereof in some other.

8ly, And because all mans indeavors without the blessing of God must needs bee fruitlesse and unsucessfull theirfore It is to be a cheif part of the schoolemasters religious care to Commend his schollers and his labours amongst them unto God by prayer, morning and evening, taking Care that his schollers doe reverendly attend during the same.

9ly, And because the Rodd of Correction is an ordinance of God necessary sometymes to bee dispenced unto Children but such as may easily be abused by overmuch severity and rigour on the one hand, or by overmuch indulgence and lenitye on the other. It is therefore ordered and agreed that the schoolemaster for the tyme beeing shall have full power to minister Correction to all or any of his schollers without respect of persons according as the nature and qualitie of the offence shall require, whereto all his schollers must bee duely subject and no parent or other of the Inhabitants shall hinder or goe about to hinder the master therein. Neverthelesse if any parent or others shall think their is just cause of Complaynt agaynst the master for to much severity, such shall have liberty freindly and lovingly to expostulate with the master about the same, and if they shall not attayne to satisfaction the matter is then to bee referred to the wardens who shall impartially judge betwixt the master and such Complaynants. And if it shall appeare to them that any parent shall make causelesse Complaynts agaynst the master in this behalf and shall persist and Continue so doeing in such case the wardens shall have power to discharge the master of the care and Charge of the Children of such parents. . . .

And because it is difficult if not Impossible to give particular rules that shall reach all cases which may fall out, therefore for a Conclusion It is ordered, and agreed, in Generall, that where particular rules are wanting there It shalbe a parte of the office and dutye of the Wardens to order and dispose of all things that Concerne the schoole, in such sort as in their wisedom and discretion they shall Judge most Conducible for the glory of God, and the trayning up of the Children of the Towne in religion, learning and Civilitie, and these orders to be Continued till the major parte of the Towne shall see cause to alter any parte thereof.[1]

82. Colonial School Laws

a. Compulsory Education, 1642

Records of the Governor and Company of Massachusetts Bay, II, 6-7.

[A General Court, May, 1642.][2]

This Court, taking into consideration the great neglect of

---

[1] Cf. also some of the entries in the extracts from the *Watertown Records*, No. 83, below.

[2] The heading is missing (by mutilation) from the *Records*.

many parents and masters in training up their children in learning and Labor and other impl[o]yments which may be proffitable to the common wealth, do hereupon order and decree, that in every towne the chosen men appointed for managing the prudentiall affayers of the same shall henceforth stand charged with the care of the redresse of this evill (so as they shalbee sufficiently punished by fines for the neglect thereof, upon presentment of the grand jury or other information or complaint in any Court . . .) And for this end they . . . shall have power to take account from time to time of all parents and masters, and of their children, concerning their calling and impl[o]yment of their children, especially of their ability to read and understand the principles of religion and the capitall lawes of this country, and to impose fines upon such as shall refuse to render such accounts to them . . . and they shall have power, with consent of any Court . . . to put forth [as] apprentices the children of such as they shall [find] not to be able and fitt to imploy and bring them up. . . .

[Connecticut copied this law in 1642, and New Haven in 1644. The Connecticut preamble, like the one above, emphasizes the civic motive: "For as much as the good education of children is of singular behoof and benefit to any commonwealth . . . it is therefore ordered," etc. Connecticut, too, was more specific as to the exact penalty for delinquent parents, — providing fines for the first two offenses, but the removal and apprenticing of the children for continued delinquency.

The Massachusetts law closed with a lengthy provision for elementary industrial training, the select men to provide materials and see that "children sett to keep cattle be set to some other imployment withall, as spinning . . . knitting, weaving tape, etc."

Plainly, this law of 1642 *assumed* that each town had a school. The next law (*b* below) expressly *provides* such schools.]

b. *A State System of Schools*
Records of Governor and Company of Massachusetts Bay, II, 203

Att a Sesion of the Generall Court, the 27th of the 8th Month, 1647, at Boston

. . . It being one cheife project of that ould deluder, Satan, to keepe men from the knowledge of the Scriptures, as in former times by keeping them in an unknowne tongue, so in these latter times by persuading from the use of tongues (that so at least the true sence and meaning of the originall might be clouded by false glosses of saint-seming deceivers), — that learning may not be buried in the grave of our fathers in the church and commonwealth, the Lord assisting our endeavors, —

It is therefore ordered . . . that every towneship in this jurisdiction, after the Lord hath increased them to the number of 50 householders, shall then forthwith appoint one within their towne to teach all such children as shall resort to him to write and reade, — whose wages shall be paid either by the parents or masters of such children, or by the inhabitants in generall, by way of supply [tax], as the major part of those that order the prudentialls of the towne shall appoint: provided, those that send their children be not oppressed by paying much more than they can have them taught for in other townes. And it is further ordered, that where any towne shall increase to the number of 100 families or householders, they shall set up a grammer schoole, the mr. thereof being able to instruct youth so farr as they may be fited for the university, provided that if any towne neglect the performance hereof above one yeare, that such towne shall pay 5 pounds to the next schoole, till they shall performe this order.

[The punctuation of this noble sentence has been somewhat classified here by the use of parentheses, dashes, and colons for the commas of the original. On this legislation, cf. *American History and Government*, § 123. The "university" was Harvard, which had been founded in 1636. The greater part of this law was adopted two years later in Connecticut.]

83. Representative Town Records

(Extracts from the *Watertown Records* for the years 1634–1678)

Watertown was the second town to set up town government. (Cf. (1), below, with No. 72, above.) The complete records of these years 1634–1678 would fill 250 pages of this volume. Note the greater illiteracy from about 1650 on, and cf. *American History and Government*, § 122.

(1) August 23, 1634. Agreed by the consent of the Freemen, that there shall be Chosen three persons to be [for] the ordering of the civill affaires in the Towne [One of them to serve as "Towne Clark"]; and [he] shall keep the Records and Acts of the Towne. The three chosen are . . .

(2) —ember 13. Agreed, by the Consent of the Freemen that Robert Seeley and Abram Browne shall measure and lay out all the Lotts that are granted.

Agreed that no man shall fell or cutt down any timber trees upon the Common, without the consent of Robert Seeley and Abram Browne, and otherwise to pay to the Towne for every tree 5s.

(3) January 3, 1635. Agreed that no man being foreigner . . . coming out of England or some other Plantation, shall have liberty to sett downe amongst us, *unless he first have the Consent of the Freemen of the Towne*.

(4) Feb. 21, 1635. Agreed by the freemen that whosoever hath a Lott in a generall Inclosure shall fence it with the rest according to proportion, and if he shall refuse, the Lott shall returne to the Towne againe. . . .

Agreed, that the towne Clark shall have six pense for every Lott of land that he shall Inroll in the towne Booke and bring the Party a note under his hand of the situation of it.[1]

(5) August 22, 1635. Agreed that whosoever being an Inhabitant in the Towne shall receive any person, or family upon

---

[1] This was a fee for a very indefinite description of title: cf. (8), below, and note.

their propriety that may prove chargeable to the Towne shall maintaine the said persons at their owne charges, to save the Towne harmeles.

(6) September 23, 1635. Agreed that (whereas there is a dayly abuse in felling of Timber upon the Common) whosoever shall offend in felling any Trees without leave, shall pay for every Tree cut downe without order, 20 shillings to the use of the Towne.

(7) November 14, 1635. . . . Agreed that John Warrin and Abram Browne shall lay out all the Highwaies, and to see that they be sufficiently repaired.

(8) — ember 30. 1635. Agreed by the Consent of the Freemen that these 11 freemen shall order all the Civill Affaires for the Towne for this yeare following, and to divide the Lands.[1] . . .

---

[1] The descriptions of such divisions of lands were exceeding vague, — illustrated by the following entry from the *Records* of the Town of Plymouth, — rather clearer than the average, but selected here because of its brevity: —
"Ordered to be Recorded pr. Thomas Southworth:
haveing order att a Townemeeting held the second day of January 1666 for the bounding of ten acrees of land graunted to Benjamine Eaton lying above the lands that was formerly George Clarkes and betwixt ffrancis Billingtons lott and the lotts that were John Cookes; have layed it out on the westward side of the swamp called Bradfords Marsh and on the south side and east end of the said land have bounded it with a swamp wood tree standing att or in the swamp: from thence the line extends nearest southwest and by west to a Red oake tree marked and standing on the westward side of the Topp of a hill; and on the north side and east end next to the swamp with a young walnutt sapling, and from the said walnut the line extends nearest southwest and by west unto a forked Red oake sapling; bounded Aprill 11th 1667 pr Will: Crow."

The following entry of a "deed" from the *Early Records of the Town of Providence* illustrates the worst cases of land titles: —

"Be it knowne unto all men by these presences that I, wissawyamake, an Ingen about the age of 23 yeares ould, now dwilling at Sekescute ner providinc, have barganed and sould unto thomas Clemenes of providinc one medow Containing about 8 Akers mor or lese, a broke at each End and a hille on the weaste sid of it and wenasbetuckit river on the other sid of it and have sould unto him the free use of the river allso, to which bargen I the sayd Ingen do hearby bine me my hayrs Exctors adminstratrs and asignes to parfforme the bargon unto Thomas Clemenes his hayrs and asignes and I the aforesaid Ingen doe here. by bind me my silfe my hayrs Exctors adminstratrs and asigns uppon the ffortner of our silves forfite unto thomas

(9) [1636] January 29. Ordered, that there shalbe 8 dayes appointed every yeare for the repayring of the Highwaies and every man that is Souldier or watchman to come at his appointed time with a wheelbarrow, mattock, spade or shovle, and for default hereof to pay for every day 5 shillings to the Towne, and a Cart for every day to pay 19 shillings.

(10) April 23, 1638. Ordered that those Freemen of the Congregation shall build and dwell upon their Lotts at the Towne plott, and not to alienate them by selling or exchanging them to any forrainer, but to Freemen of the Congregation, It being our reall intent to sitt down there close togither, and therefore these Lotts were granted to those Freemen that inhabited most remote from the meeting-house and dwell most scattered, . . .

(11) 1639. D. 31, (Mo. 10.)[1] Ordered that if any of the Freemen be absent from any Publick Towne meeting at the time appointed sufficient warning being formerly given, he shall forfett for every time to the Towne 2 shillings, 6 d.

Ordered by the Freemen that the men deputed for to order the Civill affaires shall not make any order without consent of 7 of those Freemen chosen.

(12) D. 21, (M. 2.) 1640. Ordered that if any Person shall suffer his Dog to come to the Meeting upon the Lords day he shall forfett for every time 1 s.

(13) *D. 29, (M. 10.) 1640. Ordered that all those Inhabitants that have beene by Common Consent or vote taken in amongst us, or have had Dividents granted to them shalbe accepted for Townesmen, and no others.*

(14) D. 21, (M. 7.) 1641. Ordered that George Munnings

Clemenes and to his hayrs Exstors adminstrators and asignes if I the sayd Ingen be not the right honer of the above sayd midowe and do herby warante to thomis Clemenes the fall of it agaynst all Engens and men what ever under witten this 9th day of January 1654 in the presents of Joshua ffoot"
" the mark X of
" the marke H of henry   wissowyamake "
  ffowler "

[1] Tenth month (December), thirty-first day.

is appointed to looke to the Meetinghouse, and to be free from Rates [in return for service].

(15) D. 5, (M. 5.) 1642. Ordered that Hugh Mason, Thomas Hastings, and John Shearman are appointed to set up a sufficient fence about the Burying Place with a 5-foot pale and 2 railes well nailed by the 15 of the 2 moneth, and the Towne to pay them for it.

(16) D. 6, (M. 5) 1642. Ordered that there shalbe a new Invoice taken of Mens Estates to make the *Rates*[1] by for this yeare. Also that all Lands granted by the Towne shalbe rated this yeare.

Ordered that Land broken up shall pay the Acre,	2 *lb*	10s	
Land inclosed not broken up the Acre,		10s	
The further Plaine shall pay upon the Acre,		5s	
The dividents, the remote meddows and the hither Plaine,		10s	
The land in lieu of the Towne Plott the Acre,		1s	
The Farmes shall pay upon the Acre,			6d
The home meddows shall pay the Acre,	1 *lb*	10s	
Ordered that Mares, Steeres, and Cowes are rated at	5 *lb*		
Heifers, 2 year old, at	3 *lb*		
Calves, 1 year old, at	1 *lb*	10s	
Calves, under a year, at	1 *lb*		
Goats, at		10s	
Sheep, at	2 *lb*		
Hogs, a year old, at	1 *lb*		
Pigs, 3 months old, at		6s	8d
Colts, at		17s	6d
Lambs, at		5s	
Kids, at		2s	8d

(17) D. 20, (M. 10) 1642. Ordered that there shalbe a Rate made of 100 lb for to discharge these Debts following:

Imprimis to Thomas Hastings for charges to the Poore and building the house for John Kettle	17 *lb*

---

[1] This English term for *local* taxes was used in the early colonies.

Item, to John Simson		10s
Item, for fencing the Burying place	6 lb	10s
Item, formerly due to the Officers	30 lb	
Item, for the Capitall Laws		10s
Item, for the Court Orders, 3 M 1642		11s 3d
Item, to John Knolls pastor for 1 quarter	10 lb	
Item, to George Phillips pastor for half yeare due Jan. 1	33 lb	6s 8d

(18) D. 15, (M. 6.) 1643. Ordered that John Shearman shall keepe weights and measures according to the Order of the Court for the Townes use and also to take up lost goods.

(19) [Nov. 15, 1647]. Lieu. Mason complayninge that he was burdened with the service of the Towne; the Towne did Release him: and chose Isaac Steearnes in his steade, to be one of the Seaven men.

(20) At A Generall Towne Meeting, the 17 (7) 1649.
Granted to the Ministry — 160 pounds — for this present year beginning the 24th of June last: to be gathered by Rate, and to be paied the one halfe the first weeke of December next, and the other halfe the first of march Following

agreed that there shall be a Rate of 90 pounds made for to pay Robert Saltonstall: and to Build a Schoole-house: and to Build a gallery in the Meetinghouse and to pay other debts the Towne oweth. . . .

John Sherman is apointed to procuere the Schoole house Built: and to have it built 22 foot long and 14 foot wide and 9 foot betwene Joynts — also to git a penn of one aker of ground fenced in with 4 Railes for the lodging a heard in the woods: and to procuer a small house for lodging the heardsman: and to be done in such a place as Deacon Child and himself shall thinke best, towards Sudbury Bounds

(21) the 7d. — 10 mo 1649 . . .
agreed that John Sherman Shall wright a letter, in the Townes name, unto David Mechell of Stamfourth to Certify to him the Townes desier of him to Come and keepe School in the towne

(22) At a Meeteing of the Select men at Sargeng [Seargent] Beeres the 10 December 1652.

Agreed by the towne, with the Consent of John Sherman that Willyam Barsham shall prise all the Carpenters worke aboute the scoolehouse and the Towne shall make payment akcording to his award.

Memorandum   There is 22 pounds towards it payd alredy.

(23) December 22, 1652 . . .

Mr. Norcros is to keepe ascoole upon the same pay and the same building as he had the last yeeare.

James Cuttler and John Traine are Chosen Survayers for high wayes for this yeare.

(24) At a Meeteing of the Select men the 8 (9) 1653. . . .

Ordered that the Cunstable Thomas underwood shall reserve in his hand of the Towne Rate 13 bushells of Indian Corne and 3 booshells of peaze for Thomas philpot and Deliver him every weeke one peck of Corne and every month one peck of peaze.

John Sherman did present a plot of the great dividents the 22/9/1653

[These commodities had been paid into the town treasury (as taxes), and were to be reserved by the "treasurer" (then, the Constable) for this case of "poor relief." Wages and salaries also were commonly paid in commodities (at legal rates) in New England. Thus, —

Att a Townemeeting held att the meeting house att *Plymouth* the * day of July 1667 ; It was agreed and concluded as followeth, viz :

"That the sume of fifty pounds shalbee alowed to Mr. Colton [the minister] for this present yeare and his wood To be raised by way of Rate to be payed in such as god gives, *ever onely to be minded that a considerable parte of it shalbee payed in the best pay ;* and William Clarke and William Crow are appointed by the Towne to take notice of what is payed and brought in unto him and to keep an account therof.   Joseph howland and ffrancis Combe are agreed with by the Towne to find the wood for this yeare for the sume of eight pounds."

The difficulty was to get "good pay." It is recorded in the accounts of Harvard that one student, afterward president of the college, paid his tuition with "an old cow," which, good or bad, had to be accepted at a fixed rate for coins.]

At aMeeting of the Select men
the 13 / 10 / 1653

(25) Samuel Banjamine was presented before us for Idelnes

By Mr. Norcros which Did two evidently apeare by his ragged Clothes and Divers Debts apearing, but upon his promise of amendment hee was released unto the next yeare.

(26) At apublick Towne meeting the 14 (8) 1654

Ordered by the Inhabetance that there should be anew meeting house builded

Ordered that the place where it shall stand shall be in som Convenient place betwene Sargant Brits ende fence and John Bisko his rayles.

Ordered that there shall be raysed by rate upon the inhabetance one hundred and fifty pounds this yeare for to begin the work withall

Ordered that Cambridg meeting house shall be our pattern in all poynts

Ordered the Select men shall have power to agree with John Sherman or any other person to performe tha foresaid work.

Ordered that the speaces [specie] in which workmen that Doe undertake it shall be payed in shall bee one 3d parte wheate, and the rest in rye, pease, Indecorne, and Cattell.

The Select men with the help of willyam Barsham have agreed with John Sherman to Build ameeting house Like unto Cambridg in all poynts, the Cornish and fane Excepted, and to have it finished by the Last of September in 1656; and hee is to receive of the Towne 400 pounds with the Seates of the old meeting house; which some [sum] is to be payd at 3 several payments, as by artickls of Agreement under hand and seale Dooth appeare more fully.

(27) Att a meeting of the 7 men Nov. 19. (56)

These are to Shew, that Elizabeth Braibrok widow of Watertowne in the County of Middlesex, hath putt her daughter (with the approbation of the select men) into the hands of Simont Tomson and his wife of Ipswich in the County of Essex, rope maker, to be as an apprentice, untill she come to the age of eighteene yeares, in which time the said Sarah is to serve them in all lawfull comands, and the said Simont is to teach her to reade the Englishe Tongue and to instruct her in the

knowleg of god and his wayes, and to provide for the said
Sarah, holesome meate and drink, with convenient cloathing as
the seasons doe require and he the said Simont doth ingage
himselfe and wife, to give the said Sarah at the end of her
tearme, a good cow, and an ewe sheep with convenient Cloathing, and if the said Sarah dye within one yeare before her age
pfixed, that then the said cow and sheep, shall goe to some of
the children of the said Elizabeth Brabrok.

This agreement was signed and confirmed by there markes
of each partie and witnessed as appears in two severall wright-
ings by Joshua Edmonds
and in presence of the seaven men
or the greatest part of them.
Ephraim Child in the behalfe of the rest.

(28) At a meeting of the select men at Isaak Sternes his House
January the 18th 1669

It was agreed that the select men shall take their turnes
every man his Day to site upon the gallary to looke to the
youths that they may prevent miscarigis in the time of publike
exercises on the Lords Days and also that the two Constables
shalbe desired to take their turnes to site ther also.

(29) At a meeting at Leift Beeri's march 3d 1670.

Ther comeing a complainte to us the selectmen concerneing
the poverty of Edward Sandersons famelley: that they had
not wherwith to mainetaine themselves and childeren either with
suply of provision or emplyment to earne any and considering
that it would be the charge of the towne to provide for the
wholl fameley which will be hard to doe this yeer: and not
knoweing how to suply them with provision: we considereing
if we shoulde suply them and could doe it, yet it would not
tend to the good of the children for their good eaducation and
bringeing up soe as they may be usefull in the common weall
or them selves to live comfortablly and usefuly in time to come,
We have therfore a greed to put out two of his childeren in to
sume honist famelleys wher they may be eaducated and brought
up in the knowlidge of God and sum honist calling or

labor. And therfor we doe order that Thomas Fleg and John Bigulah shall have power to binde them prentises with sume honist people with the consent of their perants if it may be hade, and if the perants shall oppose them, to use the helpe of the Magistrate: in the name and with the consent of the select men, Thomas Hastings.

(30) A ametting of the selectmen at Corparall bonds the 27th of march 1677

* * * * * * *

Agreed with leftenant shearmon to ceep an inglish scoole this year and to begin the (9th) of eaprill at the scoole house and the town to alow him twenty pounds in the town Reat that shall be raized in this yeare (77) and if the said leftenant dezireth to lay down his imployment at the years end then he shall give the town a quartur of a years warning, and if the town dezyreth to chang ther scoole master thay shall give the like warning. The select men agree allsoo that the said scoole shall be cept from the furst of may to the last of august, 8 owers in the day, to witt, to begin at seven in the morning, and not to break up untill five at night, noone time acsepted; and from the last of august untill the last of octobur 6 ouers in the day, soo allsoo in the munths of march and Eaprill and the 4 winttur munths to begin at tenn of the clock in the morning and continnue untill 2 a clock in the afternoone.

(31) At ametting of the select men at the house of gregory coock: this (7th) of Janiwary 1678:

The select men sent anoote to leftenant Shearmon and allso anoote to Mr goddard to signify to them thay had agreed with another man to ceep the scoole when thear year was oute, and that thay did thearby give them aquartur of a years warning according to the ordur upon the town Booke.

The select men agreed with mr Richard Norcros to ceep the Scoole at the Scoole house for the year foloing and to begin the 9th of Eaprill 1679, and to teach both Lattin and inglish Scollurs, so many as shall Be sent unto him from the in habitants once aweck to teach them thear catticise : only in the munths of may, June, July and august he is to teach only lattin scollurs and writturs and them at his owne house and thear to afford them all needfull help, and the other 8 munths at the scoolehouse both lattin and inglish scollurs, for which the select men agree that he shall have twenty pounds out of the town Reat to be mead for the yeare 1679, and the town at the Jenarall town metting to meak thear anuall Choyse for time to cum : this agreement Consented unto by Mr Richard norcros as witnis his hand. . . .

XIV. MASSACHUSETTS AND PERSECUTION

As long as she was permitted to do so, Massachusetts secured religious uniformity by expelling or persecuting intruders who dissented from the established order. This was the practice and theory of all states in that day except Holland. Some individuals had advanced further, however, both in England and America (cf. *American History and Government*, § 84, close, for illustrations) ; and religious freedom was the fundamental principle in the Rhode Island " experiment " (No. 90, below).

84. Puritan Arguments for and against Persecution

a. *The Simple Cobbler of Agawam, 1647*

Nathaniel Ward, minister of Ipswich (Agawam), was one of the few of the Massachusetts clergy with democratic leanings. He had been helpful in drafting the democratic *Body of Liberties* (No. 78). But like that other democratic minister, Thomas Hooker (No. 93), Ward was a strict *theocrat*. His *Simple Cobbler of Aggawamm* was published in London in 1647.

. . . FIRST, such as have given or taken any unfriendly reports of us *New-English*, should doe well to recollect themselves. Wee have beene reputed a Colluvies of wild Opinionists, swarmed into a remote wildernes to find elbow-roome for our phanatick Doctrines and practises: I trust our diligence past, and constant sedulity against such persons and courses, will plead better things for us. I dare take upon me, to bee the Herauld of *New-England* so farre, as to proclaime to the world, in the name of our Colony, that all Familists, Antinomians, Anabaptists, and other Enthusiasts *shall have free Liberty to keepe away from us*, and such as will come to be gone as fast as they can, the sooner the better.

Secondly, I dare averre, that God doth no where in his word tolerate Christian States to give Tolerations to such adversaries of his Truth, if they have power in their hands to suppresse them. . . .

Not to tolerate things meerly indifferent to weak consciences, argues a conscience too strong: pressed uniformity in these, causes much disunity: *To tolerate more then indifferents, is not to deale indifferently with God*: He that doth it, takes his Scepter out of his hand, and bids him stand by. . . .

Concerning Tolerations I may further assert.

That Persecution of true Religion, and Toleration of false, are the *Jannes* and *Jambres* to the Kingdome of Christ, *whereof the last is farre the worst.* . . .

Frederick Duke of *Saxon,* spake not one foote beyond the mark when he said. He had rather the Earth should swallow him up quick, then he should give a toleration to any opinion against any truth of God.

He that is willing to tolerate any Religion, or discrepant way of Religion, besides his own, unless it be in matters meerly indifferent, either doubts of his own, or is not sincere in it.

He that is willing to tolerate any unsound Opinion, that his own may also be tolerated, though never so sound, will for a need hang Gods Bible at the Devills girdle.

Every Toleration of false Religions or Opinions hath as many Errours and sins in it as all the false Religions and Opinions it tolerats, and one sound one more.

That State that will give Liberty of Conscience in matters of Religion, must give Liberty of Conscience and Conversation in their Morall Laws, or else the Fiddle will be out of tune, and some of the strings crack.

Experience will teach Churches and Christians, that *it is farre better to live in a State united, though a little Corrupt, then in a State, whereof some Part is incorrupt, and all the rest divided.* . . . There is talk of an universall Toleration. I would talke as loud as I could against it, did I know what more apt and reasonable Sacrifice *England* could offer to God for his late performing all his heavenly Truths then an universall Toleration *of all hellish Errors,* or how they shall make an universall

Reformation, but by making *Christs Academy* the *Divills University*, where any man may commence [graduate] Heretique *per saltum;* where he that is *filius Diabolicus*, or *simpliciter pessimus*, may have his grace to goe to Hell *cum Publico Privilegio;* and carry as many after him, as he can. . . .

It is said, Though a man have light enough himselfe to see the Truth, yet if he hath not enough to enlighten others, he is bound to tolerate them, I will engage my self, that all the Devills in *Britanie* shall sell themselves to their shirts, to purchase a Lease of this Position for three of their Lives, under the Seale of the Parliament.

It is said, That Men ought to have Liberty of their Conscience, and that it is persecution to debarre them of it: I can rather stand amazed then reply to this: it is an astonishment to think that the braines of men should be parboyl'd in such impious ignorance; Let all the wits under the Heavens lay their heads together and finde an Assertion worse then this (one excepted) I will petition to be chosen the universall Ideot of the world. . . .

The true English of all this their false Latine is nothing but *a generall Toleration of all Opinions.* . . .

b. *From the Wonder-working Providence of Sions Saviour in New England (Book III, Chapter V)*

This quaint history was printed in London in 1654, anonymously. The original manuscript has never been discovered. Tradition ascribes the authorship to Captain Edward Johnson, one of the companions of Winthrop in the migration of 1630.

. . . and in the year 1648 they [the laws] were printed, and now are to be seen of all men, to the end that none may plead ignorance, and that all who intend to transport themselves hither, may know this is no place of licentious liberty, nor will this people suffer any to trample down this Vineyard of the Lord, but with diligent execution will cut off from the city of the Lord the wicked doers, and if any man can shew wherein any of them derogate from the Word of God, very willingly will they accept thereof, and amend their imperfections (the Lord assisting) but let not any ill-affected persons find fault with them, because they suit not with their own humour, or because they meddle with matters of Religion, for it is no wrong to any man, that a people who have spent their estates, many of them, and ventured their lives for to keep faith and a pure conscience, to use all means that the Word of God allows for maintenance and continuance of the same, especially [when] they have taken up a desolate Wilderness to be their habitation, and not deluded any by keeping their profession in huggermug, but print and proclaim to all the way and course they intend, God willing, to walk in; [and] if any will yet notwithstanding seek to justle them out of their own right, let them not wonder if they meet with all the opposition a people put to their greatest straits can make; . . . but . . . it seems unreasonable, and savours too much of hypocricie, that any people should pray unto the Lord for the speedy accomplishment of his Word in the overthrow of Antichrist, and in the mean time become a Patron to sinful opinions and damnable errors that oppose the truths of Christ. . . .

c. *Discussion between Saltonstall and Cotton* (*about 1650*)

Hutchinson's *Collection of Original Papers* (1769), 401–406.

Saltonstall was the chief founder of Watertown, and one of the signers of the Cambridge Agreement (No. 58 *b*). Like his town, he was inclined to democracy in politics and to " Separation " in religion. This letter to the Boston pastors was written from England (to which he had returned in 1631) about 1650. Both letters are without dates.

(1) *Sir Richard Saltonstall to Mr. Cotton and Mr. Wilson*

Reverend and deare friends, whom I unfaynedly love and respect:

It doth not a little grieve my spirit to heare what sadd things are reported dayly of your tyranny and presecutions in New-England, — *as that you fyne, whip, and imprison men for their consciences.* First, you compell such to come into your assemblyes as you know will not joyne with you in your worship, and when they shew their dislike thereof or witnes against it, then you styrre up your magistrates to punish them for such (as you conceyve) their publicke affronts. Truely, friends, this your practice of compelling any in matters of worship to doe that whereof they are not fully persuaded, is to make them sin; for soe the apostle (Rom. 14 and 23.) tells us; and many are made hypocrites thereby, conforming in their outward man for feare of punishment. We pray for you and wish you prosperitie every way, [and] hoped the Lord would have given you so much light and love there that you might have been eyes to God's people here, and not to practice those courses in a wildernes which you went so farre to prevent. These rigid wayes have layed you very lowe in the hearts of the saynts. I doe assure you I have heard them pray in the publique assemblies that the Lord would give you meeke and humble spirits, not to stryve soe much for uniformity as [instead] to keepe the unity of the spirit in the bond of peace.

When I was in Holland about the beginning of our warres, I remember some christians there, that then had serious thoughts of planting in New-England, desired me to write to the governor thereof to know if those that differ from you in opinion, yet houlding the same foundation in religion (as Anabaptists, Seekers, Antinomians, and the like), might be permitted to live among you; to which I received this short answer from your then governour Mr. Dudley; **God forbid** (said he) **our love for the truth should be growne soe could that we should tolerate errours:** and when (for satisfaction of myself and others) I desired to know your grounds, he referred me to the books written here between the Presbyterians and Independents; — which if that had been sufficient, I needed not have sent soe farre to understand the reasons of your practice. I hope you do not assume to yourselves infallibilitie of judgment, when the most learned of the Apostles confesseth he knew but in parte and sawe but darkely as through a glass; for God is light, and no further than he doth illuminate us can we see, be our partes and learning never soe great. Oh that all those who are brethren, though yet they cannot thinke and speake the same things might be of one accord in the Lord. Now the God of patience and consolation grant you to be thus mynded towards one another, after the example of Jesus Christ our blessed Savyor, in whose everlasting armes of protection hee leaves you who will never leave to be

Your truly and much affectionate
friend in the nearest union,

RIC. SALTONSTALL.

For my reverend and worthyly much esteemed friends Mr. Cotton and Mr. Wilson, preachers to the church which is at Boston in New-England, give this.

(2) *Mr. Cotton's Answer to Sir Richard Saltonstall*

. . . You thinke to compel all men in matter of worship is to make men sinne (according to Rom. 14. 23.). If the worship be lawfull in itselfe, the magistrate compelling him to come to it compelleth him not to sinne, *but the sinne is in his will that needs to be compelled to a christian duty.* Josiah compelled all Israel, or (which is all one) made to serve the Lord their God, 2 Chron. 34. 33. yet his act herein was not blamed but recorded amongst his virtuous actions. For a governour to suffer any within his gates to prophane the sabbath, is a sinne against the 4th commandment, both in the private householder and in the magistrate; and if he requires them to present themselves before the Lord, the magistrate sinneth not, nor doth the subject sinne so great a sinne as if he did refraine to come. . . .

But (say you) it doth but make men hypocrites to compel men to conforme the outward man for feare of punishment. If it did so, yet better to be hypocrites than prophane persons. Hypocrites give God part of his due, the outward man, but the prophane person giveth God neither outward nor inward man. . . .

What you wrote out of Holland to our then governor Mr.

Dudley, in behalfe of Anabaptists, Antinomians, Seekers, and the like, it seemeth, mett with a short answer from him, but zealous; for zeal will not beare such mixtures as coldnesse or lukewarmenesse will, Revel. 2. 2. 14. 15. 20.

85. Criticism by a Moderate Episcopalian and Monarchist

Lechford's "Plaine Dealing" (1641), reprinted in *Massachusetts Historical Society Collections*, Third Series, III, 55 ff.

Thomas Lechford was in New England from 1637 to 1641. His point of view is not seriously unfriendly.

... And I doe not this, God knoweth, as delighting to lay open the infirmities of these well-affected men, many of them my friends, — but that it is necessary, at this time, for the whole Church of God, and themselves, as I take it. Besides, many of the things are not infirmities, but such as I am bound to protest against; yet I acknowledge there are some wise men among them who would help to mend things, if they were able. ... And I think that wiser men then they, going into a wildernesse to set up another strange government differing from the settled government here, might have falne into greater errors then they have done.

* * * * * * *

[After describing the method of organizing a church.] And the generall Court will not allow of any Church otherwise gathered.

Some Ministers have there heretofore, as I have heard, disclaimed the power of their Ministry, received in England, but others among them have not. Generally, for the most part, they hold the Pastors and Teachers offices to be distinct; the Teacher to minister a word of knowledg, the Pastor a word of wisdome, but some hold them all one; as in the Church of Watertowne, there are two Pastors, neither will that Church send any messengers to any other Church-gathering or ordination.[1]

---

[1] The Watertown church had strong Separatist tendencies (cf. No. 64). Hence, in part, its democratic inclination.

... Now *the most of the persons* at New-England are not admitted of their Church, and therefore are not Freemen, and when they come to be tryed there, be it for life or limb, name or estate, or whatsoever, they must bee tryed and judged too by those of the Church, who are in a sort their adversaries: how equall that hath been or may be, some by experience doe know, others may judge.

Profane swearing, drunkennesse, and beggers, are but rare in the compasse of this Patent, through the circumspection of the Magistrates, and the providence of God hitherto, the poore there living by their labours and great wages, proportionably, better then the rich by their stocks, which without exceeding great care, quickly waste. . . .

But the people begin to complain [that] they are ruled like *slaves*, and in short time shall have their children for the most part remain unbaptized: and so have little more privilege than Heathens, unlesse the discipline be amended. . . .

When I was to come away, one of the chiefest in the Country wished me to deliver him a note of what things I misliked in the Country, which I did, thus :

I doubt,

1. Whether so much time should be spent in the publique Ordinances, on the Sabbath day, because that thereby some necessary duties of the Sabbath must be needs be hindered, as visitation of the sick, and poore, and family.

2. Whether matters of offence should be publiquely handled, either before the whole Church, or strangers.

3. Whether so much time should be spent in particular catechizing those that are admitted to the communion of the Church, either men or women; or that they should make long speeches; or when they come publiquely to be admitted, any should speak contradictorily, or in recommendation of any, unlesse before the Elders, upon just occasion.

4. Whether the censures of the Church should be ordered, in publique, before all the Church, or strangers, other then the denunciation of the censures, and pronunciation of the solutions.

5. Whether any of our Nation, that is not extremely ignorant or scandalous, should bee kept from the Communion, or his children from Baptisme . . .

10. That the civill government is not so equally administered, nor can be, divers orders or bylaws considered.

11. That unlesse these things be wisely and in time prevented, many of your usefullest men will remove and scatter from you.

Certain Quaeres about Church government, planting Churches, and some other Experiments.

* * * * * * *

32. Whether or no to maintain a desired purity or perfection in the Magistracie, by election of the people, these good men of New-England, are not forced to be too strict in receiving the brethren, and to run a course tending to heathenisme?

33. Whether have not *popular elections* of chiefe Magistrates beene, and are they not, very dangerous to States and Kingdomes? Are there not some great mysteries of State and government? Is it possible, convenient, or necessary, for all men to attain to the knowledge of those mysteries, or to have the like measure of knowledge, faith, mercifulnesse, wisdome, courage, magnanimity, patience? Whence are Kings denominated, but from their skill and knowledge to rule? whereto they are even born and educated, and by long experience, and faithfull Counsellors enabled, and the grace and blessing of God upon all? Doe not the wise, good, ancient, and renowned Laws of England attribute much, yea, very much trust and confidence to the King, as to the head and supreame Governour, though much be also in the rest of the great body, heart and hands, and feete, to counsell, maintain, and preserve the whole, but especially the Head?

34. Hence what government for an Englishman but an hereditary, successive, King, the son of Nobles, well counselled and assisted?

* * * * * * *

I thank God, now I understand by experience, that there is no such government for Englishmen, or any Nation, as a Monarchy; nor for Christians, as by a lawfull Ministrie, under godly Diocesan Bishops. . . .

86. A Presbyterian Demand for the Franchise, 1646

Hutchinson's *Collection of Original Papers* (1769), 188–194. Less than half the document is given here.

To the worshipful the Governor, the Deputy Governor, and the rest of the Assistants of the Massachusets Bay in New England, together with the Deputyes of the Generall Court now assembled at Boston.

The Remonstrance and humble Petition of us whose names are underwritten, in behalfe of ourselves and divers others within this jurisdiction, humbly sheweth.

THAT we cannot but with all thankfulness acknowledge your indefategable paines, continuall care, and constant vigilancy, which, by the blessing of the Almighty, hath procured unto this wilderness the much desired fruits of peace and plenty . . . And further, that you whom the Lord hath placed at the helm . . . are best able to foresee the clouds which hang over our heads . . . *Notwithstanding, those who are under decks . . . may perceive those leaks which will inevitably sink this weake and ill compacted vessell,* if not by your wisdoms prevented . . . Not to trouble you . . . with many words, we shall briefly referre them to their heads . . .

1. Whereas this place hath been planted by the incouragement, next under God, of letters patents given and granted by his Majesty of England to the inhabitants thereof, with many privileges and immunities, viz., . . . Notwithstanding, we cannot, according to our judgments, discerne a setled forme of government according to the lawes of England, which may seeme strange to our countrymen, yea to the whole world, especially considering we are English. Neither do we understand and perceyve our owne lawes or libertyes, or any body of

lawes here so established, as that thereby there may be a sure and comfortable enjoyment of our lives, libertyes, and estates, according to our due and naturall rights, as free borne subjects of the English nation. By which, many inconveniences flow into plantations, Viz. jealousies of introducing arbitrary government, which manny are prone to beleeve, construing the procrastination of such setled lawes to proceed from an overgreedy spirit of arbitrary power (which it may be is their weaknes) such proceedings being detestable to our English nation, and to all good men, and at present the chief cause of the intestine warre in our deare country.[1] Further, it gives cause to many to thinke themselves hardly dealt with, others too much favored, and the scale of justice too much bowed and unequally balanced. From whence also proceedeth feares and jealousies of illegall committments, unjust imprisonments, taxes, rates, customes, levyes of ungrounded and undoing assessments, unjustifiable presses, undue fynes, unmeasurable expences and charges, of unconceyvable dangers through a negative or destructive vote unduly placed, and not well regulated, — in a word, of a non-certainty of all things we enjoy, whether lives, liberties, or estate; and also of undue oaths, being subject to exposition, according to the will of him or them that gives them, and not according to a due and unbowed rule of law . . .

Wherefore our humble desire and request is, that you would be pleased to consider of our present condition and upon what foundation we stand, and unanimously concurr to establish the fundamentall and wholesome lawes of our native country, and such others as are no wayes repugnant to them, unto which all of us are most accustomed; and we suppose them best agreeable to our English tempers, and yourselves obliged thereunto by the generall charter and your oathes of allegiance. . . .

2. *Whereas there are many thousands in these plantations, of the English nation, freeborne, quiett and peaceable men, righteous in their dealings, forward with hand, heart and purse, to advance the publick good, knowne friends to the honorable and victorious*

---

[1] The Civil War in England between King and Parliament.

Houses of Parliament, lovers of their nation, etc. who are debarred from all civill imployments (without any just cause that we know) not being permitted to bear the least office (though it cannot be denied but some are well qualifyed) no not so much as to have any vote in choosing magistrates, captains or other civill and military officers; notwithstanding they have here expended their youth, borne the burthen of the day, wasted much of their estates for the subsistence of these poore plantations, paid all assessments, taxes, rates, at least equall, if not exceeding others, yea when the late warre was denounced against the Narrowganset Indians, without their consent, their goods were seized on for the service, themselves and servants especially forced and impressed to serve in that warre, to the hazarding of all things most dear and near unto them, whence issue forth many great inconveniences, secret discontents, murmurings, rents in the plantations, discouragements in their callings, unsettlednes in their minds, strife, contention, and the Lord only knows to what a flame in time it may kindle; also jealousies of too much unwarranted power and dominion on the one side, and of perpetual slavry and bondage on the other, and, which is intollerable, even by those who ought to love and respect them as brethren.

We therefore desire that civill liberty and freedom be forthwith granted to all truely English, equall to the rest of their countrymen, as in all plantations is accustomed to be done, and as all freeborne enjoy in our native country (we hoping here in some things to enjoy greater liberties than elsewhere, counting it no small losse of liberty to be as it were banished from our native home, and enforced to lay our bones in a strange wildernes) without imposing any oathes or covenant on them, . . . Further, that none of the English nation, who at this time are too forward to be gone, and very backward to come hither, be banished, unles they break the known lawes of England in so high a measure, as to deserve so high a punishment; and that those few that come over may settle here without having two magistrates hands, which sometimes not being possible to obtain, hath procured a kind of banishment to some, who might have been serviceable to this place, as they have been to the state of England, etc. And we likewise desire that no greater punishments be inflicted upon offenders than are allowed and sett by the laws of our native country.

3. Whereas there are diverse sober, righteous and godly men, eminent for knowledge and other gracious gifts of the holy spirit, no wayes scandalous in their lives and conversation, members of the church of England (in all ages famous for piety and learning) not dissenting from the latest and best reformation of England, Scotland, etc. yet they and their posterity are deteined from the seales of the covenant of free grace, because, as it is supposed, they will not take these churches covenants, for which as yet they see no light in Gods word; neither can they clearly perceive what they are, every church having their covenant differing from anothers, at least in words. . . .

We therefore humbly intreat you, in whose hands it is to help and whose judicious eyes discern these great inconveniences, for the glory of God and the comfort of your brethren and countrymen, to give liberty to the members of the church of England, not scandalous in their lives and conversations (as members of these churches) to be taken into your congregation and to enjoy with you all those liberties and ordinances Christ hath purchased for them. . . . [1]

These things being granted . . . we hope to see the now contemned ordinances of God highly prized . . . To conclude, all businesses in church and commonwealth (which for many years have seemed to go backward . . .) successfully thriving . . .

    Subscribed
Robert Child [2] [and six others].

---

[1] The Church of England at this time was Presbyterian.
[2] In the reply of the General Court, Dr. Child is referred to as "a Paduan Doctor (as he is reputed), lately come into the country, who hath not so much as tasted of their grievances, nor like to doe, being a bachelor and only a sojourner, who never payd a penny to any publick charge, though (of his owne good will) he *hath* done something for publick use."

87. Punishment for not Attending "Approved" Churches, 1666

Thomas Hutchinson's *Collection of Original Papers* (1769), 399-400. Hutchinson adds in a note that the three persons here condemned were Baptists who were trying to set up a church in Boston.

At a county court held at Cambridge, on adjournment, Aprill 17. 1666.

THOMAS GOOLD, Thomas Osburne and John George being presented by the grand jury of this county for absenting themselves from the publick worship of God on the Lords dayes for one whole yeare now past, alledged respectively as followeth, viz.

Thomas Osburne answered, that the reason of his non-attendance was, that the Lord hath discovered unto him from his word and spirit of truth that the society, wherewith he is now in communion, is more agreeable to the will of God: asserted that they were a church and attended the worship of God together, and do judge themselves bound so to do, the ground whereof he said he gave in the general court.

Thomas Goold answered, that as for coming to publique worship they did meet in publique worship according to the rule of Christ, the grounds whereof they had given to the court of assistants: asserted that they were a publique meeting, according to the order of Christ Jesus gathered together.

John George answered, that he did attend the publique meetings on the Lord's dayes where he was a member; asserted that they were a church according to the order of Christ in the gospell, and with them he walked and held communion in the publique worship of God on the Lord's dayes.

Whereas at the general court in October last, and at the court of assistants in September last endeavours were used for their conviction [and that] the order of the generall court declaring the said Goold and company to be no orderly church assembly and that they stand convicted of high presumption against the Lord and his holy appoyntments was openly read to them and is on file with the records of this court: —

The court sentenced the said Thomas Goold, Thomas Osburne, and John George, for their absenting themselves from the publique worship of God on the Lords dayes, to pay foure pounds fine, each of them, to the county order. And whereas by their owne confessions they stand convicted of persisting in their schismaticall assembling themselves together, to the great dishonour of God and our profession of his holy name, contrary to the act of the generall court of October last prohibiting them therein on penalty of imprisonment, this court doth order their giving bond respectively in 20*l*. each of them, for their appearance to answer their contempt at the next court of assistants.

The abovenamed Thomas Goold, John George, and Thomas Osburne made their appeale to the next court of assistants, and refusing to put in security according to law were committed to prison.

88. Quaker Persecutions

a. *Edward Burrough's Appeal to Charles II*

Edward Burrough's *Declaration of the Sad and Great Persecution and Martyrdom of Quakers in New England* (London, 1660), 17–20. All italics in this extract are in the original.

. . . 2. TWELVE Strangers in that Country, but free-born of this Nation, *received twenty three Whippings*, the most of them being with a Whip *of three Cords*, with *Knots at the ends*, and laid on with as much strength as they could be by the Arm of their Executioner, the stripes amounting to *Three hundred and seventy*.

3. Eighteen Inhabitants of the Country, being free-born *English*, received *twenty three Whippings*, the stripes amounting to *two hundred and fifty*.

4. Sixty four Imprisonments of the Lords People, for their obedience to his Will, amounting to *five hundred and nineteen weeks*, much of it being *very cold weather*, and the Inhabitants kept in Prison *in harvest time*, which was very much to their

losse; besides many more Imprisoned, of which time we cannot give a just account.

5. Two beaten with **Pitched Ropes**, the blows amounting to **an hundred thirty nine**, by which one of them was brought near unto death, much of his body being beat **like unto a jelly**, and one of their own Doctors, a Member of their Church, who saw him, said, *It would be a Miracle if ever he recovered, he expecting the flesh should rot off the bones;* who afterwards was banished upon pain of death. There are many Witnesses of this there.

6. Also, an Innocent man, an Inhabitant of *Boston*, they **banished** from his Wife and Children, and put to seek a habitation in the Winter; and in case he returned again, he was to be kept Prisoner during his life: and for returning again, he was put in Prison, and hath been now a Prisoner above a year.

7. Twenty five **Banishments**, upon the penalties of being **whipt**, or having **their Ears cut**; or **branded in the Hand**, if they returned.

8. Fines laid upon the Inhabitants for meeting together, and edifying one another, as the Saints ever did; and **for refusing to swear**, it being contrary to Christ's Command, amounting to **about a Thousand pound**, besides what they have done since, that we have not heard of; many Families, in which there are many Children, are almost ruined, by these unmerciful proceedings.

9. Five kept *Fifteen dayes* (in all) *without food*, and *Fifty eight* dayes shut up close by the Jaylor, and had none that he knew of; and from some of them he stopt up the windows, hindring them from convenient air.

10. One laid **Neck and Heels** in Irons for *sixteen hours*.

11. One **very deeply burnt** in the right hand *with the letter* H. after he had been whipt with above *Thirty stripes*.

12. One chained the most part of Twenty dayes to a Logg of wood in an open Prison in the Winter-time.

13. Five Appeals to *England*, denied at *Boston*.

14. Three **had their right Ears** cut **by the Hangman in the**

Prison, the Door being barred, and not a Friend suffered to be present while it was doing, though some much desired it.

15. One of the Inhabitants of *Salem*, who since is banished upon pain of Death, *had one half of his House and Land seized on while he was in Prison*, a month before he knew of it.

16. At a General Court in *Boston*, they made an Order, That those who had not wherewithal to answer the Fines that were laid upon them (for their Consciences) should be sold for Bond-men, and Bond-women to Barbados, Virginia, or any of the English Plantations.

17. Eighteen of the people of God were at several times banished upon pain of Death, six of them were their own Inhabitants, two of which being very aged people, and well known among their Neighbours to be of honest Conversations, being Banished from their Houses and Families, and put upon Travelling and other hardships, soon ended their dayes; whose Death we can do no lesse than charge upon the Rulers of *Boston*, they being the occasion of it.

18. Also three of the Servants of the Lord they put to Death, all of them for obedience to the Truth, in the Testimony of it against the wicked Rulers and Laws at *Boston*.

19. And since they have banished four more, *upon pain of Death;* and twenty four of the Inhabitants of *Salem* were presented, and more Fines called for, and their Goods seized on, to the value of Forty pounds, for meeting together in the fear of God, and some for *refusing to swear*.

These things (O King) from time to time have we patiently suffered, and not for the trangression of any Just or Righteous Law, either pertaining to the Worship of God, or the Civil Government of *England*, but simply and barely for our Consciences to God, of which we can more at large give Thee (or whom thou mayest order) a full Account (if Thou wilt let us have admission to Thee, who are *Banished upon pain of Death*, and have had *our Ears cut*, who are, some of us, in *England* attending upon Thee) both of the *Causes of our Sufferings*, and *the Manner* of their disorderly and illegal Pro-

ceeding against us; who begun *with Immodesty*, went on *in
Inhumanity* and *Cruelty*, and were not satisfied until *they had
the Blood of three of the Martyrs* of JESUS: Revenge for all
which we do not seek, but lay them before Thee, considering
Thou hast been well acquainted with Sufferings, and so mayest
the better consider them that suffer, and mayest for the future
restrain the Violence of these Rulers of *New-England*, having
Power in Thy hands; they being but the Children of the
Family, of which Thou art Chief Ruler; Who have in divers
of their Proceedings *forfeited their Patent*; as upon a strict
Inquiry in many particulars will appear.

And this, O King, we are assured of, that in time to come it
will not repent Thee, if by a *Close Rebuke* Thou stoppest the
Bloody Proceedings of these *Bloody Persecutors*; for in so doing,
Thou wilt engage the hearts of many honest People unto
Thee, both there and here; and for such Works of Mercy, the
Blessing is obtained, and shewing it, is the way to prosper. . . .

b. *A Quaker Trial at Boston, 1661* [1]

Joseph Besse's *Collection of the Sufferings of the People called Quakers*
(1753), II, 222–223. Italics as in the original.

ANNO 1661. At the said next General-Court, *Wenlock Christison* was again brought to the Bar.

The Governour asked him, *What he had to say for himself, why he should not die?*

Wenlock. I have done nothing worthy of Death; if I had, I refuse not to die.

Governour. *Thou art come in among us in Rebellion, which is as the Sin of Witchcraft, and ought to be punished.*

Wenlock. I came not in among you in Rebellion, but in Obedience to the God of Heaven; not in Contempt to any of you, but in Love to your Souls and Bodies; and that you shall know one Day, when you and all Men must give an Account of your

---

[1] This document belongs chronologically in the next general division (♡), below; but it is most conveniently presented here.

Deeds done in the Body. Take heed, for you cannot escape the righteous Judgments of God.

Major-General *Adderton*. *You pronounce Woes and Judgments, and those that are gone before you pronounced Woes and Judgments; but the Judgments of the Lord God are not come upon us yet.*

Wenlock. Be not proud, neither let your Spirits be lifted up; God doth but wait till the Measure of your Iniquity be filled up, and that you have seen your ungodly Race, then will the Wrath of God come upon you to the uttermost; And as for thy part, it hangs over thy Head, and is near to be poured down upon thee, and shall come as a Thief in the Night suddenly, when thou thinkest not of it. By what Law will ye put me to Death?

Court. *We have a Law, and by our Law you are to die.*

Wenlock. So said the *Jews* of Christ, *We have a Law, and by our Law he ought to die.* Who empowered you to make that Law?

Court. *We have a* Patent, *and are* Patentees; *judge whether we have not Power to make Laws?*

Wenlock. How! Have you Power to make Laws repugnant to the Laws of *England?*

Governour. *Nay.*

Wenlock. Then you are gone beyond your Bounds, and have forfeited your *Patent*, and this is more than you can answer. Are you Subjects to the King, yea, or nay?

Secretary *Rawson*. *What will you infer from that? what Good will that do you?*

Wenlock. If you are, say so; for in your Petition to the King, you desire that he will protect you, and that you may be worthy to kneel among his loyal Subjects.

Court. *Yes.*

Wenlock. So am I, and for any thing I know, am as good as you, if not better; for if the King did but know your Hearts, as God knows them, he would see, that your Hearts are as rotten towards him, as they are towards God. Therefore seeing that you and I are Subjects to the King, I demand to be tried by the Laws of my own Nation.

Court. *You shall be tried by a Bench and a Jury.*

Wenlock. That is not the Law, but the Manner of it; for if you will be as good as your word, you must set me at Liberty, for I never heard or read of any Law that was in *England* to hang *Quakers.*

Governour. There is a Law to hang Jesuits.

Wenlock. If you put me to Death, it is not because I go under the name of a *Jesuit,* but a *Quaker,* therefore I do appeal to the Laws of my own Nation.

Court. *You are in our Hand, and have broken our Laws, and we will try you.*

Wenlock. Your Will is your Law, and what you have Power to do, that you will do: And seeing that the Jury must go forth on my Life, this I have to say to you in the Fear of the Living God: Jury, take heed what you do, for you swear by the Living God, *That you will true Trial make, and just Verdict give, according to the Evidence.* Jury, look for your Evidence: What have I done to deserve Death? Keep your Hands out of innocent Blood.

A Juryman. *It is good Counsel.*

The Jury went out, but having received their Lesson, soon returned, and brought in their Verdict *Guilty.*

Wenlock. I deny all Guilt, for my Conscience is clear in the Sight of God.

Governour. *The Jury hath condemned thee.*

Wenlock. The Lord doth justify me; who art thou that condemnest?

Then the Court proceeded to vote as to the Sentence of Death, to which several of them, *viz. Richard Russel* and others, would not consent, the Innocence and Stedfastness of the Man having prevailed upon them in his Favour. There happened also a Circumstance during this Trial, which could not but affect Men of any Tenderness or Consideration, which was, that a Letter was sent to the Court from *Edward Wharton,* signifying, *That whereas they had banished him on pain of Death, yet he was at Home in his own House in* Salem, *and therefore proposing, That they would take off their wicked Sentence from him, that he might go about his Occasions out of their Jurisdiction.* This Circumstance, however affecting to others, did only enrage *Endicot* the Governour, who was very much displeased, and in much Anger cried out, *I could find in my Heart to go Home.*

Wenlock. It were better for thee to be at Home than here, for thou art about a bloody piece of Work.

Governour. *You that will not consent, record it. I thank God, I am not afraid to give Judgment.* Wenlock Christison, *hearken to your Sentence: You must return unto the Place from whence you came, and from thence to the Place of Execution, and there you must be hanged until you be* dead, dead, dead, *upon the* 13th *Day of* June, *being the Fifth-day of the Week.*

Wenlock. The Will of the Lord be done: In whose Will I came amongst you, and in his Counsel I stand, feeling his Eternal Power, that will uphold me unto the last Gasp, I do not question it. Known be it unto you all, That if you have Power to take my Life from me, my Soul shall enter into Everlasting Rest and Peace with God, where you yourselves shall never come: And if you have Power to take my Life from me, the which I do question, I believe you shall never more take *Quakers* Lives from them: Note my Words. Do not think to weary out the Living God by taking away the Lives of his Servants: What do you gain by it? For the last Man you put to Death, here are *five* come in his Room. And if you have Power to take my Life from me, God can raise up the same Principle of Life in *ten* of his Servants, and send them among you in my Room, that you may have Torment upon Torment, which is your Portion: *For there is no Peace to the Wicked,* saith my God.

Governour. *Take him away.* . . .

XV. RHODE ISLAND TO 1660

89. A Compact in *Civil* Things Only, 1336 (?)

Early Records of the Town of Providence (1892), 1.

These *Records* were printed from the original manuscript records. In 1800, a manuscript "transcript" had been made of those records (without attempt to preserve the original spelling, and with various errors); and this transcript was followed in the first printed copy of this compact in the *Rhode Island Colony Records* (1878), I, 14.

The following entry was not dated. Apparently it was a paper presented by Williams and the first settlers to a second body of comers, probably in 1636.

We whose names are hereunder, desirous to inhabitt in the towne of providence, do promise to subject ourselves in active and passive obedience to all such orders or agreements as shall be made for publick good of our body, in an orderly way, by the major consent of the present Inhabitants, maisters of families, Incorporated together into a towne fellowship, and others whome they shall admitt unto them,

only in civill things.

Richard Scott
William X Reynolds
   mark
Abad browne
John Warner [a character, probably a "mark," follows.]
Edwarde Cope
George Rickard

Thomas Angell X *mark*
Thomas Harris
ffrancis weekes X *mark*
Benedict Arnold
Josua winsor
William Wickenden
John X ffeild
 mark

[In many ways this "compact" recalls the Mayflower Compact (No. 46); but the notable thing here is that obedience is promised in *civil* things only. "Civil" is used in contradistinction with "ecclesiastical." Obedience is promised in matters that pertain to the *state*, not in those pertaining to the church. This was the primary force of the word "civil." Observe it in the same sense in the documents that follow.]

90. Religious Freedom Consonant with Civil Order

Arnold's *History of Rhode Island*, I, 254, 255.

The town of Providence had been disturbed by tumults, and some of the inhabitants reasoned loosely that their platform of freedom of conscience forbade them to punish the transgressors. Williams then wrote the following letter to the town, defining in a masterly way the limits of civil and religious freedom. This is a good point at which to review No. 84, with the Introduction thereto.

There goes many a ship to sea, with many hundred souls in one ship, whose weal and woe is common; and [this] is a true picture of a commonwealth. . . . It hath fallen out sometimes that both Papists and Protestants, Jews and Turks, may be embarked in one ship; upon which supposal I affirm that all the liberty of conscience, that ever I pleaded for, turns upon these two hinges: that none of the Papists, Protestants Jews, or Turks, be forced to come to the ship's prayers or worship, nor compelled from their own particular prayers or worship, if they practice any. I further add that I never denied that, notwithstanding this liberty, the commander of the ship ought to command the ship's course, yea, and also command that justice, peace, and sobriety be kept and practised, both among the seamen and all the passengers. If any of the seamen refuse to perform their service, or passengers to pay their freight; if any refuse to help, in person or purse, toward the common charges or defence; if any refuse to obey the common laws and orders of the ship, concerning their common peace or preservation; if any shall mutiny and rise up against their . . . officers; if any should preach or write that there ought to be no commanders or officers because all are equal in Christ . . . I say I never denied but in such cases, whatever is pretended, the commander or commanders may judge, resist, compel, and punish such trangressors, according to their . . . merits.[1]

91. Patent of Providence Plantations, March 14/24, 1643/1644

Rhode Island Colonial Records, I, 123–146.

The Long Parliament, at the opening of its war against Charles I, created a council for colonial affairs. That body, upon petition from Williams and his friends, issued the following grant. Section I (about a page of this type) recites these facts. Practically all the rest of the document is given here. The important consideration is the repetition of the word "civil." (See note on page 267, above.)

And whereas divers well affected and industrious English Inhabitants, of the Towns of Providence, Portsmouth, and Newport in the tract aforesaid, have adventured to make a nearer neighborhood and Society with the great Body of the Narragansets, which may in Time by the blessing of God upon their Endeavours, lay a sure Foundation of Happiness to all America. And have also purchased, and are purchasing of and amongst the said Natives, some other Places, which may be convenient both for Plantations, and also for building of Ships, Supply of Pipe Staves and other Merchandize. And whereas the said English, have represented their Desire to the said Earl, and Commissioners, to have their hopeful Beginnings approved and confirmed, by granting unto them a Free Charter of **Civil** Incorporation and Government; that they may order and govern their Plantation in such a Manner as to maintain Justice and peace, both among themselves, and towards all Men with whom they shall have to do. In due Consideration of the said Premises, the said Robert Earl of Warwick, Governor in Chief, and Lord High Admiral of the said Plantations, and the greater Number of the said Commissioners, whose Names and Seals are here underwritten and subjoined, out of a Desire to encourage the good Beginnings of the said Planters, Do, by the Authority of

---

[1] The editor cannot resist the desire to add that rarely in all history has so fundamental, and at the same time so revolutionary, a truth been stated so simply and incontrovertibly.

the aforesaid Ordinance of the Lords and Commons, give, grant, and confirm, to the aforesaid Inhabitants of the Towns of Providence, Portsmouth, and Newport, a free and absolute Charter of Incorporation, to be known by the Name of the Incorporation of Providence Plantations, in the Narraganset-Bay, in New England. — Together with full Power and Authority to rule themselves, and such others as shall hereafter inhabit within any Part of the said Tract of land, by such a Form of **Civil Government,** as by voluntary consent of all, or the greater Part of them, they shall find most suitable to their Estate and Condition; and, for that End, to make and ordain such **Civil Laws** and Constitutions, and to inflict such punishments upon Transgressors, and for Execution thereof, so to place, and displace Officers of Justice, as they, or the greatest Part of them, shall by free Consent agree unto. Provided nevertheless, that the said Laws, Constitutions, and Punishments, for the **Civil Government** of the said Plantations, be conformable to the Laws of England, so far as the Nature and Constitution of the place will admit. And always reserving to the said Earl, and Commissioners, and their Successors, Power and Authority for to dispose the general Government of that, as it stands in Relation to the rest of the Plantations in America as they shall conceive from Time to Time, most conducing to the general Good of the said Plantations, the Honour of his Majesty, and the Service of the State. . . .

92. Rhode Island and the Quakers, 1657

Hutchinson's *Massachusetts Bay* (1765), App. XI.

Massachusetts had complained and threatened because Quakers, received in Rhode Island, swarmed thence into her territory.

The Government of Rhode Island to the Government of Massachusetts.

Much honoured Gentlemen,
Please you to understand, that there hath come to our view a

letter subscribed by the honour'd gentlemen commissioners of the united coloneys, the contents whereof are a request concerning certayne people caled quakers, come among us lately, etc.

Our desires are, in all things possible, to pursue after and keepe fayre and loving correspondence and entercourse with all the colloneys, and with all our countreymen in New-England; and to that purpose we have endeavoured (and shall still endeavour) to answere the desires and requests from all parts of the countrey, coming unto us, in all just and equall returnes, to which end the coloney have made seasonable provision to preserve a just and equal entercourse between the coloneys and us, by giving justice to any that demand it among us and by returning such as make escapes from you, or from the other coloneys, being such as fly from the hands of justice, for matters of crime done or committed amongst you, etc. And as concerning these quakers (so caled) which are now among us, *we have no law among us whereby to punish any for only declaring by words, etc. their mindes and understandings concerning the things and ways of God, as to salvation and an eternal condition. And we, moreover, finde that in those places where these people aforesaid, in this coloney, are most of all suffered to declare themselves freely, and are only oposed by arguments in discourse, there they least of all desire to come, and we are informed that they begin to loath this place, for that they are not opposed by the civill authority, but with all patience and meeknes are suffered to say over their pretended revelations and admonitions, nor are they like or able to gain many here to their way; and surely we find that they delight to be persecuted by civill powers, and when they are soe, they are like to gain more adherents by the conseyte of their patient sufferings, than by consent to their pernicious sayings.* And yet we conceive, that their doctrines trend to very absolute cutting downe and overturning relations and civill government among men, if generally received. But as to the dammage that may in likelyhood accrue to the neighbour colloneys by their being here entertained, we conceive it will not prove so dangerous (as else it might) in regard of the course taken by you to send them away out of the countrey, as they come among you. But, however, at present, we judge it requisitt (and doe intend) to commend the consideration of their extravagent outgoings unto the generall assembly of our coloney in March next, where we hope there will be such order taken, as may, in all honest and contientious manner, prevent the bad effects of their doctrines and endeavours; and soe, in all courtious and loving respects, and with desire of all honest and fayre commerce with you, and the rest of our honoured and beloved countreymen, we rest

    Yours in all loving respects to serve you,

BENEDICT ARNOLD, *Pres.*
From Providence, at the court of trials, held for the coloney, Oct. 13th, 1657.
WILLIAM BAULTON,
RANDALL HOWLDON,
ARTHUR FENNER,
WILLIAM FEILD,

To the much honoured, the Generall Court, sitting at Boston, the Colloney of Massachusitts.

XVI. CONNECTICUT BEFORE 1660

93. The Fundamental Orders of 1639

January 14/24, 1348/9

Connecticut Colonial Records, I, 20-25.

Cf. *American History and Government*, §§ 87-89, for the history and significance of this "first written constitution known to history that created a government." The document is printed here in full.

Forasmuch as it hath pleased the Allmighty God by the wise disposition of his divyne providence so to Order and dispose of things that we the Inhabitants and Residents of Windsor, Harteford and Wethersfield are now cohabiting and dwelling in and uppon the River of Conectecotte and the Lands thereunto adjoyneing; And well knowing where a people are gathered together the word of God requires that to mayntayne the peace and union of such a people there should be an orderly and decent Goverment established according to God, to order and dispose of the affayres of the people at all seasons as occation shall require; doe therefore assotiate and conjoyne our selves to be as one Publike State or Commonwelth; and doe, for our selves and our Successors and such as shall be adjoyned to us att any tyme hereafter, enter into Combination and Confederation togather, to mayntayne and presearve the liberty and purity of the gospell of our Lord Jesus which we now professe, as also the disciplyne of the Churches, which according to the truth of the said gospell is now practised amongst us; As also in our Civell Affaires to be guided and governed according to such Lawes, Rules, Orders and decrees as shall be made, ordered and decreed, as followeth: —

1. It is Ordered, sentenced and decreed, that there shall be yerely two generall Assemblies or Courts, the on [*one*] the second thursday in Aprill, the other the second thursday in September,

following; the first shall be called the Courte of Election, wherein shall be yerely Chosen from tyme to tyme soe many Magestrats and other publike Officers as shall be found requisitte: Whereof one to be chosen Governour for the yeare ensueing and untill another be chosen, and noe other Magestrate to be chosen for more than one yeare; provided allwayes there be sixe chosen besids the Governour; which being chosen and sworne according to an Oath recorded for that purpose shall have power to administer justice according to the Lawes here established, and for want thereof according to the rule of the word of God; which choise shall be made by all that are admitted freemen and have taken the Oath of Fidellity, and doe cohabitte within this Jurisdiction, (having beene admitted Inhabitants by the major part of the Towne wherein they live,) or the major parte of such as shall be then present.

2. It is Ordered, sentensed and decreed, that the Election of the aforesaid Magestrats shall be on this manner: every person present and quallified for choyse shall bring in (to the persons deputed to receave them) one single paper with the name of him written in yt whom he desires to have Governour, and he that hath the greatest number of papers shall be Governor for that yeare. And the rest of the Magestrats or publike Officers to be chosen in this manner: The Secretary for the tyme being shall first read the names of all that are to be put to choise and then shall severally nominate them distinctly, and every one that would have the person nominated to be chosen shall bring in one single paper written uppon, and he that would not have him chosen shall bring in a blanke: and every one that hath more written papers then blanks shall be a Magistrat for that yeare; which papers shall be receaved and told by one or more that shall be then chosen by the court and sworne to be faythfull therein; but in case there should not be sixe chosen as aforesaid, besids the Governor, out of those which are nominated, then he or they which have the most written papers shall be a Magestrate or Magestrats for the ensueing yeare, to make up the foresaid number.

THE FUNDAMENTAL ORDERS OF 1639

3. It is Ordered, sentenced and decreed, that the Secretary shall not nominate any person, nor shall any person be chosen newly into the Magestracy which was not propownded in some Generall Courte before, to be nominated the next Election; and to that end yt shall be lawfull for ech of the Townes aforesaid by their deputyes to nominate any two whom they conceave fitte to be put to Election; and the Courte may ad so many more as they judge requisitt.

4. It is Ordered, sentenced and decreed that noe person be chosen Governor above once in two yeares, and that the Governor be alwayes a member of some approved congregation, and formerly of the Magestracy within this Jurisdiction; and all the Magestrats Freemen of this Commonwelth: and that no Magestrate or other publike officer shall execute any parte of his or their Office before they are severally sworne, which shall be done in the face of the Courte if they be present, and in case of absence by some deputed for that purpose.

5. It is Ordered, sentenced and decreed, that to the aforesaid Courte of Election the severall Townes shall send their deputyes, and when the Elections are ended they may proceed in any publike searvice as at other Courts. Also the Generall Courte in September shall be for makeing of lawes, and any other publike occation, which conserns the good of the Commonwelth.

6. It is Ordered, sentenced and decreed, that the Governor shall, ether by himselfe or by the secretary, send out summons to the Constables of every Towne for the cauleing of these two standing Courts, on [*one*] month at lest before their severall tymes: And also if the Governor and the gretest parte of the Magestrats see cause uppon any spetiall occation to call a generall Courte, they may give order to the secretary soe to doe within fowerteene dayes warneing; and if urgent necessity so require, uppon a shorter notice, giveing sufficient grownds for yt to the deputyes when they meete, or els be questioned for the same; And if the Governor and [*major*] parte of Magestrats shall ether neglect or refuse to call the

two Generall standing Courts or ether of them, as also at other tymes when the occasions of the Commonwelth require, the Freemen thereof, or the Major parte of them, shall petition to them soe to doe: if then yt be ether denyed or neglected the said Freemen or the Major parte of them shall have power to give order to the Constables of the severall Townes to doe the same, and so may meete togather, and chuse to themselves a Moderator, and may proceed to do any Acte of power, which any other Generall Courte may.

7. It is Ordered, sentenced and decreed that after there are warrants given out for any of the said Generall Courts, the Constable or Constables of ech Towne shall forthwith give notice distinctly to the inhabitants of the same, in some Publike Assembly or by goeing or sending from howse to howse, that at a place and tyme by him or them lymited and sett, they meet and assemble them selves togather to elect and chuse certen deputyes to be at the General Courte then following to agitate the afayres of the commonwelth; which said Deputyes shall be chosen by all that are admitted Inhabitants in the severall Townes and have taken the oath of fidellity; provided that non be chosen a Deputy for any Generall Courte which is not a Freeman of this Commonwelth.

The foresaid deputyes shall be chosen in manner following: every person that is present and quallified as before expressed, shall bring the names of such, written in severall papers as they desire to have chosen for that Imployment, and these 3 or 4, more or lesse, being the number agreed on to be chosen for that tyme, that have greatest number of papers written for them shall be deputyes for that Courte; whose names shall be endorsed on the backe side of the warrant and returned into the Courte, with the Constable or Constables hand unto the same.

8. It is Ordered, sentenced and decreed, that Wyndsor, Hartford and Wethersfield shall have power, ech Towne, to send fower of their freemen as their deputyes to every Generall Courte; and whatsoever other Townes shall be hereafter

added to this Jurisdiction, they shall send so many deputyes as the Courte shall judge meete, a resonable proportion to the number of Freemen that are in the said Townes being to be attended therein; which deputyes shall have the power of the whole Towne to give their voats and alowance to all such lawes and orders as may be for the publike good, and unto which the said Townes are to be bownd.

9. It is ordered and decreed, that the deputyes thus chosen shall have power and liberty to appoynt a tyme and a place of meeting togather before any Generall Courte to advise and consult of all such things as may concerne the good of the publike, as also to examine their owne Elections, whether according to the order, and if they or the gretest parte of them find any election to be illegall they may seclud such for [the] present from their meeting, and returne the same and their resons to the Courte; and if yt prove true, the Courte may fyne the party or partyes so intruding and the Towne, if they see cause, and give out a warrant to goe to a newe election in a legall way, either in parte or in whole. Also the said deputyes shall have power to fyne any that shall be disorderly at their meetings, or for not comming in due tyme or place according to appoyntment; and they may returne the said fynes into the Courte if yt be refused to be paid, and the Tresurer to take notice of yt, and to estreete or levy the same as he doth other fynes.

10. It is Ordered, sentenced and decreed, that every Generall Courte, except such as through neglecte of the Governor and the greatest parte of Magestrats the Freemen themselves doe call, shall consist of the Governor, or some one chosen to moderate the Court, and 4 other Magestrats at lest, with the major parte of the deputyes of the severall Townes legally chosen; and in case the Freemen or major parte of them, through neglect or refusall of the Governor and major parte of the magestrats, shall call a Courte, it shall consist of the major parte of Freemen that are present or their deputyes, with a Moderator chosen by them: In which said Generall

Courts shall consist the supreme power of the Commonwelth, and they only shall have power to make lawes or repeale them, to graunt levyes, to admitt of Freemen, dispose of lands undisposed of, to severall Townes or persons, and also shall have power to call ether Courte or Magestrate or any other person whatsoever into question for any misdemeanour, and may for just causes displace or deale otherwise according to the nature of the offence; and also may deale in any other matter that concerns the good of this commonwelth, excepte election of Magestrats, which shall be done by the whole boddy of Freemen.

In which Courte the Governour or Moderator shall have power to order the Courte, to give liberty of spech, and silence unceasonable and disorderly speakeings, to put all things to voate, and in case the vote be equall to have the casting voice. But non of these Courts shall be adjorned or dissolved without the consent of the major parte of the Court.

11. It is ordered, sentenced and decreed, that when any Generall Courte uppon the occations of the Commonwelth have agreed uppon any summe or sommes of mony to be levyed uppon the severall Townes within this Jurisdiction, that a Committee be chosen to sett out and appoynt what shall be the proportion of every Towne to pay of the said levy, provided the Committees be made up of an equall number out of each Towne.

[Hints for Study.— 1. — This was a great democratic constitution, — the first that ever "created a state." *As a whole, it is an innovation; but very few passages in it, taken by themselves, are new.* The great bulk of the Orders came from Massachusetts' practice of the preceding five years (1634–1638), and most of it came, indeed, from express statutes of the older colony. Its peculiar democracy consisted in (1) *selecting* all the democratic features of the Massachusetts government (leaving out all the more aristocratic features), and (2) in *adding* a very few other democratic features, some of which these men had striven for in vain in Massachusetts.

a. For instances of selection :

(Article 1.) Massachusetts, during most of her history, had had "two General Courts," the Spring Court being a "Courte of Election," in which all magistrates were chosen for one year only.

(Articles 1, 2, 7, 9.) All the details of the elections of governor, magistrates, and town deputies, come from Massachusetts' *practice* in the years 1635-1638, as did also the provision for preliminary caucusing by the deputies with control over their separate meetings.

Articles 5 and 10 may be compared with the democratic legislation of Massachusetts in 1634 (No. 67 *b* (2), above).

Many minor resemblances will occur to the advanced student familiar with Massachusetts history.

b. Provisions which the democrats had wanted, but failed to secure, in Massachusetts: ineligibility of the governor for immediate reëlection (Article 4), and the method of nomination (Article 3; adopted also in Massachusetts two years later).

c. Democratic innovations: (1) making the sessions of the legislature independent of the will of the executive (Articles 6 and 10). Massachusetts had made the General Court master of its own adjournment but not of its meetings. Both the provisions were adopted by the Long Parliament in England two years later. (2) Leaving the franchise to be determined practically by the towns.

2. — Connecticut **did not reject theocracy.** Cf. the preamble and the eligibility provision for the governorship. In practice, too, the colony maintained a close union of Church and State. The restriction of the franchise to church members was rejected, not because it was theocratic, but because it was undemocratic.]

XVII. THE NEW ENGLAND CONFEDERATION

94. The Constitution

The text is printed in the *New Haven Colonial Records* and in the *Plymouth Colony Records* (IX). For the history of the formation of the Confederation, see *American History and Government*, §§ 90, 91.

ARTICLES

OF

CONFEDERATION BETWIXT THE PLANTATIONS UNDER THE GOVERNMENT OF THE *MASSACHUSETTS*, THE PLANTATIONS UNDER THE GOVERNMENT OF *PLIMOUTH*, THE PLANTATIONS UNDER THE GOVERNMENT OF *CONNECTECUT*, AND THE GOVERNMENT OF *NEW HAVEN*, WITH THE PLANTATIONS IN COMBINATION THEREWITH.

Whereas we all came into these parts of *America*, with one and the same end and ayme, namely, to advance the Kingdome of our Lord Jesus Christ, and to enjoy the liberties of the Gospel, in purity with peace; and whereas in our settling (by a wise providence of God) we are further dispersed upon the Sea-Coast, and Rivers, then was at first intended, so that we cannot (according to our desire) with convenience communicate in one Government, and Jurisdiction; and whereas we live encompassed with people of severall Nations, and strange languages, which hereafter may prove injurious to us, and our posterity: And forasmuch as the Natives have formerly committed sundry insolencies and outrages upon severall Plantations of the English, and have of late combined against us. And seeing by reason of the sad distractions in *England*, which they have heard of, and by which they know we are hindred both from that humble way of seeking advice, and reaping those comfortable fruits of protection which, at other times, we might well expect; we therefore doe conceive it our bounden duty, without delay, to enter into a present Consotiation amongst our selves, for mutuall help and strength in all our future concernments, that, as in Nation, and Religion, so, in other respects, we be, and continue, One, according to the tenour and true meaning of the ensuing Articles.

I. Wherefore it is fully Agreed and Concluded by and between the parties, or Jurisdictions above named, and they doe joyntly and severally by these presents agree and conclude, That they all be, and henceforth be called by the name of, *The United Colonies of New-England.*

II. The said United Colonies for themselves, and their posterties doe joyntly and severally hereby enter into a firm and perpetuall league of friendship and amity, for offence and defence, mutuall advice and succour, upon all just occasions, both for preserving and propagating the truth, and liberties of the Gospel, and for their own mutuall safety, and wellfare.

III. It is further agreed, That the Plantations which at present are, or hereafter shall be settled within the limits of the *Massachusets*, shall be forever under the Government of the *Massachusets*. And shall have peculiar Jurisdiction amongst themselves, as an intire body; and that *Plimouth, Connecticut,* and *New-Haven,* shall each of them, in all respects, have the like peculiar Jurisdiction, and Government within their limits. . . .

IV. It is also by these Confederates agreed, That the charge of all just Wars, whether offensive, or defensive, upon what part or Member of this Confederation soever they fall, shall both in men, provisions, and all other disbursements, be born by all the parts of this Confederation, in different proportions, according to their different abilities, in manner following, namely, That the Commissioners for each Jurisdiction, from time to time, as there shall be occasion, bring a true account and number of all the Males in each Plantation, or any way belonging to, or under their severall Jurisdictions, of what quality, or condition soever they be, from sixteen years old, to threescore, being inhabitants there. And that according to the different numbers, which from time to time shall be found in each Jurisdiction, upon a true, and just account, the service of men, and all charges of the war, be born by the poll: Each Jurisdiction, or Plantation, being left to their own just course, and custome, of rating themselves, and people, according to their different estates, with due respect to their qualities and exemptions among themselves, though the Confederation take no notice of any such priviledge. And that, according to the different charge of each Jurisdiction, and Plantation, the whole advantage of the War (if it please God so to blesse their endeavours) whether it be in Lands, Goods, or persons, shall be proportionably divided among the said Confederates.

V. It is further agreed, That if any of these Jurisdictions, or any Plantation under, or in Combination with them, be invaded by any enemy whomsoever, upon notice, and request of any three Magistrates of that Jurisdiction so invaded, The rest of the Confederates, without any further meeting or expostulation, shall forthwith send ayde to the Confederate in danger, but in different proportion, namely the *Massachusets* one hundred men sufficiently armed, and provided for such a service, and journey. And each of the rest five and forty men, so armed and provided, or any lesse number, if lesse be required, according to this proportion. . . . But none of the Jurisdictions to exceed these numbers, till by a meeting of the Commissioners . . . a greater ayde appear necessary. . . .

VI. It is also agreed, That for the managing and concluding of all affaires proper to, and concerning the whole Confederation, two Commissioners shall be chosen by, and out of the foure Jurisdictions, namely two for the *Massachusets*, two for *Plimouth*, two for *Connecticut*, and two for *New-haven*, being all in Church-fellowship with us, which shall bring full power from their severall generall Courts respectively, to hear, examine, weigh, and determine all affaires of war, or peace, leagues, aydes, charges, and numbers of men for war, division of spoyles, or whatsoever is gotten by conquest, receiving of more confederates, or Plantations into Combination with any of these Confederates, and all things of like nature, which are the proper concomitants, or consequences of such a Confederation, for amity, offence, and defence, not intermedling with the Government or any of the Jurisdictions, which by the third Article, is preserved entirely to themselves. But if these eight Commissioners when they meet, shall not all agree, yet it is concluded, **That any six of the eight agreeing, shall have power to settle and determine the businesse in question. But if six doe not agree, that then such Propositions**, with their Reasons, so far as they have been debated, **be sent, and referred to the foure Generall Courts,** *viz.* The Massachusetts, Plymouth, Connectecut, and New-haven. . . . It is further agreed, That these eight Commissioners shall meet once every year, besides extraordinary meetings, according to the fifth Article to consider, treat, and conclude of all affaires belonging to this Confederation, which meeting shall ever be the first *Thursday* in *September*. [Provision for meeting at the several capital cities in rotation.]

VII. It is further agreed, That at each meeting of these eight Commissioners, whether ordinary or extraordinary; they all, or any six of them agreeing as before, may choose their President out of themselves . . . [to secure] a comely carrying on of all proceedings in the present meeting. But he shall be invested with no such power or respect, as by which, he shall hinder the propounding or progresse of any businesse, or any way cast the scales, otherwise then in the precedent Article is agreed.

VIII. It is also agreed, That the Commissioners for this Confederation hereafter at their meetings, whether ordinary or extraordinary, as they may have Commission or opportunity, doe endeavour to frame and establish Agreements and Orders in generall cases of a civil nature, wherein all the Plantations are interested, for preserving peace amongst themselves, and preventing (as much as may be) all occasions of war, or differences with others, as about the free and speedy passage of Justice in each Jurisdiction, to all the Confederates equally, as to their own, receiving those that remove from one Plantation to another, without due Certificates, how all the Jurisdictions may carry it towards the *Indians*, that they neither grow insolent, nor be injured without due satisfaction, least War break in upon the Confederates, through such miscarriages. It is also agreed, That if any Servant run away from his Master, into any other of these Confederated Jurisdictions, That in such case, upon the Certificate of one Magistrate in the Jurisdiction, out of which the said Servant fled, or upon other due proof, the said Servant shall be delivered either to his Master, or any other that pursues, and brings such Certificate, or proof. And that upon the escape of any Prisoner whatsoever, or fugitive, for any Criminall Cause, whether breaking Prison, or getting from the Officer, or otherwise escaping, upon the Certificate of two Magistrates of the Jurisdiction out of which the escape is made, that he was a prisoner or such an offendor, at the time of the escape, the Magistrates of that Jurisdiction where for the present the said prisoner or fugitive abideth, shall forthwith grant such a Warrant as the case will bear, for the apprehending of any such person, and the delivery of him into the hand of the person who pursueth him. . . .

[IX. No one of the confederates to engage in any (offensive) war, without the vote of the commissioners, "as in the sixth Article is provided."]

XI. It is further agreed, That if any of the Confederates shall hereafter break any of these presents Articles, or be any other way injurious to any one of the other Jurisdictions, such breach of Agreement, or injury, shalbe duly considered and ordered by the Commissioners for the other Jurisdictions, that both peace, and this present Confederation, may be intirely preserved without violation.

Lastly, this perpetuall Confederation, and the severall Articles and Agreements thereof, being read and seriously considered, [statement of subscription by authority of the respective confederate governments.]

95. Massachusetts Demands More Weight

Plymouth Colony Records, I, 16–17, 118–120, 126–128.

(1) *At a meetinge of the Commissioners for the united Colonies in New England at Hartford the fift of September 1644*

. . . The Commissioners for the Massachusetts mooved that a due order might be attended in the subscriptions of the Acts and determinacions of this and any future meetings of the Commissioners for the united Colonies, and expressed not onely their owne apprehensions but the judgment of their generall Court, That by the Articles of Confederacion the first place did of Right belong to the Massachusetts, as being first named and so the other Colonies in like order. Which being taken into consideracion, and the Articles of Confederacion read, It appeared evidently to the Comissioners that no such priviledge had beene ever . . . graunted . . . by the Comissioners for the Jurisdicions in either of their former meetings, and yet the first subscription was made in the presence of the generall Court of the Massachusetts. And to prevent future inconvenience upon this occation, they thought fitt to declare that this Commission is free and may not receive any thing (not expresly agreed in the Articles) as imposed by any generall Court; yet out of their respects to the Government of the Massachusetts they did *willingly* graunt that their Comissioners [those of Massachusetts] should first subscribe after the President in this and all future meetings, and the Comissioners for the other Colonies in such order as they are named in the Articles; viz., Plymouth, Conectacutt, and New Haven.

*   *   *   *   *   *   *

(2) *At a Meting of the Commissioners of the United colonyes of New England: held at New Plymouth the 7th, 7th, 1648*

... the Comissioners for the Matathusetts presented to the Comissioners of the other Colonyes a writeing from a Comitee of theire Generall Courte desiering that a dew Consideracion may bee had thereof, in answer to the Severall pticulers. The wrighting is as Followeth. ...

" Wheareas in Cace sixe of the Comissioners shall not agree the Cause is to be refered to the fouer Generall Courtes, and by theire Joynte agrements to be determined, etc.,— to be considered if it were not more expedient to bee determined upon the agrement of any three of them. ...

" Wheareas by the .6. Article each of the Colonyes is to have two Comissioners, and the Colony of the Matathusetts beares almost five for one in the proportion of Charge with any one of the rest, they desier to have one Comissioner more; or otherwise they shall be content that any other of the Colonyes shall have the same priviledg to have three Comissioners to the other twoe, if such Colonyes will beare the Licke proporcion of Chardg with the Matathusetts. ... "

The Comissioners having perused and with dew Respect Considered the former proposicions. ...

In caces proper to the Comissioners wheareas by the sixth article, if sixe Agree not, the proposicions with the Reasons are to be Refered to the Fower Generall Courts: the Comissioners aproveing the Mocion made by the Comity of the Masachusets doe recomend it to the Fower Generall Courts that, if any ... three of the saide Courts agree ... of any such proposicion, it shall passe and bee accoumpted as the Conclusion of the united Colonyes, as it should have passed as ane act of the Comissioners if sixe of them had consented: For the 5th, sixth and seventh proposicions presented from the Comissioners of the Masachusetts, Importeing a reall Chang in the tearmes and Covenants of Confideration,— as noe alteracion Can bee made without the Consent of all and each of the Generall Courts, soe the Comissioners Feare that any of the Alteracions mencioned would prove dangerous and Inconvenient to all or som of the Colonyes. The tacken [taking]

of the Number of malles they hope need not bee frequent;
Nor, as it hath been Caryed by the Comissioners, inconvenient.
In point of the seventh proposicion they Conscaive there is a
mistack: the Lardge trade of the Masachusets, besides theire
Numbers, afford many advantages in Reference to estates
which the other Colonyes wante; but (it is from the Free
grace of god that all and each have what they have) they
diser [them] to bee thainkefull.

96. Nullification by Massachusetts

Plymouth Colony Records, X, 74–76. Cf. *American History and Government*, § 93. The following extracts from a declaration of the Massachusetts General Court put an end to the attempt of the other three colonies in the New England Confederation to force Massachusetts to join in a war against New Netherlands.

The question propounded by the General Court of the Massachusetts [June 2/12, 1653].

... Whether the Comissioners of the united Collonies have power by articles of agreement to determine the Justice of an offencive or vindictive warr and to engage the Collonies therin;

The Answare of the Committies to the question, — first more particularly from the Articles:

The whole power of Government and Jurisdiction is in the 3d and sixt Articles refered to every Collonie whoe sawe not meet to divest themselves of theire authoritie to Invest the Comissioners with any part therof being altogether unsafe and unnessesary to attaine the end of the Confeaderation;

The 9. and 10th Articles constituteth the Comissioners Judges of the Justice of a defencive warr

The 4th and 5th settle Rules for Leagues, Aides, and number in a defencive warr, and devisions of spoiles; but noe where provide for the determination of the Justice of an offencive warr, which therfore is refered wholy to the Determination of the Supreame Power of the severall Confeaderate Jurisdictions, whoe would have otherwise provided in the case.

The sixt Article, which att first view seemes to Inable the Comissioners, will evidently evince the Contrary. For, the Confederation being betwixt the Collonies, the 4th, and fift, 9, and 10th Articles provid Rules in severall Cases according to which the Confeaderates have bound themselves to Acte; And the sixt Article onely orders and appoints whoe and in what mannor the said Rules and agreements should bee executed viz. by Comissioners Improved to acte in cases specif[y]ed and regulated, — for theire number, mannor of proceeding, times and places of meeting, in the sixt and seaventh Articles; And that by nessesitie; because the supreame power of the severall Jurisdictions Could not assemble, they were enforced to Substitute deligates to order such things as were of present and urgent Nessesitie, or meerly prudenciall or polliticall or of Inferior nature, and that according to *themselves* [the Rules] prescribed by the Confeaderates. But such things [as] require the Choise Actes of Authoritie; or [are] in theire nature of Morrall Consideration and may admite of more time of Deliberation (as an offencive warr), The Wisdome of the Countrivers of the Confederacy did not Judg meete to Refere to Comissioners, and therfore [they] have not provided any Rules in such cases in these Consernments as they did in all cases of an Inferior nature;

More Generally:[1] The Comissioners of the united Collonies are not, soe fare as wee can deserne, Invested with power to Conclude an offencive warr to engage the Collonies to which they belonge to put the same in execution further then they are enabled by Comission or Instructions under the seale of theire Collonie; much lesse can it stand with the Jurisdiction and Right of Government reserved to ever[y] Collonie for six Comissioners of the other Collonies to put forth any Acte of power in a vindictive warr wherby they shall comaund the Collonie decenting to assist them in the same; neither can it

---

[1] This paragraph begins the second half of the argument, — based not on the particular Articles of Confederation, but upon the nature of such federal government in general.

NULLIFICATION BY MASSACHUSETTS

bee the meaning of the severall Collonies whoe are soe tender of theire power in Governing theire owne that they should put theire power out of theire owne hands in the most waighty points (A bondage hardly to bee borne by the most Subjective people), And cannot bee conceived soe free a people as the united Collonies should submite unto;

It can bee noe lesse then *a contradiction* to affeirme the Supreame power (which wee take to bee the Generall Courts of every Jurisdiction) can bee comaunded by others: *an absurditie in pollicye*, that an Intire Government and Jurisdiction should prostitute itselfe to the Comaund of Strangers; *a Scandall in Religion*, that a generall court of Christians should bee obliged to acte and engage upon the faith of six Delligates against theire Consience; — all which must bee admitted in case wee acknowlidg ourselves bound to undertake an offencive warr upon the bare determination of the Comissioners, whoe can not nor ever did challenge Authoritie over us, or expecte Subjection from us . . .

[Observe that the Massachusetts government did flatly nullify a decree of the federal congress of the United Colonies. However, it tried to justify itself, not by an avowal of its power, but by a constitutional argument. Massachusetts claimed first that the sixth article (which made the vote of six commissioners binding upon the whole confederation) could apply only to such matters as have been plainly referred to the Commissioners by other parts of the Constitution ; and second, that the authority claimed by the federal Congress was inconsistent with the fundamental idea of a confederation, even as it had been understood by the other confederates.

John Fiske says that this argument begins "the development of constitutional law, in the American sense," — as an attempt to interpret a written constitution. The whole debate makes an interesting prelude to the later arguments of the nullifiers and secessionists in the nineteenth century.]

C. COLONIAL AMERICA, 1660-1760

The documents selected for this period are much more isolated than those given above for the earlier colonial period. It is usually impossible in a class to do more than use a few illustrative sources for this long and difficult period; and some documents which might be expected are omitted because of the extracts given from them in the *American History and Government*.

XVIII. LIBERAL CHARTERS, 1662, 1663 [1]

97. The Connecticut Charter

April 23 / May 3, 1662

Connecticut Colonial Records, II, 3-11.

The complete document would fill some ten pages of this volume. Parts of it are plainly copied from the Massachusetts Bay charter of 1629. Indeed the whole document has the *form* of a charter to a *proprietary* "*Company*." This company, however, was a "*Corporation upon the place*," not a corporation in England managing a distant property. It was the first such corporation to receive a grant from the crown.

The parts of the charter here given are selected to show (1) the powers of self-government and (2) the inclusion of New Haven. The charter was adopted as the State Constitution in 1776, and continued in force, with very slight change, until 1818.

Charles the Second, [&c.] **Whereas** . . . Severall Lands, . . . and Plantations have byn . . . setled in that parte of . . . America called New England, and thereby the Trade . . . there hath byn of late yeares much increased, **And whereas**, We have byn informed by the humble Petition of our Trusty and welbeloved John Winthrop [and eighteen others], being

---

[1] For the conditions under which a despotic king granted these amazingly liberal charters, cf. *American History and Government*.

Persons Principally interested in our Colony . . . of Conecticutt in New England, that the same Colony . . . was purchased and obteyned for greate and valuable considerations, and thereby become a considerable enlargment and addition of our Dominions and interest there, — **Now Know yee**, that in Consideration thereof, and in regard the said Colony is remote from other the English Plantations in the Places aforesaid, And to the end the Affaires and Busines which shall from tyme to tyme happen or arise concerning the same may bee duely Ordered and managed, **Wee** . . . **Doe** Ordeine, Constitute and Declare That they, the said John Winthrop [and others] *and all such others as now are or hereafter shall bee Admitted and made free of the Company and Society of our Collony of Conecticut in America*, shall . . . bee one Body Corporate and Pollitique in fact and name, by the Name of *Governour and Company of the English Collony of Conecticut in New England in America;* . . . **And** further, wee . . . **Doe** Declare and appoint, that for the better ordering and manageing of the affairs and businesse of the said Company and their Successors, there shall be one Governour, one Deputy Governour, and Twelve Assistants, to bee from tyme to tyme Constituted, Elected and Chosen out of the Freemen of the said Company for the tyme being, in such manner and forme as hereafter in these presents is expressed. And . . . **Wee doe** . . . Constitute and appoint the aforesaid John Winthrop to bee the first and present Governour of the said Company; [appointment of Deputy Governor and Assistants]; to continue in the said severall Offices respectively untill the second Thursday which shall bee in the Moneth of October now next comeing. **And** further, wee . . . **Doe** Ordaine and Graunt that the Governour . . . for the tyme being, or, in his absence . . . the Deputy Governour . . . . . . shall and may . . . upon all occasions give Order for the assembling of the said Company . . . to Consult and advice of the businesse and Affaires of the said Company, And that for ever hereafter, Twice in every yeare, (That is to say,) on every second Thursday in October and on every second Thursday in May, or oftener, in Case it shall be requisite, The Assistants and freemen of the said Company, or such of them (not exceeding twoe Persons from each place, Towne or Citty) whoe shall bee from tyme to tyme thereunto Elected or Deputed by the major parte of the freemen of the respective Townes . . . shall have a generall meeting or Assembly, then and their to Consult and advise in and about the Affaires and businesse of the said Company; And that the Governour, or . . . Deputy Governour . . . , and such of the Assistants and freemen of the said Company as shall be soe Elected or Deputed and bee present att such meeting or Assembly, or the greatest number of them (whereof the Governour or Deputy Governour and Six of the Assistants, at least, to bee Seaven) shall be called the *Generall Assembly, and shall have full power and authority to alter and change their dayes and tymes of meeting or General Assemblies for Electing the Governour Deputy Governour and Assistants or other Officers, or any other Courts, Assemblies or meetings, and to Choose, Nominate and appoint such and soe many other Persons as they shall thinke fitt and shall bee willing to accept the same, to bee free of the said Company and Body Politique, and them into the same to Admitt and to Elect, and Constitute such Officers as they shall thinke fitt and requisite for the Ordering, mannageing, and disposeing of the Affaires of the said Governour and Company and their Successors.* And wee doe hereby . . . *Establish and Ordeine, that once in the yeare* . . . , *namely, the said Second Thursday in May, the Governour, Deputy Governour and Assistants of the said Company and other Officers of the said Company, or such of them as the said Generall Assembly shall thinke fitt, shall bee, in the said Generall Court and Assembly to bee held from that day or tyme, newly Chosen for the yeare ensuing, by such greater part of the said Company for the tyme being then and there present.* . . . And wee doe further . . . Graunt that it . . . shall . . . bee lawfull [for any General Assembly,] to Erect and make . . . Judicatories for the heareing and Determining of all Actions . , . *And alsoe from tyme to tyme to Make, Ordaine, and Establish All mannner of wholesome and reasonable Lawes, Satutes, Ordinances . . . and Instructions, not contrary to the lawes of this Realme of England . . . which they shall find needfull for the Government . . . of the said*

Colony. . . **And Knowe yee further,** That Wee . . . **Doe** give, Graunt and Confirme unto the said Governor and Company and their Successors, **All** that parte of our Dominions in New England in America bounded on the East by Norrogancett River, comonly called Norrogancett Bay, where the said River falleth into the Sea, and on the North by the lyne of the Massachusetts Plantation, and on the South by the Sea, and in longitude as the lyne of the Massachusetts Colony, runinge from East to West, (that is to say,) from the said Norrogancett Bay on the East to the South Sea on the West. . . .

98. The Rhode Island Charter

July 8/18, 1663

Rhode Island Colonial Records, II, 3–20.

John Clarke, an agent for the colony, presented a petition for a charter to Charles II in January, 1661.

. . . **Whereas** we have been informed . . . on behalf of Benjamine Arnold, William Brenton [here follow twelve names] and the rest of the purchasers and ffree inhabitants of our island, called Rhode-Island, and the rest of the colonie of Providence Plantations, in the Narragansett Bay, in New-England, in America, that they, pursueing, with peaceable and loyall mindes, their sober, serious and religious intentions, of godlie edifieing themselves, and one another, in the holie Christian ffaith and worshipp *as they were perswaded:* together with the gaineing over and conversione of the poore ignorant Indian natives, in those partes of America, to the sincere professione and obedienc of the same ffaith and worship, did, not onlie by the consent and good encouragement of our royall progenitors, transport themselves out of this kingdom of England into America, but alsoe, since their arrivall there, after their first settlement amongst other our subjects in those parts, ffor the avoideing of discorde, and those manie evills which were likely to ensue upon some of those oure subjects not beinge able to beare, in these remote partes, theire different apprehensiones in religious concernments, and in pursueance of the afforesayd ends, did once againe leave theire desireable stationes and habitationes, and with excessive labor and travell, hazard and charge, did transplant themselves into the middest of the Indian natives, who, as wee are infformed, are the most potent princes and people of all that country; where, by the good Providence of God, from whome the Plantationes have taken their name, upon theire labour and industrie, they have not onlie byn preserved to admiration, but have increased and prospered, and are seized and possessed, by purchase and consent of the said natives, to their ffull content, of such lands, islands, rivers, harbours and roades, as are verie convenient, both for plantationes and alsoe for buildinge of shipps, suplye of pype-staves, and other merchandize; and which lyes verie commodious, in manie respects, for commerce, and to accomodate oure southern plantationes, and may much advance the trade of this oure realme, and greatlie enlarge the territories thereof; they haveinge, by neare neighbourhoode to and friendlie societie with the greate bodie of the Narragansett Indians, given them encouragement, of theire owne accorde, to subject themselves, theire people and landes, unto us; whereby, as is hoped, there may, in due tyme, by the blessing of God upon theire endeavours, bee layd a sure ffoundation of happinesse to all America: And whereas, *in theire humble addresse, they have ffreely declared, that it is much on their hearts (if they may be permitted), to hold forth a livelie experiment, that a most flourishing civill state may stand and best bee maintained, and that among our English subjects, with a full libertie in religious concernements; and that true pietye rightly grounded upon gospell principles, will give the best and greatest security to sovereignetye, and will lay in the hearts of men the strongest obligations to true loyaltie:* Now know yee, *that wee beinge willinge to encourage the hopefull undertakeinge of oure sayd loyall and loveinge subjects, and to secure them in the free exercise and enjoyment of all theire civill and religious rights, appertaining to them, as our loveing subjects; and to preserve unto them that libertye, in the true Christian ffaith and worshipp of God, which*

they have sought with soe much travaill, and with peaceable myndes,
and loyall subjectione to our royall progenitors and ourselves, to enjoye ;
and because some of the people and inhabitants of the same colonie
cannot, in theire private opinions, conforme to the publique exercise of
religion, according to the litturgy, formes and ceremonyes of the Church
of England, or take or subscribe the oaths and articles made and established in that behalfe; and for that the same, by reason of the remote
distances of those places, will (as wee hope) bee noe breach of the
unitie and uniffformitie established in this nation : . . . doe hereby . . .
declare, That our royall will and pleasure is, that noe person within
the sayd colonye, at any tyme hereafter, shall bee any wise molested,
punished, disquieted, or called in question, for any differences in opinione
in matters of religion, and [i.e., if he] doe not actually disturb the
civill peace of our sayd colony ; but that all and everye person and
persons may, from tyme to tyme, and at all tymes hereafter, freelye
and fullye have and enjoye his and theire owne judgments and consciences,
in matters of religious concernments, throughout the tract of lande
hereafter mentioned ; they behaving themselves peaceablie and quietlie,
and not useing this libertie to lycentiousnesse and profanenesse, nor to
the civill injurye or outward disturbeance of others ; any lawe, statute,
or clause, therein contayned, or to bee contayned, usage or custome of
this realme, to the contrary hereof, in any wise, notwithstanding.* And
that they may bee in the better capacity to defend themselves,
in theire just rights and libertyes . . . wee . . . doe ordeyne,
. . . That they, the sayd William Brenton . . . [and others]
and all such others as now are, or hereafter shall bee admitted
and made ffree of the company and societie of our collonie of
Providence Plantations, in the Narragansett Bay, in New-England, shall bee, from tyme to tyme, and forever hereafter, a
bodie corporate and politique, . . . by the name of 𝕿𝖍𝖊 𝕲𝖔𝖇𝖊𝖗=
𝖓𝖔𝖚𝖗 𝖆𝖓𝖉 𝕮𝖔𝖒𝖕𝖆𝖓𝖞 𝖔𝖋 𝖙𝖍𝖊 𝕰𝖓𝖌𝖑𝖎𝖘𝖍 𝕮𝖔𝖑𝖑𝖔𝖓𝖎𝖊 𝖔𝖋 𝕽𝖍𝖔𝖉𝖊=𝕴𝖘𝖑𝖆𝖓𝖉 𝖆𝖓𝖉
𝕻𝖗𝖔𝖇𝖎𝖉𝖊𝖓𝖈𝖊 𝕻𝖑𝖆𝖓𝖙𝖆𝖙𝖎𝖔𝖓𝖘, 𝖎𝖓 𝕹𝖊𝖜=𝕰𝖓𝖌𝖑𝖆𝖓𝖉, 𝖎𝖓 𝕬𝖒𝖊𝖗𝖎𝖈𝖆. . . . 𝕬𝖓𝖉
𝖋𝖚𝖗𝖙𝖍𝖊𝖗, wee . . . doe declare . . . that . . . there shall bee
one Governour, one Deputie-Governour and ten Assistants, to
bee from tyme to tyme, constituted, elected and chosen, out of
the freemen of the sayd Company, for the tyme beinge, in such

manner and fforme as is hereafter in these presents expressed.
. . . [First set of magistrates named, to continue until the next Court.] And further, wee . . . doe ordeyne . . . that the Governor of the sayd Company, for the tyme being, or, in his absence, by occassion of sicknesse, or otherwise, by his leave and permission, the Deputy-Governor, ffor the tyme being, shall and may, ffrom tyme to tyme, upon all occassions, give order ffor the assemblinge of the sayd Company, and calling them together, to consult and advise of the businesse and affaires of the sayd Company. And that forever hereafter, twice in every year, that is to say, on every first Wednesday in the moneth of May, and on every last Wednesday in October, or oftener, in case it shall bee requisite, the Assistants, and such of the ffreemen of the Company, not exceedinge six persons ffor Newport, ffoure persons ffor each of the respective townes of Providence, Portsmouth and Warwicke, and two persons for each other place, towne or city, whoe shall bee, from tyme to tyme, thereunto elected or deputed by the majour parte of the ffremen of the respective townes or places . . . shall have a generall meetinge, or Assembly then and there to . . . determine . . . the affaires and businesse of the said Company and Plantations. And further, wee doe . . . give and graunt unto the sayd Governour and Company of the English collony of Rhode-Island and Providence Plantations, in New-England, in America, and theire successours, that the Governour, or, in his absence, or, by his permission, the Deputy-Governour of the sayd Company, for the tyme beinge, the Assistants, and such of the ffreemen of the sayd Company as shall bee soe as aforesayd elected or deputed, or soe many of them as shall bee present att such meetinge or assemblye, as afforesayde, shall bee called the Generall Assemblye; and that they, or the greatest parte of them present (whereof the Governour or Deputy-Governour, and sixe of the Assistants, at least to bee seven) shall have . . . ffull power [and] authority, ffrom tyme to tyme, and at all tymes hereafter, to apoynt, alter and change, such dayes, tymes and places of meetinge and Generall Assemblye, as theye shall thinke

ffitt; 𝔄n𝔡 furt𝔥𝔢𝔯 [other powers of the Assembly, as in the Connecticut Charter] . . . wee doe . . . establish and ordeyne, that yearelie, once in the yeare, forever hereafter, namely, the aforesayd Wednesday in May, and at the towne of Newport, or elsewhere, if urgent occasion doe require, the Governour, Deputy-Governour and Assistants of the sayd Company, and other officers of the sayd Company, or such of them as the Generall Assemblye shall thinke ffitt, shall bee, in the sayd Generall Court or Assembly to bee held from that daye or tyme, newly chosen for the year ensueing, by such greater part of the sayd Company, for the tyme beinge, as shall bee then and there present . . .

[Provisions for temporary government; for prevention of Indian troubles in relation to other colonies; for boundaries, etc.] 𝔄n𝔡 furt𝔥𝔢𝔯, our will and pleasure is, that in all matters of publique controversy which may fall out betweene our Collony of Providence Plantations, and the rest of our Collonies in New-England, itt shall and may bee lawful to and for the Governour and Company of the sayd Collony of Providence Plantations to make their appeals therein to us, our heirs and successours, for redresse in such cases, within this our realme of England:[1] and that itt shall be lawfull to and for the inhabitants of the sayd Collony of Providence Plantations, without let or molestation, to passe and repasse with freedome, into and through the rest of the English Collonies, upon their lawfull and civill occasions, and to converse, and hold commerce and trade, with such of the inhabitants of our other English Collonies as shall bee willing to admit them thereunto, they behaveing themselves peaceably among them; any act, clause or sentence, in any of the sayd Collonies provided, or that shall bee provided, to the contrary in anywise notwithstanding. . . .

---

[1] Observe, this is *not* an appeal from the colonial court by *an individual*. The clause has reference to the troubles, then recent, between Rhode Island and Massachusetts — the latter having threatened to exclude Rhode Island commerce.

XIX. AN ENGLISH COLONIAL SYSTEM

99. Instructions for the Councill oppointed for Forraigne Plantations (1660) by Charles II

O'Callaghan's *Documents relative to the Colonial History of New York* (1853), III, 34–36.

For the significance of this first permanent "Colonial Department," cf. *American History and Government*, § 95.

1. You shall informe yourselves by the best wayes and meanes you can of the state and condicion of all Forraigne Plantac[i]ons, and by what co[m]missions or authorities they are and have bene governed and disposed of; and are to procure either from such persons as have any graunts thereof from the Croun, or from the records themselves, the copies of all such commissions or graunts, to be transcribed and registered in a booke provided for that purpose, that you may be the better able to understand judge and administer such affaires, as by your commission and instruccions are intrusted to your care and management.

2. You shall forthwith write letters to evrie of our Governors for the time being of all our English Plantacions and to evrie such person or persons who by any Letters Pattents from us or any of our predcesors doe claime or exercise a right of governement in any of the said plantacions in which letteres you are to informe them of our gratious care and provision in their behalfe both in erecting a General Councill of Trade wherein their concernments are mingled and provided for with the rest of our dominions and especially of this particular Councell which is applyed only to the inspeccion care and conduct of Forraigne Plantacions.

3. You are in the said letters to require the said Governors and persons above mesioned, to send unto you in writeing with the advise of the Councell of evrie of the said plantacions

respectively, perticuler and exact accompt of the state of their affaires; of the nature and constitucoin of their lawes and governement and in what modell and frame they move and are disposed; what numbers of men; what fortifications and other strengths and defences are upon the place, and how furnished and provided for.

4. You are to order and settle such a continuall correspondencie that you may be able, as often as you are required thereunto, to give up to us an accompt of the Government of each Colonie; of their complaints, their wants, their abundance; of their severall growths and commodities; of every shipp trading there and its ladeing and whither consigned; and what the proceeds of that place have beene in the late yeares; that thereby the intrinsick value and the true condicion of each part and of the whole may be thoroughly understood; whereby a more steady judgement and ballance may be made for the better ordering and disposing of trade and of the proceede and improvements of the Plantacions; that soe each place within it selfe, and all of them being collected into one viewe and management here, may be regulated and ordered upon common and equall ground and principles.

5. You are to applie your selves to all prudentiall meanes for the rendering those dominions usefull to England and England helpfull to them, and for the bringing the severall Colonies and Plantacions, within themselves, into a more certaine civill and uniforme goverement and for the better ordering and distributeing of publique justice among them.

6. You are to enquire diligently into the severall governments and Councells of Colonies Plantacions and distant Dominions, belonging to other Princes or States, and to examine by what conduct and pollicies they governe or benefit them; and you are to consult and provide that if such councells be good wholsome and practiceable, they may be applied to the use of our Plantacions; or if they tend or were designed to the prejudice or disadvantage thereof or of any of our subjects or of trade or commerce, how they may be ballanced or turned back upon them.

* * * * * * *

11. You are lastly required and impowered to advise order settle and dispose of all matters relating to the good governm^t improvement and management of our Forraine Plantacôns or any of them, with your utmost skill direccôn and prudence. And in all cases wherein you shall judge that further powers and assistants shall be necessary, you are to addresse your selves to us [or] our Privy Councill for our further pleasure resolucôn and direccôns therein.

100. The Commercial Policy

a. "First"[1] Navigation Act, 1660

Statutes of the Realm, V, 246-250. The act is known as 12 Car. II, c. 18. The text would fill some ten pages of this volume. For history and references upon this and subsequent navigation acts, cf. *American History and Government*, §§ 96, 116.

AN ACT for the Encourageing and increasing of Shipping and Navigation.

[1.] For the increase of Shiping and incouragement of the Navigation of this Nation, (wherin, under the good providence and protection of God, the Wealth, Safety, and Strength of this Kingdome is soe much concerned), Bee it Enacted by the Kings most Excellent Majesty and by the Lords and Commons in this present Parliament assembled and the Authoritie therof, that from and after [December 1, 1660], and from thence forward, noe Goods or Commodities whatsoever shall be Imported into or Exported out of any Lands, Islelands, Plantations, or Territories to his Majesty belonging or in his possession or which may hereafter belong unto or be in the possession of His Majesty His Heires and Successors, in Asia, Africa, or America, in any other Ship or Ships, Vessell or Vessells what-

---

[1] The first part of this act is copied almost word for word from an act of the Long Parliament in 1651. That act, however, was not enforced. It applied only to shipping. The Act of 1660 added the "enumerating" clause (XVIII).

soever, but in such Ships or Vessels as doe truely and without fraude belong onely to the people of England or Ireland, Dominion of Wales, or Towne of Berwicke upon Tweede, or are of the built of, and belonging to any of the said Lands, Islands, Plantations, or Territories . . . and whereof the Master and three fourthes of the Marriners at least are English,[1] under the penalty of the Forfeiture [of Vessell and Cargo] . . .

[III. In like words, limits the commerce of England herself to the same shipping.]

[XVIII.] And it is further Enacted . . . That from and after . . . [April 1, 1661] . . . noe Sugars, Tobaccho, Cotton-Wool, Indicoes, Ginger, Fustick, or other dyeing wood, of the Growth, Production, or Manufacture of any English Plantations in America, Asia or Africa shall be shiped, carryed, conveyed, or transported from any of the said English Plantations to any Land, Island, Territory, Dominion, Port, or place whatsoever, other than to such other English Plantations as doe belong to His Majesty His Heires and Successors, or to the Kingdome of England or Ireland or Principallity of Wales or Towne of Berwicke upon Tweede . . . under penalty of forfeiture [as before] . . .

b. *Second Navigation Act, 1663*

Statutes of the Realm, V, 449-452 (15 Car. II, c. 7).

The act of 1660 had (1) "protected" English and colonial shipping by shutting out all other shipping from the English and colonial trade ; and (2) it had "enumerated" a few semi-tropical products which colonies could export only to England. This act of 1663 provides that all European imports to the colonies must be obtained through England.

---

[1] Question having arisen in regard to the definition of English-built ships and English mariners, these terms were defined in section V of the Act of 1662 (14 Car. II, c. 11). The portion of the section relating to mariners follows : "And whereas it is required by the said Act that in sundry cases the Master and three fourths of the Mariners are to be English, it is to be understood that any of His Majesties Subjects of England, Ireland, *and His Plantations* are to bee accounted English, and no others. . . ." — *Statutes of the Realm,* V, 395.

An Act for the Encouragement of Trade.

[IV.] And in reguard His Magesties Plantations beyond the Seas are inhabited and peopled by His Subjects of this His Kingdome of England, For the maintaining a greater correspondence and kindnesse betweene them and keepeing them in a firmer dependance upon it, and rendring them yet more beneficiall and advantagious unto it in the farther Imployment and Encrease of English Shipping and Seamen, vent of English Woollen and other Manufactures and Commodities, rendring the Navigation to and from the same more safe and cheape, and makeing this Kingdome a Staple not onely of the Commodities of those Plantations but alsoe of the Commodities of other Countryes and Places for the supplying of them, and it being the usage of other Nations to keepe their Plantation Trade to themselves, *Be it enacted*, and it is hereby enacted, That from and after [March 25, 1664], noe Commoditie of the Growth, Production, or Manufacture, of Europe, shall be imported into any Land, Island, Plantation, Colony, Territory, or Place, to His Majestie belonging, or which shall [belong hereafter] unto, or be in the Possession of His Majestie His Heires and Successors, in Asia, Africa, or America, (Tangier onely excepted) but what shall be bona fide and without fraude laden and shipped in England, Wales, [and] the Towne of Berwicke upon Tweede, and in English built Shipping, . . . and whereof the Master and three Fourthes of the Marriners at least are English, and which shall be carryed directly thence to the said Lands, Islands, Plantations, Colonyes, Territories, or Places, and from noe other place or places whatsoever, Any Law, Statute, or Usage, to the contrary notwithstanding, under the Penaltie [of forfeiture of vessel and cargo]. . .

[V.] Provided alwayes . . . That it shall and may be lawfull to shipp and lade in such Shipps, and soe navigated as in the foregoeing Clause is sett downe and expressed, *in any part of Europe*, Salt for the Fisheries of New England

and New found land, and to shipp and lade in the Medera's Wines of the Growth thereof, and to shipp and lade in the Westerne Islands or Azores Wines of the Growth of the said Islands, and to shipp [or] take in Servants or Horses in Scotland or Ireland, and to shipp or lade in Scotland all sorts of Victuall of the Growth of Production of Scotland, and to shipp or lade in Ireland all sortes of Victuall of the Growth or Production of Ireland, and the same to transport into any of the said Lands, Islands, Plantations, Colonyes, Territories, or Places, Any thing in the foregoeing Clause to the contrary in any wise notwithstanding.

[The extension of the navigation policy after 1690 to restrict American manufactures, with some additions to the "enumerated articles" in the First Navigation Act, is not illustrated in this volume. For this, with quotations from the laws, see *American History and Government*, § 116. But the following law (c) of the later period has so unique a significance that it is here inserted, out of its chronological order. Cf. *American History and Government*, § 116, note at close.]

c. Sugar Act of 1733. May 17/27, 1733

Pickering's *Statutes at Large*, XVI, 374–379 (6 Geo. II, c. 13). (Italics only as in the original.)

An act for the better securing and encouraging the trade of his Majesty's sugar colonies in America.

WHEREAS *the welfare and prosperity of your Majesty's sugar colonies in* America *are of the greatest consequence and importance to the trade, navigation and strength of this kingdom: and whereas the planters of the said sugar colonies have of late years fallen under such great discouragements, that they are unable to improve or carry on the sugar trade upon an equal footing with the foreign sugar colonies, without some advantage and relief be given to them from* Great Britain: *for remedy whereof* . . . be it enacted . . . , That from and after [December 25, 1733], there shall be raised, levied, collected and paid, unto and for the use of his Majesty . . . , upon all rum or spirits of the produce or manufacture of any of the colonies or plantations in *America,* not in the possession or under the dominion of his Majesty . . . , which at any time or times within or during the continuance of this act, shall be imported or brought into any of the colonies or plantations in *America*, which now are or hereafter may be in the possession or under the dominion of his Majesty . . . , the sum of nine pence, money of *Great Britain* . . . , for every gallon thereof, and after that rate for any greater or lesser quantity: and upon all molasses or syrups of such foreign produce or manufacture as aforesaid, which shall be imported or brought into any of the said colonies or plantations of or belonging to his Majesty, the sum of six pence of like money for every gallon thereof . . . and upon all sugars and paneles of such foreign growth, produce, or manufacture as aforesaid, which shall be imported into any of the said colonies or plantations of or belonging to his Majesty, a duty after the rate of five shillings of like money, for every hundred weight *Avoirdupoize*. . . .

[Sections II–VIII make provision for enforcing the act and for extending its provisions to Ireland.]

IX. And it is hereby further enacted . . . , That in case any sugar or paneles of the growth, produce or manufacture of any of the colonies or plantations belonging to or in the possession of his Majesty . . . , which shall have been imported into *Great Britain* after the twenty-fourth day of *June* one thousand seven hundred and thirty-three, shall at any time within one year after the importation thereof, be again exported out of *Great Britain*, and that due proof be first made, by certificate from the proper officers, of the due entry and payment of the subsidies or duties charged or payable upon the importation thereof, together with the oath of the merchant or his agent importing and exporting the same, or in case such merchant or agent shall be one of the people called *Quakers*, by his solemn affirmation to the truth thereof, and that all other requisites shall be performed that are by law to be performed in cases where any of the said subsidies or duties are to be paid by any former statute, all the residue and remainder of the subsidy or duty, by any former act or acts of parliament granted and charged on such sugar or paneles as aforesaid, shall without any delay or reward be repaid to such merchant or merchants, who do export the same, within one month after demand thereof.[1]

[X. Rebate and bounty in England upon sugar refined from brown sugar imported from English colonies.]

* * * * * * *

101. The Duke of York's Charter for New York, March 12/22, 1663/4

O'Callaghan's *Documents relating to the Colonial History of New York*, II, 295-298.

This grant was made some months before the English were in actual possession of the territory. After the loss and recapture of the Province in 1673-1674, a second grant was issued by Charles II, practically identical with this one of 1664.

CHARLES the Second, . . . [etc.] . . . Know ye that we . . . by these presents for us Our heirs and Successors Do Give and Grant unto our Dearest Brother James Duke of York his Heirs and Assigns All that part of the maine Land of New England[2] . . . [detailed bounds, the Duke to pay yearly forty beaver skins, "when they shall be demanded, or within ninety days after"]. And We do further . . . Grant unto our said Dearest Brother James Duke of York his Heirs, [etc] full and absolute power and authority to correct, punish, pardon, govern and rule all such the subjects of us Our Heirs and Successors who may from time to time adventure themselves into any the parts or places aforesaid or that shall or do at any time hereafter inhabit within the same, *according to such Laws, Orders, Ordinances, Directions and Instruments as by our said Dearest*

---

[1] The sugar from the English colonies also paid duties on admission into English ports (lower than these here prescribed for *foreign* sugars); but such duties were to be rebated, according to this section IX, upon reëxportation.

[2] The name "New England" still applied to all English America north of Delaware Bay.

Brother or his Assigns shall be established, And in defect thereof, in cases of necessity, according to the good discretions of his Deputies, Commissioners, Officers or Assigns respectively, as well in all causes and matters Capital and Criminal as civil both marine and others. So always as the said Statutes Ordinances and proceedings be not contrary to but as near as conveniently may be agreeable to the Laws, Statutes and Government of this Our Realm of England And *saving and reserving to us our Heirs and Successors the receiving, hearing and determining of the Appeal and Appeals of all or any Person or Persons of in or belonging to the territories or Islands aforesaid in or touching any Judgment or Sentence to be there made or given*[1] And further that it shall and may be lawful to and for our said Dearest Brother his Heirs and Assigns by these presents from time to time to nominate, make, constitute, ordain and confirm by such name or names stile or stiles as to him or them shall seem good and likewise to revoke, discharge, change and alter as well all and singular Governors, Officers and Ministers which hereafter shall be by him or them thought fit and needful to be made or used within the aforesaid parts and Islands And also to make, ordain and establish all manner of Orders, Laws, directions, instructions, forms and Ceremonies of Government and Magistracy fit and necessary for and Concerning the Government of the territories and Islands aforesaid, so always as the same be not contrary to the laws and statutes of this Our Realm of England but as near as may be agreeable thereunto . . . And We do further . . . Grant . . . That it shall and may be lawful to and for the said James Duke of York his heirs and Assigns in his or their discretions from time to time to admit such and so many Person and Persons to trade and traffic unto and within the Territories and Islands aforesaid and into every or any part and parcel thereof and to have possess and enjoy any Lands or Heredita-

---

[1] This was the first charter provision for appeal from a colonial court to England. The question had arisen just before in connection with the New England colonies. Cf. *American History and Government,* § 99.

ments in the parts and places aforesaid, as they shall think fit, according to the Laws, Orders, Constitutions and Ordinances by Our said Brother his Heirs, Deputies, Commissioners and Assigns from time to time to be made and established ... and under such conditions, reservations, and agreements as Our said Brother his Heirs or Assigns shall set down, order, direct and appoint, and not otherwise. ...

[Observe the absence of any provision for participation by the settlers in lawmaking. The charter does not even contain the usual guarantee of the "rights of Englishmen," though the provision for appeals to English courts would secure such rights indirectly. Cf. *American History and Government*, § 109.]

102. Penn's Grant of Pennsylvania, March 4/14, 1680/88

Charters and Laws of Pennsylvania (Harrisburg, 1879), 81-90.

Penn made the first draft of this charter from Baltimore's Maryland Charter of 1632, but the Attorney-General inserted several clauses which increased the authority of the English government, cf. *American History and Government*, § 110.

CHARLES THE SECOND [etc.]. ... *Whereas* our Trustie and well beloved Subject, William Penn, Esquire, sonn and heire of Sir William Penn, deceased, out of a commendable desire to enlarge our English Empire, and promote such usefull comodities as may bee of benefitt to us and our Dominions, as alsoe to reduce the Savage Natives by gentle and just manners to the love of civill Societie and Christian Religion hath humbley besought leave of us to transport an ample colonie unto a certaine Countrey hereinafter described in the partes of America not yet cultivated and planted. And hath likewise humbley besought our Royall Majestie to give, grant, and confirm all the said Countrey with certaine priviledges and Jurisdiccons requisite for the good Government and safetie of the said Countrey and Colonie, to him and his heirs forever. **Knowe yee,** therefore, that wee favouring the petition and good purpose of the said William Penn, and haveing regard to the memorie and meritts of his late father . . . by this Our present Charter, for us, Our heires and successors, Doe give and grant unto the said William Penn, his heires and assignes All that Tract or parte of land in America, [the long and indefinite bounding clause follows.] . . . and him the said William Penn, his heires and Assignes, Wee do, by this our Royall Charter . . . make, . . . the true and absolute Proprietaries of the Countrey aforesaid, Saving unto us . . . the Sovreignity of the aforesaid Countrey . . . To bee holden of us, our heires and Successors, Kings of England, as of our Castle of Windsor, in our County of Berks, in free and common socage by fealty only for all services, and not in Capite or by Knights services, Yeelding and paying therefore . . . two beaver Skins to bee delivered att our said Castle of Windsor, on the first day of Januarie, in every yeare; and also the fifth parte of all Gold and Silver Oare, which shall from time to time happen to be found within the Limitts aforesaid, cleare of all Charges, and . . . wee doe hereby erect the aforesaid Countrey and Islands, into a Province and Seigniorie, and doe call itt *Pensilvania* . . . , And forasmuch as wee have hereby made and ordeyned the aforesaid William Penn, his heires and assignes, the true and absolute Proprietaries of all the Lands and Dominions aforesaid. Know yee therefore, that wee reposing speciall trust and Confidence in the fidelitie, wisdome, Justice, and provident circumspeccon of the said William Penn . . . , Doe grant free, full and absolute power, by vertue of these presents to him and his heires, and to his and their Deputies, and Lieutenants, for the good and happy government of the said Countrey, to ordeyne, make, Enact, and under his and their Seales to publish, any Lawes whatsoever, for the raising money for the publick use of the said province, or for any other End apperteyning either unto the publick state, peace, or safety of the said Countrey, or unto the private utility of perticular persons, according unto their best discretions, *by and with the advice, assent, and approbacon of the freemen of the said Countrey, or the greater parte of them,*

or of their Delegates or Deputies, whom for the Enacting of the
said Lawes, when, and as often as need shall require, Wee will,
that the said William Penn, and his heires, shall assemble in such
sort and forme as to him and them shall seeme best, and the
same Lawes duely to execute unto, and upon all people within
the said Countrey and limitts thereof; And wee doe likewise give and grant unto the said William Penn, and his
heires, and to his and their Deputies and Lieutenants, such
power and authoritie to appoint and establish any Judges,
and Justices, Magistrates and Officers whatsoever, for what
Causes soever, for the probates of will and for the granting of
Administracons within the precincts aforesaid, and with what
power soever, and in such forme as to the said William Penn,
or his heires, shall seeme most convenient. Alsoe, to remitt,
release, pardon and abolish, whether before Judgement or
after, all Crimes and Offences whatsoever, comitted within the
said Countrey, against the said Lawes, Treason and wilfull
and malicious Murder onely excepted; and in those Cases, to
Grant Reprieves untill Our pleasure may bee knowne thereon,
and to doe all and every other thing and things which unto
the compleate establishment of Justice unto Courts and
Tribunals, formes of Judicature and manner of proceedings
doe belong, altho' in these presents expresse mencon bee
not made thereof; . . . Provided, Nevertheles, that the said
Lawes bee consonant to reason, and bee not repugnant or
contrarie, but as neare as conveniently may bee agreeable to
the Lawes, Statutes and rights of this our Kingdome of England, *And Saveing and reserving to us, Our heirs and Successors,
the receiving, heareing, and determining of the Appeale and
Appeales, of all or any person or persons, of, in or belonging to
the Territories aforesaid, or touching any Judgement to bee
there made or given* . . . [In emergencies, the proprietor or
his representatives may make ordinances without the consent
of the freemen; the same to be agreeable to the laws of
England with limitation as in the Maryland Charter.] And
our further will and pleasure is, that the Lawes for regulateing

and governing of Propertie, within the said Province, as well for the descent and enjoyment of lands, as likewise for the enjoyment and succession of goods and Chattells, and likewise as to felonies, shall be and continue the same as shall bee for the time being, by the general course of the Law in our Kingdome of England, untill the said Lawes shall be altered by the said William Penn, his heires or assignes, and by the freemen of the said Province, their Delegates or Deputies, or the greater part of them. And to the End the said William Penn, or heires, . . . may not att any time hereafter, by misconstrucon of the powers aforesaid, through inadvertiencie or designe, depart from that faith and due allegiance which . . . they always owe unto us, Our heires and successors, . . . by force or colour of any lawes hereafter to bee made in the said Province, . . . Our further will and pleasure is, *that a transcript or Duplicate of all lawes which shall bee soe as aforesaid, made and published within the said province, shall within five yeares after the makeing thereof, be transmitted and delivered to the privy Councell, for the time being, of us, our heires and successors;* And if any of the said Lawes within the space of six months, after that they shall be soe transmitted and delivered, bee declared by us, our heires or successors, in our or their privy Councell, inconsistent with the sovereignty or lawfull prerogative of us, our heirs or successors, or contrary to the faith and allegiance due by [*to*] the legall Government of this realme, from the said William Penn, or his heires or of the Planters and Inhabitants of the said province; and that thereupon any of the said Lawes shall bee adjudged and declared to bee void by us, our heires or successors, under our or their Privy Seale, *that then, and from thenceforth such Lawes concerning which such Judgement and declaracon shall be made, shall become voyd,* otherwise the said lawes soe transmitted, shall remaine and stand in full force according to the true intent and meaneing thereof.[1] . . .

[Grant of right to export products of the province into any

---
[1] This was the first provision for a direct English veto upon colonial laws.

English port, "and not into any other country whatsoeve," with a clause insisting upon obedience to "the Acts of Navigation."] **And Wee doe** further appoint and ordaine . . . That he the said William penn, his heires and assignes, may from time to time forever, have and enjoy the Customes and Subsidies in the ports, harbours and other Creeks, and places aforesaid, within the province aforesaid, payable or due for merchandizes and wares, there to be Laded and unladed, the said Customes and Subsidies to be reasonably assessed, upon any occasion by themselves, and the people there as aforesaid, to be assembled to whom wee Give power, by these presents for us, our heires and Successors, upon just cause, and in a due proporcon, to assesse and impose the same, *Saveing unto us, our heires and Successors, such imposicons and customes as by Act of parliament are and shall be appointed.* **And** further . . . **Wee** doe . . . grant . . . That Wee, our heeres and Successors shall att no time hereafter sett or make, or cause to be sett, any imposition, custome or other taxacon, rate or contribucon whatsoever, in and upon the dwellers and inhabitants of the aforesaid province, for their Lands, tenements, goods or chattels, within the said province, or in and upon any goods or merchandize within the said province, or to be laden or unladen within the ports or harbours of the said province, *unles the same be with the consent of the proprietary, or chiefe Governor and assembly, or by Act of parliament in England.*[1] . . . .

103. Penn's Grants to the Pennsylvanians

a. *"Laws Agreed upon in England," 1683*

Hazard's *Annals of Pennsylvania*, 568–574. Penn gave a formal charter to the settlers in 1683, prefaced by the following "laws" which constitute a bill of rights and which were to be altered only by the consent of six sevenths of the legislature. The charter of 1683 was replaced

---

[1] All italics are by the editor. The Pennsylvania charter distinctly recognized the right of Parliament to tax the colonists. These clauses, with those regarding appeals and the royal veto, were added to Penn's draft by the King's Attorney-General.

by that of 1701 (see *b*, below); but these "Lawes" were a separate instrument of government, and remained in force.

* * * * * * *

III. That all elections of members or representatives of the people . . . of the province . . . to serve in the provincial council or general assembly, to be held within the said province, shall be free and voluntary, and that the elector that shall receive any reward or gift, in meat, drink, moneys, or otherwise, shall forfeit his right to elect; and such person as shall directly or indirectly give, promise, or bestow such reward as aforesaid, to be elected, shall forfeit his election, and be thereby incapable to serve as aforesaid: and the provincial council and general assembly shall be the sole judges of the regularity or irregularity of the elections of their own respective members.

IV. That no money or goods shall be raised upon, or paid by any of the people of this province, by way of public tax, custom, or contribution, but by a law for that purpose made, and whosoever shall levy, collect, or pay any money or goods contrary thereto, shall be held a public enemy to the province, and a betrayer of the liberties of the people thereof.

V. That all courts shall be open, and justice shall neither be sold, denied, or delayed.

* * * * * * *

VII. That all pleadings, processes, and records in court, shall be short, and in English, and in an ordinary and plain character, that they may be understood, and justice speedily administered.

VIII. That all trials shall be by twelve men, and as near as may be, peers or equals, and of the neighbourhood, and men without just exception. In cases of life, there shall be first twenty-four returned by the sheriffs for a grand inquest, of whom twelve at least shall find the complaint to be true, and then the twelve men or peers, to be likewise returned by the sheriff, shall have the final judgment. But reasonable challenges shall be always admitted against the said twelve men, or any of them.

IX. That all fees in all cases shall be moderate, and settled by the provincial council and general assembly, and be hung up in a table in every respective court, and whosoever shall be convicted of taking more, shall pay twofold, and be dismissed his employment, one moiety of which shall go to the party wronged.

X. That all prisons shall be workhouses for felons, vagrants, and loose and idle persons, whereof one shall be in every county.

XI. That all persons shall be bailable by sufficient sureties, unless for capital offences, where the proof is evident, or the presumption is great.

XII. That all persons wrongfully imprisoned or prosecuted at law, shall have double damages against the informer or prosecutor.

XIII. That all prisons shall be free as to fees, food, and lodging.

XIV. That all lands and goods shall be liable to pay debts, except where there is legal issue, and then all the goods, and one-third of the land only.

XV. That all wills in writing, attested by two witnesses, shall be of the same force as to lands as other conveyances, being legally proved within forty days, either within or without the said province.

XVI. That seven years quiet possession shall give an unquestionable right, except in cases of infants, lunatics, married women, or persons beyond the seas.

* * * * * * *

XXVIII. That all children within this province, of the age of twelve years, shall be taught some useful trade or skill, to the end none may be idle, but the poor may work to live, and the rich, if they become poor, may not want.

XXIX. That servants be not kept longer than their time, and such as are careful be both justly and kindly used in their service, and put in fitting equipage at the expiration thereof, according to custom.

* * * * * *

b. Penn's Charter of Privileges to Pennsylvania, October 28/November 8, 1701

Votes and Proceedings of the House of Representatives of Pennsylvania, I, pt. II, i–iii.

A brief statement of the political conditions in the colony previous to this grant will be found in *American History and Government*, § 110. After a long absence in England, Penn returned to the colony in December, 1699, to find turmoil and confusion. After a few months, it became clear that Penn must again go back to England promptly to save his proprietary rights from attacks there; but before he left, he granted, and the Assembly accepted, this noble charter, which remained the constitution of the colony until 1776, and which the more conservative patriots of that Revolutionary day wished to have continued still longer as the constitution of the independent State.

Italics are as in the original. The editor has used **black italics** sparingly to call attention to especially important passages.

[Recital of grant of charter of 1681 to Penn, the liberal "frame of government" established by Penn in 1683, the later distractions, and Penn's promise either to restore the "frame" of 1683 or to grant a new one "better adapted to . . . the present circumstances."]

KNOW YE THEREFORE, That for the further Well-being and good Government of the said Province, and Territories; and in Pursuance of the Rights and Powers beforementioned, I the said *William Penn* do declare, grant and confirm, unto all the Freemen, Planters, and Adventurers, and other Inhabitants of this Province and Territories, these following Liberties, Franchises and Privileges, so far as in me lieth, to be held, enjoyed, and kept, by the Freemen, Planters and Adventurers, and other Inhabitants of and in the said Province, and Territories thereunto annexed, for ever.

I.

BECAUSE no People can be truly happy, tho' under the greatest Enjoyment of civil Liberties, if abridged of the Freedom of their Consciences, as to their Religious Profession and Worship: And Almighty God being the only Lord of Conscience, Father of Lights and Spirits; and the Author as well as Object of all divine Knowledge, Faith and Worship, who only doth enlighten the Minds, and persuade and convince the Understandings of People, I do hereby grant and declare, That no Person or Persons, inhabiting in this Province or Territories, who shall confess and acknowledge One almighty God, the Creator, Upholder and Ruler of the World, . . . shall be in any Case molested or prejudiced, in his or their Person or Estate, because of his or their conscientious Perswasion or Practice, nor be compelled to frequent or maintain any religious Worship, Place, or Ministry, contrary to his or their Mind, or to do or suffer any other Act or Thing, contrary to their religious Perswasion.[1]

AND that all Persons who also profess to believe in *Jesus Christ*, the Saviour of the World, shall be capable (notwithstanding their other Perswasions and Practices in Point of Conscience and Religion) to serve this Government in any Capacity, both legislatively and executively, he or they solemnly promising, when lawfully required, Allegiance to the King as Sovereign, and Fidelity to the Proprietary and Governor, . . .

II.

FOR the well governing of this Province and Territories, there shall be an Assembly yearly chosen by the Freemen thereof, to consist of Four Persons out of each County, of most Note for Virtue, Wisdom, and Ability (or of a greater Number at any Time, as the Governor and Assembly shall agree) upon the first Day of *October* for ever; and shall sit

---

[1] This grant was also in the "Laws Agreed upon in England," XXXV.

on the fourteenth Day of the same Month at *Philadelphia*, unless the Governor and Council for the Time being, shall see Cause to appoint another Place within the said Province or Territories: Which Assembly shall have Power to chuse a Speaker and other their Officers; and shall be judges of the Qualifications and Elections of their own Members; **sit upon their own Adjournments;** appoint Committees; prepare Bills, in order to pass into Laws; impeach Criminals, and redress Grievances; and shall have all other Powers and Privileges of an Assembly, according to the Rights of the Freeborn Subjects of *England*, and as is usual in any of the King's Plantations in *America*.

AND if any County or Counties, shall refuse or neglect to chuse their respective Representatives as aforesaid, or if chosen, do not meet to serve in Assembly, those who are so chosen and met, shall have the full Power of an Assembly, in as ample Manner as if all the Representatives had been chosen and met, provided they are not less than Two Thirds of the whole Number that ought to meet.

AND that the Qualifications of Electors and Elected, and all other Matters and Things relating to Elections of Representatives to serve in Assemblies, tho' not herein particularly expressed, shall be and remain as by a Law of this Government, made at *Newcastle* in the Year *One Thousand Seven Hundred*, intituled, *An Act to ascertain the Number of Members of Assembly, and to regulate the Elections.*[1]

III.

THAT the Freemen in each respective County, at the Time and Place of Meeting for Electing their Representatives to serve in Assembly, may, as often as there shall be Occasion, chuse a double Number of Persons to present to the Governor for Sheriffs and Coroners, to serve for Three Years, if so long they

---

[1] That act decreed that, in order to vote, a man must own "fifty acres of land, . . . twelve acres thereof, or more, cleared and improved; or be otherwise worth fifty pounds lawful money" above all indebtedness.

behave themselves well; out of which respective Elections and Presentments, the Governor shall nominate and commissionate one for each of the said Offices, the third Day after such Presentment, or else the first named in such Presentment, for each Office as aforesaid, shall stand and serve in that Office for the Time before respectively limited; and in case of Death or Default, such Vacancies shall be supplied by the Governor, to serve to the End of the said Term.

PROVIDED ALWAYS, That if the said Freemen shall, at any Time, neglect, or decline to chuse a Person or Persons for either or both the aforesaid Offices, then and in such Case, the Persons that are or shall be in the respective Offices of Sheriffs or Coroners, at the Time of Election, shall remain therein, until they shall be removed by another Election as aforesaid.

AND that the Justices of the respective Counties, shall or may nominate and present to the Governor three Persons, to serve for Clerk of the Peace for the said County when there is a vacancy, one of which the Governor shall commissionate within ten Days after such Presentment, or else the first nominated, shall serve in the said Office during good Behaviour.

IV.

[Style and manner of recording laws.]

V.

THAT all Criminals shall have the same Privileges of Witnesses and Council as their Prosecutors.

VI.

THAT no Person or Persons shall, or may, at any Time hereafter, be obliged to answer any Complaint, Matter or Thing whatsoever relating to Property, before the Governor and Council, or in any other Place, but in ordinary Course of Justice, unless Appeals thereunto shall be hereafter by Law appointed.

VII.

[Ordinaries and Taverns to be licensed by the Governor, on recommendation of the Justices of the counties concerned, — with power to suppress for misbehaviour.]

VIII.

IF any Person, through Temptation or Melancholy, shall destroy himself, his Estate, real and personal, shall, notwithstanding, descend to his Wife and Children, or Relations, as if he had died a natural Death;[1] and if any Person shall be destroyed or killed by Casualty or Accident, there shall be no Forfeiture to the Governor by Reason thereof.

AND no Act, Law or Ordinance whatsoever shall, at any Time hereafter, be made or done, to alter, change or diminish the Form or Effect of this Charter, or of any Part or Clause therein, contrary to the true Intent and Meaning thereof, *without the Consent of the Governor for the Time being, and Six Parts of Seven of the Assembly met.*[2]

BUT because the Happiness of Mankind depends so much upon the Enjoying of Liberty of their Consciences as aforesaid, I do hereby solemnly declare, promise and grant, for me, my Heirs and assigns, That the first Article of this Charter relating to Liberty of Conscince, and every Part and Clause therein, according to the true Intent and Meaning thereof, *shall be kept and remain, without any Alteration, inviolably for ever.*[2]

* * * * * * *

[Provision for separation of the Delaware "Territories" under their own legislature, if they so desire.]

---

[1] By the law of England, the property of a suicide, like that of a man convicted of a felony, escheated to the crown. The other half of this same paragraph abolished another ancient legal cruelty.

[2] This provision (adopted also from the "Laws Agreed upon in England") is the first attempt in a constitution to establish *a regular method of amendment.* The attempt to exclude a portion of the document from amendment, so common for long afterward, begins here also (next paragraph).

NOTWITHSTANDING which Separation of the Province and Territories, in Respect of Legislation, I do hereby promise, grant and declare, That the Inhabitants of both Province and Territories, shall separately enjoy all other Liberties, Privileges and Benefits, granted jointly to them in this Charter, any Law, Usage or Custom of this Government heretofore made and practised, or any Law made and passed by the General Assembly, to the contrary hereof notwithstanding.

104. Berkeley's Report on Virginia, 1671

Hening's *Statutes*, II, 511–517.

In 1670 the Colonial Board (No. 99, above) sent out questions, which, with the answers of Governor Berkeley for Virginia (1671), are given below. Other colonies sent like reports.

1. What councils, assemblies, and courts of judicature are within your government, and of what nature and kind?
Answer. There is a governor and sixteen counsellors, who have from his sacred majestie, a commission of *Oyer and Terminer*, who judge and determine all causes that are above fifteen pound sterling; for what is under, there are particular courts in every county, which are twenty in number. *Every year, at least the assembly is called*, before whom lye appeals, and this assembly is composed of two burgesses out of every county. These lay the necessary taxes, as the necessity of the war with the Indians, or their exigencies require.

[2. Courts of admiralty.]

3. Where the legislative and executive powers of your government are seated?
Answer. In the governor, councel and assembly, and officers substituted by them.

4. What statute laws and ordinances are now . . . in force?
Answer. The secretary of this country every year sends to the lord chancellor, or one of the principal secretaries, what laws are yearly made; which for the most part concern only our own private exigencies; for, contrary to the laws of England,

we never did, nor dare make any, only this, that no sale of land is good and legal, unless within three months after the conveyance it be recorded in the general court, or county courts.

5. What number of horse and foot are within your government, and whether they be trained bands or standing forces?

Answer. All our freemen are bound to be trained every month in their particular counties, which we suppose, and do not much mistake in the calculation, are near eight thousand horse: there are more, but it is too chargeable for poor people, as wee are, to exercise them.

6. (Castles and forts.)

7. What number of privitiers do frequent your coasts . . . the number of their men, and guns, and names of their commanders?

Answer. None to our knowledge, since the late Dutch war.

8. What is the strength of your bordering neighbors, be they Indians or others . . . ?

Answer. We have no Europeans seated nearer to us than St. Christophers or Mexico, that we know of, except some few ffrench that are beyond New England. The Indians, our neighbours, are absolutely subjected, so that there is no fear of them[1] . . .

9. (Arms, amunition, and stores . . . "sent you upon his majestys account?")

Answer. . . . His majesty in the time of the Dutch warr, sent us thirty great guns, most of which were lost in the ship that brought them. [No others sent; some *bought* by the colony.]

10. What monies have been paid . . . by his majesty, or levied within your government for and towards the buying of armes or making or maintaining of any ffortifications or castles, and how have the said monies been expended?

Answer. Besides those guns I mentioned, we never had any monies of his majesty towards the buying of ammunition or

---

[1] Five years later came an Indian uprising in which at least 300 colonists lost their lives.

building of fforts. What monies can be spared out of the publick revenue, we yearly lay out in ammunition.

11. What are the boundaries and contents of the land, within your government?

Answer. As for the boundaries of our land, it was once great, ten degrees in latitude, but now it has pleased his majesty to confine us to halfe a degree. Knowingly, I speak this. Pray God it may be for his majesty's service, but I much fear the contrary.[1]

12. What commodities are there of the production, growth and manufacture of your plantation; and particularly, what materials are there already growing, or may be produced for shipping in the same?

Answer. Commodities of the growth of our country, we never had any but tobacco, which in this yet is considerable, that it yields his majesty a great revenue; but of late, we have begun to make silk, and so many mulberry trees are planted, and planting, that if we had skilfull men from Naples or Sicily to teach us the art of making it perfectly, in less than half an age, we should make as much silk in an year as England did yearly expend three score years since; but now we hear it is grown to a greater excess, and more common and vulgar usage. Now, for shipping, we have admirable masts and very good oaks; but for iron ore I dare not say there is sufficient to keep one iron mill going for seven years.

13. Whether salt-petre is or may be produced within your plantation, and if so, at what rate may it be delivered in England?

Answer. Salt-petre, we know of none in the country.

14. What rivers, harbours or roads are there in or about your plantation and government, and of what depth and soundings are they?

Answer. Rivers, we have four, as I named before, all able, safely and severally to bear an harbour a thousand ships of the greatest burthen.

---

[1] As governor of Virginia, Berkeley is disposed to side with the colony against the English policy. Cf. 19, note, below.

15. What number of planters, servants and slaves; and how many parishes are there in your plantation?

Answer. We suppose, and I am very sure we do not much miscount, that there is in Virginia above forty thousand persons, men, women and children, and of which there are two thousand *black slaves*, six thousand *christian servants*, for a short time; the rest are born in the country or have come in to settle and seat, in bettering their condition in a growing country.

16. What number of English, Scots, or Irish have for these seven years past came yearly to plant . . . within your government; as also what *blacks* or *slaves* have been brought in . . . ?

Answer. Yearly we suppose there comes in, of servants, about fifteen hundred, of which most are English, few Scotch, and fewer Irish, and not above two or three ships of Negroes in seven years.[1]

17. [Mortality? The answer expresses inability to give exact figures, from lack of a "register office," but insists upon improvements in health of new immigrants as compared with earlier times.]

18. What number of ships to trade yearly to and from your plantations, and of what burthen are they?

Answer. English ships, near eighty, come out of England and Ireland every year for tobacco; few New England ketches; **but of our own we never had yet more than two at one time, and those not more than twenty tons burthen.**

19. What obstructions do you find to the improvement of trade and navigation . . . ?

Answer. Mighty and destructive, by that severe act of parliament which excludes us the having any commerce with any nation in Europe but our own.[2] [Navigation Acts of 1660, 1663] . . . Besides this, we cannot procure any skillfull men for our now hopefull

---

[1] Even as negroes were packed, the slaver of that time rarely carried a hundred slaves.

[2] Italicized by the editor. Cf. 11, above, and the note.

commodity, silk; for it is not lawfull for us to carry a pipe-stave or a barrel of corn to any place in Europe out of the king's dominions.[1] If this were for his majesty's service or the good of his subjects, we should not repine, whatever our sufferings . . . but on my soul, it is the contrary for both. And this is the cause why no small or great vessels are built here;[2] for we are most obedient to all laws, whilst the New England-men break through, and trade to any place that their interests lead them.

20. What advantages . . . do you observe that may be gained to your trade or navigation?

Answer. None, unless we had liberty to transport our pipe staves, timber and corn to other places besides the king's dominions.

21. What rates and duties are charged and payable upon any goods exported out of your plantation, whither of your own growth or manufacture, or otherwise, as also upon goods imported?

Answer. No goods, either exported or imported, pay any the least duties here, only two shillings the hogshead on tobacco exported, which is to defray all public charges; and this year we could not get an account of more than fifteen thousand hogsheads, out of which the king allows me a thousand yearly, with which I must maintain the part of my place, and one hundred intervening charges that cannot be put to public account. And I can knowingly affirm, that there is no government of ten years settlement, but has thrice as much allowed him. But I am supported by my hopes, that his gracious majesty will one day consider me.

22. What revenues doe or may arise to his majesty within your government, and of what nature is it; by whom is the

---

[1] This is a gross overstatement on Berkeley's part. Cf. *American History and Government*, § 96. It is notable, however, that even a courtier, like Berkeley, as a colonial governor, takes the point of view of his province against English policy. Cf. *ib.*, § 118.

[2] Then why no Virginia ships *before* 1660?

same collected, and how answered and accounted to his majesty?

Answer. There is no revenue arising to his majesty but out of the quit-rents; and this he hath given away to a deserving servant, Col. Henry Norwood.

23. What course is taken about the instructing the people, within your government in the christian religion . . . ?

Answer. The same course that is taken in England out of towns; every man according to his ability instructing his children. We have fforty eight parishes, and our ministers are well paid, and by my consent should be better *if they would pray oftener and preach less.* But of all other commodities, so of this, *the worst are sent us,* and we had few that we could boast of, since the persicution in *Cromwell's* tiranny drove divers worthy men hither. But, I thank God, *there are no free schools* nor *printing,* and I hope we shall not have these hundred years; for *learning* has brought disobedience, and heresy, and sects into the world, and *printing* has divulged them, and libels against the best government. God keep us from both!

105. The Franchise in Virginia again Restricted [1]

Hening's *Statutes at Large.*

For the general reaction of this period, *American History and Government*, §§ 103, 104.

[October, 1670.]

Act III. Whereas the usuall way of chuseing burgesses by the votes of all persons who, haveing served their tyme, are ffreemen of this country, who, haveing little interest in the country, doe oftner make tumults at the election to the disturbance of his majesties peace, then by their discretions in their votes provide for the conservasion thereof, by makeing choyse of persons fitly qualified for the discharge of soe greate a trust, **And whereas the lawes of England grant a voyce in**

---

[1] Cf. No. 35, above.

such election only to such as by their estates real or personall have interest enough to tye them to the endeavour of the publique good; It is hereby enacted, that none but ffreeholders and housekeepers who only are answerable to the publique for the levies shall hereafter have a voice in the election of any burgesses in this country; and that the election be at the court house.

["Bacon's Assembly" of 1676 repealed this restriction and restored free manhood franchise; but that act fell with the other attempted reforms of that year; Nos. 106, 109, below.]

106. "Bacon's Laws," in Virginia (Political Discontent)

Hening's *Statutes at Large*, II, 341–365.
Cf. *American History and Government*, § 105.

At a Grand Assemblie Holden at James Citie the fifth day of June, 1676.

Act I. [An act for carrying on a warre against the barbarous Indians.]

[Nearly ten pages. Declares war; Provides an army of 1000 men; decrees that captives shall be made slaves; appoints Bacon "genll. and commander in cheife."]

Act II. [Prohibits trade with Indians.]

Act III. [Reserves to the colony as a whole any deserted Indian lands.]

Act IV. [To suppress tumults.]

Act V. [Sheriffs.]

Whereas divers complaints have been made throughout the country of the abuses . . . of divers offices . . . *Bee it enacted by the governour, councell, and burgesses of this grand assembly, and by the authority of the same*, that noe person whatsoever within this country shall exercise, hold, and enjoy the office of sherriffe or under-sherriffe more than one year successively. [Penalty, 20,000 pounds of tobacco] . . . *And bee it further enacted* . . . that noe person or persons whatsoever shall hold or enjoy two of these offices hereafter named at one and the same time . . . viz. . . . sherriffs, clerke of courte, surveyor, and escheator. . . . [Three years residence necessary for eligibility to any office. . . . Provision, in much detail, against sheriffs or other officers exacting more than the legal fees.]

Act VI. [Vestries.]

Whereas the long continuance of vestries . . . is presented as a greivance, *Bee it enacted* . . . that it shall and may be lawfull . . . for the freeholders *and freemen* of every parish . . . by the majoritie of votes to elect . . . certaine freeholders or substantiall householders to the number of twelve . . . which said twelve shall be . . . the vestrie of the parish . . . and such election to be made . . . *once in every three yeares.*

Act VII [Suffrage.]

Bee it enacted . . . that the act of assembly [1770; see No. 105] . . . which forbids *freemen* to have votes in the election of burgesses be repealed, and that they be admitted, together with freeholders and householders, to vote as formerly in such elections.

Act VIII. [*To add representatives to the Board of County Justices*, except for judicial purposes.]

Whereas the justices of the county courts . . . have accustommarily sett . . . a rate or assessment upon the people of their counties . . . and whereas it hath been suspected . . . that under colour thereof many sums have bin raised . . . *for the interest of particular persons.* . . . **Bee** it enacted . . . that some of the discreetest and ableest of the inhabitants of each county, *equal in number to the number of justices* . . . be yearly chosen . . . [by parishes] by majoritie of votes of householders, ffreeholders, and ffreemen . . . which said representatives, together with the justices . . . are to meet at the usual place . . . and are hereby authorized and impowered to have equal votes with them, the said justices, *in laying county assessments and of* [in] *making wholesome by-lawes* for the good of their counties.

IX, X, XI. [Forms of procedure in collecting levies and administering estates.]

XII. [Abolition of exemptions from taxation.]

For the greater ease of the country . . . Bee it enacted that the 55th act of the printed laws [code of 1662], soe far as it relates to the honorable councill of state and ministers, bee . . . repealed, and that for the future the persons of the councill and all others of their families be liable to pay levies . . . and that the person of every minister bee exempted, . . . but all other tithable persons in his familie shall be liable to pay levies. . . .

XIII. [Permitting wolf-bounties.]

XIV. [Regarding trespass by "unrulie horses" "within another person's enclosure."]

XV. [Forbids exportation of corn until next session of the assembly.]

XVI. [For temperance reform.]

Whereas it is most apparently found that the many ordinaries [taverns] in severall parts of the couintry are very prejudiciall. . . **Bee** it therefore enacted . . . that no ordinaries, ale houses, or other tipling houses whatsoever . . . be kept in any part of the country [except "at James Citty" and "at the two great ferries" of Yorke river]; *Provided* . . . that [these exceptions] be admitted . . . to sell . . . mare's meate, horse-meate, beer, and syder, but no other strong drinke whatsoever. . . . [Penalty of 1000 pounds tobacco for selling "any sorte of drinke or liquor" *or for* "*being drunke* . . . *in his* . . . *house.*"]

XVII. XVIII. [Special Acts, relating to James City and two counties.]

Act XIX. [*General Pardon and Oblivion.*]

Act XX. [Disabling Lt. Col. Edward Hill and Lieut. John Stith. from bearing any office, civil or military, because these men had "bin the greatest instruments . . . of raiseing, promoteing, and stirring up the late differences and misunderstandings . . . between the honorable governour and his majesties good and loyal subjects," Beacon's party.]

107. Bacon's Proclamation, July 30, 1676

Massachusetts Historical Society Collections, Fourth Series, IX, 184-187.

The closing paragraphs (here given) follow some two pages of specific charges of misgovernment against Governor Berkeley and certain of "his wicked and pernicious counsellors, confederates, aides and associates against the Comonality."

The Declaracion of the People

. . . And we doe further demand that the said Sir William Berkeley with all the persons in this list be forthwith delivered up or surrender themselves within fower days after the notice hereof, Or otherwise we declare as followeth.

That in whatsoever place, howse, or ship, any of the said persons shall reside, be hidd, or protected, we declaire the owners, Masters or inhabitants of said places, to be confederates and **trayters to the people**; and the estates of them as alsoe of all the aforesaid persons to be confiscated, and this **we the Commons of Virginia**, doe declare, desiering a firme union amongst ourselves that we may joyntly and with one accord defend ourselves against the common Enimy, and lett not the faults of the guilty be the reproach of the inocent, or the faults or crimes of the oppressors devide and separate us who have suffered by theire oppressions.

These are therefore in his majesties name to command you forthwith to seize the persons above mencioned as Trayters to the King and Country and them to bring to Midle plantacon, and there to secure them untill further order, and in case of opposicion, if you want any further assistance you are forthwith to demand itt in the name of the people in all the Counties of Virginia.

Nath. Bacon.
Genll by Consent of the people.

108. Testimony of Political Discontent as a Cause of Bacon's Rebellion

Virginia Historical Magazine, II, 166–173, 289–292.

When Bacon's Rebellion had been crushed, royal commissioners arrived in the colony, with instructions to inform themselves "of all grievances." The commissioners met the inhabitants at various County Courts, and took down their complaints in writing. These complaints show some of the real causes of Bacon's Rebellion. Of course, to these royal commissioners the people as a rule would say little of infringements upon political liberty (because commissioners from Charles II could not be expected to have any sympathy with such complaints), and they *would* say much about misgovernment and economic oppression. The following extracts from the commissioners' records are selected to show that complaints regarding political oppression did find voice, even under such conditions. These entries might be greatly extended.

(1) *Gloster County*

4. That severall grievances being presented to the June Assembly [1676] upon which many good Lawes were consented to by that Assembly [No. 106] . . . they Beg those good and wholesome Lawes may be confirmed.

(2) *Lower Norfolk County*

5. Request for Liberty to Transport their Tobacco to any of his majesties Plantations without paying the Impost payable by Act of Parliament. [This request the commissioners declare "wholly mutinous."]

(3) *Surry County*

1. That the last Assembly continued many yeares . . .
10. That it has been the custome of County Courts att the laying of the levy to withdraw into a private Roome, — by which meanes the poore people, not knowing for what they paid, did admire how their taxes could be so high.
12. That, contrary to the lawes of England and this Country, high sheriffs have usually continued two years, and under

sheriffs 3 or 4 years together: wee humbly pray that for the future no person may continue sheriffe above one yeare.

14. That we have not had liberty to choose vestrymen: wee humbly desire that the wholle parish may have a free election.

15. That since his most gracious Majesty hath been most mercifully pleased to pardon our late disloyalty, wee most earnestly and humbly pray that this present grand assembly would make an Act of Oblivion,—that no person may be injured by the provoking names of Rebell, Traitor and Rogue.

(4) *Northampton County*

2. That we may have Liberty grannted us to choose a new vestery, and that every three years a new vestery may be chosen.

6. That it may be graunted us to make a free choyse of six housekeepers without Interposing of any Ruling Magistratre [to sit with the Justices of the County as a Board to assess taxes], to prevent oppressions . . . as we humbly suspect . . . to have Received heretofore.

15. That no Sheriff may officiate two years together.

(5) *Isle of Wight*

14. We desire wee may have libertie to chuse our Vestries once in three yeares, and that their may noe member of the Court [County Justices] be therein.

109. Abolition of Bacon's Reforms for Virginia

a. *The King's Orders*

Additional instructions [*from King Charles II*] *for our trusty and* **well beloved** Sir William Berkeley, Knt. *our governor of our colony of Virginia, November 13, 1676*

Hening's *Statutes*, II, 424 ff.

* * * * * *

REPEAL OF POPULAR REFORMS 331

2. You shall take care that the members of the assembly be elected only by *ffreeholders*, as being more agreeable to the custome of England, to which you are as nigh as conveniently you can to conforme yourselfe.

* * * * * * *

6. You shall declare voyd and null all the proceedings of the late assembly . . . ["Bacon's Assembly"].

b. Repeal by the Assembly, February, 1676/1677

Hening's *Statutes at Large*, II, 380.

* * * * * * *

Whereas Nathaniell Bacon . . . in the month of June, 1676 . . . did enter James Citty in a rebellious manner with a considerable number of armed men . . . environing and beseigeing the governour and councell and burgesses . . . threatening them with sudden death if they would not grant his unreasonable, unlawfull, rebellious and treasonable demands, and by his threats and . . . violence did obteine to himselfe whatsoever he soe . . . demanded; **And whereas** the kings most excellent majestie by his gratious proclamation . . . hath long since declared all the proceedings of the said assembly to be voyd in law: *Bee it therefore enacted by this present grand assembly and the authority thereof, and it is hereby enacted,* that all acts, orders, and proceedings of the said grand assembly be repealed and made null and voyd.

110. Self-government in Massachusetts Decreased

a. Randolph's Report, 1676

Hutchinson's *Collection of Original Papers* (1769), 477 ff.

Randolph had been sent to the colonies as a "commissioner" by the Lords of Trade.

* * * * * * *

Second Enquiry. What lawes and ordinances are now in force there derogatory or contrary to those of England, and what oath is prescribed by the government?

The lawes and ordinances made in that colony are no longer observed than as they stand with their convenience. The magistrates not so strictly minding the letter of the law when their publick interest is concerned, in all cases more regarding the quality and affection of the persons to their government than the nature of their offence. They see no evill in a church member, and therefore it is very difficult to get any sentence or verdict against him, tho' in the smallest matters.

No law is in force or esteeme there but such as are made by the generall court, and therefore it is accounted a breach of their privileges and a betraying of the liberties of their commonwealth to urge the observation of the lawes of England or his Majesties commands.

The lawes most derogatory and contradictory to those of England.

All persons of the age of 21 years, being excommunicate or condemned, have liberty to make wills and dispose of lands and estates.

In capital cases, dismembering or banishment; where no law is made by the generall court, or in case of defect of a law in any particular case, the offender to be tryed by the word of God and judged by the generall court.

Ministers are ordained by the people and no injunction to be put upon any church officer or member, in point of doctrine, worship or discipline, whether for substance or circumstance, besides the institution of the Lord.

Whoever shall observe christmasse day or the like festivity, by forbearing to labour, feasting or other way shall pay 5s. and whosoever shall not resort to their meeting upon the Lord's day and such days of fasting and Thanksgiving as shall be appointed by authority, shall pay 5s. no days commanded by the lawes of England to be observed or regarded.

No person shall be impressed or compelled to serve in any

wars but such as shall be enterprized by that commonwealth, by the consent of a generall court, or by authority derived from them.

No person whatsoever shall joine any persons in marriage but a magistrate, it being an honorable ordinance and therefore should be accordingly sollemnized.

All strangers professing the true christian religion that shall fly to them for succour from the tyranny or oppression of their persecutors, or for any necessary or compulsory cause, they shall be entertained and protected amongst them according to that power and prudence God shall give them. By which law Whalley and Gosse and other traytors were kindly receaved and entertained by Mr. Godkins and other magistrates.

Whosoever shall be in the possession of any land 5 years, altho' the grant of said land was to another, and the possessor have nothing to shew for the alienation thereof but his possession, the possessor shall have the land confirmed to him.

No oath shall be urged or required to be taken by any person but such oath as the generall court hath considered allowed and required.

The oaths of allegiance and supremacy are neither taken by the magistrates nor required to be taken by the inhabitants, only an oath of fidelity to the government is imposed upon all persons as well strangers as inhabitants, upon the penalty of 5 *l.* for every week they shall refuse the said oath.

b. *Second Charter of Massachusetts, October 7/17, 1691*

Acts and Resolves of the Province of Massachusetts Bay, I, 1-20.

The stubborn persistence of Massachusetts in resisting all regulation from England finally involved all New England in the despotic rule of Andros. On the overthrow of Andros (on the flight of James II and the accession of William III), Connecticut and Rhode Island continued their former charter governments; but the Massachusetts Charter of 1629 had been declared void by the English courts and had been formally surrendered. The best Massachusetts could now do was to secure a much more limited instrument. For a fuller history, cf. *American History and Government*, § 97.

[Recital of the creation of the Plymouth Council in 1620, of the grant by that Council to the Massachusetts Bay Company in 1628, of the royal charter of 1629, and of the vacating of that charter in 1684.]

And Whereas severall persons employed as Agents in behalfe of Our said Collony of the Massachusetts Bay in New England have made their humble application unto Us that Wee would be graciously pleased by Our Royall Charter to Incorporate Our Subjects in Our said Colony and to grant and confirme unto them such powers priviledges and Franchises . . . and Wee being graciously pleased to gratifie Our said Subjects. And alsoe to the end Our good Subjects within Our Collony of New Plymouth in New England aforesaid may be brought under such a forme of Government as may put them in a better Condition of defence . . .

. . . Wee doe by these presents for Us Our Heirs and Successors Will and Ordeyne that the Territories and Collonyes comonly called or known by the Names of the Collony of the Massachusetts Bay, **and Collony of New Plymouth**, the Province of Main, the Territorie called Accadia or Nova Scotia, and all that Tract of Land lying betweene the said Territories of Nova Scotia and the said Province of Main be Erected United and Incorporated . . . into one reall Province by the Name of Our Province of the Massachusetts Bay in New England And . . . [grant of territory] . . .

Provided . . . that all and every such Lands Tenements and Hereditaments and all other estates which any person or persons or Bodyes Politique or Corporate (Townes, Villages, Colledges, or Schooles) doe hold and enjoy or ought to hold and enjoy within the bounds aforesaid by or under any Grant or estate duely made or granted by any Generall Court formerly held or by vertue of the Letters Patents herein before recited or by any other lawfull Right or Title whatsoever shall be by . . . [them] . . . for ever hereafter held and enjoyed according to the purport and Intent of such respective Grant. . . . And wee doe further . . . Establish and ordeyne that . . . there shall be one Governour, One Leiutenant or Deputy Governour, and One Secretary of Our said Province or Territory, to be from time to time appointed and Commissionated by Us . . . and Eight and Twenty Assistants or Councillors to be advising and assisting to the Governour . . . for the time being as by these presents is hereafter directed and appointed, which said Councillors or Assistants are to be Constituted, Elected, and Chosen in such forme and manner as hereafter in these presents is expressed. [Appointment of first set of officers, the Assistants to continue until the last Wednesday in May, 1693.]

And Our Will and Pleasure is that the Governour . . . shall have Authority from time to time at his discretion to assemble and call together the Councillors or Assistants . . . and that the said Governour with the said Assistants or Councillors or Seaven of them at the least shall and may from time to time hold and keep a Councill for the ordering and directing the Affaires of Our said Province And Further Wee Will . . . that there shall . . . be convened . . . by the Governour . . . upon every last Wednesday in the Moneth of May every yeare for ever and at all such other times as the Governour . . . shall think fitt and appoint a great and Generall Court of Assembly Which . . . shall consist of the Governour and Councill or Assistants . . . and of such Freeholders . . . as shall be from time to time elected or deputed by the Major parte of the Freeholders and other Inhabitants of the respective Townes or Places who shall be present at such Elections . . . To which Great and Generall Court . . . Wee doe hereby . . . grant full power and authority from time to time to direct . . . what Number each County Towne and Place shall Elect and Depute to serve for and represent them respectively . . . Provided alwayes that noe Freeholder or other Person shall have a Vote in the Election of Members . . . who at the time of such Election shall not have an estate of *Freehold in Land within Our said Province or Territory to the value of Forty Shillings per Annum at the least, or other estate to the value of Forty pounds Sterling . . . and that the Governour for the time being shall have full power and Authority from time to time as he shall Judge necessary to adjourne Prorogue and dissolve all Great and Generall Courts . . . And . . . Wee doe . . . Ordeyne that yearly once in every yeare . . . the aforesaid Number of Eight and Twenty Councillors or Assistants shall be by the Generall Court . . . newly chosen . . .* [Four at least of the Assistants to come from the former Plymouth Colony and three from Maine. The General Court may remove Assistants from office, and may also fill vacancies caused by removal or death.] *And Wee doe further Grant and Ordeyne that it shall and may be lawfull for the said Governour with the advice and consent of the Councill or Assistants from time to time to nominate and appoint Judges, Commissioners of Oyer and Terminer, Sheriffs, Provosts, Marshalls, Justices of the Peace, and other Officers to Our Councill and Courts of Justice belonging,* Provided *always that noe such Nomination or Appointment of Officers be made without notice first given or summons issued out seaven dayes before such Nomination or Appointment unto such of the said Councillors or Assistants as shall be at that time resideing within Our said Province . . . and for the greater Ease and Encouragement of Our Loveing Subjects Inhabiting our said Province . . . and of such as shall come to Inhabit there Wee doe . . . Ordaine that for ever hereafter there shall be a liberty of Conscience allowed in the Worshipp of God to all Christians (Except Papists) Inhabiting . . . within our said Province . . .* [Courts for the trial of both civil and criminal cases may be established by the General Court, reserving to the governor and assistants matters of probate and administration.] And whereas *Wee judge it necessary that all our Subjects should have liberty to Appeale to us . . . in Cases that may deserve the same Wee doe . . . Ordaine that incase either party shall not rest satisfied with the Judgement or Sentence of any Judicatories or Courts within our said Province . . . in any Personall Action wherein the matter in difference doth exceed the value of three hundred Pounds Sterling that then he or they may appeale to us . . . in our . . . Privy Council Provided such Appeale be made within Fourteen dayes after the Sentence or Judgement given and that before such Appeal be allowed Security be given by the party or parties appealing in the value of the matter in Difference to pay or Answer the Debt or Damages for the which Judgement or Sentence is given With such Costs and Damages as shall be Awarded by us . . . incase the Judgement or Sentence be affirmed* [provided that no execution shall be stayed by reason of such appeal.] 𝕬𝖓𝖉 we doe further . . . grant to the said Governor and the great and Generall Court . . . full power and Authority from time to time to make . . . all manner of wholesome and reasonable Orders Laws Statutes and Ordinances Directions and Instructions either with penalties or without (soe as the same be not repugnant or contrary to the Lawes of this our Realme of England) as they shall Judge to be for the good and welfare of our said Province. . . . And for the Government and Ordering thereof and of the People Inhabiting or who shall Inhabit the same and for the necessary support and Defence of the Government thereof [and also] full power and Authority to name and settle Annually all Civill Officers within the said Province (such Officers Excepted the Election and Constitution of whome wee have by these presents reserved to us . . . or to the Governor) . . . and to Settforth the severall Duties Powers and Lymitts of every such Officer . . . and the forms of such Oathes not repugnant to the Lawes and Statutes of this our Realme of England as shall be respectively Administred unto them for the Execution of their severall Offices and places. And alsoe to impose Fines, mulcts, Imprisonments, and other Punishments; And to Impose and leavy proportionable and reasonable Assessments, Rates, and Taxes, upon the Estates and Persons of all and every the Proprietors and Inhabitants of our said Province . . . 𝔓𝔯𝔬𝔳𝔦𝔡𝔢𝔡 alwaies . . . that in the framing and passing of all such Orders . . . and in all Elections and Acts of Government whatsoever to be passed made or done by the said Generall Court . . . or in Councill, *the Governor* . . . *shall have the Negative voice, and that without his consent or Approbation signified and declared in Writing, no such Orders . . . Elections or other Acts of Government . . . shall be of any Force effect or validity . . .* And wee doe . . . Ordaine that the said Orders Laws Statutes and Ordinances be by the first opportunity after the makeing thereof sent or Transmitted unto us . . . under the Publique Seale to be appointed by us for Our . . . approbation or Disallowance *And that incase all or any of them shall, at any time within the space of three yeares next after the same shall have been presented to us . . . in Our . . . Privy Councill, be disallowed and rejected and soe signified by us . . . unto the Governor for the time being then such . . . of them as shall be soe disallowed . . . shall thenceforth cease and determine and become utterly void and of none effect.* [Laws not disallowed within the three years, to remain in force until repealed by the General Court. Grants of land by the General Court, within the limits of the former colonies of Massachusetts Bay and New Plymouth, and the Province of Maine, excepting the region north and east of the Sagadahoc, to be valid without further royal approval. The governor to direct the defense of the province, and *to exercise martial law in case of necessity*] Provided alwayes . . . That the said Governour shall not at any time hereafter by vertue of any power hereby granted or hereafter to be granted to him Transport any of the Inhabitants of Our said Province . . . or oblige them to march out of the Limitts of the same without their Free and voluntary consent or the Consent of the Great and Generall Court . . . nor grant Commissions for exercising the Law Martiall upon any the Inhabitants of Our said Province . . . without the Advice and Consent of the Councill or Assistants of the same . . . [In case of the death, removal or absence of the governor, the lieutenant-governor may take his place; failing both governor and lieutenant-governor, the council, or the major part of them, are to act.] Provided alwaies . . . that nothing herein shall extend or be taken to . . . allow the Exercise of any Admirall Court Jurisdiction Power or Authority but that the same be and is hereby reserved to Us . . . and shall from time to time be . . . exercised by vertue of Commissions to be issued under the Great Seale of England or under the Seale of the High Admirall or the Commissioners for executing the Office of High Admirall of England. . . . And lastly for the better provideing and furnishing of Masts for Our Royall Navy Wee doe hereby reserve to Us . . . all Trees of the Diameter of Twenty Four Inches and upwards of Twelve Inches from the ground growing upon any soyle or Tract of Land within Our said Province . . . not heretofore granted to any private persons.

111. Attempts by England at Closer Control after 1700

For an outline of these natural and long-continued attempts, see *American History and Government*, §§ 117, 118. The first attempt, barely avoided and only by accident, is given under *a*, below; *b* represents American feeling toward such encroachments; and *c* illustrates the activity of a New England town meeting in this field of *general* politics.

a. Recommendation from the Board of Trade to make all the Colonies into Royal Provinces. March 26/Apr. 5, 1701

North Carolina Colonial Records, I, 535.

To the King's most Excellent Majestie.
May it please, etc.

Having formerly on severall occasions humbly represented to your Majesty the state of the Government under Proprietors and Charters in America; and perceiving the irregularities of these Governments dayly to increase, to the prejudice of Trade and of your Majesties other Plantations in America, as well as of your Majesties revenue arising from the Customes here, we find ourselves obliged at present humbly to represent to your Majesty;

That those Colonies in general have no ways answered the chief design for which such large Tracts of Land and such Priviledges and Immunities were granted by the Crown.

That they have not conformed themselves to the severall acts of Parliament for regulating Trade and Navigation, to which they ought to pay the same obedience, and submit to the same Restrictions as the other Plantations, which are subject to your Majesties immediate Government; on the contrary in most of these Proprieties and Charter Governments, the Governours have not applyed themselves to your Majesty for your approbation, nor have taken the Oaths required by the acts of Trade, both which Qualifications are made necessary by the late Act for preventing frauds and regulating abuses in the Plantation Trade.

That they have assumed to themselves a power to make Laws contrary and repugnant to the Laws of England, and directly prejudicial to Trade, some of them having refused to send hither such Laws as they had enacted, and others having sent them but very imperfectly.

That diverse of them have denyed appeals to your Majesty in Councill, by which not only the Inhabitants of those Colonies but others your Majesties subjects are deprived of that benefit, enjoyed in the Plantations, under your Majesties immediate Government, and the parties agrieved are left without remedy from the arbitrary and Illegal proceedings of their Courts.

That these Colonies continue to be the refuge and retreat of Pirates and Illegal Traders, and the receptacle of Goods imported thither from foreign parts contrary to Law: In return of which Commodities those of the growth of these Colonies are likewise contrary to Law exported to Foreign parts; All which is likewise much incouraged by their not admitting appeals as aforesaide.

That by raising and lowering their coin from time to time, to their particular advantage, and to the prejudice of other Colonies, By exempting their Inhabitants from Duties and Customes to which the other Colonies are subject, and by Harbouring of Servants and fugitives, these Governments tend greatly to the undermining the Trade and Welfare of the other Plantations, and seduce and draw away the People thereof; By which Diminution of Hands the rest of the Colonies more beneficial to England do very much suffer.

That these Independent Colonies do turn the Course of Trade to the Promoting and proprogating woolen and other Manufactures proper to England, instead of applying their thoughts and Endeavours to the production of such commodities as are fit to be encouraged in these parts according to the true design and intention of such settlements.

That they do not in general take any due care for their own defence and security against an Enemy, either in Building Forts or providing their Inhabitants with sufficient Armes and Amunition, in case they should be attacked, which is every day more and more to be apprehended, considering how the French power encreases in those parts.

That this cheifly arises from the ill use they make of the powers entrusted to them by their Charters, and the Independency which they pretend to, and that each Government is obliged only to defend its self without any consideration had of their Neighbours, or of the general preservation of the whole.

That many of them have not a regular militia and some (particularly the Colonies of East and West New Jersey) are no otherwise at present than in a state of Anarchy and confusion.

And because the care of these and other great mischiefs in your Majesties Plantations and Colonies aforesaid, and the introducing such an administration of Government and fit regulation of Trade as may put them into a better State of Security and make them duly subservient and usefull to England, does every day become more and more necessary, and that your Majesties frequent Commands to them have not met with due complyance: We humbly conceive it may be expedient that the Charters of the severall Proprietors and others intitling them to absolute Government be reassumed to the Crown and these Colonies put into the same State and dependency as those of your Majesties other Plantations, without prejudice to any man's particular property and freehold. Which being no otherwise so well to be effected as by the Legislative power of this Kingdome.

Wee humbly submit the same to your Majesties Royal consideration.

b. *John Wise upon Englishmen and Tyranny*

This extract comes from a pamphlet by John Wise, minister at Ipswich, and a leader (and sufferer) against arbitrary taxation by Andros twenty years earlier, and is in the nature of a warning that the American English will not submit to political aggression.

Englishmen hate an arbitrary power (politically considered) as they hate the devil. . . . And though many of their incautelous princes have endeavored to null all their charter rights and immunities, and agrandize themselves in the servile state of the subjects, by setting up their own seperate will, for the great standard of government over the nation, yet they have all along paid dear for their attempts, both in the ruin of the nation, and in interrupting the increase of their own grandeur, and their foreign settlements and conquests.

Had the late reigns, before the accession of the great *William* and *Mary*, to the throne of England, but taken the measures of them, and [of] her present majesty,[1] in depressing vice, and advancing the union and wealth, and encouraging the prowice and bravery of the nation, they might by this time have been capable to have given laws to any monarch on earth; but spending their time in the pursuit of an absolute monarchy (contrary to the temper of the nation, and the ancient constitution of the government) through all the meanders of state craft: It has apparently kept back the glory, and dampt all the most noble affairs of the nation. And when under the midwifry of *Machiavilan* art, and cunning of a daring prince, this MONSTER, tyranny, and arbitrary government, was at last just born, upon the holding up of a finger! or upon the least signal given, ON the whole nation goes upon this HYDRA.[2]

---

[1] Queen Anne. [2] A reference to the expulsion of James II.

TOWN MEETING ACTIVITY

The very name of an arbitrary government is ready to put an Englishman's blood into a fermentation; but when it really comes, and shakes its whip over their ears, and tells them it is their master, it makes them stark mad.

c. Boston's Action Relative to the Proposed Permanent Salary for the Governor in 1729

Boston Town Records (for dates given).

The full records of the meeting are given, that the student may see how great matters of state were mingled with trivial and local business. The attempt of England to secure a fixed salary for the Governor of Massachusetts would, if successful, have made that officer wholly independent of popular control. Cf. *American History and Government*, § 118, for the whole story.

AT a Meeting of the Freeholders and Other Inhabitants of the Town of Boston Duly Qualified being Regulerly Assembled in a Publick Town meeting at the Town House Tuesday May the 6th 1729 —

After Prayer by the Revd mr Thomas Prince [and after] Elisha Cooke Esqr Chose[n] Moderator for this Meeting.

Sundry Petitions Read Vizt
About a place for the Grainery
About m. [Mr.] Peleg Wiswalls Sallary
About m. Edward Mills Sallary
m. Samuel Oakes Petition
m. Jerā [Jeremiah] Condys Petition
The Selectmens Report of Sundry things left to them
Voted to Chuse 4 Representatives
The Number of Voters were - - 192

votes.

Elisha Cooke Esqr	188	
m. Thomas Cushing -	190	Chose[n] Representatives
m. Ezekll Lewis -	190	
m. Samll Welles -	184	

Voted To Chuse a Comittee to Prepare Instructions for the Representatives for their Acting at the General Court at their Approching Session, And to Lay them befor the Meeting in the Afternoon —

Voted: That John Alford Esqr mesrs Henry Dering and Nathll Cunningham be the Said Committee —

On the Petition of Sundry Inhabitants about the Situatian of the Grainery

Voted That mr Moderator and the Selectmen be Joyned with the Comittee appointed for Building the Grainery, Be desired to View the Place, And make Return of their Opinion thereof to the Meeting after Dinner this Day —

mr John Jeffers — Excus'd
mr Thomas Moffat — Excus'd } Chosen Assessors.

Edward Maycomb - Sworn
John Spooner - - Sworn } Clerks of the Market.
Nathanll Cobbit - Sworn

Post Meridiem.

Voted That the Grainery be Erected and Set up Rainging with the Line of the Burying place on the Comon fronting Eastward, The Said Building to be not Less then [than] forty feet distant from the [South] Corner of the Brick wall of the Burying place —

mr James Pemberton - Pay [1]
mr James Watson - Sworn } Assessors.

In as much as the Gramer School at the North End of the Town of which mr Peleg Wiswall is the Master is much Increaced in the Number of the Schollers, and that no Usher is alowed to assist him in his School:

Voted That there be an Additian of Forty Pounds to the Said mr Wiswalls Salary —

Samll Oakes Petition Read and Dismist —

* * * * * * *

---

[1] Paid a fine for refusing to serve.

TOWN MEETING ACTIVITY 345

In Answer to Mr. Edward Mills His Petitian. Voted That there be an Addition of Twenty Pounds to the Said Mr. Edward Mills Sallary —

Upon A Motion made by Elisha Cook Esquire That the Dividing Line between the Towns Land in the Occupation of Mr. Nathaniel Williams and His Land on the East Side in School Street is for want of due Care become Crucked, intrenching both upon the One and the Others Land, That therefore they would Direct and Imp[o]wer the Selectmen to Rectifie that line as to them Seems Just and Equitable — And Further That they would be pleased to Accomodate him with about two feet of the Front of his Land next Mr. Williams on Such Terms as the Selectmen Shall Agree for with the Said Mr. Cooke —

Read and Voted That it be left with the Selectmen to Act therein as they Judge Meet —

On the Petition of Mr. Jeramiah Condy for Addition to his Salary.

Voted that the Consideration of Said Petition be Referred for further Consideration to the Next Town Meeting, and That in the mean time Nathaniel Green John Alford Esquires and Mr. Thomas Cushing Junior are desired to Inspect the Several Wrighting Schools within this Town at Such Time as they Shall think Avisable for the year Currant, And that they do in an Espesial Manner Vizit Mr. Condys School and Report to the Town at their Meeting the Ability and Industry of the Said Mr. Condy and the Proficiency of the Schollers under His Tuition —

The Comittee this day chosen and Appointed to Prepare Instructions for the Representatives, for their Acting at the General Court at their Approching Session And to Lay [them] before the Meeting in the afternoon — Return as Follows: Viz.

To Elisha Cooke Esquire, Messrs. Thomas Cushing, Ezekiel Lewis and Samuel Welles: —

* * * * * * *

Gentlemen —

Your known Loyalty to His Present Majesty King George, and Sincear Atachment to the Succession in the Illustrious House of Hannover, Your Hearty Love to this Your native Country, Your Singuler Value for the Liberty and Propperty of this People, your Cheerfull and Una[ni]mous Concurrance to promote our Best Intrist, And your Approved Integrity in those Publick Stations wherein you have bin Employed, Have fixed the Eyes of this Town on and Determined their Choice of you as Propper Persons to Represent them in the Next General Assembly Wherin they Expect That you behave your Selves with your Wonted Zeal and Courage in Prossecuting those good Designes which may tend to the Peace and wellfair of these His Majestys Good Subjects, and Secure those Rights and Priviledges which by the Royal Charter we have a Just claim to, and as Englishmen do of Right appertain to us, And agreable there unto we Recomend unto you in an Especial Manner —

That you Endeavor to Maintain all our Civil Rights and Propertys against any Incrochments upon them.

That you Continue to Pay a due Regard to His Excellency Our Governor, and that you Endeavor that He may have an Honourable Support, But we desire at the Same time That you use your utmost Endeavor That the Honourable House of Representatives may not be by any means Prevailed upon or brought into the Fixing a Certain Sallary for any Certain time, But that they may Improve their usual freedom in granting their Money from time to time, as they Shall Judg the Province to be able, and in Such a manner as they Shall think most for the Benefit and advantage thereof, And if your Pay Should be diverted you may Depend on all the Justice Imaginable from this Town whom you Represent: —

        John Alford
        Henry Dering } Comittee
        Nathll Cuningham

The Foregoing Return of the Committee was Presended[ted] Read Sundry times and Voted Approved.

The Report of the Selectmen upon Several Votes of the Town at their Meeting the 10th of March, 1728: were Read and Considered Viz.,

The Selectmen have Viewed the Marsh at the Bottom of the Common, and not finding any Material use that can be made of it at the present, and Considering the Present Circumstances of the Town Are of Opinion it is best to ly in the Condition it now is..

Read and the Report Accepted— . . .

As to the Proposals About Bennet Street — It is thought Convenient to be Paved if the Town thinke it Convenient to Raise Money for the Doing it at this Meeting.

Read and Refer'd for further consideration to the Next March Meeting. . . .

d. *Connecticut refuses to obey a Royal Officer appointed to command her Militia against French and Indians in 1693*

New York Colonial Documents, IV, 71.

King William III appointed Fletcher governor of the royal province of New York, and commissioned him to command the militia also of Connecticut, the neighboring charter colony, in the war usually known as King William's War. The device was eminently wise, as a military measure; but it was stubbornly resisted by Connecticut. The historians of that colony delight to tell a legend that when the governor arrived and tried to have his commission read by his secretary to the militia (drawn up in arms to repel rather than to receive him), Captain Wadsworth drowned the reading by commanding drums to beat; three times this was repeated; and the last time Wadsworth added, "If you try again, I'll make daylight shine through you." The following document gives what is probably a more accurate statement, — but one which shows equally well that Connecticut had her way. For the general conflict of which this was one incident between crown and colonies, cf. *American History and Government*, §§ 117, 118.

Governor Fletcher of New York to Mr. Southwell

Connecticute in New England
Octoer 30th '93.

Sir:

I have been in this Collony 20 dayes laboreing to perswade a stubborne people to theire dewty. I Publis'd their Majesties [William and Mary] Commission in theire General Court att Hartford. Assured them I had noe pretentions to their civell adminestration. But the mallitia being lodged in the Crowne . . . I came with commission under the greate seale to take that . . . charge. They refused all obedienc. Have sepperated not only from the Church, But Crowne of England; and allowe of noe appeale from theire Courts, nor the Lawes of England to have any force amongst them. *Some of the wiseest have saide " Wee are not permitted to vote for any members of Parliamt, and therefore [are] not lyable to theire lawes."* [Expresses military dangers due to refusal.]

I never sawe the like people. . . . I could not force obedience haveing noe Company but a few servants and two friends; nor did I think it the King's service to carry on the contest to Bloude, tho they threaten to draw mine for urging my Masters right . . . I have just now a letter from a sure freinde acquainting mee the mobb have a designe upon my life. I must not goe out of the way, tho' very thinly attended. . . .

[The following November 10, Fletcher wrote from New York to the Committee on the Colonies urging that the Connecticut Charter be proceeded against under a writ of quo warranto, with a view of uniting that colony with New York. The same letter describes in detail the serious perils from French and Indians. One paragraph should be quoted: " Our hardships grow upon us. Canada . . . hath received seven hundred men and stores of Warr from France this last Summer. Our Indians falter . . . *These small Colonies . . . are* [as] *much divided in theire interest and affection as Christian and Turk.* . . ."]

112. Commission of a Royal Governor

New Hampshire Provincial Papers, VI, 908 (edited by N. Benton).

This commission, in compact form, describes the government of a royal colony just before the Revolution. The omissions (indicated by . . .) are mainly tautological phrases.

George the Third, by the grace of God of Great Britain, France, and Ireland, King . . .

To our Trusty and well beloved Benning Wentworth Esquire, Greeting: **Know you**, that Wee, reposing especial Trust and Confidence in the Prudence, Courage, and Loyalty of you Benning Wentworth, of our Especial grace, certain Knowledge, and meer motion, Have thought fit to constitute and appoint you . . . to be our Governour and Commander-in-Chief of our Province of New Hampshire . . . with all . . . the authoritys hereby granted you . . . during our will and Pleasure:

And We do hereby require . . . you to . . . execute all things . . . that shall belong unto your said Command . . . according to the several Powers . . . granted . . . you by this Present Commission . . . or by such further powers, Instructions, and Authorities as shall at any time be granted or appointed you under our . . . sign manual . . . and according to such reasonable Laws and Statutes as now are in force or hereafter shall be made and agreed upon by you with the advice and consent of our Council and the Assembly of our said Province. . . .

And wee do hereby give . . . you full Power . . . to suspend any of the members of our said Council from sitting, Voting, and assisting therein, if you shall find just cause for so doing: and if it shall at any time happen that by the Death or Departure out of our said Province, suspension of any of our said Councillors, or otherwise, there shall be a Vacancy in our said Council (any three whereof we do hereby appoint to be a Quorum), our Will and Pleasure is that you signify the same to us by the first opportunity, that we may . . . appoint others in their stead; but that our affairs at that Distance may not suffer for want of a due number of Councillors, if ever it shall happen that there shall be less than seven of them residing in our said Province, **Wee do** hereby give . . . unto you . . . full Power . . . to choose as many Persons out of the Principal Freeholders, Inhabitants thereof, as will make up the full Number of our said Council to be seven, and no more . . .

And wee do hereby give . . . you full Power . . . with the advice and consent of our said Council from time to time, as need shall require, to summon and call General Assemblys of the said Freeholders and Planters within your Government, in manner and form according to the usage of our Province of New Hampshire:

Wee do hereby Declare that the Persons so elected and qualified shall be called and Deemed the General Assembly of our said Province . . . and that you . . . with the consent of our said Council and Assembly, or the major part of them respectively, shall have full Power . . . to make, Constitute, and ordain Laws, Statutes, and Ordinances, for the Publick Peace, Welfare, and good Government of our said Province . . . and for the Benefit of us our Heirs and Successors, — which said Laws . . . are not to be repugnant, but, as near as may be, agreeable to the laws . . . of this our Kingdom of Great Britain.

Provided that all such Statutes and Ordinances, of whatever nature and Duration soever, be, within three months . . . after the making thereof, transmitted unto us . . . for our approbation or Disallowance [as also Duplicates of the same by the next conveyance]; and in case any or all of the said Laws . . . , not before confirmed by us, shall at any time be disallowed . . . and so signified by us our Heirs or Successors . . . unto you . . . or to the Commander-in-Chief of our said Province for the time being, then such and so many of the said Laws . . . shall from thence cease, Determine, and become utterly void . . .

And to the end that nothing may be passed or done by our said Council or Assembly to the Prejudice of us, our Heirs and Successors, We will and ordain that you ... shall have ... a negative Voice in the making and Passing of all Laws and Statutes and ordinances ... **and** you shall and may ... from time to time, as you shall judge it necessary, adjourn, Prorogue, and Dissolve all General Assemblies as aforesaid. . . . .

And We do hereby authorize ... you to constitute ... Judges, and, in cases requisite, Commissioners of Oyer and Terminer, Justices of the Peace, and other necessary officers ... in our said Province for the better administration of Justice and putting the Laws in execution . . .

And we do hereby give ... you full Power ... where you shall see cause, or shall Judge any offenders ... fit objects for our mercy, to Pardon all such ... offenders, and to remit all ... fines and forfeitures, Treason and Willfull murder only excepted ... in which cases you shall likewise have Power, upon extraordinary occasions, to grant reprieves ... until ... our royal Pleasure may be known . . .

And We do hereby give ... unto you ..., by yourself or by your Captains ... by you to be authorized, full Power ... to Levy, arm, muster, command, and Employ all persons whatsoever residing within our said Province ... for the resisting and withstanding of all enemies, Pyrates, and rebels ... and to transport such forces to any of our Plantations in America, if necessity shall require, for the Defence of the same ... and to Execute martial Law in time of Invasion, or other times when by Law it may be executed, and to do and execute every other thing ... which to our Commander-in-Chief doth or ought of right to belong . . .

And We do hereby command all officers ... civil and military, and all other Inhabitants ... to be obedient aiding and assisting unto you, the said Benning Wentworth, in the Execution of this our Commission ... and in case of your Death, or absence out of our Province, unto such person as shall be appointed by us to be our Lieutenant Governor ... to whom we do therefore by these Presents give and grant all and singular the Powers and authorities aforesaid [and, if no

Lieutenant Governor has been named, then] the Eldest Councillor, whose Name is first placed in our Instructions to you . . . shall take upon him the administration of the government and Execute our said Commission . . . and the several Powers therein contained.

113. Free Speech Vindicated

(*Trial of John Peter Zenger, 1735.*)

Zenger, in 1738, published a " Brief Narrative of the Case and Tryall," somewhat in the form of a modern " Report," though he speaks in the first person. In 1735 the governor of New York removed the chief justice of the colony for personal reasons. Zenger, in his *Weekly Journal*, vigorously criticized this and *other despotic* actions of the governor. He was prosecuted for criminal libel; and the new chief justice showed a determination to secure a conviction, trying to limit the jury to deciding only whether Zenger was responsible for the publication, and reserving to himself the decision whether the words were punishable. This was the custom in English courts of the day in government prosecutions.

Italics and black-faced type are as in the original.

[The Attorney General's complaint, as Zenger reports, characterized him as " a seditious person and a frequent Printer and Publisher of false news and seditious Libels, and charged specifically that he] "did falsely, seditiously, and scandalously print and publish . . . a certain false, malicious, seditious, scandalous Libel . . . concerning His Excellency the Governour . . . [in which publication he represented a former inhabitant explaining that he had left the colony, as he doubts not others will, because, among other reasons] They . . . think . . . that their LIBER-TIES and PROPERTIES are precarious, and that SLAVERY is likely to be intailed on them and their Posterity if some past Things be not amended . . . (meaning, the past Proceedings of his Excellency the Governor . . .) . . . [and] WE . . . SEE MENS DEEDS DESTROYED, JUDGES ARBITRARILY DISPLACED, NEW COURTS ERECTED WITHOUT CONSENT OF THE LEGISLATURE. . . .

"Who then [can] call any Thing his own, or enjoy any Liberty . . . longer than those in the Administration . . . will condescend to let them ?"

[This publication, the Attorney General charges, was] to the great disturbance of the Peace of the . . . Province . . . to the Great Scandal of Our said Lord the King, of His Excellency the Governor [etc]; whereupon the said Attorney General of Our said Lord the King, for Our said Lord the King, prays . . . the due Process of the Law against him the said *John Peter Zenger* . . . in the Premises.

[The Report continues:]
To this Information the Defendant has pleaded *Not Guilty*, and we are ready to prove it. . . .

Then Mr. *Hamilton*,[1] who at the Request of some of my Friends, was so kind as to come from *Philadelphia* to assist me on the Tryal, spoke.

Mr. *Hamilton*, "May it please your Honour; I am concerned in this Cause on the Part of Mr. *Zenger* the Defendant. The Information against my Client was sent me, a few days before I left Home, with some Instructions to let me know how far I might rely upon the Truth of those Parts of the Papers set forth in the Information, and which are said to be libellous . . . I cannot think it proper for me (without doing Violence to my own Principles) to deny the Publication of a Complaint, which I think is the Right of every free-born Subject to make, when the Matters so published can be supported with Truth; and therefore I'll save Mr. Attorney the Trouble of Examining his Witnesses to that Point; and I do (for my Client) confess, that he both printed and published the two News Papers set forth in the Information, and I hope in so doing he has committed no Crime. . . ."

Mr. *Attorney*, . . . "The Case before the Court is, whether Mr. *Zenger* is guilty of Libelling his Excellency the Governor of *New-York*, and indeed the whole administration of the Gov-

---

[1] James Hamilton, an aged Pennsylvania lawyer.

ernment? Mr. *Hamilton* has confessed the Printing and Publishing, and I think nothing is plainer, than that the Words in the Information are *scandalous, and tend to Sedition, and to disquiet the Minds of the People of this Province.* And if such Papers are not Libels, I think it may be said, there can be no such Thing as a Libel."

Mr. *Hamilton*, "May it please your Honour; I cannot agree with Mr. Attorney: For tho' I freely acknowledge, that there are such Things as Libels, yet I must insist at the same Time, that what my Client is charged with, is not a Libel; and I observed just now, that Mr. Attorney in defining a Libel, made use of the Words *scandalous, seditious, and tend to disquiet the People;* but (whether with Design or not I will not say) he omitted the Word *false.*"

Mr. Attorney, I think I did not omit the Word *false:* But it has been said already, that it may be a Libel, notwithstanding it may be true.

Mr. *Hamilton*, In this I must still differ with Mr. Attorney; for I depend upon it, we are to be tried upon this Information now before the Court and Jury, and to which we have pleaded *Not Guilty,* and by it we are charged with printing and publishing, *a certain false, malicious, seditious and scandalous Libel.* This Word *false* must have some Meaning, or else how came it there? . . .

Mr. Ch. Justice, You cannot be admitted, Mr. **Hamilton,** to give the Truth of a Libel in Evidence. A Libel is not to be justified; for it is nevertheless a Libel that [i.e. tho'] it is *true.*

Mr. *Hamilton*, I am sorry the court has so soon resolved upon that Piece of Law; I expected first to have been heard to that Point. I have not in all my Reading met with an Authority that says, we cannot be admitted to give the Truth in Evidence, upon an Information for a Libel.

Mr. Ch. Justice, The Law is clear, That you cannot justify a Libel. . . .

Mr. *Hamilton*, I thank your Honour. Then, Gentlemen of the Jury, it is to you we must now appeal, for Witnesses, to the

Truth of the Facts we have offered, and are denied the Liberty to prove; and let it not seem strange, that I apply my self to you in this Manner, I am warranted so to do both by Law and Reason. The Last supposes you to be summones, *out of the Neighbourhood where the Fact is alledged to be committed;* and the Reason of your being taken out of the Neighbourhood is, *because you are supposed to have the best Knowledge of the Fact that is to be tried.* And were you to find a Verdict against my Client, you must take upon you to say, the Papers referred to in the Information, and which we acknowledge we printed and published, are *false, scandalous and seditious;* but of this I can have no Apprehension. You are Citizens of *New-York;* you are really what the Law supposes you to be, *honest and lawful Men;* and, according to my Brief, the Facts which we offer to prove were not committed in a Corner; they are notoriously known to be true; and therefore in your Justice lies our Safety. And as we are denied the Liberty of giving Evidence, to prove the Truth of what we have published, I will beg Leave to lay it down as a standing Rule in such Cases, *That the suppressing of Evidence ought always to be taken for the strongest Evidence;* and I hope it will have that Weight with you. . . .

. . . It is true in Times past it was a Crime to speak Truth, and in that terrible Court of Star-Chamber, many worthy and brave Men suffred for so doing; and yet even in that Court, and in those bad Times, a great and good Man durst say, what I hope will not be taken amiss of me to say in this Place, *to wit, the Practice of Informations for Libels is a Sword in the Hands of a wicked king and* [of] *an arrand Coward to cut down and destroy the innocent; the one cannot, because of his high station, and the other dares not, because of his Want of Courage, revenge himself in another Manner.*

Mr. *Attorney,* Pray Mr. *Hamilton,* have a Care what you say, don't go too far neither, I don't like those Liberties.

Mr. *Hamilton,* Sure, Mr. Attorney, you won't make any Applications; all Men agree that we are governed by the best of Kings, and I cannot see the Meaning of Mr. Attorney's

Caution. . . . May it please Your Honour, I was saying, That notwithstanding all the Duty and Reverence claimed by Mr. Attorney to Men in Authority, they are not exempt from observing the Rules of common Justice, either in their private or publick Capacities; the Laws of our Mother Country know no Exception. . . .

I hope to be pardon'd, Sir, for my Zeal upon this Occasion: It is an old and wise Caution, *That when our Neighbour's House is on Fire, We ought to take Care of our own.* For tho', blessed be God, I live in a Government where Liberty is well understood, and freely enjoy'd; yet Experience has shewn us all (I'm sure it has to me) that a bad Precedent in one Government, is soon set up for an Authority in another; and therefore I cannot but think it mine, and every Honest Man's Duty, that (while we pay all due Obedience to Men in Authority) we ought at the same Time to be upon our Guard against Power [i.e., arbitrary power], wherever we apprehend that it may effect Ourselves or our Fellow-Subjects.

I am truly very unequal to such an Undertaking on many Accounts. And you see I labour under the Weight of many Years, and am born down with great Infirmities of Body; yet Old and Weak as I am, I should think it my Duty, if required, to go to the utmost Part of the land, where my Service cou'd be of any Use in assisting to quench the flame of Prosecutions upon Informations, set on Foot by the Government, to deprive a People of the Right of Remonstrating (and complaining too) of the arbitrary Attempts of Men in Power. Men who injure and oppress the People under their Administration provoke them to cry out and complain; and then make that very Complaint the foundation for new Oppressions and Prosecutions. . . . But to conclude; the Question before the Court and you, Gentlemen of the Jury, is not of small nor private Concern, it is not the Cause of a poor Printer, nor of *New-York* alone, which you are now trying; No! It may in its Consequence, affect every Freeman that lives under a British Government on the Main of *America*. It is the best Cause.

It is the Cause of Liberty; and I make no Doubt but your upright Conduct, this Day, will not only entitle you to the Love and Esteem of your Fellow-Citizens; but every Man, who prefers Freedom to a Life of Slavery, will bless and honour You, as Men who have baffled the Attempt of Tyranny; and by an impartial and uncorrupt Verdict, have laid a noble Foundation for securing to ourselves, our Posterity, and our Neighbours, That to which Nature and the Laws of our Country have given us a Right,—the Liberty—both of exposing and opposing arbitrary Power (in these Parts of the World, at least) by speaking and writing Truth. . . .

Mr. Ch. Just. Gentlemen of the Jury. The great pains Mr. *Hamilton* has taken, to shew how little Regard Juries are to Pay to the Opinion of the Judges; and his insisting so much upon the Conduct of some Judges in Tryals of this kind; is done, no doubt, with a Design that you should take but very little Notice of what I may say upon this Occasion. I shall therefore only observe to you that, as the Facts or Words in the Information are confessed: The only Thing that can come in Question before you is, Whether the Words, as set forth in the Information, make a Libel. And that is a Matter of Law, no doubt, and which you may leave to the Court. But I shall trouble you no further with any Thing more of my own, but read to you the Words of a learned and upright Judge in a Case of the like Nature.

To say that corrupt Officers are appointed to administer Affairs, is certainly a Reflection on the Government. If People should not be called to account for possessing the People with an ill Opinion of the Government, no Government can subsist. For it is necessary for all Governments that the People should have a good Opinion of it. . . .

[Zenger adds]

The Jury withdrew, and in a small Time returned, and being asked by the Clerk, Whether they were agreed of their Verdict, and whether *John Peter Zenger* was guilty of Printing and Publishing the Libels in the Information mentioned?

They answered by *Thomas Hunt*, their Foreman, *Not Guilty*. Upon which there were three Huzzas in the Hall which was crowded with People, and the next Day I was discharged from my Imprisonment.

114. Franklin's "Albany Plan," July 10, 1754[1]

On the eve of the French and Indian War, in June 19, 1754, there met at Albany, on the call of the Lords of Trade, a colonial congress to agree upon measures of defense. Seven colonies were represented, — New Hampshire, Massachusetts, Rhode Island, Connecticut, New York, Pennsylvania, and Maryland, — none south of the Potomac. Massachusetts had authorized her commissioners to "enter into articles of union and confederation" with the other colonies "as well in time of peace as of war." On the sixth day of the session, the Congress voted unanimously that a union of all the colonies was "absolutely necessary for their security." A committee, representing each of the colonies present, was created to consider various plans, and, after almost daily discussions, a general plan was accepted on July 9. Franklin was appointed to draft the detailed plan, — and, the next day, a form submitted by him was adopted. Franklin afterward said of the result: "the Fate of this Plan was singular . . . The Crown disapproved it, as having too much Weight in the Democratic Part of the Constitution ; and every Assembly, as having allowed too much to Prerogative. So it was totally rejected."

The text of a number of other plans for colonial federation, between 1696 and 1754, are collected in No. 14 of the *American History Leaflets*.

a. Motives

The following extract is part of the "introduction" to the Plan afterward drawn up by Franklin and printed in his *Works* (Smyth edition, III, 203–204).

The commissioners from a number of the northern colonies, being met at Albany, and considering the difficulties that have always attended the most necessary general measures for the common defence, or for the annoyance of the enemy, when they were to be carried through the several particular Assemblies of all the colonies; some Assemblies being before at

---

[1] The "New Style" chronology was adopted by England in 1752.

variance with their governors or councils, and the several branches of the government not on terms of doing business with each other: others taking the opportunity, when their concurrence is wanted, to push for favorite laws, powers, or points, that they think could not at other times be obtained, and so creating disputes and quarrels; one Assembly waiting to see what another will do, being afraid of doing more than its share, or desirous of doing less, or refusing to do anything because its country is not at present so much exposed as others, or because another will reap more immediate advantage; from one or other of which causes, the Assemblies of six out of seven colonies applied to, had granted no assistance to Virginia when lately invaded by the French, though purposely convened, and the importance of the occasion earnestly urged upon them; — considering moreover, that one principal encouragement to the French, in invading and insulting the British American dominions, was their knowledge of our disunited state, and of our weakness arising from such want of union; and that from hence different colonies were, at different times, extremely harassed, and put to great expense both of blood and treasure, who would have remained in peace, if the enemy had had cause to fear the drawing on themselves the resentment and power of the whole; — the said commissioners, considering also the present encroachments of the French, and the mischievous consequences that may be expected from them, if not opposed with our [united] force, came to an unanimous resolution; *That a union of the colonies is absolutely necessary for their preservation.*

b. The Plan

Broadhead's Documents relative to the Colonial History of New York, VI, 589-591.

Plan of a proposed Union of the several Colonies of Massachusetts Bay, New Hampshire, Connecticut, Rhode Island, New York, New Jerseys, Pennsylvania, Maryland, Virginia, North

Carolina, and South Carolina,[1] *for their mutual defence and security, and for extending the British Settlements in North America.*

That humble application be made for an Act of the Parliament of Great Brittain, by virtue of which, one General Government may be formed in America, including all the said Colonies, within and under which Government each Colony may retain its present Constitution, except in the particulars wherein a [*change*] may be directed by the said Act, as hereafter follows.

That the said General Government be administered by a president General, to be appointed and supported by the Crown, and a grand Council *to be chosen by the representatives of the people of the severall Colonies,* [*met*] in their respective Assemblies.[2]

[Provision for election of first grand council, of forty-eight members, — Massachusetts and Virginia to have *seven* each, Pennsylvania *six*, Connecticut *five*, New York, Maryland,

---

[1] Georgia was not included. Franklin seems originally to have contemplated a union of the northern colonies only.

[2] In Franklin's comments upon the sections of this plan (*Works*, Smyth edition, III, 208 ff.), he adds to this section: " . . . it being proposed by the gentlemen of the Council of New York . . . to alter the plan in this particular, and *to give the governors and council* of the several provinces a share in the choice of the grand council [or at least a veto upon the selections], it was said, . . .

"That it is essential to English liberty, that the subject should not be taxed but by his own consent, or the consent of his elected representatives.

"That taxes to be laid and levied by this proposed constitution will be proposed and agreed to by the representatives of the people, if the plan in this particular be preserved.

"But if the proposed alteration should take place, it seemed as if matters may be so managed as that the crown shall finally have the appointment, not only of the president-general, but of a majority of the grand Council. . . .

"And so the people in all the colonies would in effect be taxed by their governors.

[Some three pages more of like argument.]

" Upon the whole the commissioners were of opinion that the choice was most properly placed in the representatives of the people."

North Carolina, and South Carolina each *four*, New Jersey *three*, New Hampshire and Rhode Island each *two*.]

Who shall meet for the present time at the City of Philadelphia in Pennsylvania, being called by the President General as soon as conveniently may be after his appointment.

That there shall be a New Election of the Members of the Grand Council every three years, and on the death or resignation of any Member, his place should be supplyed by a new choice at the next sitting of the Assembly of the Colony he represented.

That after the first three years, when the proportion of money arising out of each Colony to the General Treasury can be known, the number of Members to be chosen, for each Colony shall from time to time in all ensuing Elections be regulated by that proportion (yet so as that the Number to be chosen by any one province be not more than seven nor less than two).

That the Grand Council shall meet once in every year, and oftener if occasion require, at such time and place as they shall adjourn to at the last preceding meeting, or as they shall be called to meet at by the President General, on any emergency, he having first obtained in writing the consent of seven of the Members to such call, and sent due and timely notice to the whole.

That the Grand Council have power to chuse their speaker, and *shall neither be dissolved prorogued, nor continue sitting longer than six weeks at one time without their own consent,*[1] *or the special command of the Crown.*

That the Members of the Grand Council shal be allowed for their service ten shillings sterling per diem, during their Ses-

---

[1] Franklin's comment was (see note above): "Governors have sometimes wantonly exercised the power of . . . continuing the sessions of Assemblies, merely to harass the members and compel a compliance; and sometimes dissolve them on slight disgusts." This provision may have been suggested to Franklin by the fact that in his own colony the legislative sittings were independent of the governor's will (No. 103, *b*, above).

sions or [*and*] Journey to and from the place of Meeting; twenty miles to be reckoned a days Journey.

That the Assent of the President General be requisite to all Acts of the Grand Council, and that it be his Office and duty to cause them to be carried into execution.

That the President General with the advice of the Grand Council, hold or direct all Indian Treaties in which the general interest of the Colonys may be concerned; and make peace or declare War with Indian Nations. That they make such Laws as they judge necessary for the regulating all Indian Trade. That they make all purchases from Indians for the Crown, of lands not [now] within the bounds of particular Colonies, or that shall not be within their bounds when some of them are reduced to more convenient dimensions. That they make new settlements on such purchases by granting Lands, [in the King's name] reserving a Quit rent to the Crown, for the use of the General Treasury.

That they make Laws for regulating and governing such new settlements, till the Crown shall think fit to form them into particular Governments.

That they raise and pay Soldiers, and build Forts for the defence of any of the Colonies, and equip vessels of Force to guard the Coasts and protect the Trade on the Ocean, Lakes, or great Rivers; but they shall not impress men in any Colonies without the consent of its Legislature. That for these purposes they have power to make Laws and lay and Levy such general duties, imposts or taxes, as to them shall appear most equal and just, considering the ability and other circumstances of the Inhabitants in the several Colonies, and such as may be collected with the least inconvenience to the people, rather discouraging luxury, than loading Industry with unnecessary burthens.— That they might appoint a General Treasurer and a particular Treasurer in each Government when necessary, and from time to time may order the sums in the Treasuries of each Government, into the General Treasury, or draw on them for special payments as they find most convenient; yet no money to issue but by joint orders of the President General and Grand Council, except where sums have been appropriated to particular purposes, and the President General is previously impowered by an Act to draw for such sums.

That the General accounts shall be yearly settled and reported to the several Assemblies.

That a Quorum of the Grand Council impowered to act with the President General, do consist of twenty five Members, among whom there shall be one or more from a majority of the Colonies. That the laws made by them for the purposes aforesaid, shall not be repugnant, but as near as may be agreeable to the Laws of England, and shall be transmitted to the King in Council for approbation, as soon as may be after their passing, and if not disapproved within three years after presentation to remain in Force.

That in case of the death of the President General, the Speaker of the Grand Council for the time being shall succeed, and be vested with the same powers and authority, to continue until the King's pleasure be known.

[Commissions, military and civil, for officers acting under this constitution, to be issued jointly by President-General and Grand Council.] — That the particular Military as well as Civil establishments in each Colony remain in their present State this General constitution notwithstanding. And that on sudden emergencies any Colony may defend itself, and lay the accounts of expence, thence arisen, before the President General and Grand Council, who may allow and order payment of the same if judged reasonable.

[In 1789 Franklin wrote, with good reason, that the adoption of the Albany Plan would have probably delayed the separation of the colonies from England, "perhaps during another century." There would have been a central legislature to vote supplies and prepare defense against Indians and French, and the British reasons for the Stamp Act would not have existed.]

XX. HARSH PHASES OF COLONIAL SOCIETY[1]

115. Legal Punishment in Virginia, 1662-1748

Hening's *Statutes*, II, 75. The following statute was enacted in March, 1662. It was reënacted, in similar words, in 1705 and in 1748 (*ib.* 367-368 and 507-508), and was in force at the opening of the Revolution.

Whereas many offences are punishable by the laws of England and of this country with corporall punishments, for executeing whereof noe such provision hath been made as the said laws doe require; *Be it therefore enacted*, that, in every county, the court cause to be sett up a pillory, a pair of stocks, and a whipping post, neere the courthouse, and a ducking-stoole in such a place as they shall think convenient . . . And the courts not causeing the said pillory and whipping post, stocks and ducking stoole to be erected within six months, after the date of this act shall be fined five thousand pounds of tobacco to the use of the publique.

116. White Servants in 1774

William Eddes, *Letters from America*.
These *Letters*, written in 1774, were printed in London in 1792. Eddes was a customs official at Annapolis.

Persons in a state of servitude are under four distinct denominations: negroes, who are the entire property of their respective owners: convicts, who are transported from the mother country for a limited term: indented servants, who are engaged for five years previous to their leaving England; and free-willers, who are supposed, from their situation, to possess superior advantages. . . .

Persons convicted of felony, and in consequence transported to this continent, if they are able to pay the expence of passage, are free to pursue their fortune agreeably to their inclinations or abilities. Few, however, have means to avail themselves of

---
[1] Cf. *American History and Government*, §§ 120-124.

this advantage. These unhappy beings are, generally, consigned to an agent, who classes them suitably to their real or supposed qualifications; advertises them for sale, and disposes of them, for seven years, to planters, to mechanics, and to such as choose to retain them for domestic service.

* * * * * * *

The generality of the inhabitants in this province are very little acquainted with those fallacious pretences, by which numbers are continually induced to embark for this continent. On the contrary, they too generally conceive an opinion that the difference is merely nominal between the indented servant and the convicted felon: nor will they readily believe that people, who had the least experience in life, and whose characters were unexceptionable, would abandon their friends and families, and their ancient connexions, for a servile situation, in a remote appendage to the British Empire. From this persuasion they rather consider the convict as the more profitable servant, his term being for seven, the latter only for five years; and, I am sorry to observe, that there are but few instances wherein they experience different treatment. Negroes being a property for life, the death of slaves, in the prime of youth or strength, is a material loss to the proprietor; they are, therefore, almost in every instance, under more comfortable circumstances than the miserable European, over whom the rigid planter exercises an inflexible severity. They [white servants] are strained to the utmost to perform their allotted labour. . . .

The situation of the free-willer is, in almost every instance more to be lamented than either that of the convict or the indented servant; the deception which is practised on those of this description being attended with circumstances of greater duplicity and cruelty. . . . They are told, that their services will be eagerly solicited, in proportion to their abilities; that their reward will be adequate to the hazard they encounter by courting fortune in a distant region; and that the parties with whom they engage will readily advance the sum agreed on for their passage; which, being averaged at about nine pounds sterling, they will speedily be enabled to repay, and to enjoy, in a state of liberty, a comparative situation of ease and affluence. . . . It is, therefore, an article of agreement with these deluded victims, that if they are not successful in obtaining situations, on their own terms, within a certain number of days after their arrival in the country, they are then to be sold, in order to defray the charges of passage. . . .

117. Runaway Servants and Apprentices

From "Newspaper Extracts," 1770–1771, in *New Jersey Archives*, First Series, XXVII. The editor of this volume is responsible for the italics.

Trenton Goal, December 28, 1769.

This is to give notice, there was committed to my custody, by William Clayton, Esq., as a runaway apprentice on the 24th day of October last, THOMAS SANDAMAN. This is to inform his master or sheriff that he run away from, that they come and pay charges and take him away, *or he will be sold* to pay cost and charges, on Saturday the 20th day of January, 1770, by me

PETER HANKINSON, *Goaler.*
— *The Pennsylvania Journal, No. 1413, January 4, 1770.*

THREE POUNDS REWARD

Run-away on Friday the 12th Inst. from the Subscriber at Hunterdon County, in New-Jersey, an Apprentice, named DAVID COX, about Twenty Years of Age, a Carpenter and Joiner by Trade, but its likely he may pass for a Mill-Wright, as he has two Brothers of that Trade, that works near Albany. He is about 5 Feet 10 Inches high, large boned, knock kneed, of a dark Complexion, down Look, black Eyes, black Hair, and wears it tied. Had on when he went away, a grey coloured Coat and Jacket, pretty much worn, with Horn Buttons on them, new Leather Breeches, with black Horn Buttons, Russia Shirt, black Yarn Stockings, new Shoes, also a rusty Castor Hat, wears it cocked: It is also suspected he has stole his Indentures, and will very likely show them for a Pass, as he is near of Age. Whoever apprehends said Apprentice, and secures him in any Goal, so that his Master may have Notice thereof, shall have the above Reward, paid by me.

JAMES TAYLOR.

N. B. Perhaps he may change his Cloaths, that he may not be discovered.

— *The N. Y. Gazette, or Weekly Post Boy, No. 1412, January 22, 1770.*

New Jersey, November 24, 1769.

Run-away the 22d September, from the Subscriber, living in Monmouth County, in the Township of Shrewsbury, in the Province of East New-Jersey; an indented Servant Man, named Walter Clark, *born in the Jerseys*, about Twenty-four Years of Age, a Black-Smith by trade, and understands farming Business; he is about six Feet high, has black curled Hair, and keeps his Mouth much open: He took several Suits of Apparel with him, all of a brownish Colour, some Broad Cloth, and some thin Stuff; also one striped double-breasted Jacket. Whoever takes up the above said Servant and delivers him to me the Subscriber, shall have Three Pounds Reward, and reasonable Charges paid, by me.

BENJAMIN JACKSON.

— *The N. Y. Journal or General Advertiser, No. 1412, January 25, 1770.*

Run away from the subscriber, living near Morris-Town, in New-Jersey, on Christmas-day last, a servant man, named Thomas Clay, a Cooper by trade, *near 50 years of age*, about 5 feet 10 inches high, brown curled hair, will drink to excess, and then is noisy, likes to sing songs; had on, when he went away, a blue great coat, and jacket of the same, leather breeches, and felt hat. Whoever takes up and secures said servant, so that his master may have him again, shall have Three Pounds Reward, and reasonable charges, paid by

DANIEL GERARD, junior.

— *Pennsylvania Gazette*, No. 2146, February 8, 1770.

BURLINGTON, December 3, 1770.

This Day was committed to the Goal of this City, a certain Thomas Gearn, *upon suspicion of being a runaway Servant*; he says that he belongs to William Withers, living in Cecil County, Maryland, and that he left his said Master about 14 or 15 Weeks ago. Said Servant is about 20 Years of Age, and says when he left his Master he had *an Iron Collar on his Neck*, but soon got it off. Whoever owns the said Thomas Gearn, is desired to come or send; pay Charges immediately, and take him away. — EPHRAIM PHILLIPS, *Goaler*.

GLOUCESTER COUNTY GOAL, September 12, 1771.

Taken up *on suspicion*, as a runaway servant and now confined here, a young man about 5 feet 6 inches high, marked with the small-pox, has on a blue coat, homespun shirt, and check trousers, says his name is Hugh M'Cage, and that he belongs to one William or John Miller, living near Lancaster. His master, if any he has, is desired to fetch him away, *and pay charges*; otherwise he will be *sold out* in 3 weeks from the date hereof.

RICHARD JOHNSON, *Goaler*.

— *Pennsylvania Gazette*, Sept. 12, 1771.

[These advertisements all relate to *White* men. Like entries continue through the early Revolutionary days, often in the same column with flaming expressions of the spirit of political liberty, in a manner somewhat amazing to a modern reader. This one volume of newspaper extracts for the years 1770–1771, has *seventy-seven* such advertisements of run-away White servants for New Jersey alone, — many times as many as there were for runaway Negroes.]

D. THE REVOLUTION

XXI. PRELIMINARY PERIOD — TO 1774

On the history and subdivisions of this period, cf. *American History and Government*, §§ 126-144. Many documents which might be expected for the Revolution are omitted in this volume because of the short quotations from them in *American History and Government*.

118. Sugar Act of 1764

Pickering's *Statutes at Large*, XXVI, 33-52 (4 Geo. III, c. 15). On the bearing of this and the Stamp Act (following) upon the Revolution, cf. *American History and Government*, §§ 131, 132.

An act for granting certain duties in the British colonies and plantations in America; for continuing, amending, and making perpetual, an act passed in the sixth year of the reign of his late Majesty King George the Second, (intituled, An act for the better securing and encouraging the trade of his Majesty's sugar colonies in America;) *for applying the produce of such duties, and of the duties to arise by virtue of the said act, towards defraying the expences of defending, protecting, aud securing the said colonies and plantations ;* ... *and for altering and disallowing several drawbacks on exports from this kingdom, and more effectually preventing the clandestine conveyance of goods to and from the said colonies and plantations, and improving and securing the trade between the same and Great Britain.*

WHEREAS *it is expedient that new provisions and regulations should be established for improving the revenue of this Kingdom, and for extending and securing the navigation and commerce between* Great Britain *and your Majesty's dominions in* America, *which, by the peace, have been so happily enlarged: and whereas it is just and necessary, that a revenue be raised, in your Maj-*

esty's said dominions in America, *for defraying the expences of defending, protecting, and securing the same* . . . be it enacted . . . , That from and after [September 29, 1764], there shall be raised, levied, collected, and paid, unto his Majesty . . . , for and upon all white or clayed sugars of the produce or manufacture of any colony or plantation in *America*, not under the dominion of his Majesty . . . ; for and upon indico, and coffee of foreign produce or manufacture; for and upon all wines (except *French* wine;) for and upon all wrought silks, bengals, and stuffs, mixed with silk or herba, of the manufacture of *Persia, China,* or *East India,* and all callico painted, died, printed, or stained there; and for and upon all foreign linen cloth called *Cambrick* and *French* Lawns, which shall be imported or brought into any colony or plantation in *America* . . . under the dominion of his Majesty . . . , the several rates and duties following; that it to say,

For every hundred weight avoirdupois of such foreign white or clayed sugars, one pound two shillings, over and above all other duties imposed by any former act of parliament. . . .

For every hundred weight avoirdupois of such foreign coffee, which shall be imported from any place except *Great Britain*, two pounds, nineteen shillings, and nine pence.

For every ton of wine of the growth of the *Madeiras,* or of any other island or place from whence such wine may be lawfully imported . . . , the sum of seven pounds.

For every ton of *Portugal, Spanish,* or any other wine (except *French* wine) imported from *Great Britian,* the sum of ten shillings.

For every pound weight avoirdupois of wrought silks, bengals, and stuffs, mixed with silk or herba, of the manufacture of *Persia, China,* or *East India,* imported from *Great Britain,* two shillings.

For every piece of callico painted, dyed, printed, or stained, in *Persia, China,* or *East India,* imported from *Great Britain,* two shillings and six pence.

For every piece of foreign linen cloth, called *Cambrick*, imported from *Great Britain*, three shillings. . . .

II. And it is hereby further enacted . . . That from and after [September 29, 1764] there shall also be raised, levied, collected, and paid, unto his Majesty . . . , for and upon all coffee and pimento of the growth and produce of any *British* colony or plantation in *America*, which shall be there laden on board any *British* ship or vessel, to be carried out from thence or any other place whatsoever, except *Great Britain*, the several rates and duties following; that is to say,

III. For every hundred weight avoirdupois of such *British* coffee, seven shillings.

For every pound weight avoirdupois of such *British* pimento, one half penny. . . .

[IV, V, VI. The Sugar Act of 1733 (No. 100*c*) to continue in force perpetually with a decrease of one half in the rate upon imports from British colonies.]

* * * * * * *

XI. And it is further enacted . . . That all the monies which . . . shall arise by the several rates . . . herein . . . granted . . . shall be paid into the receipt of his Majesty's Exchequer, **and shall be entered separate and apart from all other monies paid or payable to his Majesty . . . : and shall be there reserved, to be, from time to time, disposed of by parliament, towards defraying the necessary expences of defending, protecting, and securing, the *British* colonies and plantations in *America*.**

* * * * * * *

XVIII. And be it further enacted . . . , That from and after . . . [September 29, 1764] . . . , no rum or spirits of the produce or manufacture of any of the colonies or plantations in *America*, not in the possession or under the dominion of his Majesty . . . , shall be imported or brought into any of the colonies or plantations in *America* which now are, or hereafter may be, in the possession or under the dominion of his Majesty . . . upon forfeiture of all such rum or spirits, together with the ship or vessel in which the same shall be imported, with the tackle, apparel, and furniture thereof; to be seized by any officer or officers of his Majesty's customs, and prosecuted in such manner and form as herein is after expressed; any law, custom, or usage, to the contrary notwithstanding.

* * * * . * * *

XXVII. And it is hereby further enacted . . . , That from and after . . . [September 29, 1764] . . . , all coffee, pimento, cocoa nuts, whale fins, raw silk, hides, and skins, pot and pearl ashes, of the growth, production, or manufacture, of any *British* colony or plantation in *America*, shall be imported directly from thence into this kingdom, or some other *British* colony or plantation.

[XXVIII Adds iron and lumber of all sorts to the "enumerated" list of articles to be exported by the colonies only to Great Britain.]

[Most of the omitted sections of this long act have to do with providing a costly but efficient machinery of bonds, inspectors, etc., to enforce the navigation laws. The stringent section, XXXV, designed to prevent any trade whatever with the French West Indies is added.]

XXXV. And, in order to prevent any illicit trade or commerce between his Majesty's subjects in *America*, and the subjects of the crown of *France* in the islands of *Saint Pierre* and *Miquelon*, it is hereby further enacted . . . , That from and after [September 29, 1764], if any *British* ship or vessel *shall be found standing into, or coming out from, either of those islands, or hovering or at anchor within two leagues of the coasts thereof*, or shall be discovered to have taken any goods or merchandizes on board at either of them, or to have been there for that purpose; such ship or vessel, and all the goods so taken on board there, shall be forfeited and lost, and shall and may be seized and prosecuted by any officer of his Majesty's customs; and the master or other person having the charge of such ship or vessel, and every person concerned in taking any such goods on board, shall forfeit treble the value thereof.

119. Stamp Act

March 22, 1765

Pickering's *Statutes at Large*, XXVI, 179–204 (5 Geo. III, c. 12).

An act for granting and applying certain stamp duties, and other duties, in the British *colonies and plantations in* America, *towards further defraying the expences of defending, protecting, and securing the same;* . . .

WHEREAS . . . it is just and necessary, that provision be made for raising a further revenue within your Majesty's dominions in America, towards defraying the . . . expences [of the colonies] . . . be it enacted . . . , That from and after the first day of *November,* one thousand seven hundred and sixty five, there shall be raised, levied, collected, and paid unto his Majesty, his heirs, and successors, throughout the colonies and plantations in *America* . . .

For every skin or piece of vellum or parchment, or sheet or piece of paper, on which shall be ingrossed, written or printed, any declaration, plea, replication, rejoinder, demurrer, or other pleading, or any copy thereof, in any court of law within the *British* colonies and plantations in *America,* a stamp duty of three pence.

[Fifty-five paragraphs follow, each imposing a duty (varying from a penny to several pounds) for different legal or governmental papers, or upon the sale of certain articles, or upon pamphlets, with many pages of provisions for the enforcement of the law.]

LIV. And be it further enacted . . . , That all the monies which shall arise by the several rates and duties hereby granted (except the necessary charges of raising, collecting, recovering, answering, paying, and accounting for the same, and the necessary charges from time to time incurred in relation to this act, and the execution thereof) shall be paid into the receipt of his Majesty's exchequer, and shall be entered separate and apart from all other monies, and shall be there reserved to be from time to time disposed of by parliament, *towards further defraying the necessary expences of defending, protecting, and securing, the said colonies and plantations.*

* * * * * * *

120. Reception of the Stamp Act in America

a. Patrick Henry's Resolutions, May 27, 1765

Journals of the Virginia House of Burgesses, 1761–1765, lxvi–lxvii.
The text below gives the resolutions as approved in committee of the whole, May 27. The last two failed to pass the House, May 28; and May 29 the last of the others was expunged from the record. The full text was published by newspapers, however, and it was generally supposed that Virginia had approved them all as here given.

Whereas, The Honorable House of Commons, in *England,* have of late drawn into question how far the General Assembly of this colony hath power to enact laws for laying of taxes and imposing duties payable by the people of this, his Majesty's most ancient colony; for settling and ascertaining the same to all future times, the House of Burgesses of this present General Assembly have come to the following resolves.

Resolved, That the first adventurers, settlers of this his Majesty's colony and dominion of *Virginia,* brought with them and transmitted to their posterity, and all other his Majesty's subjects, since inhabiting in this his Majesty's colony, all the privileges and immunities that have at any time been held, enjoyed, and possessed by the people of *Great Britain.*

Resolved, That by two royal charters, granted by King *James* the First, the colony aforesaid are declared and entitled to all privileges, and immunities of natural born subjects, to all intents and purposes as if they had been abiding and born within the realm of *England.*

Resolved, That his Majesty's liege people of this ancient colony have enjoyed the right of being thus governed by their own Assembly in the article of taxes and internal police, and that the same have never been forfeited, or any other way yielded up, but have been constantly recognized by the King and people of *Great Britain.*

Resolved, Therefore, that the General Assembly of this colony, together with his Majesty or his substitutes, have, in their representative capacity, the only exclusive right and power to lay taxes and imposts upon the inhabitants of this colony; and that every attempt to vest such power in any other person or persons whatever than the General Assembly aforesaid, is illegal, unconstitutional, and unjust, and has a manifest tendency to destroy *British* as well as *American* liberty.

Resolved, That his Majesty's liege people, the inhabitants of this colony, are not bound to yield obedience to any law or ordinance whatever, designed to impose any taxation whatsoever upon them, other than the laws or ordinances of the General Assembly aforesaid.

Resolved, That any person who shall, by speaking or writing, assert or maintain that any person or persons, other than the General Assembly of this colony, have any right or power to impose or lay any taxation on the people here, shall be deemed an enemy to his Majesty's colony.

[The sixth and seventh resolutions point to *forcible resistance,* not merely to *protest.* This is the peculiarity which marks off this document from many others of the time. A few months later, that tone was common. Cf. *b,* below.]

b. *An Association against the Stamp Act in a Virginia County, 1766*

Journals of the House of Burgesses, 1761–1765, lxxii. These Resolutions were drawn by Richard Henry Lee.

[County] resolutions passed at *Leedstown,* on the 27th day of February 1766:

... We, who subscribe this paper, have associated, and do bind ourselves to each other, to God, and to our country, by the firmest ties that religion and virtue can frame, most sacredly and punctually to stand by, and with our lives and fortunes, to support, maintain, and defend each other in the observance and execution of these following articles. . . .

* * * * * * *

Thirdly. As the Stamp Act does absolutely direct the property of the people to be taken from them without their consent expressed by their representatives, and as in many cases it deprives the *British American* subject of his right to trial by jury; we do determine, at every hazard, and, paying no regard to danger or to death, we will exert every faculty, to prevent the execution of the said Stamp Act in any instance whatsoever within this Colony. And every abandoned wretch, who shall be so lost to virtue and public good, as wickedly to contribute to the introduction or fixture of the Stamp Act in this Colony, by using stampt paper, or by any other means, we will, with the utmost expedition, convince all such profligates that immediate danger shall attend their prostitute purpose.

Fourthly. That the last article may most surely and effectually be executed, we engage to each other, that whenever it shall be known to any of this association, that any person is so conducting himself as to favor the introduction of the Stamp Act, that immediate notice shall be given to as many of the association as possible; and that every individual so informed, shall, with expedition, repair to a place of meeting to be appointed as near the scene of action as may be. . . .

Sixthly. If any attempt shall be made on the liberty or property of any associator for any action or thing to be done in consequence of this engagement, we do most solemnly bind ourselves by the sacred engagements above entered into, at the utmost risk of our lives and fortunes, to restore such associate to his liberty, and to protect him in the enjoyment of his property. . . .

[One hundred and fifteen names are signed, — among them, a Washington and six Lees.]

c. Resignation of Stamp Distributor in Virginia, 1765
(Letter of the Governor to the Lords of Trade)

Journals of the House of Burgesses, 1762–1765, lxviii–lxxi.

WILLIAMSBURG Nov. 3d 1765.

MY LORDS,

The present unhappy state of this Colony, will, to my great concern, oblige me to trouble Your Lordships with a long and very disagreeable letter. We were for some time in almost daily expectations of the arrival of Colonel Mercer with the Stamps for the use of this Colony, and rumours were industriously thrown out that at the time of the General Court parties would come down from most parts of the country to seize on and destroy all Stamped Papers. . . .

Very unluckily, Colonel Mercer arrived at the time this town was the fullest of Strangers. On Wednesday the 30th October he came up to town. I then thought proper to go to the Coffee house . . . that I might be an eye witness of what did really pass, and not receive it by relation from others. The mercantile people were all assembled as usual. The first word I heard was "One and all"; upon which, as at a word agreed on before between themselves, they all quitted the place to find Colonel Mercer at his Father's lodgings where it was known he was. This concourse of people I should call a mob, did I not know that *it was chiefly if not altogether composed of gentlemen of property* in the Colony, some of them at the head of their respective Counties, *and the merchants of the country*, whether English, Scotch or Virginian; for few absented themselves. They met Colonel Mercer on the way, just at the Capitol: there they stopped and demanded of him an answer whether he would resign or act in this office as Distributor of the Stamps. He said it was an affair of great moment to him; he must consult his friends; and promised to give them an answer at 10 o'clock on Friday morning at that place. This did not satisfy them; and they followed him to the Coffee house, in the porch of which I had seated myself with many of the Council and the

Speaker, who had posted himself between the crowd and myself. We all received him with the greatest marks of welcome; with which, if one may be allowed to judge by their countenances, they [the "mob"] were not well pleased, tho' they remained quiet and were silent. Now and then a voice was heard from the crowd that Friday was too late; the Act would take place, they would have an answer tomorrow. Several messages were brought to Mr. Mercer by the leading men of the crowd, to whom he constantly answered he had already given an answer and he would have no other extorted from him. After some little time a cry was heard, "let us rush in." Upon this we that were at the top of the [steps], knowing the advantage our situation gave us to repell those who should attempt to mount them, advanced to the edge of the Steps, of which number I was one. I immediately heard a cry, "See the Governor, take care of him." Those who before were pushing up the steps, immediately fell back, and left a small space between me and them. If your Lordships will not accuse me of vanity I would say that I believe this to be partly owing to the respect they bore to my character and partly to the love they bore to my person. After much entreaty of some of his friends, Mr. Mercer was, against his own inclination, prevailed upon to promise them an answer at the Capitol the next evening at five. The crowd did not yet disperse; it was growing dark, and I did not think it safe to have to leave Mr. Mercer behind me, so I again advanced to the edge of the steps and said aloud I believed no man there would do me any hurt, and turned to Mr. Mercer and told him if he would walk with me through the people I believed I could conduct him safe to my house; and we accordingly walked side by side through the thickest of the people, who did not molest us, tho' there was some little murmurs. By me thus taking him under my protection, I believe I saved him from being insulted at least. When we got home we had much discourse on the subject. . . . He left me that night in a state of uncertainty what part he should act.

Accordingly Mr. Mercer appeared at the Capitol at 5, as he

had promised. The number of people assembled there was much increased, by messengers having been sent into the neighborhood for that purpose. Colonel Mercer then read to them the answer which is printed in the Supplement of the Gazette, of which I enclose your Lordships a copy, to which I beg leave to refer.[1] . . .

[Mercer offered to resign his commission to the governor—who refused to accept the resignation.] If I accepted the resignation, I must appoint another, and I was well convinced I could not find one to accept of it, in those circumstances, which would render the office cheap. Besides if I left Mr. Mercer in possession of the place he would be always ready to distribute the Stamped papers, whenever peoples eyes should be opened and they should come to their senses, so as to receive them. . . .

FRANCIS FAUQUIER.

Colonel Mercer has informed me that he proposes to apply to the Commanders of His Majesty's ships of War, to take the Stamped Papers on board their ships for His Majesty's service: it being the place of the greatest if not the only security for them: for I am convinced, as well as himself, that it would be extremely dangerous to attempt to land them during the present fermented state of the Colony. If these Gentlemen should refuse to take charge of them, and Mr. Mercer should apply to me, I will do my duty to His Majesty and save them from being destroyed, to the best of my power, tho' I can by no means answer for the success of my endeavors. . . .

I am with the greatest respect and esteem, my Lords
    Your Lordships most obedient
        and devoted Servant.

FRANCIS FAUQUIER.

---

[1] Mercer promised not to act unless first he should have secured permission from the Virginia Assembly. He was then borne in triumph to his lodgings by the joyful "mob."

d. Terrorizing the Respecters of the Law in New Jersey

The New York Gazette or Weekly Post Boy, February 27, 1766; reproduced in *New Jersey Archives*, First Series, XXV, 38.

A large Gallows was erected in Elizabeth-Town last Week, with a Rope ready fixed thereto; and the Inhabitants there vow and declare that the first Person that either distributes and [or] takes out [*i.e.*, uses] Stamped Paper, shall be hung thereon without Judge or Jury.

121. Origin of the Virginia Non-importation Agreement

a. Protest of the Burgesses against the Proposal of the English Government to send Americans, accused of Treason, to England for Trial.

Journals of the House of Burgesses, 1766–1769, 212–218.

Tuesday, the 16th of May. 9 Geo. III. 1769.

* * * * * * *

... The Order of the Day being read, for the House to resolve itself into a Committee of the whole House, to consider of the present State of the Colony;

Ordered, That ... one other Statute made in the Thirty-fifth Year of the same King's Reign [Henry VIII], entituled, *An Act for the Trial of Treasons committed out of the King's Dominions*, be referred to the said Committee.

Then the House resolved itself into the said Committee.

Mr. *Speaker* left the Chair.

Mr. *Blair* took the Chair of the Committee.

Mr. *Speaker* resumed the Chair.

Mr. *Blair* reported, from the Committee, that they had come to several Resolutions; which he read in his Place, and afterwards delivered in at the Clerk's Table, where the same were read, and are as followeth, *viz.*

[Resolutions I and II repeat familiar clauses as to right of taxation only by the Virginia Assembly, and as to right of petition for redress of grievances.]

[III] *Resolved*, That it is the Opinion of this committee, that all Trials for Treason, Misprison of Treason, or for any Felony or Crime whatsoever, committed and done in this his Majesty's said Colony and Dominion, by any Person or Persons residing therein, ought of Right to be had, and conducted in and before his Majesty's Courts, held within the said Colony, according to the fixed and known Course of Proceeding; and that the seizing any Person or Persons, residing in this Colony, suspected of any Crime whatsoever, committed therein, and sending such Person, or Persons, to Places beyond the Sea, to be tried, is highly Derogatory of the Rights of *British* Subjects; as thereby the inestimable Privilege of being tried by a *Jury from a Vicinage* as well as the Liberty of summoning and producing Witnesses on such Trial, will be taken away from the Party accused. . . .

[A fourth resolution declared the purpose of memorializing King George upon the matter of the third resolution.]

The said *Resolutions* being severally read a second Time;

Resolved, Nemine Contradicente,

That this House doth agree with the Committee in the said Resolutions.

* * * * * * *

Resolved, That this House will, To-morrow, resolve itself into a Committee of the whole House, to consider further of the present State of the Colony.

Ordered, That the Speaker of this House do transmit without Delay, to the Speakers of the several Houses of Assembly, on this Continent, a Copy of the Resolutions now agreed to by this House, requesting their Concurrence therein.

Ordered, That a Committee be appointed to draw up an Address, to be presented to his Majesty, upon the fourth Resolution of the Committee of the whole House, this Day reported, and agreed to by the House.

* * * * * * *

Wednesday. the 17th of May. 9 Geo. III. 1769.

* * * * * * *

Ordered, That the Resolutions of the Committee of the whole House, Yesterday reported to the House, and by them agreed to, be printed in the *Virginia Gazette*.

* * * * * * *

[Mr. Blair, previously appointed to draft an address to the King, read the address, as follows.]

When we consider, that by the established Laws and Constitution of this Colony, the most ample Provision is made for apprehending and punishing all those who shall dare to engage in any treasonable Practices against your Majesty, or disturb the Tranquility of Government, we cannot, without Horror, think of the new, unusual, and permit us, with all Humility, to add, unconstitutional and illegal Mode, recommended to your Majesty, of seizing and carrying beyond the Sea, the Inhabitants of America, suspected of any Crime; and of trying such Persons in any other Manner than by the ancient and long established Course of Proceeding: For how truly deplorable must be the Case of a wretched American, who, having incurred the Displeasure of any one in Power, is dragged from his native Home, and his dearest domestick Connections, thrown into Prison, not to await his Trial before a Court, Jury, or Judges, from a Knowledge of whom he is encouraged to hope for speedy Justice; but to exchange his Imprisonment in his own Country, for Fetters amongst Strangers? Conveyed to a distant Land, where no Friend, no Relation, will alleviate his Distresses, or minister to his Necessities; and where no Witness can be found to testify his Innocence; shunned by the reputable and honest, and consigned to the Society and Converse of the wretched and the abandoned; he can only pray that he may soon end his Misery with his Life. . . .

The said *Address* being read a second Time;

Resolved, Nemine Contradicente,

That the House doth agree with the Committee, in the said Address, to be presented to his Majesty.

Ordered, That Mr. *Speaker* do transmit the said Address to the Agent for this Colony, with Directions to cause the same to be presented to his Most Excellent Majesty; and afterwards to be printed and published in the *English* Papers.

*   *   *   *   *   *   *

A Message from the Governor, by Mr. *Walthoe:*

"Mr. Speaker, the Governor commands the immediate Attendance of your House in the Council Chamber."

Accordingly, Mr. *Speaker,* with the House, went up to attend the Governor in the Council Chamber; where his Excellency was pleased to say to them:

"Mr. Speaker, and Gentlemen of the House of Burgesses, I have heard of your Resolves and augur ill of their Effect: You have made it my Duty to dissolve you; and you are dissolved accordingly."

b. *Association of the Ex-Burgesses, May 18, 1769*

Journals of House of Burgesses, 1766–1769, xxxix ff.

"The late representatives of the people" then judging it necessary that some action should be taken to relieve their "distressed situation, and for preserving the true and essential interests of the Colony, resolved upon a meeting" and at once repaired to the house of *Mr. Anthony Hay,* when it was proposed that such matters as demanded attention might be considered. This body, according to adjournment, met next day and continued its session. The minutes of both meetings, not being included in the regular Journals of the House of Burgesses, were ordered by the Burgesses to be printed, as follows.

Williamsburg
Wednesday. the 17th May. 1769.

About 12 o'Clock his Excellency the Governor was pleased, by his Messenger, to command the Attendance of the House of Burgesses in the Council Chamber, whereupon, in Obedience to his Lordship's Command, the House, with their Speaker, immediately waited upon his Excellency, when he thought fit to dissolve the General Assembly.

The late Representatives of the People then judging it necessary that some Measures should be taken in their distressed Situation, for preserving the true and essential Interests of the Colony, resolved upon a Meeting for that very salutary Purpose, and therefore, immediately, with the greatest Order and Decorum, repaired to the House of Mr. Anthony Hay in this City, where being assembled, it was first proposed, for the more decent and regular Discussion of such Matters as might be taken into Consideration, that a Moderator should be appointed, and, on the Question being put, Peyton Randolph, Esq; *late Speaker of the House of Burgesses*, was unanimously elected.

The true state of the Colony, being then opened and fully explained, and it being proposed that a regular Association should be formed, a Committee was appointed to prepare the necessary and most proper Regulations for that Purpose, and they were ordered to make their Report to the General Meeting the next Day at 10 o'clock.

Thursday. May 18.

At a farther Meeting, according to Adjournment, the Committee appointed Yesterday, made their Report, which being read, seriously considered and approved, was signed by a great Number of the Principal Gentlemen of the Colony then present, and is as follows:

We his Majesty's most dutiful Subjects, the late Representatives of all the Freeholders of the Colony of Virginia, avowing our inviolable and unshaken Fidelity and Loyalty to our most gracious Sovereign, our Affection for all our Fellow Subjects of Great Britain protesting against every Act or Thing which may have the most distant Tendancy to interrupt, or in any wise disturb his Majesty's Peace, and the good Order of his Government in this Colony, which we are resolved, at the Risque of our Lives and Fortune, to maintain and defend; but at the same Time, being deeply affected with the Grievances and Distresses with which his Majesty's American Subjects are oppressed, and dreading the Evils which threaten the ruin of ourselves and our posterity, by reducing us from a free and happy People, to a wretched and miserable State of Slavery; and having taken into our most serious Consideration the present State of the Trade of this Colony, and of the American Commerce in general, observe with Anxiety, that the Debt due Great Britain for Goods imported from thence is very great, and that the Means of paying this Debt, in the present Situation of Affairs, are likely to become more and more precarious; that the Difficulties, under which we now labour, are owing to Restrictions, Prohibitions, and ill advised Regulations in several late Acts of Parliament of Great Britain; in particular, that the late unconstitutional Act, imposing Duties on Tea, Paper, Glass, etc., for the sole Purpose of raising a Revenue in America, is injurious to Property, and destructive to Liberty, hath a necessary Tendency to prevent the Payment of the Debt due from this Colony to Great Britain, and is, of Consequence, ruinous to Trade; that, notwithstanding the many earnest Applications already made, there is little reason to expect a Redress of those Grievances: Therefore, in Justice to ourselves and our Posterity, as well as to the Traders of Great Britain concerned in the American Commerce, we, the Subscribers, have voluntarily and unanimously entered into the following Resolutions, in Hopes that our Example will induce the good People of this Colony to be frugal in the Use and Consumption of British Manufactures, and that the Merchants and Manufacturers of Great Britain may, from Motives of Interest, Friendship, and Justice, be engaged to exert themselves to obtain for us a Redress of those Grievances, under which the Trade and Inhabitants of America at present labour: We do therefore most earnestly recommend this our Association to the serious inhabitants of this Colony, in Hopes, that they will very readily and cordially accede thereto.

First, It is UNANIMOUSLY agreed on and resolved this 18th day of May, 1769, that the Subscribers, as well by their own Example, as all other legal Ways and Means in their Power, will promote and encourage Industry and Frugality, and discourage all Manner of Luxury and Extravagance.

Secondly, That they will not at any Time hereafter, directly or indirectly import, or cause to be imported, any Manner of Goods, Merchandise, or Manufactures, which are, or shall thereafter be taxed by Act of Parliament, for the Purpose of raising a Revenue in *America* (except Paper, not exceeding Eight Shillings Sterling per Reem, and except such Articles only, as Orders have been already sent for) nor purchase any such after the First Day of September next, of any Person whatsoever, but that they will always consider such Taxation, in every Respect, as an absolute Prohibition, and in all future Orders, direct their Correspondents to ship them no Goods whatever, taxed as aforesaid, except as is above excepted. . . .[1]

[Present
    89 members.]

The business being finished, the following TOASTS were drank, and Gentlemen retired.

The KING,

The QUEEN and ROYAL FAMILY,

His Excellency Lord BOTETOURT [the Governor], and Prosperity to VIRGINIA.

The speedy and lasting Union between Great Britain and her Colonies.

The constitutional British Liberty in America, and all true Patriots, the Supporters thereof. . . .

---

[1] George Washington and George Mason (as their preserved letters show) had been in correspondence regarding such a non-importation agreement for some weeks. Mason drew the resolutions; Washington was to have presented them to the Assembly. Now he did so (in person or by deputy) to the informal meeting at Mr. Hay's. See Washington's *Writings*, first edition, II, 263; and *Mason's Life and Correspondence*, I, 136 ff.

122. The Origin of Massachusetts Town-Committees of Correspondence, 1772

Boston Town Records, 1770–1777 (*Report* of the Record Commissioners, 1887), pp. 90–93.

A Boston town meeting of October 28 had been concerned with the report that "Stipends are affixed by order of the Crown to the offices of the Judges of Superior Court." This action had been taken by the British government to render the judges independent of the Assembly and of public opinion in Massachusetts. The meeting had voted that "a decent . . . Application" be made to the governor asking for information as to the truth of the report. The Governor's refusal appears in the first part of the document. This crisis, and the refusal of Governor Hutchinson (below) to permit the Assembly to meet, brought about the organization of committees of correspondence. Cf. *American History and Government*, § 140.

Fryday October 30, 10 O'Clock Before Noon, Met according to Adjournment.

The Committee to present the Governor an Address Reported the following answer which his Excellency delivered to them in Writing — Viz —

Gentlemen

It is by no means proper for me to lay before the Inhabitants of any Town whatsoever in consequence of their Votes and Proceedings in a Town Meeting any part of my Correspondence as Governor of this Province or to acquaint them whether I have or have not received any advice relating to the public Affairs of the Government. This reason alone if your Address to me had been in other respects unexceptionable, would have been sufficient to restrain me from complying with your desire —

I shall always be ready to gratify the Inhabitants of the Town of Boston upon every regular Application to me on business of public concernment to the Town as far as I shall have it in my power consistent with fidelity to the trust which his Majesty has reposed in me —

T. Hutchinson.

The aforegoing answer, having been considered — It was moved and the Question put — Whether application shall be now made to his Excellency by the Town that he would be pleased to permit the General Assembly to meet at the time to which they stand prorogued, which passed in the Affirmative *Nem Con.* — It was then Voted, that

    The Honorable James Otis, Esq.
    Mr. Samuel Adams
    The Honorable Thomas Cushing, Esq.

be a Committee to prepare a Petition to his Excellency for the purpose aforesaid —

The Petition of a number of the Inhabitants — "That another public School may be Established at the South part of the Town," was read, and after debate had thereon — the Question was put — Whether the Consideration of the same shall be referred to March Meeting — Passed in the affirmative.

The Committee appointed by the Town at a late Meeting to consider what was proper to be done to prevent the ruin of Beacon Hill, were desired to make Report as soon as may be.

Voted, that the Town Clerk be directed to lay the Original Grant of Beacon Hill before the Town at their adjournment.

Upon a Motion made — Voted, that the Selectmen be added to the Committee relative to Beacon Hill —

The Committee chosen to prepare a Petition to the Governor, relative to the Meeting of the General Court — Reported the following Draft — Viz —

The Petition of the Freeholders and other Inhabitants of the Town of Boston legally Assembled by Adjournment in Faneuil Hall on Fryday 30 of October 1772 —

Humbly Sheweth —

That your Petitioners are still greatly alarmed at the Report which has been prevalent of late Viz. That Stipends are affixed to the Offices of the Judges of the Superior Court of Judicature of this Province by Order of the Crown for their support —

Such an Establishment is contrary not only to the plain and

obvious sense of the Charter of this Province but also some of the fundamental Principles of the Common Law, to the benefit of which all British Subjects, wherever dispersed throughout the British Empire, are indubitably entitled — . . .

It is therefore their earnest and humble request that your Excellency would be pleased to allow the General Assembly to meet at the time to which they now stand prorogued; in order that in that *Constitutional* Body, with whom it is to enquire into Grievances and Redress them, the Joint Wisdom of the Province may be employed, in deliberating and determining on a matter so important and alarming —

The Town having considered the foregoing Draft of a Petition to Governor Hutchinson — It was Voted, that the same be accepted, *Nem. Con.* Also Voted, that [seven names] be a Committee to present the Petition to his Excellency —

Voted, that this Meeting be Adjourned to Monday next 3. O'Clock P.M.

Monday November 2d 3. O'Clock P.M. Met According to Adjournment.

The Committee appointed to present a Petition To his Excellency the Governor of this Province, Reported and laid before the Town the following Reply which his Excellency had been pleased to deliver them in writing — Viz. [A firm claim that the town-meeting was meddling with matters that were beyond its province, and a refusal to call the Assembly.]

The foregoing Reply having been read several times and duly considered; it was moved and the Question accordingly put Whether the same be satisfactory to the Town; which passed in the Negative *Nem. Con.* And thereupon —

Resolved as the Opinion of the Inhabitants of this Town that they have ever had, and ought to have, a right to Petition the King or his Representatives for the Redress of such Grievances as they feel or for preventing of such as they have reason to apprehend, and to communicate their Sentiment to other Towns.

It was then moved by Mr. Samuel Adams, That a Committee of

Correspondence be appointed to consist of twenty-one Persons — to state the Rights of the Colonists and of this Province in particular, as Men, as Christians, and as Subjects; to communicate and publish the same to the several Towns in this Province and to the World as the sense of this Town, with the Infringements and Violations thereof that have been, or from time to time may be made — Also requesting of each Town a free communication of their Sentiments on this Subject — And the Question being accordingly put — Passed in the Affirmative. *Nem. Con.* — Also Voted, that [a list headed with the names of Samuel Adams, James Otis, and Joseph Warren] be and hereby are appointed a Committee for the purpose aforesaid, and that they be desired to Report to the Town as soon as may be — . .

Then the Meeting was dissolved.

123. Creation of Standing Intercolonial Committees of Correspondence, 1773

This was the most important step in America between the Stamp Act Congress and the First Continental Congress. Cf. *American History and Government*, § 140.

a. Jefferson's Account of the Origin of the Movement (written at a Later Date)

Ford's *Writings of Jefferson*, I, 7, 8.

Not thinking our old and leading members up to the point of forwardness and zeal which the times required, *Mr. Henry, Richard Henry Lee, Francis L. Lee, Mr. Carr* and myself agreed to meet in the evening in a private room of the *Raleigh*, to consult on the state of things. There may have been a member or two more whom I do not recollect. We were all sensible that the most urgent of all measures was that of coming to an understanding with all the other colonies, to consider the British claims as a common cause to all, and to produce a unity of action; and for this purpose that a committee of correspondence in each colony would be the best instrument for intercommunication; and that their first measure would probably be, to propose a meeting of deputies from every colony, at some central place, who should be charged with the direction of the measures which should be taken by all. We therefore drew up the resolutions. The consulting members proposed to me to move them, but I urged that it should be done by *Mr. Carr*, my friend and brother in law, then a member, to whom I wished an opportunity should be given of making known to the house his great worth and talents. It was so agreed; he moved them. They were agreed to *nem. con.*, and a committee of correspondence appointed, of whom Peyton Randolph, the Speaker, was chairman.

b. *The Action of the Virginia Burgesses*

Journals of the House of Burgesses, 1775–1776, 26–28.

Friday, the 12th of March, 13 Geo. III. 1773.

* * * * * * *

The House resolved itself into a Committee of the whole House, upon the State of the Colony.

Mr. *Speaker* left the chair.

Mr. *Bland* took the Chair of the Committee.

Mr. *Speaker* resumed the Chair.

Mr. *Bland* reported from the Committee, that they had directed him to make the following Report to the House, *viz.*[1]

Whereas, the minds of his Majesty's faithful Subjects in this Colony have been disturbed, by various Rumours and Reports of proceedings tending to deprive them of their ancient, legal and constitutional Rights.

And *whereas*, the affairs of this Colony are frequently connected with those of Great Britain, as well as of the neighboring *Colonies*, which renders a Communication of Sentiments necessary; in Order therefore to remove the Uneasiness, and to quiet the minds of the People, as well as for the other good purposes above mentioned:

---

[1] Only the *result* of the action of the Committee of the Whole goes on record. Cf. No. 121.

Be it *resolved*, that a standing Committee of Correspondence and inquiry be appointed, to consist of eleven Persons, to wit, the Honourable *Peyton Randolph*, Esquire, *Robert Carter Nicholas*, *Richard Bland*, *Richard Henry Lee*, *Benjamin Harrison*, *Edmund Pendleton*, *Patrick Henry*, *Dudley Digges*, *Dabney Carr*, *Archibald Cary*, and *Thomas Jefferson*, Esquires, any six of whom to be a Committee, whose business it shall be to obtain the most early and authentic intelligence of all such Acts and *Resolutions* of the *British Parliament*, or proceedings of Administration, as may relate to or affect the British Colonies in America, and to keep up and maintain a Correspondence and Communication with our Sister Colonies, respecting these important Considerations; and the result of such their proceedings, from Time to Time, to lay before this House.

Resolved, that it be an instruction to the said Committee, that they do, without delay, inform themselves particularly of the principles and Authority, on which was constituted a *Court of Inquiry*, said to have been lately held in *Rhode Island*, with Powers to transmit Persons, accused of Offences committed in America, to places beyond the Seas, to be tried.

The said *Resolutions*, being severally read a second Time, were upon the Question severally put thereupon agreed to by the House, *nemine contradicente*.

Resolved, that the Speaker of this House do transmit to the Speakers of the different Assemblys of the British Colonies, on the Continent, Copies of the said Resolutions, and desire that they will lay them before their respective Assemblies; and request them to appoint some Person or Persons, of their respective Bodies, to communicate, from Time to Time, with the said Committee.

c. *Letters received by the Virginia Committee of Correspondence, 1773*

Journals *of the House of Burgesses of Virginia, 1773–1767*, 47–50.

* * * * * * *

(1) Rhode Island.
New Port, May 15th, 1773.
SIR:

I had the Pleasure of receiving your Favour of the 19th of March with the Resolves of the House of Burgesses of Virginia; which with the Letter from your Committee of Correspondence I laid before the House of Deputies of this Colony at their meeting the last Week.

The House thoroughly convinced that a firm Union of the Colonies is absolutely necessary for the Preservation of their ancient, legal and constitutional Rights, and that the Measures proposed by your House of Burgesses will greatly promote so desirable an End, came, Nemine contradicente, into the Resolutions of which I have the honor now to enclose you a Copy.

I am desired to inform you that the Committee apointed by our House of Deputies, will, as soon as possible, transmit to the Committee of Correspondence of Virginia, the best Accounts they shall be able to obtain, respecting the Court of Inquiry lately held in this Colony.

I am with great Respect, your most obedient Servant,
Metcalf Bowler [Speaker].

[The Resolves inclosed, as follows.]
May 7th 1773. In the House of Deputies.

Resolved that a standing *Committee of Correspondence and Inquiry* be appointed to consist of seven Persons, *to wit* the honorable *Stephen Hopkins*, Esquire, *Metcalf Bowler, Moses Brown, John Cole, William Bradford, Henry Ward,* and *Henry Merchant* Esquires, and four of whom to be a Committee, whose Business it shall be to obtain the most early and authentick Intelligence of all such Acts and Resolutions of the British Parliament or Proceedings of Administration as may relate to or affect the British Colonies in America, and to keep up and maintain a Correspondence with our Sister Colonies respecting these important Considerations; and the Result of such their Proceedings from Time to Time to lay before this House.

Voted Per Order J. Lyndon, Clerk.

The above written is a true *Copy* of a Vote of the House of Deputies of Lower House of Assembly of the Colony of *Rhode Island*.

* * * * * * *

May 7th 1773. In the House of Deputies.

Resolved, that the *Speaker* of this House be requested to write to the *Speaker* of the House of Burgesses in *Virginia*, and to all other *Speakers* of Assemblies in North America, informing them of the Proceedings of this House relating to the Preservation of the Rights of the Colonies.

Voted Per Order J. Lyndon, Clerk.

* * * * * * *

(2)   From a Massachusetts Legislative Committee.

Province of Massachusetts Bay, June 3d., 1773.

Sir:

The very judicious and important Resolves entered into by the House of Burgesses of his Majesty's most ancient Colony of Virginia on the 12th March last, together with your obliging Letter inclosing the same, have been laid before the house of Representatives of this Province.

The Wisdom of the Measures proposed in those Resolves, and the great and good Effects that may reasonably be expected to flow from them, not only to the Colonies but the Parent State, were so obvious, that the House immediately adopted them; and appointed a Committee to keep up and maintain a free Communication with Virginia and the Rest of the Sister Colonies.

* * * * * * *

[Similar replies from other colonies.]

124. Tea Riots

From a Philadelphia Handbill to the Delaware Pilots, September, 1773, given in Scharf and Westcott's *History of Philadelphia*, I, 286.

... We need not point out to you the steps you ought to take if the tea-ship falls in your way. You cannot be at a loss how to prevent, or if that cannot be done, how to give the merchants of the city timely notice of her arrival. But this you may depend upon, that whatever pilot brings her into the river, such pilot will be marked for his treason. . . . Like Cain, he will be hung out as a spectacle to the nations, and be forever recorded as the *damned traitorous pilot who brought up the tea-ship.* . . .

(Signed) THE COMMITTEE FOR TARRING AND FEATHERING.

[Another broadside was addressed as a warning to Captain Ayers of the expected tea-ship. "What think you, Captain, of a Halter round your Neck, ten gallons of liquid Tar decanted on your Pate, with the feathers of a doxen wild Geese lain over that, to enliven your appearance?"

All this activity preceded the Boston "Tea-Party." The Philadelphia ship, however, did not arrive until some weeks after she was expected — on Christmas Day at Gloucester Point, near the city. The Captain was escorted to the city, where a mass meeting of 8000 people persuaded him to sail at once for England, without breaking cargo.]

XXII. RISE OF REVOLUTIONARY GOVERNMENTS

The colonies between 1768 and 1773 had each organized, more or less perfectly, local committees — town or county — to enforce non-importation agreements, and these committees often acted as "committees of correspondence" to organize the province as a unit for action. Then in 1773 the Intercolonial Committees (No. 123) gave the germ of a standing continental union.

"The next step toward revolutionary government was to develop from the local committees the *Provincial* Congresses in individual colonies, and from the intercolonial committees of the continent a *Continental* Congress. These things developed *in the summer and fall of 1774*, as the result of *three events :* (1) the attempt of the ministry to force taxed tea down the throats of the colonists [see § 121 for colonial resistance]; (2) the rather animated protest of the Boston Tea Party; and (3) the punishment of Boston by the Port Bill." (*American History and Government*, § 141. Cf. remainder of the same section for additional explanation.)

The documents for this period are very numerous, and many of the most valuable are not suitable for condensation and are too long for insertion here. It has seemed well to draw primarily upon one colony; and Virginia has been selected, partly because of her leadership, partly because her documents excel in form.

125. The Virginia Burgesses suggest an Annual Continental Congress

A detailed account is given in *American History and Government*, § 141.

a. Extract from a Letter by a Member of the Assembly to a London Friend

Force's *American Archives*, Fourth Series, I, 340. The Assembly had met May 6. Very little business had been transacted when the news of the Boston Port Bill arrived; but Virginia had been in high good humor with her governor, and the Burgesses had appointed May 30 for a great state ball, in honor of the governor's wife, the Lady Countess of Dunmore, just arrived from England.

WILLIAMSBURG, May 20, 1774.

Infinite astonishment, and equal resentment, has seized every one here on account of the war sent to Boston. It is the universal determination to stop the exportation of tobacco, pitch, tar, lumber, etc., and to stop all importation from *Britain* while this act of hostility continues. We every day expect an express from *Boston,* and it appears to me incontestabl[y] certain, that the above measures will be universally adopted. We see with concern, that this plan will be most extensively hurtful to our fellow-subjects in *Britain;* nor would we have adopted it, if *Heaven* had left us any other way to secure our *liberty*, and prevent the total ruin of ourselves and our posterity to endless ages. A wicked Ministry must answer for all the consequences. I hope the wise and good on your side will pity and forgive us. The House is now pushing on the public business for which we were called here at this time; but before we depart, our measures will be settled and agreed on. The plan proposed is extensive; it is wise, and I hope, under *God*, it will not fail of success. *America* possesses virtue unknown and unfelt by the abominable sons of corruption who planned this weak and wicked enterprise.

b. Thomas Jefferson's Account of the Feeling aroused by News of the Port Bill, and of the Action taken Thereon

Works, Washington edition, I, 6, 7. The *Autobiography* in which this passage occurs was composed many years after the event.

The lead in the House . . . being no longer left to the old members, Mr. Henry, R. H. Lee, Fr. L. Lee, three or four other members whom I do not recollect, and myself, agreeing that we must boldly take an unequivocal stand in the line with Massachusetts, determined to meet and consult on proper measures . . . We were under conviction of the necessity of arousing our people . . . and thought that . . . a day of general fasting and prayer would be most likely to . . . alarm their attention. No example of such a solemnity had existed since . . .

our distresses in the war of of '55, since which a new generation had grown up. With the help, therefore, of Rushworth [*Historical Collections*], whom we rummaged over for the revolutionary precedents and forms of the Puritans of that day [England, in the Seventeenth century], we cooked up a resolution, somewhat modernizing the phrases, for appointing the first day of June, on which the Port Bill was to commence, as a day of fasting, humiliation, and prayer. . . . To give greater emphasis to our proposition, we agreed to wait the next morning on Mr. Nicholas, whose grave and religious character was more in unison with the tone of our resolution, and to solicit him to move it . . . He moved it the same day . . . and it passed without opposition [c, below.]

c. *Resolution of the Burgesses*

Journals of the House of Burgesses, 1773–1776, 123–136.

Tuesday, the 24th of May. 14 Geo. III. 1774.

* * * * * * *

This House, being deeply impressed with apprehension of the great dangers, to be derived to british *America*, from the hostile Invasion of the City of *Boston*, in our Sister Colony of *Massachusetts* bay, whose commerce and harbour are, on the first Day of June next, to be stopped by an Armed force, deem it highly necessary that the said first day of June be set apart, by the Members of this House, as a day of Fasting, Humiliation, and Prayer, devoutly to implore the divine interposition for averting the heavy Calamity which threatens destruction to our Civil Rights, and the Evils of civil War; to give us one heart and one Mind firmly to oppose, by all just and proper means, every injury to American Rights; and that the Minds of his Majesty and his Parliament, may be inspired from above with Wisdom, Moderation, and Justice, to remove from the loyal People of America all cause of danger from a continued pursuit of Measures pregnant with their ruin.

* * * * * * *

d. Dissolution

Thursday, the 26th of May. 14 Geo. III. 1774.
The Order of the Day being read;
Mr. *Speaker* laid before the House the Letters from the Speakers of the lower Houses of Assembly of the british Colonies in *America*, with other Papers, upon the subject matter, which were referred to the standing Committee of Correspondence and Inquiry.

And the said *Letters* and *Papers* were read.

Resolved, that the said Letters and Papers be taken into Consideration upon this Day Sevenight. . . .

A *Message* from the Governor by Mr. *Blair:*

"Mr. *Speaker:* the Governor commands this House to attend his Excellency immediately, in the Council Chamber."

Accordingly Mr. *Speaker* with the House, went up to attend his Excellency in the Council Chamber, where his Excellency was pleased to say to them.

"Mr. Speaker and Gentlemen of the House of Burgesses,

"I have in my hand a Paper published by Order of your House, conceived in such Terms as reflect highly upon his Majesty and the Parliament of Great Britain; which makes it necessary for me to dissolve you; and you are dissolved accordingly."

e. *Virginia Ex-burgesses propose an Annual Continental Congress*

Journals of the House of Burgesses, 1773–1776, xiii, xiv.
This is the first such proposal by any body of men so nearly approaching a "government."

. . . *an Association signed by eighty nine members of the House of Burgesses, in session in the old Raleigh Tavern in Williamsburg, on May 27th, 1774:*

We his Majesty's most dutiful and loyal subjects, the late

representatives of the good people of this country, having been deprived by the sudden interposition of the executive part of this government from giving our countrymen the advice we wished to convey to them in a legislative capacity, find ourselves under the hard necessity of adopting this, the only method we have left, of pointing out to our countrymen such measures as in our opinion are best fitted to secure our dearest rights and liberty from destruction, by the heavy hand of power now lifted against *North America:* With much grief we find that our dutiful applications to *Great Britain* for security of our ancient and constitutional rights, have been not only disregarded, but that a determined system is formed and pressed for reducing the inhabitants of *British America* to slavery by subjecting them to the payment of taxes imposed without the consent of the people or their representatives; and that in pursuit of this system, we find an act of the British parliament, lately passed, for stopping the harbour and commerce of the town of *Boston*, in our sister colony of *Massachusetts Bay,* until the people there submit to the payment of such unconstitutional taxes, and which act most violently and arbitrarily deprives them of their property, in wharfs erected by private persons, at their own great and proper expense, which act is, in our opinion, a most dangerous attempt to destroy the constitutional liberty and rights of all *North America.* It is further our opinion, that as Tea, on its importation into *America,* is charged with a duty imposed by parliament for the purpose of raising a revenue, without the consent of the people, it ought not to be used by any person who wishes well to the constitutional rights and liberty of British America. And *whereas* the *India Company* have ungenerously attempted the ruin of *America* by sending many ships loaded with tea into the colonies, thereby intending to fix a precedent in favor of arbitrary taxation, we deem it highly proper, and do accordingly recommend it strongly to our countrymen, not to purchase or use any kind of *East India* commodity whatsoever, **except salt-**

petre and spices, until the grievances of *America* are redressed. We are further clearly of opinion, that an attack, made on one of our sister colonies to compel submission to arbitrary taxes, is an attack made on all British America, and threatens ruin to the rights of all, unless the united wisdom of the whole be applied. **And for this purpose it is recommended to the Committee of Correspondence, that they communicate, with their several corresponding committees, on the expediency of appointing deputies from the several colonies of British America, to meet in general congress, at such place** *annually* **as shall be thought most convenient;** there to deliberate on those general measures which the united interests of America may from time to time require.[1]

f. Letters from the Virginia Committee of Correspondence, according to direction above

Journals of the House of Burgesses, *1773–1776*, 138.

At a Committee of Correspondence held in Williamsburg on Saturday the 28th May, 1774.

Present

The honorable *Peyton Randolph*, Esquire
Robert C. Nicholas, Richard Bland,
Edmund Pendleton, Benjamin Harrison,
Richard Henry Lee, Dudley Digges
and *Thomas Jefferson*, Esquires.

Ordered, that Letters be prepared to the several Committees of Correspondence requesting their Sentiments on the Appointments of Deputies from the several Colonies to meet annually in general Congress. . . . A Letter was accordingly prepared to the Committee of Correspondence for *Maryland*, which being read and approved of the Committee is as follows:

---

[1] A letter from Richard Henry Lee to Samuel Warren (June 23) states that he had intended to present such a resolution in the Assembly, but, on advice of friends, waited for the completion of important business, — and then came the dissolution. Washington went from this meeting, over which he had presided, to dine with Lord and Lady Dunmore. The tone of Virginia intercourse with the governor remains suave for some time.

Williamsburg, May 28th 1774.
Gentlemen.

The inclosed Papers will explain to you our present political State here, with respect to the unhappy Dispute with our Mother Country. The Propriety of appointing Deputies from the several Colonies of British America to meet annually in general Congress, appears to be a Measure extremely important and extensively useful, as it tends so effectually to obtain the united Wisdom of the Whole, in every Case of General Concern. We are desired to obtain your Sentiments on this Subject which you will be pleased to furnish us with. Being very desirous of communicating to you the Opinion and Conduct of the late Representatives on the present Posture of American Affairs as quickly as possible we beg Leave to refer you to a future Letter on these Subjects.

We are, with great Respect,
Your most obedient Servants,
Peyton Randolph.
Robert C. Nicholas.
Dudley Digges.

To the Committee of Correspondence for Maryland.

Also Letters of the same Import, to the Committe of Correspondence for Pennsylvania, New Jersey, Massachuset's Bay, Connecticut, New Hampshire, Rhode Island, [Delaware], North Carolina, South Carolina, and Georgia.

Ordered, that the said Letters be sent by this Day's Post.

[On the arrival of these letters in Maryland, a Baltimore town meeting (May 31) called a Provincial Assembly, to appoint delegates to the proposed Continental Congress. Other counties took like action; and (June 22, before the time set for the Virginia Convention), the Maryland Convention met and named representatives. Two days earlier still, action had been taken in Rhode Island, after receipt of the Virginia suggestion, as appears below.]

VIRGINIA SUGGESTS ANNUAL CONGRESSES

*Answer to Virginia from the Rhode Island Assembly
[with Appointment of Delegates]*
Journals of the House of Burgesses, 1773–1776, 152–153.

New Port June 20. 1774.

Sir,

Agreeable to the Directions of the General Assembly I have the honor to inclose you a Copy of certain Resolutions entered into by them respecting the very alarming Situation of the Colonies.

I have also to inform you that upon this Occasion the Assembly have adjourned to the fourth Monday in August next.

I am with very great Regard,
Sir, your most humble Servant.
Metcalf Bowler.
Speaker.

Resolutions inclosed.

At the general Assembly of the Governor and Company of the English colony of *Rhode Island* and Providence Plantations in *New England* in America begun and holden by Adjournment at *Newport* within and for the said Colony on the second *Monday* in *June* in the Year of our LORD one thousand seven hundred and seventy four and fourteenth of the Reign of his most sacred Majesty *George* the third by the grace of GOD king of Great Britain etc.

This Assembly taking into the most serious Consideration several Acts of the British Parliament for levying Taxes upon his Majesty's Subjects in America without their Consent, and particularly an Act lately passed for blocking up the Port of *Boston*, which Act even upon the Supposition that the People of *Boston* had justly deserved Punishment, is scarcely to be parallelled in History for the Severity of the Vengeance executed upon them; and also considering to what a deplorable State this and the other Colonies are reduced, when by an Act of Parliament in which the Subjects in *America* have not a single Voice, and without being heard, they may be divested of Property and deprived of Liberty, do upon mature Deliberation, *resolve*

That it is the Opinion of this Assembly that a firm and inviolable Union of all the Colonies in Counsels and Measures is absolutely necessary for the preservation of their Rights and Liberties; and that for that purpose, a Convention of the Representatives from all the Colonies ought to be holden in some suitable Place, as soon as may be, in Order to consult upon proper Measures to obtain a Repeal of the said Act, and to establish the Rights and Liberties of the Colonies upon a just and solid Foundation.

That the honorable *Stephen Hopkins* and the honorable *Samuel Ward* Esquires be and they are hereby appointed by this Assembly to represent the People of this Colony in a general Congress of Representatives from the other Colonies at such Time and place as shall be agreed upon by the major part of the Committees appointed or to be appointed by the Colonies in general.

That they consult and advise with the Representatives of the other Colonies who shall meet in such Congress upon a loyal and dutiful Petition and Remonstrance to be presented to his Majesty as the united Voice of his faithful Subjects in *America* setting forth the grievances they labour under, and praying his gracious Interposition for their Relief: *And* that in Case a major part of the Representatives of all the Colonies shall agree upon such Petition and Remonstrance they be empowered to sign the same on behalf of this Colony.

That they also consult upon all such reasonable and lawful Measures as may be expedient for the Colonies, in an united Manner to persue in Order to procure a Redress of their Grievances, and to ascertain and establish their Rights and Liberties.

That they also endeavor to Procure a regular annual Convention of Representatives from all the Colonies to consider of Proper Means for the preservation of the Rights and Liberties of the Colonies. . . .[1]

(Witnessed) Henry Ward, *Sect'y*.

---

[1] The resolutions so reported on June 20 to the Virginia committee, had been adopted on the 15th. Rhode Island, therefore, was the first colony to ap-

126. Another "Call" for the Continental Congress

June 17, 1774, the Massachusetts House of Representatives, under the lead of Samuel Adams (and after a carefully planned, secret campaign), adopted the following resolutions.

That a meeting of committees from the several colonies on this continent is highly expedient and necessary, to consult upon the present state of the colonies, and the miseries to which they are and must be reduced by the operation of certain acts of Parliament respecting America, and to deliberate and determine upon wise and proper measures, to be by them recommended to all the colonies, for the recovery and establishment of their just rights and liberties, civil and religious, and the restoration of union and harmony between Great Britain and the colonies, most ardently desired by all good men : Therefore, resolved, that the Hon. James Bowdoin, Esq., the Hon. Thomas Cushing, Esq., Mr. Samuel Adams, John Adams and Robert Treat Paine, Esqrs., be, and they are hereby appointed a committee on the part of this province, for the purposes aforesaid, any three of whom to be a quorum, to meet such committees or delegates from the other colonies as have been or may be appointed, either by their respective houses of burgesses or representatives, or by convention, or by the committees of correspondence appointed by the respective houses of assembly, in the city of Philadelphia, or any other place that shall be judged most suitable by the committee, on the 1st day of September next; and that the speaker of the house be directed, in a letter to the speakers of the houses of burgesses or representatives in the several colonies, to inform them of the substance of these resolves.

[This is often referred to as " the call " for the Continental Congress. It was the first action by a colonial legislature in regular session. It did not, however, have " legal " validity under the Charter to which the men of Massachusetts constantly appealed. That charter (1691) required the

---

point delegates. The resolutions, of course, are given also in the *Rhode Island Colonial Records*.

assent of the upper House and the approval of the governor for every resolution and every appointment ; and these elements, of course, were lacking. The dramatic story of Sam Adams' plot is well told in many places, — notably in Dr. Hosmer's *Samuel Adams*.]

127. A Virginia County Suggests a Continental Congress and a General Association

Force, *American Archives*, Fourth Series, I, 392–393.

At a Meeting of the Freeholders and other Inhabitants of the County of *Frederick*, in *Virginia* . . . the 8th day of June, 1774 [to consider the Boston Port Bill].

The Reverend Charles M. Thurston, Moderator.

A Committee of the following gentlemen, viz: the Reverend Charles M. Thurston, Isaac Zane, George Rootes, Angus McDonald, Alexander White, George Johnston, and Samuel Beall, 3d, were appointed to draw up Resolves suitable to the same occasion, who, withdrawing for a short time, returned with the following votes, viz:

Voted, 1st. That we will always cheerfully pay due submission to such Acts of Government as his Majesty has a right **by law** to exercise over his subjects, as Sovereign of the *British* Dominions, **and to such only.**

2d. That it is the inherent right of *British* subjects to be governed and taxed by Representatives chosen by themselves only; and that every Act of the British Parliament respecting the internal policy of North America, is a daring and unconstitutional invasion of our said rights and privileges.

3d. That the Act of Parliament above mentioned is not only in itself repugnant to the fundamental law of natural justice, in condemning persons for a supposed crime unheard, but also **a despotic exertion of unconstitutional power,** calculated to enslave a free and loyal people.

4th. *That the enforcing the execution of the said Act of Parliament by a military power, will have a necessary tendency to raise a civil war, thereby dissolving that union which has so long happily subsisted between the mother country and her Colonies;* . . .

5th. It is the unanimous opinion of this meeting, that a joint resolution of all the Colonies to stop all importations from *Great Britain*, and exportations to it, till the said Act shall be repealed, will prove the salvation of North America and her liberties. . . .

7th. That it is the opinion of this meeting that Committees ought to be appointed for the purpose of effecting a general Association, that the same measures may be pursued through the whole Continent. That the Committees ought to correspond with each other, and to meet at such places and times as shall be agreed on, in order to form such General Association, and that when the same shall be formed and agreed on by the several Committees, we will strictly adhere thereto; and till the general sense of the Continent shall be known, we do pledge ourselves to each other and our country, that we will inviolably adhere to the votes of this day.

8th. That Charles M. Thurston, Isaac Zane, Angus McDonald, Samuel Beall, 3d, Alexander White, and George Rootes, be appointed a Committee for the purposes aforesaid; and that they or any three of them, are hereby fully empowered to act.

Which being read, were unanimously assented to and subscribed.

[This meeting *makes no reference* to the action of the ex-Burgesses at Williamsburg some ten days before, but probably it originated from that action.]

128. The First Call for a Provincial Convention (Virginia)

a. *Suggestion from the Ex-Burgesses (May 30, 1774)*

Force, *American Archives*, Fourth Series, I, p. 351.

The ex-Burgesses, many of them, remained in Williamsburg to attend the state ball on the 30th and for the day of prayer, June 1 (cf. No. 122 *c*). On the day after the call for a Continental Congress (May 29), letters arrived from committees of correspondence in the northern colonies, as below noted; and the following day, twenty-five of the ex-Burgesses called a meeting of the whole number for August 1, as below. That meeting was expanded into a true representative convention by modifications in the plan indicated in *b* and *c* below. Force does not indicate the source of the following statement; but presumably it was printed by order of the meeting in the Williamsburg papers. Such proceedings were ordered printed in almost every case by the various county meetings; but the clause referring to printing is usually omitted in these extracts.

... Immediately upon receipt of these letters the Honorable Peyton Randolph, Esquire, moderator of the Committee of the late House of Representatives, thought it proper to convene all the members that were then in town; who on considering those important papers [suggesting the need of uniform action in the various colonies], came to a resolution to call together several other members near this city, to whom notice could be given. [Twenty-five of them met next day, Monday, May 30, at ten o'clock, when] it was unanimously agreed to refer the further consideration of this matter to *the first day of August next;* at which time it is expected there will be a very general attendance of the late members of the House. ...

[This notice is referred to in a letter of June 23 by Richard Henry Lee to Samuel Adams as follows, after describing the meeting of the ex-Burgesses on May 27 — No. 125, *e.*] ... "Most of the members, myself among the rest, had left Williamsburg before your message from Boston arrived. Twenty-five of them, however, were assembled to consider that message, and they determined to invite a general meeting of the whole body on the first of August." (Force, Fourth Series, I, 446.)

[Presumably the committee of correspondence sent out a circular letter to the various counties. The editor of this volume has not been able to find any such letter, but some of the documents just following assume such action. After June 1, the remaining ex-Burgesses at Williamsburg departed home, in order to arouse their respective counties to appoint delegates for the August convention.]

b. Sample Notice to a Virginia County by an Ex-Burgess

Force, *American Archives*, Fourth Series, I, 418. Thomas Mason writes from Williamsburg on June 16, portraying the situation, through several pages. Only the close of the letter is given here.

If the governour should be restrained by the instructions of a wicked Minister from relieving the distresses of the Colony

VIRGINIA'S FIRST PROVINCIAL CONVENTION 409

by calling an Assembly, immediately, and writs should not be issued for that purpose before the 1st day of July, I advise the freeholders of each county in the Colony to convene themselves and choose two of the most able and discreet of their inhabitants to accompany and assist their late Representatives at the meeting at Williamsburg, on the 1st of August; and let the whole Colony unanimously support whatever may be there resolved upon.

[Lord Dunmore did issue writs that same day for a new Assembly, to meet August 11. No doubt he hoped this would induce the Virginia counties not to appoint delegates to the meeting called for August 1. Such a purpose was suspected and defeated. (See below, § 129, *a*).

Some counties sent only their ex-burgesses to the August Convention; some elected new burgesses for the Assembly called for August 11, but instructed them to attend the Convention also on the 1st; and some (as Mason suggested) sent not only their "burgesses," but also certain additional deputies.]

c. *Sample Call for a County Meeting to give Instructions for the August Convention*

Force, *American Archives*, Fourth Series, I, 451.

At a meeting of the Committee of Correspondence for Norfolk . . . held at the Court House, on Monday, the 27th day of June, 1774. Present [six names].

Voted That the Freeholders and Inhabitants of the County and Borough of Norfolk be earnestly requested to attend at the Court House of the said County on Wednesday, the 6th day of July next, at ten o'clock in the forenoon, that the late Burgesses may collect their sentiments previous to the meeting appointed to be held at Williamsburg, on the 1st day of August next.

William Davis, *Clerk.*

As late Burgesses for Norfolk . . . we heartily concur . . . with the Committee of Correspondence, and propose to attend at the time appointed. [Signatures of the ex-burgesses for the County.]

[The meeting was held at the appointed time (Force, IV, 1, 518), and adopted ten resolutions — directing "our late Burgesses" to attend the Williamsburg Convention on August 1; to try to secure a "general association" there for the Colony of Virginia, "against all importations and exportations (medicines excepted) to and from Great Britain"; to try to extend such association against every part of the colonies which should refuse to accept the measure; and to secure the appointment in each County of Virginia of a Committee " of respectable men . . . to prevent any breach of such . . . Association as may be adopted."]

129. Typical Virginia County Instructions to Delegates to the First Provincial Convention

Force has preserved records of meetings in thirty-one Virginia counties, to appoint and instruct delegates to the Provincial Convention called for the 1st of August. Many of these sets of instructions rank as great state papers, quite equal in logic, rhetoric, and statesmanship to the documents put forth by the Continental Congress three months later at Philadelphia. The Fairfax County resolutions, which are given in about a third part below, seem to have been in exceptional degree the model for the resolutions adopted by the August Convention, which, in turn, with the same Fairfax document, must have been before the committees of the Continental Congress which drew up the famous documents issued by that body.

Brief extracts from a few other Virginia county resolutions follow the main document (*a*), to show the drift of feeling in certain plain matters. When the exact location in Force is omitted, to save space, it can readily be found from the index to that work.

Virginia Counties appoint Delegates to the First Virginia Convention

a. Westmoreland County (Virginia) Resolutions

Force, *American Archives*, Fourth Series, I, 437, 438.

At a respectable Meeting of the Freeholders **and other Inhabitants** of the County of Westmoreland, assembled on due notice, at the Court House of the said County, on Wednesday, the 22d of June, 1774.

[The Reverend Mr. Thomas Smith, having been appointed

Moderator], Several papers containing the Proceedings of the late House of Burgesses of this Colony, and the subsequent determinations of the late Representatives after the House was dissolved, together with extracts of several Resolves of the Provinces of Massachusetts Bay, Maryland, etc., being read, the meeting proceeded seriously to consider the present dangerous and truly alarming crisis, when ruin is threatened to the ancient constitutional rights of *North America*, and came to the following Resolves:

* * * * * * *

7th. This meeting do heartily concur with the late Representative body of this country, to disuse tea, and not purchase any other commodity of the East Indies, *except saltpetre*, until the grievances of *America* are redressed. (Cf. No. 125 *e*, above.)

8th. We do most heartily concur in these preceding Resolves, and will, to the utmost of our power, take care that they are carried into execution; and that we will regard every man as infamous who now agree[s] to, and shall hereafter make a breach of all or any of them; subject however to such future alterations as shall be judged expedient, at a general meeting of Deputies from the several parts of this Colony, or a general Congress of all the Colonies.

9th. We do appoint *Richard Henry Lee*, and *Richard Lee*, Esquires, the late Representatives of this county, to attend the general meeting of Deputies from all the counties [August 1]; and we desire that they do exert their best abilities to get these, our earnest desires for the security of public liberty, assented to.

10th. And as it may happen that the Assembly now called to meet on the 11th of August, may be prorogued to a future day, and many of the Deputies appointed to meet on the 1st of August, trusting to the certainty of meeting in Assembly on the 11th may fail to attend on the first, by which means decisive injury may arise to the common cause of liberty, by the general sense of the country not being early known at this dangerous crisis of *American* freedom, we do, therefore, direct that our Deputies now chosen fail not to attend at Williamsburg, on the said 1st of August; and it is our earnest wish that the Deputies from other counties be directed to do the same, for the reasons above assigned.

[Other counties responded to this wish. Thus, seven days later, a "respectable meeting of Freeholders **and Freemen** of the County of Richmond," called to choose and instruct delegates to the August Convention, did so with the following caution:

* * * * * * *

"8th. This meeting do appoint Robert Wormeley Carter and Francis L. Lee, gentlemen, as their Deputies for the purposes afore said; and they do request them that they fail not to attend in Williamsburg on the said first day of August, and do not trust to meeting in Assembly on the 11th ... as it is in the power of Government either to prorogue the Assembly to a future day, or dissolve the same, — by which means the sense of this Colony may not be known." (Force, IV, 1, 492, 493.)]

b. *Fairfax County (Virginia) Resolutions*

Force, *American Archives*, Fourth Series, I, 597–602.

At a General Meeting of the Freeholders and other Inhabitants of the County of Fairfax, at the Court House in the Town of Alexandria, on Monday, the 18th day of July, 1774.

George Washington, Esquire, *Chairman*, and

Robert Harrison, Gentleman, *Clerk*.

Resolved, That this Colony and Dominion of Virginia cannot be considered as a conquered country, and, if it was, that the present inhabitants are the descendants, not of the conquered, but of the conquerors. That the same was not settled at the national expense of England, but at the private expense of the adventurers, our ancestors ... [and] that our ancestors ... brought with them, even if the same had not been confirmed by Charters, the civil Constitution and form of Government of the country they came from, and were by the laws of nature and Nations entitled to all its privileges, immunities, and advantages, which have descended to us, their posterity ...

Resolved, That the most important and valuable part of the British Constitution, upon which its very existence depends, is the fundamental principle of the people's being governed by no laws to which they have not given their consent by Representatives freely chosen by themselves, **who are affected by the laws they enact equally with their constituents, to whom they are accountable and whose burthens they share.**

[The colonies "are not, and from their situation, cannot be, represented in the British Parliament"; and therefore "legislative power here can, *of right*, be exercised only by our Provincial Assemblies, or **Parliaments**, subject to the assent or negative of the British crown . . . "; but it is recognized as reasonable that the British Parliament should, *in practice*, regulate trade "for the general good of that great body politick of which we are a part, although in some degree repugnant to the principles of the Constitution," but only when such power is exercised "with wisdom and moderation."]

Resolved, That the claim lately assumed and exercised by the *British* Parliament, for making all such laws as they think fit to govern the people of these Colonies, and to extort from us our money without our consent, is not only diametrically contrary to the first principles of the Constitution and the original compacts by which we are dependent upon the *British* Crown and Government, but is totally incompatible with the privileges of a free people and the natural rights of mankind, will render our own Legislatures merely nominal and nugatory, and is calculated to reduce us from a state of freedom and happiness to slavery and misery.

Resolved, That taxation and representation are in their nature inseparable; that the right of withholding, or of giving and granting their own money, is the only effectual security to a free people against the encroachments of despotism and tyranny; and that whenever they yield the one, they must quickly fall a prey to the other.

Resolved, That the powers over the people of America, now claimed by the British House of Commons, — **in whose election we have no share; in whose determinations we have no influence; whose information must be always defective, and often false; who in many instances may have a separate, and in some an opposite** interest to ours ; and who are removed from those impressions of tenderness and compassion, arising from personal intercourse and connection, which soften the rigours of the most despotick Government, must, if continued, establish the most grievous and intolerable species of tyranny and oppression that ever was inflicted upon mankind.

Resolved, That it is our greatest wish and inclination, as well as interest, to continue our connection with, and dependence upon, the British Government; but though we are its subjects, we will use every means which Heaven hath given us to prevent our becoming its slaves.

* * * * * * *

Resolved, That the several Acts of Parliament for raising a revenue upon the people of America without their consent; the erecting new and dangerous jurisdictions here [the "special commissions"]; the taking away our trials by jury; the ordering persons, on criminal accusations, to be tried in another country than that in which the fact is charged to have been committed; the Act inflicting Ministerial vengeance upon the town of Boston; the two Bills lately brought into Parliament for abrogating the charter of Massachusetts Bay, and **for the protection and encouragement of murderers** in the said Province,[1] are part of the above-mentioned iniquitous system . . .

* * * * * * *

Resolved, That nothing will so much contribute to defeat the pernicious designs of the common enemies of Great Britain and her Colonies, as a firm union of the latter, who ought to regard every act of violence or oppression inflicted upon any one of them, as aimed at all; and to effect this desirable purpose, **that a Congress should be appointed, to consist of Deputies from all the Colonies**, to concert a general and uniform plan for

---

[1] This final clause refers to a provision withdrawing from trial in colonial courts any servants of the government accused of violence in the performance of duty. The list of offending statutes is repeated, somewhat less impressively but more specifically, in the Continental Congress's **Declaration** (130 *c*).

the defence and preservation of our common rights, and continuing the connection and dependence of the said Colonies upon Great Britain, under a just, lenient, permanent, and constitutional form of Government.

* * * * * * *

Resolved, That . . . all manner of luxury and extravagance ought immediately to be laid aside, as totally inconsistent with the threatening and gloomy prospect before us; that it is the indispensable duty of all the gentlemen and men of fortune to set examples of temperance, fortitude, frugality, and industry . . . [and] that great care and attention should be had to the cultivation of flax, cotton, and other materials for manufactures; and we recommend it to such of the inhabitants as have large stocks of sheep, to sell to their neighbors at a moderate price, as the most certain means of speedily increasing our breed of sheep and quantity of wool.[1]

[Some pages of resolves as to non-importation with much of the detail afterward copied by the Continental Congress — especially the following provisions: —

" That the merchants and vendors of goods ought not to take advantage of our present distress, but continue to sell the goods and merchandise which they now have, or which may be shipped to them before the 1st of September next [when non-importation was recommended to begin], at the same rates and prices they have been accustomed to do within one year past; and that if any person shall sell such goods on any

---

[1] Upon this passage was based the Sixth Article of the Virginia Association, recommended August 1, by the Convention as follows: —

"6th. We will endeavor to improve our breed of sheep, and increase their number to the utmost extent; and to this end, we will be as sparing as we conveniently can, in killing sheep, especially those of the most profitable kind; and if we should at any time be overstocked, or can conveniently spare any, we will dispose of them to our neighbors, especially the poorer sort of people, on moderate terms."

In time, this passage was copied even more closely in the Association of the Continental Congress at Philadelphia (No. 130 *d*).

other terms . . . that no inhabitant of this colony should, at any time forever thereafter, deal with him, his agent, factor, or storekeeper, for any commodity whatsoever"; with provisions for depositing goods of later shippings with the committees of their counties, *i.e.*, as adopted by the Continental Congress; resolutions against importing slaves, and against exporting lumber to the West Indies, and, after November 1, 1775 (unless redress of grievances should come), against *all* exports to Great Britain. "And . . . as the people will thereby be disabled from paying their debts, that no judgments should be rendered by the Courts . . . for any debt, after imformation of the said measures being determined upon."]

* * * * * * *

***Resolved*, That *George Washington*, Esquire, and *Charles Broadwater*, Gentleman, lately elected our Representatives to serve in the General Assembly, attend the Convention at Williamsburg, on the first day of August next, and present these Resolves as the sense of the people of this county upon measures proper to be taken in the present alarming and dangerous situation of America.**

***Resolved*, That George Washington Esquire, [and 24 others] be a Committee for this county; that they, or a majority of them, on any emergency, have power to call a general meeting, and to concert and adopt such measures as may be thought most expedient and necessary.**

***Resolved*, That a copy of these Proceedings be transmitted to the Printer at Williamsburg, to be published.**

[It is possible to find in these instructions by Fairfax County to its delegates to Williamsburg almost every provision of the "Association" adopted three months later by the Continental Congress at Philadelphia. For a very large part of the two documents, the language is almost identical. Much alike as many such papers of the time were, it is impossible to read these two together without being convinced that the committee which framed the Association at Philadelphia had a copy of the Fairfax instructions before them.]

c. *Nansemond County* (*July 11*)

[10] Resolved that very kind of luxury, dissipation, and extravagance, ought to be banished from amongst us. . . .

[12] Resolved That the African [Negro] trade is injurious to this Colony, obstructs the population of it by freemen, prevents manufactures and useful emigrants from Europe from settling amongst us and occasions an annual increase of the balance of trade against the colony.[1]

[14] Resolved that to be clothed in manufactures fabricated in this Colony ought to be considered as a badge and distinction of respect and true patriotism.

d. *York County* (*July 18*)

[Instructions to delegates for the August Convention, after urging appointment of Virginia delegates to a "General Congress of America," continue: —]

"That these Representatives be instructed to form a Declaration of American Rights [a page of suggestions follows].

[That *imports* be stopped at once, and that *exports* be regulated by the General Congress when it comes.]

"**That industry and frugality be adopted, in their largest extent, throughout this Colony; and that horse-racing, and every species of expensive amusement, be laid aside, as unsuitable to the situation of the country, and unbecoming men who feel for its distress.**"

e. *Middlesex County* (*July 15*)

[This county alone takes a royalist tone.]

Resolved, That we do not approve of the conduct of the people of Boston in destroying the tea . . . and notwithstanding the tax on tea must be esteemed a violent infringement of one of the fundamental privileges . . . yet we apprehend violence cannot justify violence. . . . A desistance from the consumption of tea, and a confidence in the virtue of our countrymen, whose sense of the spirit of the law will no doubt induce a total disuse of it, are much more eligible means, and more probably will work a repeal of the Act, than disorders, outrages, and tumults.

---

[1] This resolution is found in identical words in the resolutions of Caroline County (Virginia), July 14, 1774; and the sentiment, in more varied forms, appears often in the county meetings. Thus Hanover (Patrick Henry's county) declared: "The African trade for slaves we consider most dangerous to virtue and the welfare of this country. We therefore most earnestly wish to see it totally discouraged."

130. The First Continental Congress

a. *Method of Voting*, etc.

John Adams' "Diary" (*Works*, II, 365 ff.).

[Sept.] 5. Monday. At ten the delegates all met at the City Tavern, and walked to the Carpenters' Hall, where they took a view of the room, and of the chamber where is an excellent library; there is also a long entry where gentlemen may walk, and a convenient chamber opposite to the library. The general cry was, that this was a good room, and the question was put, whether we were satisfied with this room? and it passed in the affirmative. A very few were for the negative, and they were chiefly from Pennsylvania and New York. Then Mr. Lynch arose, and said there was a gentleman present who had presided with great dignity over a very respectable society, greatly to the advantage of America, and he therefore proposed that the Honorable Peyton Randolph, Esquire, one of the delegates from Virginia, and the late Speaker of their House of Burgesses, should be appointed Chairman, and he doubted not it would be unanimous.

The question was put, and he was unanimously chosen.

Mr. Randolph then took the chair, and the commissions of the delegates were all produced and read.

Then Mr. Lynch proposed that Mr. Charles Thomson, a gentleman of family, fortune, and character in this city, should be appointed Secretary, which was accordingly done without opposition, though Mr. Duane and Mr. Jay discovered at first an inclination to seek further.

Mr. Duane then moved that a committee should be appointed to prepare regulations for this Congress. Several gentlemen objected.

I then arose and asked leave of the President to request of the gentleman from New York an explanation, and that he would point out some particular regulations which he had in his mind. He mentioned particularly the method of voting, whether it should be by Colonies, or by the poll, or by interests.

Mr. Henry then rose, and said this was the first General Congress which had ever happened; that no former Congress could be a precedent; that we should have occasion for more general congresses, and therefore that a precedent ought to be established now; that it would be great injustice if a little Colony should have the same weight in the councils of America as a great one, and therefore he was for a committee.

Major Sullivan [from New Hampshire] observed that a little Colony had its all at stake as well as a great one. . . .

Mr. Henry. Government is dissolved. Fleets and armies and the present state of things show that government is dissolved. Where are your landmarks, your boundaries of Colonies? We are in a state of nature, sir. . . .

The distinctions between Virginians, Pennsylvanians, New Yorkers, and New Englanders, are no more. I am not a Virginian, but an American.

Slaves are to be thrown out of the question, and if the freemen can be represented according to their numbers, I am satisfied.

Mr. Lynch. I differ in one point from the gentleman from Virginia, that is, in thinking that numbers only ought to determine the weight of Colonies. I think that property ought to be considered, and that it ought to be a compound of numbers and property that should determine the weight of the Colonies.[1]

I think it cannot be now settled.

* * * * * * *

Mr. Lee. But one reason . . . prevails with me [for favoring one vote to each colony] . . . that we are not at this time provided with proper materials [to assign proper proportions] . . .

Mr. Gadsen. I can't see any way of voting but by Colonies.

---

[1] Mr. Lynch was from South Carolina. This position here taken as to "numbers *and* property" was taken thirteen years later by South Carolina delegates in the Convention which framed our present Constitution.

Mr. Pendleton. If the committee should find themselves unable to ascertain the weight of the Colonies, by their numbers and property, they will report this, and this will lay the foundation for the Congress to take some other steps to procure evidence of numbers and property at some future time.

Mr. Henry. I agree that authentic accounts cannot be had, if by authenticity is meant attestations of officers of the Crown.

I go upon the supposition that government is at an end. All distinctions are thrown down. All America is thrown into one mass. We must aim at the minutiæ of rectitude.

* * * * * * *

The argument that the delegates lacked information (such as a census would have provided) to arrange a proper apportionment of votes to different colonies prevailed. October 10, the Connecticut delegates wrote to the governor of their colony : " The mode of voting . . . was first resolved upon ; which was that each colony should have one voice ; but, as this was objected to as unequal, an entry was made in the journals to prevent its being drawn into precedent in future. "

b. *John Adams' Impressions toward the Close*

Diary, as above.

[Oct.]10. Monday. The deliberations of the Congress are spun out to an immeasurable length. There is so much wit, sense, learning, acuteness, subtlety, eloquence, etc., among fifty gentlemen, each of whom has been habituated to lead and guide in his own Province, that an immensity of time is spent unnecessarily.

* * * * * * *

24. Monday. In Congress, nibbling and quibbling as usual. There is no greater mortification than to sit with half a dozen wits, deliberating upon a petition, address, or memorial. These great wits, these subtle critics, these refined geniuses, these learned lawyers, these wise statesmen, are so fond of showing their parts and powers, as to make their consultations very tedious. Young Ned Rutledge is a perfect Bob-o-Lincoln, —

a swallow, a sparrow, a peacock; excessively vain, excessively weak, and excessively variable and unsteady; jejune, inane, and puerile. Mr. Dickinson is very modest, delicate, and timid. Spent the evening at home. Colonel Dyer, Judge Sherman, and Colonel Floyd came in, and spent the evening with Mr. [Samuel] Adams and me. Mr. Mifflin and General Lee came in. Lee's head is running upon his new plan of a battalion. . . .

26. Wednesday. Dined at home. This day the Congress finished. Spent the evening together at the City Tavern; all the Congress, and several gentlemen of the town. . . .

28. Friday. Took our departure, in a very great rain, from the happy, the peaceful, the elegant, the hospitable, and polite city of Philadelphia. It is not very likely that I shall ever see this part of the world again, but I shall ever retain a most grateful, pleasing sense of the many civilities I have received in it, and shall think myself happy to have an opportunity of returning them.

[Delegates from eleven colonies to the First Continental Congress assembled at Philadelphia, September 5, 1774. Delegates from North Carolina appeared on the 14th. Georgia was not represented. For elections and credentials, cf. *American History and Government*, § 141.]

c. *Declaration of Rights*

Journals of the Continental Congress (Ford edition), I, 63 ff. A committee, appointed on September 7, reported on the 22d. The report was taken up October 12, and adopted October 14.

Whereas, since the close of the last war, the British parliament, claiming a power, of right, to bind the people of America by statutes in all cases whatsoever, hath, in some acts, expressly imposed taxes on them, and in others, under various pretences, but in fact for the purpose of raising a revenue, hath imposed rates and duties payable in these colonies, established a board of commissioners, with unconstitutional powers, and extended the jurisdiction of courts of admiralty, not only for collecting the said duties, but for the trial of causes merely arising within the body of a county.

And whereas, in consequence of other statutes, judges, who before held only estates at will in their offices, have been made dependant on the crown alone for their salaries, and standing armies kept in times of peace: And whereas it has lately been resolved in parliament, that by force of a statute, made in the thirty-fifth year of the reign of King Henry the Eighth, colonists may be transported to England, and tried there upon accusations for treasons and misprisions, or concealments of treasons committed in the colonies, and by a late statute, such trials have been directed in cases therein mentioned:

And whereas, in the last session of parliament, three statutes were made; one entitled, "An act to discontinue, in such manner and for such time as are therein mentioned, the landing and discharging, lading, or shipping of goods, wares and merchandize, at the town, and within the harbour of Boston, in the province of Massachusetts-Bay in North-America;" another entitled, "An act for the better regulating the government of the province of Massachusetts-Bay in New England;" and another entitled, "An act for the impartial administration of justice, in the cases of persons questioned for any act done by them in the execution of the law, or for the suppression of riots and tumults, in the province of the Massachusetts-Bay in New England;" and another statute was then made, "for making more effectual provision for the government of the province of Quebec, etc." All which statutes are impolitic, unjust, and cruel, as well as unconstitutional, and most dangerous and destructive of American rights:

And whereas, assemblies have been frequently dissolved, contrary to the rights of the people, when they attempted to deliberate on grievances; and their dutiful, humble, loyal, and reasonable petitions to the crown for redress, have been repeatedly treated with contempt, by his Majesty's ministers of state:

The good people of the several colonies of New-Hampshire, Massachusetts-Bay, Rhode-Island and Providence Plantations, Connecticut, New-York, New-Jersey, Pennsylvania, Newcastle, Kent, and Sussex on Delaware, Maryland, Virginia, North-

THE FIRST CONTINENTAL CONGRESS 423

Carolina, and South-Carolina, justly alarmed at these arbitrary proceedings of parliament and administration, have severally elected, constituted, and appointed deputies to meet, and sit in general Congress, in the city of Philadelphia, in order to obtain such establishment, as that their religion, laws, and liberties, may not be subverted: Whereupon the deputies so appointed being now assembled, in a full and free representation of these colonies, taking into their most serious consideration, the best means of attaining the ends aforesaid, do, in the first place, as Englishmen, their ancestors in like cases have usually done, for asserting and vindicating their rights and liberties, DECLARE,

That the inhabitants of the English colonies in North-America, by the immutable laws of nature, the principles of the English constitution, and the several charters or compacts, have the following RIGHTS:

Resolved, N. C. D. 1. That they are entitled to life, liberty and property: and they have never ceded to any foreign power whatever, a right to dispose of either without their consent.

Resolved, N. C. D. 2. That our ancestors, who first settled these colonies, were at the time of their emigration from the mother country, entitled to all the rights, liberties, and immunities of free and natural-born subjects, within the realm of England.

Resolved, N. C. D. 3. That by such emigration they by no means forfeited, surrendered, or lost any of those rights, but that they were, and their descendants now are, entitled to the exercise and enjoyment of all such of them, as their local and other circumstances enable them to exercise and enjoy.

Resolved, 4. That the foundation of English liberty, and of all free government, is a right in the people to participate in their legislative council: and as the English colonists are not represented, and from their local and other circumstances, cannot properly be represented in the British parliament, they are entitled to a free and exclusive power of legislation in their several provincial legislatures, where their right of representation can alone be preserved, in all cases of taxation and internal polity, subject only to the negative of their sovereign, in such manner as has been heretofore used and accustomed: But, from the necessity of the case, and a regard to the mutual interest of both countries, we cheerfully consent to the operation of such acts of the British parliament, as are, *bona fide*, restrained to the regulation of our external commerce, for the purpose of securing the commercial advantages of the whole empire to the mother country, and the commercial benefits of its respective members; excluding every idea of taxation internal or external, for raising a revenue on the subjects, in America, without their consent.

Resolved, *N. C. D.* 5. That the respective colonies are entitled to the common law of England, and more especially to the great and inestimable privilege of being tried by their peers of the vicinage, according to the course of that law.

Resolved, 6. That they are entitled to the benefit of such of the English statutes, as existed at the time of their colonization; and which they have, by experience, respectively found to be applicable to their several local and other circumstances.

Resolved, *N. C. D.* 7. That these, his majesty's colonies, are likewise entitled to all the immunities and privileges granted and confirmed to them by royal charters, or secured by their several codes of provincial laws.

Resolved, *N. C. D.* 8. That they have a right peaceably to assemble, consider of their grievances, and petition the king; and that all prosecutions, prohibitory proclamations, and commitments for the same, are illegal.

Resolved, *N. C. D.* 9. That the keeping a standing army in these colonies, in times of peace, without the consent of the legislature of that colony, in which such army is kept, is against law.

Resolved, *N. C. D.* 10. It is indispensably necessary to good government, and rendered essential by the English constitution, that the constituent branches of the legislature be independent of each other; that, therefore, the exercise of legislative power in several colonies by a council appointed, during pleasure, by the crown, is unconstitutional, dangerous and destructive to the freedom of American legislation.

All and each of which the aforesaid deputies, in behalf of themselves, and their constituents, do claim, demand, and insist on, as their indubitable rights and liberties; which cannot be legally taken from them, altered or abridged by any power whatever, without their own consent, by their representatives in their several provincial legislatures.

In the course of our inquiry, we find many infringements and violations of the foregoing rights, which, from an ardent desire that harmony and mutual intercourse of affection and interest may be restored, we pass over for the present, and proceed to state such acts and measures as have been adopted since the last war, which demonstrate a system formed to enslave America.

Resolved, N. C. D. That the following acts of parliament are infringements and violations of the rights of the colonists; and that the repeal of them is essentially necessary, in order to restore harmony between Great-Britain and the American colonies, viz.

The several acts of 4 Geo. III. ch. 15. and ch. 34. — 5 Geo. III. ch. 25. — 6 Geo. III. ch. 52. — 7 Geo. III. ch. 41. and ch. 46. — 8 Geo. III. ch. 22. which impose duties for the purpose of raising a revenue in America, extend the power of the admiralty courts beyond their ancient limits, deprive the American subject of trial by jury, authorise the judges certificate to indemnify the prosecutor from damages, that he might otherwise be liable to, requiring oppressive security from a claimant of ships and goods seized, before he shall be allowed to defend his property, are subversive of American rights.

Also 12 Geo. III. ch. 24. intituled, "An act for the better securing his majesty's dockyards, magazines, ships, ammunition, and stores," which declares a new offence in America, and deprives the American subject of a constitutional trial by jury of the vicinage, by authorising the trial of any person, charged with the committing any offence described in the said act, out of the realm, to be indicted and tried for the same in any shire or county within the realm.

Also the three acts passed in the last session of parliament, for stopping the port and blocking up the harbour of Boston, for altering the charter and government of Massachusetts-Bay, and that which is entitled, "An act for the better administration of justice, etc."

Also the act passed in the same session for establishing the Roman Catholic religion, in the province of Quebec, abolishing, the equitable system of English laws, and erecting a tyranny there, to the great danger, (from so total a dissimilarity of religion, law and government) of the neighbouring British colonies, by the assistance of whose blood and treasure the said country was conquered from France.

Also the act passed in the same session, for the better providing suitable quarters for officers and soldiers in his majesty's service, in North-America.

Also, that the keeping a standing army in several of these colonies, in time of peace, without the consent of the legislature of that colony in which such army is kept, is against law.

To these grievous acts and measures, Americans cannot submit, but in hopes their fellow subjects in Great-Britain will, by a revision of them, restore us to that state, in which both countries found happiness and prosperity, we have for the present, only resolved to pursue the following peaceable measures: 1. To enter into a non-importation, non-consumption, and non-exportation agreement or association. 2. To prepare an address to the people of Great-Britain, and a memorial to the inhabitants of British America: and 3. To prepare a loyal address to his majesty, agreeable to resolutions already entered into.

[This "Declaration" confines itself almost wholly, it will be observed, to "concrete" English rights, which had been infringed by recent acts of government. There is little suggestion of the more general principles soon to appear, first in the Virginia bill of rights and then in the Declaration of Independence. Advanced students will find in John Adams' *Works* (II, 373 ff.) an autobiographical extract, *composed in 1804*, giving Adams' recollections of the drawing up of the Declaration.]

d. *The Association*

(October 20, 1774)

Journals of Congress (Ford edition), I, 75 ff. For conflict between this plan and Galloway's moderate proposal, cf. *American History and Government*, 141. The wording of much of the plan, and the efficient machinery for putting it in operation (Eleventh Article), were common property by this time. In particular, cf. No. 129 *b*, above, and comment at close.

WE, his majesty's most loyal subjects, the delegates of the several colonies of New-Hampshire, Massachusetts-Bay, Rhode-Island, Connecticut, New-York, New-Jersey, Pennsylvania, the three lower counties of Newcastle, Kent and Sussex on Delaware,[1] Maryland, Virginia, North-Carolina, and South-Carolina, deputed to represent them in a continental Congress, held in the city of Philadelphia, on the fifth day of September, 1774, avowing our allegiance to his majesty, our affection and regard for our fellow-subjects in Great Britain and elsewhere, affected with the deepest anxiety, and most alarming apprehensions, at those grievances and distresses with which his majesty's American subjects are oppressed; and having taken under our most serious deliberation the state of the whole continent, find, that the present unhappy situation of our affairs is occasioned by a ruinous system of colony administration, adopted by the British ministry about the year 1763, evidently calculated for inslaving these colonies, and, with them, the British Empire. In prosecution of which system, various acts of parliament have been passed, for raising a revenue in America, for depriving the American subjects, in many instances, of the constitutional trial by jury, exposing their lives to danger, by directing a new and illegal trial beyond the seas, for crimes alleged to have been committed in America: And in prosecution of the same system, several late, cruel, and oppressive acts have been passed, respecting the town of Boston and the Massachusetts-Bay, and also an act

---

[1] This was the "style" of the three "counties" soon to form the state of Delaware.

for extending the province of Quebec, so as to border on the western frontiers of these colonies, establishing an arbitrary government therein, and discouraging the settlement of British subjects in that wide extended country; thus, by the influence of civil principles and ancient prejudices, to dispose the inhabitants to act with hostility against the free Protestant colonies, whenever a wicked ministry shall chuse so to direct them.

To obtain redress of these grievances, which threaten destruction to the lives, liberty, and property of his majesty's subjects, in North-America, we are of opinion, that a non-importation, non-consumption, and non-exportation agreement, faithfully adhered to, will prove the most speedy, effectual, and peaceable measure: And, therefore, we do, for ourselves, and the inhabitants of the several colonies, whom we represent, firmly agree and associate, under the sacred ties of virtue, honour and love of our country, as follows:

First, That from and after the first day of December next, we will not import, into British America, from Great-Britain or Ireland, any goods, wares, or merchandize whatsoever, or from any other place, any such goods, wares, or merchandize, as shall have been exported from Great-Britain or Ireland; nor will we, after that day, import any East-India tea from any part of the world; nor any molasses, syrups, paneles, coffee, or pimento, from the British plantations or from Dominica; nor wines from Madeira, or the Western Islands; nor foreign indigo.

Second, We will neither import nor purchase, any slave imported after the first day of December next; after which time, we will wholly discontinue the slave trade, and will neither be concerned in it ourselves, nor will we hire our vessels, nor sell our commodities or manufactures to those who are concerned in it.

Third, As a non-consumption agreement, strictly adhered to, will be an effectual security for the observation of the non-importation, we, as above, solemnly agree and associate, that

THE FIRST CONTINENTAL CONGRESS 429

from this day, we will not purchase or use any tea, imported on account of the East-India company, or any on which a duty hath been or shall be paid; and from and after the first day of March next, we will not purchase or use any East-India tea whatever; nor will we, nor shall any person for or under us, purchase or use any of those goods, wares, or merchandize, we have agreed not to import, which we shall know, or have cause to suspect, were imported after the first day of December, except such as come under the rules and directions of the tenth article hereafter mentioned.

Fourth, The earnest desire we have not to injure our fellow-subjects in Great-Britain, Ireland, or the West-Indies, induces us to suspend a non-exportation, until the tenth day of September, 1775; at which time, if the said acts and parts of acts of the British parliament herein after mentioned, are not repealed, we will not directly or indirectly, export any merchandize or commodity whatsoever to Great-Britain, Ireland, or the West-Indies, except rice to Europe.

Fifth, Such as are merchants, and use the British and Irish trade, will give orders, as soon as possible, to their factors, agents and correspondents, in Great-Britain and Ireland, not to ship any goods to them, on any pretence whatsoever, as they cannot be received in America; and if any merchant, residing in Great-Britain or Ireland, shall directly or indirectly ship any goods, wares or merchandize, for America, in order to break the said non-importation agreement, or in any manner contravene the same, on such unworthy conduct being well attested, it ought to be made public; and, on the same being so done, we will not, from thenceforth, have any commercial connexion with such merchant.

Sixth, That such as are owners of vessels will give positive orders to their captains, or masters, not to receive on board their vessels any goods prohibited by the said non-importation agreement, on pain of immediate dismission from their service.

Seventh, We will use our utmost endeavours to improve the breed of sheep, and increase their number to the greatest extent; and to that end, we will kill them as seldom as may be, especially those of the most profitable kind; nor will we export any to the West-Indies or elsewhere; and those of us, who are or may become overstocked with, or can conveniently spare any sheep, will dispose of them to our neighbours, especially to the poorer sort, on moderate terms.

Eighth, We will, in our several stations, encourage frugality, œconomy, and industry, and promote agriculture, arts and the manufactures of this country, especially that of wool; and will discountenance and discourage every species of extravagance and dissipation, especially all horse-racing, and all kinds of gaming, cock fighting, exhibitions of shews, plays, and other expensive diversions and entertainments; and on the death of any relation or friend, none of us, or any of our families, will go into any further mourning-dress than a black crape or ribbon on the arm or hat, for gentlemen, and a black ribbon and necklace for ladies, and we will discontinue the giving of gloves and scarves at funerals.

Ninth, Such as are venders of goods or merchandize will not take advantage of the scarcity of goods that may be occasioned by this association, but will sell the same at the rates we have been respectively accustomed to do, for twelve months last past. — And if any vender of goods or merchandize shall sell such goods on higher terms, or shall, in any manner, or by any device whatsoever, violate or depart from this agreement, no person ought, nor will any of us deal with any such person, or his or her factor or agent, at any time thereafter, for any commodity whatever.

Tenth, In case any merchant, trader, or other person, shall import any goods or merchandize, after the first day of December, and before the first day of February next, the same ought forthwith, at the election of the owner, to be either re-shipped or delivered up to the committee of the county or town, wherein they shall be imported, to be stored at the risque of the importer, until the non-importation agreement shall cease, or be sold under the direction of the committee aforesaid;

and in the last-mentioned case, the owner or owners of such goods shall be reimbursed out of the sales, the first cost and charges, the profit, if any, to be applied towards relieving and employing such poor inhabitants of the town of Boston, as are immediate sufferers by the Boston port-bill; and a particular account of all goods so returned, stored, or sold, to be inserted in the public papers; and if any goods or merchandizes shall be imported after the said first day of February, the same ought forthwith to be sent back again, without breaking any of the packages thereof.

Eleventh, That a committee be chosen in every county, city, and town, by those who are qualified to vote for representatives in the legislature, whose business it shall be attentively to observe the conduct of all persons touching this association; and when it shall be made to appear, to the satisfaction of a majority of any such committee, that any person within the limits of their appointment has violated this association, that such majority do forthwith cause the truth of the case to be published in the gazette; to the end, that all such foes to the rights of British-America may be publicly known, and universally contemned as the enemies of American liberty; and thenceforth we respectively will break off all dealings with him or her.

Twelfth, That the committee of correspondence, in the respective colonies, do frequently inspect the entries of their custom-houses, and inform each other, from time to time, of the true state thereof, and of every other material circumstance that may occur relative to this association.

Thirteenth, That all manufactures of this country be sold at reasonable prices, so that no undue advantage be taken of a future scarcity of goods.

Fourteenth, And we do further agree and resolve, that we will have no trade, commerce, dealings or intercourse whatsoever, with any colony or province, in North-America, which shall not accede to, or which shall hereafter violate this association, but will hold them as unworthy of the rights of freemen, and as inimical to the liberties of their country.

And we do solemnly bind ourselves and our constituents, under the ties aforesaid, to adhere to this association, until such parts of the several acts of parliament, passed since the close of the last war, as impose or continue duties on tea, wine, molasses, syrups, paneles, coffee, sugar, pimento, indigo, foreign paper, glass, and painters colours, imported into America, and extend the powers of the admiralty courts beyond their ancient limits, deprive the American subject of trial by jury, authorise the judge's certificate to indemnify the prosecutor from damages, that he might otherwise be liable to, from a trial by his peers, require oppressive security from a claimant of ships or goods seized, before he shall be allowed to defend his property, are repealed. — And until that part of the act of the 12. G. 3. ch. 24. entitled, "An act for the better securing his majesty's dock-yards, magazines, ships, ammunition, and stores," by which any persons charged with committing any of the offences therein described, in America, may be tried in any shire or county within the realm, is repealed — and until the four acts, passed the last session of parliament, viz. that for stopping the port and blocking up the harbour of Boston — that for altering the charter and government of the Massachusetts-Bay — and that which is entitled, "An act for the better administration of justice, etc." — and that "For extending the limits of Quebec, etc." are repealed. And we recommend it to the provincial conventions, and to the committees in the respective colonies, to establish such farther regulations as they may think proper, for carrying into execution this association.

131. Prince William County (Virginia) Committee, Approval of the Association

Force, *American Archives*, Fourth Series, I, 1034.

In consequence of the eleventh Resolution of the Continental Congress, the Freeholders of the County of Prince William, being convened at the house of William Reno on Monday, the

9th day of December, 1774, proceeded to elect the following gentlemen as a Committee for the said County: [25 names].

[Notice of the organization of the Committee by election of its chairman and clerk — and then a series of six resolutions adopted by it. Four of them are given below.]

Resolved, That the thanks of the Committee are due to the Deputies of this Colony, for their wise, firm, and patriotick conduct in the late Continental Congress.

Resolved, That whenever there appears . . . cause to suspect that any Merchant . . . of this County has violated the Association . . . by raising the price of his Goods, such Trader be called upon to show his day-books and invoices, to clear up such suspicion; and that, in case of refusal, he be deemed guilty . . . and subject to the penalties in such case provided. . . .

Resolved, That all publick Balls and Entertainments be discountenanced in this county from this time, as contrary to the sentiments of the Continental Congress. . . .

Resolved, That no person in this County ought to purchase more Goods in one year than he has been accustomed to do . . . that the poor . . . may not be distressed by wealthy designing men.

By order —   Evan Williams, *Clerk.*

132. Virginia County "Conventions" become De Facto Governments

Force, *American Archives,* Fourth Series, I, 1145.

For the occasion for the "second conventions" in the various colonies in the winter of 1774–5, cf. *American History and Government,* § 143.

The Virginia Convention of August 1–6, 1774, had appointed delegates to the Continental Congress to be held in September at Philadelphia, and adjourned after authorizing its chairman to call another convention when necessary. *It was only an informal conference.*

In December, a *Second Maryland Convention* virtually became a *de facto* government, arming the province for defense against England. This example was followed promptly in single *counties* in Virginia, — first in George Washington's County.

[*Extracts from the Proceedings of the Committee of Fairfax County, on the 17th of January 1775.*]

George Washington, Esquire, *Chairman,*
Robert H. Harrison, *Clerk:*

Resolved, That the defenceless state of this County renders it indispensably neccessary that a quantity of Ammunition should be immediately provided; and as the same will be for the common benefit, protection, and defence of the inhabitants thereof, it is but just and reasonable that the expenses incurred in procuring the same should be defrayed by a general and equal contribution. It is therefore recommended that the sum of three Shillings per poll, for the purpose aforesaid, be paid by and for every tithable person in this County, to the Sheriff, or such other Collector as may be appointed, who is to render the same to this Committee, with a list of the names of such persons as shall refuse to pay the same, if any such there be.

Resolved, That this Committee do concur in opinion with the Provincial Committee of the Province of Maryland, that a well regulated Militia, composed of gentlemen freeholders, and other freemen, is the natural strength and only stable security of a free Government, and that such Militia will relieve our mother country from any expense in our protection and defence, will obviate the pretence of a necessity for taxing us on that account, and render it unnecessary to keep Standing Armies among us — ever dangerous to liberty ; and therefore it is recommended to such of the inhabitants of this County as are from sixteen to fifty years of age, to form themselves into Companies of sixty-eight men; to choose a Captain, two Lieutenants, an Ensign, four Sergeants, four Corporals, and one Drummer, for each Company; that they provide themselves with good Firelocks, and use their utmost endeavours to make themselves masters of the Military Exercise, published by order of his Majesty in 1764, and recommended by the Provincial Congress of the Massachusetts Bay, on the 29th of October last.

133. Virginia Provincial Conventions become Governments
(March–July, 1775)

a. *County Instructions to Delegates*

Force, *American Archives*, Fourth Series, II, 3.

Instructions from the Freeholders of Cumberland County Virginia.

To John Mayo and William Fleming, Gentlemen [Delegates of Cumberland County to the Second Virginia Convention, to be held in March, 1775.]

We, the Freeholders of Cumberland County, having elected you to represent us in a Provincial Convention,[1] to be held in the Town of Richmond, on Monday, the 20th of this instant, and being convinced that the safety and happiness of British America depend upon the unanimity, firmness and joint efforts of all the Colonies, we expect you will, on your parts, let your measures be as much for the common safety as the peculiar interests of this Colony will permit, and that you, in particular, comply with the recommendation of the Continental Congress, in appointing Delegates to meet in the City of Philadelphia, in May next.

The means of Constitutional legislation in this Colony being now interrupted, and entirely precarious, and being convinced that some rule is necessary for speedily putting the Colony in a state of defence, we, in an especial manner, recommend this matter to your consideration in Convention; and you may depend that any general tax, by that body imposed, for such purposes, will be cheerfully submitted to, and paid by the inhabitants of this County.[2]

---

[1] This convention had finally been called in January by Peyton Randolph, chairman of the preceding convention, according to authorization by body. Cf. introduction to No. 137, above. The work of the Convention is given in No. 139.

[2] Observe the authorization to raise money by taxation, — a special prerogative of government.

b. The Second Virginia Convention (March 20-27, 1775) arms the Colony for War

Force, *American Archives*, Fourth Series, II, 165-172.

At a Convention of Delegates for the Counties and Corporations in the Colony of Virginia, at the Town of Richmond, in the County of Henrico, on Monday, the 20th of March, 1775. [Present: 120 names.] . . .

* * * * * * *

The Honourable *Peyton Randolph*, Esquire, was unanimously elected President of this Convention, and *Mr. John Tazewell*, Clerk thereof.

The President then recommended it to the Convention to proceed in the deliberation and discussion of the several important matters which should come before them, with that prudence, decency, and order which had distinguished their conduct on all former occasions; and laid before the Convention the proceedings of the Continental Congress. . . .

Resolved, That this Convention will observe, in their debates, the same rules and orders as are established in the House of Burgesses in this Colony.

Adjourned till to-morrow 10 o'clock.

March 21. . . . *Resolved unanimously*, **That this Convention doth entirely and cordially approve the Proceedings and Resolutions of the *American* Continental Congress [the "First Continental Congress"], and that they consider this whole Continent as under the highest obligations to that very respectable body, for the wisdom of their counsels, and their unremitted endeavours to maintain and preserve inviolate the just rights and liberties of His Majesty's dutiful and loyal subjects in *America*.**

Resolved unanimously, That the warmest thanks of this Convention, and all the inhabitants of this Colony, whom they represent, are particularly due, and that this just tribute of applause be presented, to the Honourable *Peyton Randoph*, Esquire, *Richard Henry Lee*, *George Washington*, *Patrick*

Henry, Junior, *Richard Bland, Benjamin Harrison*, and *Edmund Pendleton*, Esquires, the worthy Delegates deputed by a former Convention to represent this Colony in General Congress, for their cheerful undertaking, and faithful discharge of the very important trust reposed in them.

Adjourned till to-morrow 10 o'clock.

March 22. . . . *Resolved,* **That a well regulated Militia, composed of Gentlemen and Yeomen, is the natural strength, and only security of a free Government; that such a Militia in this Colony would for ever render it unnecessary for the Mother Country to keep among us, for the purpose of our defence, any Standing Army of mercenary forces, always subversive of the quiet, and dangerous to the liberties of the people, and would obviate the pretext of taxing us for their support.**

That the establishment of such a Militia is at this time peculiarly necessary, by the state of our laws for the protection and defence of the Country, some of which have already expired, and others will shortly do so; and that the known remissness of Government, in calling us together in a legislative capacity renders it too insecure, in this time of danger and distress to rely, that opportunity will be given of renewing them in General Assembly, or making any provision to secure our inestimable rights and liberties from those farther violations with which they are threatened.

Resolved therefore, That this Colony be immediately put into a posture of defence; and that Patrick Henry, Richard Henry Lee, Robert Carter Nicholas, Benjamin Harrison, Lemuel Riddick, George Washington, Adam Stephen, Andrew Lewis, William Christian, Edmund Pendleton, Thomas Jefferson, and Isaac Zane, Esquires, be a Committee to prepare a plan for the embodying, arming, and disciplining such a number of men as may be sufficient for that purpose.

Adjourned till to-morrow 10 o'clock. . . .

Saturday, March 25, 1775. . . . *Resolved,* As the opinion of this Convention, that, on account of the unhappy disputes between Great Britain and the Colonies, and the unsettled state of this Country, the lawyers, suitors, and witnesses ought not to attend the prosecution or defence of civil suits at the next General Court; and it is recommended to the several Courts of Justice not to proceed to the hearing or determination of suits on their dockets, except attachments; nor to give judgments but in the case of Sheriffs or other collectors for Money or Tobacco received by them; in other cases, where such judgment shall be voluntarily confessed; or upon such amicable proceedings as may become necessary for the settlement, division, or distribution of estates. And, during this suspension of the administration of justice, it is earnestly recommended to the people to observe a peaceable and orderly behaviour; to all creditors to be as indulgent to their debtors as may be; to all debtors to pay as far as they are able; and where differences may arise which cannot be adjusted between the parties, that they refer the decision thereof to judicious neighbours, and abide by their determination.

The Convention then took into their consideration, according to the order of yesterday, the plan for embodying, arming and disciplining the Militia; which, being read, and amended, was unanimously agreed to, as follows:

* * * * * * *

The committee are further of opinion that, as from the expiration of the above-mentioned latter laws, and various other causes, the legal and necessary disciplining the Militia has been much neglected, and a proper provision of Arms and Ammunition has not been made, to the evident danger of the community in case of invasion or insurrection, **it be recommended to the inhabitants of the several Counties of this Colony that they form one or more volunteer Companies of Infantry and Troops of Horse, in each County, and to be in constant training and readiness to act on any emergency.**

* * * * * * *

That, in order to make a further and more ample provision of Amunition, it be recommended to the Committees of the several

Counties, that they collect from their Constituents, in such manner as shall be most agreeable to them, so much money as will be sufficient to purchase half a pound of Gunpowder, one pound of Lead, necessary Flints and Cartridge Paper, and dispose thereof, when procured, in such place or places of safety as they may think best; and it is earnestly recommended to each individual to pay such proportion of the money necessary for these purposes as by the respective Committees shall be judged requisite.

That as it may happen that some Counties, from their situation, may not be apprized of the most certain and speedy method of procuring the articles before-mentioned, one General Committee should be appointed, whose business it should be to procure, for such Counties as may make application to them, such articles, and so much thereof as the moneys wherewith they shall furnish the said Committee with purchase, after deducting the charges of transportation, and other necessary expenses.

Resolved, That Robert Carter Nicholas, Thomas Nelson, and Thomas Whiting, Esquires, or any two of them, be a Committee for the purpose afore-mentioned.

. . . *Resolved*, That *Robert Carter Nicholas, Richard Bland, James Mercer, Edmund Pendleton, Archibald Cary, Charles Carter* of *Stafford, Benjamin Harrison, Richard Henry Lee, Josias Clapham, George Washington, Patrick Henry, James Holt,* and *Thomas Newton,* Esquires, be a Committee to prepare a plan for the encouragement of Arts and Manufactures in this Colony.

The Convention then proceeded to the election of Delegates by ballot, to represent this Colony in General Congress, to be held at the City of *Philadelphia,* on the 10th day of *May* next; when the Honourable *Peyton Randolph,* Esquire, *George Washington, Patrick Henry, Richard Henry Lee, Edmund Pendleton, Benjamin Harrison, and Richard Bland,* Esquires, were chosen for that purpose.

Resolved, That *Robert Carter Nicholas,* Esquire, be desired to lay before the Convention, on Monday next, an account of the Money received from the several Counties and Corporations in this Colony, for the use of the Delegates sent to represent this Colony in General Congress.

Adjourned till Monday, 10 o'clock.

March 27 . . . *Resolved unanimously*, That from and after the first day of *May* next, no person or persons whatever ought to use, in his or their families, unless in case of necessity, and on no account to sell to butchers, or kill for market, any Sheep under four years old; and where there is necessity for using any mutton in his, her, or their families, it is recommended to kill such only as are least profitable to be kept.

Resolved unanimously, That the setting up and promoting Woollen, Cotton, and Linen Manufactures ought to be encouraged in as many different branches as possible, especially Coating, Flannel, Blankets, Rugs, or Coverlids, Hosiery, and coarse Cloths, both broad and narrow.

* * * * * * *

Resolved unanimously, As Salt is a daily and indispensable necessary of life, and the making of it amongst ourselves must be deemed a valuable acquisition, it is therefore recommended that the utmost endeavours be used to establish Salt Works, and that proper encouragement be given to Mr. *James Tait*, who hath made proposals, and offered a scheme to the publick, for so desirable a purpose.

Resolved unanimously, That Saltpetre and Sulphur, *being articles of great and necessary use*, the making, collecting, and refining them to the utmost extent, be recommended, the Convention being of opinion that it may be done to great advantage.

Resolved unanimously, That the making of Gunpowder be recommended.

Resolved unanimously, That the manufacturing of iron into Nails and Wire, and other necessary articles, be recommended.

Resolved unanimously, That the making of Steel ought to be largely encouraged, as there will be a great demand for this article.

Resolved unanimously, That the making of different kinds of Paper ought to be encouraged; and as the success of this branch depends on a supply of old Linen and Woollen Rags, the inhabitants of this Colony are desired, in their respective families, to preserve these articles.

Resolved unanimously, That whereas Wool Combs, Cotton and Wool Cards, Hemp and Flax Heckles, have been for some time made to advantage in some of the neighbouring Colonies, and are necessary for carrying on Linen and Woollen Manufactures, the establishing such Manufactures be recommended.

Resolved unanimously, That the erecting Fulling Mills and mills for breaking, swingling, and softening Hemp and Flax, and also the making Grindstones be recommended.

Resolved unanimously, That the brewing Malt Liquors in this Colony would tend to render the consumption of foreign Liquors less necessary. It is therefore recommended that proper attention be given to the cultivation of Hops and Barley.

Resolved unanimously, That it be recommended to all the inhabitants of this Colony, that they use, as the Convention engageth to do, our own Manufactures, and those of other Colonies, in preference to all others.

* * * * * * *

The Members of the Convention then, in order to encourage Mr. *James Tait*, who is about to erect Salt Works, undertook, for their respective Counties, to pay the sum of Ten Pounds to *Robert Carter Nicholas*, Esquire, for the use of the said *James Tait*, on or before the 10th day of *May* next.

* * * * * * *

Resolved, That this Convention doth consider the delegation of its members as now at an end; and that it is recommended to the People of this Colony to choose Delegates to represent them in Convention *for one year*, as soon as they conveniently can.

Peyton Randolph, President.
John Tazewell, Clerk of the Convention.

c. [*The Third Virginia Convention*, pursuant to the call in the closing recommendation of the Second, met July 17, 1775, and adopted the forms of a legislative body, giving bills three readings, etc. The first resolution read . . .

"That this Convention will observe, in their debates *and proceedings*, the same Rules and Orders as are established in the House of Burgesses of this Colony." Cf. with the corresponding Resolution of the Second Convention above ; note significance of the two additional words. That significance is brought out clearly in the postscript of a letter from George Mason to a friend, August 22:

"P. S. Every ordinance goes thro' all the Formalities of a Bill in the House of Burgesses, has three Readings, etc. before it is passed, and in every respect wears the Face of Law, — Resolves, as recommendations, being no longer trusted to. . . ." (Virginia Calendar of State Papers, I, 269.)

Thus the Third Convention was a "government" in style as well as in fact. It held two busy sessions ; and, in January, 1776, though its "year" was not up, it adjourned, to give place to a new Convention freshly instructed from the people.]

XXIII. INDEPENDENCE

Cf. *American History and Government* (§§ 146–150) for additional comment and narrative, and suggestions as to bibliography, on each of the following numbers, 134–139. Many short extracts are there given from documents which, on that account, are not reproduced here,— notably from Paine's *Common Sense*.

134. Virginia County Instructions for Independence, April 23, 1776

Force, *American Archives*, Fourth Series, V, 1034–1035.

The following instructions from a county meeting of Charlotte County, Virginia, to delegates for the next Virginia Convention [to meet May 6] show that that body was at least partially authorized to take its momentous action of adopting a State constitution and of instructing the Virginia delegates at Philadelphia to move for independence. Note that the King, to whom all earlier documents had professed loyalty, is here coupled with the ministry and parliament. Other counties gave similar instruction. Cf. Force, V, 1046.

To Paul Carrington, and Thomas Read, Esq's.:

Gentlemen: When we consider the despotick plan adopted by the King, Ministry and Parliament of *Great Britain*, insidiously pursued for these twelve years past, to enslave *America;* when we consider that they have turned a deaf ear to the repeated petitions and remonstrances of this and our sister Colonies, and that they have been equally inattentive to the rights of freemen and the British Constitution; and when we consider that they have for some time been endeavouring to enforce their arbitrary mandates by fire and sword, and likewise encouraging, by every means in their power, our savage neighbours, and our more savage domesticks, to spill the blood of our wives and children; and to crown the whole, they have added insult to their injustice and cruelty, by repeatedly pretending to hold out the olive branch of peace in such a way as teacheth us that they are determined to persist in their hellish designs, and that nothing is intended for us but the most abject slavery. . . .

Therefore despairing of any redress of our grievances from the King and Parliament of *Great Britain,* and all hopes of a reconciliation between her and the United Colonies being now at an end, and being concious that their treatment has been such as loyal subjects did not deserve, and to which as freemen, we are determined not to submit; by the unanimous approbation and direction of the whole freeholders, and all the other inhabitants of this County, we advise and instruct you, cheerfully to concur and give your best assistance in our Convention, to push to the utmost a war offensive and defensive until you are certified that such proposals of peace are made to our General Congress as shall by them be judged just and friendly. And because the advantages of a trade will better enable us to pay the taxes, and procure the necessaries for carrying on a war, and in our present circumstances this cannot be had without a Declaration of Independence; therefore, if no such proposals of peace shall be made, we judge it to be a dictate of the first law of nature, to continue to oppose every attempt on our lives and properties; and we give it you in charge, to use your best endeavours **that the Delegates which are sent to the General Congress be instructed immediately to cast off the *British* yoke**, and to enter into a commercial alliance with any nation or nations friendly to our cause. And as King George the Third of Great Britain etc., has manifested deliberate enmity towards us, and under the character of a parent persists in behaving as a tyrant, that they, in our behalf renounce allegiance to him for ever; **and that, taking God of Heaven to be our King, and depending upon His protection and assistance, they plan out that form of Government which may the more effectually secure to us the enjoyment of our civil and religious rights and privileges, to the latest posterity.** . . .

Ordered, That the above Resolves be published in the *Virginian Gazette.*

By order: William Jameson, Clerk.

135. Instructions for Independence in the Virginia Convention (and Resolutions for an Independent State Government), May 15, 1776 [1]

Force, *American Archives*, Fourth Series, VI, 461–462.

The Fourth Virginia Convention met May 6, elected on the recommendation of the preceding Convention (see No. 133 c, close). On the 9th the Convention voted to go next day into Committee of the Whole to consider the state of the colony (which meant to take up the matter of independence and a State government). Military needs, however, delayed the consideration until the 14th. On that day and the 15th, the questions were debated, and, on the 15th, the Committee rose and reported to the Convention the resolutions below, which were unanimously adopted. For a more detailed story, see *American History and Government*, § 148; but it should be seen here clearly that the Convention instructed its delegates in the Continental Congress to secure a *general* declaration of Independence for all the colonies, and that, at the same time, it began the work of a permanent independent constitution for Virginia.

[The first half of the document is a preamble stating the grievances of the colonies.] . . . In this state of extreme danger, we have no alternative left but an abject submission to the will of those overbearing tyrants or a total separation from the crown and government of Great Britain, uniting and exerting the strength of all America for defence, and forming alliances with foreign powers for commerce and aid in war: Wherefore, appealing to the Searcher of Hearts for the sincerity of former declarations expressing our desire to preserve the connection with that nation, and that we are driven from that inclination by their wicked councils and the eternal laws of self-preservation;

Resolved, unanimously, That the delegates appointed to represent this colony in General Congress be instructed to propose to that respectable body to declare the United Colonies free and independent States, absolved from all allegiance

---

[1] For the recommendation of Congress, on this same day, regarding setting up State governments, cf. *American History and Government*, § 148. (For earlier recommendations as to temporary governments, cf. *ib.*) This action, of course, was not known in Virginia when this Convention took action regarding independence and a permanent State constitution.

to or dependence upon the Crown or parliament of Great Britain; and that they give the assent of this colony to such declaration, and to whatever measures may be thought proper and necessary by the Congress for forming foreign alliances and a confederation of the colonies, at such time, and in such manner, as to them shall seem best: Provided that the power of forming government for, and the regulation of, the internal concerns of each colony, be left to the respective colonial legislatures.

Resolved unanimously, That a committee be appointed to prepare a DECLARATION OF RIGHTS and such a plan of government as will be most likely to maintain peace and order in this colony, and secure substantial and equal liberty to the people.

136. The Virginia Bill of Rights, June 12, 1776

Poore, *Charters and Constitutions*, II, 1908-1909. Cf. No. 135 for history. This bill of rights was reported by a committee to the Virginia Convention on May 27, and adopted unanimously on June 12. It was the model, often followed closely, for similar bills in other states. See comment at close.

A declaration of rights made by the representatives of the good people of Virginia, assembled in full and free convention; which rights do pertain to them and their posterity, as the basis and foundation of government.

SECTION 1. That all men are by nature equally free and independent, and have certain inherent rights, of which, when they enter into a state of society, they cannot, by any compact, deprive or divest their posterity; namely, the enjoyment of life and liberty, with the means of acquiring and possessing property, and pursuing and obtaining happiness and safety.

SECTION 2. That all power is vested in, and consequently derived from, the people; that magistrates are their trustees and servants, and at all times amenable to them.

SECTION 3. That government is, or ought to be, instituted for the common benefit, protection, and security of the people, nation, or community; of all the various modes and forms of government, that is best which is capable of producing the greatest degree of happiness and safety, and is most effectually secured against the danger of maladministration; and that, when any government shall be found inadequate or contrary to these purposes, a majority of the community hath an indubitable, inalienable, and indefeasible right to reform, alter, or abolish it in such manner as shall be judged most conducive to the public weal.

SECTION 4. That no man, or set of men, are entitled to exclusive or separate emoluments or privileges from the community, but in consideration of public services; which, not being descendible, neither ought the offices of magistrate, legislator, or judge to be hereditary.

SECTION 5. That the legislative and executive powers of the State should be separate and distinct from the judiciary; and that the members of the two first may be restrained from oppression, by feeling and participating in the burdens of the people, they should, at fixed periods, be reduced to a private station, return into that body from which they were originally taken, and the vacancies be supplied by frequent, certain, and regular elections, in which all, or any part of the former members to be again eligible, or ineligible, as the laws shall direct.

SECTION 6. That elections of members to serve as representatives of the people, in assembly, ought to be free; and that all men, having sufficient evidence of permanent common interest with, and attachment to, the community, have the right of suffrage, and cannot be taxed or deprived of their property for public uses, without their own consent, or that of their representatives so elected, nor bound by any law to which they have not, in like manner, assented, for the public good.[1]

---

[1] The sixth article seems to have been designed by George Mason, who drew it, as an argument for extending the franchise to heads of families. Mason drew also a plan for the *frame of government*, which the convention in the main adopted on *June 29*. In this plan he proposed to "extend" the franchise to leaseholders with seven-year terms, and to any "housekeeper"

SECTION 7. That all power of suspending laws, or the execution of laws, by any authority, without consent of the representatives of the people, is injurious to their rights, and ought not to be exercised.

SECTION 8. That in all capital or criminal prosecutions a man hath a right to demand the cause and nature of his accusation, to be confronted with the accusers and witnesses, to call for evidence in his favor, and to a speedy trial by an impartial jury of twelve men of his vicinage, without whose unanimous consent he cannot be found guilty; nor can he be compelled to give evidence agaist himself; that no man be deprived of his liberty, except by the law of the land or the judgment of his peers.

SECTION 9. That excessive bail ought not to be required, nor excessive fines imposed, nor cruel and unusual punishments inflicted.

SECTION 10. That general warrants, whereby an officer or messenger may be commanded to search suspected places without evidence of a fact committed, or to seize any person or persons not named, or whose offence is not particularly de-

---

who was also the father of three children (Article V of Mason's Plan; printed in full in Kate Mason Rowland's *Life and Correspondence of George Mason*, I, 444 ff.). The convention, however, left the franchise as "now established by law"—on a freehold basis (*American History and Government*, §§ 105, 107). Mason, in his plan, suggested graded landed qualifications for holding office: £500 freehold to act as a member of his proposed electoral college to choose state senators; £1000 freehold to sit in the lower House; £2000 freehold to sit in the upper House.

It is often said that Mason proposed a £1000-freehold qualification for the franchise. The language of Section III of his "plan," *taken by itself*, would so indicate. But the clauses III and IV are very loosely worded and punctuated; and, when they are read in conjunction with Section V, the only possible conclusion is the one stated above. In proposing so liberal a franchise, however, Mason stood alone in Virginia in his day. Even Jefferson's plan for a Virginia constitution called for "a freehold of ¼ of an acre of land in a town, or 25 acres in the country" (*Works*, Ford edition, II, 7 ff.).

Eleven years later at the Philadelphia convention, Mason used the same language as in the Virginia bill of rights, in opposing a real-estate qualification for the national franchise; but he still advocated a landed qualification for membership in even the lower House of Congress.

VIRGINIA BILL OF RIGHTS, JUNE 12, 1776

scribed and supported by evidence, are grievous and oppressive, and ought not to be granted.

SECTION 11. That in controversies respecting property, and in suits between man and man, the ancient trial by jury is preferable to any other, and ought to be held sacred.

SECTION 12. That the freedom of the press is one of the great bulwarks of liberty, and can never be restrained but by despotic governments.

SECTION 13. That a well-regulated militia, composed of the body of the people, trained to arms, is the proper, natural, and safe defence of a free State; that standing armies, in time of peace, should be avoided, as dangerous to liberty; and that in all cases the military should be under strict subordination to, and governed by, the civil power.

SECTION 14. That the people have a right to uniform government; and, therefore, that no government separate from, or independent of the government of Virginia, ought to be erected or established within the limits thereof.

SECTION 15. That no free government, or the blessings of liberty, can be preserved to any people, but by a firm adherence to justice, moderation, temperance, frugality, and virtue, and by frequent recurrence to fundamental principles.

SECTION 16. That religion, or the duty which we owe to our Creator, and the manner of discharging it, can be directed only by reason and conviction, not by force or violence; and therefore all men are equally entitled to the free exercise of religion, according to the dictates of conscience; and that it is the mutual duty of all to practise Christian forbearance, love and charity towards each other.

[The failure of historians to give due credit to this bill of rights is remarkable. I call attention to two illustrations.

(1) Cushing's *Transition from Provincial to Commonwealth Government in Massachusetts* (Columbia University Studies, VII, 1896) states incorrectly (p. 246, note 1) that the constitution of Virginia contained no preamble (cf. No. 137 below): and,

on page 247 and notes, it quotes precedents from the Maryland bill of rights instead of from the Virginia document from which the Maryland statement was taken; while page 248, in referring to "others [than Massachusetts that] realized keenly the vital importance of a clear and abiding statement of the immunities and privileges of man in civil society," adds the note: "A Declaration of Rights was adopted by Delaware, Maryland, New Hampshire (1784), North Carolina, Pennsylvania, Vermont, *and* Virginia" (!) The order of statement is ingeniously misleading. All the others named drew mainly from the one named last.

(2) Merriam's *History of American Political Theories* (1902) contains several such misleading statements. On page 49, to illustrate the fact that some State constitutions (as well as the Declaration of Independence) asserted the doctrine of "inalienable rights," including "life, liberty, and the pursuit of happiness," reference is made in detail to the New Hampshire bill of rights (eight years later than the Declaration), but not at all to the Virginia bill of rights, which preceded the Continental Declaration. So, too, especially on page 153, a footnote is inserted expressly to show how the idea of "frequent recurrence to fundamental principles" was often expressed in Revolutionary State constitutions, as follows: "Massachusetts (1780), Art. 18; Pensylvania (1776), Art. 14; New Hampshire, Art. 38; North Carolina, Art. 21; Vermont, Art. 16." Would it not have been well to recognize in such a list the State in whose constitution the phrase was first used?]

137. The First Declaration of Independence by a State
Preamble to the Virginia Constitution, June 29, 1776

The Virginia constitution, adopted on June 29, 1776, consisted of three parts: (1) a declaration of independence; (2) the bill of rights; (3) the frame of government. The original intention (No. 135, close) had been to include the last two only, and to leave the declaration of independence to Congress. But on June 24, when the convention had nearly completed its consideration of the constitution, it received from Jefferson a draft of a constitution prefaced by a declaration of independence. Of the adoption of this preface, Jefferson wrote in 1825:

"I was then at Philadelphia . . . knowing that the Convention of Virginia was engaged in forming a plan of government, I turned my mind to the same subject, and drew a sketch . . . of a Constitution with a preamble, which I sent to Mr. Pendleton, president of the Convention . . . He informed me . . . that he received it on the day on which the Committee of the Whole had reported to the House the plan they had agreed to; and that it had been so long in hand, so disputed inch by inch . . . that they were worried with the contentions it had produced, and could not, from mere lassitude, have been induced to open the instrument again; but that, being pleased with the Preamble to mine, they adopted it in the House, by way of amendment to the report of the committee [June 29]; and thus my Preamble was tacked to the work of George Mason, . . . *The Preamble was prior in composition to the Declaration* [of July 4]." [1]

Whereas George Guelf, king of Great Britain . . . and heretofore entrusted with the exercise of the kingly office in this government [Virginia], hath endeavored to pervert the same into a detestable and insupportable tyranny:

> by putting his negative on laws the most wholesome and necessary for the public good;
> by . . . [21 indictments follow — similar to the charges in the Declaration soon after adopted at Philadelphia] by which several acts of mis-rule the said George Guelf has forfeited the kingly office, and has rendered it necessary for the preservation of the people that he should be immediately deposed from the same. . . .

Be it therefore enacted by the authority of the people that

---

[1] Jefferson's plan was indorsed. " . . . It is proposed that this bill, after correction by the Convention, shall be referred by them to the people, to be assembled in their respective counties; and that the suffrages of two-thirds the counties shall be necessary to establish it." Jefferson always contended that the Virginia constitution, since it was not so submitted to popular ratification, was not a "fundamental law," but was subject to repeal, like any other statute, by ordinary legislative action. Cf. *American History and Government*, § 152.

the said George Guelf be, and he hereby is deposed from the kingly office within this government, and absolutely divested of all its rights, powers, and prerogatives: and that he and his descendants, and all persons acting by or through him, and all other persons whatsoever, shall be and forever remain incapable of the same: and that the said office shall henceforth cease, and never more either in name or substance be reestablished within this colony.

138. Revolutionary State Governments

a. Recommendation of Congress, May 15, 1776

Journals of Congress (Ford edition), V, 357 ff.

IN CONGRESS, May 15, 1776.

Whereas, his Britanic majesty, in conjunction with the lords and commons of Great Britain, has, by a late act of parliament, excluded the inhabitants of these united colonies from the protection of his crown — And whereas no answer whatever to the humble petitions of the colonies for redress of grievances and reconciliation with Great Britain, has been, or is likely to be given, but the whole force of that kingdom, aided by foreign mercenaries, is to be exerted for the destruction of the good people of these colonies — and whereas it appears absolutely irreconcilable to reason and good conscience, for the people of these colonies NOW to take the oaths and affirmations necessary for the support of any government under the crown of Great Britain; **and it is necessary that the exercise of every kind of authority under the said crown should be totally suppressed, and all the powers of government exerted under the authority of the people of the colonies,** for the preservation of internal peace, virtue, and good order, as well as for the defence of their lives, liberties and properties, against the hostile invasions and cruel depredations of their enemies — Therefore,

Resolved, That it be recommended to the respective assemblies, and conventions, of the united colonies, where no government sufficient to the exigencies of their affairs has been heretofore established, to adopt such government as shall, in the opinion of the representatives of the people, best conduce to the happiness and safety of their constituents in particular, and America in general.

b. *John Adams' Comment upon the Bearing of that Action* (a *above*) *upon Independence*

Letters of John Adams to His Wife, I, 109–111. Adams had been the special champion of the action finally recommended by Congress as above. On the following Sunday, he wrote as follows of that memorable action, and of the earlier action in South Carolina in adopting a *temporary* government of its own.

John Adams to Abigail Adams
Philadelphia, May 17, 1776.

I have this morning heard Mr. Duffield, upon the signs of the times. . . . He concluded, that the course of events indicated strongly the design of Providence, that we should be separated from Great Britain, etc. . . .

Is it not a saying of Moses, "who am I, that I should go in and out before this great people?" When I consider the great events which are passed, and those greater which are rapidly advancing, and that I may have been instrumental in touching some springs, and turning some small wheels, which have had and will have such effects, I feel an awe upon my mind, which is not easily described. Great Britain has at last driven America to the last step, a complete separation from her; a total absolute independence, not only of her Parliament, but of her crown, *for such is the amount of the resolve of the 15th. Confederation among ourselves, or alliances with foreign nations, are not necessary to a perfect separation from Britain. That is effected by extinguishing all authority under the crown, Parliament, and nation, as the resolution for instituting governments has done, to all intents and purposes.*

Confederation will be necessary for our internal concord, and alliances may be so for our external defence.

I have reasons to believe that no colony, which shall assume a government under the people, will give it up. There is something very unnatural and odious in a government a thousand leagues off. A whole government of our own choice, managed by persons whom we love, revere, and can confide in, has charms in it, for which men will fight. Two young gentlemen from South Carolina in this city, who were in Charlestown when their new constitution was promulgated, and when their new Governor and Council and Assembly walked out in procession, attended by the guards, company of cadets, light horse, etc., told me, that they were beheld by the people with transports and tears of joy. The people gazed at them with a kind of rapture. They both told me, that the reflection, that these were gentlemen whom they all loved, esteemed and revered, gentlemen of their own choice, whom they could trust, and whom they could displace, if any of them should behave amiss, affected them so, that they could not help crying. *They say, their people will never give up this government.* . . .

139. Instructions by "State" Conventions *against* Independence (January–May, 1776)

Proceedings of the Conventions of Maryland in 1774, 1775, and 1776, pages 82–84, 140–142, 176.

Similar instructions were given in Pennsylvania and New Jersey.

(1) *In Convention, January 12th,*

To the honorable Matthew Tilgham, Esq., Thomas Jefferson, jr., Robert Goldsborough, William Paca, Samuel Chase, Thomas Stone, Robert Alexander, and John Rogers, Esquires.

The convention taking into their most serious consideration the present state of the unhappy dispute between Great Britain and the united colonies, think it proper to deliver you their sentiments, and to instruct you in certain points, relative to your conduct in congress, as representatives of this province.

INSTRUCTIONS AGAINST INDEPENDENCE

The experience we and our ancestors have had of the mildness and equity of the English constitution, under which we have grown up to and enjoyed a state of felicity, not exceeded among any people we know of, until the grounds of the present controversy were laid by the ministry and parliament of Great Britain, has most strongly endeared to us that form of government from whence these blessings have been derived, and makes us ardently wish for a reconciliation with the mother country, upon terms that may insure to these colonies an equal and permanent freedom.

To this constitution we are attached, not merely by habit, but by principle, being in our judgments persuaded [that] it is of all known systems best calculated to secure the liberty of the subject, to guard against despotism on the one hand, and licentiousness on the other.

Impressed with these sentiments, we warmly recommend to you, to keep constantly in your view the avowed end and purpose for which these colonies originally associated, — the redress of American grievances and [the] securing the rights of the colonists.

* * * * * * *

We further instruct you, *that you do not without the previous knowledge and approbation of the convention of this province, assent to any proposition to declare these colonies independent of the crown of Great Britain, nor to any proposition for making or entering into alliance with any foreign power, nor to any union or confederation of these colonies,* which may necessarily lead to a separation from the mother country, unless in your judgments of any four of you, or of a majority of the whole of you, if all shall be then attending in congress, it shall be thought absolutely necessary for the preservation of the liberties of the united colonies; and *should a majority of the colonies in congress, against such your judgment, resolve to declare these colonies independent of the crown of Great Britain, or to make or enter into alliance with any foreign power, or into any union or confederation of these colonies, which may neces-*

sarily lead to a separation from the mother country, then we instruct you immediately to call the convention of this province, and repair thereto with such proposition and resolve, and lay the same before the said convention, for their consideration, and this convention will not hold this province bound by such majority in congress, until the representative body of the province in convention assent thereto.

Desirous as we are of peace with Great Britain upon safe and honourable terms, we wish you nevertheless, and instruct you to join with the other colonies in such military operations as may be judged proper and necessary for the common defence, until such a peace can be happily obtained.

[May 15, came the recommendation of Congress for extinguishing all authority under the British crown and the setting up of state governments (No. 138a above), and also the instructions of the Virginia Convention for Independence and Confederation. The response in Maryland was merely a repetition of her previous instructions, in the passage given below. Note the jealous disposition to deny authority to Congress and to resent the wording of its recommendations.]

(2) *Tuesday, May 21, 1776*

* * * * * * *

The convention took into their consideration the report from the committee appointed to report on the resolution of congress of the 15th instant, and thereupon came to the following resolutions.

Resolved unanimously, That the people of this province have the sole and exclusive right of regulating the internal government and police of this province.

* * * * * * *

Resolved unanimously, That this province has hitherto exerted itself, and will upon all occasions continue to exert itself, with cheerfulness and alacrity, in the common cause, agreeable to the faith pledged in the union of the colonies: and *if it shall appear to this province* necessary to enter into a further compact for the preservation of the constitutional rights of America, this province will enter into such further engagement for that purpose.

Resolved unanimously, That this convention, by a resolution of the 15th day of this instant, hath made sufficient provision to prevent a necessity for any person within this province now taking the oaths for the support of government under the crown of Great Britain, and that it is the opinion of this convention, that *it is not necessary that the exercise of every kind of authority under the said crown should be now totally suppressed* in this province, and all the powers of government exerted under the authority of the people.

* * * * * * *

Resolved unanimously, That as this convention is firmly persuaded that a re-union with Great Britain on constitutional principles would most effectually secure the rights and liberties, and increase the strength and promote the happiness of the whole empire, objects which this province hath ever had in view, *the said deputies are bound and directed to govern themselves by the instructions given to them by this convention in its session of December*[1] *last, in the same manner as if the said instructions were particularly repeated.*

[These instructions continued in force until revoked on *June 28* as follows:]

(3) *Resolved unanimously,* That the instructions given by the convention of December last (and renewed by the convention in May) to the deputies of this colony in Congress be recalled, and the restrictions therein contained removed; and that the deputies of this colony attending in Congress . . . be authorized and empowered to concur with the *other*[2] united colonies, or a majority of them, in declaring the united colonies free and independent states, in forming such further compact and confederation between them, in making foreign alliances, and in adopting such other measures as shall be judged necessary for securing

---

[1] The action of January 12 in (1) above belonged to the session beginning in December.

[2] Is the following word "united" then, in this place, part of a proper noun, or merely an adjective?

the liberties of America; and this colony will hold itself bound [1] by the resolutions of a majority of the united colonies in the premises: provided the sole and exclusive right of regulating the internal government and police of this colony be reserved to the people thereof.

140. Motion in Congress for Independence

Journals of Congress, V, 425. In obedience to the instructions from the Virginia Convention, Richard Henry Lee, on June 7, moved in Congress the following resolutions. After delays, to permit certain delegates to secure permission for their colonial assemblies, the resolution was finally adopted July 2, by the vote of all colonies but New York. For further detail, cf. *American History and Government*, § 150.

That these united colonies are, and of right ought to be, free and independent States; that they are absolved from all allegiance to the British Crown; and that all political connection between them and the State of Great Britain is, and ought to be, totally dissolved.

That it is expedient forthwith to take the most effectual measures for forming foreign alliances.

That a plan of confederation be prepared and transmitted to the respective colonies for their consideration.

141. The Continental Declaration of Independence

While the debate was proceeding on Lee's resolutions (No. 140), to save time, in case those resolutions should be adopted, Congress appointed a committee (Thomas Jefferson, John Adams, Benjamin Franklin, Roger Sherman, and R. R. Livingston) to draft a full "Declaration of Independence." Jefferson, the member from the colony which had moved the resolution,[2] was naturally made chairman and drew the document, which with slight modification was presented to Congress on June 28. After the adoption of the resolutions on July 2, this formal Declaration was taken

---

[1] Would that colony have felt itself "bound" *before* it gave them instructions, if Congress had acted on these matters? Cf. *American History and Government*, § 187, for a discussion of this and allied points.

[2] Lee was about to return to Virginia, and so was not placed on the committee.

DECLARATION OF INDEPENDENCE

up by Congress, considered on the 2d, 3d, and 4th of July, and passed. August 2, a copy, engrossed on parchment, was signed by the members of Congress there present. Other signatures were added later until all thirteen States were represented. The following capitalization, paragraphing, and punctuation follow the original parchment.

In Congress, July 4, 1776
The Unanimous Declaration of the Thirteen United States of America

When in the Course of human events, it becomes necessary for one people to dissolve the political bands which have connected them with another, and to assume among the powers of the earth, the separate and equal station to which the Laws of Nature and of Nature's God entitle them, a decent respect to the opinions of mankind requires that they should declare the causes which impel them to the separation. — We hold these truths to be self-evident, that all men are created equal, that they are endowed by their Creator with certain unalienable Rights, that among these are Life, Liberty and the pursuit of Happiness. — That to secure these rights, Governments are instituted among Men, deriving their just powers from the consent of the governed. — That whenever any Form of Government becomes destructive of these ends, it is the Right of the People to alter or to abolish it, and to institute new Government, laying its foundation on such principles and organizing its powers in such forms, as to them shall seem most likely to effect their Safety and Happiness. Prudence, indeed, will dictate that Governments long established should not be changed for light and transient causes; and accordingly all experience hath shewn, that mankind are more disposed to suffer, while evils are sufferable, than to right themselves by abolishing the forms to which they are accustomed. But when a long train of abuses and usurpations, pursuing invariably the same Object evinces a design to reduce them under absolute Despotism, it is their right, it is their duty, to throw off such Government, and to provide new Guards for their future security. — Such has been the patient sufferance of these Colonies; and such is now the necessity which constrains them to alter their former Systems of Government. The history of the present King of Great Britain is a history of repeated injuries and usurpations, all having in direct object the establishment of an absolute Tyranny over these States. To prove this, let Facts be submitted to a candid world. — He has refused his Assent to Laws, the most wholesome and necessary for the public good. — He has forbidden his Governors to pass Laws of immediate and pressing importance, unless suspended in their operation till his Assent should be obtained; and when so suspended, he has utterly neglected to attend to them. — He has refused to pass other Laws for the accommodation of large districts of people, unless those people would relinquish the right of Representation in the Legislature, a right inestimable to them and formidable to tyrants only. — He has called together legislative bodies at places unusual, uncomfortable, and distant from the depository of their Public Records, for the sole purpose of fatiguing them into compliance with his measures. — He has dissolved Representative Houses repeatedly, for opposing with manly firmness his invasions on the rights of the people. — He has refused for a long time, after such dissolutions, to cause others to be elected; whereby the Legislative Powers, incapable of Annihilation, have returned to the People at large for their exercise; the State remaining in the mean time exposed to all the dangers of invasion from without, and convulsions within. — He has endeavoured to prevent the population of these States; for that purpose obstructing the Laws for Naturalization of Foreigners; refusing to pass others to encourage their migration hither, and raising the conditions of new Appropriations of Lands. — He has obstructed the Administration of Justice, by refusing his Assent to Laws for establishing Judiciary Powers. — He has made Judges dependent on his will alone, for the tenure of their offices, and the amount and payment of their salaries. — He has erected a multitude of New Offices, and sent hither swarms of Officers to harass our People, and eat out their substance. — He has kept among us, in times of peace, Standing Armies without the Consent of our legislature. — He has affected to render the Military independent of and superior to the Civil Power. — He has combined with others to subject us to a jurisdiction foreign to our constitution, and unacknowledged by our laws; giving his Assent to their acts of pretended legislation: — For quartering large bodies of armed troops among us: — For protecting them, by a mock Trial, from Punishment for any Murders which they should commit on the Inhabitants of these States: — For cutting off our Trade with all parts of the world: — For imposing taxes on us without our Consent: — For depriving us in many cases, of the benefits of Trial by Jury: — For transporting us beyond Seas to be tried for pretended offence: — For abolishing the free System of English Laws in a neighbouring Province, establishing therein an Arbitrary government, and enlarging it Boundaries so as to render it at once an example and fit instrument for introducing the same absolute rule into these Colonies: — For taking away our Charters, abolishing our most valuable Laws, and altering fundamentally the Forms of our Governments: — For suspending our own Legislature, and declaring themselves invested with Power to legislate for us in all cases whatsoever. — He has abdicated Government here, by declaring us out of his Protection and waging War against us. — He has plundered our seas, ravaged our Coasts, burnt our towns, and destroyed the lives of our people. — He is at this time transporting large armies of foreign mercenaries to compleat the works of death, desolation and tyranny, already begun with circumstances of Cruelty & perfidy scarcely paralleled in the most barbarous ages, and totally unworthy the Head of a civilized nation. — He has constrained our fellow Citizens taken Captive on the high Seas to bear Arms against their Country, to become the executioners of their friends and Brethren, or to fall themselves by their Hands. — He has excited domestic insurrections amongst us, and has endeavoured to bring on the inhabitants of our frontiers, the merciless Indian Savages, whose known rule of warfare, is an undistinguished destruction of all ages, sexes and conditions. In every stage of these Oppressions We have Petitioned for Redress in the most humble terms: Our repeated Petitions have been answered only by repeated injury. A Prince, whose character is thus marked by every act which may define a Tyrant, is unfit to be the ruler of a free people. Nor have We been wanting in attentions to our Brittish brethren. We have warned them from time to time of attempts by their legislature to extend an unwarrantable jurisdiction over us. We have reminded them of the circumstances of our emigration and settlement here. We have appealed to their native justice and magnanimity, and we have conjured them by the ties of common kindred to disavow these usurpations, which would inevitably interrupt our connections and correspondence. They too have been deaf to the voice of justice and of consanguinity. We must, therefore, acquiesce in the necessity, which denounces our Separation, and hold them, as we hold the rest of mankind, Enemies in War, in Peace Friends. —

We, therefore, the Representatives of the **united States of America,** in General Congress, Assembled, appealing to the Supreme Judge of the world for the rectitude of our intentions, do, in the Name, and by Authority of the good People of these Colonies, solemnly publish and declare, That these United Colonies are, and of Right ought to be, **Free and Independent States;** that they are Absolved from all Allegiance to the British Crown, and that all political connection between them and the State of Great Britain, is and ought to be totally dissolved; and that as FREE and INDEPENDENT STATES, they have full Power to levy War, conclude Peace, contract Alliances, establish Commerce, and to do all other Acts and Things which INDEPENDENT STATES may of right do. — And for the support of this Declaration, with a firm reliance on the protection of divine Providence, we mutually pledge to each other our Lives, our Fortunes and our sacred Honor.

JOHN HANCOCK.

[Signatures of the other representatives of the thirteen States.]

142. Anti-Social Tendencies of the Pre-Revolutionary Measures

a. *Closing of the Courts*

From " Passages from an Autobiography " in John Adams' *Works* (II, 420–421).

The passage illustrates one of the forces that drove many of the respectable classes into Tory ranks.

* * * * * * *

An event of the most trifling nature in appearance, and fit only to excite laughter in other times, struck me into a profound reverie, if not a fit of melancholy. I met a man who had sometimes been my client, and sometimes I had been against him. He, though a common horse-jocky, was sometimes in the right, and I had commonly been successful in his favor in our courts of law. He was always in the law, and had been sued in many actions at almost every court. As soon as he saw me, he came up to me, and his first salutation to me was, "Oh! Mr. Adams, what great things have you and your colleagues done for us! We can never be grateful enough to you. There are no courts of justice now in this Province and I hope there never will be another." Is this the object for which I have been contending? said I to myself, for I rode along without any answer to this wretch. Are these the sentiments of such people, and how many of them are there in the country? Half the nation, for what I know; for half the nation are debtors, if not more, and these have been, in all countries, the sentiments of debtors. If the power of the country should get into such hands, and there is great danger that it will, to what purpose have we sacrificed our time, health and every thing else? Surely we must guard against this spirit and these principles, or we shall repent of all our conduct. However, the good sense and integrity of the majority of the great body of the people came into my thoughts, for my relief, and the last resource was after all in a good Providence.

b. Mob Violence, to enforce the "Association"

From an anonymous parody, expressing the loyalist's dilemma, in Moore's *Diary of the American Revolution*, I, 169.

> To sign, or not to sign! — That is the question:
> Whether 'twere better for an honest man
> To sign — and so be safe; or to resolve,
> Betide what will, against 'associations'
> And, by retreating, shun them. To fly — I reck
> Not where — and by that flight to 'scape
> Feathers and tar, and thousand other ills
> That Loyalty is heir to. 'Tis a consummation
> Devoutly to be wished. To fly — to want —
> To want — perchance to starve! Ay there's the rub!

* * * * * * *

c. Correspondence between a Tory and a Committee

Niles' *Principles and Acts of the Revolution*, 260–261.

I acknowledge to have wrote a piece, and did not sign it, since said to be an extract of a letter from Kent county, on Delaware, published in Humphreys' Ledger, No. 3. It was not dated from any place, and is some altered from the original. I folded it up and directed the same to J. F. and Sons. I had no intention to have it published; and further, I let them know the author thought best it should not be published; nor did I think they would. — I am sincerely sorry I ever wrote it, as also for its being published, and hope I shall be excused for this, my first breach in this way, and I intend it shall be the last.

R. H.

To the committee of correspondence for Kent county, on Delaware. May 2d, 1775.

SIR. — The president of the committee of correspondence, by and with the advice of such other of the members of that committee as he was able to collect and consult, this day laid before the committee of inspection for this county, your letter wherein you confess yourself to be the author of the Kentish letter (commonly so called) published in 3d No. of Humphreys' Ledger.

The committee took the same into consideration, and have unanimously resolved that it is unsatisfactory, and you are requested to attend the committee at their next meeting on Tuesday the 9th inst. at French Battell's, in Dover and render such satisfaction to the committee, as will enable them to clear the good people of this county from the aspersions of that letter, and justify them in the eyes of the public.

Signed by order of the committee.

To R. H.

GENTLEMEN. — With sorrow and contrition for my weakness and folly, I confess myself the author of the letter, from which an extract was published in the 3d No. of Humphreys' Ledger, said to be from Kent county, on Delaware; but at the same time to declare it was published without my consent, and not without some alterations.

I am now convinced that the political sentiments therein contained, were founded on the grossest error; more especially that malignant insinuation, that "if the king's standard were now erected, nine out of ten would repair to it," could not have been suggested, but from the deepest infatuation. True indeed it is, the people of this county have ever shewn a zealous attachment to his majesty's person and government, and whenever he raised his standard in a just cause, were ready to flock to it: but let the severe account I now render to an injured people, witness to the world, that none are more ready to oppose tyranny or to be first in the cause of liberty, than the inhabitants of Kent county.

Conscious that I can render no satisfaction adequate to the injury I have done my country, I can only beg the forgiveness of my countrymen, upon those principles of humanity, which may induce them to consider the frailty of human nature — and I do profess and promise, that I will never again oppose those laudable measures, necessarily adopted by my countrymen, for the preservation of American freedom: but will co-operate with them to the utmost of my abilities, in their virtuous struggle for liberty (so far as is consistent with my religious principles). R. H.

Resolved unanimously, that the committee do think the above recantation fully satisfactory.

THO'S. NIXON, Jr. Clerk.

May 9th, 1775.

143. An Oath of Allegiance to a New State, 1777

A facsimile from Scharf and Westcott's *History of Philadelphia*, I, 338.

I DO hereby CERTIFY, That Francis Hopkinson of the City of Philad. Esquire hath voluntarily taken and subscribed the Oath or Affirmation of Allegiance and Fidelity, as directed by an Act of General Assembly of Pennsylvania, passed the 13th day of June, A.D. 1777. Witness my hand and seal, the first day of July A.D. 1777.

(L.S.)

PRINTED BY JOHN DUNLAP.

144. A Loyalist's Suggestion of the Danger to American Liberty in the French Alliance, 1779

Tyler's *Literary History of the Revolution*, II, 75–76. The extracts come from a keen pamphlet by a Tory, with the style of a "diary" of the year 1789 — ten years later than the publication, to intimate what would then be the condition in America under French rule.

Boston, November 10, 1789. — His Excellency, Count Tyran, has this day published, by authority from his majesty, a proclamation for the suppresion of heresy and establishment of the inquisition in this town, which has already begun its functions in many other places of the continent under his majesty's dominion.

The use of the Bible in the vulgar tongue is strictly prohibited, on pain of being punished by discretion of the inquisition.

November 11. — The Catholic religion is not only outwardly professed, but has made the utmost progress among all ranks of people here, owing, in a great measure, to the unwearied labors of the Dominican and Franciscan friars, who omit no opportunity of scattering the seeds of religion, and converting the wives and daughters of heretics. We hear that the building formerly called the Old South Meeting, is fitting up for a cathedral, and that several other old meeting-houses are soon to be repaired for convents.

November 12. — This day being Sunday, the famous Samuel Adams read his recantation of heresy, after which he was present at mass, and we hear he will soon receive priest's orders to qualify him for a member of the American Sorbonne. . . .

The king has been pleased to order that five thousand of the inhabitants of Massachusetts Bay should be drafted to supply his garrisons in the West Indies; the officers for them are already arrived from France.

* * * * * * *

New York, November 15. — The edict for prohibiting the use of the English language, and establishing that of the French in all law proceedings, will take place on the 20th instant. At the same time, the ordinance for abolishing trials by juries, and introducing the imperial law, will begin to take effect. . . .

November 17. — A criminal of importance, who has been long imprisoned in the New Bastille, was this day privately beheaded. He commanded the American forces against Great Britain for a considerable time, but was confined by order of the government on suspicion of possessing a dangerous influence in a country newly conquered, and not thoroughly settled.[1] . . .

The king has been pleased to parcel out a great part of the lands in America to noblemen of distinction, who will grant them again to the peasantry upon leases at will, with the reservation of proper rents and services.

His majesty has been graciously pleased to order that none of the natives of America shall keep any firearms in their possession, upon pain of being sentenced to the galleys. . . .

November 22. — We hear from Williamsburg, in Virginia, that some commotions took place there when the new capitation tax was first executed. But the regiment of Bretagne, being stationed in that neighborhood, speedily suppressed them by firing upon the populace, and killing fifty on the spot. It is hoped that this example will prevent any future insurrection in that part of the country.

November 23. — His majesty has directed his viceroy to send five hundred sons of the principal inhabitants of America, to be educated in France, where the utmost care will be taken to imbue them with a regard for the Catholic faith, and a due sense of subordination to government.

145. How the Revolution set free Social Forces

David Ramsey's *History of the American Revolution* (1789), II, 315 ff. Dr. Ramsey was a citizen of South Carolina.

When the war began, the Americans were a mass of hus-

---

[1] The student will see that Washington is here designated.

bandmen, merchants, mechanics, and fishermen; but the necessities of the country gave a *spring* to the active powers of the inhabitants, and set them on thinking, speaking, and acting, in a line far beyond that to which they had been accustomed. The difference between nations is not so much owing to nature, as to education and circumstances. While the Americans were guided by the leading strings of the mother country, they had no scope nor encouragement for exertion. All the departments of government were established and executed *for* them, but not *by* them. In the years 1775 and 1776, the country, being suddenly thrown into a situation that needed the abilities of all its sons, these generally took their places, each according to the bent of his inclination. As they severally pursued their objects with ardor, *a vast expansion of the human mind speedily followed*. This displayed itself in a variety of ways. It was found that the talents for great stations did not differ in kind, but only in degree, from those which were necessary for the proper discharge of the ordinary business of civil society. . . .

E. CONFEDERATION AND CONSTITUTION

XXIV. THE ARTICLES OF CONFEDERATION

146. Debates in the Continental Congress on the Articles of Confederation

John Adams (*Works*, II, 492–502) preserved fairly full notes upon part of the discussion on the Articles. The parts dealing with western lands, with basis of taxation, and with the equality of the States in Congress are reproduced here. The form is rather fragmentary; and, in some cases, allusions are made which it would take too long to explain here. But the student can at least get the general drift and the alignment of the States on the opposing sides.

In Committee of the Whole

1776. July 25. Article 14 of the confederation. Terms in this Article equivocal and indefinite.[1]

Jefferson. The limits of the Southern Colonies are fixed. Moves an amendment, that all purchases of lands, not within the boundaries of any Colony, shall be made by Congress of the Indians in a great Council.

Sherman seconds the motion.

Chase [Maryland]. The intention of this Article is very obvious and plain. The Article appears to me to be right and the amendment wrong. It is the intention of some gentlemen to limit the boundaries of particular States. No Colony has a right to go to the South Sea; they never had; they can't have. It would not be safe to the rest. It would be destructive to her sisters and to herself.

---

[1] The draft then read: "No purchases of lands hereafter to be made of the Indians, by Congress or private persons, before the limits of the Colonies are ascertained, to be valid." The purpose was to prevent Virginia and other large States from selling their western lands for their private profit. This was part of the "Small-State" plan, and was not adopted.

ARTICLE 15. *Jefferson.* What are reasonable limits? What security have we, that the Congress will not curtail the present settlements of the States? I have no doubt that the Colonies will limit themselves.

Wilson. Every gentleman has heard much of claims to the South Sea. They are extravagant. The grants were made upon mistakes. They were ignorant of the Geography. They thought the South Sea within one hundred miles of the Atlantic Ocean. It was not conceived that they extended three thousand miles. Lord Camden considers the claims to the South Sea, as what never can be reduced to practice. Pennsylvania has no right to interfere in those claims, but she has a right to say, that she will not confederate unless those claims are cut off. I wish the Colonies themselves would cut off those claims. . . .

July 30. Article 17. "In determining questions, each Colony shall have one vote."

Dr. Franklin. Let the smaller Colonies give equal money and men, and then have an equal vote. But if they have an equal vote without bearing equal burthens, a confederation upon such iniquitous principles will never last long.

Dr. Witherspoon [New Jersey]. We all agree that there must and shall be a confederation for this war. . . . The greatest danger we have, is of disunion among ourselves. Is it not plausible that the small States will be oppressed by the great ones? The Spartans and the Helotes. The Romans and their dependents. Every Colony is a distinct person. . . .

Clark. We must apply for pardons if we don't confederate.

Wilson. We should settle upon some plan of representation.

* * * * * * *

Wilson. If the war continues two years, each soul will have forty dollars to pay of the public debt. It will be the greatest encouragement to continue slave-keeping and to increase it, that can be, to exempt them from the numbers which are to vote and pay. Slaves are taxables in the Southern

Colonies. It will be partial and unequal. Some Colonies have as many black as white; these will not pay more than half what they ought.[1] Slaves prevent freemen from cultivating a country. It is attended with many inconveniences.

Lynch [South Carolina]. If it is debated, whether their slaves are their property, there is an end of the confederation. Our slaves being our property, why should they be taxed more than the land, sheep, cattle, horses, etc.?

Freemen cannot be got to work in our Colonies; it is not in the ability or inclination of freemen to do the work that the negroes do. Carolina has taxed their negroes; so have other Colonies their lands.

Dr. Franklin. Slaves rather weaken than strengthen the State, and there is therefore some difference between them and sheep; sheep will never make any insurrections.

Rutledge. I shall be happy to get rid of the idea of slavery. The slaves do not signify property; the old and young cannot work. The property of some Colonies is to be taxed, in others, not. The Eastern Colonies will become the carriers for the Southern; they will obtain wealth for which they will not be taxed.

August 1. *Hooper.* North Carolina is a striking exception to the general rule that was laid down yesterday, that the riches of a country are in proportion to the numbers of inhabitants. A gentleman of three or four hundred negroes don't raise more corn than feeds them. A laborer can't be hired for less than twenty-four pounds a year in Massachusetts Bay. The net profit of a negro is not more than five or six pounds per annum. I wish to see the day that slaves are not necessary. Whites and negroes cannot work together. Negroes are goods and chattels are property. A negro works under the impulse of fear, has no care of his master's interest.[2]

---

[1] The plan then was that the colonies should contribute money in proportion to their white population. This was afterward amended. See *Articles*.

[2] Mr. Chase's amendment (to count slaves in apportioning representatives in Congress) was lost. Seven States, New Hampshire, Massachusetts, Rhode

The Consideration of the Seventeenth Article resumed

Article 17. *Dr. Franklin* moves that votes should be in proportion to numbers. *Mr. Middleton* moves that the vote should be according to what they pay.

Sherman thinks we ought not to vote according to numbers. We are representatives of States, not individuals. States of Holland. The consent of every one is necessary. Three Colonies would govern the whole, but would not have a majority of strength to carry those votes into execution. **The vote should be taken two ways; call the Colonies, and call the individuals, and have a majority of both.**[1]

Dr. Rush. Abbé Raynal has attributed the ruin of the United Provinces [Netherlands] to three causes. The principal one is, that the consent of every State is necessary; the other, that the members are obliged to consult their constituents upon all occasions. We lose an equal representation; we represent the people. It will tend to keep up colonial distinctions. We are now a new nation. . . . If we vote by numbers, liberty will be always safe. Massachusetts is contiguous to two small Colonies, Rhode Island and New Hampshire; Pennsylvania is near New Jersey and Delaware; Virginia is between Maryland and North Carolina. . . . Montesquieu pronounces the confederation of Lycia the best that ever was made; the cities had different weights in the scale. . . . I would not have it understood that I am pleading the cause of Pennsylvania; when I entered that door, I considered myself a citizen of America.

* * * * * * *

G. Hopkins [Rhode Island]. A momentous question; many difficulties on each side; four larger, five lesser, four stand

---

Island, Connecticut, New York, New Jersey, and Pennsylvania voted against it. Delaware, Maryland, Virginia, North and South Carolina voted for it. Georgia was divided.

[1] A suggestion almost of a two-house Congress, similar to the "Connecticut Compromise" adopted for our present Constitution.

indifferent. Virginia, Massachusetts, Pennsylvania, Maryland, make more than half the people.

. . . It can't be expected that nine Colonies will give way to be governed by four. The safety of the whole depends upon the distinctions of Colonies.

Dr. Franklin. I hear many ingenious arguments to persuade us that an unequal representation is a very good thing. If we had been born and bred under an unequal representation, we might bear it; but to set out with an unequal representation is unreasonable. It is said the great Colonies will swallow up the less. Scotland said the same thing at the union.

* * * * * * *

August 2. "Limiting the bounds of States, which by charter, &c. extend to the South Sea."

Sherman thinks the bounds ought to be settled. A majority of States have no claim to the South Sea. Moves this amendment to be substituted in place of this clause, and also instead of the fifteenth article; — "No lands to be separated from any State, which are already settled, or become private property."

Chase [Maryland] denies that any Colony has a right to go to the South Sea.

Harrison [Virginia]. How came Maryland by its land, but by its charter? By its charter, Virginia owns to the South Sea. Gentlemen shall not pare away the Colony of Virginia. Rhode Island has more generosity than to wish the Massachusetts pared away. Delaware does not wish to pare away Pennsylvania.

Huntington. Admit there is danger from Virginia, does it follow that Congress has a right to limit her bounds? The consequence is, not to enter into confederation. . . .

Stone [Maryland] . . . Is it meant that Virginia shall sell these lands for their own emolument? All the Colonies have defended these lands against the King of Britain, and at the expense of all. Does Virginia intend to establish quit rents? . . .

Jefferson. I protest against the right of Congress to decide upon the right of Virginia. Virginia has released all claims to the land settled by Maryland, &c.

[This clause, as to limiting the western claims, was stricken out in committee. The subsequent history of the struggle is well known, terminating in the acts of cession of claims to the western territory. For details, cf. *American History and Government*, §§ 179–180.

Jefferson's Notes on this same debate (*Journals of Congress*, VI, 1104, — from a MS. of Jefferson's) contain the following additional item: "*John Adams* advocated voting in proportion to numbers. He said that we stand here as representatives of the people; that in some States the people are many, in others they are few . . . that the individuality of the colonies is a mere sound. . . . **It has been said we are independent individuals making a bargain together: the question is not what we are now, but what we ought to be when our bargain shall be made.** The Confederacy IS TO MAKE US ONE individual only; it is to form us, like separate parcels of metal, into one common mass. . . ."[1]]

147. Articles of Confederation.

November 15, 1777
March 2, 1781

Text from *Revised Statutes* of 1878. For history, cf. *American History and Government*, §§ 179, 186–188 ff. The editor has used black-faced type to indicate a few passages especially important for study.

The Articles were adopted by Congress, and recommended to the States, November 15, 1777. The delegates from the several States signed as follows: New Hampshire, Massachusetts Bay, Rhode Island and Providence Plantations, Connecticut, New York, Pennsylvania, Virginia, and South Carolina, July 9, 1778; North Carolina, July 21, 1778; Georgia, July 24, 1778; New Jersey, Nov. 26, 1778; Delaware, May 5, 1779; Maryland, March 1, 1781. Congress met under the Articles, March 2, 1781.

To all to whom these Presents shall come, we the undersigned Delegates of the States affixed to our Names send greeting

Whereas the Delegates of the United States of America in Congress assembled did on the fifteenth day of November in

---

[1] Did Adams then think that, *before* the new Articles should have been accepted, the states were constitutionally one nation or thirteen? Cf. *American History and Government*, § 187 and notes.

the year of our Lord One Thousand Seven Hundred and Seventy-seven, and in the Second Year of the Independence of America, agree to certain articles of Confederation and perpetual Union between the States of Newhampshire, Massachusetts-bay, Rhodeisland and Providence Plantations, Connecticut, New York, New Jersey, Pennsylvania, Delaware, Maryland, Virginia, North-Carolina, South-Carolina and Georgia in the Words following, viz.

Articles of Confederation and perpetual Union between the States of Newhamshire, Massachusetts-bay, Rhodeisland and Providence Plantations, Connecticut, New York, New Jersey, Pennsylvania, Delaware, Maryland, Virginia, North Carolina, South Carolina, and Georgia.

ARTICLE I. — The stile of this Confederacy shall be, "The United States of America."

Art. II. — *Each State retains its sovereignty, freedom, and independence, and every power, jurisdiction, and right, which is not by this Confederation expressly delegated to the United States, in Congress assembled.*

Art. III. — The said States hereby severally enter into a *firm league of friendship with each other,* for their common defence, the security of their liberties, and their mutual and general welfare, binding themselves to assist each other against all force offered to, or attacks made upon them, or any of them, on account of religion, sovereignty, trade, or any other pretence whatever.

Art. IV. — The better to secure and perpetuate mutual friendship and intercourse among the people of the States in this Union, *the free inhabitants of each of these states,* paupers, vagabonds, and fugitives from justice excepted, *shall be entitled to all privileges and immunities of free citizens in the several States;* and the people of each State shall have free ingress and egress to and from any other State, and shall enjoy therein all the privileges of trade and commerce subject to the same duties, impositions, and restrictions as the inhabitants thereof respectively; provided that such restrictions shall not extend so far as to prevent the removal of property imported into any State to any other State of which the owner is an inhabitant: provided also that no imposition, duties, or restriction shall be laid by any State on the property of the United States, or either of them.

If any person guilty of, or charged with treason, felony, or other high misdemeanor in any State, shall flee from justice, and be found in any of the United States, he shall upon demand of the Governor or Executive power of the State from which he fled, be delivered up and removed to the State having jurisdiction of his offence.

Full faith and credit shall be given in each of these States to the records, acts, and judicial proceedings of the courts and magistrates of every other State.

ARTICLE V. — For the more convenient management of the general interest of the United States, delegates shall be annually appointed **in such manner as the legislature of each State shall direct,** to meet in Congress on the first Monday in November, in every year, **with a power reserved to each State, to recall its delegates,** or any of them, at any time within the year, and to send others in their stead, for the remainder of the year.

No State shall be represented in Congress by less than two, nor by more than seven members; and no person shall be capable of being a delegate for more than three years in any term of six years; nor shall any person, being a delegate, be capable of holding any office under the United States, for which he, or another for his benefit, receives any salary, fees or emolument of any kind.

Each State shall maintain its own delegates in a meeting of the States, and while they act as members of the committee of the States.

In determining questions in the United States, in Congress assembled, each State shall have one vote.

Freedom of speech and debate in Congress shall not be impeached or questioned in any court, or place out of Congress, and the members of Congress shall be protected in their persons from arrests and im-

prisonments, during the time of their going to and from, and attendance on Congress, except for treason, felony, or breach of the peace.

Article VI. No State without the consent of the United States in Congress assembled, shall send any embassy to, or receive any embassy from, or enter into any conference, agreement, alliance or treaty with any king, prince or state; nor shall any person holding any office of profit or trust under the United States, or any of them, accept of any present, emolument, office or title of any kind whatever from any king, prince or foreign state; nor shall the United States in Congress assembled, or any of them, grant any title of nobility.

No two or more States shall enter into any treaty, confederation or alliance whatever between them, without the consent of the United States in Congress assembled, specifying accurately the purposes for which the same is to be entered into, and how long it shall continue.

No state shall lay any imposts or duties, which may interfere with any stipulations in treaties entered into by the United States, in Congress assembled, with any king, prince, or state, in pursuance of any treaties already proposed by Congress to the courts of France and Spain.

No vessel of war shall be kept up in time of peace by any State, except such number only as shall be deemed necessary by the United States, in Congress assembled, for the defence of such State or its trade, nor shall any body of forces be kept up by any State in time of peace, except such number only as, in the judgment of the United States, in Congress assembled, shall be deemed requisite to garrison the forts necessary for the defence of such State; but every State shall always keep up a well-regulated and disciplined militia, sufficiently armed and accoutred, and shall provide and constantly have ready for use in public stores a due number of field-pieces and tents, and a proper quantity of arms, ammunition, and camp equipage.

No State shall engage in any war without the consent of the United States, in Congress assembled, unless such State be actually invaded by enemies, or shall have received certain advice of a resolution being formed by some nation of Indians to invade such State, and the danger is so imminent as not to admit of a delay till the United States, in Congress assembled, can be consulted; nor shall any State grant commissions to any ships or vessels of war, nor letters of marque or reprisal, except it be after a declaration of war by the United States, in Congress assembled, and then only against the kingdom or state, and the subjects thereof, against which war has been so declared, and under such regulations as shall be established by the United States, in Congress assembled, unless such State be infested by pirates, in which case vessels of war may be fitted out for that occasion, and kept so long as the danger shall continue, or until the United States, in Congress assembled, shall determine otherwise.

ART. VII. — When land forces are raised by any State for the common defence, all officers of or under the rank of Colonel shall be appointed by the Legislature of each State respectively by whom such forces shall be raised, or in such manner as such State shall direct, and all vacancies shall be filled up by the States which first made the appointment.

ART. VIII. — All charges of war, and all other expenses that shall be incurred for the common defence or federal welfare, and allowed by the United States in Congress assembled, shall be defrayed out of a common treasury, which shall be supplied by the several States, in proportion to the value of all land within each State, granted to or surveyed for any person, as such land and the buildings and improvements thereon shall be estimated according to such mode as the United States in Congress assembled, shall from time to time direct and appoint.

The taxes for paying that proportion shall be laid and levied by the authority and direction of the Legislatures of the several States within the time agreed upon by the United States in Congress assembled.

ARTICLE IX.[1] — The United States in Congress assembled, shall have the sole and exclusive right and power of determining on peace and war, except in the cases mentioned in the

---

[1] Summarize briefly the enumeration of powers in this Article.

sixth article — of sending and receiving ambassadors — entering into treaties and alliances, provided that no treaty of commerce shall be made whereby the legislative power of the respective States shall be restrained from imposing such imposts and duties on foreigners, as their own people are subjected to, or from prohibiting the exportation or importation of any species of goods or commodities whatsoever — of establishing rules for deciding in all cases, what captures on land or water shall be legal, and in what manner prizes taken by land or naval forces in the service of the United States shall be divided or appropriated — of granting letters of marque and reprisal in times of peace — appointing courts for the trial of piracies and felonies committed on the high seas and establishing courts for receiving and determining finally appeals in all cases of captures, provided that no member of Congress shall be appointed a judge of any of the said courts.

The United States in Congress assembled shall also be the last resort on appeal in all disputes and differences now subsisting or that hereafter may arise between two or more States concerning boundary, jurisdiction or any other cause whatever; which authority shall always be exercised in the manner following. [A long passage as to method of constituting commissioners to decide such contests.]

The United States in Congress assembled shall also have the sole and exclusive right and power of regulating the alloy and value of coin struck by their own authority, or by that of the respective States — fixing the standard of weights and measures throughout the United States — regulating the trade and managing all affairs with the Indians, not members of any of the States, provided that the legislative right of any State within its own limits be not infringed or violated — establishing and regulating post-offices from one State to another, throughout all the United States, and exacting such postage on the papers passing thro' the same as may be requisite to defray the expenses of the said office — appointing all officers of the land forces, in the service of the United States, excepting regimental officers — appointing all the officers of the naval forces, and commissioning all officers whatever in the service of the United States — making rules for the government and regulation of the said land and naval forces, and directing their operations.

The United States in Congress assembled shall have authority to appoint a committee, to sit in the recess of Congress, to be denominated "a Committee of the States," and to consist of one delegate from each State; and to appoint such other committees and civil officers as may be necessary for managing the general affairs of the United States under their direction — to appoint one of their number to preside, provided that no person be allowed to serve in the office of president more than one year in any term of three years; to ascertain the necessary sums of money to be raised for the service of the United States, and to appropriate and apply the same for defraying the public expenses — to borrow money, or emit bills on the credit of the United States, transmitting every half year to the respective States an account of the sums of money so borrowed or emitted, — to build and equip a navy — to agree upon the number of land forces, and to make requisitions from each State for its quota, in proportion to the number of white inhabitants in such State; **which requisition shall be binding;** and thereupon the Legislature of each State shall appoint the regimental officers, raise the men, and clothe, arm, and equip them in a soldier-like manner, at the expense of the United States; and the officers and men so clothed, armed, and equipped shall march to the place appointed, and within the time agreed on by the United States, in Congress assembled; but if the United States, in Congress assembled, shall, on consideration of circumstances, judge proper that any State should not raise men, or should raise a smaller number than its quota, and that any other State should raise a greater number of men than the quota thereof, such extra number shall be raised, officered, clothed, armed, and equipped in the same manner as the quota of such State, unless the Legislature of such State shall judge that such extra number cannot be safely spared out of the same, in which case they shall raise, officer, clothe, arm, and equip as many of such extra number as they judge can be safely spared, and the officers and men so clothed, armed, and equipped shall march to the place appointed, and within the time agreed on by the United States, in Congress assembled.

The United States, in Congress assembled, shall never engage in a war, nor grant letters of marque and reprisal in time of peace, nor enter into any treaties or alliances, nor coin money, nor regulate the value thereof, nor ascertain the sums and expenses necessary for the defence and welfare of the United States, or any of them, nor emit bills, nor borrow money on the credit of the United States, nor appropriate money, nor agree upon the number of vessels of war to be built or purchased, or the number of land or sea forces to be raised, nor appoint a commander-in-chief of the army or navy, **unless nine States assent to the same;** nor shall a question on any other point, except for adjourning from day to day, be determined, unless by the votes of a majority of the United States, in Congress assembled.

The Congress of the United States shall have power to adjourn to any time within the year, and to any place within the United States, so that no period of adjournment be for a longer duration than the space of six months, and shall publish the journal of their proceedings monthly, except such parts thereof relating to treaties, alliances, or military operations as in their judgment require secrecy; and the yeas and nays of the delegates of each State, on any question shall be entered on the journal, when it is desired by any delegate; and the delegates of a State, or any of them, at his or their request shall be furnished with a transcript of the said journal, except such parts as are above excepted, to lay before the Legislatures of several States.

ARTICLE X. — The committee of the States, or any nine of them, shall be authorized to execute, in the recess of Congress, such of the powers of Congress as the United States in Congress assembled, by the consent of nine States, shall from time to time think expedient to vest them with; provided that no power be delegated to the said committee, for the exercise of which, by the articles of confederation, the voice of nine States in the Congress of the United States assembled is requisite.

Article XI. — Canada acceding to this confederation, and joining in the measures of the United States, shall be admitted into, and entitled to all the advantages of this Union : but no other colony shall be admitted into the same, unless such admission be agreed to by nine States.

Article XII. — All bills of credit emitted, monies borrowed and debts contracted by, or under the authority of Congress, before the assembling of the United States, in pursuance of the present confederation, shall be deemed and considered as a charge against the United States, for payment and satisfaction whereof the said United States, and the public faith are hereby solemnly pledged.

Article XIII. — Every State shall abide by the determinations of the United States in Congress assembled, on all questions which by this confederation are submitted to them. And the articles of this confederation shall be inviolably observed by every State, and the Union shall be perpetual ; nor shall any alteration at any time hereafter be made in any of them ; unless such alteration be agreed to in a Congress of the United States, and be afterwards confirmed by the Legislatures of every State.

And whereas it hath pleased the Great Governor of the World to incline the hearts of the Legislatures we respectively represent in Congress, to approve of, and to authorize us to ratify the said **articles of confederation and perpetual union**. Know ye that we the undersigned delegates, by virtue of the power and authority to us given for that purpose, do by these presents, in the name and in behalf of our respective constituents, fully and entirely ratify and confirm each and every of the said articles of confederation and **perpetual union**, and all and singular the matters and things therein contained.

And we do further solemnly plight and engage the faith of our respective constituents, that they shall abide by the determinations of the United States, in Congress assembled, on all questions which by the said Confederation are submitted to them; and that the Articles thereof shall be inviolably observed by the States we respectively represent, and that the Union shall be perpetual.

> In witness whereof we have hereunto set our hands in Congress. Done at Philadelphia in the State of Pennsylvania the ninth day of July in the year of our Lord one thousand seven hundred and seventy-eight, and in the third year of the independence of America.

[The signatures follow. Cf. introduction, on p. 475, for the dates.]

XXV. THE NATIONAL DOMAIN

148. Desire for Statehood; Self-confidence of the West

Early in 1784, North Carolina ceded her western territory (afterward Tennessee) to Congress, giving that body two years in which to accept. The Westerners, already bitterly dissatisfied, now complained loudly that the mother State had cast them off; they would not wait two years, in anarchy, for possible action by the dilatory Congress; they would take their fate at once into their own hands. Accordingly, the three counties of eastern Tennessee (the outgrowth of the Watauga settlement, numbering now some 10,000 souls) established themselves for a time as the State of Frankland ("Land of the Freemen").

The militia had been organized by territorial units, each "company" from one group of hamlets, or "stations." Each "company" now chose delegates to a central convention. This "preliminary" convention recommended the people to choose another "constitutional convention,"[1] with full powers to set up a government. August 23, 1784, this second convention, composed of forty delegates with John Sevier as president, resolved on immediate statehood, and put forth an interesting address to justify that action. The following passage from that address illustrates the wild hopes of the West as to immediate development. (Cf. also *American History and Government*, §§ 173-175.)

"If we should be so happy as to have a separate government, vast numbers from different quarters, with a little encouragement from the public, would fill up our frontier; which would strengthen us, improve agriculture, perfect manufactures, encourage literature and everything truly laudable. The seat of government being among ourselves would evidently tend, not only to keep a circulating medium in gold and silver among us,[2] but would draw it from many individuals living in

---

[1] These quoted phrases are the modern terms, of course. The Franklanders called both meetings merely conventions.

[2] This was a matter of supreme moment. The first legislature of the new State found it necessary to fix a "currency in kind," as legal-tender, in which all business transactions should be carried on, and all government

other States, who claim large quantities of land that would lie within the bounds of the new State."

[A constitution was adopted by yet a third convention, and government instituted under it. North Carolina, however, repealed her cession before Congress had accepted it, and reasserted her authority over "Frankland," not without long and bitter conflict.]

149. Organization by Congress

a. *A Plan for a Temporary Government of the Western Territory. April 23, 1784*

Journals of Congress (1801 edition), IX, 109–110.

This act is usually known as Jefferson's Territorial Ordinance of 1784. For history, cf. *American History and Government*, § 181. It is given here mainly for comparison with the Ordinance of 1787 (No. 149*b*), and, *by most students, it can be read to best advantage after a study of that document.*

"Resolved that so much of the territory **ceded or to be ceded** by individual states to the United States [the rest of this paragraph provides for division into two tiers of states, bounded by alternate parallels of latitude, with some rather obscure provisions for fragmentary pieces of territory on the north and east, cf. *American History and Government*, § 181.]

"That the settlers on any territory so purchased, and offered for sale, shall, either on their own petition or order of Congress, receive authority from them, with appointments of time and place, for their free males of full age within the limits of their state to meet together, for the purpose of establishing a temporary government, to adopt the constitution and laws of any one of the original states; so that such laws nevertheless shall be subject to alteration by their ordinary legislature; and to erect, subject to a like alteration, counties, townships, or other divisions, for the election of members for their legislature.

"That when any such state shall have acquired 20,000 free inhabitants, on giving due proof thereof to Congress, they shall receive from them authority, with appointments of time and place, to call a convention of

---

salaries paid. A pound of sugar was to pass for one shilling; a fox or raccoon skin for two shillings; a gallon of peach brandy for three shillings; and an otter or a deer skin for six shillings. Easterners, even Benjamin Franklin, indulged in much laughter at this "money which could not be counterfeited," forgetting how their own fathers had used similar currency.

representatives to establish a permanent constitution and government for themselves. Provided that both the temporary and permanent governments be establisted on these principles as their basis :

"1st. That they shall for ever remain a part of this confederacy of the United States of America.

"2d. That they shall be subject to the articles of confederation in all those cases in which the original states shall be so subject, and to all the acts and ordinances of the United States in Congress assembled, conformable thereto.

"3d. That they in no case shall interfere with the primary disposal of the soil by the United States in Congress assembled, nor with the ordinances and regulations which Congress may find necessary, for securing the title in such soil to the *bona fide* purchasers.

"4th. That they shall be subject to pay a part of the federal debts contracted or to be contracted, to be apportioned on them by Congress, according to the same common rule and measure by which apportionments thereof shall be made on the other states.

"5th. That no tax shall be imposed on lands, the property of the United States.

"6th. That their respective governments shall be republican.

"7th. That the lands of non-resident proprietors shall, in no case, be taxed higher than those of residents within any new state, before the admission thereof to a vote by its delegates in Congress.

"That whensoever any of the said states shall have, of free inhabitants, as many as shall then be in any one the least numerous of the thirteen original states, such state shall be admitted by its delegates into the Congress of the United States, on an equal footing with the said original states; provided the consent of so many states in Congress is first obtained as may at the time be competent to such admission. (And in order to adapt the said articles of confederation to the state of Congress when its numbers shall be thus increased, it shall be proposed to the legislatures of the states, originally parties thereto, to require the assent of two-thirds of the United States in Congress assembled, in all those cases wherein by the said articles, the assent of nine states is now required, which being agreed to by them, shall be binding on the new states.) Until such admission by their delegates into Congress, any of the said states after the establishment of their temporary government shall have authority to keep a member in Congress, with a right of debating but not of voting.

"That measures not inconsistent with the principles of the confederation, and necessary for the preservation of peace and good order among the settlers in any of the said new States, until they shall assume a temporary government as aforesaid, may from time to time, be taken by the United States in Congress assembled.[1]

"That the preceding articles shall be formed into a charter of compact . . . [provision for promulgation] and shall stand as fundamental constitutions between the thirteen original States and each of the several States now newly described, unalterable . . . but by the joint consent of the United States in Congress assembled and of the particular State within which such alteration is proposed to be made."

b. *The Northwest Ordinance* (*July 13, 1787*)

Journals of Congress (1801 edition), XII, 58 ff.

For history of this document, cf. *American History and Government*, § 182. The documents relating to the *acquisition* of a "Public Domain" are quoted so extensively in that work that they are omitted in this collection. Cf., however, No. 146 above for discussions in Congress.

An Ordinance for the government of the territory of the United States Northwest of the River Ohio

Be it ordained by the United States in Congress Assembled that the said territory for the purposes of temporary government be one district, subject however to be divided into two districts as future circumstances may in the opinion of Congress make it expedient.

Be it ordained by the authority aforesaid, that the estates both of resident and non resident proprietors in the said territory dying intestate shall descend to and be distributed among their children and the descendants of a deceased child **in equal parts;** the descendants of a deceased child or grandchild to take the share of their deceased parent in equal parts among them; and where there shall be no children or descendants then in equal parts to the next of kin in equal degree; and among collaterals the children of a deceased brother or sister of the intestate shall

---

[1] This paragraph was added by amendment (proposed by Mr. Gerry) at the last moment. A more stringent proposition was lost, — viz.: "That *until* such time as the settlers shall have adopted the constitution and laws of some one of the original states . . . the settlers shall be ruled by magistrates to be appointed by the United States in Congress assembled, and under such laws and regulations as the United States, in Congress assembled, shall direct."

have in equal parts among them their deceased parent's share and there shall in no case be a distinction between kindred of the whole and half blood; saving in all cases to the widow of the intestate her third part of the real estate for life, and one third part of the personal estate: and this law relative to descents and dower shall remain in full force until altered by the legislature of the district. And until the governor and judges shall adopt laws as herein after mentioned, estates in the said territory may be devised or bequeathed by wills in writing signed and sealed by him or her in whom the estate may be, being of full age, and attested by three witnesses, and real estates may be conveyed by lease and release or bargain and sale, signed, sealed and delivered by the person being of full age in whom the estate may be, and attested by two witnesses, provided such wills be duly proved and such conveyances be acknowledged or the excution there of duly proved, and be recorded within one year after proper magistrates, courts and registers shall be appointed for that purpose; and personal property may be transferred by delivery saving however to the french and canadian inhabitants and other settlers of the Kaskaskies, Saint Vincents and the neighbouring villages, who have hereto fore professed themselves citizens of Virginia, their laws and customs now in force among them, relative to the descent and conveyance of property.

Be it ordained by the authority aforesaid, that there shall be appointed, from time to time, by Congress, a governor, whose commission shall continue in force for the term of three years, unless sooner revoked by Congress; he shall reside in the district, and have a freehold estate therein in 1000 acres of land, while in the exercise of his office.

There shall be appointed, from time to time, by Congress, a secretary, whose commission shall continue in force for four years unless sooner revoked; he shall reside in the district, and have a freehold estate therein in 500 acres of land, while in the exercise of his office; it shall be his duty to keep and preserve the acts and laws passed by the legislature, and the public records of the district, and the proceedings of the governor in his Executive department; and transmit authentic copies of such acts and proceedings, every six months, to the Secretary of Congress: There shall also be appointed a court to consist of three judges, any two of whom to form a court, who shall have a common law jurisdiction, and reside in the district, and have each therein a freehold estate in 500 acres of land while in the exercise of their offices; and their commissions shall continue in force during good behavior.

The governor and judges, or a majority of them, shall adopt and publish in the district such laws of the original States, criminal and civil, as may be necessary and best suited to the circumstances of the district, and report them to Congress from time to time: which laws shall be in force in the district until the organization of the General Assembly therein, unless disapproved of by Congress; but, afterwards, the legislature shall have authority to alter them as they shall think fit.

The governor, for the time being, shall be commander-in-chief of the militia, appoint and commission all officers in the same below the rank of general officers; all general officers shall be appointed and commissioned by Congress.

Previous to the organization of the General Assembly, the governor shall appoint such magistrates and other civil officers, in each county or township, as he shall find necessary for the preservation of the peace and good order in the same. After the General Assembly shall be organized, the powers and duties of the magistrates and other civil officers shall be regulated and defined by the said Assembly; but all . . . civil officers not herein otherwise directed shall during the continuance of this temporary government be appointed by the governor.

For the prevention of crimes and injuries the laws to be adopted or made shall have force in all parts of the district; and for the execution of process criminal and civil, the governor shall make proper divisions thereof, and he shall proceed from time to time as circumstances may require to lay out the parts of the District in which the indian titles shall have been extinguished into counties and townships subject however to such alterations as may thereafter be made by the legislature.

So soon as there shall be five thousand free male inhabitants of full age in the district, upon giving proof thereof to the governor, they shall receive authority with time and place to elect representatives from their counties or townships to represent them in the general Assembly, provided that for every five hundred free male inhabitants there shall be one representative; and so on progressively with the number of free male inhabitants shall the right of representation encrease until the number of representatives shall amount to twenty five, after which the number and proportion of representatives shall be regulated by the legislature; provided that no person be eligible or qualified to act as a representative unless he shall have been a citizen of one of the United States three years and be a resident in the district or unless he shall have resided in the district three years, and in either case shall likewise hold in his own right in fee simple two hundred acres of land within the same; provided also that a freehold in fifty acres of land in the district having been a citizen of one of the states and being resident in the district, or the like freehold and two years residence in the district shall be necessary to qualify a man as an elector of a representative.

The representatives thus elected shall serve for the term of two years, and in case of the death of a representative or removal from office, the governor shall issue a writ to the county or township for which he was a member, to elect another in his stead to serve for the residue of the term.

The general Assembly or legislature shall consist of the governor, legislative council and a house of representatives. The legislative council shall consist of five members to continue in Office five years unless sooner removed by Congress, any three of whom to be a quorum and the members of the council shall be nominated and appointed in the following manner, to wit: As soon as representatives shall be elected, the governor shall appoint a time and place for them to meet together; and, when met, they shall nominate ten persons, residents in the district, and each possessed of a freehold in 500 acres of land, and return their names to Congress; five of whom Congress shall appoint and commission to serve as aforesaid; and, whenever a vacancy shall happen in the council, by death or removal from office, the house of representatives shall nominate two persons, qualified as aforesaid, for each vacancy, and return their names to Congress; one of whom Congress shall appoint and commission for the residue of the term. And every five years, four months at least before the expiration of the time of service of the members of council, the said house shall nominate ten persons, qualified as aforesaid, and return their names to Congress; five of whom Congress shall appoint and commission to serve as members of the council five years, unless sooner removed. And the governor, legislative council, and house of representatives, shall have authority to make laws in all cases, for the good government of the district, not repugnant to the principles and articles in this ordinance established and declared. And all bills, having passed by a majority in the house, and by a majority in the council, shall be referred to the governor for his assent; but no bill, or legislative act whatever, shall be of any force without his assent. The governor shall have power to convene, prorogue, and dissolve the General Assembly, when, in his opinion, it shall be expedient.

The governor, judges, legislative council, secretary, and such other officers as Congress shall appoint in the district, shall take an oath or affirmation of fidelity and of office; the governor before the President of Congress, and all other officers before the governor. As soon as a legislature shall be formed in the district, the council and house assembled in one room, shall have authority, by joint ballot, to elect a delegate to Congress, who shall have a seat in Congress, with a right of debating but not of voting during this temporary government.

And, for extending the fundamental principles of civil and religious liberty, which form the basis whereon these republics, their laws and constitutions are erected; to fix and establish those principles as the basis of all laws, constitutions, and governments, which forever hereafter shall be formed in the said territory: to provide also for the establishment of States, and permanent Government therein, and for their admission to a Share in the federal Councils on an equal footing with the original States, at as early periods as may be consistent with the general interest —

It is hereby Ordained and declared by the authority aforesaid, That the following Articles shall be considered as Articles of compact between the Original States and the People and States in the said territory, and forever remain unalterable, unless by common consent, *to wit,*

Article the First. No Person demeaning himself in a peaceable and orderly manner shall ever be molested on account of his mode of worship or religious sentiments in the said territory —

Article the Second. The Inhabitants of the said territory shall always be entitled to the benefits of the writ of Habeas Corpus, and of the trial by jury; of a proportionate representation of the people in the legislature, and of judicial proceedings according to the course of the common law; all Persons shall be bailable unless for capital offences, where the proof shall be evident, or the presumption great; all fines shall be moderate, and no cruel or unusual punishments shall be inflicted; no man shall be deprived of his liberty or property but by the judgment of his Peers, or the law of the land; and should the Public exigencies make it necessary for the common preservation to take any person's property, or to demand his particular Services, full compensation shall be made for the same, — and in the just preservation of rights and property it is understood and declared, that no law ought ever to be made, or have force in the said territory, that shall in any manner whatever interfere with or affect private Contracts or engagements, bona fide and without fraud previously formed.

Article the Third. Religion, Morality and knowledge being necessary to good Government and the happiness of mankind, Schools and the means of education shall forever be encouraged. The utmost good faith shall always be observed towards the Indians; their lands and property shall never be taken from them without their consent; and in their property, rights and liberty, they never shall be invaded or disturbed, unless in just and lawful wars authorized by Congress; but laws founded in justice and humanity shall from time to time be made, for preventing wrongs being done to them, and for preserving peace and friendship with them —

Article the Fourth. The said Territory, and the States which may be formed therein, shall forever remain a part of this Confederacy . . . subject to the Articles of Confederation, and to such alterations therein as shall be constitutionally made; and to all the acts and ordinances of the United States in Congress assembled, comfortable thereto. The inhabitants and settlers in the said territory shall be subject to pay a part of the federal debts contracted or to be contracted, and a proportional part of the expenses of government, to be apportioned on them by Congress according to the same common rule and measure by which apportionments thereof shall be made on the other States; and the taxes, for paying their proportion, shall be laid and levied by the authority and direction of the legislatures of the district or districts, or new States, as in the original States within the time agreed upon by the United States in Congress assembled. The legislatures of those districts or new States shall never interfere with the primary disposal of the soil by the United States in Congress assembled, nor with any regulations Congress may find necessary for securing the title in such soil to the *bona fide* purchasers. No tax shall be imposed on lands the property of the United States; and, in no case, shall non-resident proprietors be taxed higher than residents. The navigable waters leading into the Mississippi and St. Lawrence, and the carrying places between the same, shall be common highways, and forever free, as well to the inhabitants of the said territory as to the citizens of the United States, and those of any other States that may be admitted into the Confederacy, without any tax, impost, or duty, therefor.

Article the Fifth. There shall be formed in the said territory, not less than three nor more than five States; and the boundaries of the States, as soon as Virginia shall alter her act of cession, and consent to the same, shall become fixed and established as follows, to wit: The Western State in the said territory, shall be bounded by the Mississippi, the Ohio, and Wabash rivers; a direct line drawn from the Wabash and Post St. Vincent's, due North, to the territorial line between the United States and Canada; and, by the said territorial line, to the Lake of the Woods and Mississippi. The middle State shall be bounded by the said direct line, the Wabash from Post Vincent's, to the Ohio; by the Ohio, by a direct line, drawn due North from the mouth of the Great Miami, to the said territorial line, and by the said territorial line. The Eastern State shall be bounded by the last mentioned direct line, the Ohio, Pennsylvania, and the said territorial line: *Provided however*, and it is further understood and declared, that the boundaries of these three States shall be subject so far to be altered, that, if Congress shall hereafter find it expedient, they shall have authority to form one or two States in that part of the said territory which lies North of an East and West line drawn through the Southerly bend or extreme of lake Michigan. And, whenever any of the said States shall have 60,000 free inhabitants therein, such State shall be admitted, by its delegates, into the Congress of the United States, on an equal footing with the original States in all respects whatever, and shall be at liberty to form a permanent constitution and State government: *Provided*, the constitution and government, so to be formed, shall be republican, and in conformity to the principles contained in these articles; and, so far as it can be consistent with the general interest of the confederacy, such admission shall be allowed at an earlier period, and when there may be a less number of free inhabitants in the State than 60,000.

Article the Sixth. There shall be neither slavery nor involuntary servitude in the said territory, otherwise than in the punishment of crimes, whereof the party shall have been duly convicted: Provided, always, That any person escaping into the same, from whom labor or service is lawfully claimed in any one of the original States, such fugitive may be lawfully reclaimed and conveyed to the person claiming his or her labor or service as aforesaid.

Be it ordained by the authority aforesaid, That the resolutions of the 23d of April, 1784, relative to the subject of this ordinance, be, and the same are hereby, repealed and declared null and void.[1]

Done by the United States, in Congress assembled, the 13th day of July, in the year of our Lord 1787, and of their sovereignty and independence the twelfth.

[The great Sixth Article has rendered this Ordinance immortal. This anti-slavery provision, however, has been spoken of sometimes in terms more rhetorical than exact. Senator Hoar, in a centennial memorial oration at Marietta, in 1888, said: "Here was the first human government under which absolute civil and religious liberty has always prevailed. . . . Here no slave was ever born, or dwelt." The student may compare *American History and Government*, § 333, close. But Daniel Webster was the historian rather than merely the orator when he said: "I doubt whether one single law of any lawgiver, ancient or modern, has produced effects of more distinct, marked, and lasting character, than the Ordinance of 1787."

August 7, 1789, the First Congress under the Constitution passed a *Confirmatory Act*, reënacting the Northwest Ordinance, with the provision that the appointments therein referred to Congress should be made by the President, subject to confirmation by the Senate.]

---

[1] For this earlier ordinance, cf. No. 149a.

XXVI. DRIFTING TOWARD ANARCHY

150. Danger (or Hope) of a Military Dictator (1783)

Gouverneur Morris to John Jay

Life and Works of Morris (Sparks' edition), I, 249. If this letter is taken in conjunction with the army plots, it would seem that Morris was not averse to a military revolution as a step toward aristocratic rule.

PHILADELPHIA, January 1, 1783.

. . . The army have swords in their hands. *You know enough of the history of mankind to know much more than I have said, — and possibly much more than they themselves yet think of. I will add, however, that I am glad to see things in this present train. Depend on it; good will arise from the situation to which we are hastening.* . . . Although I think it probable that much of convulsion will ensue, yet it must terminate in giving to government that power without which government is but a name.

151. Shays' Rebellion

a. A temperate statement of real grievances leading to the "Rebellion"

Minot's *History of the Insurrection in Massachusetts*, pages 34–37.

The following "schedule of grievances" was adopted by a mass convention of Hampshire County, Massachusetts, in 1786. For the general narrative, cf. *American History and Government*, § 188–192.

At a meeting of the delegates from *fifty* towns in the county of Hampshire, in convention held at Hatfield, in said county, on Tuesday, the 22d day of August instant [1786], and continued by adjournments until the twenty fifth, etc. *Voted, that this meeting is constitutional.*

497

The convention from a thorough conviction of great uneasiness, subsisting among the people of this county and Commonwealth, then went into an inquiry for the cause; and, upon mature consideration, deliberation, and debate, were of opinion, *that many grievances and unnecessary burdens now lying upon the people, are the source of that discontent so evidently discoverable throughout this Commonwealth.* Among which the following articles were voted as such, viz.

1st. *The existence of the Senate.*[1]

2d. *The present mode of representation.*

3d. The officers of government not being annually dependent on the representatives of the people, in General Court assembled, for their salaries.

4th. All the civil officers of government, not being annually elected by the Representatives of the people, in General Court assembled.

5th. The existence of the Courts of Common Pleas, and General Sessions of the Peace.

6th. *The Fee Table as it now stands.*

7th. The present mode of appropriating the impost and excise.

8th. *The unreasonable grants made to some of the officers of government.*

9th. The supplementary aid.

10th. The present mode of paying the governmental securities.

11th. The present mode adopted for the payment and speedy collection of the last tax.

12th. *The present mode of taxation, as it operates unequally between the polls and estates, and between landed and mercantile interests.*

13th. *The present method of practice of the attornies at law.*

14th. *The want of a sufficient medium of trade, to remedy the mischiefs arising from the scarcity of money.*

---

[1] Which was so constituted as to represent wealth rather than men, cf. *American History and Government,* § 154 and note.

15th. The General Court sitting in the town of *Boston*.

16th. The present embarrassments on the press.

17th. The neglect of the settlement of important matters depending between the Commonwealth and Congress, relating to monies and averages.

18th. Voted, This convention recommend to the several towns in this country that they instruct their Representatives, to use their influence in the next General Court, to have emitted *a bank of paper money, subject to a depreciation; making it a tender in all payments, equal to silver and gold*, to be issued in order to call in the Commonwealth's securities.

19th. *Voted, That whereas several of the above articles of grievances arise from defects in the constitution; therefore a revision of the same ought to take place.*

20th. Voted, That it be recommended by this convention to the several towns in this county, that they petition the Governour to call the General Court immediately together, in order that the other grievances complained of, may, by the legislature, be redressed.

21st. **Voted, That this convention recommend it to the inhabitants of this county, that they abstain from all mobs and unlawful assemblies, until a constitutional method of redress can be obtained.**

22d. Voted, That Mr. Caleb West be desired to transmit a copy of the proceedings of this convention to the convention of the County of Worcester.

23d. Voted, That the chairman of the convention be desired to transmit a copy of the proceedings of this convention to the county of Berkshire.

24th. Voted, That the chairman of this convention be directed to notify a county convention, upon any motion made to him for that purpose, if he judge the reasons offered be sufficient, giving such notice together with the reasons therefor, in the publick papers of this county.

25th. Voted, That a copy of the proceedings of this convention be sent to the press in Springfield for publication.

b. Washington's Alarm

(1) George Washington to Henry Lee.

Washington's *Writings* (Ford edition), XI, 76–78. Lee was a Virginia delegate in the Continental Congress. Washington's letter is in reply to one received from Lee.

MOUNT VERNON, October 31, 1786.

. . . The picture which you have exhibited . . . of the commotions and temper of numerous bodies in the eastern States, are equally to be lamented and deprecated. They exhibit a melancholy proof of what our transatlantic foe has predicted; and of another thing perhaps, which is still more to be regretted, and is yet more unaccountable, **that mankind, when left to themselves, are unfit for their own government.** I am mortified beyond expression when I view the clouds that have spread over the brightest morn that ever dawned upon any country. In a word, I am lost in amazement when I behold what intrigue, the interested views of desperate characters, ignorance, and jealously of the minor part, are capable of effecting, as a scourge on the major part of our fellow citizens of the Union; for it is hardly to be supposed, that the great body of the people, though they will not act can be so shortsighted or enveloped in darkness, as not to see rays of a distant sun through all this mist of intoxication and folly.

You talk, my good Sir, of employing influence to appease the present tumults in Massachusetts. I know not where that influence is to be found, or, if attainable, that it would be a proper remedy for the disorders. *Influence* is no *government*. Let us have one by which our lives, liberties, and properties will be secured, or let us know the worst at once. Under these impressions, my humble opinion is, that there is a call for decision. Know precisely what the insurgents aim at. If they have *real* grievances, redress them if possible; or acknowledge the justice of them, and your inability to do it in the present moment. If they have not, employ the force of government against them at once. If this is inadequate, *all* will be convinced, that the superstructure is bad, or wants support. To be more exposed in the eyes of the world, and more contemptible than we already are, is hardly possible. To delay one or the other of these, is to exasperate . . . or to give confidence, and will add to their numbers; for, like snow-balls, such bodies increase by every moment unless there is something in the way to obstruct and crumble them before the weight is too great and irresistible. . . .

(2) *George Washington, to James Madison.*

Writings (Ford edition), XI, 80, 81. Note especially the extracts quoted from General Lincoln, in command against the rebels.

November 5, 1786.

I thank you for the communications in your letter of the 1st instant. . . . Fain would I hope that the great and most important of all subjects, the *federal government,* may be considered with . . . calm and deliberate attention. . . . No morn ever dawned more favorably than ours did; and no day was ever more clouded than the present. Wisdom and good examples are necessary at this time to rescue the political machine from the impending storm. Virginia has now an opportunity to set the latter, and has enough of the former, I hope, to take the lead in promoting this great and arduous work. Without an alteration in our political creed, the superstructure we have been seven years in raising, at the expense of so much treasure and blood, must fall. We are fast verging to anarchy and confusion.

. . . a letter which I have received from General Knox, who had just returned from Massachusetts, whither he had been sent by Congress consequent of the commotions in that State, is replete with melancholy accounts of the temper and designs of a considerable part of that people. Among other things he says:

" Their creed is, that the property of the United States has been protected from the confiscation of Britain by the joint exertions of *all ;* and therefore ought to be the *common property of all;* and he that attempts opposition to this creed, is an enemy to equity and justice, and ought to be swept from off the face of the earth." Again: "They are determined to annihilate all debts, public and private, and have agrarian laws, which are easily effected by the means of unfunded paper money, which shall be a tender in all cases whatever." He adds: "The number of these people amount in Massachusetts to about one fifth part of several populous counties, and to them may be collected people of similar sentiments from the States of Rhode Island, Connecticut, and New Hampshire, so as to constitute a body of about twelve or fifteen thousand desperate and unprincipled men. They are chiefly of the young and active part of the community."

How melancholy is the reflection, that in so short a space we should have made such large strides towards fulfilling the predictions of our transatlantic foes! "Leave them to themselves, and their government will soon dissolve." Will not the wise and good strive hard to avert this evil? Or will their supineness suffer ignorance, and the arts of self interested, designing, disaffected, and desperate characters, to involve this great country in wretchedness and contempt? What stronger evidence can be given of the want of energy in our government, than these disorders? If there is not power in it to check them, what security has a man for life, liberty, or property? To you I am sure I need not add aught on this subject. The consequences of a lax or inefficient government are too obvious to be dwelt upon. Thirteen sovereignties pulling against each other, and all tugging at the federal head, will soon bring ruin on the whole; whereas a liberal and energetic constitution, well guarded and closely watched to prevent encroachments, might restore us to that degree of respectability and consequence to which we had a fair claim. . . .

152. A Shrewd Foreign Observer's View of the Social Conflict over the Adoption of a New Constitution

Louis Guillaume Otto to Vergennes[1]

George Bancroft's *History of the Constitution* (1882), II, Appendix, 399 ff.

---

[1] Otto was the French minister to the United States; Vergennes was the French minister in charge of foreign affairs at Paris.

PHILADELPHIA, October 10, 1786.

[The letter first describes the failure of the Annapolis Convention.]

The people are not ignorant that the natural consequences of an increase of power in the government would be a regular collection of taxes, a strict administration of justice, extraordinary duties on imports, *rigorous executions against debtors —* in short, *a marked preponderance of rich men and of large proprietors.*

It is, however, for the interest of the people to guard as much as possible the absolute freedom granted them in a time when no other law was known but necessity, and when an English army, as it were, laid the foundations of the political constitution.

In those stormy times *it was necessary* to agree that all power ought to emanate only from the people; that everything was subject to its supreme will, and that the magistrates were only its servants.

Although there are no nobles in America, there is a class of men denominated "gentlemen," who, by reason of their wealth, their talents, their education, their families, or the offices they hold, *aspire to a pre-eminence which the people refuse to grant them;* and, although many of these men have betrayed the interests of their order to gain popularity, *there reigns among them a connection so much the more intimate as they almost all of them dread the efforts of the people to despoil them of their possessions, and, moreover, they are creditors,* and therefore interested in strengthening the government, and watching over the execution of the laws. . . .

The majority of them being merchants, it is for their interest to establish the credit of the United States in Europe on a solid foundation by the exact payment of debts, and to grant to congress powers extensive enough to compel the people to contribute for this purpose. The attempt, my lord, has been vain, by pamphlets and other publications, to spread notions of justice and integrity, and to deprive the people of a freedom which they have so misused. By proposing a new organization of the federal government all minds would have been revolted; circumstances ruinous to the commerce of America have happily arisen to furnish the reformers with a pretext for introducing innovations.

They represented to the people that the American name had become opprobrious among all the nations of Europe; that the flag of the United States was everywhere exposed to insults and annoyance. . . .

[Otto continues at length to represent that the gentry sought to secure a stronger government by inflaming the common people against foreign powers. He then declares that it was never intended that the Annapolis convention should do anything; that it was only one step in a "plot" to secure a more unfettered convention.]

The measures were so well taken that at the end of September no more than five states were represented at Annapolis, and the commissioners from the northern states tarried several days at New York, in order to retard their arrival.

The states which assembled, after having waited nearly three weeks, separated under the pretext that they were not in sufficient numbers to enter on business, and, to justify this dissolution, they addressed to the different legislatures and to congress a report, the translation of which I have the honor to enclose to you [i.e., the paper reproduced in No. 153].

In this paper the commissioners employ an infinity of circumlocutions and ambiguous phrases to show to their constituents the impossibility of taking into consideration a general plan of commerce and the powers pertaining thereto, without at the same time touching upon other objects closely connected with the prosperity and national importance of the United States.

Without enumerating these objects, the commissioners enlarge upon the present crisis of public affairs, upon the dangers to which the confederation is exposed, upon the want of credit of the United States abroad, and upon the necessity of uniting, under a single point of view, the interests of all the states.

They close by proposing, for the month of May next, a new

assembly of commissioners, instructed to deliberate not only upon a general plan of commerce, but upon other matters which may concern the harmony and welfare of the states, and upon the means of rendering the federal government adequate to the exigencies of the union.

In spite of the obscurity of this document, you will perceive, my lord, that the commissioners were unwilling to take into consideration the grievances of commerce, which are of exceeding interest for the people, without at the same time perfecting the fundamental constitution of congress.

XXVII. MAKING THE CONSTITUTION

153. Call issued by the Annapolis Convention

Documentary History of the Constitution, I, 1–6. For a narrative of the circumstances, cf. *American History and Government*, § 199.

Sundry of the States having in Consequence of a Resolution and Circular Letter from the State of Virginia appointed Commissioners to meet at such time and Place as should be agreed upon by them the said Commissioners, to take into Consideration the Trade and Commerce of the United States etc:— the Commissioners of Virginia, Delaware, Pennsylvania, New Jersey and New York, met at the City of Annapolis on the 11th of September 1786, but did not think it advisable to proceed on the Business of their Mission. They therefore broke up after making a Report to the States by which they had been appointed and transmitting to Congress a Copy thereof which is as follows.

To the Honorable the Legislatures of Virginia, Delaware, Pennsylvania, New Jersey and New York.

The Commissioners from the said States respectively Assembled at the City of Annapolis, humbly beg leave to Report:

That, pursuant to their several Appointments, they met at Annapolis in the State of Maryland, on the eleventh day of September Instant, and, having proceeded to a communication of their Powers, they found that the States of New York, Pennsylvania and Virginia had, in substance, and nearly in the same terms, authorized their respective Commissioners "to meet such Commissioners as were or might be appointed by the other States in the Union, at such time and Place as should be agreed upon by the said Commissioners, to take into Consideration the trade and Commerce of the United States, to consider how far an uniform System in their commercial intercourse and regulations might be necessary to their common interest and permanent harmony, and *to report, to the several States,* such an Act relative to this great Object, *as when unanimously ratified by them,* would enable the United States in Congress Assembled effectually to provide for the same."

That the State of Delaware had given similar Powers to their Commissioners, with this difference only, that the Act to be framed in virtue of those Powers, is required to be reported "to the United States in Congress Assembled to be agreed to by them and Confirmed by the Legislatures of every State."

That the State of New Jersey has enlarged the Object of their Appointment, empowering their Commissioners, "to consider how far an uniform System in their Commercial Regulations, and *other important matters,* might be necessary to the common interest and permanent harmony of the several States;" and to "report such an Act on the Subject, as when ratified by them" would "enable the United States in Congress Assembled effectually to provide *for the exigencies of the Union."*

That appointments of Commissioners have also been made by the States of New Hampshire, Massachusetts, Rhode Island and North Carolina, none of whom have however attended, but that no information has been received by your Commissioners of any Appointment having been made by the States of Connecticut, Maryland, South-Carolina or Georgia.

That the express terms of the Powers to your Commissioners supposing a Deputation from *all* the States, and having for Object *the trade and Commerce of the United States,* your Commissioners did not conceive it adviseable to proceed on the business of their Mission, under the Circumstance of so partial and defective a Representation.

Deeply impressed however with the magnitude and importance of the Object confided to them on this Occasion, your Commissioners cannot forbear to indulge an expression of their earnest and unanimous wish that speedy measures may be taken to effect a general meeting of the States in a future Convention, for the same, and such other Purposes, as the situation of Public Affairs may be found to require.

If in expressing this wish, or in intimating any other Sentiment, your Commissioners should seem to exceed the strict bounds of their Appointment, they entertain a full Confidence that a Conduct dictated by an anxiety for the welfare of the United States, will not fail to receive an indulgent Construction.

In this persuasion, your Commissioners submit an Opinion, that the Idea of extending the Powers of their Deputies to other Objects than those of Commerce, which has been adopted by the State of New Jersey, was an improvement on the original Plan, and will deserve to be incorporated into that of a future Convention. They are the more naturally led to which Conclusion, as in the course of the Reflections on the Subject, they have been induced to think, that the Power of regulating Trade, is of such comprehensive extent, and will enter so far into the General System of the Fœderal Government, that to give it efficacy, and to obviate questions and doubts concerning its precise nature and limits, may require a corresponding adjustment of other Parts of the Fœderal System.

That there are important defects in the System of the Fœderal Government, is acknowledged by the Acts of those States which have concurred in the present Meeting. That the defects, upon a closer examination may be found greater and more numerous than even these Acts imply, is at least so far probable from the embarrassments which characterize the present state of our National Affairs, foreign and domestic, as may reasonably be supposed to merit a deliberate and candid discussion, in some mode, which will unite the Sentiments and Councils of all the States. In the choice of the mode, your Commissioners are of Opinion that a Convention of Deputies from the different States, for the special and sole purpose of entering into this investigation and digesting a Plan for supplying such defects as may be discovered to exist, will be entitled to a preference, from Considerations which will occur without being particularized.

THE ANNAPOLIS CALL

Your Commissioners decline an enumeration of those National Circumstances on which their Opinion respecting the Propriety of a future Convention with more enlarged Powers is founded; as it would be an useless intrusion of facts and Observations, most of which have been frequently the Subject of Public Discussion, and none of which can have escaped the penetration of those to whom they would in this instance be addressed. They are however of a nature so serious as, in the View of your Commissioners, to render the situation of the United States delicate and critical, calling for an exertion of the united Virtue and Wisdom of all the Members of the Confederacy.

Under this Impression Your Commissioners, with the most respectful deference, beg leave to suggest *their unanimous conviction that it may essentially tend to advance the interests of the Union, if the States by whom they have been respectively delegated would themselves concur, and use their endeavours to procure the concurrence of the other States, in the Appointment of Commissioners to meet at Philadelphia on the second Monday in May next, to take into Consideration the situation of the United States, to devise such further Provisions as shall appear to them necessary to render the Constitution of the Fœderal Government adequate to the exigencies of the Union; and to report such an Act for that purpose to the United States in Congress Assembled, as when " agreed to by them and afterwards confirmed by the Legislatures of every State " will effectually provide for the same.*

Though your Commissioners could not with propriety address these Observations and Sentiments to any but the States they have the honor to Represent, they have nevertheless concluded, from motives of respect, to transmit Copies of this Report, to the United States in Congress Assembled, and to the Executives of the other States.

By Order of the Commissioners
John Dickinson, Chairman

Dated at Annapolis
    September 14th 1786.

154. Appointment of Delegates: Credentials (Georgia)

Records of the Federal Convention (Farrand), III, 576–577.

Georgia is here selected for illustration, because of the emphasis upon the sovereignty of the State in the forms used.

GEORGIA

By the Honorable GEORGE MATHEWS Esquire, Captain General, Governor and Commander in Chief, in and over the said State aforesaid.

To all to whom these Presents shall come Greeting.

KNOW YE that JOHN MILTON Esquire, who hath certified the annexed Copy of an Ordinance intitled "An Ordinance for the appointment of Deputies from this State for the purpose of revising the Fœderal Constitution"—is Secretary of the said State in whose Office the Archives of the same are deposited. Therefore all due faith, Credit and Authority are and ought to be had and given the same.

IN TESTIMONY whereof I have hereunto set my hand and caused the Great Seal of the said State to be put and affixed at *Augusta*, this Twenty fourth day of April in the Year of our Lord One thousand seven hundred and eighty seven and of *our* Sovereignty and Independence the Eleventh.

GEO: (Seal) MATHEWS.

By his Honor's Command
J. MILTON Secy

AN ORDINANCE for the appointment of Deputies from this State for the purpose of revising the Fœderal Constitution.

BE IT ORDAINED by the Representatives of the Freemen of the State of Georgia in General Assembly met and by the Authority of the same, that WILLIAM FEW, ABRAHAM BALDWIN, WILLIAM PIERCE, GEORGE WALTON, WILLIAM HOUSTOUN and NATHANIEL PENDLETON ESQUIRES, Be, and they are hereby appointed Commissioners, who, *or any two or more of them* are hereby authorized as Deputies from this State to meet such deputies as may be appointed and authorized by other States to assemble in Convention at Philadelphia and to join with them in devising and discussing all such Alterations and farther Provisions as may be necessary to render the Federal Constitution adequate to the exigencies of the Union, and in reporting such an Act for that purpose to the United States in Congress Assembled as *when agreed to by them, and duly confirmed by the several States* will effectually provide for the same. In case of the death of any of the said Deputies, or of their declining their appointments, the Executive are hereby authorized to supply such Vacancies.

  By Order of the House
    (signed) WM GIBBONS Speaker.
Augusta the 10th February 1787.

 Georgia.
 Secretary's Office
 The above is a true Copy from the Original Ordinance deposited in my Office.

  Augusta ⎫
 24 April 1787. ⎬ J. MILTON, Secretary.

The State of Georgia by the grace of God free, Sovereign and Independent

  To the Honorable WILLIAM PIERCE, Esquire.

WHEREAS you, the said William Pierce, are in and by an Ordinance of the General Assembly of our said State Nominated and Appointed a Deputy to represent the same in a Convention of the United States to be assembled at Philadelphia, for the Purposes of devising and discussing such Alterations and farther Provisions as may be necessary to render the Fœderal Constitution adequate to the exigencies of the Union.

You are therefore hereby Commissioned to proceed on the duties required of you in virtue of the said Ordinance

Witness our trusty and well beloved *George Mathews* Esquire, our[1] Captain General, Governor, and Commander in Chief, under his hand and our Great Seal at Augusta this Seventeenth day of April in the Year of our Lord one thousand seven hundred and eighty seven and of our Sovereignty and Independence the Eleventh.[2]

GEO: MATHEWS (Seal)

By His Honor's Command.
J. Milton. Secy.

[Like commissions for the other delegates.]

155. George Mason on the Preliminaries at Philadelphia

George Mason to George Mason, Jr.

Records of the Federal Convention (Farrand), III, 22–24.

PHILADELPHIA, May 20th, 1787.

. . . Upon our arrival here on Thursday evening, seventeenth May, I found only the States of Virginia and Pennsylvania fully represented; and there are at this time only five — New York, the two Carolinas, and the two before mentioned. All the States, Rhode Island excepted, have made their appointments; but the members drop in slowly; some of the deputies from the Eastern States are here, but none of them have yet a sufficient representation, and it will probably be several days before the Convention will be authorized to proceed to business. The expectations and hopes of all the Union centre in this Convention. God grant that we may be able to concert effectual means of preserving our country from the evils which threaten us.

---

[1] This was an old royal form, now used by the *State* instead of by the King.

[2] Some States dated: "in the year of the Sovereignty and Independence of the United States the Eleventh." Others were even more specific than Georgia; as, "in the Eleventh year of the Independence of the Delaware State"; or, as in New York, — "the Eleventh year of the Independence of the Said State."

The Virginia deputies (who are all here) meet and confer together two or three hours every day, in order to form a proper correspondence of sentiments; and for form's sake, to see what new deputies are arrived, and to grow into some acquaintance with each other, we regularly meet every day at three o'clock. These and some occasional conversations with the deputies of different States and with some of the general officers of the late army (who are here upon a general meeting of the Cincinnati), are the only opportunities I have hitherto had of forming any opinion upon the great subject of our mission, and, consequently, a very imperfect and indecisive one. Yet, upon the great principles of it, I have reason to hope there will be greater unanimity and less opposition, except from the little States, than was at first apprehended. The most prevalent idea in the principal States seems to be a total alteration of the present federal system, and substituting a great national council or parliament, consisting of two branches of the legislature, founded upon the principles of equal proportionate representation, with full legislative powers upon all the subjects of the Union; and an executive: and to make the several State legislatures subordinate to the national, by giving the latter the power of a negative upon all such laws as they shall judge contrary to the interest of the federal Union . . . and what is a very extraordinary phenomenon, we are likely to find the republicans, on this occasion, issue from the Southern and Middle States, and the anti-republicans from the Eastern; however extraordinary this may at first seem, it may, I think be accounted for from a very common and natural impulse of the human mind. Men disappointed in expectations too hastily and sanguinely formed, tired and disgusted with the unexpected evils they have experienced, and anxious to remove them as far as possible, are very apt to run into the opposite extreme; and the people of the Eastern States, setting out with more republican principles, have consequently been more disappointed than we have been. . . .

156. The Virginia Plan

Records of the Federal Convention (Farrand), I, 20–22, for May 29. For history of the plan, cf. *American History and Government*, § 202. On the opening day of the Philadelphia Convention for business Mr. Randolph, after a brilliant speech, introduced the following resolutions in behalf of the Virginia delegation.

1. Resolved that the articles of Confederation ought to be so corrected and enlarged as to accomplish the objects proposed by their institution; namely, "common defence, security of liberty and general welfare."

2. Resd. therefore that the rights of suffrage in the National Legislature ought to be proportioned to the Quotas of contribution, or to the number of free inhabitants, as the one or the other rule may seem best in different cases.

3. Resd. that the National Legislature ought to consist of two branches.

4. Resd. that the members of the first branch of the National Legislature ought to be elected by the people of the several States every —— for the term of ——; to be of the age of —— years at least; to receive liberal stipends by which they may be compensated for the devotion of their time to public service; to be ineligible to any office established by a particular State, or under the authority of the United States, except those peculiarly belonging to the functions of the first branch, during the term of service, and for the space of —— after its expiration; to be incapable of re-election for the space of —— after the expiration of their term of service, and to be subject to recall.

5. Resold. that the members of the second branch of the National Legislature ought to be elected by those of the first, out of a proper number of persons nominated by the individual Legislatures, to be of the age of —— years at least; to hold their offices for a term sufficient to ensure their independency; to receive liberal stipends, by which they may be compensated for the devotion of their time to public service; and to be ineligible to any office established by a particular

State, or under the authority of the United States, except those peculiarly belonging to the functions of the second branch, during the term of service, and for the space of —— after the expiration thereof.

6. Resolved that each branch ought to possess the right of originating Acts; that the National Legislature ought to be impowered to enjoy the Legislative Rights vested in Congress by the Confederation and moreover to legislate in all cases to which the separate states are incompetent, or in which the harmony of the United States may be interrupted by the exercise of individual Legislation; to negative all laws passed by the several States, contravening in the opinion of the National Legislature the articles of Union; and to call forth the force of the Union against any member of the Union failing to fulfill its duty under the articles thereof.

7. Resd. that a National Executive be instituted; to be chosen by the National Legislature for the term of —— years, to receive punctually at stated times, a fixed compensation for the services rendered, in which no increase or diminution shall be made so as to affect the Magistracy existing at the time of increase or dimunition, and to be ineligible a second time; and that besides a general authority to execute the National laws, it ought to enjoy the Executive rights vested in Congress by the Confederation.

8. Resd. that the Executive and a convenient number of the National Judiciary, ought to compose a council of revision with authority to examine every act of the National Legislature before it shall operate, and every act of a particular Legislature before a Negative thereon shall be final; and that the dissent of the said Council shall amount to a rejection, unless the Act of the National Legislature be again passed, or that of a particular Legislature be again negatived by —— of the members of each branch.

9. Resd. that a National Judiciary be established to consist of one or more supreme tribunals, and of inferior tribunals to be chosen by the National Legislature, to hold their offices

during good behaviour; and to receive punctually at stated times fixed compensation for their services, in which no increase or diminution shall be made so as to affect the persons actually in office at the time of such increase or diminution that the jurisdiction of the inferior tribunals shall be to hear and determine in the first instance, and of the supreme tribunal to hear and determine in the dernier resort, all piracies and felonies of the high seas, captures from an enemy; cases in which foreigners or citizens of other States applying to such jurisdiction may be interested, or which respect the collection of the National revenue; impeachments of any National officers, and questions which may involve the national peace and harmony.

10. Resolvd. that provision ought to be made for the admission of States lawfully arising within the limits of the United States, whether from a voluntary junction of Government and Territory or otherwise, with the consent of a number of voices in the National legislature less than the whole.

11. Resd. that a Republican Government and the territory of each State, except in the instance of a voluntary junction of Government and territory, ought to be guaranteed by the United States to each State.

12. Resd. that provision ought to be made for the continuance of Congress and their authorities and privileges, until a given day after the reform of the articles of Union shall be adopted, and for the completion of all their engagements.

13. Resd. that provision ought to be made for the amendment of the Articles of Union whensoever it shall seem necessary; and that the assent of the National Legislature ought not to be required thereto.

14. Resd. that the Legislative Executive and Judiciary powers within the several States ought to be bound by oath to support the articles of Union.

15. Resd. that the amendments which shall be offered to the Confederation by the Convention, ought at a proper time, or times, after the approbation of Congress to be submitted to an assembly or assemblies of Representatives, recommended by

the several Legislatures to be expressly chosen by the people to consider and decide thereon.

157. George Mason on the Convention and its Aristocratic Tendencies (June, 1787)

George Mason to George Mason, Jr.

Records of the Federal Convention (Farrand), III, 32–33

PHILADELPHIA, June 1, 1787.

. . . Virginia has had the honor of presenting the outlines of the plan upon which the convention is proceeding; but so slowly that it is impossible to judge when the business will be finished, most probably not before August — *festina lente* may very well be called our motto. *When I first came here, judging from casual conversations with gentlemen from the different States, I was very apprehensive that, soured and disgusted with the unexpected evils we had experienced from the democratic principles of our governments, we should be apt to run into the opposite extreme and in endeavoring to steer too far from Scylla, we might be drawn into the vortex of Charybdis, of which I still think there is some danger,*[1] though I have the pleasure to find in the convention, many men of fine republican principles. America has certainly, upon this occasion, drawn forth her first characters; there are upon this Convention many gentlemen of the most respectable abilities, and so far as I can discover, of the purest intentions. The eyes of the United States are turned upon this assembly, and their expectations raised to a very anxious degree. . . .

All communications of the proceedings are forbidden during the sitting of the Convention; this I think was a necessary precaution to prevent misrepresentations or mistakes; there being a material difference between the appearance of a subject in its first crude and undigested shape, and after it shall have been properly matured and arranged.

---

[1] Later, Mason became again convinced there was much such danger. Cf. No. 161 below.

158. The New Jersey Plan

Records of the Federal Convention (Farrand), I, 242-245 (for June 15). The Convention, in committee of the whole, in two weeks of debate, had adopted nineteen resolutions based upon the fifteen in the Virginia Plan above. Action upon this report of the committee of the whole was then interrupted by the presentation of the following plan on which the "Small States" had now agreed.

Mr. Patterson [New Jersey] laid before the Convention the plan which he said several of the deputations wished to be substituted in place of that proposed by Mr. Randolph. After some little discussion of the most proper mode of giving it a fair deliberation it was agreed that it should be referred to a Committee of the Whole, and that in order to place the two plans in due comparison, the other should be recommitted. At the earnest desire of Mr. Lansing [New Jersey], and some other gentlemen, it was also agreed that the Convention should not go into Committee of the whole on the subject till tomorrow, by which delay the friends of the plan proposed by Mr. Patterson wd. be better prepared to explain and support it, and all would have an opportunity of taking copies. —

The propositions from N. Jersey moved by Mr. Patterson were in the words following.

1. Resd. that the articles of Confederation ought to be so revised, corrected and enlarged as to render the federal Constitution adequate to the exigencies of Government, and the preservation of the Union.

2. Resd. that in addition to the powers vested in the U. States in Congress, by the present existing articles of Confederation, they be authorized to pass acts for raising a revenue, by levying a duty or duties on all goods and merchandizes of foreign growth or manufacture, imported into any part of the U. States, by Stamps on paper, vellum or parchment, and by a postage on all letters or packages passing through the general post-Office, to be applied to such federal purposes as they shall deem proper and expedient; to make rules and regulations for the collection thereof; and the same from time to time to alter and amend in

such manner as they shall think proper : to pass Acts for the regulation of trade and commerce as well with foreign nations as with each other : provided that all punishments, fines, forfeitures and penalties, to be incurred for contravening such acts rules and regulations shall be adjudged by the Common law judiciarys of the State in which any offence contrary to the true intent and meaning of such Acts rules and regulations shall have been committed or perpetrated, with liberty of commencing in the first instance all suits and prosecutions for that purpose in the superior Common law Judiciary in such State, subject nevertheless, for the correction of all errors, both in law and fact in rendering judgment, to an appeal to the Judiciary to the U. States.

3. Resd. that whenever requisitions shall be necessary, instead of the rule for making requisitions mentioned in the articles of Confederation, the United States in Congs. be authorized to make such requisitions in proportion to the whole number of white and other free citizens and inhabitants of every age sex and condition including those bound to servitude for a term of years and three fifths of all other persons not comprehended in the foregoing description, except Indians not paying taxes; that if such requisitions be not complied with, in the time specified therein, to direct the collection thereof in the non complying States and for that purpose to devise and pass acts directing and authorizing the same; provided that none of the powers hereby vested in the U. States in Congs. shall be exercised without the consent of at least ——— States, and in that proportion, if the number of Confederated States should hereafter be increased or diminished.

4. Resd. that the U. States in Congs. be authorized to elect a federal Executive to consist of ——— persons, to continue in office for the term of ——— years, to receive punctually at stated times a fixed compensation for their services, in which no increase or diminution, shall be made so as to affect the persons composing the Executive at the time of such increase or diminution, to be paid out of the federal treasury; to be incapable of holding any other office or appointment during their time

of service and for ——— years thereafter; to be ineligible a second time, and removeable by Congs. on application by a majority of the Executives of the several States; that the Executives besides their general authority to execute the federal acts ought to appoint all federal officers not otherwise provided for, and to direct all military operations; provided that none of the persons composing the federal Executive shall on any occasion take command of any troops, so as personally to conduct any enterprise as General, or in other capacity.

5. Resd. that a federal judiciary be established to consist of a supreme Tribunal the Judges of which to be appointed by the Executive, and to hold their offices during good behaviour, to receive punctually at stated times a fixed compensation for their services in which no increase or diminution shall be made, so as to affect the persons actually in office at the time of such increase or diminution; that the Judiciary so established shall have authority to hear and determine in the first instance on all impeachments of federal officers, and *by way of appeal, in the dernier resort, in all cases touching the rights of Ambassadors, in all cases of captures from an enemy, in all cases of piracies and felonies on the high seas, in all cases in which foreigners may be interested, in the construction of any treaty or treaties, or which may arise on any of the Acts for regulation of trade, or the collection of the federal Revenue:* that none of the Judiciary shall during the time they remain in Office be capable of receiving or holding any other office or appointment during their time of service, or for ——— thereafter.

6. Resd. that all Acts of the U. States in Congs. made by virtue and in pursuance of the powers hereby and by the articles of confederation vested in them, and all Treaties made and ratified under the authority of the U. States shall be the supreme law of the respective States so far forth as those Acts or Treaties shall relate to the said States or their Citizens, and *that the Judiciary of the several States* shall be bound thereby in their decisions, any thing in the respective laws of the individual States to the contrary notwithstanding; and that if any State or any body of men in

any State shall oppose or prevent the carrying into execution such acts or treaties, the federal Executive shall be authorized to call forth the power of the Confederated States, or so much thereof as may be necessary to enforce and compel an obedience to such Acts or an Observance of such Treaties.

7. Resd. that provision be made for the admission of new States into the Union.

8. Resd. the rule for naturalization ought to be the same in every State.

9. Resd. that a Citizen of one State committing an offence in another State of the Union, shall be deemed guilty of the same offence as if it had been committed by a Citizen of the State in which the Offence was committed.

Adjourned

159. Hamilton's Plan

On June 18, Hamilton occupied nearly the whole session with an argument for a government stronger and more centralized even than the Virginia Plan — to meet the advocates of the New Jersey Plan by taking high ground. During this address he presented his own Plan (not what he thought attainable, but desirable). The paper given below (from Hamilton's *Works*, Federalist edition, I, 401 ff.) seems to have been prepared to assist the delivery of this address, as a sort of brief. The address itself is reported by Madison (*Journal*, for June 18) much more at length, but with many of the same phrases. The student would do well to compare the two. Copious extracts from that speech, and from other words of Hamilton in the Convention, are quoted in *American History and Government*, § 200.

All communities divide themselves into the few and the many. The first are the rich and well-born; the other, the mass of the people. . . . The people are turbulent and changing; they seldom judge or determine right. Give therefore to the first class [the few] a distinct *permanent* share in the government. They will check the unsteadiness of the second; and, as they cannot receive any advantage by a change, they therefore will ever maintain good government. . . . Nothing but a *permanent* body can check the imprudence of democracy.

Their turbulent and uncontrollable disposition requires checks. . . .

It is admitted that you cannot have a good Executive upon a democratic plan. See the excellency of the British Executive. He is placed above temptation. He can have no distinct interests from the public welfare. **Nothing short of such an executive can be efficient.** . . . **Let one body of the Legislature be constituted during good behavior or life.** Let one Executive be appointed who dares execute his powers. It may be asked: Is this a republican system? It is strictly so, as long as they remain elective. And let me observe that an Executive is less dangerous to the liberties of the people when in office during life, than for seven years. . . . **Let electors be appointed in each of the States to elect the Legislature,** to consist of two branches; and I would give them [the national legislature] the *unlimited power of passing all laws, without exception.* The Assembly to be elected for three years by the people in districts. The Senate to be elected by electors to be chosen for that purpose by the people, and to remain in office during life. *The Executive to have the power of negativing all laws;* to make war and peace, with their [Senate's] advice, but to have sole direction of all military operations, and to send ambassadors, and appoint all military officers; and to pardon all offenders, treason excepted, unless by advice of the Senate . . . Supreme judicial officers to be appointed by the Executive and the Senate.

The Legislature to appoint courts in each State, *so as to make the State governments unnecessary to it.* All state laws which contravene the general laws to be absolutely void. *An officer to be appointed in each State to have a negative on all State laws.* . . .

160. Character Sketches of Delegates by William Pierce

Records of the Federal Convention, III, 87 ff.

Pierce was a delegate from Georgia. It is not known just when he composed these sketches.

From New Hampshire.

Mr. Langdon is a man of considerable fortune. . . .

From Massachusetts.

Rufus King, Natl. Gorham, Gerry and Jno. [Caleb] Strong Esquires.

Mr. King is a Man much distinguished for his eloquence and great parliamentary talents. He was educated in Massachusetts and is said to have good classical as well as legal knowledge. He has served for three years in the Congress of the United States with great and deserved applause, and is at this time high in the confidence and approbation of his Countrymen. This Gentleman is about thirty three years of age, about five feet ten Inches high, well formed, an handsome face, with a strong expressive Eye, and a sweet high toned voice. In his public speaking there is something peculiarly strong and rich in his expression, clear, and convincing in his arguments, rapid and irresistible at times in his eloquence but he is not always equal. His action is natural, swimming and graceful, but there is a rudeness of manner sometimes accompanying it. But take him *tout en semble*, he may with propriety be ranked among the Luminaries of the present Age.

Mr. Gorham is a Merchant in Boston. . . .

Mr. Gerry's character is marked for integrity and perseverance. He is a hesitating and laborious speaker;—possesses a great degree of confidence and goes extensively into all subjects that he speaks on, without respect to elegance or flower of diction. He is connected and sometimes clear in his arguments, conceives well, and cherishes as his virtue, a love for his Country. Mr. Gerry is very much of a Gentleman in his principles and manners;—he has been engaged in the mercantile line and is a Man of property. He is about 37 years of age.

From Connecticut.

Saml. Johnson, Roger Sherman, and W. [Oliver] Elsworth Esquires.

* * * * * * * *

Mr. Sherman exhibits the oddest shaped character I ever remember to have met with. He is awkward, un-winning, and unaccountably strange in his manner. But in his train of thinking there is something regular, deep and comprehensive; yet the oddity of his address, the vulgarisms that accompany his public speaking, and that strange New England cant that runs through his public as well as his private speaking make everything that is connected with him grotesque and laughable; — and yet he deserves infinite praise, — no Man has a better Heart or a clearer Head. If he cannot embellish he can furnish thoughts that are wise and useful. He is an able politician and extremely artful in accomplishing any particular object; — and it is remarked that he seldom fails. I am told he sits on the bench in Connecticut, and is very correct in the discharge of his Judicial functions. In the early part of his life he was a Shoe-maker; — but despising the lowness of his condition, he turned Almanack maker, and so progressed upwards to a Judge. He has been several years a Member of Congress, and discharged the duties of his Office with honor and credit to himself, and advantage to the State he represented. He is about 60.

Mr. Elsworth is a Judge of the Supreme Court in Connecticut; — he is a Gentleman of a clear, deep, and copious understanding; eloquent, and connected in public debate; and always attentive to his duty. He is very happy in a reply, and choice in selecting such parts of his adversary's arguments as he finds make the strongest impressions, — in order to take off the force of them, so as to admit the power of his own. Mr. Elsworth is about 37 years of age, a Man much respected for his integrity, and venerated for his abilities.

From New York.

Alexander Hamilton, [Robert] Yates, and W. [John] Lansing Esquires.

Colo. Hamilton is deservedly celebrated for his talents. He is a practitioner of the Law, and reputed to be a finished Scholar. To a clear and strong judgment he unites the ornaments of fancy, and whilst he is able, convincing, and engaging in his eloquence the Heart and Head sympathize in approving him. Yet there is something too feeble in his voice to be equal to the strains of oratory; — it is my opinion that he is rather a convincing Speaker, that [than] a blazing Orator. Colo. Hamilton requires time to think, — he enquires into every part of his subject with the searchings of phylosophy, and when he comes forward he comes highly charged with interesting matter. There is no skimming over the surface of a subject with him, he must sink to the bottom to see what foundation it rests on. — His language is not always equal, sometimes didactic like Bolingbroke's at others light and tripping like Stern's. His eloquence is not so defusive as to trifle with the senses, but he rambles just enough to strike and keep up the attention. He is about 33 years old, of small stature, and lean. His manners are tinctured with stiffness, and sometimes with a degree of vanity that is highly disagreeable.

Mr. Yates is said to be an able Judge. He is a Man of great legal abilities, but not distinguished as an Orator. Some of his Enemies say he is an anti-federal Man, but I discovered no such disposition in him. He is about 45 years old, and enjoys a great share of health.

Mr. Lansing is a practicing Attorney at Albany, and Mayor of that Corporation. He has a hesitation in his speech, that will prevent his being an Orator of any eminence;— his legal knowledge I am told is not extensive, nor his education a good one. He is however a Man of good sense, plain in his manners, and sincere in his friendships. He is about 32 years of age.

From New Jersey.

Wm. Livingston, David Brearly, Wm. Patterson, and Jonn. Dayton, Esquires.

Governor Livingston is confessedly a Man of the first rate talents, but he appears to me rather to indulge a sportiveness of wit, than a strength of thinking. He is however equal to anything, from the extensiveness of his education and genius. His writings teem with satyr and a neatness of style. But he is no Orator, and seems little acquainted with the guiles of policy. He is about 60 years old, and remarkably healthy.

Mr. Brearly is a man of good, rather than of brilliant parts. He is a Judge of the Supreme Court of New Jersey, and is very much in the esteem of the people. As an Orator he has little to boast of, but as a Man he has every virtue to recommend him. Mr. Brearly is about 40 years of age.

M. Patterson is one of those kind of Men whose powers break in upon you, and create wonder and astonishment. He is a Man of great modesty, with looks that bespeak talents of no great extent, — but he is a Classic, a Lawyer, and an Orator; — and of a disposition so favorable to his advancement that every one seemed ready to exalt him with their praises. He is very happy in the choice of time and manner of engaging in a debate, and never speaks but when he understands his subject well. This Gentleman is about 34 years of age, of a very low stature.

Capt. Dayton is a young Gentleman of talents, with ambition to exert them. He possesses a good education, and some reading; he speaks well, and seems desirous of improving himself in Oratory. There is an impetuosity in his temper that is injurious to him; but there is an honest rectitude about him that makes him a valuable Member of Society, and secures to him the esteem of all good Men. He is about 30 years old, served with me as a Brother Aid to General Sullivan in the Western expedition of '79.

From Pennsylvania.

Benja. Franklin, Thos. Mifflin, Robt. Morris, Geo. Clymer, Thomas Fitzsimmons, Jared Ingersol, James Wilson, Governeur Morris.

Dr. Franklin is well known to be the greatest phylosopher of the present age; — all the operations of nature he seems to understand, — the very heavens obey him, and the Clouds yield up their Lightning to be imprisoned in his rod. But what claim he has to the politician posterity must determine. It is certain that he does not shine much in public Council, — he is no Speaker, nor does he seem to let politics engage his attention. He is, however, a most extraordinary Man, and tells a story in a style more engaging that anything I ever heard. Let his Biographer finish his character. He is 82 years old, and possesses an activity of mind equal to a youth of 25 years of age.

* * * * * * *

Robert Morris is a merchant of great eminence and wealth; an able Financier, and a worthy Patriot. He has an understanding equal to any public object, and possesses an energy of mind that few Men can boast of. Although he is not learned, yet he is as great as those who are. I am told that when he speaks in the Assembly of Pennsylvania, that he bears down all before him. What could have been his reason for not Speaking in the Convention I know not,— but he never spoke on any point. This Gentleman is about 50 years of age. . . .

Mr. Fitzsimmons is a Merchant of considerable talents. . . .

* * * * * * *

Mr. Ingersol is a very able Attorney, and possesses a clear legal understanding. He is well educated in the Classic's and is a Man of very extensive reading. Mr. Ingersol speaks well, and comprehends his subject fully. There is a modesty in his character that keeps him back. He is about 36 years old.

Mr. Wilson ranks among the foremost in legal and political knowledge. He has joined to a fine genius all that can set him off and show him to advantage. He is well acquainted with Man, and understands all the passions that influence him.

Government seems to have been his peculiar Study, all the political institutions of the World he knows in detail, and can trace the causes and effects of every revolution from the earliest stages of the Greecian commonwealth down to the present time. No man is more clear, copious, and comprehensive than Mr. Wilson, yet he is no great Orator. He draws the attention not by the charm of his eloquence, but by the force of his reasoning. He is about 45 years old.

Mr. Governeur Morris is one of those Genius's in whom every species of talents combine to render him conspicuous and flourishing in public debate: — He winds through all the mazes of rhetoric, and throws around him such a glare that he charms, captivates, and leads away the senses of all who hear him. With an infinite streach of fancy he brings to view things when he is engaged in deep argument, that render all the labor of reasoning easy and pleasing. But with all these powers he is fickle and inconstant, — never pursuing one train of thinking, — nor ever regular. He has gone through a very extensive course of reading, and is acquainted with all the sciences. No Man has more wit, — nor can any one engage the attention more than Mr. Morris. He was bred to the Law, but I am told he disliked the profession, and turned merchant. He is engaged in some great mercantile matters with his namesake Mr. Robt Morris. This Gentleman is about 38 years old, he has been unfortunate in losing one of his Legs, and getting all the flesh taken off his right arm by a scald, when a youth.

From Delaware.

John Dickinson, Gunning Bedford, Geo: Richd. Bassett, and Jacob Broom Esquires.

Mr. Dickinson has been famed through all America, for his Farmers Letters; he is a Scholar, and said to be a Man of very extensive information. When I saw him in the Convention I was induced to pay the greatest attention to him whenever he spoke. I had often heard that he was a great Orator, but I found him an indifferent Speaker. With an affected air of wisdom he labors to produce a trifle, — his language is irregular and incorrect, — his flourishes (for he sometimes attempts them), are like expiring flames, they just shew themselves and go out; — no traces of them are left on the mind to chear or animate it. He is, however, a good writer and will ever be considered one of the most important characters in the United States. He is about 55 years old, and was bred a Quaker.

Mr. Bedford was educated for the Bar, and in his profession I am told has merit. He is a bold and nervous Speaker, and has a very commanding and striking manner; — but he is warm and inpetuous in his temper, and precipitate in his judgment. [Cf. No. 161.] Mr. Bedford is about 32 years old, and very corpulant.

* * * * * * *

From Maryland.

Luther Martin, Jas. McHenry, Daniel of St. Thomas, Jenifer, and Daniel Carrol Esquires.

Mr. Martin was educated for the Bar, and is Attorney general for the State of Maryland. This Gentleman possesses a good deal of information, but he has a very bad delivery, and so extremely prolix, that he never speaks without tiring the patience of all who hear him. He is about 34 years of age.

Mr. Jenifer is a Gentleman of fortune. . . .

Mr. Carroll is a Man of large fortune. . . .

From Virginia.

Genl. Geo: Washington, Geo: Wythe, Geo: Mason, Jas. Maddison junr. Jno. Blair, Edmd. Randolph, and James Mc.Lurg.

* * * * * * *

Mr. Mason is a Gentleman of a remarkable strong powers, and possesses a clear and copious understanding. He is able and convincing in debate, steady and firm in his principles, and undoubtedly one of the best politicians in America. Mr. Mason is about 60 years old, with a fine strong constitution.

Mr. Maddison is a character who has long been in public life; and what is very remarkable every Person seems to acknowledge his greatness. He blends together the profound politician, with the Scholar. In the management of every great question he evidently took the lead in the Convention, and tho' he cannot be called an Orator, he is a most agreable, eloquent, and convincing Speaker. From a spirit of industry and application which he possesses in a most eminent degree, he always comes forward the best informed Man of any point in debate. The affairs of the United States, he perhaps, has the most correct knowledge of, of any Man in the Union. He has been twice a Member of Congress, and was always thought one of the ablest Members that ever sat in that Council. Mr. Maddison is about 37 years of age, a Gentleman of great modesty, — with a remarkable sweet temper. He is easy and unreserved among his acquaintances, and has a most agreable style of conversation.

Mr. Blair is one of the most respectable Men in Virginia both on account of his Family as well as his fortune. . . .

Mr. Randolph is Governor of Virginia, — a young Gentleman in whom unite all the accomplishments of the Scholar, and the States-man. He came forward with the postulata or first principles, on which the Convention acted, and he supported them with a force of eloquence and reasoning that did him great honor. He has a most harmonious voice, a fine person and striking manners. Mr. Randolph is about 32 years of age.

*　　*　　*　　*　　*　　*　　*

North Carolina.

Wm. Blount, Richd. Dobbs Spaight, Hugh Williamson, Wm. Davey, and Jno. [Alexander] Martin Esquires.

Mr. Blount is a character strongly marked for integrity and honor. He has been twice a Member of Congress, and in that office discharged his duty with ability and faithfulness. He is no Speaker, nor does he possess any of those talents that make Men shine; — he is plain, honest, and sincere. Mr. Blount is about 36 years of age.

Mr. Spaight is a worthy Man, of some abilities, and fortune. Without possessing a Genius to render him brilliant, he is able to discharge any public trust that his Country may repose in him. He is about 31 years of age. . . .

MEN OF THE CONVENTION

South Carolina.

Jno. Rutledge, Chs. Cotesworth Pinckney, Charles Pinckney, and Pierce Butler Esquires.

Mr. Rutledge is one of those characters who was highly mounted at the commencement of the late revolution; his reputation in the first Congress gave him a distinguished rank among the American Worthies. He was bred to the Law, and now acts as one of the Chancellors of South Carolina. This Gentleman is much famed in his own State as an Orator, but in my opinion he is too rapid in his public speaking to be denominated an agreeable Orator. He is undoubtedly a man of abilities, and a Gentleman of distinction and fortune. Mr. Rutledge was once Governor of South Carolina. He is about 48 years of age.

Mr. Chas. Cotesworth Pinckney is a Gentleman of Family and fortune. . . .

Mr. Charles Pinckney is a young Gentleman of most promising talents. He is, altho only 24 years of age, in possession of a very great variety of knowledge. Government, Law, History, and Philosophy are his favorite studies, but he is intimately acquainted with many species of polite learning. . . .

* * * * * * *

For Georgia.

Wm. Few, Abraham Baldwin, Wm. Pierce, and Wm. Houstoun Esqrs.

Mr. Few possesses a strong natural Genius, and from application has acquired some knowledge of legal matters; and he practices at the bar of Georgia, and speaks tolerably well in the Legislature. He has been twice a Member of Congress, and served in that capacity with fidelity to his State, and honor to himself. Mr. Few is about 35 years of age.

Mr. Baldwin is a Gentleman of superior abilities, and joins in a public debate with great art and eloquence. Having laid the foundation of a compleat classical education at Harvard College, he pursues every other study with ease. He is well acquainted with Books and Characters, and has an accomodating turn of mind, which enables him to gain the confidence of Men, and to understand them. He is a practicing Attorney in Georgia, and has been twice a Member of Congress. Mr. Baldwin is about 38 years of age.

Mr. Houstoun is an Attorney at Law. . . . He is a Gentleman of Family, and was educated in England. As to his legal or political knowledge, he has very little to boast of. Nature seems to have done more for his corporeal than mental powers. His person is striking. . .

161. One Day in the Philadelphia Convention

Madison's *Journal.* The day chosen was the closing day of debate on the "Connecticut Compromise" proposition, when the Convention came near disruption. For the narrative, cf. *American History and Government,* § 203.

SATURDAY, JUNE 30th

In Convention, — Mr. BREARLY [New Jersey][1] moved that the President write to the Executive of New Hampshire, informing it that the business depending before the Convention was of such a nature as to require the immediate attandance of the Deputies of that State. In support of his motion, he observed that the difficulties of the subject, and the diversity of opinions called for all the assistance we could possibly obtain. (It was well understood that the object was to add New Hampshire to the number of States opposed to the doctrine of proportional representation, which it was presumed, from her relative size, she must be adverse to.)

Mr. PATTERSON [New Jersey] seconded the motion.

Mr. RUTLEDGE [South Carolina] could see neither the necessity nor propriety of such a measure. They are not unapprized of the meeting, and can attend if they choose.

---

[1] Observe the motion was a "small-State" move, opposed by the "large States" in debate as in vote.

Rhode Island might as well be urged to appoint and send deputies. Are we to suspend the business until the Deputies arrive? If we proceed, he hoped all the great points would be adjusted before the letter could produce its effect.

Mr. KING [Massachusetts] said he had written more than once as a private correspondent, and the answer gave him every reason to expect that State would be represented very shortly, if it should be so at all. Circumstances of a personal nature had hitherto prevented it. A letter could have no effect.

Mr. WILSON [Pennsylvania] wished to know, whether it would be consistent with rule or reason of secrecy, to communicate to New Hampshire that the business was of such a nature as the motion described. It would spread a great alarm. Besides he doubted the propriety of soliciting any State on the subject, the meeting being merely voluntary.

On motion of Mr. BREARLY.

New York, New Jersey, aye — 2; Massachusetts, Connecticut, Virginia, North Carolina, South Carolina, no — 5; Maryland divided; Pennsylvania, Delaware, Georgia, not on the floor.

The motion of Mr. ELLSWORTH being resumed, for allowing each State an equal vote in the second branch, — [1]

Mr. WILSON did not expect such a motion after the establishment of the contrary principle in the first branch; and considering the reasons which would oppose it, even if an equal vote had been allowed in the first branch. The gentleman from Connecticut (Mr. ELLSWORTH) had pronounced, that if the motion should not be acceded to, of all the States north of Pennsylvania one only would agree to any General Government. He entertained more favourable hopes of Connecticut and of the other Northern States. He hoped the alarms exceeded their cause, and that they would not abandon

---

[1] This motion had been made the day before. The Convention had previously agreed that voting in the "first branch" should be in proportion to population.

a country to which they were bound by so many strong and endearing ties. But should the deplored event happen, it would neither stagger his sentiments nor his duty. *If the minority of the people of America refuse to coalesce with the majority on just and proper principles; if a separation must take place, it could never happen on better grounds.* The votes of yesterday against the just principle of representation were as twenty-two to ninety of the people of America. Taking the opinions to be the same on this point, and he was sure, if there was any room for change, it could not be on the side of the majority, the question will be, shall less than one-fourth of the United States withdraw themselves from the Union, or shall more than three-fourths renounce the inherent, indisputable and unalienable rights of men, in favor of the artificial system of States? If issue must be joined, it was on this point he would choose to join it. The gentleman from Connecticut, in supposing that the preponderance secured to the majority in the first branch had removed the objections to an equality of votes in the second branch for the security of the minority, narrowed the case extremely. Such an equality will enable the minority to control, in all cases whatsoever, the sentiments and interests of the majority. Seven States will control six: seven States, according to the estimates that had been used, composed twenty-four ninetieths of the whole people. It would be in the power, then, of less than one-third to overrule two-thirds, whenever a question should happen to divide the States in that manner. . . .

Mr. ELLSWORTH. The capital objection of Mr. WILSON, "that the minority will rule the majority," is not true. **The power is given to the few to save them from being destroyed by the many.** If an equality of votes had been given to them in both branches, the objection might have weight. Is it a novel thing that the few should have a check on the many? Is it not the case in the British Constitution, the wisdom of which so many gentlemen have united in applauding? Have not the House of Lords, who form so small a proportion of the nation, a negative on the laws, as a necessary defence of their peculiar rights against the encroachments of the Commons? No instance of a confederacy has existed in which an equality of voices has not been exercised by the members of it. We are running from one extreme to another. We are razing the foundations of the building, when we need only repair the roof. No salutary measure has been lost for want of *a majority of the States* to favor it. If security be all that the great States wish for, the first branch secures them. The danger of combinations among them is not imaginary. Although no particular abuses could be foreseen by him the possibility of them would be sufficient to alarm him. But he could easily conceive cases in which they might result from such combinations. Suppose, that, in pursuance of some commercial treaty or arrangement, three or four free ports and no more were to be established, would not combinations be formed in favor of Boston, Philadelphia, and some port of the Chesapeake? A like concert might be formed in the appointment of the great offices. He appealed again to *the obligations of the Federal compact* [Articles of Confederation] *in force,* and which had been entered *into with so much solemnity; persuading himself that some regard would still be paid to the plighted faith under which each State, small as well as great, held an equal right of suffrage in the general councils.* His remarks were not the result of partial or local views. The State he represented (Connecticut) held a middle rank.

Mr. MADISON did justice to the able and close reasoning of Mr. ELLSWORTH, but must observe that it did not always accord with itself. On another occasion, the large States were described by him as the aristocratic States, ready to oppress the small. Now the small are the House of Lords, requiring a negative to defend them against the more numerous Commons. Mr. ELLSWORTH had also erred in saying that no instance had existed in which confederated states had not retained to themselves a perfect equality of suffrage. Passing over the German system, in which the King of Prussia has nine voices, he reminded Mr. ELLSWORTH of the Lycian confederacy, in which the component members had votes proportioned to their importance, and which Montesquieu recommends as the fittest model for that form of government. Had the fact been as stated by Mr. ELLSWORTH, it would have been of little avail to him, or rather would have strengthened the arguments against him; the history and fate of the several confederacies, modern as well as ancient, demonstrating some radical vice in their structure. In reply to the appeal of Mr. ELLSWORTH to the faith plighted in the existing federal compact, he remarked, that the party claiming from others an adherence to a common engagement, ought at least to be guiltless itself of a violation. Of all the States, however, Connecticut was perhaps least able to urge this plea. Besides the various omissions to perform the stipulated acts, from which no State was free, the Legislature of that State had, by a pretty recent vote, *positively refused* to pass a law for complying with the requisitions of Congress, and transmitted a copy of the vote to Congress.[1] It was urged, he said, continually, that an equality of votes in the second branch was not only necessary to secure the small, but would be perfectly safe to the large ones; whose majority in the first branch was an effectual bulwark. But notwithstanding this apparent defence, the majority of States might still injure the majority of the people. . . . He admitted that every peculiar interest, whether in any class of citizens or any description of States, ought to be secured as far as possible. Wherever there is danger of attack, there ought to be given a constitutional power of defence. **But he contended that the States were divided into different interests, not by their difference of size, but other circumstances; the most material of which resulted partly from climate, but principally from the effects of their having or not having slaves. These two causes concurred in forming the great division of interests in the United States. It did not lie between the large and small States. It lay between the Northern and Southern.** . . .

Mr. ELLSWORTH assured the House, that, whatever might be

---

[1] This begins the rather unhappy " personalities " of the debate.

thought of the Representatives of Connecticut, the State was entirely Federal in her disposition. He appealed to her great exertions during the war, in supplying both men and money. *The muster-rolls would show she had more troops in the field than Virginia.*[1] If she had been delinquent, it had been from inability, and not more so than other States.

Mr. SHERMAN. MR. MADISON animadverted on the delinquency of the States, when his object required him to prove that the constitution of Congress was faulty. Congress is not to blame for the faults of the States. Their measures have been right, and the only thing wanting has been a further power in Congress to render them effectual.

Mr. DAVIE [North Carolina] was much embarrassed, and wished for explanations. The Report of the Committee [of the Whole], allowing the Legislatures to choose the Senate, and establishing a proportional representation in it, seemed to be impracticable. There will, according to this rule, be ninety members in the outset, and the number will increase as new States are added. It was impossible that so numerous a body could possess the activity and other qualities required in it. Were he to vote on the comparative merits of the Report, as it stood, and the amendment, he should be constrained to prefer the latter. . . . Under this view of the subject, he could not vote for any plan for the Senate yet proposed. He thought that, in general, there were extremes on both sides. *We were partly federal, partly national, in our union;* and he did not see why the Government might not in some respects operate on the States, in others on the people.

Mr. WILSON admitted the question concerning the number of Senators to be embarrassing. If the smallest States be allowed one, and the others in proportion, the Senate will certainly be too numerous. He looked forward to the time when the smallest States will contain a hundred thousand souls at least. Let there be then one Senator in each, for every hundred thousand souls, and let the States not having

---

[1] Cf. note above.

that number of inhabitants be allowed one. He was willing himself to submit to this temporary concession to the small States; and threw out the idea as a ground of compromise. . . .

Doctor FRANKLIN. The diversity of opinions turns on two points. If a proportional representation takes place, the small States contend that their liberties will be in danger. If an equality of votes is to be put in its place, the large States say their money will be in danger. When a broad table is to be made, and the edges of planks do not fit, the artist takes a little from both, and makes a good joint. In like manner, here, both sides must part from some of their demands, in order that they may join in some accommodating proposition. He had prepared one which he would read, that it might lie on the table for consideration. The proposition was in the words following:

"That the Legislatures of the several States shall choose and send an equal number of delegates, namely . . . , who are to compose the second branch of the General Legislature.

"That in all cases or questions wherein the sovereignty of individual States may be affected, or whereby their authority over their own citizens may be diminished, or the authority of the General Government within the several States augmented, each State shall have equal suffrage.

"That in the appointment of all civil officers of the General Government, in the election of whom the second branch may by the constitution have part, each State shall have equal suffrage.

"That in fixing the salaries of such officers, and in all allowances for public services, and generally in all appropriations and disposition of money to be drawn out of the general Treasury; and in all laws for supplying that Treasury, the Delegates of the several States shall have suffrage in proportion to the sums which their respective States do actually contribute to the Treasury."

Where a ship had many owners, this was the rule of deciding on her expedition. He had been one of the ministers from this country to France during the joint war, and would have been very glad if allowed to vote in distributing the money to carry it on.

Mr. KING observed, that the simple question was, whether

each State should have an equal vote in the second branch; that it must be apparent to those gentlemen who liked neither the motion for this quality, nor the Report as it stood, that the Report was as susceptible of melioration as the motion; that a reform would be nugatory and nominal only, if we should make another Congress of the proposed Senate; that if the adherence to an equality of votes was fixed and unalterable, there could not be less obstinacy on the other side; and that *we were in fact cut asunder already, and it was in vain to shut our eyes against it.* That he was, however, filled with astonishment, that, if we were convinced that every *man* in America was secured in all his rights, we should be ready to sacrifice this substantial good to the phantom of *State* sovereignty. That his feelings were more harrowed and his fears more agitated for his country than he could express; that he conceived this to be the last opportunity of providing for its liberty and happiness: that he could not, therefore, but repeat his amazement, that when a just government, founded on a fair representation of the *People* of America, was within our reach, we should renounce the blessing, from an attachment to the ideal freedom and importance of *States*. That should this wonderful illusion continue to prevail, his mind was prepared for any event, rather than sit down under a Government founded on a vicious principle of representation, and which must be as short-lived as it would be unjust. He might prevail on himself to accede to some such expedient as had been hinted by Mr. WILSON; but *he never could listen to an equality of votes, as proposed in the motion.*

Mr. DAYTON. *When assertion is given for proof, and terror substituted for argument, he presumed they would have no effect, however eloquently spoken.* It should have been shown that the evils we have experienced have proceeded from the equality now objected to; and that the seeds of dissolution for the State Governments are not sown in the General Government. He considered the system on the table [Virginia Plan] as a novelty, an amphibious monster; and was persuaded that it never would be received by the people.

Mr. Martin [Maryland] *would never confederate, if it could not be done on just principles* [*i.e.*, giving small States equal voice in at least one House].

Mr. Madison would acquiesce in the concession hinted by Mr. Wilson, on condition that a due independence should be given to the Senate. The plan in its present shape makes the Senate absolutely dependent on the States. The Senate, therefore, is only another edition of Congress. He knew the faults of that body, and had used a bold language against it. Still he would preserve the State rights as carefully as the trial by jury.

Mr. Bedford [Delaware] contended, that there was no middle way between a perfect consolidation, and a mere confederacy of the States. The first is out of the question; and in the latter they must continue, if not perfectly, yet *equally*, sovereign. If political societies possess ambition, avarice, and all the other passions which render them formidable to each other, ought we not to view them in this light here? Will not the same motives operate in America as elsewhere? If any gentleman doubts it, let him look at the votes. Have they not been dictated by interest, by ambition? *Are not the large States evidently seeking to aggrandize themselves at the expense of the small?* They think, no doubt, that they have right on their side, but interest has blinded their eyes. Look at Georgia. Though a small State at present, she is actuated by the prospect of soon being a great one. South Carolina is actuated both by present interest, and future prospects. She hopes, too, to see the other States cut down to her own dimensions. North Carolina has the same motives of present and future interest. Virginia follows. Maryland is not on that side of the question. Pennsylvania has a direct and future interest. Massachusetts has a decided and palpable interest in the part she takes. . . . *The three large States have a common interest to bind them together in commerce.* But whether a combination, as we supposed, shall take place among them, in either case the small States must be ruined.

We must, like Solon, make such a government as the people will approve. Will the smaller States ever agree to the proposed degradation of them? It is not true that the people will not agree to enlarge the powers of the present Congress. The language of the people has been, that Congress ought to have the power of collecting an impost, and of coercing the States where it may be necessary. On the first point they have been explicit, and, in a manner, unanimous in their declarations. And must they not agree to this, and similar measures, if they ever mean to discharge their engagements? The little States are willing to observe their engagements, *but will meet the large ones on no ground but that of the Confederation. We have been told, with dictatorial air, this is the last moment for a fair trial in favor of a good government. It will be the last, indeed, if the propositions reported from the Committee go forth to the people. He was under no apprehensions. The large States dare not dissolve the Confederation. If they do, the small ones will find some foreign ally, of more honour and good faith, who will take them by the hand, and do them justice.* He did not mean, by this, to intimidate or alarm. It was a natural consequence, which ought to be avoided by enlarging the Federal powers, not annihilating the Federal system. This is what the people expect. All agree in the necessity of a more efficient government, and why not make such an one as they desire?

Mr. ELLSWORTH. Under a National Government, he should participate in the national security, as remarked by Mr. KING; but that was all. What he wanted was domestic happiness. The National Government could not descend to the local objects on which this depended. It could only embrace objects of a general nature. He turned his eyes, therefore, for the preservation of his rights, to the State Governments. From these alone he could derive the greatest happiness he expects in this life. His happiness depends on their existence, as much as a new-born infant on its mother for nourishment. If this reasoning was not satisfactory, he had nothing to add that could be so.

Mr. KING was for preserving the States in a subordinate degree, and as far as they could be necessary for the purposes stated by Mr. ELLSWORTH. He did not think a full answer had been given to those who apprehended a dangerous encroachment on their jurisdictions. . . . He could not sit down without taking some notice of the language of the honorable gentleman from Delaware (Mr. BEDFORD). It was not he [King] that had uttered a dictatorial language. This intemperance had marked the honorable gentleman himself. It was not he [King] who, with a vehemence unprecedented in that House, had declared himself ready to turn his hopes from our common country, and court the protection of some foreign hand. This, too, was the language of the honorable member himself. He was grieved that such an expression had dropped from his lips. The gentleman could only excuse it to himself on the score of passion. For himself, **whatever might be his distress, he would never court relief from a foreign power.**

Adjourned.

[The vote, taken on the opening of the next session, is recorded as follows :

"*In Convention*, — On the question for allowing each State one vote in the second branch, as moved by Mr. ELLSWORTH, it was lost, by an equal division of votes, — Connecticut, New York, New Jersey, Delaware, Maryland, aye — 5 ; Massachusetts, Pennsylvania, Virginia, North Carolina, South Carolina, no — 5 ; Georgia, divided (Mr. Baldwin aye, Mr. Houston, no)."

This was a tie, intentionally made so by the Georgia delegate who voted last. For this and for the final victory of the " Compromise," cf. *American History and Government*, § 203.]

XXVIII. RATIFYING THE CONSTITUTION[1]

162. George Mason's Objections to the Constitution, 1787

Kate Mason Rowland's *Life of George Mason* (1892), II, 387–390.

Mason had been one of the most enthusiastic of the Philadelphia Convention in its early stages, writing to his son, after a few weeks, that he would "bury my bones in Philadelphia" rather than injure the business by leaving prematurely, though his private affairs were pressing. But he was more democratic than the Convention, and, before its close, he came to look upon the results with suspicion. He refused to sign the completed constitution, and afterward he opposed its ratification in Virginia. Mason was the chief author of the Virginia Bill of Rights of 1776 (No. 136 above). Cf. also No. 163.

There is no Declaration of Rights, and, the laws of the general government being paramount to the laws and constitution of the several States, the Declaration of Rights in the separate States are no security. *Nor are the people secured even in the enjoyment of the benefit of the common law.*

In the House of Representatives there is not the substance but the shadow only of representation; which can never produce proper information in the legislature, or inspire confidence in the people; the laws will therefore be generally made by men little concerned in, and unacquainted with their effects and consequences.

The Senate have the power of altering all money bills, and of originating appropriations of money, and the salaries of the officers of their own appointment, in conjunction with the president of the United States, although they are not the representatives of the people or amenable to them.

---

[1] The Federalist side is presented in books which should be accessible in reference libraries, much more fully than can possibly be reproduced here. Space is given for only three documents which indicate something of the opposition.

These with their other great powers (viz. : their power in the appointment of ambassadors and all public officers; in making treaties, and in trying all impeachments; their influence upon and connection with the supreme Executive from these causes; their duration of office and their being a constantly existing body, almost continually sitting; joined with their being one complete branch of the legislature) will destroy any balance in the government, and enable them to accomplish what usurpations they please upon the rights and liberties of the people.

The Judiciary of the United States is so constructed and extended, as to absorb and destroy the judiciaries of the several States; thereby rendering law as tedious, intricate and expensive, and justice as unattainable, by a great part of the community, as in England, and enabling the rich to oppress and ruin the poor.

The President of the United States has no Constitutional Council, a thing unknown in any safe and regular government. He will therefore be unsupported by proper information and advice, and will generally be directed by minions and favorites; or he will become a tool to the Senate — or a Council of State will grow out of the principal officers of the great departments; the worst and most dangerous of all ingredients for such a Council in a free country. From this fatal defect has arisen the improper power of the Senate in the appointment of public officers, and the alarming dependence and connection between that branch of the legislature and the supreme Executive.

Hence also sprung that unnecessary officer the Vice-President, who for want of other employment is made president of the Senate, thereby dangerously blending the executive and legislative powers, besides always giving to some one of the States an unnecessary and unjust preëminence over the others.

The President of the United States has the unrestrained power of granting pardons for treason, which may be sometimes exercised to screen from punishment those whom he had secretly instigated to commit the crime, and thereby prevent a discovery of his own guilt.

By declaring all treaties supreme laws of the land, the Executive and the Senate have, in many cases, an exclusive power of legislation; which might have been avoided by proper distinctions with respect to treaties, and requiring the assent of the House of Representatives, where it could be done with safety.

By requiring only a majority to make all commercial and navigation laws, the five Southern States, whose produce and circumstances are totally different from that of the eight Northern and Eastern States, may be ruined, for such rigid and premature regulations may be made as will enable the merchants of the Northern and Eastern States not only to demand an exhorbitant freight, but to monopolize the purchase of the commodities at their own price, for many years, to the great injury of the landed interest, and impoverishment of the people; and the danger is the greater as the gain on one side will be in proportion to the loss on the other. Whereas requiring two-thirds of the members present in both Houses would have produced mutual moderation, promoted the general interest, and removed an insuperable objection to the adoption of this government.

Under their own construction of the general clause, at the end of the enumerated powers,[1] the Congress may grant monopolies in trade and commerce, constitute new crimes, inflict unusual and severe punishments, and extend their powers as far as they shall think proper; so that the State legislatures have no security for the powers now presumed to remain to them, or the people for their rights.

There is no declaration of any kind, for preserving the liberty of the press, or the trial by jury in civil causes; nor against the danger of standing armies in time of peace.

---

[1] "Necessary and proper." Mason almost alone saw the possibilities of change in this clause. Cf. No. 164 below.

The State legislatures are restrained from laying export duties on their own produce.

Both the general legislature and the State legislature are expressly prohibited making *ex post facto* laws; though there never was nor can be a legislature but must and will make such laws, when necessity and the public safety require them; which will hereafter be a breach of all the constitutions in the Union, and afford precedents for other innovations.

This government will set out a moderate aristocracy: it is at present impossible to foresee whether it will, in its operation, produce a monarchy, or a corrupt, tyrannical aristocracy; it will most probably vibrate some years between the two, and then terminate in the one or the other.

The general legislature is restrained from prohibiting the further importation of slaves for twenty odd years; though such importations render the United States weaker, more vulnerable, and less capable of defence.

163. Mason's Explanation of the Preparation of his "Objections" (and Accusation of "Railroading" through the Plan of the Majority)

George Mason to Thomas Jefferson [in France]

Records of the Federal Convention, III, 304–305.

VIRGINIA, GUNSTON HALL, May 26, 1788.

I make no Doubt that You have long ago received Copys of the new Constitution. . . . Upon the most mature consideration I was capable of, and from Motives of sincere Patriotism, I was under the Necessity of refusing my Signature, as one of the Virginia Delegates; and drew up some general Objections; which I intended to offer, by way of Protest; but was discouraged from doing so, by the precipitate and intemperate, not to say indecent, Manner, in which the Business was conducted during the last week of the Convention, after the Patrons of this New Plan formed they had a decided Majority in their Favour: which was obtained by a Compromise between the Eastern and the two Southern States, to permit the latter to continue the Importation of Slaves for twenty odd years; a more favorite Object with them than the Liberty and Happiness of the People.

164. An Unfriendly Account of Hancock's Support of the Constitution in the Massachusetts Ratifying Convention of 1788

Writings of Laco, VII, 23 ff. (a series of "Letters" published by Stephen Higginson and other Federalists, in 1789, to defeat Hancock in his candidacy for reëlection to the governorship). Higginson was a Boston merchant, and a leading Federalist. The "plan" he refers to as placed in Hancock's hands, favored the adoption of the Constitution with a list of amendments to be adopted later by the new government.

There are men in every free society, who have not a common interest with the community at large; and who rely wholly on the popular affection in their favour, to give them promotion and support in publick life. . . . Without abilities to make them really useful in publick life, and devoid of principles or merits that can command respect, they have no dependence but upon popular attention to bring them into view; and, having been long attentive to the popular pulse, and always acquainted with the darling object with the multitude for the time, they rarely fail to touch the right string, and to make the people subserve their own selfish and private views . . . There cannot be found within the compass of our memory, an instance, so strongly verifying the preceding observation, as that of Mr. H. and his adhering dependents. . . .

. . . The course of his conduct from his reassuming the chair, to the meeting of our State Convention, for considering and adopting the new form of government for the Union, was nothing more than a renewed exhibition of the same levities, and a uniform preference of his own private interest, to that of the public.

A scene now opens upon us, very interesting and important: — The objects which [were] then presented for our consideration, were so novel, and of such magnitude, as deservedly engrossed the feelings and the attention of every man. No one could remain mute and indifferent, while the question as to the New Constitution was pending; and every one, who felt no other bias than a regard to the safety and happiness of our country, . . . was most anxiously solicitous for its adoption. But the popular demagogues, and those [who] were very much embarrassed in their affairs, united to oppose it with all their might; and they laboured incessantly, night and day, to alarm the simple and credulous, by insinuating, that, however specious its appearance, and that of its advocates, tyranny and vassalage would result from its principles. The former of those descriptions were conscious, that a stable and efficient government would deprive them of all future importance, or support from the publick; and the latter of them knew, that nothing but weakness and convulsions in government could screen them from payment of their debts. How far Mr. H. was influenced by either, or both of those motives, it is not easy to determine; but no one, who recollects his general habits, who knows his situation and views, and was acquainted with the open conversation and conduct of his cabinet counsellors, can have a doubt of his being opposed to it. We all know, that Mr. Quondam, and Mr. Changeling, as well as the *once venerable old Patriot* [Samuel Adams], who, by a notable defection, has lately thrown himself into the arms of Mr. H. in violation of every principle; and for the paltry privilege of sharing in his smiles, has, at the eve of life, cast an indelible stain over his former reputation — it is well known, I say, that these men do not dare to speak in publick a language opposite to that of their patron; and it is equally notorious, that they were open in their opposition to the Constitution — They even went so far as to vilify its compilers, that they might thence draw an argument to support their suggestions of its containing the seeds of latent tyranny and oppression. They endeavoured by every possible mean in their power, to create a popular clamour against the Constitution; but they failed in their attempt; and Mr. H. and his friends were obliged, upon their own principles to grow more cautious in their opposition. The good sense of the *Mechanicks of Boston* had produced some manly and spirited resolutions, which effectually checked Mr. H. and his followers in their opposition to the Constitution; and eventually occasioned *four* votes in its favour, which otherwise would have been most certainly against it. Had those resolutions not made their appearance, Mr. H. and three others of our Delegates would have been in the negative; but it was thought necessary by them, after they had appeared, to vote in favour of it. Having settled this point, the next thing was to do it with a good grace, and to profit as much by it as they could; and Mr. H. accordingly intimated to the advocates for the adoption, that he would appear in its favour, if they would make it worth his while. This intimation was given through a common friend, who assured the friends of the Constitution, that nothing more would be required on the part of Mr. H. than a promise to support him in the chair at the next election. This promise, though a bitter pill, was agreed to be given; for such was the state of things, that they were very much afraid to decide upon the question, whilst he was opposed to it. The famous conciliatory proposition of Mr. H. as it was called, was then prepared by the advocates, and adopted by him; but the truth is, he never was consulted about it, nor knew its contents, before it was handed to him to bring forward in Convention. At the appointed time, Mr. H. with all the parade of an Arbiter of States, came out with the motion, not only in the words, but the very original paper that was given him; and, with a confidence astonishing to all who were in the secret, he called it his own, and said it was the result of his own reflections on the subject, in the short intervals of ease which he had enjoyed, during a most painful disorder. In this pompous and farcical manner did he make that famous proposition, upon which he and his adherents have arrogated so much; but neither he nor they have any other merit in the case, than an attempt to deceive both parties can fairly entitle them. For, at the very time he was buoying up the hopes of the advocates, he was assuring the opposers of the Constitution, by his emissaries, that he was really adverse to it; and upon the strictest scrutiny we cannot find that any one vote was gained by his being ostensibly in favour of it. The votes of the Old Patriot, and Mr. Changeling, and Mr. Joyce, jun. we know were determined in its favour by the resolutions of the Mechanicks; but the votes of many others, who used implicitly to follow Mr. H. were in the negative, which were counted upon by the friends of the Constitution, as being certain on their side. This is a strong confirmation that Mr. H. was then playing a game, which these people well understood; and indeed they, some of them, explicitly declared it at the time. His subsequent conduct, in regard to amendments, is a clear proof also, that by appearing in its favour in Convention, he did not mean to support it; and that he was not serious when he declared his proposition to be only conciliatory, and not to remedy any defects existing in his mind in the constitution as reported, which he explicitly declared at the time was the case.

165. The Federal Constitution

Recommended by the Philadelphia Convention to the States, September 17, 1787; ratified by the ninth State, June 21, 1788; in effect, April 30, 1789 (*American History and Government*, §§ 210, 212). The text is that authorized by the Department of State and printed in the *Revised Statutes* (1878), except for the footnote references and the brackets used in a few instances to inclose portions of the document no longer effective, and for the omission of numbers for the paragraphs. Interpolated explanatory matter is in the same type as this paragraph, and is placed within marks of parenthesis.

We the People [1] of the United States, in Order to form a more perfect Union, establish Justice, insure domestic Tranquillity, provide for the common defence, promote the general Welfare,[2] and secure the Blessings of Liberty to ourselves and our Posterity, do ordain and establish this CONSTITUTION for the United States of America.

ARTICLE I

SECTION 1. All legislative Powers herein granted shall be vested in a Congress of the United States, which shall consist of a Senate and House of Representatives.

SECTION 2. The House of Representatives shall be composed of Members chosen every second Year by the People of the several States, and the Electors in each State shall have the Qualifications requisite for electors of the most numerous Branch of the State Legislature.[3]

No Person shall be a Representative who shall not have attained to the Age of twenty five Years, and been seven Years a Citizen of the United States, and who shall not, when elected, be an Inhabitant of that State in which he shall be chosen.

Representatives and direct Taxes shall be apportioned among the several States which may be included within this Union,

---

[1] Cf. *American History and Government*, § 211.

[2] *Ib.*, § 204 a.

[3] Modified by the Fifteenth Amendment; and cf. *American History and Government*, § 209.

according to their respective numbers [which shall be determined by adding to the whole Number of free Persons, including those bound to Service for a Term of Years], and excluding Indians not taxed, [three fifths of all other Persons].[1] The actual Enumeration shall be made within three Years after the first Meeting of the Congress of the United States, and within every subsequent Term of ten Years, in such Manner as they shall by Law direct.[2] The number of Representatives shall not exceed one for every thirty Thousand,[3] but each State shall have at Least one Representative; [and until such enumeration shall be made, the State of New Hampshire shall be entitled to chuse three, Massachusetts eight, Rhode-Island and Providence Plantations one, Connecticut five, New-York six, New Jersey four, Pennsylvania eight, Delaware one, Maryland six, Virginia ten, North Carolina five, South Carolina five, and Georgia three].

When vacancies happen in the Representation from any State, the Executive Authority thereof shall issue Writs of Election to fill such Vacancies.

The House of Representatives shall chuse their Speaker and other Officers; and shall have the sole Power of Impeachment.

SECTION 3. The Senate of the United States shall be composed of two Senators from each State, chosen [by the Legislature thereof],[4] for six Years; and each Senator shall have one Vote.

[Immediately after they shall be assembled in Consequence of the first Election, they shall be divided as equally as may be into three Classes. The Seats of the Senators of the first Class shall be vacated at the Expiration of the second Year, of

---

[1] The abolition of slavery has rendered obsolete the clauses within brackets in this paragraph.

[2] Cf. *American History and Government*, § 205 b. The first census was taken in 1790, the second year of the new government, and one has been taken in the closing year of each decade since.

[3] The First Congress made the number 33,000. It is now (1911) 193,284.

[4] Superseded by the Seventeenth Amendment.

THE FEDERAL CONSTITUTION   553

the second Class at the Expiration of the fourth Year, and of the third Class at the Expiration of the sixth Year], so that one third may be chosen every second Year;[1] and if Vacancies happen by Resignation, or otherwise, during the Recess of the Legislature of any State, the Executive thereof may make temporary Appointments until the next Meeting of the Legislature, which shall then fill such Vacancies.

No Person shall be a Senator who shall not have attained to the Age of thirty Years, and been nine Years a Citizen of the United States, and who shall not, when elected, be an Inhabitant of that State for which he shall be chosen.

The Vice President of the United States shall be President of the Senate, but shall have no Vote, unless they[2] be equally divided.

The Senate shall chuse their other Officers, and also a President pro tempore, in the Absence of the Vice President, or when he shall exercise the Office of President of the United States.

The Senate shall have the sole Power to try all Impeachments. When sitting for that Purpose, they shall be on Oath or Affirmation. When the President of the United States is tried, the Chief Justice shall preside: And no Person shall be convicted without the Concurrence of two thirds of the Members present.

Judgment in Cases of Impeachment shall not extend further than to removal from Office, and disqualification to hold and enjoy any Office of honor, Trust, or Profit under the United States: but the Party convicted shall nevertheless be liable and subject to Indictment, Trial, Judgment, and Punishment, according to Law.

SECTION 4. The Times, Places, and Manner of holding Elections for Senators and Representatives shall be prescribed in

---

[1] Precedents for this principle of "partial renewals" were found in several State Constitutions.
[2] What is the antecedent?

each State by the Legislature thereof; but the Congress may at any time by Law make or alter such Regulations, except as to the Places of chusing Senators.[1]

The Congress shall assemble at least once in every Year, and such Meeting shall be on the first Monday in December, unless they shall by Law appoint a different Day.

SECTION 5. Each House shall be the Judge of the Elections, Returns, and Qualifications of its own Members, and a Majority of each shall constitute a Quorum to do Business; but a smaller Number may adjourn from day to day, and may be authorized to compel the Attendance of absent Members, in such Manner, and under such Penalties as each House may provide.

Each House may determine the Rules of its Proceedings, punish its Members for disorderly Behaviour, and, with the Concurrence of two thirds, expel a member.

Each House shall keep a Journal of its Proceedings, and from time to time publish the same, excepting such Parts as may in their Judgment require Secrecy; and the Yeas and Nays of the Members of either House on any question shall, at the Desire of one fifth of those Present, be entered on the Journal.

Neither House, during the Session of Congress, shall, without the Consent of the other, adjourn for more than three days, nor to any other Place than that in which the two Houses shall be sitting.

SECTION 6. The Senators and Representatives shall receive a Compensation for their Services, to be ascertained by Law,

---

[1] A law of 1872 requires all Representatives to be chosen on "the Tuesday next after the first Monday in November" in each even-numbered year; and a law of 1871 had already ordered that all such elections should be by ballot. An Act of 1866 provided a uniform method of electing Senators: the legislation of each state (in which such an election is to be made) to vote first *in separate Houses*, and, if no one candidate received a majority in each House, then thereafter in *joint* session, taking at least one ballot daily until some candidate received a majority, or until the legislative session came to an end without an election. Forty-seven years later (1913), this law was superseded by the Seventeenth Amendment.

and paid out of the Treasury of the United States.[1] They shall in all Cases, except Treason, Felony, and Breach of the Peace, be privileged from Arrest during their Attendance of the Session of their respective Houses, and in going to and returning from the same; and for any Speech or Debate in either House, they shall not be questioned in any other Place.

No Senator or Representative shall, during the Time for which he was elected, be appointed to any civil Office under the Authority of the United States, which shall have been created, or the Emoluments whereof shall have been encreased during such time; and no Person holding any Office under the United States, shall be a Member of either House during his Continuance in Office.[2]

SECTION 7. All Bills for raising Revenue shall originate in the House of Representatives; but the Senate may propose or concur with Amendments as on other Bills.

Every Bill which shall have passed the House of Representatives and the Senate, shall, before it become a Law, be presented to the President of the United States; If he approve he shall sign it, but if not he shall return it, with his Objections, to that House in which it shall have originated, who shall enter the Objections at large on their Journal, and proceed to reconsider it. If after such Reconsideration two thirds of that House shall agree to pass the Bill, it shall be sent, together with the Objections, to the other House, by which it shall likewise be reconsidered, and if approved by two thirds of that House, it shall become a Law. But in all such Cases the Votes of both Houses shall be determined by Yeas and Nays, and the Names of the Persons voting for and against the Bill shall be entered on the Journal of each House respectively. If any Bill shall not be returned by the President within ten Days (Sundays excepted) after it shall have been presented to him,

---

[1] How does this compare with the rule of the Articles of Confederation?

[2] This paragraph, designed to prevent corruption by direct use of the executive patronage, was vehemently opposed by Hamilton and Gouverneur Morris. See also a similar clause in Articles of Confederation.

the Same shall be a law, in like Manner as if he had signed it, unless the Congress by their Adjournment prevent its Return, in which Case it shall not be a Law.[1]

Every Order, Resolution, or Vote to which the Concurrence of the Senate and House of Representatives may be necessary (except on a question of Adjournment) shall be presented to the President of the United States; and before the Same shall take Effect, shall be approved by him, or being disapproved by him, shall be repassed by two thirds of the Senate and House of Representatives, according to the Rules and Limitations prescribed in the Case of a Bill.

---

[1] The first veto provision in a State Constitution (New York, 1777) ran as follows: —

"Section III. And whereas laws inconsistent with the spirit of this constitution, or with the public good, may be hastily and unadvisedly passed: Be it ordained that the governor for the time being, the chancellor, and the judges of the supreme court, or any two of them together with the governor, shall be and hereby are constituted a council to revise all bills about to be passed into laws by the legislature. . . . [Provision for veto procedure and reconsideration in language essentially the same as in Massachusetts provision given below.]

"And in order to prevent unnecessary delays, be it further ordained that if any bill shall not be returned by the council within ten days after it shall have been presented, the same shall be a law, unless the Legislature shall, by their adjournment, render a return of the said bill within ten days impracticable; in which case the bill shall be returned on the first day of the Legislature after the expiration of the ten days."

The Veto Provision in the Massachusetts Constitution of 1780 ran: —

"Article II. No bill or resolve of the senate or house of representatives shall become a law, and have force as such, until it shall have been laid before the governor for his revisal; and if he, upon such revision, approve thereof, he shall signify his approbation by signing the same. But if he have any objection to the passing of such bill or resolve, he shall return the same, together with his objections thereto, in writing, to the senate or house of representatives, in whatsoever the same shall have originated, who shall enter the objections sent down by the governor, at large, on their records, and proceed to reconsider the said bill or resolve; but if after such reconsideration, two-thirds of the said senate or house of representatives shall, notwithstanding the objections, agree to pass the same, it shall, together with the objections, be sent to the other branch of the legislature, when it shall also be reconsidered, and if approved by two-thirds of the members present, shall have the force of law; but in all such cases, the vote of both houses shall be determined

THE FEDERAL CONSTITUTION

SECTION 8. The Congress shall have Power To lay and collect Taxes, Duties, Imposts, and Excises, to pay the Debts and provide for the common Defence and general Welfare of the United States;[1] but all Duties, Imposts, and Excises shall be uniform throughout the United States;

To borrow Money on the Credit of the United States;

To regulate Commerce with foreign Nations, and among the several States, and with the Indian Tribes;

To establish an uniform Rule of Naturalization,[2] and

---

by yeas and nays; and the names of the persons voting for or against the said bill or resolve shall be entered upon the public records of the Commonwealth.

"And in order to prevent unnecessary delays, if any bill or resolve shall not be returned by the governor within five days after it shall have been presented, the same shall have the force of law."

The Virginia Plan recommended essentially the New York method. The Massachusetts delegates at Philadelphia, however, contended strenuously for the plan in use in their State, and finally carried their point. The "pocket-veto" clause (the last provision of the text above) was original in the Federal Constitution.

[1] Observe punctuation and paragraphing; and see for comment *American History and Government*, § 204 a.

[2] Citizenship, in practice, comes by birth or by admission by a court of record under authority of a law of Congress. Two classes of people are citizens by birth: (1) according to the Fourteenth Amendment, all who are born within the limits of the United States (except children of official representatives of foreign states, of a foreign army occupying part of our territory); (2) according to a law of Congress, all who are born of parents who are American citizens but who were temporarily residing abroad. No one not included in one of the above classes can become a citizen except by (1) a special Act of Congress, or (2) by admission by a court of record under authority of the general law passed by Congress. That law has varied from time to time (cf. index, for some of the more important variations); but the usual period of residence required for an alien, previous to admission, has been five years, — which is also the present requirement (1913). The present law (passed in 1906) requires also a two years' previous "notice of intention," and excludes all who cannot "speak" English (unless homesteaders), all polygamists, and all who disbelieve in "organized government." Some States, however, permit aliens to vote after receiving their "first papers," — *i.e.*, after making the preliminary "declaration of intention," before a clerk of court. The final admission rests with a judge, — who *may* make his examination of the applicant rigid or a mere matter of form. The power has been sometimes abused for political purposes, both in excluding and in admitting unfit aliens.

uniform Laws on the subject of Bankruptcies throughout the United States;

To coin Money, regulate the Value thereof, and of foreign Coin, and fix the Standard of Weights and Measures;

To provide for the Punishment of counterfeiting the Securities and current Coin of the United States;

To establish Post Offices and post Roads;

To promote the Progress of Science and useful Arts, by securing for limited Times to Authors and Inventors the exclusive Right to their respective Writings and Discoveries;

To constitute Tribunals inferior to the supreme Court;

To define and punish Piracies and Felonies committed on the high Seas, and Offences against the Law of Nations;

To declare War, grant Letters of Marque and Reprisal, and make Rules concerning Captures on Land and Water;

To raise and support Armies, but no Appropriation of Money to that Use shall be for a longer Term than two Years;

To provide and maintain a Navy;

To make Rules for the Government and Regulation of the land and naval Forces;

To provide for calling forth the Militia to execute the Laws of the Union, suppress Insurrections and rebel Invasions;

To provide for organizing, arming, and disciplining, the Militia, and for governing such Part of them as may be employed in the Service of the United States, reserving to the States respectively, the Appointment of the Officers, and the Authority of training the Militia according to the discipline prescribed by Congress;

To exercise exclusive Legislation in all Cases whatsoever, over such District (not exceeding ten Miles square) as may, by Cession of particular States, and the Acceptance of Congress, become the Seat of the Government of the United States, and to exercise like Authority over all Places purchased by the Consent of the Legislature of the State in which the same shall be, for the Erection of Forts, Magazines, Arsenals, dock-Yards, and other needful Buildings;— And

To make all Laws which shall be necessary and proper[1] for carrying into Execution the foregoing Powers, and all other Powers vested by this Constitution in the Government of the United States, or in any Department or Officer thereof.

SECTION 9. [The Migration or Importation of such Persons as any of the States now existing shall think proper to admit, shall not be prohibited by the Congress prior to the Year one thousand eight hundred and eight, but a Tax or duty may be imposed on such Importation, not exceeding ten dollars for each Person.]

The Privilege of the Writ of Habeas Corpus shall not be suspended, unless when in Cases of Rebellion or Invasion the public Safety may require it.

No Bill of Attainder or ex post facto Law shall be passed.

No Capitation, or other direct,[2] Tax shall be laid, unless in Proportion to the Census or Enumeration herein before directed to be taken.

No Tax or Duty shall be laid on Articles exported from any State.

No Preference shall be given by any Regulation of Commerce or Revenue to the Ports of one State over those of another: nor shall Vessels bound to, or from, one State, be obliged to enter, clear, or pay Duties in another.[3]

No Money shall be drawn from the Treasury, but in Consequence of Appropriations made by Law; and a regular Statement and Account of the Receipts and Expenditures of all public Money shall be published from time to time.

No Title of Nobility shall be granted by the United States: And no Person holding any Office of Profit or Trust under them, shall, without the Consent of the Congress, accept of any

---

[1] For comment and reference, see *American History and Government*, §§ 204 b, 222, 280 b. Cf. also with enumeration of powers in Articles of Confederation.

[2] Modified, so far as "direct" income taxes are concerned, by the Sixteenth Amendment.

[3] With what clause in Section 8 might this paragraph have been combined?

present, Emolument, Office, or Title, of any kind whatever, from any King, Prince, or foreign State.

SECTION 10. No State shall enter into any Treaty, Alliance, or Confederation; grant Letters of Marque and Reprisal; coin Money; emit Bills of Credit; make any Thing but gold and silver Coin a Tender in Payment of Debts; pass any Bill of Attainder, ex post facto Law, or Law impairing the Obligation of Contracts, or grant any Title of Nobility.

No State shall, without the Consent of the Congress, lay any Imposts or Duties on Imports or Exports, except what may be absolutely necessary for executing its inspection Laws: and the net Produce of all Duties and Imposts, laid by any State on Imports or Exports, shall be for the Use of the Treasury of the United States; and all such Laws shall be subject to the Revision and Controul of the Congress.

No State shall, without the Consent of Congress, lay any Duty of Tonnage, keep Troops, or Ships of War in time of Peace, enter into any Agreement or Compact with another State, or with a foreign Power, or engage in War, unless actually invaded, or in such imminent Danger as will not admit of delay.[1]

(**Exercise on Article One.** — Are the names in Section 1 new in American history? Can Congress constitutionally provide for woman suffrage by law? If a Senator from your State were to die to-morrow, how would his place be filled? Would it have been filled differently, if it had happened at any other time during the year? How long would the new Senator keep his seat? (The same questions as to a Representative.) How many Representatives has your State? When did it last gain or lose one? How many has the largest State in the Union (cf. World Almanac)? How many has the smallest State? Do you need a World Almanac to answer the last question? Under what possible conditions can the presiding officer of the Senate vote even when there is no tie? With what provision in Section 9 is the last paragraph of Section 3 logically connected?

---

[1] Additional prohibitions upon the States are contained in the Thirteenth, Fourteenth, and Fifteenth Amendments, just as certain additional prohibitions upon Congress are contained in Amendments 1–8. Compare with Section 10 the summary of prohibitions upon the State in the Articles of Confederation.

If a Representative utters plain treason on the floor of the House, can he be punished? How? Commit to memory Section 8. Make two questions upon naturalization and citizenship, based upon the note on page 556. *Write appropriate headings for each section; e.g.*, for Section 8, " Powers of Congress.")

ARTICLE II

SECTION 1. The executive Power shall be vested in a President of the United States of America. He shall hold his Office during the Term of four Years, and, together with the Vice President, chosen for the same Term, be elected, as follows

Each State shall appoint, in such Manner as the Legislature thereof may direct, a Number of Electors, equal to the whole Number of Senators and Representatives to which the State may be entitled in the Congress: but no Senator or Representative, or Person holding an Office of Trust or Profit under the United States, shall be appointed an Elector.

[The Electors shall meet in their respective States, and vote by Ballot for two Persons, of whom one at least shall not be an Inhabitant of the same State with themselves. And they shall make a List of all the Persons voted for, and of the Number of Votes for each; which List they shall sign and certify, and transmit sealed to the Seat of the Government of the United States, directed to the President of the Senate. The President of the Senate shall, in the Presence of the Senate and House of Representatives, open all the Certificates, and the Votes shall then be counted. The Person having the greatest Number of Votes shall be the President, if such Number be a Majority of the whole Number of Electors appointed; and if there be more than one who have such Majority, and have an equal Number of Votes, then the House of Representatives shall immediately chuse by Ballot one of them for President; and if no Person have a Majority, then from the five highest on the List the said House shall in like Manner chuse the President. But in chusing the President, the Votes shall be taken by States, the Representation from each State having one Vote; A quorum for this Purpose shall consist of a Member or Members from two thirds of the States, and a Majority of all the States shall be necessary to a Choice. In every Case, after the Choice of the President, the Person having the greatest Number of Votes of the Electors shall be the Vice President. But if there should remain two or more who have equal Votes, the Senate shall chuse from them by Ballot the Vice President.]¹

The Congress may determine the Time of chusing the Electors, and the Day on which they shall give their Votes; which Day shall be the same throughout the United States.

No Person except a natural born Citizen, or a Citizen of the United States, at the time of the Adoption of this Constitution, shall be eligible to the Office of President; neither shall any Person be eligible to that Office who shall not have attained to the Age of thirty five Years, and been fourteen Years a Resident within the United States.

In Case of the Removal of the President from Office, or of his Death, Resignation, or Inability to discharge the Powers and Duties of the said Office, the Same shall devolve on the Vice President, and the Congress may by Law provide for the Case of Removal, Death, Resignation, or Inability, both of the President and Vice President, declaring what Officer shall then act as President, and such Officer shall act accordingly, until the Disability be removed, or a President shall be elected.²

The President shall, at stated Times, receive for his Services,

---

[1] Superseded by Twelfth Amendment, which might have been *substituted* for this paragraph in the body of the document.

[2] In 1792, Congress provided that the president pro tem of the Senate should be next in succession, and after him the Speaker of the House. In 1886 (Jan. 19), this undesirable law was supplanted by a new one, placing the succession (after the Vice President) in the following order: Secretary of State, Secretary of the Treasury, Secretary of War, Attorney-General, Postmaster-General, Secretary of the Navy, Secretary of the Interior. Cannot the student see on what ground these officers are named in this order? Cf. *American History and Government*, § 215 and note. This provides securely against any interregnum, and (what is almost as important) against a transfer by accident to an opposite political party.

a Compensation, which shall neither be encreased nor diminished during the Period for which he shall have been elected, and he shall not receive within that Period any other Emolument from the United States, or any of them.[1]

Before he enter on the Execution of his Office, he shall take the following Oath or Affirmation: —

"I do solemnly swear (or affirm) that I will faithfully execute the Office of President of the United States, and will to the best of my Ability, preserve, protect, and defend the Constitution of the United States."

SECTION 2. The President shall be Commander in Chief of the Army and Navy of the United States, and of the Militia of the several States, when called into the actual Service of the United States; he may require the Opinion, in writing, of the principal Officer in each of the executive Departments, upon any Subject relating to the Duties of their respective Offices,[2] and he shall have Power to grant Reprieves and Pardons for Offences against the United States, except in Cases of Impeachment.

He shall have Power, by and with the Advice and Consent of the Senate, to make Treaties, provided two thirds of the Senators present concur; and he shall nominate, and by and with the Advice and Consent of the Senate,[3] shall appoint Ambassadors, other public Ministers and Consuls, Judges of the supreme Court, and all other Officers of the United States, whose Appointments are not herein otherwise provided for, and which shall be established by Law: but the Congress may by Law

---

[1] What is the antecedent of "them"? The salary of George Washington was fixed by the First Congress at $25,000. This amount remained unchanged until 1871, when it was made $50,000. In 1909, the salary was raised to $75,000. Large allowances are made also, in these latter days, for expenses of various sorts, — one item of $25,000 for instance, for traveling expenses, — which is the reason the salary is commonly referred to as $100,000.

[2] For the development of the "Cabinet," cf. *American History and Government*, § 215.

[3] *Ib.*, § 214, for different views, at the beginning of the government, as to this clause, and for the settlement in practice.

vest the Appointment of such inferior Officers, as they think proper, in the President alone, in the Courts of Law, or in the Heads of Departments.

The President shall have Power to fill up all Vacancies that may happen during the Recess of the Senate, by granting Commissions which shall expire at the End of their next Session.

SECTION 3. He shall from time to time give to the Congress Information of the State of the Union, and recommend to their Consideration such Measures as he shall judge necessary and expedient; he may, on extraordinary Occasions, convene both Houses, or either of them, and in Case of Disagreement between them, with Respect to the Time of Adjournment, he may adjourn them to such Time as he shall think proper; he shall receive Ambassadors and other public Ministers; he shall take Care that the Laws be faithfully executed, and shall Commission all the Officers of the United States.

SECTION 4. The President, Vice President, and all civil Officers of the United States shall be removed from office on Impeachment for, and conviction of, Treason, Bribery, or other high Crimes and Misdemeanours.

ARTICLE III

SECTION 1. The judicial Power of the United States, shall be vested in one supreme Court, and in such inferior Courts as the Congress may from time to time ordain and establish. The Judges, both of the supreme and inferior Courts, shall hold their Offices during good Behavior, and shall, at stated Times, receive for their Services, a Compensation, which shall not be diminished during their Continuance in Office.

SECTION 2. The judicial Power shall extend to all Cases, in Law and Equity, arising under this Constitution, the Laws of the United States, and Treaties made, or which shall be made, under their Authority; — to all Cases affecting Ambassadors, other public Ministers and Consuls; — to all Cases of admiralty and maritime Jurisdiction; — to Controversies to which the United States shall be a Party; — to Controversies between two or more States; — between a State and Citizens or another State;[1] — between Citizens of different States, — between Citizens of the same State claiming lands under Grants of different States, — and between a State, or the Citizens thereof, and foreign States, Citizens or Subjects.

In all Cases affecting Ambassadors, other public Ministers and Consuls, and those in which a State shall be Party, the supreme Court shall have original Jurisdiction. In all the other Cases before mentioned, the supreme Court shall have appellate Jurisdiction, both as to Law and Fact, with such Exceptions, and under such Regulations as the Congress shall make.

The trial of all Crimes, except in Cases of Impeachment, shall be by Jury; and such Trial shall be held in the State where the said Crimes shall have been committed; but when not committed within any State, the Trial shall be at such Place or Places as the Congress may by Law have directed.

SECTION 3. Treason against the United States, shall consist only in levying War against them, or in adhering to their Enemies, giving them Aid and Comfort. No Person shall be convicted of Treason unless on the Testimony of two Witnesses to the same overt Act, or on Confession in open Court.

The Congress shall have Power to declare the Punishment of Treason, but no attainder of Treason shall work Corruption of Blood, or Forfeiture except during the Life of the Person attainted.[2]

(On the appellate jurisdiction, cf. *American History and Government*, §§ 207 *a* and 217. Section 25 of the Judiciary Act of 1789, still in force, defines that jurisdiction as follows:

"*And be it further enacted*, That a final judgment or decree in any suit, in the highest court of law or equity of a State in which a decision

---

[1] Limited by the Eleventh Amendment to cases begun by a State as plaintiff. Cf. *American History and Government*, § 218.

[2] The last three paragraphs of this section might have been included advantageously in a "bill of rights." What preceding paragraphs might have been so disposed of?

in the suit could be had, when is drawn in question the validity of a treaty or statute of, or an authority exercised under, the United States, and the decision is against their validity; or when is drawn in question the validity of a statute of, or an authority exercised under, any State, on the ground of their being repugnant to the Constitution, treaties, or laws of the United States, and the decision is in favor of such their validity; or when is drawn in question the construction of any clause of the Constitution, or of a treaty, or statute of, or commission held under, the United States, and the decision is against the title, right, privilege, or exemption, especially set up or claimed . . . under such clause of the said Constitution, treaty, statute, or commission, may be re-examined, and revised or affirmed in the Supreme Court of the United States upon a writ of error . . . "

On the establishment of "inferior courts," cf. *American History and Government*, § 217. Such courts at present (1913) are from the bottom up: —

1. *District Courts.* Over ninety in 1911; the law of 1789 provided for thirteen.

2. *Circuit Courts.* Nine, each three justices. The first law, 1789, provided three circuit courts, but no special circuit judges; a circuit court then consisted of a justice of the Supreme Court " or circuit " and one or more judges of district courts included within the circuit. This remained the rule with a brief attempt at change in 1801, as described in § 240, until 1866, when separate circuit justices were provided.

3. *Circuit Courts of Appeals.* One for each of the nine circuits, composed of a justice of the Supreme Court and of other Federal judges — not less than three in all, and not including any justice from whose decision the appeal is taken. This order of courts was instituted in 1891, to relieve the Supreme Court which was then hopelessly overburdened with appeals from lower courts. In most cases, now, the decision of the circuit court of appeals is final.

4. *The Supreme Court.* One Chief Justice and eight Associate Justices. Its business now is confined very largely to those supremely important matters specified in the Constitution and in the law of 1789 quoted above.

There are also three special courts, somewhat outside this system: (1) the Federal *Court of Claims*, to determine money claims against the United States, established in 1855; (2) *Court of Customs Appeals*, established in 1909; and (3) *the Commerce Court*, created in 1910, to revise the work of the Interstate Commerce Commission.)

ARTICLE IV

SECTION 1. Full Faith and Credit shall be given in each State to the public Acts, Records, and judicial Proceeding of every other State. And the Congress may by general Laws prescribe the Manner in which such Acts, Records and Proceedings shall be proved, and the Effect thereof.

SECTION 2. The Citizens of each State shall be entitled to all Privileges and immunities of Citizens in the several States.[1]

A Person charged in any State with Treason, Felony, or other Crime, who shall flee from Justice, and be found in another State, shall on Demand of the executive Authority of the State from which he fled, be delivered up, to be removed to the State having Jurisdiction of the Crime.

[No Person held to Service or Labour in one State, under the Laws thereof, escaping into another, shall, in Consequence of any Law or Regulation therein, be discharged from such Service or Labour, but shall be delivered up on claim of the Party to whom such Service or Labour may be due.][2]

SECTION 3. New States may be admitted by the Congress into this Union; but no new State shall be formed or erected within the Jurisdiction of any other State; nor any State be formed by the Junction of two or more States, or Parts of States, without the consent of the Legislatures of the States concerned as well as of the Congress.

The Congress shall have Power to dispose of and make all needful Rules and Regulations respecting the Territory or other Property belonging to[3] the United States; and nothing in this Constitution shall be so construed as to Prejudice any Claims of the United States, or of any particular State.

SECTION 4. The United States shall guarantee to every State in this Union a Republican Form of Government, and

---

[1] Extended by Fourteenth Amendment.

[2] Superseded by Thirteenth Amendment so far as it relates to slaves.

[3] On the significance of this language as to Territory, cf. *American History and Government*, § 260 c.

shall protect each of them against Invasion; and on Application of the Legislature, or of the Executive (when the Legislature cannot be convened) against domestic Violence.

ARTICLE V[1]

The Congress, whenever two thirds of both Houses shall deem it necessary, shall propose Amendments to this Constitution, or, on the Application of the Legislatures of two thirds of the several States, shall call a Convention for proposing Amendments, which, in either Case, shall be valid to all Intents and Purposes, as Part of this Constitution, when ratified by the Legislatures of three fourths of the several States, or by Conventions in three fourths thereof, as the one or the other Mode of Ratification may be proposed by the Congress; Provided [that no Amendment which may be made prior to the Year One thousand eight hundred and eight shall in any Manner affect the first and fourth Clauses in the Ninth Section of the first Article; and] that no State, without its Consent, shall be deprived of its equal Suffrage in the Senate.

ARTICLE VI

All Debts contracted and Engagements entered into, before the Adoption of this Constitution, shall be as valid against the United States under this Constitution, as under the Confederation.

This Constitution, and the Laws of the United States which shall be made in Pursuance thereof; and all Treaties made, or which shall be made, under the Authority of the United States, shall be the supreme Law of the Land; and the Judges

---

[1] Article V, as far as to the brackets, should be committed to memory. Note the *four* varieties of amendment provided. Only one has ever been used (1913). Congress has always proposed, and State legislatures ratified. On the amending clause in general, cf. index to *American History and Government*.

in every State shall be bound thereby, any Thing in the Constitution or Laws of any State to the Contrary notwithstanding.[1]

The Senators and Representatives before mentioned, and the Members of the several State Legislatures, and all executive and judicial Officers, both of the United States and of the several States, shall be bound by Oath or Affirmation, to support this Constitution; but no religious Test shall ever be required as a Qualification to any Office or public Trust under the United States.

ARTICLE VII

The Ratification of the Conventions of nine States, shall be sufficient for the Establishment of this Constitution between the States so ratifying the Same.

(Exercise. — Write headings for each Article in the Constitution. Restate Sections 1 and 2 of Article IV in form appropriate for insertion in Section 10 of Article I. Cf. with corresponding provisions in the Articles of Confederation and in the Constitution of the New England Confederation. Can you restate Sections 3 and 4 so as to fit them for insertion under any preceding Article? Observe that Articles I, II, III, and V give the framework. Article VII, highly important at the time, had but temporary significance.)

AMENDMENTS

[i] [2]

Congress shall make no law respecting an establishment of religion, or prohibiting the free exercise thereof; or abridging the freedom of speech, or of the press; or the right of the people peaceably to assemble, and to petition the Government for a redress of grievances.

[ii]

A well regulated Militia, being necessary to the security of a free State, the right of the people to keep and bear Arms, shall not be infringed.

---

[1] On the history of this clause, cf. § 207 a.
[2] Originally, the first twelve amendments were not numbered in the official manuscripts.

[iii]

No Soldier shall, in time of peace be quartered in any house, without the consent of the Owner, nor in time of war, but in a manner to be prescribed by Law.

[iv]

The right of the people to be secure in their persons, houses, papers, and effects, against unreasonable searches and seizures, shall not be violated, and no Warrants shall issue, but upon probable cause, supported by Oath or affirmation, and particularly describing the place to be searched, and the persons or things to be seized.

[v]

No person shall be held to answer for a capital, or otherwise infamous crime, unless on a presentment or indictment of a Grand Jury except in cases arising in the land or naval forces, or in the Militia, when in actual service in time of war or public danger; nor shall any person be subject for the same offence to be twice put in jeopardy of life or limb; nor shall be compelled in any criminal case to be a witness against himself, nor be deprived of life, liberty, or property, without due process of law; nor shall private property be taken for public use, without just compensation.

[vi]

In all criminal prosecutions the accused shall enjoy the right to a speedy and public trial, by an impartial jury of the State and district wherein the crime shall have been committed, which district shall have been previously ascertained by law, and to be informed of the nature and cause of the accusation; to be confronted with the witnesses against him; to have compulsory process for obtaining witnesses in his favor, and to have the Assistance of Counsel for his defence.

THE FEDERAL CONSTITUTION

[vii]

In suits at common law, where the value in controversy shall exceed twenty dollars, the right of trial by jury shall be preserved, and no fact tried by a jury shall be otherwise re-examined in any Court of the United States, than according to the rules of the common law.

[viii]

Excessive bail shall not be required, nor excessive fines imposed, nor cruel and unusual punishments inflicted.

[ix]

The enumeration in the Constitution, of certain rights, shall not be construed to deny or disparage others retained by the people.

[x][1]

The powers not delegated to the United States by the Constitution, nor prohibited by it to the States, are reserved to the States respectively or to the people.

[xi][2]

The Judicial power of the United States shall not be construed to extend to any suit in law or equity, commenced or prosecuted against one of the United States by Citizens of another State, or by Citizens or Subjects of any Foreign State.

[xii][3]

The Electors shall meet in their respective States, and vote by ballot for President and Vice President, one of whom, at

---

[1] These first ten amendments were in force after November 3, 1791. Cf. comment in *American History and Government*, § 216. They are usually referred to as the Bill of Rights. It is a suggestive exercise to rewrite the "bill of rights," incorporating all those features of that character which are included in the body of the Constitution.

[2] Proclaimed to be in force January 8, 1798. For the history, cf. *Ib.*, § 217.

[3] Proclaimed in force September 25, 1804. Cf. *Ib.*, § 241.

least, shall not be an inhabitant of the same State with themselves; they shall name in their ballots the person voted for as President, and in distinct ballots the person voted for as Vice President, and they shall make distinct lists of all persons voted for as President, and of all persons voted for as Vice President, and of the number of votes for each, which lists they shall sign and certify, and transmit sealed to the seat of the government of the United States, directed to the President of the Senate; — The President of the Senate shall, in the presence of the Senate and House of Representatives, open all the certificates and the votes shall then be counted; — The person having the greatest number of votes for President, shall be the President, if such number be a majority of the whole number of Electors appointed; and if no person have such majority, then from the persons having the highest numbers not exceeding three on the list of those voted for as President, the House of Representatives shall choose immediately, by ballot, the President. But in choosing the President, the votes shall be taken by States, the representation from each State having one vote; a quorum for this purpose shall consist of a member or members from two-thirds of the States, and a majority of all the States shall be necessary to a choice. And if the House of Representatives shall not choose a President whenever the right of choice shall devolve upon them, before the fourth day of March next following, then the Vice President shall act as President, as in the case of the death or other constitutional disability of the President. — The person having the greatest number of votes as Vice President, shall be the Vice President, if such number be a majority of the whole number of Electors appointed, and if no person have a majority, then from the two highest numbers on the list, the Senate shall choose the Vice President; a quorum for the purpose shall consist of two-thirds of the whole number of Senators, and a majority of the whole number shall be necessary to a choice. But no person constitutionally ineligible to the office of President shall be eligible to that of Vice President of the United States.

THE FEDERAL CONSTITUTION

[xiii][1]

SECTION 1. Neither slavery nor involuntary servitude, except as a punishment for crime whereof the party shall have been duly convicted, shall exist within the United States, or any place subject to their jurisdiction.

SECTION 2. Congress shall have power to enforce this article by appropriate legislation.

[xiv][2]

SECTION 1. All persons born or naturalized in the United States, and subject to the jurisdiction thereof, are citizens of the United States and of the State wherein they reside. No State shall make or enforce any law which shall abridge the privileges or immunities of citizens of the United States: nor shall any State deprive any person of life, liberty, or property, without due process of law; nor deny to any person within its jurisdiction the equal protection of the laws.

SECTION 2. Representatives shall be apportioned among the several States according to their respective numbers, counting the whole number of persons in each State, excluding Indians not taxed. But when the right to vote at any election for the choice of electors for President and Vice President of the United States, Representatives in Congress, the Executive and Judicial offices of a State, or the members of the Legislature thereof, is denied to any of the male inhabitants of such State, being twenty one years of age, and citizens of the United States, or in any way abridged, except for participation in rebellion, or other crime, the basis of representation therein shall be reduced in the proportion which the number of such male citizens shall bear to the whole number of male citizens twenty one years of age in such State.

SECTION 3. No person shall be a Senator or Representative in Congress, or elector of President and Vice President, or

---

[1] Proclaimed in force December 18, 1865. On Amendments Thirteen to Fifteen inclusive, cf. *Ib.*, §§ 377, 385 ff.

[2] Proclaimed in force July 28, 1868.

hold any office, civil or military, under the United States, or under any State, who, having previously taken an oath, as a member of Congress, or as an officer of the United States, or as a member of any State legislature, or as an executive or judicial officer of any State, to support the Constitution of the United States, shall have engaged in insurrection or rebellion against the same, or given aid or comfort to the enemies thereof. But Congress may by a vote of two-thirds of each House, remove such disability.

SECTION 4. The validity of the public debt of the United States, authorized by law, including debts incurred for payment of pensions and bounties for services in suppressing insurrection or rebellion, shall not be questioned. But neither the United States nor any State shall assume or pay any debt or obligation incurred in aid of insurrection or rebellion against the United States, or any claim for the loss or emancipation of any slave; but all such debts, obligations and claims shall be held illegal and void.

SECTION 5. The Congress shall have power to enforce, by appropriate legislation, the provisions of this article.

[xv][1]

SECTION 1. The right of citizens of the United States to vote shall not be denied or abridged by the United States or by any State on account of race, color, or previous condition of servitude.

SECTION 2. The Congress shall have power to enforce this article by appropriate legislation.

[xvi][2]

The Congress shall have power to lay and collect taxes on incomes, from whatever source derived, without apportionment among the States, and without regard to any census or enumeration.

---

[1] Proclaimed in force March 30, 1870.
[2] Ratified in 1913, while these pages were at press.

[xvii][1]

The Senate of the United States shall be composed of two Senators from each State, elected by the people thereof for six years; and each Senator shall have one vote. The electors in each State shall have the qualifications requisite for electors of the most numerous branch of the State Legislatures.

When vacancies happen in the representation of any State in the Senate, the executive authority of such State shall issue writs of election to fill vacancies: Provided, that the Legislature of any State may empower the executive thereof to make temporary appointments until the people fill the vacancies by election as the legislature may direct.

This amendment shall not be so construed as to affect the election or term of any Senator chosen before it becomes valid as a part of the Constitution.

---

[1] Ratified in 1913, while these pages were at press.

INDEX OF SOURCES

The *Writings* of statesmen or the *Records* of a colony are sometimes indexed twice, — once by title, under the name of the subject, and once by the name of the editor. The latter is done, however, only in cases where it is customary to quote the work with the editor's name, as with **Hening's** *Statutes*. Authors' and editors' names, when standing first, are in **heavy-faced type**. Titles, even when the work is indexed by title rather than by editor, are in *italics*. Each entry closes with a list of the selections in this volume which are based upon it. In many cases the introduction to the first number in each such list contains additional bibliographical material, when it seems worth while to present such material anywhere.

Adams, John, The Works of (Boston; 10 vols.; edited by Charles Francis Adams). Nos. 130 a, b, c, 146.

Adams, John, Letters of, addressed to his Wife (Boston; 2 vols.). No. 138 b.

Arber, Edward (editor), *The Story of the Pilgrim Fathers* (London). No. 48 a.

Arnold, Samuel Greene, *History of Rhode Island* (Providence; 2 vols.). No. 90.

"Aspinwall Papers," the, in *Massachusetts Historical Society Collections*, 4th series, IX. No. 31 b.

Bacon (editor), *The Laws of Maryland*. See *Maryland*.

Bancroft, George, *History of the Constitution* (New York, 2 vols.). No. 162.

Besse, Joseph, *A Collection of the Sufferings of the People called Quakers* (London; 1753). No. 88.

Boston Town Records (Report of the Record Commissioners for 1887). No. 122.

Bradford, William, *Plymouth Plantation* ("Original Narratives" edition). Nos. 43, 44, 45.

British Record Office, The manuscript *Charter* of the Company of Westminster for the Plantation of Providence Isle. No. 55.

Brown, Alexander, *The First Republic in America* (Houghton). No. 3, note.

—— *Genesis of the United States* (Houghton; 2 vols.). Nos. 4, 5, 7, 10, 18, 22.

Burroughs, Edward, *A Declaration of the Sad and Great Persecution and Martyrdom of Quakers in New England* (London; 1660). No. 88 b.

Calendar of State Papers, Colonial Series, 1574–1660 (W. Noel Sainsbury, editor). No. 55.

Calvin, John, *Institutes* (the translation of 1813, London). No. 61.

Congress, Journals of the Continental (Ford edition). Nos. 130 c, d, 138 a, 140, 141.

INDEX OF SOURCES

Ib. (Philadelphia edition, 1801). No. 148, *a*, *b*.

Connecticut, Colonial Records of (Hartford; 15 vols.). Nos. 93, 97.

Documentary History of the Constitution (Washington; Government Printing Office; 4 vols.). No. 153.

Dorchester Town Records (edited by the Boston Record Commissioners). Nos. 66, 81.

Drayton, Michael, *Poems* (London; 1619). No. 4.

Eddes, William, *Letters from America* (London; 1792). No. 116.

Federal Convention, The Records of the (edited by Farrand). 3 vols. Nos. 155, 156, 157, 158, 160, 163.

Force, Peter (editor), *American Archives, Fourth Series* (Washington; 6 vols.). Nos. 125 *a*, 127, 128 *a*, *b*, *c*, 129 *a*, *b*, *c*, *d*, *e*, 131, 132 *a*, *b*, 134, 135.

—— *Historical Tracts* (Washington; 1836; 4 vols.). Nos. 6, 9, 23, 26, 62 *c*.

Franklin, Benjamin, The Works of (Smyth edition; Putnam's; 10 vols.). No. 114 *a*.

"Goodspeed to Virginia" (in Brown's *Genesis of the United States*). No. 5.

Gorges, Sir Ferdinando, "Briefe Narration," *Massachusetts Historical Society Collections*, 3d series, VI. Nos. 51 *a*, 53 note.

Hakluyt, Richard, *Voyages . . . and Discoveries of the English Nation* (published in 1589; quoted here from the Goldschmid edition). Nos. 2, 15.

—— *A Discourse on Western Planting* (republished in the *Maine Historical Society Collections*, 2d series, II). No. 3.

Hamilton, Alexander, *The Works of* (Federalist edition; Putnam's; 12 vols.). No. 159.

Hazard, Ebenezer (editor), *Historical Collections of State Papers.* (Commonly quoted as Hazard's *State Papers*. Washington, 1792; 2 vols.). Nos. 29, 30, 39 *a*, *b*, 42, 46 addendum, 51 *a*.

Hazard, Samuel (editor); *Annals of Pennsylvania* (Philadelphia). No. 103.

Hening, William W. (editor), *Statutes at Large, being a Collection of the Laws of Virginia.* (Richmond, 1823; 13 vols.) Nos. 17, 31, 33, 34, 35, 105, 106, 109.

Higginson, Francis, "Relation of New England's Plantation" (1629; reprinted in Young's *Chronicles of Massachusetts Bay*). No. 59 *d*.

Holinshed, Raphael, *Chronicles of England, Scotland, and Ireland* (London; 1577). No. 1.

Hutchinson, Thomas (editor), *Collection of Original Papers* (published as a third volume, in the nature of an appendix, of his *History of Massachusetts Bay*). Nos. 53, 58 *b*, 59 *a*, 76 *a*, 86, 110.

—— *History of Massachusetts Bay* (London; 1769). Nos. 60 *a*, 75, 76 *b*, 92.

Jefferson, Thomas, The Writings of (Ford edition; Putnams; 10 vols.). Nos. 123 *a*, 136 addendum.

Jefferson, Thomas, The Works of (Washington edition; 9 vols.). No. 125 *b*.

Johnson, Captain Edward, *The Wonder-working Providence of Sions Saviour in New England* (London; 1654). No. 54 *b*.

Kingsbury, Susan (editor), *Records of the Virginia Company of Lon-*

don (Washington, 1906). See *Virginia*.

Lechford, Thomas, *Plaine Dealing* (1641; republished in *Massachusetts Historical Society Collections*). No. 85.

Madison, James, *Journal of the Philadelphia Convention* (also in Farrand's *Records of the Federal Convention*). Nos. 159, 161.

Marston, John, *Eastward Hoe!* (London; 1605). No. 8.

Maryland, Proceedings of the Conventions of (Baltimore). No. 139.

Mason, George, *Life and Correspondence of* (by Kate Mason Rowland; 2 vols.). Nos. 121 note, 136 addendum, 162.

Massachusetts, Colonial Records of (Boston; 7 vols.; edited by Nathaniel Shurtleff). Nos. 53, 57, 58 a, c, 65, 72, 75 b, 80 addendum, 82.

Massachusetts, Historical Society Collections. Nos. 31 b, 41, 47, 53, 85, 107.

Massachusetts Bay, Acts and Resolves of the Province of (Boston; 7 vols.) 110 b.

Minot, George Richards, *History of the Insurrections in Massachusetts in the Year MDCCLXXXVI* (Worcester; 1788). No. 151 b.

Moore, Frank (editor), *Diary of the American Revolution* (Scribner's; 2 vols.). No. 142 b.

Morris, Gouverneur, *Life and Writings of* (Sparks' edition; 3 vols.). No. 150.

Neill, Edward D., *The Virginia Company* (Albany, N. Y.; 1869). No. 18.

—— *Virginia and Virginiola* (Albany, N. Y.; 1878). No. 11.

New Hampshire, Provincial Papers of (Concord; by a series of editors). No. 110.

New Haven, Colonial Records of (Hartford, 2 vols.). No. 94.

New Jersey Archives, First Series, Vols. XXV and XXVII ("Newspaper Extracts" for 1769-1770 and 1770-1771). Nos. 117, 120 d.

New York, Documents relative to the Colonial History of (by a series of editors). Nos. 99, 101, 111 d, 114 b.

Niles, Hezekiah, *Principles and Acts of the Revolution in America* (Baltimore; 1822). No. 142 c.

North Carolina, Colonial Records of (Raleigh; 10 vols.; edited by W. L. Saunders). No. 111 a.

Nova Britannia (London; 1609; republished in Force's *Historical Tracts*). Nos. 6, 20.

Peckham, Sir George, *True Report* [of Gilbert's Voyage], (1582; republished in Hakluyt's *Voyages*). No. 2.

Pennsylvania, Charters and Laws of (Harrisburg; 1879). No. 102.

Plymouth Colony, Records of (Boston; 12 vols.). Nos. 94, 95, 96.

Poore, Benjamin Perley (editor), *Charters and Constitutions* (Washington; Government Printing Office). No. 15.

Purchas, Samuel, *Purchas his Pilgrimes* (1625; London; 4 vols.). No. 19 a.

Ramsey, David, *History of the American Revolution* (1789; 2 vols.). No. 145.

Rhode Island, Colonial Records of (Providence; 10 vols.). Nos. 91, 98.

Rowland, Kate Mason, *Life and Correspondence of George Mason* (New York; 2 vols.). See *George Mason*.

INDEX OF SOURCES

Scharf, J. Thomas, *History of Maryland* (Philadelphia; 3 vols.). Nos. 36, 38.

Scharf and Westcott, *History of Philadelphia* (Philadelphia; 3 vols.). Nos. 124, 143.

Smith, Captain John, *Complete Works of* (Birmingham edition). Nos. 13, 14, 48 b, 60 b.

Statutes at Large, from Magna Carta to 1869 (Cambridge, 110 vols.; commonly quoted, from the editor, as Pickering's *Statutes*). Nos. 100 c, 118, 119.

Stith, William, *History of Virginia*, (1747; edited by Sabin and reprinted in 1865). Nos. 16, 20, 21.

Thorpe, Francis (editor), *American Charters and Constitutions* (Washington; Government Printing Office; 7 vols.). No. 15.

Tyler, Moses Coit, *Literary History of the American Revolution* (Putnam's; 2 vols.). 144.

United States, *Revised Statutes of* (1878). No. 147.

Virginia, *Calendar of State Papers of* (Richmond; 11 vols.). No. 133.

Virginia, *Colonial Records of* (edited by Wynne and Gilman). No. 25.

Virginia, *Journals of the House of Burgesses of* (Putnam's; 10 vols.). Nos. 120 a, b, c, 123 b, 125 c, d, e, f.

Virginia Company of London, *Records of the* (Washington; 1906; 2 vols.; edited by Susan Kingsbury). Nos. 12, 24, 26 28.

Virginia Magazine of History and Biography (Richmond). Nos. 31 b, 37 a, b, c, 108.

Ward, Nathaniel, *The Simple Cobbler of Aggawamm* (London; 1647). No. 84 a.

Washington, George, *The Writings of* (Washington edition). Nos. 121 b, 151 b.

Watertown, *Records of the Town of*. No. 83.

White, John, *Brief Relation* (1630; reprinted in Young's *Chronicles*). No. 56.

Whitmore, W. H., *Bibliographical Sketch of the Laws of the Massachusetts Colony* (Boston). No. 78.

Winthrop, John, *History of New England* ("Original Narratives" edition). Nos. 62, 64, 67, 68, 69, 70, 71, 73, 74, 77, 79, 80.

Winthrop, John, *Life and Letters of* (Boston; 2 vols.; edited by Robert C. Winthrop). Nos. 59 a, b, c, 62 b.

Writings of Lace (a series of letters from Federalists attacking John Hancock in the campaign of 1789). No. 164.

Young, Alexander (editor), *Chronicles of Massachusetts* (Boston; 1846). Nos. 56, 59 d.

Zenger, John Peter, *Brief Narrative of the Case and Tryall of John Peter Zenger* (New York; 1738). No. 113.

SUBJECT INDEX

The references are to the numbers of selections, not to pages.

Adams, John, account of debates in Continental Congress, 130 a; impressions of First Continental Congress, 130 b; on resolution of Congress of May 15, 1776, for State governments 138 b; on first independent government in South Carolina, ib.; on anti-social tendencies of pre-Revolutionary measures (the horse-jockey client), 142.

Aggawamm, the Simple Cobbler of, see *Ward*.

Albany Plan, the, for union of colonies, 114 a and b.

Albion, Charter of the Province of (1634), representative feature, 39.

Annapolis Convention, the, regarded as part of an aristocratic plot, 152; its call for the Federal Convention, 153.

Avalon, Baltimore's colony of, 36; charter the first royal grant recognizing popular government, 38, 39.

Bacon, Nathaniel, Rebellion, 106–109; "Bacon's laws," 106; Bacon's Proclamation, 107; causes of rebellion, 108; reforms of, abolished, 109.

Ballot, used by London Company in England, 23, 28 (2), 28 (3); used in Massachusetts first, 67 a, note; adopted legally for general elections in Massachusetts General Court, 70; used for secrecy in a Boston town election, 71; develops from "proxies," 73.

Baltimore, First Lord, the, letter from Avalon to Charles I, 36.

Berkeley, Sir William, Commission of 1641 authorizing the Assembly, 32 a; report of 1671 on conditions in Virginia, 104. See *Bacon*.

Bill of Rights, the first, in Virginia (June, 1776), 136.

"Body of Liberties," the (of Massachusetts), 77, 78.

Boston Port Bill, effect in Virginia, 125.

Boston town meeting, and colonial politics, 111 c; 122.

Bradford, William, charter from New England Council, 49; surrender of charter to colonists, 50.

Cambridge Agreement, the, 58 b.

Charter colonies, recommendation of Board of Trade to abolish, 111 a.

Charters, *Royal to Proprietors*; Gilbert's, of 1578 (and Raleigh's of 1584), 15; Baltimore's for Maryland, 37; for Avalon, 38; for New Albion and Maine, 39; Duke of York's for New York, 101; Penn's for Pennsylvania, 102. *Royal to proprietary corporations in England:* First Virginia Charter (to London and Plymouth branches of a colonizing company), 16; Second Charter, 20; Third Charter, 21; to New England Council (1620), 42; to Massachusetts Bay Company, 53; to Company of Westminster for Providence Isle, 55. *Royal to "corporations upon the place":* parliamentary to Williams in 1648, 91; Connecticut Charter of 1662, 97; Rhode Island (1663), 98;

SUBJECT INDEX

The references are to the numbers of selections.

Massachusetts (1691), 110. *From proprietary corporations or proprietors to settlers:* Virginia Company of London to Virginians, 25, 27; to intending Pilgrim settlers (Wincob charter), 43, 45; New England Council to Pierce for Plymouth, 47; to Bradford, 49; to Robert Gorges as proprietor in Massachusetts, 51; Penn's grants to Pennsylvanians — Laws agreed upon in England, 103 *a*; Charter of 1701, 103 *b*.

Child, Robert, demand for the franchise in Massachusetts for Presbyterians, 86.

Christison, Wenlock, trial as a Quaker, 88 *b*.

Colonial Department (English), established, 99.

Colonization, hardships, of Baltimore in Avalon, 36; at Jamestown, 19; in Massachusetts Bay, 62 *a*, *b*, *c*.

Committees of Correspondence (Revolutionary), towns in Massachusetts, 122; intercolonial — Jefferson's account of creation, 123; resolution of Virginia, Burgesses for, 123 *b*; correspondence of, 123 *c*; and regarding call for Continental Congress, 125 *f*.

Confederation, New England, 94, 95, 96; Franklin's "Albany Plan," 114; Continental Congress, 125 ff.; debates in Congress regarding character of, 146; the Articles, 147; anarchy under, 150, 151.

Connecticut, Fundamental Orders, 93; charter, 97; refusal to accept a royal commander of militia, 111 *d*.

Connecticut Compromise, in the Federal Convention, 161.

Constitution, the Federal, Annapolis Convention, 152; call for Philadelphia Convention, 153; credentials of delegates, 154; George Mason on preliminaries and on aristocratic forces in, 155, 157; Virginia Plan, 156; New Jersey Plan, 158; Hamilton's Plan, 159; the critical day's debate on the Connecticut Compromise, 161; ratification, 162 ff.; document and amendments, 165.

Continental Congress, the First, proposed by Virginia ex-Burgesses, 125 *e*; Rhode Island appoints delegates, 125 *f*; "called" by Massachusetts, 126; suggested also by Virginia county, 127; method of voting decided, 130 *a*; Adams' impressions of, 130 *b*; Declaration of Rights, 130 *c*; and the Association, 130 *d*.

Cotton, Rev. John, denounces democracy, 67 *a*, 71, 75 (addendum); letter to English lords on Massachusetts conditions, 75; on rules of fair trade, 79; against toleration, 84 *c*.

Crashaw, "Daily Prayer," for use in Virginia, 9; sermon before Delaware's expedition (on players), 10.

Cushman, Robert, to Pastor Robinson, 43.

Dale, Sir Thomas, to London Company, on glories of Virginia, 12.

Dates, New Style and Old, 21.

Democracy, decried by Puritan leaders: Calvin, 61; Cotton and Winthrop, 67 *a*, 71, 75 (addendum), 77, 80; and sumptuary legislation in Massachusetts, 75 *b*; denounced by Hamilton in Federal Convention, 159; establishes government by town meeting, 66.

Dorchester, school code, 81.

Drayton, *Ode to the Virginian Voyage*, 4.

Ducking stool, the, 115.

Dudley, Thomas, to Countess of Lincoln on first winter in Massachusetts, 62 *c*.

"Eastward Hoe!", 8.

Exeter, "Combination of Settlers" at, 46 (addendum).

SUBJECT INDEX

The references are to the numbers of selections.

Fairfax County (Virginia), resolutions for First Continental Congress, 129 *b*; for Revolutionary militia, 132.

Fauquier, Francis (Governor of Virginia), to Lords of Trade, on resignation of Mercer, Stamp Distributor, 120 *c*.

Fletcher (Governor of New York), and Connecticut militia, 111 *d*.

Franchise, in Virginia, 35, 105, 107, 109; in Massachusetts, denied to Presbyterians, 86.

Frankland, State of, 148.

Franklin, Benjamin, Albany plan of, 114 *a* and *b*; characterized in Federal Convention by Pierce, 160.

Free speech, denied in Massachusetts in 1635, 69, 77; vindicated in New York in Zenger trial, 113.

French Alliance, the Conservatives' fear of, 144.

"Gentlemen," in 16th century England, 1; in early Virginia, 19 *b*; in colonial Massachusetts, 75 *a* and *b*.

Georgia, credentials of delegates to Federal Convention, 154.

Gilbert, Sir Humphrey, charter, 15.

"Goodspeed to Virginia," on motives for colonization, 5.

Gorges, Sir Ferdinando, and grant of Massachusetts, 39 *b*; and reorganization of Plymouth Council, 42; "Briefe Narration" of, 51 *a*, 53 note.

Gorges, Robert, grant from Plymouth Council (representative features), 51 *a*, 53 note.

Hakluyt, Rev. Richard, on motives for colonization, 3.

Hamilton, Alexander, plan for the Constitution (denunciation of democracy), 159; character sketch of, in Federal Convention, 160.

Hamilton, James, and the Zenger trial, 113.

Hancock, John, and inducement to favor the Constitution, 164.

Harvey, Sir John, "Propositions for Virginia," suggesting restoration of the Assembly, 32 *a*.

Henry, Patrick, Stamp Act Resolutions, 120 *a*; creation of Committees of Correspondence, 123 *a*; and call for First Continental Congress, 125 *b*; in debates in Congress ("I am not a Virginian"), 130 *a*.

Higginson, Rev. Francis, Agreement with Massachusetts Company, 56; *Relation,* 59 *d*.

Higginson, Stephen, on John Hancock and ratification of Constitution, 164.

Hutchinson, Thomas, and Boston town meeting, 122.

Indentured servants, see *White servants.*

Independence, Virginia county instructions for, 134; Virginia Convention, instructions for, 135; Virginia Declaration of, 137; Congressional resolutions for independent State governments, 138 *a* and *b*; State instructions against, 139; Lee's motion for in Congress, 140; the Declaration, 140; sets free social forces, 145.

Industry in common, in early Virginia, 17, 18; in Plymouth, 44.

James I, instructions to Jamestown expedition, 17; attempts to control elections in London Company, 28.

Jefferson, Thomas, proposition for the franchise in first Virginia constitution, 136 (addendum); and Virginia declaration of independence, 137; and Declaration of July 4, 141; and Ordinance of 1784, 148 *a*.

Keayne, Captain Robert, and exorbitant trading profits, 79; and

SUBJECT INDEX

The references are to the numbers of selections.

the "sow business" in Massachusetts, 80.

Laborers, in England, 1; in Massachusetts and wage legislation, 65; condition of White servants in 1774, 116, 117.

Laws, of Virginia in 1619, 25; Plymouth code of 1636, 50; of early Massachusetts, 65; sumptuary discrimination against classes below the gentry, 75; the "Body of Liberties," 78; later Virginian, 105, 106; late colonial, regarding White servants, 117.

Lee, Richard Henry, and county resolutions against Stamp Act, 120 *b*; and creation of Committees of Correspondence, 123 *a*; and call for First Continental Congress, 125 *b*; and Westmoreland County resolutions, 129 *a*; and motion for independence, 140.

Local Government, see *Town meeting.*

London Company, see *Virginia Company.*

Loyalists (in Revolution), parody "to sign or not to sign," 142 *b*; correspondence with a committee of safety, 143; pretended diary to show danger in French alliance, 144. See *Mob violence.*

Maine, grant of to Gorges (representative government), 39 *b*.

Maryland, early, 36, 37, 38, 39, 40; Second Provincial Convention of, a government, 132 (introduction); instructions against independence, 139.

Mason, George, and Virginia non-importation agreement of 1769, 121 *b*, note; declares the Third Virginia Convention a government, 133 *c*; and Virginia Bill of Rights, 136 (addendum); on democratic and aristocratic forces in the Federal Convention, 155, 157; objections to signing the Constitution, 162, 163.

Massachusetts, to 1660, 41 ff.; early beginnings at Salem, 52; charter of 1629, 53; docket of charter, 54; question of transfer of charter to America, 55 (and addendum); decision to transfer the charter, 58; decision of Puritan gentlemen to remove to Massachusetts, 59; early hardships and religious matters, 62; oligarchic usurpations, 63; Watertown protest and some democratic gains, 64; aristocratic legislation, 65; beginning of town government, 66; establishment of representative government, 67; religious controversies, 74; social conditions, 75; danger of English interference, 76; demand for written laws, 77; social conditions as shown in town legislation, 83; and religious persecution, 84, 85, 86, 88; English relations after 1660, 100; charter of 1691, 110 *b*; in the Revolution, 122 ff. (See Table of Contents.)

Mayflower Compact, the, 46.

Mercer, Colonel, induced to resign as Stamp Distributor, 120 *c*.

Ministers in Virginia, not to "give themselves to excesse of drinking," 33.

Mob violence, pre-Revolutionary, 120 *c, d*, 124; after Declaration of Independence, 142 *a, b, c*.

Morris, Gouverneur, on the hope for a military dictator, 150; character sketch in Federal Convention, 160.

Navigation Acts, 100 *a, b, c*; 118.

New England Confederation, constitution, 94; Massachusetts demands more weight in, 95; nullification by Massachusetts, 96.

New England Council, 42. See *Plymouth Council.*

New Hampshire, commission of royal governor of, 112.

SUBJECT INDEX

The references are to the numbers of selections.

New Jersey, advertisements for runaway (White) servants, 117.

New Jersey Plan, in Federal Convention, 158.

"New Style," in dates, 21, note.

New York, charter to Duke of York, 101.

North Sea passage, to be sought for by first Virginia expedition, 18.

Northwest Ordinance, the, 149 b.

Nullification, in New England Confederation, 96.

"Old Style," dates, 21, note.

Ordinance of 1621, for Virginia, 27.

Ordinance of 1784, for organizing the National Domain, 149 a.

Ordinance of 1789, for the Northwest, 149 b.

Otto, Louis Guillaume, to Vergennes, on Annapolis Convention as a plot of the aristocratic classes, 152.

Parody, a Tory's, on Hamlet's soliloquy, 142 b.

Peirce, John, charter for Plymouth, 47.

Penn, William, grant of Pennsylvania, 102; grants to the settlers, 103 a and b.

Percy, Master George, "Discourse," on first weeks in Jamestown, 19 a.

Pierce, William, character sketches by, of men of the Federal Convention, 160.

Pillory, the, 115.

Plymouth Council, a branch of the first Virginia Company, 16 (section v); reorganized by charter of 1620, 42; grants to the Pilgrims, 47, 49; to Gorges, for Massachusetts, 51.

Plymouth Plantation, delay in securing Wincob charter, 43; articles of partnership with London merchants, 44; a "body politic" before sailing, 45; Mayflower Compact, 46; the Peirce charter, 47; early history, 48 a and b; the Bradford charter, 49; surrender of the same to the colony, 50; first code of laws, 50.

Presbyterians, excluded from the franchise in early Massachusetts, 86.

Providence Isle, charter to Company of Westminster for plantation of, 55.

Puritans (Massachusetts), political principles of, 61; not Separatists, 52, 60, 62.

Quakers, persecution in Massachusetts, 88; and Rhode Island, 92.

Randolph, Edmund, *Report* of 1676 on Massachusetts, 110.

Religious freedom, toleration in Maryland, 40; persecution in Massachusetts, 84, 85, 86, 87, 88; freedom in Rhode Island, 89, 90, 91, 92; in Pennsylvania, 103.

Representative government, first representative assembly (Virginia), 25; preserved in Virginia against James and Charles, 29, 30, 31, 32; first royal authorization of (Maryland charter), 37; also in charters for Avalon and Maine, 38, 39; in Gorges grant of 1623, 51; established in Massachusetts, 61–67.

Revolution, the, pre-Revolutionary agitation, 114–124; rise of Revolutionary governments, 125–133; Independence, 134–144; social forces set free by, 145.

Rhode Island, religious freedom, 89–92.

Robinson, Pastor John, on the terms of partnership between Pilgrims and London merchants, 44, note; farewell letter, 45.

SUBJECT INDEX 585

The references are to the numbers of selections.

Rogers, Rev. Ezekiel, champion of democracy in Early Massachusetts, 77 (addendum).

Sabbath in Virginia, no traveling on, 33 (4).

Salem, White's *Relation* of the beginning of, 52.

Saltonstall, Richard, signer of Cambridge Agreement, 58 *b*; letter urging religious freedom, 84 *c*.

Sandys, Sir Edwin, letter to stockholders of London Company, 11; and the Company's Declaration of 1620, 26; and interference of King James against reëlection, 28 (1); and Plymouth Colony, 43.

Schools, in Massachusetts: Dorchester regulations, 81; compulsory education, 82 *a*; State system, 82 *b*. In Virginia (Berkeley's *Report*), 104.

Selectmen, first established at Dorchester, 66.

"Servants," see *White servants*.

Shays' Rebellion, Hampshire County Grievances, 151 *a*; and Washington's alarm, 151 *b*.

Smith, Captain John, on the London Company (not mercenary), 13; last plea for colonization (for Massachusetts), 14; on "gentlemen" in Virginia, 19 *b*; on Plymouth in 1624, 48 *b*; Massachusetts Puritans not Separatists, 60 *b*.

Spain, and English colonization, 3 (ch. v.), 5, 6; danger of Spanish attack on Jamestown, 22.

Stamp Act, the, 119; reception in America: Henry's resolutions, 120 *a*; Virginia county resolutions against, 120 *b*; Virginia Stamp Distributor induced to resign, 120 *c*; mob violence, 120 *d*.

Stoughton, Israel, disfranchised for criticizing Massachusetts government, 69.

Sugar Act, of 1733, 100 *c*; of 1764, 118.

Sydney, Sir Philip, on American colonization, 3, note.

Tea riots, 124.

Town meeting, establishment at Dorchester, 66, and at Watertown, 83; use of ballot in, 73 *b*; recognized in "Body of Liberties," 78; typical records of from Watertown (illustrating New England society), 83; at Boston, political activity in affairs of the province, 111 *c*, and pre-Revolutionary (town committees of correspondence), 122.

Two-House legislature, evolution of in Massachusetts, 68, 69, 80.

Virginia, motives for colonization, patriotic and religious, 2, 3, 4, 5, 6, 7, 9, 10, 11, 13, 14; ridiculed (*Eastward Hoe*), 8; praised by Dale, 12; classes of colonists, 7; "gentlemen" in, 19 *b*; under King and Company, 16–19; Charter of 1609 (under the Company), 20; Charter of 1612, 21; danger from Spain, 22; under the liberal London Company (which see), 23–28; first Representative Assembly, 25; a royal province, 29–33; royal commissions ignoring Assembly, 29, 30; Assembly's declaration, "No taxation without representation," 31 *a*; protests in favor of Assembly, 31 *b*; restoration of Assembly, 32; legislation, moral and financial, 33: under the Commonwealth, 34–35; franchise, 35, 105, 106, 109; under the second Stuarts — Bacon's Rebellion and suppression of reforms, 105–109; in pre-Revolutionary agitation, 121 ff.; non-importation agreement, 121 *a* and *b*; originates intercolonial Committees, 123 *a* and *b*; suggests Continental Congress, 125 *a*, *b*, *c*, *d*, *e*, *f*, *g*; calls

SUBJECT INDEX

The references are to the numbers of selections.

provincial convention, 128 *a* and *b*; county meetings — instructions to delegates to provincial convention, 128 *c*, 129 *a*, *b*, *c*, *d*, *e*; county approval of Continental Congress' Associations, 131; county conventions become governments (Fairfax County), 132, 133 *a*; Second Provincial Convention a government de facto, 133 *b*; Third Convention (July, 1775), a government in form also, 133 *c*; Charlotte County instructions for independence, 134; Convention instructs delegates in Continental Congress to move for independence, 135; resolves upon an independent State constitution, *ib.*; Bill of Rights, 136; State declaration of independence, 137.

Virginia Company, the, pamphlets in favor of, 5, 6; "True and Sincere Declaration" of, 7; Smith's vindication of, 13; charter of 1606, 15; instructions from King James, 17; instructions from the Council in England, 18; charter of 1609, 20; charter of 1612, 21; rules adopted by the liberal management in 1619, 23; "Order" recognizing right of settlers to share in government, 24; first charter to settlers (noticed in records of Assembly), 25; "Declaration" of 1620, 26; Ordinance of 1621, 27; struggle with the King for right of free election, 28.

Virginia Plan, the, in Federal Convention, 156.

Ward, Rev. Nathaniel, argument against religious toleration, 84.

Washington, George, and Virginia's non-importation association of 1769, 121 *b*, note; and Fairfax County resolutions of 1774, 129 *b*; and Fairfax County organization of Revolutionary militia, 132; and Shays' Rebellion, 151 *b*.

Watertown Protest, the, 64.

Watertown Records, extracts from, illustrating social conditions, 83.

Western territory, debates on in Continental Congress, 146; desire for Statehood, 148; Ordinance of 1784, 149 *a*; Northwest Ordinance, 149 *b*.

Weymouth, Captain George, record of voyage to Maine, 41.

Wheelwright, Rev. John, and petition for free speech, 74.

White, Rev. John, account of beginnings of Massachusetts, 52.

White "servants," corporal punishment, 65; classified (in 1774), 116; advertisements for runaways (1769, 1774), 117.

Williams, Roger, on religious freedom, 90.

Winslow, Edward, letter to friend in England on the beginnings of Plymouth, 48 *a*.

Winthrop, John, signer of Cambridge Agreement, 58 *b*; argument for making Massachusetts a Puritan settlement, 59; reasons for coming to America, 59 *b*; farewell letter to the Church of England, 60 *a*; on early hardships in the colony, 62 *a* and *b*; decries democracy, 64, 67, 71, 73, 77; denies free speech, 69; denies right of petition, 77.

Winthrop, John, Jr., decision to come to Massachusetts, 59 *c*.

Wise, Rev. John, on Englishmen's dislike for arbitrary government, 111 *b*.

Written laws, demand for in Massachusetts, 77.

Yeardley, Sir George, and Virginia Representative Assembly, 25.

Yeomen, English, in 16th century, 1.

Zenger, John Peter, and free speech, 113.

Date Due

PRINTED IN U. S. A.